Mastering ROS for Robotics Programming
Second Edition

Design, build, and simulate complex robots using the Robot Operating System

Lentin Joseph

Jonathan Cacace

Packt>

BIRMINGHAM - MUMBAI

I0034660

Mastering ROS for Robotics Programming
Second Edition

Copyright © 2018 Packt Publishing

All rights reserved. No part of this book may be reproduced, stored in a retrieval system, or transmitted in any form or by any means, without the prior written permission of the publisher, except in the case of brief quotations embedded in critical articles or reviews.

Every effort has been made in the preparation of this book to ensure the accuracy of the information presented. However, the information contained in this book is sold without warranty, either express or implied. Neither the author, nor Packt Publishing or its dealers and distributors, will be held liable for any damages caused or alleged to have been caused directly or indirectly by this book.

Packt Publishing has endeavored to provide trademark information about all of the companies and products mentioned in this book by the appropriate use of capitals. However, Packt Publishing cannot guarantee the accuracy of this information.

Commissioning Editor: Vijin Boricha
Acquisition Editor: Divya Poojari
Content Development Editor: Eisha Dsouza
Technical Editor: Naveenkumar Jain
Copy Editor: Safis Editing
Project Coordinator: Kinjal Bari
Proofreader: Safis Editing
Indexer: Pratik Shirodkar
Graphics: Jisha Chirayil
Production Coordinator: Arvindkumar Gupta

First published: December 2015
Second edition: February 2018

Production reference: 1220218

Published by Packt Publishing Ltd.
Livery Place
35 Livery Street
Birmingham
B3 2PB, UK.

ISBN 978-1-78847-895-3

www.packtpub.com

Mapt

mapt.io

Mapt is an online digital library that gives you full access to over 5,000 books and videos, as well as industry leading tools to help you plan your personal development and advance your career. For more information, please visit our website.

Why subscribe?

- Spend less time learning and more time coding with practical eBooks and Videos from over 4,000 industry professionals

- Improve your learning with Skill Plans built especially for you

- Get a free eBook or video every month

- Mapt is fully searchable

- Copy and paste, print, and bookmark content

PacktPub.com

Did you know that Packt offers eBook versions of every book published, with PDF and ePub files available? You can upgrade to the eBook version at www.PacktPub.com and as a print book customer, you are entitled to a discount on the eBook copy. Get in touch with us at service@packtpub.com for more details.

At www.PacktPub.com, you can also read a collection of free technical articles, sign up for a range of free newsletters, and receive exclusive discounts and offers on Packt books and eBooks.

Contributors

About the authors

Lentin Joseph is an author and robotics entrepreneur from India. He runs a robotics software company called Qbotics Labs in India. He has 7 years of experience in the robotics domain especially in Robot Operating System, Open-CV, and PCL.

He has authored three books in ROS, namely, *Learning Robotics using Python*, *Mastering ROS for Robotics Programming*, and *ROS Robotics Projects*.

He is currently pursuing his masters in Robotics from India and is also doing research in Robotics Institute, CMU, USA.

Jonathan Cacace was born in Naples, Italy, on December 13, 1987. He received his Master's degree in computer science, and a Ph.D. degree in Information and Automation Engineering, from the University of Naples Federico II.
Currently, he is a postdoc at the PRISMA Lab of the University of Naples Federico II. He is involved in different research projects focused on industrial and service robotics in which he has developed several ROS-based applications integrating robot perception and control.

I would like to express my thanks and gratitude to my friends, my parents and all the people I met during my life who contributed to enrich my life and my knowledge.

About the reviewer

Ruixiang Du is a PhD candidate in Mechanical Engineering at Worcester Polytechnic Institute (WPI). He currently works in the Autonomy, Control and Estimation Laboratory with a research focus on the motion planning and control of autonomous mobile robots. He received a bachelor's degree in Automation from North China Electric Power University in 2011 and a master's degree in Robotics Engineering from WPI in 2013.

Ruixiang has general interests in robotics and in real-time and embedded systems. He has worked on various robotic projects with robot platforms ranging from medical robots, unmanned aerial/ground vehicles, to humanoid robots. He was a member of Team WPI-CMU for the DARPA Robotics Challenge.

Packt is searching for authors like you

If you're interested in becoming an author for Packt, please visit `authors.packtpub.com` and apply today. We have worked with thousands of developers and tech professionals, just like you, to help them share their insight with the global tech community. You can make a general application, apply for a specific hot topic that we are recruiting an author for, or submit your own idea.

Table of Contents

Preface

Robot Operating System is robotic middleware that helps developers to program robotic applications, and is widely used in robotics companies, research centers, and universities. *Mastering ROS for Robotics Programming, Second Edition* presents advanced concepts of the ROS framework and is particularly suitable for users who are already familiar with the basic concepts of ROS. However, a brief introduction of the basic ROS concepts is proposed in the first chapter in order to help new developers start with the examples in the book. Readers will be guided through the creation, the modeling model and design, new robots, as well as simulating and interfacing them with the ROS framework. They will use advanced simulation software to use ROS tools that allow robot navigation, manipulation, and sensor elaboration. Finally, the reader will learn how to handle important concepts such as ROS low-level controllers, nodelets, and plugins. The readers can work with almost all of the examples of the book using only a standard computer without any special hardware requirements. However, additional hardware components will be used in some chapters of the book to discuss how to use ROS with external sensors, actuators, and I/O boards.

The book is organized as follows. After an introduction to the basic concepts of ROS, how to model and simulate a robot is discussed. Gazebo and the V-REP software simulator will be used to control and interact with the modeled robot. These simulators will be used to connect the robots with MoveIt! and navigation ROS package. ROS plugins, controllers, and nodelets are then discussed. Finally, the book discusses how to connect Matlab and Simulink software with ROS.

Who this book is for

This book is meant to be used by passionate robotics developers or researchers who want to fully exploit the features of ROS. The book is also good for all the users who already are familiar with typical robotics applications or who want to start learning how to develop the world of ROS in an advanced manner, learning how to model, build, and control their own robots. A basic knowledge of GNU/Linux and C++ programming is strongly recommended if you want to easily comprehend the contents of the book.

What this book covers

Chapter 1, *Introduction to ROS*, gives you an understanding of the core underlying concepts of ROS.

Chapter 2, *Getting Started with ROS Programming*, explains how to work with ROS packages.

Chapter 3, *Working with 3D Robot Modeling in ROS*, discusses the design of two robots; one is a seven Degree of Freedom (DOF) manipulator and the other is a differential drive robot.

Chapter 4, *Simulating Robots Using ROS and Gazebo*, discusses the simulation of a *seven DOF arm*, differential wheeled robots, and ROS controllers that help control robot joints in Gazebo.

Chapter 5, *Simulating Robots Using ROS and V-REP*, introduces using the V-REP simulator and vrep_plugin to connect ROS with the simulation scene. Then the control of a seven DOF arm and a differential mobile robot is discussed.

Chapter 6, *Using the ROS MoveIt! and Navigation Stack*, interfaces out-of-the-box functionalities such as robot manipulation and autonomous navigation using ROS MoveIt! and Navigation stack.

Chapter 7, *Working with Pluginlib, Nodelets, and Gazebo Plugins*, shows some of the advanced concepts in ROS, such as ROS pluginlib, nodelets, and Gazebo plugins. We will discuss the functionalities and application of each concept and can practice one example to demonstrate its working.

Chapter 8, *Writing ROS Controllers and Visualization Plugins*, shows how to write a basic ROS controller for PR2 robots and robots similar to PR2. After creating the controller, we will run the controller using the PR2 simulation in Gazebo. We will also see how to create plugin for RViz.

Chapter 9, *Interfacing I/O Boards, Sensor, and Actuators to ROS*, discusses interfacing some hardware components, such as sensors and actuators, with ROS. We will see the interfacing of sensors using I/O boards, such as Arduino, Raspberry Pi, and Odroid-XU4, with ROS.

Chapter 10, *Programming Vision Sensors Using ROS, Open-CV and PCL*, discusses how to interface various vision sensors with ROS and program it using libraries such as Open Source Computer Vision (OpenCV) and Point Cloud Library (PCL), and working with *AR Markers*.

Chapter 11, *Building and Interfacing Differential Drive Mobile Robot Hardware in ROS*, helps you to build autonomous mobile robot hardware with differential drive configuration and interface it with ROS. This chapter aims to give you an idea of building a custom mobile robot and interfacing it with ROS.

Chapter 12, *Exploring the Advanced Capabilities of ROS-MoveIt!*, discusses the capabilities of MoveIt! such as collision avoidance, perception using 3D sensors, grasping, picking, and placing. After that, we can see how to interface of a robotic manipulator hardware with MoveIt!

Chapter 13, *Using ROS in Matlab and Simulink*, discusses how to connect Matlab and Simulink software with ROS.

Chapter 14, *ROS for Industrial Robots*, helps you understand and install ROS-Industrial packages in ROS. We can see how to develop an MoveIt! IKFast plugin for an industrial robot.

Chapter 15, *Troubleshooting and Best Practices in ROS*, discusses how to set the ROS development environment in Eclipse IDE, best practices in ROS, and troubleshooting tips in ROS.

To get the most out of this book

In order to run the examples in this book, you need a standard PC running Linux OS. Ubuntu 16.04 is the suggested Linux distribution, but Debian 8 is supported as well. The suggested PC configuration requires at least 4 GB of RAM and a modern processor (Intel i-family) to execute Gazebo simulations and image processing algorithms.

Readers can even work in a virtual environment setup installing Linux OS on a virtual machine, using Virtual box or VMware software hosted on a Windows system. The disadvantage of this choice is that more computational power is needed to work with the examples and the reader could face issues when interfacing ROS with real hardware.

The software needed to follow the book is ROS and Kinetic Kame. Additional software required is V-REP simulator, Git, Matlab, and Simulink.

Finally, some chapters help readers to interface ROS with commercial hardware such as I/O boards (Arduino, Odroid, and Raspberry Pi computers), vison sensors (Kinect/Asus Xition Pro), and actuators. These are special hardware components that must be bought to run some examples of the book but are not strictly required to learn ROS.

Download the example code files

You can download the example code files for this book from your account at `www.packtpub.com`. If you purchased this book elsewhere, you can visit `www.packtpub.com/support` and register to have the files emailed directly to you.

You can download the code files by following these steps:

1. Log in or register at `www.packtpub.com`.
2. Select the **SUPPORT** tab.
3. Click on **Code Downloads & Errata**.
4. Enter the name of the book in the **Search** box and follow the onscreen instructions.

Once the file is downloaded, please make sure that you unzip or extract the folder using the latest version of:

- WinRAR/7-Zip for Windows
- Zipeg/iZip/UnRarX for Mac
- 7-Zip/PeaZip for Linux

The code bundle for the book is also hosted on GitHub at `https://github.com/PacktPublishing/Mastering-ROS-for-Robotics-Programming-Second-Edition`. In case there's an update to the code, it will be updated on the existing GitHub repository.

We also have other code bundles from our rich catalog of books and videos available at `https://github.com/PacktPublishing/`. Check them out!

Download the color images

We also provide a PDF file that has color images of the screenshots/diagrams used in this book. You can download it here: `http://www.packtpub.com/sites/default/files/downloads/MasteringROSforRoboticsProgrammingSecondEdition_ColorImages.pdf`.

Conventions used

There are a number of text conventions used throughout this book.

`CodeInText`: Indicates code words in text, database table names, folder names, filenames, file extensions, pathnames, dummy URLs, user input, and Twitter handles. Here is an example: "Mount the downloaded `WebStorm-10*.dmg` disk image file as another disk in your system."

A block of code is set as follows:

```
<launch>
 <group ns="/">
  <param name="rosversion" command="rosversion roslaunch" />
  <param name="rosdistro" command="rosversion -d" />
  <node pkg="rosout" type="rosout" name="rosout" respawn="true"/>
 </group>
</launch>
```

Any command-line input or output is written as follows:

```
$ rostopic list
$ cd
```

Bold: Indicates a new term, an important word, or words that you see onscreen. For example, words in menus or dialog boxes appear in the text like this. Here is an example: "On the main toolbar, select **File | Open Workspace**, and choose the directory representing the ROS workspace."

Warnings or important notes appear like this.

Tips and tricks appear like this.

Get in touch

Feedback from our readers is always welcome.

General feedback: Email `feedback@packtpub.com` and mention the book title in the subject of your message. If you have questions about any aspect of this book, please email us at `questions@packtpub.com`.

Errata: Although we have taken every care to ensure the accuracy of our content, mistakes do happen. If you have found a mistake in this book, we would be grateful if you would report this to us. Please visit `www.packtpub.com/submit-errata`, selecting your book, clicking on the Errata Submission Form link, and entering the details.

Piracy: If you come across any illegal copies of our works in any form on the Internet, we would be grateful if you would provide us with the location address or website name. Please contact us at `copyright@packtpub.com` with a link to the material.

If you are interested in becoming an author: If there is a topic that you have expertise in and you are interested in either writing or contributing to a book, please visit `authors.packtpub.com`.

Reviews

Please leave a review. Once you have read and used this book, why not leave a review on the site that you purchased it from? Potential readers can then see and use your unbiased opinion to make purchase decisions, we at Packt can understand what you think about our products, and our authors can see your feedback on their book. Thank you!

For more information about Packt, please visit `packtpub.com`.

1
Introduction to ROS

The first two chapters of this book introduce basic ROS concepts and its package management system in order to refresh your memory about concepts you should already know. In this first chapter, we will go through ROS concepts such as the ROS Master, the ROS nodes, the ROS parameter server, ROS messages and services discussing what we need to install ROS and how to get started with the ROS master.

In this chapter, we will cover the following topics:

- Why should we learn ROS?
- Why should we prefer or should not prefer ROS for robots?
- Getting started with the ROS filesystem level and its computation graph level.
- Understanding ROS framework elements.
- Getting started with the ROS master.

Why should we learn ROS?

Robot Operating System (ROS) is a flexible framework, providing various tools and libraries to write robotic software. It offers several powerful features to help developers in such tasks as message passing, distributing computing, code reusing, and implementation of state-of-the-art algorithms for robotic applications.

The ROS project was started in 2007, with the name *Switchyard*, by Morgan Quigley (`http://wiki.osrfoundation.org/morgan`), as part of the Stanford STAIR robot project. The main development of ROS happened at Willow Garage (`https://www.willowgarage.com/`).

The ROS community is growing very fast, and there are many users and developers worldwide. Most of the high-end robotics companies are now porting their software to ROS. This trend is also visible in industrial robotics, in which companies are switching from proprietary robotic applications to ROS.

The ROS industrial movement has gained momentum in the past few years, owing to the large amount of research done in that field. ROS Industrial can extend the advanced capabilities of ROS to manufacturing. The increasing applications of ROS can generate a lot of job opportunities in this field. So, after some years, a knowledge of ROS will be an essential requirement for a robotics engineer.

Why we prefer ROS for robots

Imagine that we are going to build an autonomous mobile robot. Here are some of the reasons why people choose ROS over other robotic platforms, such as Player, YARP, Orocos, MRPT, and so on:

- **High-end capabilities**: ROS comes with ready-to-use capabilities. For example, **Simultaneous Localization and Mapping (SLAM)** and **Adaptive Monte Carlo Localization (AMCL)** packages in ROS can be used for performing autonomous navigation in mobile robots, and the MoveIt package can be used for motion planning of robot manipulators. These capabilities can directly be used in our robot software without any hassle. These capabilities are its best form of implementation, so writing new code for existing capabilities is like reinventing the wheel. Also, these capabilities are highly configurable; we can fine-tune each capability using various parameters.
- **Tons of tools**: ROS is packed with tons of tools for debugging, visualizing, and performing a simulation. The tools, such as rqt_gui, RViz, and Gazebo, are some of the strong open source tools for debugging, visualization, and simulation. A software framework that has these many tools is very rare.
- **Support for high-end sensors and actuators**: ROS is packed with device drivers and interface packages of various sensors and actuators in robotics. The high-end sensors include Velodyne-LIDAR, Laser scanners, Kinect, and so on, and actuators such as DYNAMIXEL servos. We can interface these components to ROS without any hassle.

- **Inter-platform operability**: The ROS message-passing middleware allows communication between different nodes. These nodes can be programmed in any language that has ROS client libraries. We can write high-performance nodes in C++ or C and other nodes in Python or Java. This kind of flexibility is not available in other frameworks.

- **Modularity**: One of the issues that can occur in most of the standalone robotic applications is that if any of the threads of main code crash, the entire robot application can stop. In ROS, the situation is different; we are writing different nodes for each process, and if one node crashes, the system can still work. Also, ROS provides robust methods to resume operations even if any sensors or motors are dead.

- **Concurrent resource handling**: Handling a hardware resource via more than two processes is always a headache. Imagine we want to process an image from a camera for face detection and motion detection; we can either write the code as a single entity that can do both, or we can write a single-threaded code for concurrency. If we want to add more than two features in threads, the application behavior will get complex and will be difficult to debug. But in ROS, we can access the devices using ROS topics from the ROS drivers. Any number of ROS nodes can subscribe to the image message from the ROS camera driver, and each node can perform different functionalities. It can reduce the complexity in computation and also increase the debug ability of the entire system.

- **Active community**: When we choose a library or software framework, especially from an open source community, one of the main factors that needs to be checked before using it is its software support and developer community. There is no guarantee of support from an open source tool. Some tools provide good support and some tools don't. In ROS, the support community is active. There is a web portal to handle the support queries from users too (`http://answers.ros.org`). It seems that the ROS community has a steady growth in developers worldwide.

There are many reasons to choose ROS other than the preceding points.

Next, we can check the various reasons why people don't use ROS. Here are some of the existing reasons.

Why some do not prefer ROS for robots

Here are some of the reasons why some people do not prefer ROS for their robotic projects:

- **Difficulty in learning**: ROS can be difficult to learn. It has a steep learning curve and developers should become familiar with many new concepts to get benefits from the ROS framework.

- **Difficulties in starting with simulation**: The main simulator in ROS is Gazebo. Even though Gazebo works well, to get started with Gazebo is not an easy task. The simulator has no inbuilt features to program. Complete simulation is done only through coding in ROS. When we compare Gazebo with other simulators, such as V-REP and Webots, they have inbuilt functionalities to prototype and program the robot. They also have a rich GUI toolset support a wide variety of robots and have ROS interfaces too. These tools are proprietary but can deliver a decent job. The toughness of learning simulation using Gazebo and ROS is a reason for not using it in projects.

- **Difficulties in robot modeling**: The robot modeling in ROS is performed using URDF, which is an XML-based robot description. In short, we need to write the robot model as a description using URDF tags. In V-REP, we can directly build the 3D robot model in the GUI itself, or we can import the mesh. In ROS, we should write the robot model definitions using URDF tags. There is a SolidWorks plugin to convert a 3D model from SolidWorks to URDF, but if we use other 3D CAD tools, there are no options at all. Learning to model a robot in ROS will take a lot of time, and building using URDF tags is also time-consuming compared to other simulators.

- **Potential limitations**: Current ROS versions have some limitations. For example, there is a lack of a native real-time application development support or the complexity to implement robust multi-robot distributed applications.

- **ROS in commercial robot products**: When we deploy ROS on a commercial product, a lot of things need to be taken care of. One thing is the code quality. ROS code follows a standard coding style and keeps best practices for maintaining the code too. We have to check whether it satisfies the quality level required for our product. We might have to do additional work to improve the quality of the code. Most of the code in ROS is contributed by researchers from universities, so if we are not satisfied with the ROS code quality, it is better to write our own code, which is specific to the robot and only use the ROS core functionalities if required.

We now know where we have to use ROS and where we do not. If ROS is really required for your robot, let's start discussing ROS in more detail. First, we can see the underlying core concepts of ROS. There are mainly three levels in ROS: the filesystem level, computation graph level, and community level. We will briefly have a look at each level.

Understanding the ROS filesystem level

ROS is more than a development framework. We can refer to ROS as a meta-operating system, since it offers not only tools and libraries but even OS-like functions, such as hardware abstraction, package management, and a developer toolchain. Like a real operating system, ROS files are organized on the hard disk in a particular manner, as depicted in the following figure:

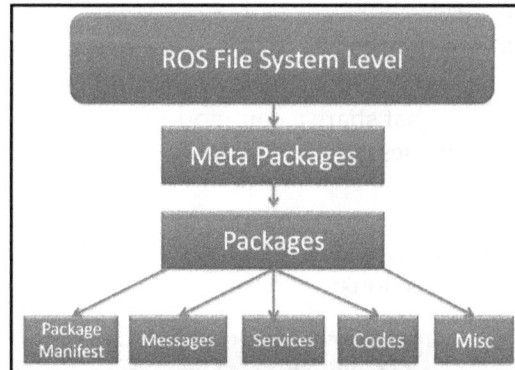

Figure 1: ROS filesystem level

Here are the explanations for each block in the filesystem:

- **Packages**: The ROS packages are the most basic unit of the ROS software. They contain one or more ROS programs (nodes), libraries, configuration files, and so on, which are organized together as a single unit. Packages are the atomic build item and release item in the ROS software.
- **Package manifest**: The package manifest file is inside a package that contains information about the package, author, license, dependencies, compilation flags, and so on. The `package.xml` file inside the ROS package is the manifest file of that package.

- **Metapackages**: The term metapackage refers to one or more related packages which can be loosely grouped together. In principle, metapackages are virtual packages that don't contain any source code or typical files usually found in packages.
- **Metapackages manifest**: The metapackage manifest is similar to the package manifest, the difference being that it might include packages inside it as runtime dependencies and declare an `export` tag.
- **Messages** (`.msg`): The ROS messages are a type of information that is sent from one ROS process to the other. We can define a custom message inside the `msg` folder inside a package (`my_package/msg/MyMessageType.msg`). The extension of the message file is `.msg`.
- **Services** (`.srv`): The ROS service is a kind of request/reply interaction between processes. The reply and request data types can be defined inside the `srv` folder inside the package (`my_package/srv/MyServiceType.srv`).
- **Repositories**: Most of the ROS packages are maintained using a **Version Control System** (**VCS**), such as Git, Subversion (svn), Mercurial (hg), and so on. The collection of packages that share a common VCS can be called repositories. The package in the repositories can be released using a catkin release automation tool called `bloom`.

The following screenshot gives you an idea of the files and folders of a package that we are going to create in the upcoming sections:

```
ros_pkg
├── action
│   └── demo.action
├── CMakeLists.txt
├── include
│   └── ros_pkg
│       └── demo.h
├── msg
│   └── message.msg
├── src
│   └── demo.cpp
└── srv
    └── service.srv
```

Figure 2: List of files inside the exercise package

ROS packages

A typical structure of an ROS package is shown here:

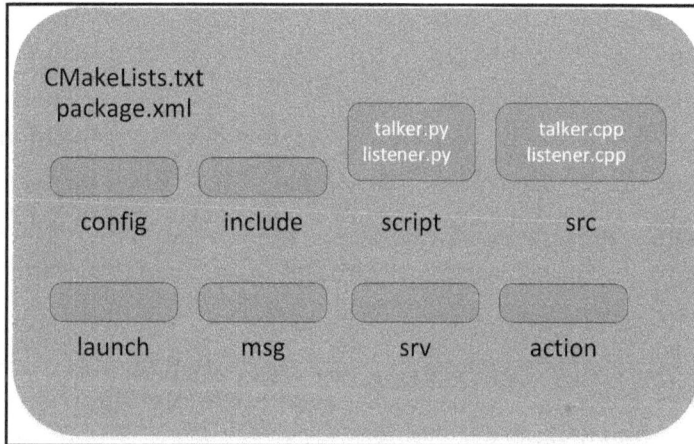

Figure 3: Structure of a typical C++ ROS package

We can discuss the use of each folder as follows:

- `config`: All configuration files that are used in this ROS package are kept in this folder. This folder is created by the user and it is a common practice to name the folder `config` to keep the configuration files in it.
- `include/package_name`: This folder consists of headers and libraries that we need to use inside the package.
- `script`: This folder keeps executable Python scripts. In the block diagram, we can see two example scripts.
- `src`: This folder stores the C++ source codes.
- `launch`: This folder keeps the launch files that are used to launch one or more ROS nodes.
- `msg`: This folder contains custom message definitions.
- `srv`: This folder contains the services definitions.
- `action`: This folder contains the action files. We will see more about these kind of files in the next chapter.
- `package.xml`: This is the package manifest file of this package.
- `CMakeLists.txt`: This files contains the directives to compile the package.

We need to know some commands to create, modify, and work with the ROS packages. Here are some of the commands used to work with ROS packages:

- `catkin_create_pkg`: This command is used to create a new package
- `rospack`: This command is used to get information about the package in the filesystem
- `catkin_make`: This command is used to build the packages in the workspace
- `rosdep`: This command will install the system dependencies required for this package

To work with packages, ROS provides a bash-like command called `rosbash` (`http://wiki.ros.org/rosbash`), which can be used to navigate and manipulate the ROS package. Here are some of the `rosbash` commands:

- `roscd`: This command is used to change the current directory using a package name, stack name, or a special location. If we give the argument a package name, it will switch to that package folder.
- `roscp`: This command is used to copy a file from a package.
- `rosed`: This command is used to edit a file using the *vim* editor.
- `rosrun`: This command is used to run an executable inside a package.

The definition of `package.xml` of a typical package is shown in the following screenshot:

```xml
<?xml version="1.0"?>
<package>
  <name>hello_world</name>
  <version>0.0.1</version>
  <description>The hello_world package</description>
  <maintainer email="jonathan.cacace@gmail.com">Jonathan Cacace</maintainer>

  <buildtool_depend>catkin</buildtool_depend>
  <build_depend>roscpp</build_depend>
  <build_depend>rospy</build_depend>
  <build_depend>std_msgs</build_depend>

  <run_depend>roscpp</run_depend>
  <run_depend>rospy</run_depend>
  <run_depend>std_msgs</run_depend>

  <export>
  </export>
</package>
```

Figure 4: Structure of `package.xml`

The `package.xml` file consists of the package name, version of the package, the package description, author details, package build dependencies, and runtime dependencies. The `<build_depend></build_depend>` tag includes the packages that are necessary to build the source code of the package. The packages inside the `<run_depend></run_depend>` tags are necessary during runtime of the package node.

ROS metapackages

Metapackages are specialized packages in ROS that only contain one file, that is, a `package.xml` file. They don't contain folders and files like a normal package.

Metapackages simply group a set of multiple packages as a single logical package. In the `package.xml` file, the metapackage contains an `export` tag, as shown here:

```
<export>
  <metapackage/>
</export>
```

Also, in metapackages, there are no `<buildtool_depend>` dependencies for `catkin`; there are only `<run_depend>` dependencies, which are the packages grouped in the metapackage.

The ROS navigation stack is a good example of metapackages. If ROS and its navigation package are installed, we can try the following command, by switching to the navigation metapackage folder:

```
$ roscd navigation
```

Open `package.xml` using your favorite text editor (`gedit` in the following case):

```
$ gedit package.xml
```

This is a lengthy file; here is a stripped-down version of it:

```xml
<?xml version="1.0"?>
<package>
    <name>navigation</name>
    <version>1.14.0</version>
    <description>
        A 2D navigation stack that takes in information from odometry, sensor
        streams, and a goal pose and outputs safe velocity commands that are sent
        to a mobile base.
    </description>
    ...
    <url>http://wiki.ros.org/navigation</url>
    ...
    <buildtool_depend>catkin</buildtool_depend>

    <run_depend>amcl</run_depend>
    ...
    <export>
        <metapackage/>
    </export>
</package>
```

Figure 5: Structure of meta-package `package.xml`

ROS messages

The ROS nodes can write or read data that has a different type. The types of data are described using a simplified message description language, also called ROS messages. These datatype descriptions can be used to generate source code for the appropriate message type in different target languages.

The data type description of ROS messages is stored in `.msg` files in the `msg` subdirectory of a ROS package. Even though the ROS framework provides a large set of robotic-specific messages already implemented, developers can define their own message type inside their nodes.

The message definition can consist of two types: `fields` and `constants`. The field is split into field types and field names. The field type is the data type of the transmitting message and field name is the name of it. The constants define a constant value in the `message` file.

Here is an example of message definitions:

```
int32 number
string name
float32 speed
```

Here, the first part is the field type and the second is the field name. The field type is the data type and the field name can be used to access the value from the message. For example, we can use `msg.number` for accessing the value of the number from the message.

Here is a table showing some of the built-in field types that we can use in our message:

Primitive type	Serialization	C++	Python
bool(1)	Unsigned 8-bit int	uint8_t(2)	bool
int8	Signed 8-bit int	int8_t	int
uint8	Unsigned 8-bit int	uint8_t	int (3)
int16	Signed 16-bit int	int16_t	int
uint16	Unsigned 16-bit int	uint16_t	int
int32	Signed 32-bit int	int32_t	int
uint32	Unsigned 32-bit int	uint32_t	int
int64	Signed 64-bit int	int64_t	long
uint64	Unsigned 64-bit int	uint64_t	long
float32	32-bit IEEE float	float	float
float64	64-bit IEEE float	double	float
string	ascii string(4)	std::string	string
time	secs/nsecs unsigned 32-bit ints	ros::Time	rospy.Time
duration	secs/nsecs signed 32-bit ints	ros::Duration	rospy.Duration

Other kinds of messages are designed to cover a specific application necessity, such as exchanging common geometrical (geometry_msgs) or sensor (sensor_msgs) information. A special type of ROS message is called a message header. Headers can carry information, such as time, frame of reference or frame_id, and sequence number. Using headers, we will get numbered messages and more clarity in who is sending the current message. The header information is mainly used to send data such as robot joint transforms (TF). Here is an example of the message header:

```
uint32 seq
time stamp
string frame_id
```

The rosmsg command tool can be used to inspect the message header and the field types. The following command helps to view the message header of a particular message:

```
$ rosmsg show std_msgs/Header
```

This will give you an output like the preceding example message header. We will look at the rosmsg command and how to work with custom message definitions further in the upcoming sections.

The ROS services

The ROS services are a type request/response communication between ROS nodes. One node will send a request and wait until it gets a response from the other. The request/response communication is also using the ROS message description.

Similar to the message definitions using the ".msg" file, we have to define the service definition in another file called ".srv", which has to be kept inside the srv subdirectory of the package. Similar to the message definition, a service description language is used to define the ROS service types.

An example service description format is as follows:

```
#Request message type
string str
---
#Response message type
string str
```

The first section is the message type of the request that is separated by --- and in the next section is the message type of the response. In these examples, both Request and Response are strings.

In the upcoming sections, we will look at how to work with ROS services.

Understanding the ROS computation graph level

The computation in ROS is done using a network of a process called ROS nodes. This computation network can be called the computation graph. The main concepts in the computation graph are ROS **Nodes**, **Master**, **Parameter server**, **Messages**, **Topics**, **Services**, and **Bags**. Each concept in the graph is contributed to this graph in different ways.

The ROS communication-related packages including core client libraries, such as `roscpp` and `rospython` , and the implementation of concepts, such as topics, nodes, parameters, and services are included in a stack called `ros_comm` (http://wiki.ros.org/ros_comm).

This stack also consists of tools such as `rostopic`, `rosparam`, `rosservice`, and `rosnode` to introspect the preceding concepts.

The `ros_comm` stack contains the ROS communication middleware packages and these packages are collectively called the **ROS Graph layer**:

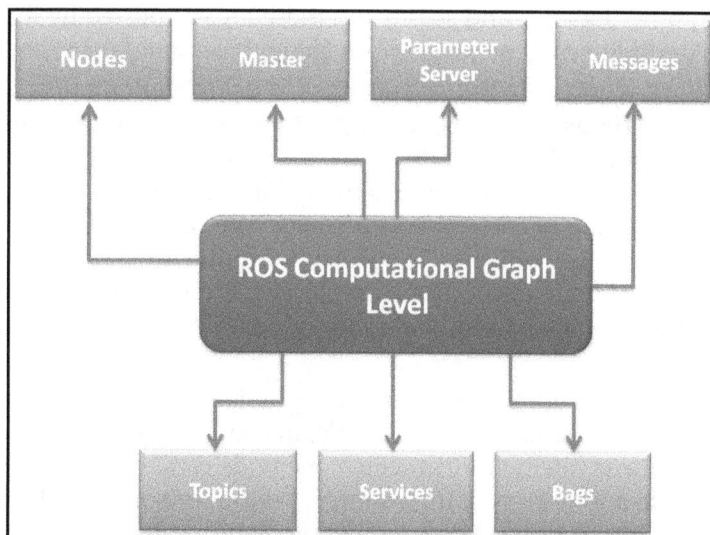

Figure 6: Structure of the ROS Graph layer

The following are abstracts of each graph's concepts:

- **Nodes**: Nodes are the process that perform computation. Each ROS node is written using ROS client libraries. Using client library APIs, we can implement different ROS functionalities, such as the communication methods between nodes, which is particularly useful when different nodes of our robot must exchange information between them. Using the ROS communication methods, they can communicate with each other and exchange data. One of the aims of ROS nodes is to build simple processes rather than a large process with all the functionality. Being a simple structure, ROS nodes are easy to debug.

- **Master**: The ROS Master provides the name registration and lookup to the rest of the nodes. Nodes will not be able to find each other, exchange messages, or invoke services without a ROS Master. In a distributed system, we should run the master on one computer, and other remote nodes can find each other by communicating with this master.

- **Parameter server**: The parameter server allows you to keep the data to be stored in a central location. All nodes can access and modify these values. The parameter server is a part of the ROS Master.

- **Messages**: Nodes communicate with each other using messages. Messages are simply a data structure containing the typed field, which can hold a set of data, and that can be sent to another node. There are standard primitive types (integer, floating point, Boolean, and so on) and these are supported by ROS messages. We can also build our own message types using these standard types.

- **Topics**: Each message in ROS is transported using named buses called topics. When a node sends a message through a topic, then we can say the node is publishing a topic. When a node receives a message through a topic, then we can say that the node is subscribing to a topic. The publishing node and subscribing node are not aware of each other's existence. We can even subscribe a topic that might not have any publisher. In short, the production of information and consumption of it are decoupled. Each topic has a unique name, and any node can access this topic and send data through it as long as they have the right message type.

- **Services**: In some robot applications, the publish/subscribe communication model may not be suitable. For example, in some cases, we need a kind of request/response interaction, in which one node can ask for the execution of a fast procedure to another node; for example, asking for some quick calculation. The ROS service interaction is like a remote procedure call.

- **Logging**: ROS provides a logging system for storing data, such as sensor data, which can be difficult to collect but is necessary for developing and testing robot algorithms: the bagfiles. Bagfiles are very useful features when we work with complex robot mechanisms.

The following graph shows how the nodes communicate with each other using topics. The topics are mentioned in a rectangle and the nodes are represented in ellipses. The messages and parameters are not included in this graph. These kinds of graphs can be generated using a tool called `rqt_graph` (`http://wiki.ros.org/rqt_graph`):

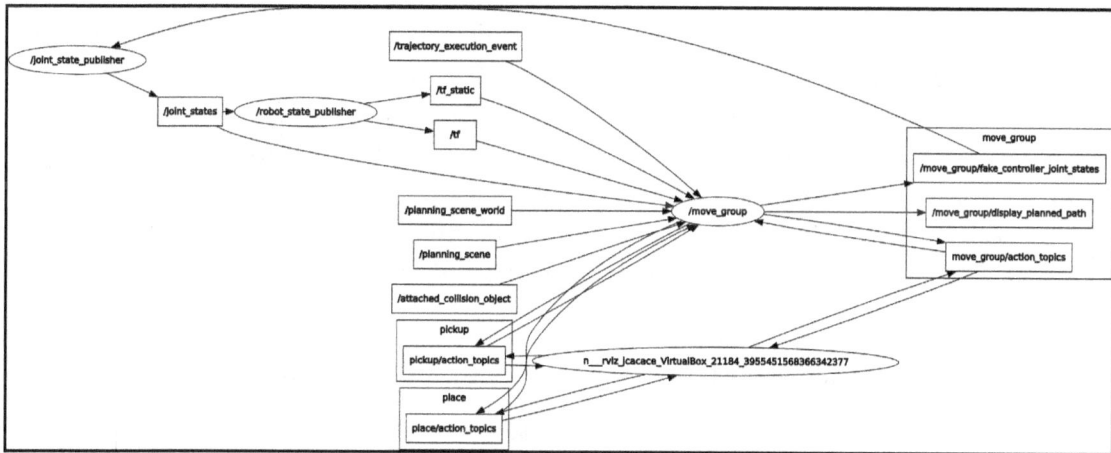

Figure 7: Graph of communication between nodes using topics

ROS nodes

ROS nodes are a process that perform computation using ROS client libraries such as `roscpp` and `rospy`. One node can communicate with other nodes using ROS Topics, Services, and Parameters.

A robot might contain many nodes; for example, one node processes camera images, one node handles serial data from the robot, one node can be used to compute odometry, and so on.

Using nodes can make the system fault tolerant. Even if a node crashes, an entire robot system can still work. Nodes also reduce the complexity and increase debug-ability compared to monolithic code because each node is handling only a single function.

All running nodes should have a name assigned to identify them from the rest of the system. For example, `/camera_node` could be a name of a node that is broadcasting camera images.

There is a `rosbash` tool to introspect ROS nodes. The `rosnode` command can be used to get information about a ROS node. Here are the usages of `rosnode`:

- `$ rosnode info [node_name]`: This will print the information about the node
- `$ rosnode kill [node_name]`: This will kill a running node
- `$ rosnode list`: This will list the running nodes
- `$ rosnode machine [machine_name]`: This will list the nodes running on a particular machine or a list of machines
- `$ rosnode ping`: This will check the connectivity of a node
- `$ rosnode cleanup`: This will purge the registration of unreachable nodes

We will look at example nodes using the `roscpp` client and will discuss the working of ROS nodes that use functionalities such ROS Topics, Service, Messages, and actionlib.

ROS messages

ROS nodes communicate with each other by publishing messages to a topic. As we discussed earlier, messages are a simple data structure containing field types. The ROS message supports standard primitive datatypes and arrays of primitive types.

Nodes can also exchange information using service calls. Services are also messages. The service message definitions are defined inside the `srv` file.

We can access the message definition using the following method. For example, to access `std_msgs/msg/String.msg`, we can use `std_msgs/String`. If we are using the `roscpp` client, we have to include `std_msgs/String.h` for the string message definition.

In addition to message data type, ROS uses an MD5 checksum comparison to confirm whether the publisher and subscriber exchange the same message data types.

ROS has inbuilt tools called `rosmsg` to get information about ROS messages. Here are some parameters used along with `rosmsg`:

- `$ rosmsg show [message]`: This shows the message description
- `$ rosmsg list`: This lists all messages
- `$ rosmsg md5 [message]`: This displays `md5sum` of a message
- `$ rosmsg package [package_name]`: This lists messages in a package
- `$ rosmsg packages [package_1] [package_2]`: This lists packages that contain messages

ROS topics

ROS topics are named buses in which ROS nodes exchange messages. Topics can anonymously publish and subscribe, which means that the production of messages is decoupled from the consumption. The ROS nodes are not interested in knowing which node is publishing the topic or subscribing topics; they only look for the topic name and whether the message types of the publisher and subscriber are matching.

The communication using topics are unidirectional. If we want to implement a request/response, such as communication, we have to switch to ROS services.

The ROS nodes communicate with topics using TCP/IP-based transport known as **TCPROS**. This method is the default transport method used in ROS. Another type of communication is **UDPROS**, which has low-latency, loose transport, and is only suited for teleoperations.

The ROS topic tool can be used to get information about ROS topics. Here is the syntax of this command:

- `$ rostopic bw /topic`: This command will display the bandwidth used by the given topic.
- `$ rostopic echo /topic`: This command will print the content of the given topic in a human readable format. Users can use the "-p" option to print data in a csv format.
- `$ rostopic find /message_type`: This command will find topics using the given message type.
- `$ rostopic hz /topic`: This command will display the publishing rate of the given topic.

- `$ rostopic info /topic`: This command will print information about an active topic.
- `$ rostopic list`: This command will list all active topics in the ROS system.
- `$ rostopic pub /topic message_type args`: This command can be used to publish a value to a topic with a message type.
- `$ rostopic type /topic`: This will display the message type of the given topic.

ROS services

When we need a request/response kind of communication in ROS, we have to use the ROS services. ROS topics can't implement natively such kind of communication because it is unidirectional. The ROS services are mainly used in a distributed system.

The ROS services are defined using a pair of messages. We have to define a request datatype and a response datatype in a `srv` file. The `srv` files are kept in a `srv` folder inside a package.

In ROS services, one node acts as a ROS server in which the service client can request the service from the server. If the server completes the service routine, it will send the results to the service client. For example, consider a node able to provide the sum of two numbers received in input, implementing this functionality through a ROS service. The other nodes of our system might request the sum of two numbers via this service. Differently, topics are used to stream continuous data flow.

The ROS service definition can be accessed by the following method; for example, if `my_package/srv/Image.srv` can be accessed by `my_package/Image`.

In ROS services also, there is an MD5 `checksum` that checks in the nodes. If the sum is equal, then only the server responds to the client.

There are two ROS tools to get information about the ROS service. The first tool is `rossrv`, which is similar to `rosmsg`, and is used to get information about service types. The next command is `rosservice`, which is used to list and query about the running ROS services.

The following explain how to use the `rosservice` tool to get information about the running services:

- `$ rosservice call /service args`: This tool will call the service using the given arguments
- `$ rosservice find service_type`: This command will find services in the given service type
- `$ rosservice info /services`: This will print information about the given service
- `$ rosservice list`: This command will list the active services running on the system
- `$ rosservice type /service`: This command will print the service type of a given service
- `$ rosservice uri /service`: This tool will print the service ROSRPC URI

ROS bags

A bag file in ROS is for storing ROS message data from topics and services. The `.bag` extension is used to represent a bag file.

Bag files are created using the `rosbag` command, which will subscribe one or more topics and store the message's data in a file as it's received. This file can play the same topics as they are recorded from or it can remap the existing topics too.

The main application of `rosbag` is data logging. The robot data can be logged and can visualize and process offline.

The `rosbag` command is used to work with `rosbag` files. Here are the commands to record and playback a bag file:

- `$ rosbag record [topic_1] [topic_2] -o [bag_name]`: This command will record the given topics into a bag file that is given in the command. We can also record all topics using the `-a` argument.
- `$ rosbag play [bag_name]`: This will playback the existing bag file.

Further details about this command can be found at:
`http://wiki.ros.org/rosbag/Commandline`

There is a GUI tool to handle the record and playback of bag files called `rqt_bag`. To learn more about `rqt_bag`, go to: `http://wiki.ros.org/rqt_bag`.

The ROS Master

The ROS Master is much like a DNS server, associating unique names and IDs to ROS elements active in our system. When any node starts in the ROS system, it will start looking for the ROS Master and register the name of the node in it. So, the ROS Master has the details of all the nodes currently running on the ROS system. When any details of the nodes change, it will generate a callback and update with the latest details. These node details are useful for connecting with each node.

When a node starts publishing a topic, the node will give the details of the topic, such as name and data type, to the ROS Master. The ROS Master will check whether any other nodes are subscribed to the same topic. If any nodes are subscribed to the same topic, the ROS Master will share the node details of the publisher to the subscriber node. After getting the node details, these two nodes will interconnect using the TCPROS protocol, which is based on TCP/IP sockets. After connecting to the two nodes, the ROS Master has no role in controlling them. We might be able to stop either the publisher node or the subscriber node according to our requirement. If we stop any nodes, it will check with the ROS Master once again. This same method is used for the ROS services.

The nodes are written using the ROS client libraries, such as `roscpp` and `rospy`. These clients interact with the ROS Master using **XML Remote Procedure Call** (**XMLRPC**)-based APIs, which act as the backend of the ROS system APIs.

The `ROS_MASTER_URI` environment variable contains the IP and port of the ROS Master. Using this variable, ROS nodes can locate the ROS Master. If this variable is wrong, the communication between nodes will not take place. When we use ROS in a single system, we can use the IP of a localhost or the name `localhost` itself. But in a distributed network, in which computation is on different physical computers, we should define `ROS_MASTER_URI` properly; only then will the remote nodes be able find each other and communicate with each other. We need only one Master in a distributed system, and it should run on a computer in which all other computers can ping it properly to ensure that remote ROS nodes can access the Master.

The following diagram shows an illustration of how the ROS Master interacts with a publishing and subscribing node, with the publisher node publishing a string type topic with a `Hello World` message and the subscriber node subscribing to this topic:

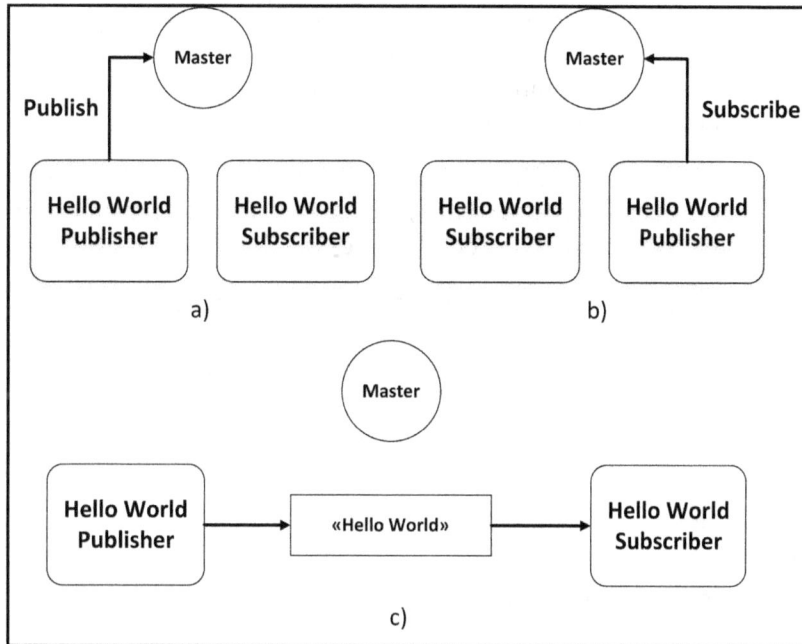

Figure 8: Communication between the ROS Master and Hello World publisher and subscriber

When the publisher node starts publishing the `Hello World` message in a particular topic, the ROS Master gets the details of the topic and details of the node. It will search whether any node is subscribing to the same topic. If there are no nodes subscribing to the same topic at that time, both nodes remain unconnected. If the publisher and subscriber nodes run at the same time, the ROS Master exchanges the details of the publisher to the subscriber and they will connect and can exchange data through ROS messages.

Using the ROS parameter

When programming a robot, we might have to define robot parameters, such as robot controller gains P, I, and D. When the number of parameters increases, we might need to store them as files. In some situations, these parameters have to share between two or more programs too. In this case, ROS provides a parameter server, which is a shared server in which all ROS nodes can access parameters from this server. A node can read, write, modify, and delete parameter values from the parameter server.

We can store these parameters in a file and load them into the server. The server can store a wide variety of data types and can even store dictionaries. The programmer can also set the scope of the parameter, that is, whether it can be accessed by only this node or all the nodes.

The parameter server supports the following XMLRPC datatypes:

- 32-bit integers
- Booleans
- Strings
- Doubles
- ISO8601 dates
- Lists
- Base64-encoded binary data

We can also store dictionaries on the parameter server. If the number of parameters is high, we can use a YAML file to save them. Here is an example of the YAML file parameter definitions:

```
/camera/name : 'nikon'  #string type
/camera/fps : 30      #integer
/camera/exposure : 1.2  #float
/camera/active : true  #boolean
```

The `rosparam` tool is used to get and set the ROS parameter from the command line. The following are the commands to work with ROS parameters:

- `$ rosparam set [parameter_name] [value]`: This command will set a value in the given parameter
- `$ rosparam get [parameter_name]`: This command will retrieve a value from the given parameter

- `$ rosparam load [YAML file]`: The ROS parameters can be saved into a YAML file and it can load to the parameter server using this command
- `$ rosparam dump [YAML file]`: This command will dump the existing ROS parameters to a YAML file
- `$ rosparam delete [parameter_name]`: This command will delete the given parameter
- `$ rosparam list`: This command will list existing parameter names

The parameters can be changed dynamically during the execution of the node that uses these parameters, using the `dyamic_reconfigure` package (`http://wiki.ros.org/dynamic_reconfigure`).

ROS community level

These are ROS resources that enable a new community for ROS to exchange software and knowledge. The various resources in these communities are as follows:

- **Distributions**: Similar to the Linux distribution, ROS distributions are a collection of versioned metapackages that we can install. The ROS distribution enables easier installation and collection of the ROS software. The ROS distributions maintain consistent versions across a set of software.
- **Repositories**: ROS relies on a federated network of code repositories, where different institutions can develop and release their own robot software components.
- **The ROS Wiki**: The ROS community Wiki is the main forum for documenting information about ROS. Anyone can sign up for an account and contribute their own documentation, provide corrections or updates, write tutorials, and more.
- **Bug ticket system**: If we find a bug in the existing software or need to add a new feature, we can use this resource.
- **Mailing lists**: The ROS-users mailing list is the primary communication channel about new updates to ROS, as well as a forum to ask questions about the ROS software.
- **ROS Answers**: This website resource helps to ask questions related to ROS. If we post our doubts on this site, other ROS users can see this and give solutions.
- **Blog**: The ROS blog updates with news, photos, and videos related to the ROS community (`http://www.ros.org/news`).

What are the prerequisites for starting with ROS?

Before getting started with ROS and trying the code in this book, the following prerequisites should be met:

- **Ubuntu 16.04 LTS / Ubuntu 15.10 / Debian 8**: ROS is officially supported by Ubuntu and Debian operating systems. We prefer to stick with the LTS version of Ubuntu, that is, Ubuntu 16.04.
- **ROS kinetic desktop full installation**: Install the full desktop installation of ROS. The version we prefer is ROS kinetic, the latest stable version. The following link gives you the installation instruction of the latest ROS distribution: `http://wiki.ros.org/kinetic/Installation/Ubuntu`. Choose the `ros-kinetic-desktop-full` package from the repository list.

Running the ROS Master and the ROS parameter server

Before running any ROS nodes, we should start the ROS Master and the ROS parameter server. We can start the ROS Master and the ROS parameter server by using a single command called `roscore`, which will start the following programs:

- ROS Master
- ROS parameter server
- `rosout` logging nodes

The `rosout` node will collect log messages from other ROS nodes and store them in a log file, and will also re-broadcast the collected log message to another topic. The `/rosout` topic is published by ROS nodes by using ROS client libraries such as `roscpp` and `rospy`, and this topic is subscribed by the `rosout` node which rebroadcasts the message in another topic called `/rosout_agg`. This topic has an aggregate stream of log messages. The `roscore` command is a prerequisite before running any ROS node. The following screenshot shows the messages printing when we run the `roscore` command in a Terminal.

The following is a command to run `roscore` on a Linux Terminal:

```
$ roscore
```

```
... logging to /home/jcacace/.ros/log/d0cdf7da-6667-11e7-a0a0-0800278bc65c/roslaunch-robot-31486.log
Checking log directory for disk usage. This may take awhile.                                      1
Press Ctrl-C to interrupt
Done checking log file disk usage. Usage is <1GB.

started roslaunch server http://robot:35683/
ros_comm version 1.12.7                                                                            2


SUMMARY
========

PARAMETERS
 * /rosdistro: kinetic
 * /rosversion: 1.12.7                                                                             3

NODES

auto-starting new master
process[master]: started with pid [31498]
ROS_MASTER_URI=http://robot:11311/                                                                 4

setting /run_id to d0cdf7da-6667-11e7-a0a0-0800278bc65c
process[rosout-1]: started with pid [31511]
started core service [/rosout]                                                                     5
```

Figure 9: Terminal messages while running the ГOSCOГe command

The following are explanations of each section when executing `roscore` on the Terminal:

- In **section 1**, we can see a log file is created inside the `~/.ros/log` folder for collecting logs from ROS nodes. This file can be used for debugging purposes.
- In **section 2**, the command starts a ROS launch file called `roscore.xml`. When a launch file starts, it automatically starts the `rosmaster` and the ROS parameter server. The `roslaunch` command is a Python script, which can start `rosmaster` and the ROS parameter server whenever it tries to execute a launch file. This section shows the address of the ROS parameter server within the port.
- In **section 3**, we can see the parameters such as `rosdistro` and `rosversion` displayed on the Terminal. These parameters are displayed when it executes `roscore.xml`. We look at `roscore.xml` and its details further in the next section.
- In **section 4**, we can see the `rosmaster` node is started using `ROS_MASTER_URI`, which we defined earlier as an environment variable.
- In **section 5**, we can see the `rosout` node is started, which will start subscribing the `/rosout` topic and rebroadcasting into `/rosout_agg`.

The following is the content of `roscore.xml`:

```
<launch>
 <group ns="/">
  <param name="rosversion" command="rosversion roslaunch" />
  <param name="rosdistro" command="rosversion -d" />
  <node pkg="rosout" type="rosout" name="rosout" respawn="true"/>
 </group>
</launch>
```

When the `roscore` command is executed, initially, the command checks the command-line argument for a new port number for the `rosmaster`. If it gets the port number, it will start listening to the new port number; otherwise, it will use the default port. This port number and the `roscore.xml` launch file will pass to the `roslaunch` system. The `roslaunch` system is implemented in a Python module; it will parse the port number and launch the `roscore.xml` file.

In the `roscore.xml` file, we can see the ROS parameters and nodes are encapsulated in a group XML tag with a / namespace. The group XML tag indicates that all the nodes inside this tag have the same settings.

The two parameters called `rosversion` and `rosdistro` store the output of the `rosversionroslaunch` and `rosversion-d` commands using the `command` tag, which is a part of the ROS `param` tag. The `command` tag will execute the command mentioned on it and store the output of the command in these two parameters.

The `rosmaster` and parameter server are executed inside `roslaunch` modules by using the `ROS_MASTER_URI` address. This is happening inside the `roslaunch` Python module. The `ROS_MASTER_URI` is a combination of the IP address and port in which `rosmaster` is going to listen. The port number can be changed according to the given port number in the `roscore` command.

Checking the roscore command output

Let's check the ROS topics and ROS parameters created after running `roscore`. The following command will list the active topics on the Terminal:

```
$ rostopic list
```

The list of topics is as follows, as per our discussion on the `rosout` node subscribe `/rosout` topic. This has all the log messages from the ROS nodes and `/rosout_agg` will rebroadcast the log messages:

```
/rosout
/rosout_agg
```

The following command lists the parameters available when running `roscore`. The following is the command to list the active ROS parameter:

```
$ rosparam list
```

The parameters are mentioned here; they have the ROS distribution name, version, address of the `roslaunch` server and `run_id`, where `run_id` is a unique ID associated with a particular run of `roscore`:

```
/rosdistro
/roslaunch/uris/host_robot_virtualbox__51189
/rosversion
/run_id
```

The list of the ROS service generated during the running `roscore` can be checked using the following command:

```
$ rosservice list
```

The list of services running is as follows:

```
/rosout/get_loggers
/rosout/set_logger_level
```

These ROS services are generated for each ROS node for setting the logging levels.

Questions

After going through the chapter, you should now be able to answer the following questions:

- Why should we learn ROS?
- How does ROS differ from other robotic software platforms?
- What are the basic elements of ROS framework?
- What is the internal working of `roscore`?

Summary

ROS is now a trending software framework among roboticists. Gaining knowledge in ROS is essential in the upcoming years if you are planning to build your career as a robotics engineer. In this chapter, we have gone through the basics of ROS, mainly to refresh the concepts if you have already learned ROS. We discussed the necessity of learning ROS and how it excels among the current robotics software platforms. We went through the basic concepts, such as the ROS Master, the parameter server, and `roscore`, and looked at the explanation of the working of `roscore`. In the next chapter, we will introduce the ROS package management, discussing some practical examples of the ROS communication system.

2
Getting Started with ROS Programming

After discussing the basics of the ROS Master, the parameter server, and `roscore`, we can now start to create and build a ROS package. In this chapter, we will create different ROS nodes implementing the ROS communication system. Working with ROS packages, we will also refresh the concepts of ROS nodes, topics, messages, services, and actionlib.

We will cover the following list of topics:

- Creating, compiling and running ROS packages.
- Working with standard and custom ROS messages.
- Working with ROS services and actionlib.
- Maintaining and releasing your ROS packages.
- Creating a wiki page for ROS packages.

Creating a ROS package

The ROS packages are the basic unit of the ROS system. We can create a ROS package, build it, and release it to the public. The current distribution of ROS we are using is kinetic. We are using the `catkin` build system to build ROS packages. A build system is responsible for generating 'targets' (executable/libraries) from a raw source code that can be used by an end user. In older distributions, such as Electric and Fuerte, `rosbuild` was the build system. Because of the various flaws of `rosbuild`, `catkin` came into existence, which is basically based on **Cross Platform Make (CMake)**. This has a lot of advantages, such as porting the package into another operating system, such as Windows. If an OS supports CMake and Python, `catkin`-based packages can be easily ported into it.

The first requirement work with ROS packages is to create a ROS `catkin` workspace. After installed ROS, we can create and build a `catkin_workspace` called `catkin_ws`:

```
$ mkdir -p ~/catkin_ws/src
```

To compile the workspace, we should source the ROS environment, in order to get access to ROS functions:

```
$ source /opt/ros/kinetic/setup.bash
```

Switch to the source, `src` folder previously created.

```
$ cd ~/catkin_ws/src
```

Initialize a new `catkin` workspace:

```
$ catkin_init_workspace
```

We can build the workspace even if there are no packages. We can use the following command to switch to the workspace folder:

```
$ cd ~/catkin_ws
```

The `catkin_make` command will build the following workspace:

```
$ catkin_make
```

This last command will create a `devel` and a `build` directory in the catkin workspace. Inside the `devel` folder different setup files are located. To add the created ROS workspace to the ROS environment, we should source one of this file. In addition, we can source the setup file of this workspace every time that a new `bash` session starts with the following command:

```
$ echo "source ~/catkin_ws/devel/setup.bash" >> ~/.bashrc
$ source ~/.bashrc
```

After setting the `catkin` workspace, we can create our own package that has sample nodes to demonstrate the working of ROS topics, messages, services, and actionlib. The `catkin_create_pkg` command is used to create a ROS package. This command is used to create our package, in which we are going to create demos of various ROS concepts.

Switch to the `catkin` workspace `src` folder and create the package, using the following command:

```
$ catkin_create_pkg package_name [dependency1] [dependency2]
```

> **Source code folder:** All ROS packages, either created from scratch or downloaded from other code repositories, must be placed in the src folder of the ROS workspace, otherwise they can not be recognized by the ROS system and compiled.

Here is the command to create the sample ROS package:

```
$ catkin_create_pkg mastering_ros_demo_pkg roscpp std_msgs
actionlib actionlib_msgs
```

The dependencies in the packages are as follows:

- roscpp: This is the C++ implementation of ROS. It is a ROS client library which provides APIs to C++ developers to make ROS nodes with ROS topics, services, parameters, and so on. We are including this dependency because we are going to write a ROS C++ node. Any ROS package which uses the C++ node must add this dependency.
- std_msgs: This package contains basic ROS primitive data types, such as integer, float, string, array, and so on. We can directly use these data types in our nodes without defining a new ROS message.
- actionlib: The actionlib metapackage provides interfaces to create preemptible tasks in ROS nodes. We are creating actionlib -based nodes in this package. So we should include this package to build the ROS nodes.
- actionlib_msgs: This package contains standard message definitions needed to interact with the action server and action client.

After package creation, additional dependencies can be added manually by editing the CMakeLists.txt and package.xml files. We will get the following message if the package has been successfully created:

```
Created file mastering_ros_v2_pkg/package.xml
Created file mastering_ros_v2_pkg/CMakeLists.txt
Created folder mastering_ros_v2_pkg/include/mastering_ros_v2_pkg
Created folder mastering_ros_v2_pkg/src
Successfully created files in /home/jcacace/mastering_ros_v2_pkg. Pleas
e adjust the values in package.xml.
```

Figure 1: Terminal messages while creating a ROS package

After creating this package, build the package without adding any nodes, using the `catkin_make` command. This command must be executed from the `catkin` workspace path. The following command shows you how to build our empty ROS package:

```
~/catkin_ws $ catkin_make
```

After a successful build, we can start adding nodes to the `src` folder of this package.

The build folder in the CMake build files mainly contains executables of the nodes that are placed inside the `catkin` workspace `src` folder. The `devel` folder contains bash script, header files, and executables in different folders generated during the build process. We can see how to make ROS nodes and build using `catkin_make`.

Working with ROS topics

Topics are the basic way of communicating between two nodes. In this section, we can see how the topics works. We are going to create two ROS nodes for publishing a topic and subscribing the same. Navigate to the `mastering_ros_demo_pkg` folder, joining the `/src` subdirectory for the source code. `demo_topic_publisher.cpp` and `demo_topic_subscriber.cpp` are the two sets of code that we are going to discuss.

Creating ROS nodes

The first node we are going to discuss is `demo_topic_publisher.cpp`. This node will publish an integer value on a topic called `/numbers`. Copy the current code into a new package or use this existing file from the code repository.

Here is the complete code:

```cpp
#include "ros/ros.h"
#include "std_msgs/Int32.h"
#include <iostream>
int main(int argc, char **argv)
{
  ros::init(argc, argv,"demo_topic_publisher");
  ros::NodeHandle node_obj;
  ros::Publisher number_publisher =
node_obj.advertise<std_msgs::Int32>("/numbers",10);
  ros::Rate loop_rate(10);
  int number_count = 0;
  while (ros::ok())
  {
```

```
    std_msgs::Int32 msg;
    msg.data = number_count;
    ROS_INFO("%d",msg.data);
    number_publisher.publish(msg);
    ros::spinOnce();
    loop_rate.sleep();
    ++number_count;
  }
  return 0;
}
```

Here is the detailed explanation of the preceding code:

```
#include "ros/ros.h"
#include "std_msgs/Int32.h"
#include <iostream>
```

The ros/ros.h is the main header of ROS. If we want to use the roscpp client APIs in our code, we should include this header. The std_msgs/Int32.h is the standard message definition of the integer datatype.

Here, we are sending an integer value through a topic. So we should need a message type for handling the integer data. std_msgs contains the standard message definition of primitive datatypes. std_msgs/Int32.h contains the integer message definition:

```
    ros::init(argc, argv,"demo_topic_publisher");
```

This code will initialize a ROS node with a name. It should be noted that the ROS node should be unique. This line is mandatory for all ROS C++ nodes:

```
    ros::NodeHandle node_obj;
```

This will create a Nodehandle object, which is used to communicate with the ROS system:

```
    ros::Publisher number_publisher =
  node_obj.advertise<std_msgs::Int32>("/numbers",10);
```

This will create a topic publisher and name the topic /numbers with a message type std_msgs::Int32. The second argument is the buffer size. It indicates how many messages need to be put in a buffer before sending. It should be set to high if the data sending rate is high:

```
    ros::Rate loop_rate(10);
```

This is used to set the frequency of sending data:

```
while (ros::ok())
{
```

This is an infinite `while` loop, and it quits when we press *Ctrl* + *C*. The `ros::ok()` function returns zero when there is an interrupt; this can terminate this `while` loop:

```
std_msgs::Int32 msg;
msg.data = number_count;
```

The first line creates an integer ROS message, and the second line assigns an integer value to the message. Here, `data` is the field name of the `msg` object:

```
ROS_INFO("%d",msg.data);
```

This will print the message data. This line is used to log the ROS information:

```
number_publisher.publish(msg);
```

This will publish the message to the topics `/numbers`:

```
ros::spinOnce();
```

This command will read and update all ROS topics. The node will not publish without a `spin()` or `spinOnce()` function:

```
loop_rate.sleep();
```

This line will provide the necessary delay to achieve a frequency of 10 Hz.

After discussing the publisher node, we can discuss the subscriber node, which is `demo_topic_subscriber.cpp`. Copy the code to a new file or use the existing file.

Here is the definition of the subscriber node:

```
#include "ros/ros.h"
#include "std_msgs/Int32.h"
#include <iostream>
void number_callback(const std_msgs::Int32::ConstPtr& msg) {
    ROS_INFO("Received [%d]",msg->data);
}

int main(int argc, char **argv) {
    ros::init(argc, argv,"demo_topic_subscriber");
    ros::NodeHandle node_obj;
    ros::Subscriber number_subscriber =
```

```
node_obj.subscribe("/numbers",10,number_callback);
    ros::spin();
    return 0;
}
```

Here is the code explanation:

```
#include "ros/ros.h"
#include "std_msgs/Int32.h"
#include <iostream>
```

This is the header needed for the subscribers:

```
void number_callback(const std_msgs::Int32::ConstPtr& msg) {
    ROS_INFO("Recieved [%d]",msg->data);
}
```

This is a `callback` function that will execute whenever a data comes to the `/numbers` topic. Whenever a data reaches this topic, the function will call and extract the value and print it on the console:

```
ros::Subscriber number_subscriber =
node_obj.subscribe("/numbers",10,number_callback);
```

This is the subscriber, and here we are giving the topic name needed to subscribe, the buffer size, and the `callback` function. We are subscribing the `/numbers` topic and we have already seen the `callback` function in the preceding section:

```
ros::spin();
```

This is an infinite loop in which the node will wait in this step. This code will fasten the callbacks whenever a data reaches the topic. The node will quit only when we press the *Ctrl + C* key.

Building the nodes

We have to edit the `CMakeLists.txt` file in the package to compile and build the source code. Navigate to `mastering_ros_demo_pkg` to view the existing `CMakeLists.txt` file. The following code snippet in this file is responsible for building these two nodes:

```
include_directories(
    include
    ${catkin_INCLUDE_DIRS}
    ${Boost_INCLUDE_DIRS}
)
```

```
#This will create executables of the nodes
add_executable(demo_topic_publisher src/demo_topic_publisher.cpp)
add_executable(demo_topic_subscriber src/demo_topic_subscriber.cpp)

#This will generate message header file before building the target
add_dependencies(demo_topic_publisher
mastering_ros_demo_pkg_generate_messages_cpp)
add_dependencies(demo_topic_subscriber
mastering_ros_demo_pkg_generate_messages_cpp)

#This will link executables to the appropriate libraries
target_link_libraries(demo_topic_publisher ${catkin_LIBRARIES})
target_link_libraries(demo_topic_subscriber ${catkin_LIBRARIES})
```

We can add the preceding snippet to create a new a CMakeLists.txt file for compiling the two codes.

The catkin_make command is used to build the package. We can first switch to a workspace:

```
$ cd ~/catkin_ws
```

Build mastering_ros_demo_package as follows:

```
$ catkin_make
```

We can either use the preceding command to build the entire workspace, or use the the – DCATKIN_WHITELIST_PACKAGES option. With this option, it is possible to set one or more packages to compile:

```
$ catkin_make –DCATKIN_WHITELIST_PACKAGES="pkg1,pkg2,..."
```

Note that is necessary to revert this configuration to compile other packages or the entire workspace. This can be done using the following command:

```
$ catkin_make –DCATKIN_WHITELIST_PACKAGES=""
```

If the building is done, we can execute the nodes. First, start roscore:

```
$ roscore
```

Now run both commands in two shells. In the running publisher:

```
$ rosrun mastering_ros_demo_package demo_topic_publisher
```

In the running subscriber:

```
$ rosrun mastering_ros_demo_package demo_topic_subscriber
```

We can see the output as shown here:

```
jcacace@robot:~$ rosrun mastering_ros_demo_pkg demo_topic_pub jcacace@robot:~$ rosrun mastering_ros_demo_pkg demo_topic_sub
lisher                                                         scriber
[ INFO] [1500276155.757008571]: 0                             [ INFO] [1500276156.057591945]: Recieved  [3]
[ INFO] [1500276155.857052842]: 1                             [ INFO] [1500276156.157553762]: Recieved  [4]
[ INFO] [1500276155.957062454]: 2                             [ INFO] [1500276156.257991575]: Recieved  [5]
[ INFO] [1500276156.057095824]: 3                             [ INFO] [1500276156.358034728]: Recieved  [6]
[ INFO] [1500276156.157087268]: 4                             [ INFO] [1500276156.457377162]: Recieved  [7]
[ INFO] [1500276156.257505796]: 5                             [ INFO] [1500276156.557647552]: Recieved  [8]
[ INFO] [1500276156.357532737]: 6                             [ INFO] [1500276156.658285212]: Recieved  [9]
```

Figure 2: Running topic publisher and subscriber

The following diagram shows how the nodes communicate with each other. We can see that the demo_topic_publisher node publishes the /numbers topic and then subscribes to the demo_topic_subscriber node:

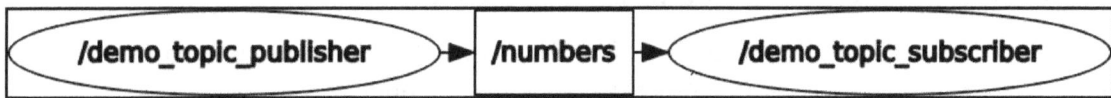

Figure 3: Graph of the communication between publisher and subscriber nodes

We can use the rosnode and rostopic tools to debug and understand the working of two nodes:

- $ rosnode list: This will list the active nodes.
- $ rosnode info demo_topic_publisher: This will get the info of the publisher node.
- $ rostopic echo /numbers: This will display the value sending through the /numbers topic.
- $ rostopic type /numbers: This will print the message type of the /numbers topic.

Adding custom msg and srv files

In this section, we will look at how to create custom messages and services definitions in the current package. The message definitions are stored in a `.msg` file and the service definitions are stored in a `.srv` file. These definitions inform ROS about the type of data and name of data to be transmitted from a ROS node. When a custom message is added, ROS will convert the definitions into equivalent C++ codes, which we can include in our nodes.

We can start with message definitions. Message definitions have to be written in the `.msg` file and have to be kept in the `msg` folder, which is inside the package. We are going to create a message file called `demo_msg.msg` with the following definition:

```
string greeting
int32 number
```

Until now, we have worked only with standard message definitions. Now, we have created our own definitions and can see how to use them in our code.

The first step is to edit the `package.xml` file of the current package and uncomment the lines `<build_depend>message_generation</build_depend>` and `<exec_depend>message_runtime</exec_depend>`.

Edit the current `CMakeLists.txt` and add the `message_generation` line, as follows:

```
find_package(catkin REQUIRED COMPONENTS
 roscpp
 rospy
 std_msgs
 actionlib
 actionlib_msgs
 message_generation
 )
```

Uncomment the following line and add the custom message file:

```
add_message_files(
    FILES
    demo_msg.msg
)
## Generate added messages and services with any dependencies listed here
generate_messages(
    DEPENDENCIES
    std_msgs
    actionlib_msgs
)
```

After these steps, we can compile and build the package:

```
$ cd ~/catkin_ws/
$ catkin_make
```

To check whether the message is built properly, we can use the rosmsg command:

```
$ rosmsg show mastering_ros_demo_pkg/demo_msg
```

If the content shown by the command and the definition are the same, the procedure is correct.

If we want to test the custom message, we can build a publisher and subscriber using the custom message type named demo_msg_publisher.cpp and demo_msg_subscriber.cpp. Navigate to the mastering_ros_demo_pkg/1 folder for these code.

We can test the message by adding the following lines of code in CMakeLists.txt:

```
add_executable(demo_msg_publisher src/demo_msg_publisher.cpp)
add_executable(demo_msg_subscriber src/demo_msg_subscriber.cpp)

add_dependencies(demo_msg_publisher
mastering_ros_demo_pkg_generate_messages_cpp)
add_dependencies(demo_msg_subscriber
mastering_ros_demo_pkg_generate_messages_cpp)

target_link_libraries(demo_msg_publisher ${catkin_LIBRARIES})
target_link_libraries(demo_msg_subscriber ${catkin_LIBRARIES})
```

Build the package using `catkin_make` and test the node using the following commands.

- Run `roscore`:

```
$ roscore
```

- Start the custom message publisher node:

```
$ rosrun mastering_ros_demo_pkg demo_msg_publisher
```

- Start the custom message subscriber node:

```
$ rosrun mastering_ros_demo_pkg demo_msg_subscriber
```

The publisher node publishes a string along with an integer, and the subscriber node subscribes the topic and prints the values. The output and graph are shown as follows:

```
jcacace@robot:~$ rosrun mastering_ros_demo_pkg demo_msg_publisher jcacace@robot:~$ rosrun mastering_ros_demo_pkg demo_msg_subscriber
[ INFO] [1500276387.166778705]: 0                          [ INFO] [1500276387.467496520]: Recieved  greeting [hello world ]
[ INFO] [1500276387.166861438]: hello world               [ INFO] [1500276387.467579254]: Recieved  [3]
[ INFO] [1500276387.267694471]: 1                          [ INFO] [1500276387.567331442]: Recieved  greeting [hello world ]
[ INFO] [1500276387.267855187]: hello world               [ INFO] [1500276387.567382312]: Recieved  [4]
[ INFO] [1500276387.368803935]: 2                          [ INFO] [1500276387.668345874]: Recieved  greeting [hello world ]
[ INFO] [1500276387.368898128]: hello world               [ INFO] [1500276387.668564167]: Recieved  [5]
[ INFO] [1500276387.466853659]: 3                          [ INFO] [1500276387.768672445]: Recieved  greeting [hello world ]
[ INFO] [1500276387.466933039]: hello world               [ INFO] [1500276387.768753221]: Recieved  [6]
```

Figure 4: Running publisher and subscriber using custom message definitions.

The topic in which the nodes are communicating is called `/demo_msg_topic`. Here is the graph view of the two nodes:

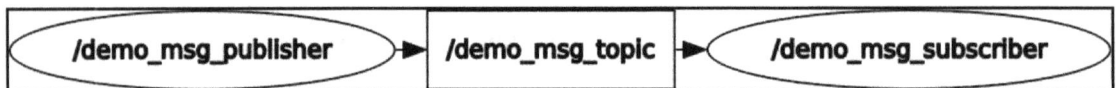

Figure 5: Graph of the communication between message publisher and subscriber

Next, we can add `srv` files to the package. Create a new folder called `srv` in the current package folder and add a `srv` file called `demo_srv.srv`. The definition of this file is as follows:

```
string in
---
string out
```

Here, both the `Request` and `Response` are strings.

In the next step, we need to uncomment the following lines in `package.xml` as we did for the ROS messages:

```
<build_depend>message_generation</build_depend>
<exec_depend>message_runtime</exec_depend>
```

Take `CMakeLists.txt` and add `message_runtime` in `catkin_package()`:

```
catkin_package(
    CATKIN_DEPENDS roscpp rospy std_msgs actionlib actionlib_msgs
message_runtime
)
```

We need to follow the same procedure in generating services as we did for the ROS message. Apart from that, we need additional sections to be uncommented, as shown here:

```
## Generate services in the 'srv' folder
add_service_files(
    FILES
    demo_srv.srv
  )
```

After making these changes, we can build the package using `catkin_make` and using the following command, we can verify the procedure:

```
$ rossrv show mastering_ros_demo_pkg/demo_srv
```

If we see the same content as we defined in the file, we can confirm it's working.

Working with ROS services

In this section, we are going to create ROS nodes, which can use the services definition that we defined already. The service nodes we are going to create can send a string message as a request to the server and the server node will send another message as a response.

Navigate to `mastering_ros_demo_pkg/src`, and find nodes with the names `demo_service_server.cpp` and `demo_service_client.cpp`.

The `demo_service_server.cpp` is the server, and its definition is as follows:

```cpp
#include "ros/ros.h"
#include "mastering_ros_demo_pkg/demo_srv.h"
#include <iostream>
#include <sstream>
using namespace std;

bool demo_service_callback(mastering_ros_demo_pkg::demo_srv::Request &req,
      mastering_ros_demo_pkg::demo_srv::Response &res) {
 std::stringstream ss;
 ss << "Received Here";
 res.out = ss.str();
 ROS_INFO("From Client [%s], Server says
[%s]",req.in.c_str(),res.out.c_str());
 return true;
}

int main(int argc, char **argv)
{
 ros::init(argc, argv, "demo_service_server");
 ros::NodeHandle n;
 ros::ServiceServer service = n.advertiseService("demo_service",
demo_service_callback);
 ROS_INFO("Ready to receive from client.");
 ros::spin();
 return 0;
}
```

Let's see an explanation of the code:

```cpp
#include "ros/ros.h"
#include "mastering_ros_demo_pkg/demo_srv.h"
#include <iostream>
#include <sstream>
```

Here, we included `ros/ros.h`, which is a mandatory header for a ROS CPP node. The `mastering_ros_demo_pkg/demo_srv.h` header is a generated header, which contains our service definition and we can use this in our code. The `sstream.h` is for getting string streaming classes:

```cpp
bool demo_service_callback(mastering_ros_demo_pkg::demo_srv::Request &req,
      mastering_ros_demo_pkg::demo_srv::Response &res)
{
```

This is the server callback function executed when a request is received on the server. The server can receive the request from clients with a message type of `mastering_ros_demo_pkg::demo_srv::Request` and sends the response in the `mastering_ros_demo_pkg::demo_srv::Response` type:

```
std::stringstream ss;
ss << "Received Here";
res.out = ss.str();
```

In this code, the string data `"Received Here"` is passing to the service `Response` instance. Here, `out` is the field name of the response that we have given in `demo_srv.srv`. This response will go to the service client node:

```
ros::ServiceServer service = n.advertiseService("demo_service",
demo_service_callback);
```

This creates a service called `demo_service` and a callback function is executed when a request comes to this service. The callback function is `demo_service_callback`, which we saw in the preceding section.

Next, we can see how `demo_service_client.cpp` is working.

Here is the definition of this code:

```
#include "ros/ros.h"
#include <iostream>
#include "mastering_ros_demo_pkg/demo_srv.h"
#include <iostream>
#include <sstream>
using namespace std;

int main(int argc, char **argv)
{
 ros::init(argc, argv, "demo_service_client");
 ros::NodeHandle n;
 ros::Rate loop_rate(10);
 ros::ServiceClient client =
n.serviceClient<mastering_ros_demo_pkg::demo_srv>("demo_service");
 while (ros::ok())
 {
  mastering_ros_demo_pkg::demo_srv srv;
  std::stringstream ss;
  ss << "Sending from Here";
  srv.request.in = ss.str();
  if (client.call(srv))
  {
```

```
    ROS_INFO("From Client [%s], Server says
[%s]",srv.request.in.c_str(),srv.response.out.c_str());

  }
  else
  {
   ROS_ERROR("Failed to call service");
   return 1;
  }

 ros::spinOnce();
 loop_rate.sleep();

 }
 return 0;
}
```

Let's explain the code:

```
    ros::ServiceClient client =
    n.serviceClient<mastering_ros_demo_pkg::demo_srv>("demo_service");
```

This line creates a service client that has the message type
mastering_ros_demo_pkg::demo_srv and communicates to a ROS service named
demo_service:

```
    mastering_ros_demo_pkg::demo_srv srv;
```

This line will create a new service object instance:

```
    std::stringstream ss;
    ss << "Sending from Here";
    srv.request.in = ss.str();
```

Fill the request instance with a string called "Sending from Here":

```
    if (client.call(srv))
    {
```

This will send the service call to the server. If it is sent successfully, it will print the response
and request; if it failed, it will do nothing:

```
    ROS_INFO("From Client [%s], Server says
[%s]",srv.request.in.c_str(),srv.response.out.c_str());
```

If the response is received, then it will print the request and the response.

After discussing the two nodes, we can discuss how to build these two nodes. The following code is added to CMakeLists.txt to compile and build the two nodes:

```
add_executable(demo_service_server src/demo_service_server.cpp)
add_executable(demo_service_client src/demo_service_client.cpp)

add_dependencies(demo_service_server
mastering_ros_demo_pkg_generate_messages_cpp)
add_dependencies(demo_service_client
mastering_ros_demo_pkg_generate_messages_cpp)

target_link_libraries(demo_service_server ${catkin_LIBRARIES})
target_link_libraries(demo_service_client ${catkin_LIBRARIES})
```

We can execute the following commands to build the code:

```
$ cd ~/catkin_ws
$ catkin_make
```

To start the nodes, first execute roscore and use the following commands:

```
$ rosrun mastering_ros_demo_pkg demo_service_server
$ rosrun mastering_ros_demo_pkg demo_service_client
```

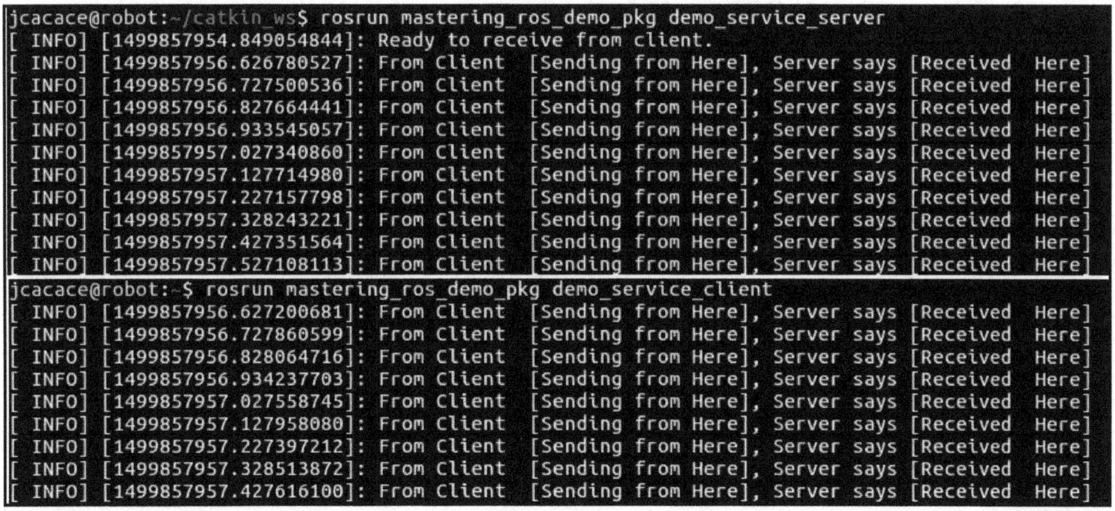

Figure 6: Running ROS service client and server nodes.

We can work with `rosservice` using the `rosservice` command:

- `$ rosservice list`: This will list the current ROS services
- `$ rosservice type /demo_service`: This will print the message type of `/demo_service`
- `$ rosservice info /demo_service`: This will print the information of `/demo_service`

Working with ROS actionlib

In ROS services, the user implements a request/reply interaction between two nodes, but if the reply takes too much time or the server is not finished with the given work, we have to wait until it completes, blocking the main application while waiting for the termination of the requested action. In addition, the calling client could be implemented to monitor the execution of the remote process. In these cases, we should implement our application using `actionlib`. This is another method in ROS in which we can preempt the running request and start sending another one if the request is not finished on time as we expected. Actionlib packages provide a standard way to implement these kinds of preemptive tasks. Actionlib is highly used in robot arm navigation and mobile robot navigation. We can see how to implement an action server and action client implementation.

There is another method in ROS in which we can preempt the running request and start sending another one if the request is not finished on time as we expected. Actionlib packages provide a standard way to implement these kinds of preemptive tasks. Actionlib is highly used in robot arm navigation and mobile robot navigation. We can see how to implement an action server and action client implementation.

Like ROS services, in `actionlib`, we have to specify the action specification. The action specification is stored inside the action file having an extension of `.action`. This file must be kept inside the `action` folder, which is inside the ROS package. The `action` file has the following parts:

- **Goal**: The action client can send a goal that has to be executed by the action server. This is similar to the request in the ROS service. For example, if a robot arm joint wants to move from 45 degrees to 90 degrees, the goal here is 90 degrees.

- **Feedback**: When an action client sends a goal to the action server, it will start executing a callback function. Feedback is simply giving the progress of the current operation inside the callback function. Using the feedback definition, we can get the current progress. In the preceding case, the robot arm joint has to move to 90 degrees; in this case, the feedback can be the intermediate value between 45 and 90 degrees in which the arm is moving.
- **Result**: After completing the goal, the action server will send a final result of completion, it can be the computational result or an acknowledgment. In the preceding example, if the joint reaches 90 degrees it achieves the goal and the result can be anything indicating it finished the goal.

We can discuss a demo action server and action client here. The demo action client will send a number as the goal. When an action server receives the goal, it will count from 0 to the goal number with a step size of 1 and with a 1 second delay. If it completes before the given time, it will send the result; otherwise, the task will be preempted by the client. The feedback here is the progress of counting. The action file of this task is as follows. The action file is named `Demo_action.action`:

```
#goal definition
int32 count
---
#result definition
int32 final_count
---
#feedback
int32 current_number
```

Here, the count value is the goal in which the server has to count from zero to this number. `final_count` is the result, in which the final value after completion of a task and `current_number` is the feedback value. It will specify how much the progress is.

Navigate to `mastering_ros_demo_pkg/src` and you can find the action server node as `demo_action_server.cpp` and action client node as `demo_action_client.cpp`.

Creating the ROS action server

In this section, we will discuss `demo_action_server.cpp`. The action server receives a goal value that is a number. When the server gets this goal value, it will start counting from zero to this number. If the counting is complete, it will successfully finish the action, if it is preempted before finishing, the action server will look for another goal value.

This code is a bit lengthy, so we can discuss the important code snippet of this code.

Let's start with the header files:

```
#include <actionlib/server/simple_action_server.h>
#include "mastering_ros_demo_pkg/Demo_actionAction.h"
```

The first header is the standard action library to implement an action server node. The second header is generated from the stored action files. It should include accessing our action definition:

```
class Demo_actionAction
{
```

This class contains the action server definition:

```
actionlib::SimpleActionServer<mastering_ros_demo_pkg::Demo_actionAction>
as;
```

Create a simple action server instance with our custom action message type:

```
mastering_ros_demo_pkg::Demo_actionFeedback feedback;
```

Create a feedback instance for sending feedback during the operation:

```
mastering_ros_demo_pkg::Demo_actionResult result;
```

Create a result instance for sending the final result:

```
Demo_actionAction(std::string name) :
  as(nh_, name, boost::bind(&Demo_actionAction::executeCB, this, _1),
false),
  action_name(name)
```

This is an action constructor, and an action server is created here by taking an argument such as `Nodehandle`, `action_name`, and `executeCB`, where `executeCB` is the action callback where all the processing is done:

```
as.registerPreemptCallback(boost::bind(&Demo_actionAction::preemptCB,
this));
```

This line registers a callback when the action is preempted. The `preemtCB` is the callback name executed when there is a preempt request from the action client:

```
void executeCB(const mastering_ros_demo_pkg::Demo_actionGoalConstPtr
&goal)
{
if(!as.isActive() || as.isPreemptRequested()) return;
```

This is the callback definition which is executed when the action server receives a `goal` value. It will execute callback functions only after checking whether the action server is currently active or it is preempted already:

```
for(progress = 0 ; progress < goal->count; progress++){
//Check for ros
if(!ros::ok()){
```

This loop will execute until the goal value is reached. It will continuously send the current progress as feedback:

```
if(!as.isActive() || as.isPreemptRequested()){
 return;
 }
```

Inside this loop, it will check whether the action server is active or it is preempted. If it occurs, the function will return:

```
if(goal->count == progress){
 result.final_count = progress;
 as.setSucceeded(result);
 }
```

If the current value reaches the goal value, then it publishes the final result:

```
Demo_actionAction demo_action_obj(ros::this_node::getName());
```

In `main()`, we create an instance of `Demo_actionAction`, which will start the action server.

Creating the ROS action client

In this section, we will discuss the workings of an action client. `demo_action_client.cpp` is the action client node that will send the goal value consisting of a number which is the goal. The client is getting the goal value from the command-line arguments. The first command-line argument of the client is the goal value, and the second is the time of completion for this task.

The goal value will be sent to the server and the client will wait until the given time, in seconds. After waiting, the client will check whether it completed or not; if it is not complete, the client will preempt the action.

The client code is a bit lengthy, so we will discuss the important sections of the code:

```
#include <actionlib/client/simple_action_client.h>
#include <actionlib/client/terminal_state.h>
#include "mastering_ros_demo_pkg/Demo_actionAction.h"
```

In the action client, we need to include `actionlib/client/simple_action_client.h` to get the action client APIs, which are used to implement action clients:

```
actionlib::SimpleActionClient<mastering_ros_demo_pkg::Demo_actionAction>
ac("demo_action", true);
```

This will create an action client instance:

```
ac.waitForServer();
```

This line will wait for an infinite time if there is no action server running on the system. It will exit only when there is an action server running on the system:

```
mastering_ros_demo_pkg::Demo_actionGoal goal;
goal.count = atoi(argv[1]);
ac.sendGoal(goal);
```

Create an instance of a goal, and send the goal value from the first command line argument:

```
bool finished_before_timeout =
ac.waitForResult(ros::Duration(atoi(argv[2])));
```

This line will wait for the result from the server until the given seconds:

```
ac.cancelGoal();
```

If it is not finished, it will preempt the action.

Building the ROS action server and client

After creating these two files in the `src` folder, we have to edit the `package.xml` and `CMakeLists.txt` to build the nodes.

The `package.xml` file should contain message generation and runtime packages, as we did for ROS service and messages.

We have to include the `Boost` library in `CMakeLists.txt` to build these nodes. Also, we have to add the action files that we wrote for this example:

```
find_package(catkin REQUIRED COMPONENTS
 roscpp
 rospy
 std_msgs
 actionlib
 actionlib_msgs
 message_generation
 )
```

We should pass `actionlib`, `actionlib_msgs`, and `message_generation` in `find_package()`:

```
## System dependencies are found with CMake's conventions
find_package(Boost REQUIRED COMPONENTS system)
```

We should add `Boost` as a system dependency:

```
## Generate actions in the 'action' folder
 add_action_files(
   FILES
   Demo_action.action
   )
```

We need to add our action file in `add_action_files()`:

```
## Generate added messages and services with any dependencies listed here
 generate_messages(
   DEPENDENCIES
   std_msgs
   actionlib_msgs
   )
```

We have to add `actionlib_msgs` in `generate_messages()`:

```
catkin_package(
 CATKIN_DEPENDS roscpp rospy std_msgs actionlib actionlib_msgs
message_runtime
)

include_directories(
 include
 ${catkin_INCLUDE_DIRS}
 ${Boost_INCLUDE_DIRS}
)
```

We have to add `Boost` to include the directory:

```
##Building action server and action client

add_executable(demo_action_server src/demo_action_server.cpp)
add_executable(demo_action_client src/demo_action_client.cpp)

add_dependencies(demo_action_server
mastering_ros_demo_pkg_generate_messages_cpp)
add_dependencies(demo_action_client
mastering_ros_demo_pkg_generate_messages_cpp)

target_link_libraries(demo_action_server ${catkin_LIBRARIES} )
target_link_libraries(demo_action_client ${catkin_LIBRARIES})
```

After `catkin_make`, we can run these nodes using the following commands:

- Run `roscore`:

    ```
    $ roscore
    ```

- Launch the action server node:

    ```
    $rosrun mastering_ros_demo_pkg demo_action_server
    ```

- Launch the action client node:

    ```
    $rosrun mastering_ros_demo_pkg demo_action_client 10 1
    ```

The output of these process is shown as follows:

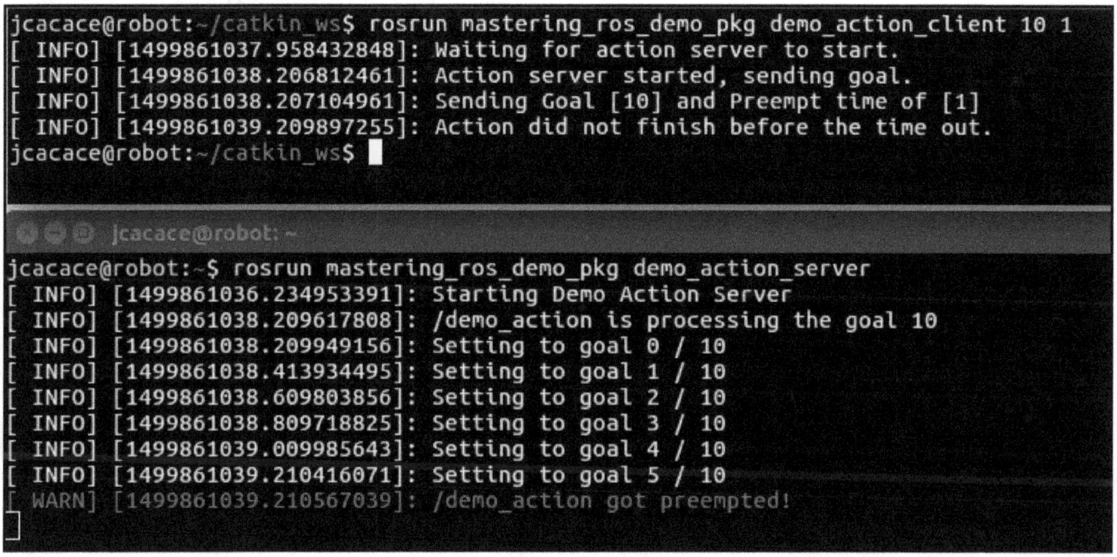

```
jcacace@robot:~/catkin_ws$ rosrun mastering_ros_demo_pkg demo_action_client 10 1
[ INFO] [1499861037.958432848]: Waiting for action server to start.
[ INFO] [1499861038.206812461]: Action server started, sending goal.
[ INFO] [1499861038.207104961]: Sending Goal [10] and Preempt time of [1]
[ INFO] [1499861039.209897255]: Action did not finish before the time out.
jcacace@robot:~/catkin_ws$

    jcacace@robot: ~
jcacace@robot:~$ rosrun mastering_ros_demo_pkg demo_action_server
[ INFO] [1499861036.234953391]: Starting Demo Action Server
[ INFO] [1499861038.209617808]: /demo_action is processing the goal 10
[ INFO] [1499861038.209949156]: Setting to goal 0 / 10
[ INFO] [1499861038.413934495]: Setting to goal 1 / 10
[ INFO] [1499861038.609803856]: Setting to goal 2 / 10
[ INFO] [1499861038.809718825]: Setting to goal 3 / 10
[ INFO] [1499861039.009985643]: Setting to goal 4 / 10
[ INFO] [1499861039.210416071]: Setting to goal 5 / 10
[ WARN] [1499861039.210567039]: /demo_action got preempted!
```

Figure 7: Running ROS actionlib server and client.

Creating launch files

The launch files in ROS are a very useful feature for launching more than one node. In the preceding examples, we have seen a maximum of two ROS nodes, but imagine a scenario in which we have to launch 10 or 20 nodes for a robot. It will be difficult if we run each node in a terminal one by one. Instead, we can write all nodes inside an XML-based file called launch files and, using a command called **roslaunch**, we can parse this file and launch the nodes.

The roslaunch command will automatically start the ROS Master and the parameter server. So, in essence, there is no need to start the roscore command and individual node; if we launch the file, all operations will be done in a single command.

Let's start creating launch files. Switch to the package folder and create a new launch file called `demo_topic.launch` to launch two ROS nodes that are publishing and subscribing an integer value. We keep the launch files in a `launch` folder, which is inside the package:

```
$ roscd mastering_ros_demo_pkg
$ mkdir launch
$ cd launch
$ gedit demo_topic.launch
```

Paste the following content into the file:

```
<launch>
  <node name="publisher_node" pkg="mastering_ros_demo_pkg"
type="demo_topic_publisher" output="screen"/>

  <node name="subscriber_node" pkg="mastering_ros_demo_pkg"
type="demo_topic_subscriber" output="screen"/>
</launch>
```

Let's discuss what is in the code. The `<launch></launch>` tags are the root element in a `launch` file. All definitions will be inside these tags.

The `<node>` tag specifies the desired node to launch:

```
  <node name="publisher_node" pkg="mastering_ros_demo_pkg"
type="demo_topic_publisher" output="screen"/>
```

The `name` tag inside `<node>` indicates the name of the node, `pkg` is the name of the package, and `type` is the name of executable we are going to launch.

After creating the launch file `demo_topic.launch`, we can launch it using the following command:

```
$ roslaunch mastering_ros_demo_pkg demo_topic.launch
```

Here is the output we get if the launch is successful:

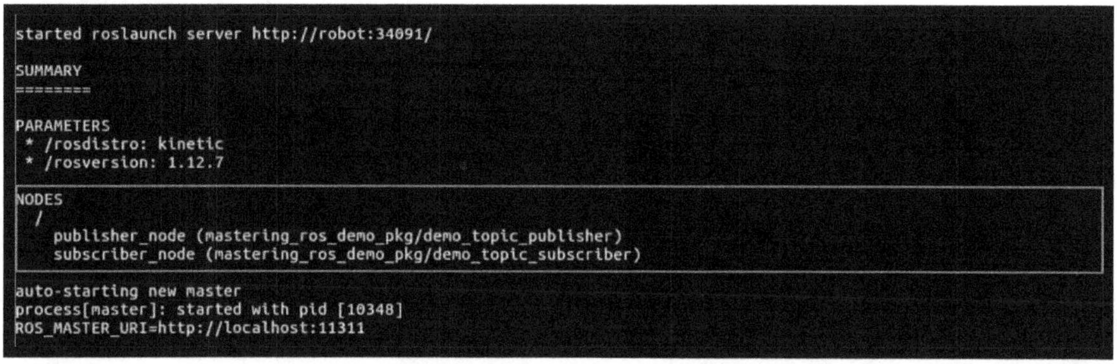
started roslaunch server http://robot:34091/
SUMMARY
========
PARAMETERS
* /rosdistro: kinetic
* /rosversion: 1.12.7
NODES
/
publisher_node (mastering_ros_demo_pkg/demo_topic_publisher)
subscriber_node (mastering_ros_demo_pkg/demo_topic_subscriber)
auto-starting new master
process[master]: started with pid [10348]
ROS_MASTER_URI=http://localhost:11311

Figure 8: Terminal messages while launching the `demo_topic`.launch file.

We can check the list of nodes using:

```
$ rosnode list
```

We can also view the log messages and debug the nodes using a GUI tool called `rqt_console`:

```
$ rqt_console
```

We can see the logs generated by two nodes in this tool, as shown here:

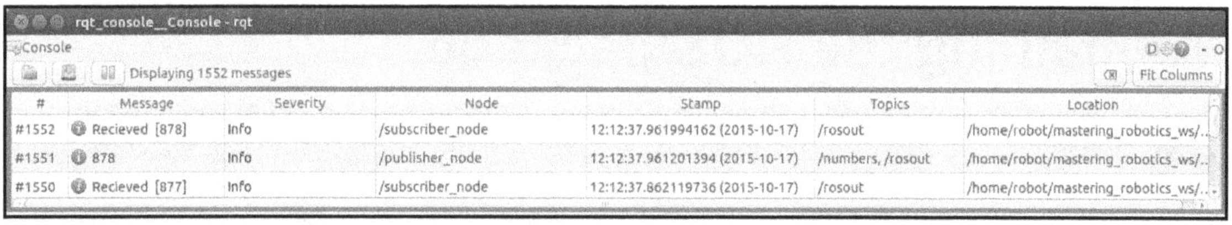
rqt_console__Console - rqt
Console
Displaying 1552 messages
Fit Columns
| Message | Severity | Node | Stamp | Topics | Location
#1552 | Recieved [878] | Info | /subscriber_node | 12:12:37.961994162 (2015-10-17) | /rosout | /home/robot/mastering_robotics_ws/...
#1551 | 878 | Info | /publisher_node | 12:12:37.961201394 (2015-10-17) | /numbers, /rosout | /home/robot/mastering_robotics_ws/...
#1550 | Recieved [877] | Info | /subscriber_node | 12:12:37.862119736 (2015-10-17) | /rosout | /home/robot/mastering_robotics_ws/...

Figure 9: Logging using the `rqt_console` tool.

Applications of topics, services, and actionlib

Topics, services, and actionlib are used in different scenarios. We know topics are a unidirectional communication method, services are a bidirectional request/reply kind of communication, and actionlib is a modified form of ROS services in which we can cancel the executing process running on the server whenever required.

Here are some of the areas where we use these methods:

- **Topics**: Streaming continuous data flow, such as sensor data. For example, stream joypad data to teleoperate a robot, publish robot odometry, publish video stream from a camera.
- **Services**: Executing procedures that terminate quickly. For example, save calibration parameter of sensors, save a map generated by the robot during its navigation, or load a parameter file.
- **Actionlib**: Execute long and complex actions managing their feedback. For example, navigate towards a target or plan a motion path.

The complete source code of this project can be cloned from the following Git repository. The following command will clone the project repository:

```
$ git clone https://github.com/jocacace/mastering_ros_demo_pkg.git
```

Maintaining the ROS package

Most ROS packages are maintained using a **Version Control System** (**VCS**) such as Git, Subversion (svn), Mercurial (hg), and so on. A collection of packages that share a common VCS can be called a repository. The package in the repository can be released using a catkin release automation tool called bloom. Most ROS packages are released as open source with the BSD license. There are active developers around the globe who are contributing to the ROS platform. Maintaining packages is important for all software, especially open source applications. Open source software is maintained and supported by a community of developers. Creating a version control system for our package is essential if we want to maintain and accept a contribution from other developers.

The preceding package is already updated in GitHub, and you can view the source code of the project at https://github.com/jocacace/mastering_ros_demo_pkg.

Releasing your ROS package

After creating a ROS package in GitHub, we can officially release our package. ROS provides detailed steps to release the ROS package using a tool called bloom (`http://ros-infrastructure.github.io/bloom/`). Bloom is a release automation tool, designed to make platform-specific releases from the source projects. Bloom is designed to work best with the catkin project.

The prerequisites for releasing the package are as follows:

- Install the Bloom tool
- Create a Git repository for the current package
- Create an empty Git repository for the release

The following command will install bloom in Ubuntu:

```
$ sudo apt-get install python-bloom
```

Create a Git repository for the current package. The repository that has the package is called the upstream repository. Here, we already created a repository at `https://github.com/jocacace/mastering_ros_demo_pkg`.

Create an empty repository in Git for the release package. This repository is called the `release` repository. We have created a package called `demo_pkg-release`.

After meeting these prerequisites, we can start to create the release of the package. Navigate to the `mastering_ros_demo_pkg` local repository where we push our package code to Git. Open a terminal inside this local repository and execute the following command:

```
$ catkin_generate_changelog
```

The purpose of this command is to create a `CHANGELOG.rst` file inside the local repository. After executing this command, it will show this option:

Continue without -all option [y/N]. Give y here

It will create a `CHANGELOG.rst` in the local repository.

After the creation of the log file, we can update the Git repository by committing the changes:

```
$ git add -A
$ git commit -m 'Updated CHANGELOG.rst'
$ git push -u origin master
```

Preparing the ROS package for the release

In this step, we will check whether the package contains change logs, versions, and so on. The following command makes our package consistent and recommended for release.

This command should execute from the local repository of the package:

```
$ catkin_prepare_release
```

The command will set a version tag if there is no current version, and commit the changes in the upstream repository.

Releasing our package

The following command starts the release. The syntax of this command is as follows:

```
bloom-release --rosdistro <ros_distro> --track <ros_distro> repository_name
$ bloom-release --rosdistro kinetic --track kinetic mastering_ros_demo_pkg
```

When this command is executed, it will go to the rosdistro (https://github.com/ros/rosdistro) package repository to get the package details. The rosdistro package in ROS contains an index file, which contains a list of all the packages in ROS. Currently, there is no index for our package because this is our first release, but we can add our package details to this index file called distributions.yaml.

The following message will be displayed when there is no reference of the package in rosdistro:

```
ROS Distro index file associate with commit '43659b6409dcb545fd3d25c6d977f195cdf
f886a'
New ROS Distro index url: 'https://raw.githubusercontent.com/ros/rosdistro/43659
b6409dcb545fd3d25c6d977f195cdff886a/index.yaml'
Specified repository 'mastering_ros_demo_pkg' is not in the distribution file lo
cated at 'https://raw.githubusercontent.com/ros/rosdistro/43659b6409dcb545fd3d25
c6d977f195cdff886a/kinetic/distribution.yaml'
Could not determine release repository url for repository 'mastering_ros_demo_pk
g' of distro 'kinetic'
You can continue the release process by manually specifying the location of the
RELEASE repository.
To be clear this is the url of the RELEASE repository not the upstream repositor
y.
For release repositories on GitHub, you should provide the `https://` url which
should end in `.git`.
Here is the url for a typical release repository on GitHub: https://github.com/r
os-gbp/rviz-release.git
==> Looking for a release of this repository in a different distribution...
A previous distribution, 'indigo', released this repository.
Release repository url [https://github.com/qboticslabs/demo_pkg-release.git]: ht
tps://github.com/jocacace/demo_pkg-release.git
```

Figure 10: Terminal messages when there is no reference of the package in rosdistro

We should give the release repository in the terminal that is marked in red in the preceding screenshot. In this case, the URL was https://github.com/jocacace/demo_pkg-release:

```
Given track 'kinetic' does not exist in release repository.
Available tracks: []
Create a new track called 'kinetic' now [Y/n]? Y
Creating track 'kinetic'...
Repository Name:
  upstream
    Default value, leave this as upstream if you are unsure
  <name>
    Name of the repository (used in the archive name)
  ['upstream']: mastering_ros_demo_pkg
Upstream Repository URI:
  <uri>
    Any valid URI. This variable can be templated, for example an svn url
    can be templated as such: "https://svn.foo.com/foo/tags/foo-:{version}"
    where the :{version} token will be replaced with the version for this releas
e.
  [None]: https://github.com/jocacace/mastering_ros_demo_pkg.git
```

Figure 11: Inputting the release repository URL

In the upcoming steps, the wizard will ask for the repository name, upstream, URL, and so on. We can give these options and, finally, a pull request to `rosdistro` will be submitted, which is shown in the following screenshot:

```
==> Pulling latest rosdistro branch
remote: Counting objects: 99872, done.
remote: Compressing objects: 100% (38/38), done.
remote: Total 99872 (delta 35), reused 48 (delta 20), pack-reused 99809
Receiving objects: 100% (99872/99872), 29.62 MiB | 4.71 MiB/s, done.
Resolving deltas: 100% (64655/64655), done.
From https://github.com/ros/rosdistro
 * branch            master       -> FETCH_HEAD
==> git reset --hard 43659b6409dcb545fd3d25c6d977f195cdff886a
HEAD is now at 43659b6 Merge pull request #15521 from trainman419/bloom-diagnost
ics-32
==> Writing new distribution file: kinetic/distribution.yaml
==> git add kinetic/distribution.yaml
==> git commit -m "mastering_ros_demo_pkg: 0.0.3-0 in 'kinetic/distribution.yaml
' [bloom]"
[bloom-mastering_ros_demo_pkg-0 763d941] mastering_ros_demo_pkg: 0.0.3-0 in 'kin
etic/distribution.yaml' [bloom]
 1 file changed, 6 insertions(+)
==> Pushing changes to fork
Counting objects: 4, done.
Delta compression using up to 2 threads.
Compressing objects: 100% (3/3), done.
Writing objects: 100% (4/4), 458 bytes | 0 bytes/s, done.
Total 4 (delta 2), reused 0 (delta 0)
remote: Resolving deltas: 100% (2/2), completed with 2 local objects.
To https://7454b673dc9f5564070690111b8f170187884d73:x-oauth-basic@github.com/joc
acace/rosdistro.git
 * [new branch]      bloom-mastering_ros_demo_pkg-0 -> bloom-mastering_ros_demo_
pkg-0
<== Pull request opened at: https://github.com/ros/rosdistro/pull/15526
```

Figure 12: Sending a pull request to rosdistro

The `pull` request for this package can be viewed at `https://github.com/ros/rosdistro/pull/15526`.

If it is accepted, it will merge to `kinetic/distribution.yaml`, which contains the index of all packages in ROS.

The following screenshot displays the package as an index in
`kinetic/distribution.yaml`:

```
6 ▨▨▨▨▨ kinetic/distribution.yaml

  ⊹          @@ -3531,6 +3531,12 @@ repositories:
3531  3531              release: release/kinetic/{package}/{version}
3532  3532            url: https://github.com/MarvelmindRobotics/marvelmind_nav-release.git
3533  3533            version: 1.0.6-0
      3534  +  mastering_ros_demo_pkg:
      3535  +    release:
      3536  +      tags:
      3537  +        release: release/kinetic/{package}/{version}
      3538  +      url: https://github.com/jocacace/mastering_ros_demo_pkg.git
      3539  +      version: 0.0.3-0
3534  3540    mav_comm:
3535  3541      release:
3536  3542        packages:
```

Figure 13: The distribution.yaml file of ROS kinetic.

After this step, we can confirm that the package is released and officially added to the ROS index.

Creating a Wiki page for your ROS package

ROS wiki allows users to create their own home pages to showcase their package, robot, or sensors. The official wiki page of ROS is `wiki.ros.org`. Now, we are going to create a wiki page for our package.

Downloading the example code:
You can download the example code files from your account at: `http://www.packtpub.com` for all the Packt Publishing books you have purchased. If you purchased this book elsewhere, you can visit: `http://www.packtpub.com/support` and register to have the files emailed directly to you. You can also download chapter codes from: `https://github.com/jocacace/mastering_ros_2nd_ed.git`; this code repository contains the link to all other code repositories used in this book.

The first step is to register in wiki using your e-mail address. Go to `wiki.ros.org`, and click on the **Login** button, as shown in the screenshot:

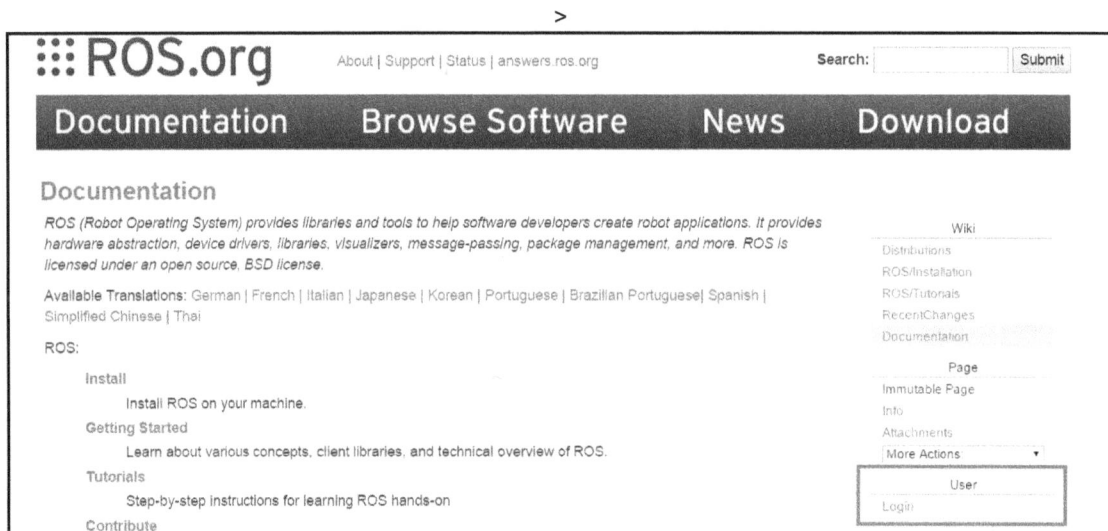

Figure 14: Locating the login option from ROS wiki

After clicking on **Login**, you can register or directly log in with your details if you are already registered. After **Login**, press the username link on the right side of the wiki page, as shown in the following screenshot:

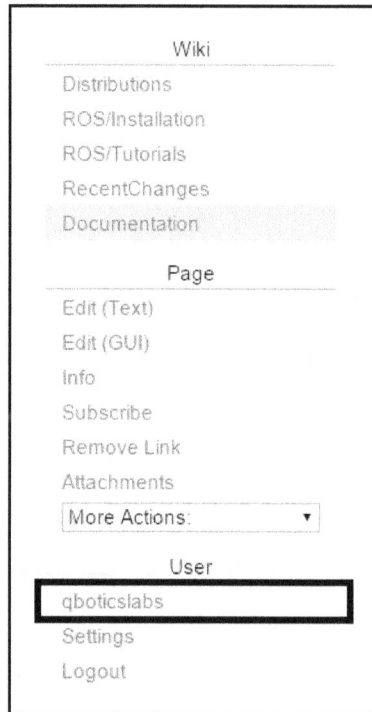

Figure 15: Locating the user account button from ROS wiki

After clicking on this link, you will get a chance to create a home page for your package; you will get a text editor with GUI to enter data into. The following screenshot shows you the page we created for this demo package:

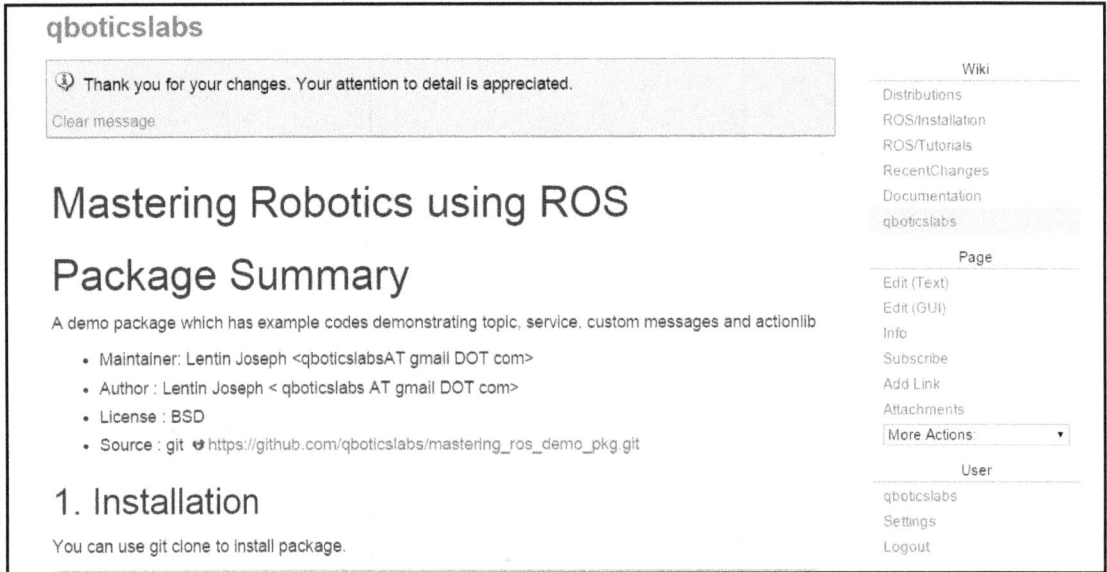

qboticslabs

> ⚓ Thank you for your changes. Your attention to detail is appreciated.
>
> Clear message

Mastering Robotics using ROS

Package Summary

A demo package which has example codes demonstrating topic, service, custom messages and actionlib

- Maintainer: Lentin Joseph <qboticslabsAT gmail DOT com>
- Author : Lentin Joseph < qboticslabs AT gmail DOT com>
- License : BSD
- Source : git ⚙ https://github.com/qboticslabs/mastering_ros_demo_pkg.git

1. Installation

You can use git clone to install package.

Wiki
Distributions
ROS/Installation
ROS/Tutorials
RecentChanges
Documentation
qboticslabs

Page
Edit (Text)
Edit (GUI)
Info
Subscribe
Add Link
Attachments
More Actions ▾

User
qboticslabs
Settings
Logout

Figure 16: Creating a new wiki page.

Questions

After going through the chapter, you should now be able to answer the following questions:

- Which kind of communication protocols between nodes are supported by ROS?
- What is the difference between `rosrun` and `roslaunch` commands?
- How do ROS topics and services differ in their operations?
- How do ROS services and `actionlib` differ in their operations?

Summary

In this chapter, we provided different examples of ROS nodes in which ROS features such as ROS topics, services, and actions were implemented. We discussed how to create and compile ROS packages using custom and standard messages. After demonstrating the workings of each concept, we uploaded the package to GitHub and created a wiki page for the package.

In the next chapter, we will discuss ROS robot modeling using URDF and `xacro`, and will design some robot models.

3
Working with 3D Robot Modeling in ROS

The first phase of robot manufacturing is design and modeling. We can design and model a robot using CAD tools such as AutoCAD, SOLIDWORKS, and Blender. One of the main purposes of robot modeling is simulation.

The robotic simulation tool can check for critical flaws in the robot's design and can confirm that the robot will work before it goes to the manufacturing phase.

The virtual robot model must have all the characteristics of the real hardware. The shape of a robot may or may not look like the actual robot, but it must be abstract, which has all the physical characteristics of the actual robot.

In this chapter, we are going to discuss the designing of two robots. One is a seven **Degrees of Freedom** (**DOF**) manipulator, and the other is a differential drive robot. In the upcoming chapters, we will look at simulation, how to build the real hardware, and interfacing with ROS.

If we are planning to create the 3D model of the robot and simulate it using ROS, you need to learn about some ROS packages that help in robot designing. Creating a model for our robot in ROS is important for different reasons. For example, we can use this model to simulate and control the robot, visualize it, or use ROS tools to get information on the robotic structure and its kinematics.

ROS has a standard meta package for designing and creating robot models called `robot_model`, which consists of a set of packages, some of which are called `urdf`, `kdl_parser`, `robot_state_publisher`, and `collada_urdf`. These packages help us create the 3D robot model description with the exact characteristics of the real hardware.

In this chapter, we will cover the following topics:

- ROS packages for robot modeling
- Creating the ROS package for the robot description
- Understanding robot modeling using URDF
- Understanding robot modeling using xacro
- Converting xacro to URDF
- Creating a robot description for a seven DOF robot manipulator
- Working with the joint state publisher and robot state publisher
- Creating robot description for a differential wheeled robot

ROS packages for robot modeling

ROS provides some good packages that can be used to build 3D robot models.
In this section, we will discuss some of the important ROS packages that are commonly used to build and model a robot:

- urdf: The most important ROS package to model the robot is the urdf package. This package contains a C++ parser for the **Unified Robot Description Format (URDF)**, which is an XML file representing a robot model. Other different components make up urdf:
  - urdf_parser_plugin: This package implements methods to fill URDF data structures
  - urdfdom_headers: This component provides core data structure headers to use the urdf parser
  - collada_parser: This package populates data structures by parsing a Collada file
  - urdfdom: This component populates data structures by parsing URDF files
  - collada-dom: This is a stand-alone component to convert Collada documents with 3D computer graphics software such as *Maya, Blender,* and *Soft image*

We can define a robot model, sensors, and a working environment using URDF, and we can parse it using URDF parsers. We can only describe a robot in URDF that has a tree-like structure in its links, that is, the robot will have rigid links and will be connected using joints. Flexible links can't be represented using URDF. The URDF is composed using special XML tags, and we can parse these XML tags using parser programs for further processing. We can work on URDF modeling in the upcoming sections:

- `joint_state_publisher`: This tool is very useful when designing robot models using URDF. This package contains a node called `joint_state_publisher`, which reads the robot model description, finds all joints, and publishes joint values to all nonfixed joints using GUI sliders. The user can interact with each robot joint using this tool and can visualize using RViz. While designing URDF, the user can verify the rotation and translation of each joint using this tool. We will talk more about the `joint_state_publisher` node and its usage in the upcoming section.

- `kdl_parser`: **Kinematic and Dynamics Library** (KDL) is an ROS package that contains parser tools to build a KDL tree from the URDF representation. The kinematic tree can be used to publish the joint states and also to forward and inverse the kinematics of the robot.

- `robot_state_publisher`: This package reads the current robot joint states and publishes the 3D poses of each robot link using the kinematics tree build from the URDF. The 3D pose of the robot is published as the `tf` (transform) ROS. The `tf` ROS publishes the relationship between the coordinates frames of a robot.

- `xacro`: Xacro stands for (XML Macros), and we can define how `xacro` is equal to URDF plus add-ons. It contains some add-ons to make URDF shorter and readable, and can be used for building complex robot descriptions. We can convert `xacro` to URDF at any time using ROS tools. We will learn more about `xacro` and its usage in the upcoming sections.

Understanding robot modeling using URDF

We have discussed the `urdf` package. In this section, we will look further into the URDF XML tags, which help to model the robot. We have to create a file and write the relationship between each link and joint in the robot and save the file with the `.urdf` extension.

URDF can represent the kinematic and dynamic description of the robot, the visual representation of the robot, and the collision model of the robot.

The following tags are the commonly used URDF tags to compose a URDF robot model:

- `link`: The `link` tag represents a single link of a robot. Using this tag, we can model a robot link and its properties. The modeling includes the size, the shape, and the color, and it can even import a 3D mesh to represent the robot link. We can also provide the dynamic properties of the link, such as the inertial matrix and the collision properties.

    The syntax is as follows:

    ```
    <link name="<name of the link>">
    <inertial>...........</inertial>
      <visual> ............</visual>
      <collision>..........</collision>
    </link>
    ```

    The following is a representation of a single link. The **Visual** section represents the real link of the robot, and the area surrounding the real link is the **Collision** section. The **Collision** section encapsulates the real link to detect collision before hitting the real link:

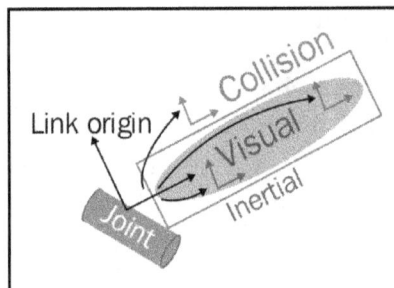

Figure 1: Visualization of a URDF link

- `joint`: The `joint` tag represents a robot joint. We can specify the kinematics and the dynamics of the joint, and set the limits of the joint movement and its velocity. The `joint` tag supports the different types of joints, such as **revolute, continuous, prismatic, fixed, floating,** and **planar**.

    The syntax is as follows:

    ```
    <joint name="<name of the joint>">
      <parent link="link1"/>
      <child link="link2"/>
      <calibration .... />
    ```

```
<dynamics damping ..../>
<limit effort .... />
</joint>
```

A URDF joint is formed between two links; the first is called the **Parent** link, and the second is called the **Child** link. The following is an illustration of a joint and its link:

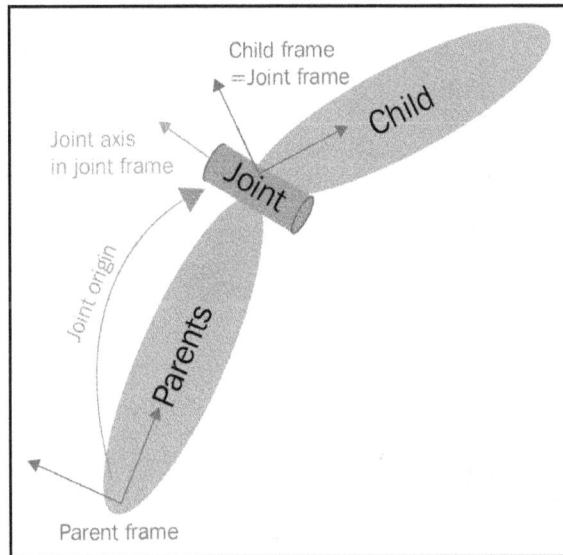

Figure 2: Visualization of a URDF joint

- robot: This tag encapsulates the entire robot model that can be represented using URDF. Inside the robot tag, we can define the name of the robot, the links, and the joints of the robot.

  The syntax is as follows:

  ```
  <robot name="<name of the robot>"
      <link>  ..... </link>
      <link> ...... </link>

      <joint> ....... </joint>
      <joint> ........</joint>
  </robot>
  ```

A robot model consists of connected links and joints. Here is a visualization of the robot model:

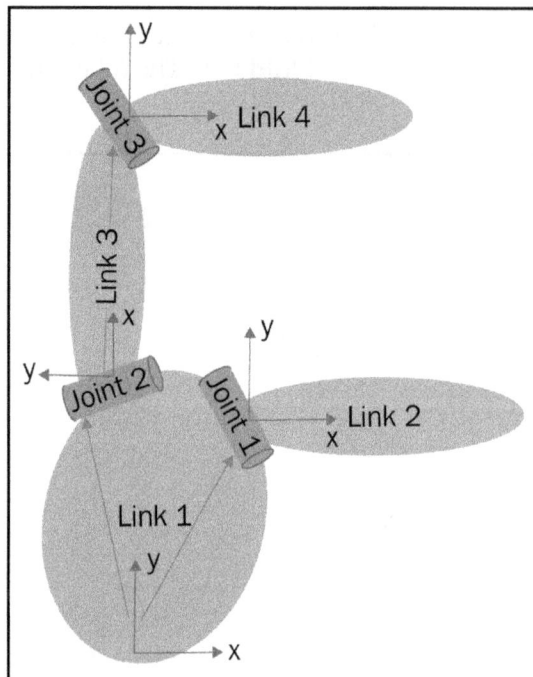

Figure 3: Visualization of a robot model having joints and links

- gazebo: This tag is used when we include the simulation parameters of the Gazebo simulator inside the URDF. We can use this tag to include gazebo plugins, gazebo material properties, and so on. The following shows an example using gazebo tags:

```
<gazebo reference="link_1">
    <material>Gazebo/Black</material>
</gazebo>
```

You can find more URDF tags at http://wiki.ros.org/urdf/XML.

Creating the ROS package for the robot description

Before creating the URDF file for the robot, let's create an ROS package in the `catkin` workspace so that the robot model keeps using the following command:

```
$ catkin_create_pkg mastering_ros_robot_description_pkg roscpp tf
  geometry_msgs urdf rviz xacro
```

The package mainly depends on the `urdf` and `xacro` packages. If these packages have not been installed on to your system, you can install them using the package manager:

```
$sudo apt-get install ros-kinetic-urdf
$sudo apt-get install ros-kinetic-xacro
```

We can create the `urdf` file of the robot inside this package and create launch files to display the created `urdf` in RViz. The full package is available on the following Git repository; you can clone the repository for a reference to implement this package, or you can get the package from the book's source code:

```
$ git clone
https://github.com/jocacace/mastering_ros_robot_description_pkg.git
```

Before creating the `urdf` file for this robot, let's create three folders called `urdf`, `meshes`, and `launch` inside the package folder. The `urdf` folder can be used to keep the `urdf` and `xacro` files that we are going to create. The `meshes` folder keeps the meshes that we need to include in the `urdf` file, and the `launch` folder keeps the ROS launch files.

Creating our first URDF model

After learning about URDF and its important tags, we can start some basic modeling using URDF. The first robot mechanism that we are going to design is a pan-and-tilt mechanism, as shown in the following figure.

There are three links and two joints in this mechanism. The base link is static, and all the other links are mounted on it. The first joint can pan on its axis, and the second link is mounted on the first link, and it can tilt on its axis. The two joints in this system are of a revolute type:

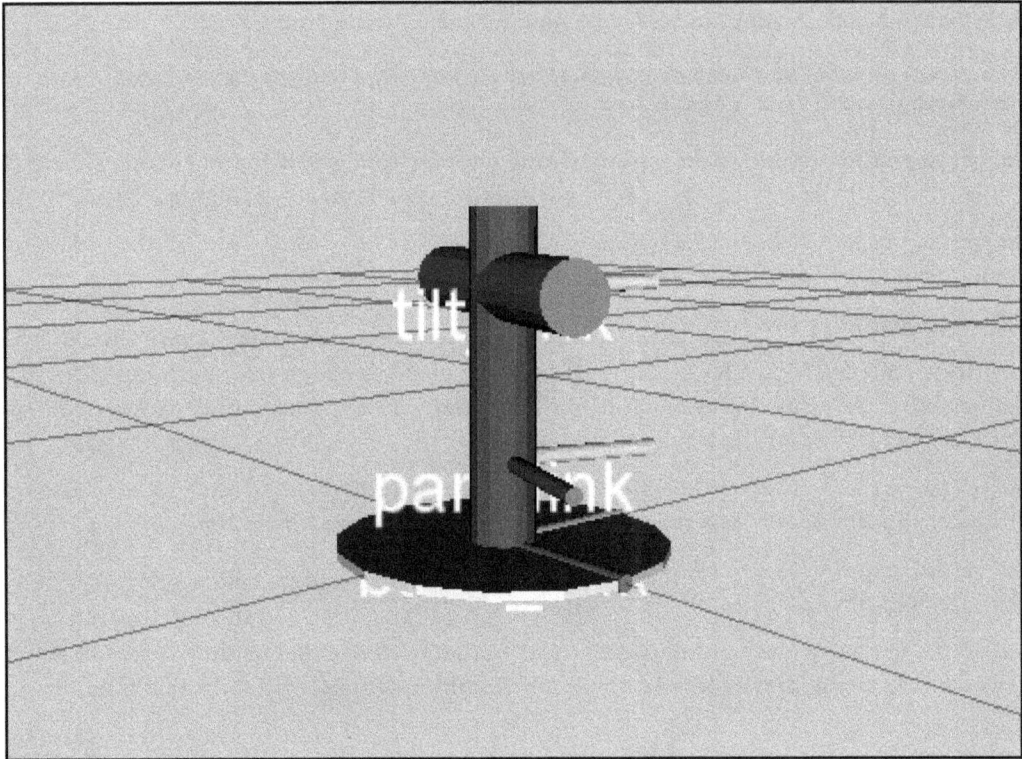

Figure 4: Visualization of a pan-and-tilt mechanism in RViz

Let's see the URDF code of this mechanism. Navigate to the `mastering_ros_robot_description_pkg/urdf` directory and open `pan_tilt.urdf`:

```xml
<?xml version="1.0"?>
<robot name="pan_tilt">
  <link name="base_link">
    <visual>
      <geometry>
      <cylinder length="0.01" radius="0.2"/>
      </geometry>
      <origin rpy="0 0 0" xyz="0 0 0"/>
```

```xml
      <material name="yellow">
        <color rgba="1 1 0 1"/>
      </material>
    </visual>
  </link>
  <joint name="pan_joint" type="revolute">
    <parent link="base_link"/>
    <child link="pan_link"/>
    <origin xyz="0 0 0.1"/>
    <axis xyz="0 0 1" />
  </joint>
  <link name="pan_link">
    <visual>
      <geometry>
      <cylinder length="0.4" radius="0.04"/>
      </geometry>
      <origin rpy="0 0 0" xyz="0 0 0.09"/>
      <material name="red">
        <color rgba="0 0 1 1"/>
      </material>
    </visual>
  </link>
  <joint name="tilt_joint" type="revolute">
    <parent link="pan_link"/>
    <child link="tilt_link"/>
    <origin xyz="0 0 0.2"/>
    <axis xyz="0 1 0" />
  </joint>
  <link name="tilt_link">
    <visual>
      <geometry>
  <cylinder length="0.4" radius="0.04"/>
      </geometry>
      <origin rpy="0 1.5 0" xyz="0 0 0"/>
      <material name="green">
        <color rgba="1 0 0 1"/>
      </material>
    </visual>
  </link>
</robot>
```

Explaining the URDF file

When we check the code, we can add a `<robot>` tag at the top of the description:

```
<?xml version="1.0"?>
<robot name="pan_tilt">
```

The `<robot>` tag defines the name of the robot that we are going to create. Here, we named the robot `pan_tilt`.

If we check the sections after the `<robot>` tag definition, we can see link and joint definitions of the pan-and-tilt mechanism:

```
<link name="base_link">
  <visual>
    <geometry>
    <cylinder length="0.01" radius="0.2"/>
    </geometry>
    <origin rpy="0 0 0" xyz="0 0 0"/>
    <material name="yellow">
      <color rgba="1 1 0 1"/>
    </material>
  </visual>
</link>
```

The preceding code snippet is the `base_link` definition of the pan-and-tilt mechanism. The `<visual>` tag describes the visual appearance of the link, which is shown on the robot simulation. We can define the link geometry (`cylinder`, `box`, `sphere`, or `mesh`) and the material (`color` and `texture`) of the link using this tag:

```
<joint name="pan_joint" type="revolute">
  <parent link="base_link"/>
  <child link="pan_link"/>
  <origin xyz="0 0 0.1"/>
  <axis xyz="0 0 1" />
</joint>
```

In the preceding code snippet, we define, a joint with a unique name and its joint type. The joint type we used here is `revolute`, and the parent and child links are `base_link` and `pan_link`, respectively. The joint origin is also specified inside this tag.

Save the preceding URDF code as `pan_tilt.urdf` and check whether the `urdf` contains errors using the following command:

```
$ check_urdf pan_tilt.urdf
```

The `check_urdf` command will parse the `urdf` tag and show an error, if there are any. If everything is OK, it will output the following:

```
robot name is: pan_tilt
---------- Successfully Parsed XML ---------------
  root Link: base_link has 1 child(ren)
    child(1):  pan_link
      child(1):  tilt_link
```

If we want to view the structure of the robot links and joints graphically, we can use a command tool called `urdf_to_graphiz`:

```
$ urdf_to_graphiz pan_tilt.urdf
```

This command will generate two files: `pan_tilt.gv` and `pan_tilt.pdf`. We can view the structure of this robot using this command:

```
$ evince pan_tilt.pdf
```

We will get the following output:

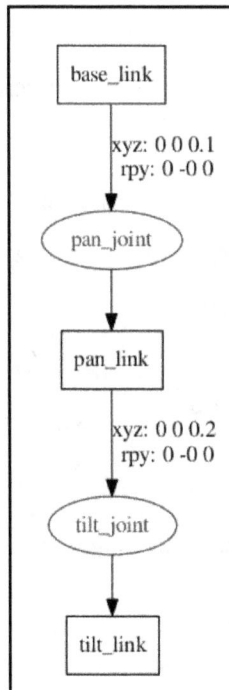

Figure 5: Graph of joint and links in the pan-and-tilt mechanism

Visualizing the 3D robot model in RViz

After designing the URDF, we can view it on RViz. We can create a `view_demo.launch` launch file and put the following code into the `launch` folder. Navigate to the `mastering_ros_robot_description_pkg/launch` directory for the code:

```
<launch>
  <arg name="model" />
  <param name="robot_description" textfile="$(find
mastering_ros_robot_description_pkg)/urdf/pan_tilt.urdf" />
  <param name="use_gui" value="true"/>
  <node name="joint_state_publisher" pkg="joint_state_publisher"
type="joint_state_publisher" />
  <node name="robot_state_publisher" pkg="robot_state_publisher"
type="state_publisher" />
  <node name="rviz" pkg="rviz" type="rviz" args="-d $(find
mastering_ros_robot_description_pkg)/urdf.rviz" required="true" />
</launch>
```

We can launch the model using the following command:

```
$ roslaunch mastering_ros_robot_description_pkg view_demo.launch
```

If everything works fine, we will get a pan-and-tilt mechanism in RViz, as shown here:

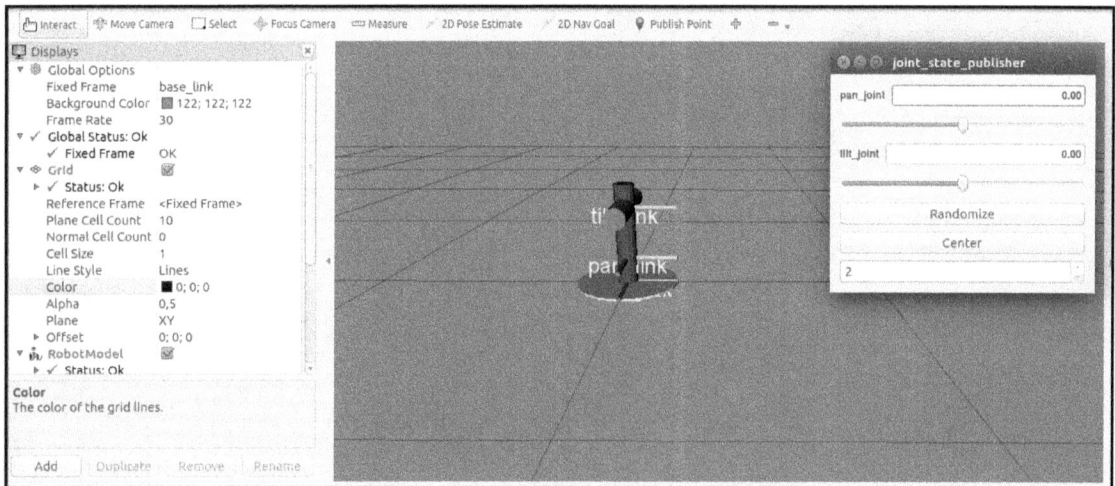

Figure 6: Joint level of pan-and-tilt mechanism

Interacting with pan-and-tilt joints

We can see that an extra GUI came along with RViz; it contains sliders to control the pan joints and the tilt joints. This GUI is called the Joint State Publisher node, from the `joint_state_publisher` package:

```
<node name="joint_state_publisher" pkg="joint_state_publisher"
type="joint_state_publisher" />
```

We can include this node in the `launch` file, using this statement. The limits of pan-and-tilt should be mentioned inside the `joint` tag:

```
<joint name="pan_joint" type="revolute">
  <parent link="base_link"/>
  <child link="pan_link"/>
  <origin xyz="0 0 0.1"/>
  <axis xyz="0 0 1" />
  <limit effort="300" velocity="0.1" lower="-3.14" upper="3.14"/>
  <dynamics damping="50" friction="1"/>
</joint>
```

`<limit effort="300" velocity="0.1" lower="-3.14" upper="3.14"/>` defines the limits of effort, the velocity, and the angle limits. The effort is the maximum force supported by this joint; `lower` and `upper` indicate the lower and upper limit of the joint in the radian for the revolute type joint, and meters for prismatic joints. The velocity is the maximum joint velocity:

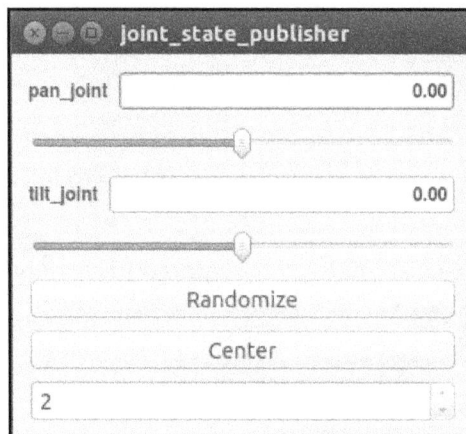

Figure 7: Joint level of pan-and-tilt mechanism

The preceding screenshot shows the GUI of `joint_state_publisher`, with sliders and current joint values shown in the box.

Adding physical and collision properties to a URDF model

Before simulating a robot in a robot simulator, such as Gazebo or V-REP, we need to define the robot link's physical properties, such as geometry, color, mass, and inertia, as well as the collision properties of the link.

We will only get good simulation results if we define all these properties inside the robot model. URDF provides tags to include all these parameters and code snippets of `base_link` contained in these properties, as given here:

```
<link>
......
<collision>
     <geometry>
     <cylinder length="0.03" radius="0.2"/>
     </geometry>
     <origin rpy="0 0 0" xyz="0 0 0"/>
</collision>

<inertial>
<mass value="1"/>
<inertia ixx="1.0" ixy="0.0" ixz="0.0" iyy="1.0" iyz="0.0" izz="1.0"/>
</inertial>
..........
</link>
```

Here, we define the collision geometry as cylinder and the mass as 1 kg, and we also set the inertial matrix of the link.

The `collision` and `inertia` parameters are required in each link, otherwise Gazebo will not load the robot model properly.

Understanding robot modeling using xacro

The flexibility of URDF reduces when we work with complex robot models. Some of the main features that URDF is missing are simplicity, reusability, modularity, and programmability.

If someone wants to reuse a URDF block 10 times in his robot description, he can copy and paste the block 10 times. If there is an option to use this code block and make multiple copies with different settings, it will be very useful while creating the robot description.

The URDF is a single file and we can't include other URDF files inside it. This reduces the modular nature of the code. All code should be in a single file, which reduces the code's simplicity.

Also, if there is some programmability, such as adding variables, constants, mathematical expressions, and conditional statements, in the description language, it will be more user-friendly.

The robot modeling using xacro meets all of these conditions. Some of the main features of xacro are as follows:

- **Simplify URDF**: The xacro is the cleaned-up version of URDF. It creates macros inside the robot description and reuses the macros. This can reduce the code length. Also, it can include macros from other files and make the code simpler, more readable, and more modular.
- **Programmability**: The xacro language supports a simple programming statement in its description. There are variables, constants, mathematical expressions, conditional statements, and so on that make the description more intelligent and efficient.

We can say that xacro is an updated version of URDF, and we can convert the xacro definition to URDF whenever it is necessary, using some ROS tools.

We can talk about the same description of pan-and-tilt using xacro. Navigate to `mastering_ros_robot_description_pkg/urdf`, and the file name is `pan_tilt.xacro`. Instead of `.urdf`, we need to use the `.xacro` extension for xacro files. Here is the explanation of the xacro code:

```xml
<?xml version="1.0"?>
<robot xmlns:xacro="http://www.ros.org/wiki/xacro" name="pan_tilt">
```

These lines specify a namespace that is needed in all xacro files for parsing the xacro file. After specifying the namespace, we need to add the name of the xacro file.

Using properties

Using xacro, we can declare constants or properties that are the named values inside the xacro file, which can be used anywhere in the code. The main use of these constant definitions is, instead of giving hardcoded values on links and joints, we can keep constants, and it will be easier to change these values rather than finding the hardcoded values and replacing them.

An example of using properties is given here. We declare the base link and the pan link's length and radius. So, it will be easy to change the dimension here rather than changing the values in each one:

```
<xacro:property name="base_link_length" value="0.01" />
<xacro:property name="base_link_radius" value="0.2" />
<xacro:property name="pan_link_length" value="0.4" />
<xacro:property name="pan_link_radius" value="0.04" />
```

We can use the value of the variable by replacing the hardcoded value with the following definition:

```
<cylinder length="${pan_link_length}"
radius="${pan_link_radius}"/>
```

Here, the old value, `"0.4"`, is replaced with `"{pan_link_length}"`, and `"0.04"` is replaced with `"{pan_link_radius}"`.

Using the math expression

We can build mathematical expressions inside `${}` using basic operations such as +, −, * , / , unary minus, and parenthesis. Exponentiation and modulus are not supported yet. The following is a simple math expression used inside the code:

```
<cylinder length="${pan_link_length}"
radius="${pan_link_radius+0.02}"/>
```

Using macros

One of the main features of xacro is that it supports macros. We can use xacro to reduce the length of complex definitions. Here is a `xacro` definition we used in our code for inertial:

```
<xacro:macro name="inertial_matrix" params="mass">
  <inertial>
      <mass value="${mass}" />
        <inertia ixx="0.5" ixy="0.0" ixz="0.0"
        iyy="0.5" iyz="0.0" izz="0.5" />
  </inertial>
</xacro:macro>
```

Here, the macro is named `inertial_matrix`, and its parameter is mass. The mass parameter can be used inside the inertial definition using `${mass}`. We can replace each inertial code with a single line, as given here:

```
<xacro:inertial_matrix mass="1"/>
```

The xacro definition improved the code readability and reduced the number of lines compared to `urdf`. Next, we will look at how to convert xacro to a URDF file.

Converting xacro to URDF

After designing the xacro file, we can use the following command to convert it to a URDF file:

```
$ rosrun xacro xacro pan_tilt.xacro --inorder > pan_tilt_generated.urdf
```

The `--inorder` option has been recently introduced in ROS to increase the power of the conversion tool. It allows us to process the document in read order, adding more features than there were in older ROS versions.

We can use the following line in the ROS launch file for converting xacro to URDF and use it as a `robot_description` parameter:

```
<param name="robot_description" command="$(find xacro)/xacro --inorder
$(find mastering_ros_robot_description_pkg)/urdf/pan_tilt.xacro"
/>
```

We can view the xacro of pan-and-tilt by making a launch file, and it can be launched using the following command:

```
$ roslaunch mastering_ros_robot_description_pkg
view_pan_tilt_xacro.launch
```

Creating the robot description for a seven DOF robot manipulator

Now, we can create some complex robots using URDF and xacro. The first robot we are going to deal with is a seven DOF robotic arm, which is a serial link manipulator with multiple serial links. The seven DOF arm is kinematically redundant, which means it has more joints and DOF than required to achieve its goal position and orientation. The advantage of redundant manipulators is that we can have more joint configuration for a desired goal position and orientation. It will improve the flexibility and versatility of the robot movement and can implement effective collision-free motion in a robotic workspace.

Let's start creating the seven DOF arm; the final output model of the robot arm is shown here (the various joints and links in the robot are also marked on the image):

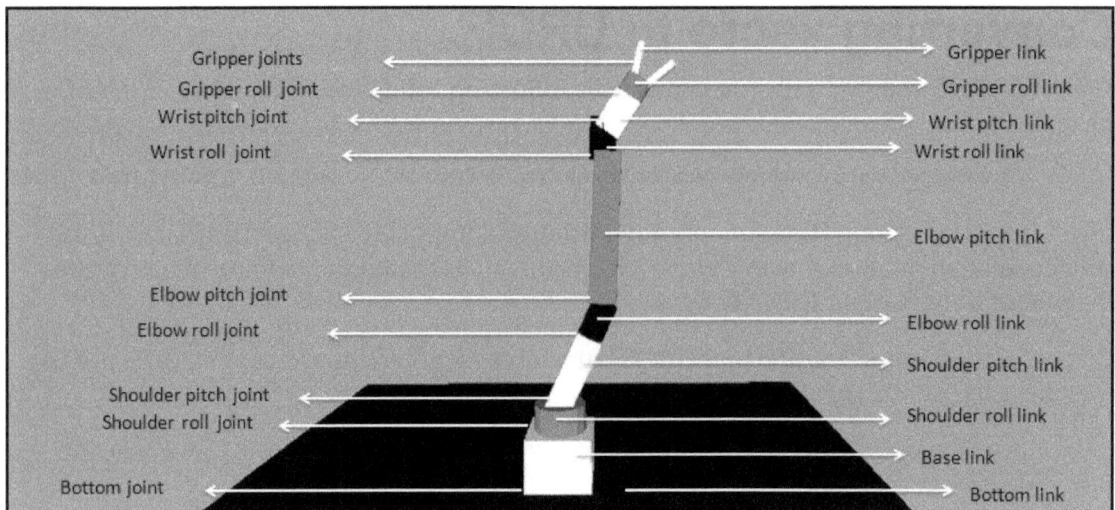

Figure 8: Joints and Links of seven DOF arm robot

The preceding robot is described using xacro. We can take the actual description file from the cloned repository. We can navigate to the `urdf` folder inside the cloned package and open the `seven_dof_arm.xacro` file. We will copy and paste the description to the current package and discuss the major section of this robot description.

Arm specification

Here is the robot arm specification of this seven DOF arm:

- Degrees of freedom: 7
- Length of the arm: 50 cm
- Reach of the arm: 35 cm
- Number of links: 12
- Number of joints: 11

Type of joints

Here is the list of joints containing the joint name and its type of robot:

Joint number	Joint name	Joint type	Angle limits (in degrees)
1	`bottom_joint`	Fixed	--
2	`shoulder_pan_joint`	Revolute	-150 to 114
3	`shoulder_pitch_joint`	Revolute	-67 to 109
4	`elbow_roll_joint`	Revolute	-150 to 41
5	`elbow_pitch_joint`	Revolute	-92 to 110
6	`wrist_roll_joint`	Revolute	-150 to 150
7	`wrist_pitch_joint`	Revolute	92 to 113
8	`gripper_roll_joint`	Revolute	-150 to 150
9	`finger_joint1`	Prismatic	0 to 3 cm
10	`finger_joint2`	Prismatic	0 to 3 cm

We design the xacro of the arm using the preceding specifications; next up is the explanation of the xacro arm file.

Explaining the xacro model of the seven DOF arm

We will define ten links and nine joints on this robot, and two links and two joints in the robot gripper.

Let's start by looking at the xacro definition:

```
<?xml version="1.0"?>
<robot name="seven_dof_arm" xmlns:xacro="http://ros.org/wiki/xacro">
```

Because we are writing a xacro file, we should mention the xacro namespace to parse the file.

Using constants

We use constants inside this xacro to make robot descriptions shorter and more readable. Here, we define the degree to the radian conversion factor, PI value, length, height, and width of each of the links:

```
<property name="deg_to_rad" value="0.01745329251994329577"/>
<property name="M_PI" value="3.14159"/>
<property name="elbow_pitch_len" value="0.22" />
<property name="elbow_pitch_width" value="0.04" />
<property name="elbow_pitch_height" value="0.04" />
```

Using macros

We define macros in this code to avoid repeatability and to make the code shorter. Here are the macros we have used in this code:

```
<xacro:macro name="inertial_matrix" params="mass">
   <inertial>
     <mass value="${mass}" />
     <inertia ixx="1.0" ixy="0.0" ixz="0.0" iyy="0.5" iyz="0.0"
izz="1.0" />
   </inertial>
</xacro:macro>
```

This is the definition of the `inertial matrix` macro, in which we can use `mass` as its parameter:

```
<xacro:macro name="transmission_block" params="joint_name">
 <transmission name="tran1">
   <type>transmission_interface/SimpleTransmission</type>
   <joint name="${joint_name}">
     <hardwareInterface>PositionJointInterface</hardwareInterface>
   </joint>
   <actuator name="motor1">
     <hardwareInterface>PositionJointInterface</hardwareInterface>
     <mechanicalReduction>1</mechanicalReduction>
   </actuator>
 </transmission>
</xacro:macro>
```

In the section of the code, we can see the definition using the `transmission` tag.

The `transmission` tag relates a joint to an actuator. It defines the type of transmission that we are using in a particular joint, as well as the type of motor and its parameters. It also defines the type of hardware interface we use when we interface with the ROS controllers.

Including other xacro files

We can extend the capabilities of the robot xacro by including the xacro definition of sensors using the `xacro:include` tag. The following code snippet shows how to include a sensor definition in the robot xacro:

```
<xacro:include filename="$(find
mastering_ros_robot_description_pkg)/urdf/sensors/xtion_pro_live.urdf.xacro
"/>
```

Here, we include a xacro definition of a sensor called **Asus Xtion pro**, and this will be expanded when the xacro file is parsed.

Using "`$(find mastering_ros_robot_description_pkg)/urdf/sensors/xtion_pro_live.urdf.xacro`", we can access the xacro definition of the sensor, where `find` is to locate the current `mastering_ros_robot_description_pkg` package.

We will talk more about vision-processing in `Chapter 10`, *Building and Interfacing Differential Drive Mobile Robot Hardware in ROS*.

Using meshes in the link

We can insert a primitive shape in to a link, or we can insert a mesh file using the `mesh` tag. The following example shows how to insert a mesh into the vision sensor:

```
<visual>
  <origin xyz="0 0 0" rpy="0 0 0"/>
  <geometry>
    <mesh filename=
"package://mastering_ros_robot_description_pkg/meshes/sensors/xtion_pro_liv
e/xtion_pro_live.dae"/>
  </geometry>
<material name="DarkGrey"/>
</visual>
```

Working with the robot gripper

The gripper of the robot is designed for the picking and placing of blocks; the gripper is in the simple linkage category. There are two joints for the gripper, and each joint is prismatic. Here is the `joint` definition of one gripper joint:

```
<joint name="finger_joint1" type="prismatic">
<parent link="gripper_roll_link"/>
<child link="gripper_finger_link1"/>
<origin xyz="0.0 0 0" />
<axis xyz="0 1 0" />
  <limit effort="100" lower="0" upper="0.03" velocity="1.0"/>
  <safety_controller k_position="20"
                     k_velocity="20"
                     soft_lower_limit="${-0.15 }"
                     soft_upper_limit="${ 0.0 }"/>
<dynamics damping="50" friction="1"/>
</joint>
```

Here, the first gripper joint is formed by `gripper_roll_link` and `gripper_finger_link1`, and the second joint is formed by `gripper_roll_link` and `gripper_finger_link2`.

The following graph shows how the gripper joints are connected in `gripper_roll_link`:

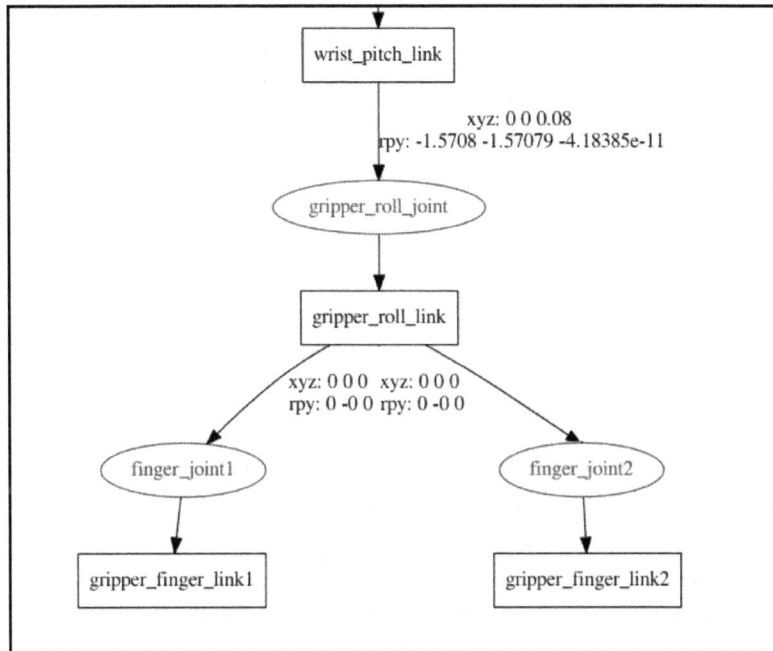

Figure 9: Graph of the end effector section of the seven DOF arm robot

Viewing the seven DOF arm in RViz

After talking about the robot model, we can view the designed xacro file in **RViz** and control each joint using the `joint state publisher` node and publish the robot state using `Robot State Publisher`.

The preceding task can be performed using a launch file called `view_arm.launch`, which is inside the `launch` folder of this package:

```
<launch>
  <arg name="model" />

  <!-- Parsing xacro and loading robot_description parameter -->
  <param name="robot_description" command="$(find xacro)/xacro --inorder
$(find mastering_ros_robot_description_pkg)/urdf/ seven_dof_arm.xacro " />

  <!-- Setting gui parameter to true for display joint slider, for getting
```

```
joint control -->
  <param name="use_gui" value="true"/>

  <!-- Starting Joint state publisher node which will publish the joint
values -->
  <node name="joint_state_publisher" pkg="joint_state_publisher"
type="joint_state_publisher" />

  <!-- Starting robot state publish which will publish current robot joint
states using tf -->
  <node name="robot_state_publisher" pkg="robot_state_publisher"
type="state_publisher" />

  <!-- Launch visualization in rviz -->
  <node name="rviz" pkg="rviz" type="rviz" args="-d $(find
mastering_ros_robot_description_pkg)/urdf.rviz" required="true" />
</launch>
```

Create the following launch file inside the `launch` folder, and build the package using the `catkin_make` command. Launch the `urdf` using the following command:

$ roslaunch mastering_ros_robot_description_pkg view_arm.launch

The robot will be displayed on RViz, with the joint state publisher GUI:

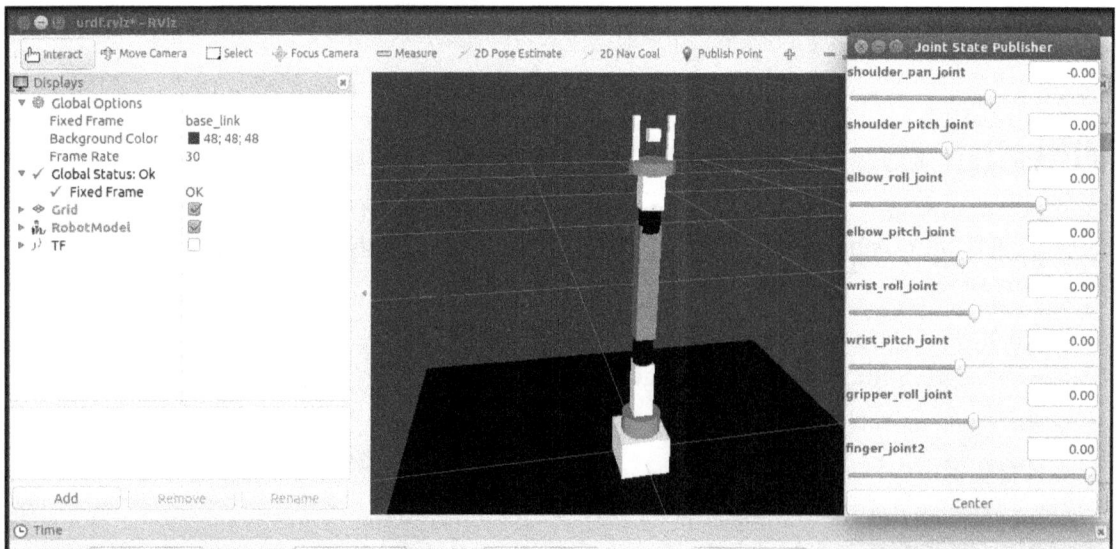

Figure 10: Seven DOF arm in RViz with joint_state_publisher

We can interact with the joint slider and move the joints of the robot. Next, we will talk about what `joint state publisher` can do.

Understanding joint state publisher

Joint state publisher is one of the ROS packages that is commonly used to interact with each joint of the robot. The package contains the `joint_state_publisher` node, which will find the nonfixed joints from the URDF model and publish the joint state values of each joint in the `sensor_msgs/JointState` message format.

In the preceding launch file, `view_arm.launch`, we started the `joint_state_publisher` node and set a parameter called `use_gui` to `true`, as follows:

```
<param name="use_gui" value="true"/>

<!-- Starting Joint state publisher node which will publish the joint values -->
<node name="joint_state_publisher" pkg="joint_state_publisher"
type="joint_state_publisher" />
```

If we set `use_gui` to `true`, the `joint_state_publisher` node displays a slider-based control window to control each joint. The lower and upper value of a joint will be taken from the lower and upper values associated with the `limit` tag used inside the `joint` tag. The preceding screenshot shows the robot model in RViz, along with a user interface to change the position of robot joints, which states with the `use_gui` parameter set to `true`.

We can find more on the `joint state publisher` package at http://wiki.ros.org/joint_state_publisher.

Understanding robot state publisher

The `robot state publisher` package helps to publish the state of the robot to `tf`. This package subscribes to joint states of the robot and publishes the 3D pose of each link using the kinematic representation from the URDF model. We can implement the `robot state publisher` node using the following line inside the launch file:

```
<!-- Starting robot state publish which will publish tf -->
<node name="robot_state_publisher" pkg="robot_state_publisher"
type="state_publisher" />
```

In the preceding launch file, `view_arm.launch`, we started this node to publish the `tf` of the arm. We can visualize the transformation of the robot by clicking the `tf` option on RViz, shown as follows:

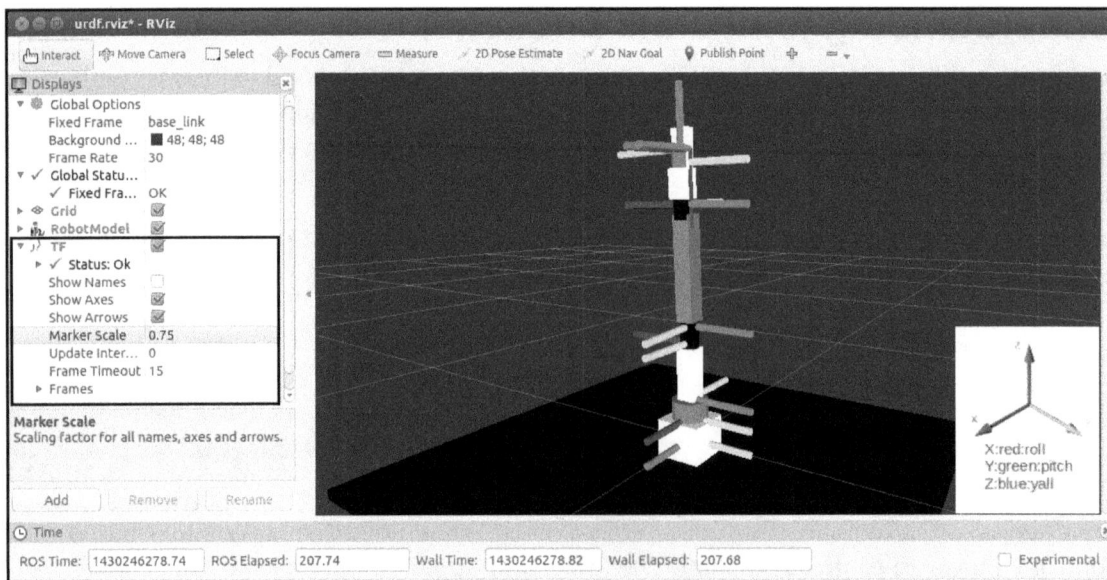

Figure 11: TF view of seven DOF arm in RViz

The `joint_state_publisher` and `robot_state_publisher` packages are installed along with the ROS desktop's installations.

After creating the robot description of the seven DOF arm, we can talk about how to make a mobile robot with differential wheeled mechanisms.

Creating a robot model for the differential drive mobile robot

A differential wheeled robot will have two wheels connected on opposite sides of the robot chassis, which is supported by one or two caster wheels. The wheels will control the speed of the robot by adjusting individual velocity. If the two motors are running at the same speed, the wheels will move forward or backward. If one wheel is running slower than the other, the robot will turn to the side of the lower speed. If we want to turn the robot to the left side, we reduce the velocity of the left wheel, and vice versa.

There are two supporting wheels, called caster wheels, that will support the robot and rotate freely based on the movement of the main wheels.

The URDF model of this robot is present in the cloned ROS package. The final robot model is shown here:

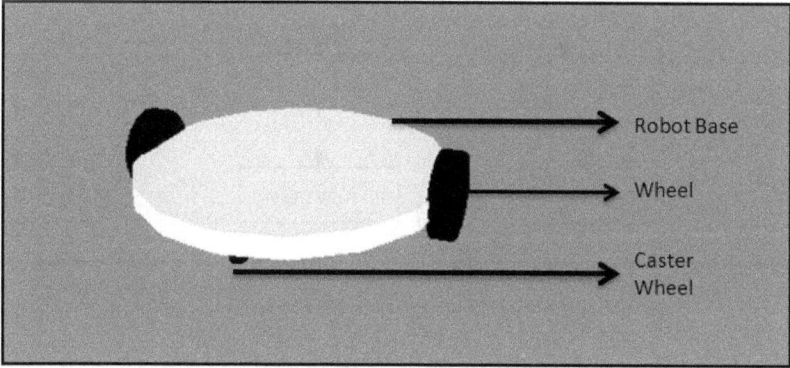

Figure 12: Differential drive mobile robot

The preceding robot has five joints and links. The two main joints connect the wheels to the robot, while the others are fixed joints connecting the caster wheels and the base footprint to the body of the robot.

The preceding robot has five joints and five links. The two main joints are two-wheel joints, and the other three joints are two fixed joints by caster wheels, and one fixed joint by base foot print to the base link of the robot. Here is the connection graph of this robot:

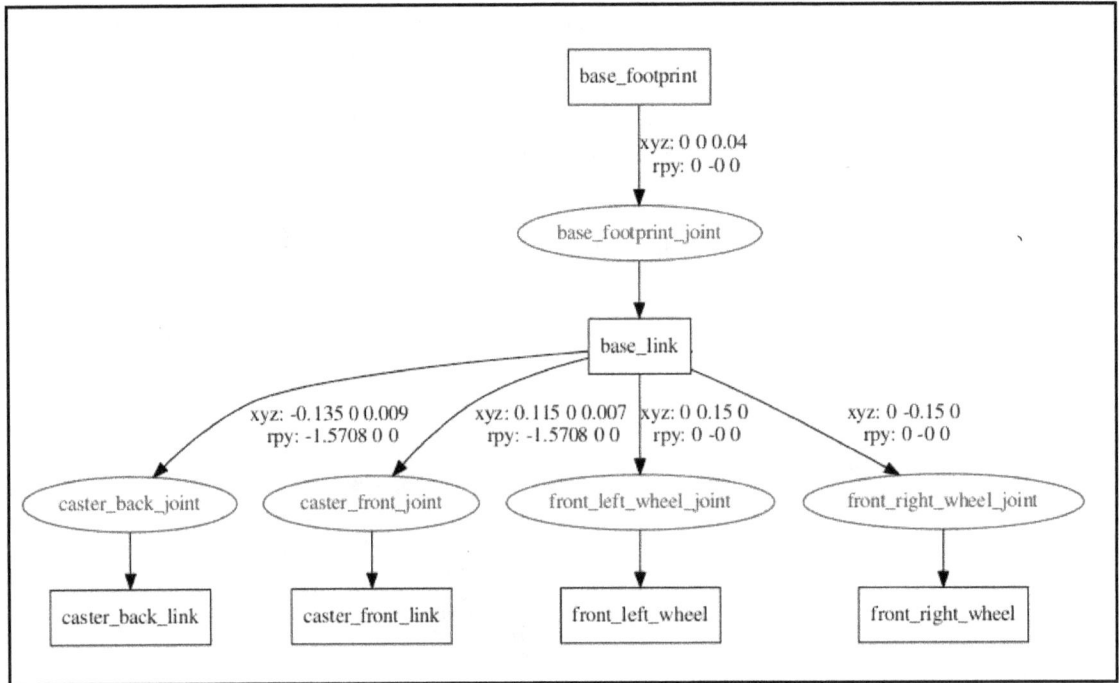

Figure 13: Graphical representation of links and joints for the differential drive mobile robot

We can go through the important section of code in the URDF file. The URDF file, called `diff_wheeled_robot.xacro`, is placed inside the `urdf` folder of the cloned ROS package.

The first section of the URDF file is given here. The robot is named `differential_wheeled_robot`, and it also includes a URDF file, called `wheel.urdf.xacro`. This xacro file contains the definition of the wheel and its transmission; if we use this xacro file, then we can avoid writing two definitions for the two wheels. We use this xacro definition because the two wheels are identical in shape and size:

```
<?xml version="1.0"?>
<robot name="differential_wheeled_robot"
xmlns:xacro="http://ros.org/wiki/xacro">

  <xacro:include filename="$(find
mastering_ros_robot_description_pkg)/urdf/wheel.urdf.xacro">
```

The definition of a wheel inside `wheel.urdf.xacro` is given here. We can mention whether the wheel has to be placed to the left, right, front, or back. Using this macro, we can create a maximum of four wheels but, for now, we require only two:

```
<xacro:macro name="wheel" params="fb lr parent translateX translateY
flipY"> <!--fb : front, back ; lr: left, right -->
    <link name="${fb}_${lr}_wheel">
```

We also mention the Gazebo parameters required for simulation. Mentioned here are the Gazebo parameters associated with a wheel. We can mention the frictional co-efficient and the stiffness co-efficient using the `gazeboreference` tag:

```
<gazebo reference="${fb}_${lr}_wheel">
  <mu1 value="1.0"/>
  <mu2 value="1.0"/>
  <kp  value="10000000.0" />
  <kd  value="1.0" />
  <fdir1 value="1 0 0"/>
  <material>Gazebo/Grey</material>
  <turnGravityOff>false</turnGravityOff>
</gazebo>
```

The joints that we define for a wheel are continuous joints because there is no limit in the `wheel` joint. The `parent link` here is the robot base, and the `child link` is each wheel:

```
<joint name="${fb}_${lr}_wheel_joint" type="continuous">
  <parent link="${parent}"/>
  <child link="${fb}_${lr}_wheel"/>
  <origin xyz="${translateX *
```

We also need to mention the `transmission` tag of each wheel; the macro of the wheel is as follows:

```
<!-- Transmission is important to link the joints and the controller -
->
<transmission name="${fb}_${lr}_wheel_joint_trans">
  <type>transmission_interface/SimpleTransmission</type>
  <joint name="${fb}_${lr}_wheel_joint" />
  <actuator name="${fb}_${lr}_wheel_joint_motor">
    <hardwareInterface>EffortJointInterface</hardwareInterface>
    <mechanicalReduction>1</mechanicalReduction>
  </actuator>
</transmission>
</xacro:macro>
</robot>
```

In `diff_wheeled_robot.xacro`, we can use the following lines to use the macros defined inside `wheel.urdf.xacro`:

```
<wheel fb="front" lr="right" parent="base_link" translateX="0"
translateY="-0.5" flipY="-1"/>
<wheel fb="front" lr="left" parent="base_link" translateX="0"
translateY="0.5" flipY="-1"/>
```

Using the preceding lines, we define the wheels on the left and right of the robot base. The robot base is cylindrical, as shown in the preceding figure. The inertia calculating macro is given here. This xacro snippet will use the mass, radius, and height of the cylinder to calculate inertia using this equation:

```
<!-- Macro for calculating inertia of cylinder -->
<macro name="cylinder_inertia" params="m r h">
  <inertia  ixx="${m*(3*r*r+h*h)/12}" ixy = "0" ixz = "0"
            iyy="${m*(3*r*r+h*h)/12}" iyz = "0"
            izz="${m*r*r/2}" />
</macro>
```

The launch file definition for displaying this root model in RViz is given here. The launch file is named `view_mobile_robot.launch`:

```
<launch>
  <arg name="model" />
  <!-- Parsing xacro and setting robot_description parameter -->
  <param name="robot_description" command="$(find xacro)/xacro --inorder
$(find mastering_ros_robot_description_pkg)/urdf/diff_wheeled_robot.xacro"
/>
  <!-- Setting gui parameter to true for display joint slider -->
  <param name="use_gui" value="true"/>
```

```
<!-- Starting Joint state publisher node which will publish the joint
values -->
  <node name="joint_state_publisher" pkg="joint_state_publisher"
type="joint_state_publisher" />
  <!-- Starting robot state publish which will publish tf -->
  <node name="robot_state_publisher" pkg="robot_state_publisher"
type="state_publisher" />
  <!-- Launch visualization in rviz -->
  <node name="rviz" pkg="rviz" type="rviz" args="-d $(find
mastering_ros_robot_description_pkg)/urdf.rviz" required="true" />
</launch>
```

The only difference between the arm URDF file is the change in the name; the other sections are the same.

We can view the mobile robot using the following command:

```
$ roslaunch mastering_ros_robot_description_pkg view_mobile_robot.launch
```

The screenshot of the robot in RViz is as follows:

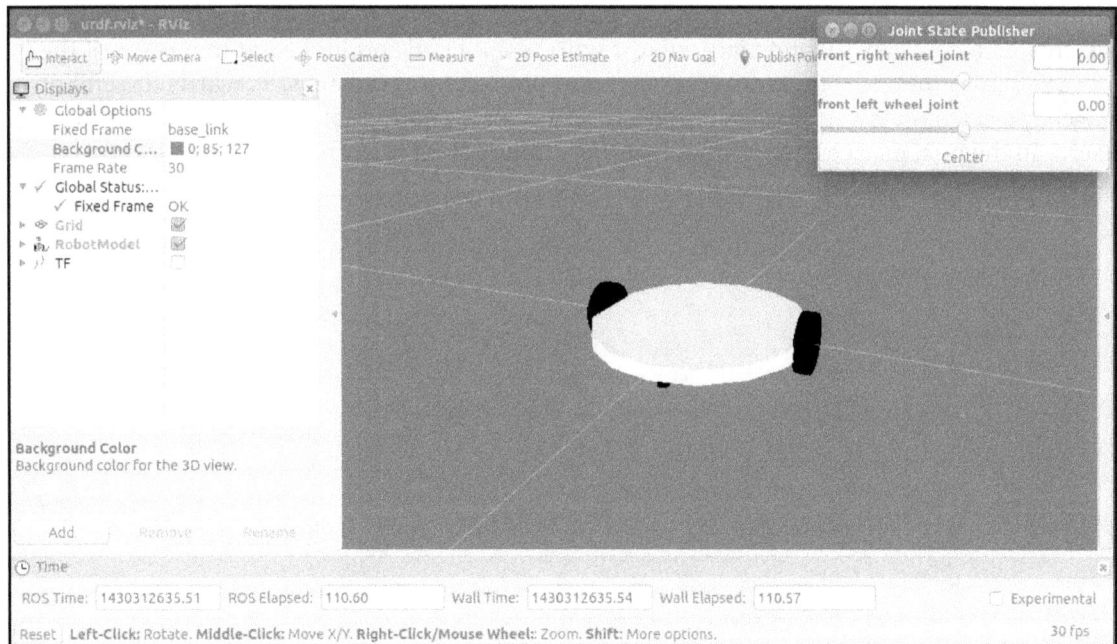

Figure 14: Visualizing mobile robot in RViz with joint state publisher

Questions

- What are the packages used for robot modeling in ROS?
- What are the important URDF tags used for robot modeling?
- What are the reasons for using xacro over URDF?
- What is the function of the joint state publisher and robot state publisher packages?
- What is the function of the transmission tag in URDF?

Summary

In this chapter, we mainly looked at the importance of robot modeling and how we can model a robot in ROS. We talked more about the `robot_model` meta package and the packages inside `robot_model`, such as `urdf`, `xacro`, and `joint_state_publisher`. We discussed URDF, xacro, and the main URDF tags that we are going to use. We also created a sample model in URDF and xacro and discussed the difference between the two. After that, we created a complex robotic manipulator with seven DOF and looked at the usage of the `joint state publisher` and `robot state publisher` packages. Towards the end of the chapter, we reviewed the designing procedure of a differential drive mobile robot using xacro. In the next chapter, we will look at the simulation of these robots using Gazebo.

4
Simulating Robots Using ROS and Gazebo

After designing the 3D model of a robot, the next phase is its simulation. Robot simulation will give you an idea about the working of robots in a virtual environment.

We are going to use the Gazebo (`http://www.gazebosim.org/`) simulator to simulate the seven DOF arms and the mobile robot.

Gazebo is a multi-robot simulator for complex indoor and outdoor robotic simulation. We can simulate complex robots, robot sensors, and a variety of 3D objects. Gazebo already has simulation models of popular robots, sensors, and a variety of 3D objects in their repository (`https://bitbucket.org/osrf/gazebo_models/`). We can directly use these models without having to create new ones.

Gazebo has a good interface in ROS, which exposes the whole control of Gazebo in ROS. We can install Gazebo without ROS, and we should install the ROS-Gazebo interface to communicate from ROS to Gazebo.

In this chapter, we will discuss the simulation of seven DOF arms and differential wheeled robots. We will discuss ROS controllers that help to control the robot's joints in Gazebo.

We will cover the following topics in this chapter:

- Understanding robotic simulation and Gazebo
- Simulation a model of a robotic arm for Gazebo
- Simulating the robotic arm with an *rgb-d* sensor
- Moving robot joints using ROS controllers in Gazebo
- Simulating a differential wheeled robot in Gazebo
- Teleoperating a mobile robot in Gazebo

Simulating the robotic arm using Gazebo and ROS

In the previous chapter, we designed a seven-DOF arm. In this section, we will simulate the robot in Gazebo using ROS.

Before starting with Gazebo and ROS, we should install the following packages to work with Gazebo and ROS:

```
$ sudo apt-get install ros-kinetic-gazebo-ros-pkgs ros-kinetic-gazebo-msgs
ros-kinetic-gazebo-plugins ros-kinetic-gazebo-ros-control
```

The default version installed from kinetic ROS packages is Gazebo 7.0. The use of each package is as follows:

- `gazebo_ros_pkgs`: This contains wrappers and tools for interfacing ROS with Gazebo
- `gazebo-msgs`: This contains messages and service data structures for interfacing with Gazebo from ROS
- `gazebo-plugins`: This contains Gazebo plugins for sensors, actuators, and so on.
- `gazebo-ros-control`: This contains standard controllers to communicate between ROS and Gazebo

After installation, check whether Gazebo is properly installed using the following commands:

```
$ roscore & rosrun gazebo_ros gazebo
```

These commands will open the Gazebo GUI. If we have the Gazebo simulator, we can proceed to develop the simulation model of the seven-DOF arm for Gazebo.

Creating the robotic arm simulation model for Gazebo

We can create the simulation model for a robotic arm by updating the existing robot description by adding simulation parameters.

We can create the package needed to simulate the robotic arm using the following command:

```
$ catkin_create_pkg seven_dof_arm_gazebo gazebo_msgs gazebo_plugins
gazebo_ros gazebo_ros_control mastering_ros_robot_description_pkg
```

Alternatively, the full package is available in the following Git repository; you can clone the repository for a reference to implement this package, or you can get the package from the book's source code:

```
$ git clone  https://github.com/jocacace/seven_dof_arm_gazebo.git
```

You can see the complete simulation model of the robot in the `seven_dof_arm.xacro` file, placed in the `mastering_ros_robot_description_pkg/urdf/` folder.

The file is filled with URDF tags, which are necessary for the simulation. We will define the sections of collision, inertial, transmission, joints, links, and Gazebo.

To launch the existing simulation model, we can use the `seven_dof_arm_gazebo` package, which has a launch file called `seven_dof_arm_world.launch`. The file definition is as follows:

```
<launch>

  <!-- these are the arguments you can pass this launch file, for example
paused:=true -->
  <arg name="paused" default="false"/>
  <arg name="use_sim_time" default="true"/>
  <arg name="gui" default="true"/>
  <arg name="headless" default="false"/>
  <arg name="debug" default="false"/>

  <!-- We resume the logic in empty_world.launch -->
  <include file="$(find gazebo_ros)/launch/empty_world.launch">
    <arg name="debug" value="$(arg debug)" />
    <arg name="gui" value="$(arg gui)" />
    <arg name="paused" value="$(arg paused)"/>
    <arg name="use_sim_time" value="$(arg use_sim_time)"/>
    <arg name="headless" value="$(arg headless)"/>
  </include>

  <!-- Load the URDF into the ROS Parameter Server -->
  <param name="robot_description" command="$(find xacro)/xacro --inorder
'$(find mastering_ros_robot_description_pkg)/urdf/seven_dof_arm.xacro'" />

  <!-- Run a python script to the send a service call to gazebo_ros to
spawn a URDF robot -->
  <node name="urdf_spawner" pkg="gazebo_ros" type="spawn_model"
respawn="false" output="screen"
  args="-urdf -model seven_dof_arm -param robot_description"/>
</launch>
```

Launch the following command and check what you get:

```
$ roslaunch seven_dof_arm_gazebo seven_dof_arm_world.launch
```

You can see the robotic arm in Gazebo, as shown in the following figure; if you get this output, without any errors, you are done:

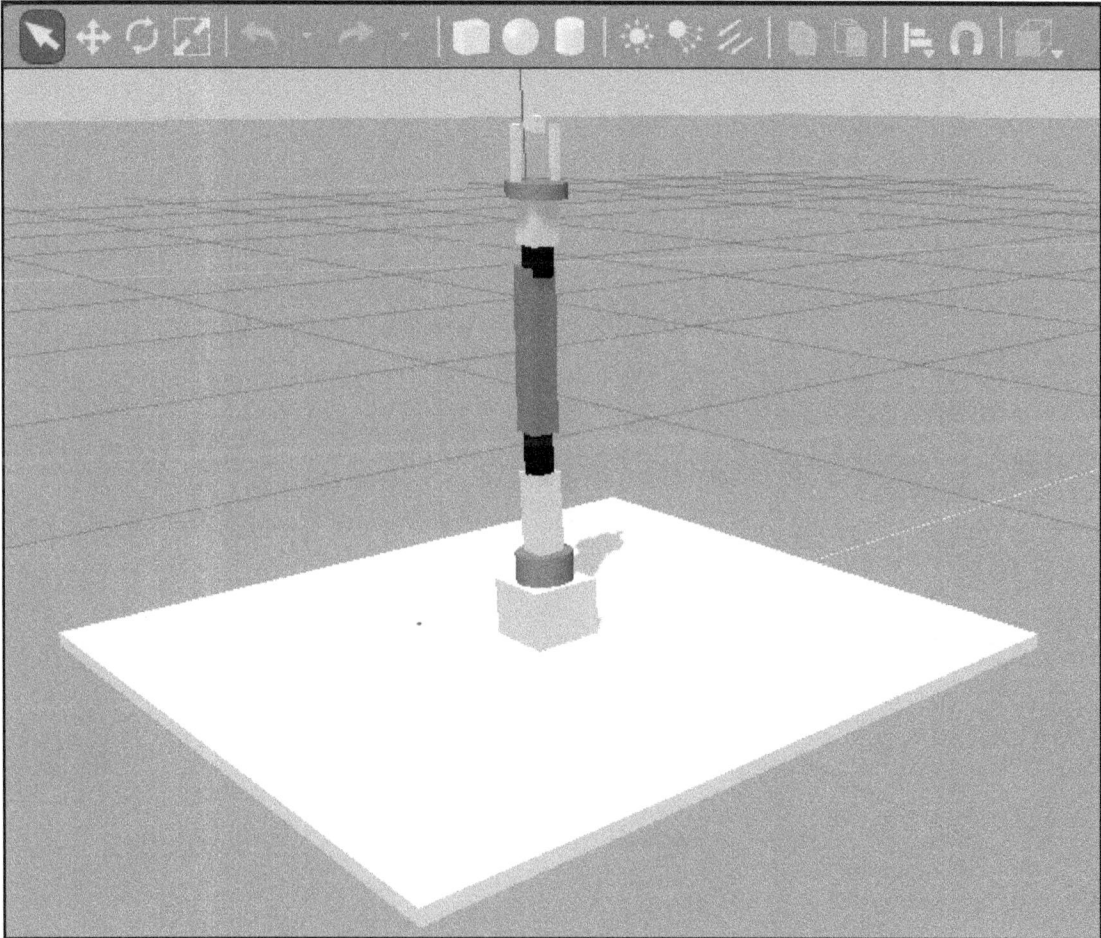

Figure 1: Simulation of seven-DOF arm in Gazebo

Let's discuss the robot simulation model files in detail.

Adding colors and textures to the Gazebo robot model

We can see in the simulated robot that each link has different colors and textures. The following tags inside the xacro file provide textures and colors to robot links:

```
<gazebo reference="bottom_link">
  <material>Gazebo/White</material>
</gazebo>
<gazebo reference="base_link">
  <material>Gazebo/White</material>
</gazebo>
<gazebo reference="shoulder_pan_link">
  <material>Gazebo/Red</material>
</gazebo>
```

Adding transmission tags to actuate the model

To actuate the robot using ROS controllers, we should define the `<transmission>` element to link actuators to joints. Here is the macro defined for transmission:

```
<xacro:macro name="transmission_block" params="joint_name">
  <transmission name="tran1">
    <type>transmission_interface/SimpleTransmission</type>
    <joint name="${joint_name}">
<hardwareInterface>hardware_interface/PositionJointInterface</hardwareInterface>
    </joint>
    <actuator name="motor1">
     <mechanicalReduction>1</mechanicalReduction>
    </actuator>
  </transmission>
</xacro:macro>
```

Here, `<joint name = "">` is the joint in which we link the actuators. The `<type>` element is the type of transmission. Currently, `transmission_interface/SimpleTransmission` is only supported. The `<hardwareInterface>` element is the type of hardware interface to load (position, velocity, or effort interfaces). In the proposed example, a position control hardware interface has been used. The hardware interface is loaded by the `gazebo_ros_control` plugin; we look at this plugin in the next section.

Adding the gazebo_ros_control plugin

After adding the transmission tags, we should add the `gazebo_ros_control` plugin in the simulation model to parse the transmission tags and assign appropriate hardware interfaces and the control manager. The following code adds the `gazebo_ros_control` plugin to the xacro file:

```
<!-- ros_control plugin -->
<gazebo>
  <plugin name="gazebo_ros_control" filename="libgazebo_ros_control.so">
    <robotNamespace>/seven_dof_arm</robotNamespace>
  </plugin>
</gazebo>
```

Here, the `<plugin>` element specifies the plugin name to be loaded, which is `libgazebo_ros_control.so`. The `<robotNamespace>` element can be given as the name of the robot; if we are not specifying the name, it will automatically load the name of the robot from the URDF. We can also specify the controller update rate (`<controlPeriod>`), the location of `robot_description` (URDF) on the parameter server (`<robotParam>`), and the type of robot hardware interface (`<robotSimType>`). The default hardware interfaces are `JointStateInterface`, `EffortJointInterface`, and `VelocityJointInterface`.

Adding a 3D vision sensor to Gazebo

In Gazebo, we can simulate the robot movement and its physics; we can also simulate sensors too.

To build a sensor in Gazebo, we must model the behavior of that sensor in Gazebo. There are some prebuilt sensor models in Gazebo that can be used directly in our code without writing a new model.

Here, we are adding a 3D vision sensor (commonly known as an *rgb-d* sensor) called the Asus Xtion Pro model in Gazebo. The sensor model is already implemented in the `gazebo_ros_pkgs/gazebo_plugins` ROS package, which we have already installed in our ROS system.

Each model in Gazebo is implemented as a Gazebo-ROS plugin, which can be loaded by inserting it into the URDF file.

Here is how we include a Gazebo definition and a physical robot model of Xtion Pro in the `seven_dof_arm_with_rgbd.xacro` robot xacro file:

```
<xacro:include filename="$(find
mastering_ros_robot_description_pkg)/urdf/sensors/xtion_pro_live.urdf.xacro
"/>
```

Inside `xtion_pro_live.urdf.xacro`, we can see the following lines:

```
<?xml version="1.0"?>
<robot xmlns:xacro="http://ros.org/wiki/xacro">
  <xacro:include filename="$(find
mastering_ros_robot_description_pkg)/urdf/sensors/xtion_pro_live.gazebo.xac
ro"/>
...................
  <xacro:macro name="xtion_pro_live" params="name parent *origin
*optical_origin">
...................
    <link name="${name}_link">
      ....................
  <visual>
        <origin xyz="0 0 0" rpy="0 0 0"/>
        <geometry>
          <mesh
filename="package://mastering_ros_robot_description_pkg/meshes/sensors/xtio
n_pro_live/xtion_pro_live.dae"/>
        </geometry>
        <material name="DarkGrey"/>
    </visual>
    </link>

</robot>
```

Here, we can see it includes another file called `xtion_pro_live.gazebo.xacro`, which consists of the complete Gazebo definition of Xtion Pro.

We can also see a macro definition named `xtion_pro_live`, which contains the complete model definition of Xtion Pro, including links and joints:

```
<mesh
filename="package://mastering_ros_robot_description_pkg/meshes/sensors/xtio
n_pro_live/xtion_pro_live.dae"/>
```

In the macro definition, we are importing a mesh file of the Asus Xtion Pro, which will be shown as the camera link in Gazebo.

In the `mastering_ros_robot_description_pkg/urdf/sensors/xtion_pro_live.gazebo.xacro` file, we can set the Gazebo-ROS plugin of Xtion Pro. Here, we will define the plugin as macro with RGB and depth camera support. Here is the plugin definition:

```
        <plugin name="${name}_frame_controller"
 filename="libgazebo_ros_openni_kinect.so">
        <alwaysOn>true</alwaysOn>
        <updateRate>6.0</updateRate>
        <cameraName>${name}</cameraName>
        <imageTopicName>rgb/image_raw</imageTopicName>

    </plugin>
```

The plugin filename of Xtion Pro is `libgazebo_ros_openni_kinect.so`, and we can define the plugin parameters, such as the camera name, image topics, and so on.

Simulating the robotic arm with Xtion Pro

Now that we have learned about the camera plugin definition in Gazebo, we can launch the complete simulation using the following command:

```
$ roslaunch seven_dof_arm_gazebo seven_dof_arm_with_rgbd_world.launch
```

We can see the robot model with a sensor on the top of the arm, as shown here:

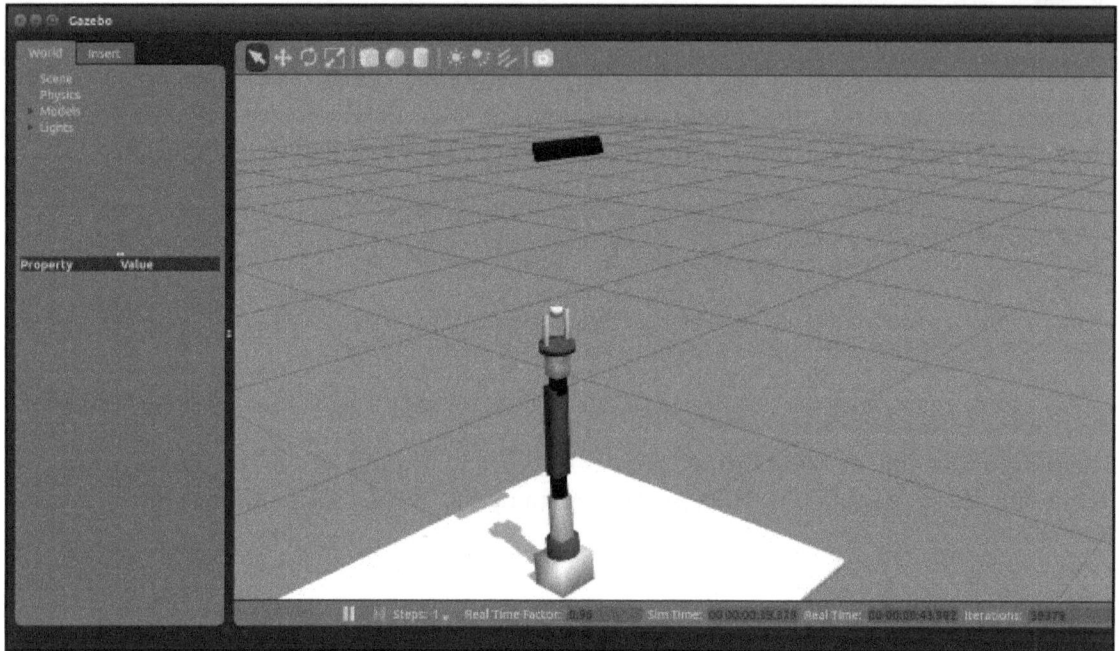

Figure 2: Simulation of seven-DOF arm with Asus Xtion Pro in Gazebo

We can now work with the simulated *rgb-d* sensor as if it were directly plugged into our computer. So we can check whether it provides the correct image output.

Visualizing the 3D sensor data

After launching the simulation using the preceding command, we can check topics generated by the sensor plugin:

```
jcacace@robot:~$ rostopic list
/rgbd_camera/depth/image_raw
/rgbd_camera/ir/image_raw
/rgbd_camera/rgb/image_raw
```

Figure 3: *rgb-d* image topics generated by Gazebo

Let's view the image data of a 3D vision sensor using the following tool called `image_view`:

- View the RGB raw image:

```
$ rosrun image_view image_view image:=/rgbd_camera/rgb/image_raw
```

- View the IR raw image:

```
$ rosrun image_view image_view image:=/rgbd_camera/ir/image_raw
```

- View the depth image:

```
$ rosrun image_view image_view image:=/rgbd_camera/depth/image_raw
```

Here is the screenshot with all these images:

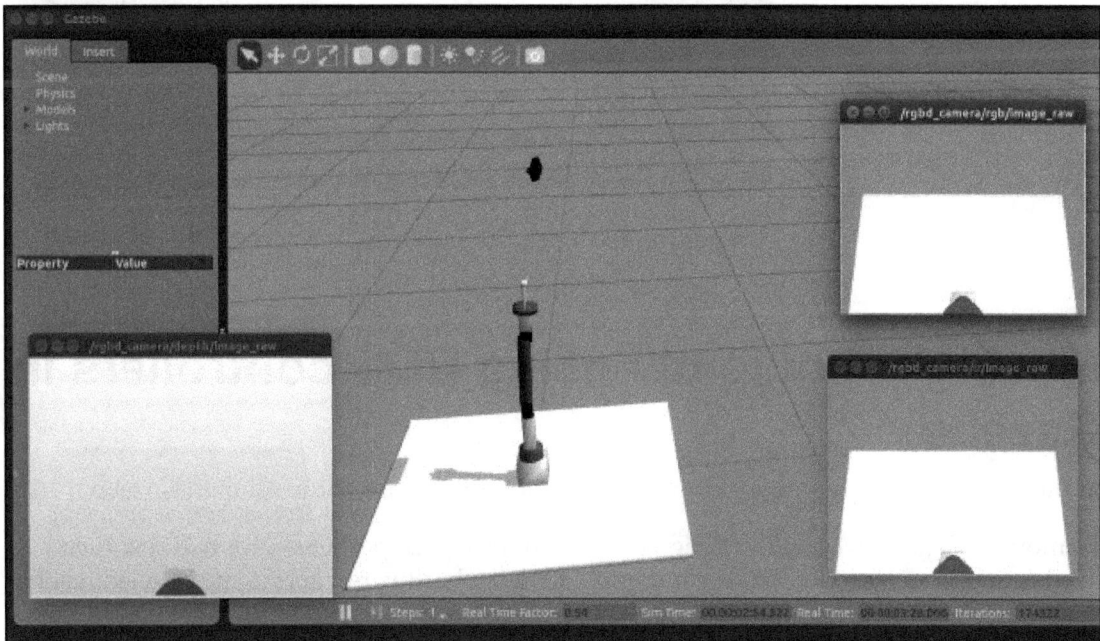

Figure 4: Viewing images of the *rgb-d* sensor in Gazebo

We can also view the point cloud data of this sensor in RViz.

Launch RViz using the following command:

```
$ rosrun rviz rviz -f /rgbd_camera_optical_frame
```

Add a **PointCloud2** display type and set the **Topic** as `/rgbd_camera/depth/points`. We will get a point cloud view as follows:

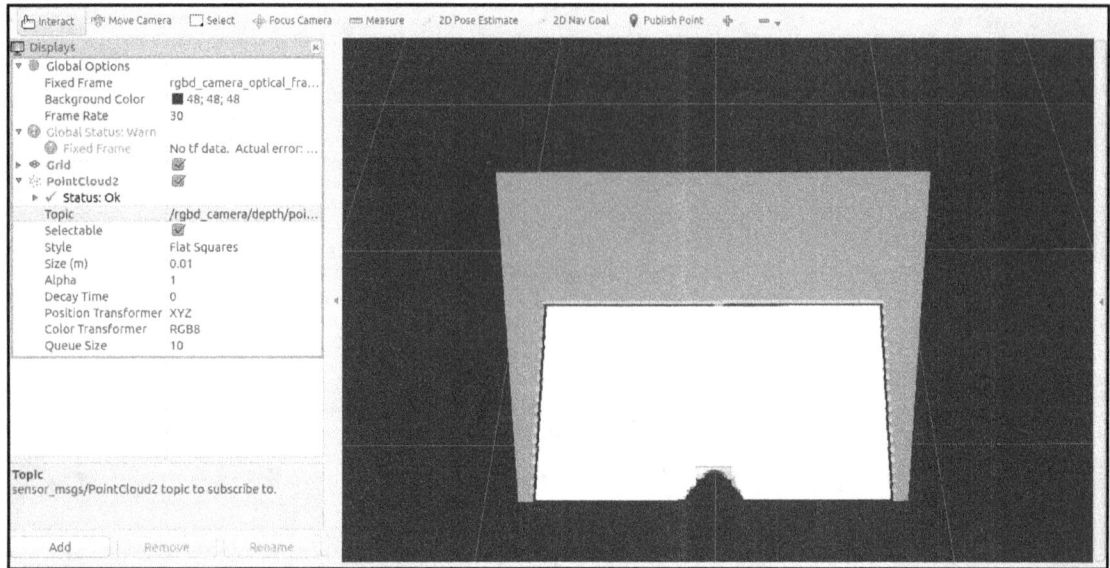

Figure 5: Viewing point cloud data from an *rgb-d* sesor in RViz

Moving robot joints using ROS controllers in Gazebo

In this section, we are going to discuss how to move each joint of the robot in Gazebo.

To move each joint, we need to assign an ROS controller. In particular, for each joint we need to attach a controller that is compatible with the hardware interface mentioned inside the `transmission` tags.

An ROS controller mainly consists of a feedback mechanism that can receive a set point and control the output using the feedback from the actuators.

The ROS controller interacts with the hardware using the hardware interface. The main function of the hardware interface is to act as a mediator between ROS controllers and the real or simulated hardware, allocating the resources to control it considering the data generated by the ROS controller.

In this robot, we have defined the position controllers, velocity controllers, effort controllers, and so on. The ROS controllers are provided by a set of packages called `ros_control`.

For a proper understanding of how to configure ROS controllers for the arm, we should understand its concepts. We will discuss more on the `ros_control` packages, different types of ROS controllers, and how an ROS controller interacts with the Gazebo simulation.

Understanding the ros_control packages

The `ros_control` packages have the implementation of robot controllers, controller managers, hardware interfaces, different transmission interfaces, and control toolboxes. The `ros_controls` packages are composed of the following individual packages:

- `control_toolbox`: This package contains common modules (PID and Sine) that can be used by all controllers
- `controller_interface`: This package contains the `interface` base class for controllers
- `controller_manager`: This package provides the infrastructure to `load`, `unload`, `start`, and `stop` controllers
- `controller_manager_msgs`: This package provides the message and service definition for the controller manager
- `hardware_interface`: This contains the base class for the hardware interfaces
- `transmission_interface`: This package contains the interface classes for the `transmission` interface (differential, four bar linkage, joint state, position, and velocity)

Different types of ROS controllers and hardware interfaces

Let's see the list of ROS packages that contain the standard ROS controllers:

- `joint_position_controller`: This is a simple implementation of the joint position controller
- `joint_state_controller`: This is a controller to publish joint states
- `joint_effort_controller`: This is an implementation of the joint effort (force) controller

The following are some of the commonly used hardware interfaces in ROS:

- `Joint Command Interfaces`: This will send the commands to the hardware
- `Effort Joint Interface`: This will send the `effort` command
- `Velocity Joint Interface`: This will send the `velocity` command
- `Position Joint Interface`: This will send the `position` command
- `Joint State Interfaces`: This will retrieve the joint states from the actuators encoder

How the ROS controller interacts with Gazebo

Let's see how an ROS controller interacts with Gazebo. The following figure shows the interconnection of the ROS controller, robot hardware interface, and simulator/real hardware:

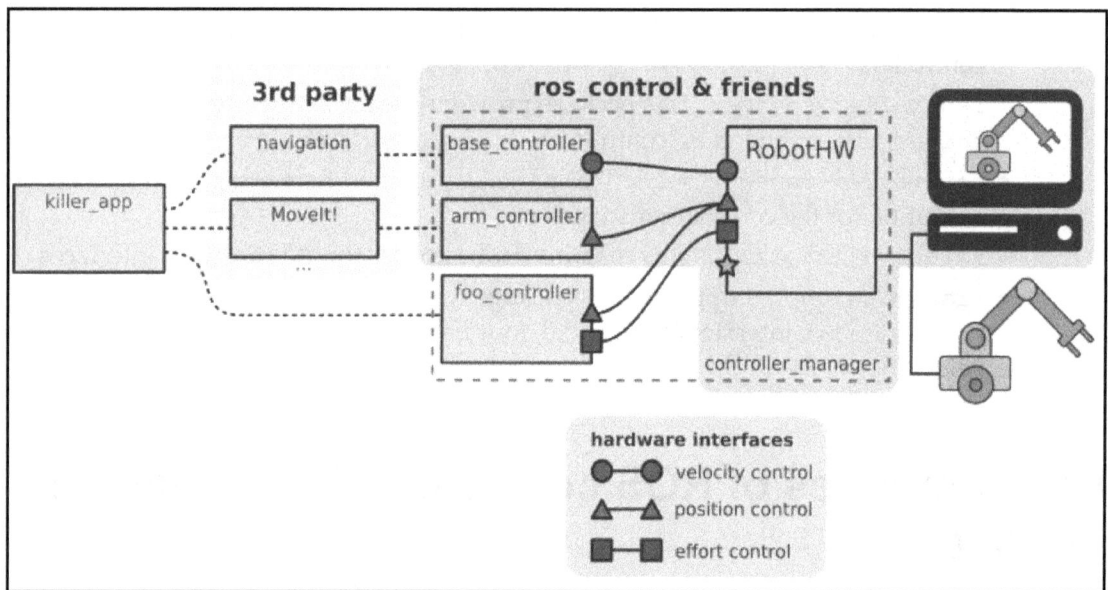

Figure 6: Interacting ROS controllers with Gazebo

We can see the third-party tools, the `navigation` and `MoveIt` packages. These packages can give the goal (set point) to the mobile robot controllers and robotic arm controllers. These controllers can send the position, velocity, or effort to the robot hardware interface.

The hardware interface allocates each resource to the controllers and sends values to each resource. The communications between the robot controllers and robot hardware interfaces are shown in the following diagram:

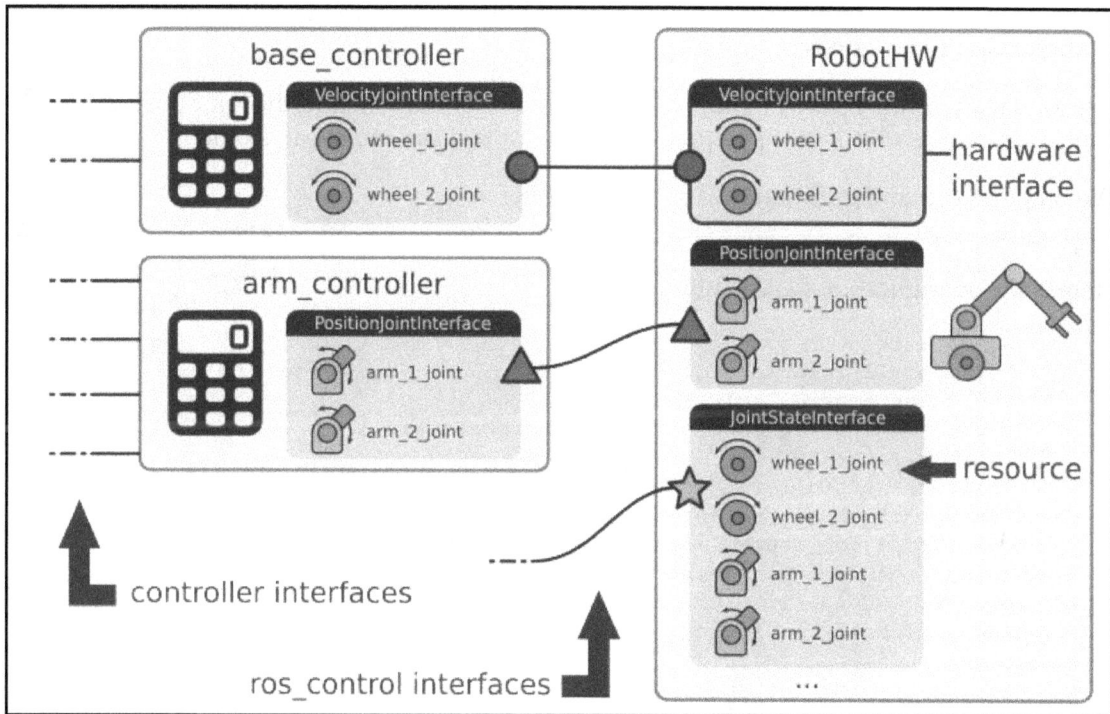

Figure 7: Illustration of ROS controllers and hardware interfaces.

The hardware interface is decoupled from actual hardware and simulation. The values from the hardware interface can be fed to Gazebo for simulation or to the actual hardware itself.

The hardware interface is a software representation of the robot and its abstract hardware. The resource of the hardware interfaces are actuators, joints, and sensors. Some resources are read-only, such as joint states, IMU, force-torque sensors, and so on, and some are read and write compatible, such as position, velocity, and effort joints.

Interfacing joint state controllers and joint position controllers to the arm

Interfacing robot controllers to each joint is a simple task. The first task is to write a configuration file for two controllers.

The joint state controllers will publish the joint states of the arm and the joint position controllers can receive a goal position for each joint and can move each joint.

We will find the configuration file for the controller at seven_dof_arm_gazebo_control.yaml in the seven_dof_arm_gazebo/config folder.

Here is the configuration file definition:

```
seven_dof_arm:
  # Publish all joint states ----------------------------------
  joint_state_controller:
    type: joint_state_controller/JointStateController
    publish_rate: 50
  # Position Controllers --------------------------------------
  joint1_position_controller:
    type: position_controllers/JointPositionController
    joint: shoulder_pan_joint
    pid: {p: 100.0, i: 0.01, d: 10.0}
  joint2_position_controller:
    type: position_controllers/JointPositionController
    joint: shoulder_pitch_joint
    pid: {p: 100.0, i: 0.01, d: 10.0}
  joint3_position_controller:
    type: position_controllers/JointPositionController
    joint: elbow_roll_joint
    pid: {p: 100.0, i: 0.01, d: 10.0}
  joint4_position_controller:
    type: position_controllers/JointPositionController
    joint: elbow_pitch_joint
    pid: {p: 100.0, i: 0.01, d: 10.0}
  joint5_position_controller:
    type: position_controllers/JointPositionController
    joint: wrist_roll_joint
    pid: {p: 100.0, i: 0.01, d: 10.0}
  joint6_position_controller:
    type: position_controllers/JointPositionController
    joint: wrist_pitch_joint
    pid: {p: 100.0, i: 0.01, d: 10.0}
  joint7_position_controller:
    type: position_controllers/JointPositionController
```

```
joint: gripper_roll_joint
pid: {p: 100.0, i: 0.01, d: 10.0}
```

We can see that all the controllers are inside the namespace `seven_dof_arm`, and the first line represents the joint state controllers, which will publish the joint state of the robot at the rate of 50 Hz.

The remaining controllers are joint position controllers, which are assigned to the first seven joints, and they also define the PID gains.

Launching the ROS controllers with Gazebo

If the controller configuration is ready, we can build a launch file that starts all the controllers along with the Gazebo simulation. Navigate to the `seven_dof_arm_gazebo/launch` directory and open the `seven_dof_arm_gazebo_control.launch` file:

```
<launch>
  <!-- Launch Gazebo  -->
  <include file="$(find
seven_dof_arm_gazebo)/launch/seven_dof_arm_world.launch" />


  <!-- Load joint controller configurations from YAML file to parameter
server -->
  <rosparam file="$(find
seven_dof_arm_gazebo)/config/seven_dof_arm_gazebo_control.yaml"
command="load"/>


  <!-- load the controllers -->
  <node name="controller_spawner" pkg="controller_manager" type="spawner"
respawn="false"
  output="screen" ns="/seven_dof_arm" args="joint_state_controller
          joint1_position_controller
          joint2_position_controller
          joint3_position_controller
          joint4_position_controller
          joint5_position_controller
          joint6_position_controller
          joint7_position_controller"/>


  <!-- convert joint states to TF transforms for rviz, etc -->
  <node name="robot_state_publisher" pkg="robot_state_publisher"
```

```
type="robot_state_publisher"
  respawn="false" output="screen">
    <remap from="/joint_states" to="/seven_dof_arm/joint_states" />
  </node>

</launch>
```

The launch files start the Gazebo simulation of the arm, load the controller configuration, load the joint state controller and joint position controllers, and, finally, run the robot state publisher, which publishes the joint states and TF.

Let's check the controller topics generated after running this launch file:

```
$ roslaunch seven_dof_arm_gazebo seven_dof_arm_gazebo_control.launch
```

If the command is successful, we can see these messages in the Terminal:

```
[ INFO] [1503389354.607765795, 0.155000000]: Loaded gazebo_ros_control.
[INFO] [1503389354.726844, 0.274000]: Controller Spawner: Waiting for service controll
er_manager/switch_controller
[INFO] [1503389354.728599, 0.276000]: Controller Spawner: Waiting for service controll
er_manager/unload_controller
[INFO] [1503389354.730271, 0.277000]: Loading controller: joint_state_controller
[INFO] [1503389354.812192, 0.355000]: Loading controller: joint1_position_controller
[INFO] [1503389354.896451, 0.433000]: Loading controller: joint2_position_controller
[INFO] [1503389354.905462, 0.442000]: Loading controller: joint3_position_controller
[INFO] [1503389354.914256, 0.451000]: Loading controller: joint4_position_controller
[INFO] [1503389354.921049, 0.458000]: Loading controller: joint5_position_controller
[INFO] [1503389354.928891, 0.466000]: Loading controller: joint6_position_controller
[INFO] [1503389354.935862, 0.473000]: Loading controller: joint7_position_controller
[INFO] [1503389354.944609, 0.482000]: Controller Spawner: Loaded controllers: joint_st
ate_controller, joint1_position_controller, joint2_position_controller, joint3_positio
n_controller, joint4_position_controller, joint5_position_controller, joint6_position_
controller, joint7_position_controller
[INFO] [1503389354.947569, 0.485000]: Started controllers: joint_state_controller, joi
nt1_position_controller, joint2_position_controller, joint3_position_controller, joint
4_position_controller, joint5_position_controller, joint6_position_controller, joint7_
position_controller
```

Figure 8: Terminal messages while loading the ROS controllers of seven-DOF arm

Here are the topics generated from the controllers when we run this launch file:

```
/seven_dof_arm/joint1_position_controller/command
/seven_dof_arm/joint2_position_controller/command
/seven_dof_arm/joint3_position_controller/command
/seven_dof_arm/joint4_position_controller/command
/seven_dof_arm/joint5_position_controller/command
/seven_dof_arm/joint6_position_controller/command
/seven_dof_arm/joint7_position_controller/command
```

Figure 9: Position controller command topics generated by the ROS-controllers

Moving the robot joints

After finishing the preceding topics, we can start commanding positions to each joint.

To move a robot joint in Gazebo, we should publish a desired joint value with a message type `std_msgs/Float64` to the joint position controller command topics.

Here is an example of moving the fourth joint to 1.0 radians:

```
$ rostopic pub /seven_dof_arm/joint4_position_controller/command
std_msgs/Float64 1.0
```

Figure 10: Moving a joint of the arm in Gazebo

We can also view the joint states of the robot by using the following command:

```
$ rostopic echo /seven_dof_arm/joint_states
```

Simulating a differential wheeled robot in Gazebo

We have seen the simulation of the robotic arm. In this section, we can set up the simulation for the differential wheeled robot that we designed in the previous chapter.

You will get the `diff_wheeled_robot.xacro` mobile robot description from the `mastering_ros_robot_description_pkg/urdf` folder.

Let's create a launch file to spawn the simulation model in Gazebo. As we did for the robotic arm, we can create a ROS package to launch a Gazebo simulation using the same dependencies of the `seven_dof_arm_gazebo` package, clone the entire package from the following Git repository, or get the package from the book's source code:

```
$ git clone  https://github.com/jocacace/diff_wheeled_robot_gazebo.git
```

Navigate to the `diff_wheeled_robot_gazebo/launch` directory and take the `diff_wheeled_gazebo.launch` file. Here is the definition of this launch:

```
<launch>
  <!-- these are the arguments you can pass this launch file, for example
paused:=true -->
  <arg name="paused" default="false"/>
  <arg name="use_sim_time" default="true"/>
  <arg name="gui" default="true"/>
  <arg name="headless" default="false"/>
  <arg name="debug" default="false"/>

  <!-- We resume the logic in empty_world.launch -->
  <include file="$(find gazebo_ros)/launch/empty_world.launch">
    <arg name="debug" value="$(arg debug)" />
    <arg name="gui" value="$(arg gui)" />
    <arg name="paused" value="$(arg paused)"/>
    <arg name="use_sim_time" value="$(arg use_sim_time)"/>
    <arg name="headless" value="$(arg headless)"/>
  </include>

  <!-- urdf xml robot description loaded on the Parameter Server-->
  <param name="robot_description" command="$(find xacro)/xacro --inorder
'$(find
mastering_ros_robot_description_pkg)/urdf/diff_wheeled_robot.xacro'" />

  <!-- Run a python script to the send a service call to gazebo_ros to
spawn a URDF robot -->
  <node name="urdf_spawner" pkg="gazebo_ros" type="spawn_model"
```

```
respawn="false" output="screen"
  args="-urdf -model diff_wheeled_robot -param robot_description"/>

</launch>
```

To launch this file, we can use the following command:

```
$ roslaunch diff_wheeled_robot_gazebo diff_wheeled_gazebo.launch
```

You will see the following robot model in Gazebo. If you get this model, you have successfully finished the first phase of the simulation:

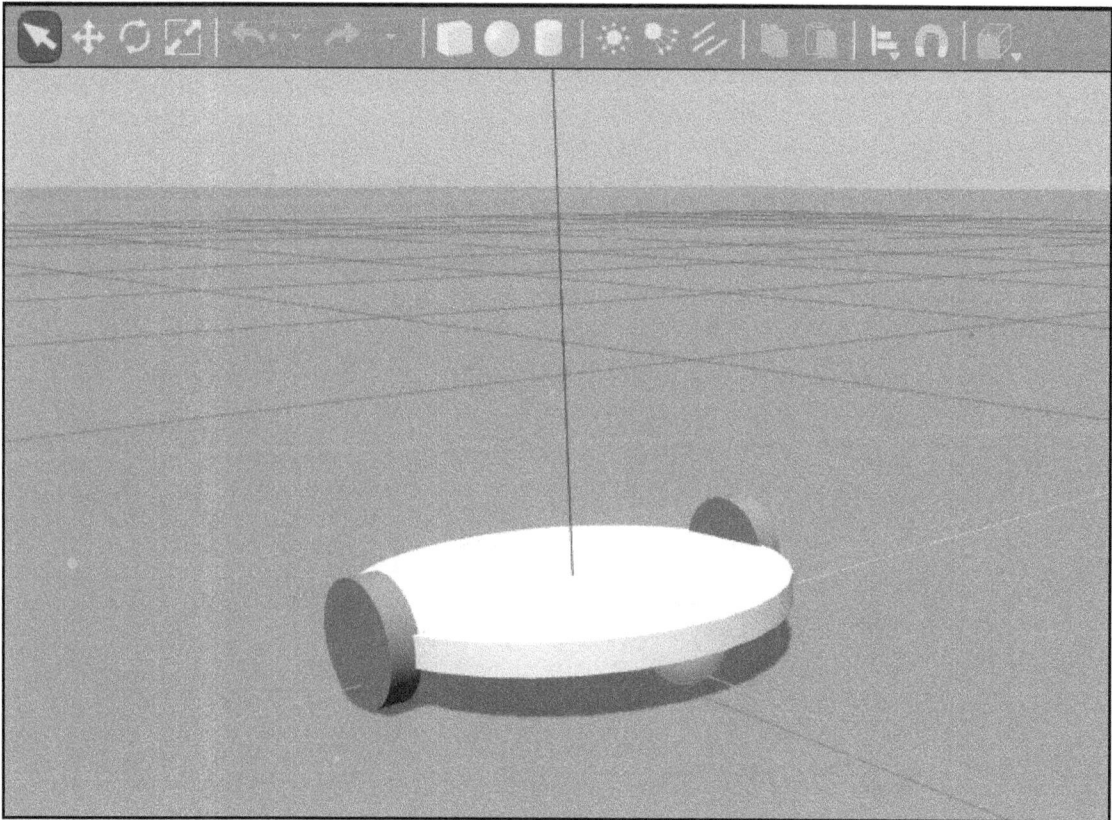

Figure 11: Differential wheeled robot in Gazebo

After successful simulation, let's add the laser scanner to the robot.

Adding the laser scanner to Gazebo

We add the laser scanner on the top of Gazebo to perform high-end operations, such as autonomous navigation or map creation using this robot. Here, we should add the following extra code section to `diff_wheeled_robot.xacro` to add the laser scanner to the robot:

```
<link name="hokuyo_link">
  <visual>
    <origin xyz="0 0 0" rpy="0 0 0" />
    <geometry>
      <box size="${hokuyo_size} ${hokuyo_size} ${hokuyo_size}"/>
    </geometry>
    <material name="Blue" />
  </visual>
</link>
<joint name="hokuyo_joint" type="fixed">
  <origin xyz="${base_radius - hokuyo_size/2} 0
${base_height+hokuyo_size/4}" rpy="0 0 0" />
  <parent link="base_link"/>
  <child link="hokuyo_link" />
</joint>
<gazebo reference="hokuyo_link">
  <material>Gazebo/Blue</material>
  <turnGravityOff>false</turnGravityOff>
  <sensor type="ray" name="head_hokuyo_sensor">
    <pose>${hokuyo_size/2} 0 0 0 0 0</pose>
    <visualize>false</visualize>
    <update_rate>40</update_rate>
    <ray>
      <scan>
        <horizontal>
          <samples>720</samples>
          <resolution>1</resolution>
          <min_angle>-1.570796</min_angle>
          <max_angle>1.570796</max_angle>
        </horizontal>
      </scan>
      <range>
        <min>0.10</min>
        <max>10.0</max>
        <resolution>0.001</resolution>
      </range>
    </ray>
    <plugin name="gazebo_ros_head_hokuyo_controller"
filename="libgazebo_ros_laser.so">
      <topicName>/scan</topicName>
```

```
        <frameName>hokuyo_link</frameName>
      </plugin>
    </sensor>
  </gazebo>
```

In this section, we use the Gazebo ROS plugin file called `libgazebo_ros_laser.so` to simulate the laser scanner. The complete code can be found in the `diff_wheeled_robot_with_laser.xacro` description file in the `mastering_ros_robot_description_pkg/urdf/` directory.

We can view the laser scanner data by adding some objects in the simulation environment. Here, we add some cylinders around the robot and can see the corresponding laser view in the next section of the figure:

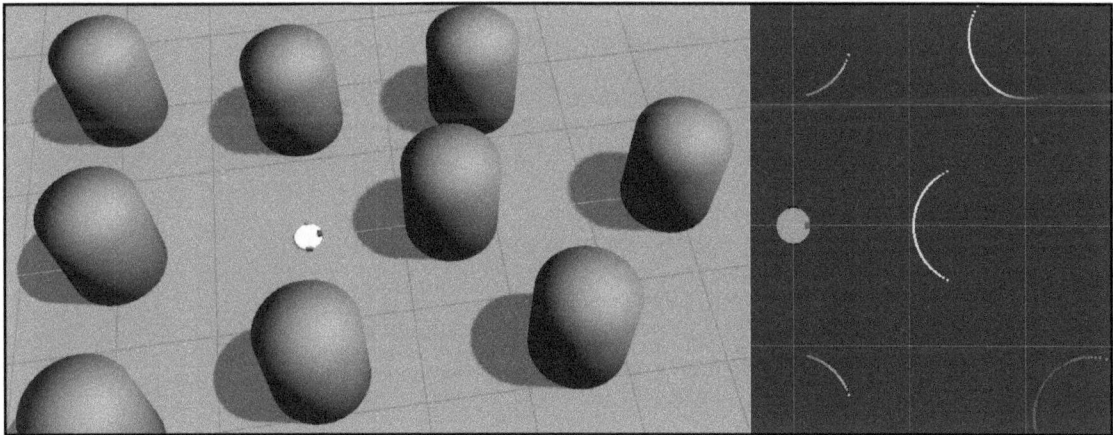

Figure 12: Differential drive robot in random object in Gazebo

The laser scanner plugin publishes laser data (`sensor_msgs/LaserScan`) into the `/scan` topic.

Moving the mobile robot in Gazebo

The robot we are working with is a differential robot with two wheels and two caster wheels. The complete characteristics of the robot should model as the Gazebo-ROS plugin for the simulation. Luckily, the plugin for a basic differential drive is already implemented.

To move the robot in Gazebo, we should add a Gazebo-ROS plugin file called `libgazebo_ros_diff_drive.so` to get the differential drive behavior in this robot.

Here is the complete code snippet of the definition of this plugin and its parameters:

```
<!-- Differential drive controller  -->
<gazebo>
  <plugin name="differential_drive_controller"
filename="libgazebo_ros_diff_drive.so">

    <rosDebugLevel>Debug</rosDebugLevel>
    <publishWheelTF>false</publishWheelTF>
    <robotNamespace>/</robotNamespace>
    <publishTf>1</publishTf>
    <publishWheelJointState>false</publishWheelJointState>
    <alwaysOn>true</alwaysOn>
    <updateRate>100.0</updateRate>

    <leftJoint>front_left_wheel_joint</leftJoint>
    <rightJoint>front_right_wheel_joint</rightJoint>

    <wheelSeparation>${2*base_radius}</wheelSeparation>
    <wheelDiameter>${2*wheel_radius}</wheelDiameter>
    <broadcastTF>1</broadcastTF>
    <wheelTorque>30</wheelTorque>
    <wheelAcceleration>1.8</wheelAcceleration>
    <commandTopic>cmd_vel</commandTopic>
    <odometryFrame>odom</odometryFrame>
    <odometryTopic>odom</odometryTopic>
    <robotBaseFrame>base_footprint</robotBaseFrame>


  </plugin>
</gazebo>
```

We can provide the parameters such as the wheel joints of the robot (joints should be of a continuous type), wheel separation, wheel diameters, odometry topic, and so on, in this plugin.

An important parameter that we need to move the robot is:

```
<commandTopic>cmd_vel</commandTopic>
```

This parameter is the command velocity topic to the plugin, which is basically a `Twist` message in ROS (sensor_msgs/Twist). We can publish the `Twist` message into the /cmd_vel topic, and we can see the robot start to move from its position.

Adding joint state publishers in the launch file

After adding the differential drive plugin, we need to join state publishers to the existing launch file, or we can build a new one. You can see the new final launch file, `diff_wheeled_gazebo_full.launc`, in `diff_wheeled_robot_gazebo/launch`.

The launch file contains joint state publishers, which help to visualize in RViz. Here are the extra lines added in this launch file for the joint state publishing:

```
<node name="joint_state_publisher" pkg="joint_state_publisher"
type="joint_state_publisher" ></node>
  <!-- start robot state publisher -->
  <node pkg="robot_state_publisher" type="robot_state_publisher"
name="robot_state_publisher" output="screen" >
    <param name="publish_frequency" type="double" value="50.0" />
  </node>
```

Adding the ROS teleop node

The ROS teleop node publishes the ROS `Twist` command by taking keyboard inputs. From this node, we can generate both linear and angular velocity, and there is already a standard teleop node implementation available; we can simply reuse the node.

The teleop is implemented in the `diff_wheeled_robot_control` package. The script folder contains the `diff_wheeled_robot_key` node, which is the teleop node. As per usual, you can get this package from the code provided with the book or download it from the following link:

```
$ git clone  https://github.com/jocacace/diff_wheeled_robot_control.git
```

To successfully compile and use this package, you may need to install the `joy_node` package:

```
$ sudo apt-get install ros-kinetic-joy
```

Here is the launch file called `keyboard_teleop.launch` to start the teleop node:

```
<launch>
  <!-- differential_teleop_key already has its own built in velocity
smoother -->
  <node pkg="diff_wheeled_robot_control" type="diff_wheeled_robot_key"
name="diff_wheeled_robot_key"  output="screen">

    <param name="scale_linear" value="0.5" type="double"/>
    <param name="scale_angular" value="1.5" type="double"/>
    <remap from="turtlebot_teleop_keyboard/cmd_vel" to="/cmd_vel"/>
  </node>
</launch>
```

Let's start moving the robot.

Launch Gazebo with complete simulation settings, using the following command:

```
$ roslaunch diff_wheeled_robot_gazebo diff_wheeled_gazebo_full.launch
```

Start the teleop node:

```
$ roslaunch diff_wheeled_robot_control keyboard_teleop.launch
```

Start RViz to visualize the robot state and laser data:

```
$ rosrun rviz rviz
```

Add `Fixed Frame : /odom`, add `Laser Scan`, and the topic as `/scan` to view the laser scan data, and add the `Robot model` to view the robot model.

In the teleop terminal, we can use some keys (U, I, O, J, K, L, M, ",", ".") for direction adjustment and other keys (q, z, w, x, e, c, k, space key) for speed adjustments. Here is the screenshot showing the robot moving in Gazebo using the teleop and its visualization in RViz.

We can add primitive shapes from the Gazebo toolbar to the robot environment or we can add objects from the online library, which is on the left-side panel:

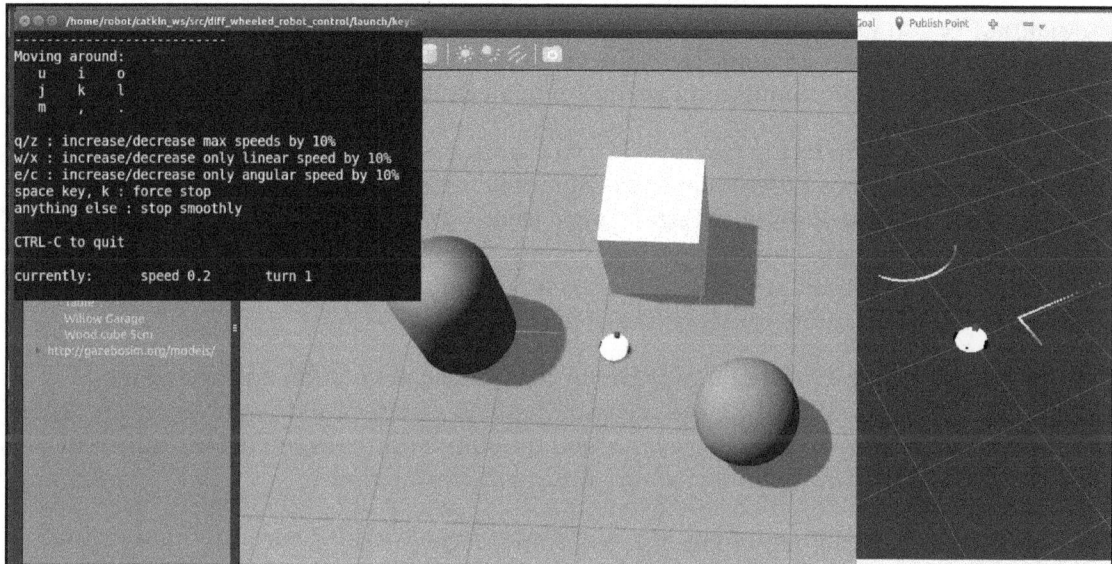

Figure 13: Moving differential drive robot in Gazebo using teleoperation

The robot will only move when we press the appropriate key inside the teleop node terminal. If this terminal is not active, pressing the key will not move the robot. If everything works well, we can explore the area using the robot and visualizing the laser data in RViz.

Questions

- Why do we perform robotic simulation?
- How can we add sensors into a Gazebo simulation?
- What are the different types of ROS controllers and hardware interfaces?
- How can we move the mobile robot in a Gazebo simulation?

Summary

After designing the robot, the next phase is its simulation. There are a lot of uses in simulation. We can validate a robot design, and at the same time, we can work with a robot without having its real hardware. There are some situations when we need to work without having a robot hardware. Simulators are useful in all these situations.

In this chapter, we were trying to simulate two robots, one was a robotic arm with seven-DOF and the other was a differential wheeled mobile robot. We started with the robotic arm, and discussed the additional Gazebo tags needed to launch the robot in Gazebo. We discussed how to add a 3D vision sensor to the simulation. Later, we created a launch file to start Gazebo with a robotic arm and discussed how to add controllers to each joint. We added the controllers and worked with each joint.

Like the robotic arm, we created the URDF for the Gazebo simulation and added the necessary Gazebo-ROS plugin for the laser scanner and differential drive mechanism. After completing the simulation model, we launched the simulation using a custom launch file. Finally, we looked at how to move the robot using the teleop node.

We can learn more about the robotic arm and mobile robots, which are supported by ROS, from the following link: `http://wiki.ros.org/Robots`.

In the next chapter, we will see how to simulate robots using another famous robotics simulation: *V-REP*.

5
Simulating Robots Using ROS and V-REP

Having learned how to simulate robots with Gazebo, in this chapter, we will discuss how to use another powerful and famous simulation software: V-REP (Virtual Robot Experimentation Platform, `http://www.coppeliarobotics.com`).

V-REP is a multi-platform robotic simulator developed by Coppelia Robotics. It offers many simulation models of popular industrial and mobile robots ready to be used, and different functionalities that can be easily integrated and combined through a dedicated API. In addition, V-REP can operate with ROS using a communication interface that allows us to control the simulation scene and the robots via topics and services. Like Gazebo, V-REP can be used as a standalone software, while an external plugin must be installed to work with ROS.

In this chapter, we will learn how to set up the V-REP simulator and install the ROS communication bridge, discussing some initial codes to understand how it works. We will show how to interact with V-REP using services and topics and how to import and interface a new robot model using the URDF file. Finally, we will discuss how to interact with popular mobile robots imported from the V-REP model database, enriching it with additional sensors.

We will cover the following topics in this chapter:

- Setting up V-REP with ROS
- Understanding `vrep_plugin`
- Interacting with V-REP using ROS
- Importong a robot model using an URDF file
- Implementing a ROS interface to simulate a robotic arm in V-REP
- Controlling a mobile robot using V-REP
- Adding additional sensors to simulated robots

Setting up V-REP with ROS

Before starting to work with V-REP, we need to install it in our system and compile the ROS packages needed to establish the communication bridge between ROS and the simulation scene. V-REP is a cross-platform software, available for different operating systems, such as Windows, macOS, and Linux. It is developed by *Coppelia Robotics GmbH* and is distributed with both free educational and commercial licenses. Download the last version of the V-REP simulator from the *Coppelia Robotics* download page: `http://www.coppeliarobotics.com/downloads.html`, choosing the Linux version of the V-REP PRO EDU software.

In this chapter, we will refer to the V-REP version `v3.4.0`. You can download this version, if already available on the website, using the following command in any desired directory:

```
$ wget
http://coppeliarobotics.com/files/V-REP_PRO_EDU_V3_4_0_Linux.tar.gz
```

After completing the download, extract the archive:

```
$ tar -zxvf V-REP_PRO_EDU_V3_4_0_Linux.tar.gz
```

To easily access V-REP resources, it is convenient to set the `VREP_ROOT` environmental variable that points to the V-REP main folder:

```
$ echo "export VREP_ROOT=/path/to/v_rep/folder >> ~/.bashrc"
```

V-REP offers the following modes to control simulated robots from external applications:

- **Remote API**: The V-REP remote API is composed of several functions that can be called from external applications developed in C/C++, Python, Lua, or Matlab. The remote API interacts with V-REP over the network, using socket communication. You can integrate the remote API in your C++ or Python nodes, in order to connect ROS with the simulation scene. The list of all remote APIs available in V-REP can be found on the *Coppelia Robotics* website: http://www.coppeliarobotics.com/helpFiles/en/remoteApiFunctions.htm. To use the remote API, you must implement both client and server sides:
    - **V-REP Client:** The client side resides in the external application. It can be implemented in a ROS node or in a standard program written in one of the supported programming languages.
    - **V-REP Server:** This side is implemented in V-REP scripts and allows the simulator to receive external data to interact with the simulation scene.
- **RosPlugin**: The V-REP RosPlugin implements a high-level abstraction that directly connects the simulated object scene with the ROS communication system. Using this plugin, you can automatically apply subscribed messages and publish topics from scene objects to get information or control simulated robots.
- **RosInterface**: Introduced in the latest versions of V-REP, this interface will substitute the RosPlugin in the future versions. Differently from the RosPlugin, this module duplicates the C++ API functions to allow ROS and V-REP communication.

In this book, we will discuss how to interact with V-REP using the RosPlugin. The first thing to do is to compile the ROS communication bridge. We must add two packages to our ROS workspace: `vrep_common` and `vrep_plugin`. As usual, you can clone the entire package from the following GitHub repository or obtain the package from the book's source code:

```
$ git clone https://github.com/jocacace/vrep_common.git
$ git clone https://github.com/jocacace/vrep_plugin.git
```

Compile the packages with the `catkin_make` command. If everything goes right, the compilation will create the `vrep_plugin` shared library: `libv_repExtRos.so`. This file is located in the `devel/lib/` directory in the ROS workspace. To enable V-REP to use this library, we need to copy it into the main `vrep` folder:

```
$ cp devel/lib/libv_repExtRos.so $VREP_ROOT
```

This library allows V-REP to connect with an active instance of roscore at startup, transforming it in a ROS node linked to the framework. So, to connect V-REP with ROS, an instance of roscore must be executed before launching V-REP. To test that everything is working properly, start `roscore` and launch the V-REP software:

```
$ roscore & $VREP_ROOT/vrep.sh
```

During the startup, all V-REP plugins installed in the system will be loaded. We can check if the `vrep_plugin` is loaded, as shown in the following figure:

```
jcacace@robot:~$ $VREP_ROOT/vrep.sh
Using the default Lua library.
Loaded the video compression library.
Add-on script 'vrepAddOnScript-addOnScriptDemo.lua' was loaded.
Simulator launched.
Plugin 'BubbleRob': loading...
Plugin 'BubbleRob': load succeeded.
Plugin 'Collada': loading...
Plugin 'Collada': load succeeded.
Plugin 'RemoteApi': load succeeded.
Plugin 'Ros': loading...
Plugin 'Ros': load succeeded.
```

Figure 1: Plugins loading during V-REP startup

In addition, after starting the V-REP program, a new topic is published containing information about the simulation status. Listing the active topics, we can check that the `/vrep/info` topic is published. As shown in the next figure, this message provides information about the state of the simulation, if it is running or not, and information about the simulation time:

```
---
headerInfo:
  seq: 823
  stamp:
    secs: 1504261442
    nsecs: 363384144
  frame_id: ''
simulatorState:
  data: 1
simulationTime:
  data: 41.1496582031
timeStep:
  data: 0.0500000007451
---
```

Figure 2: Content of /vrep/info message

To explore `vrep_plugin` functionalities, we can have a look at the `plugin_publisher_subscriber.ttt` scene, located in the `vrep_demo_pkg/scene` folder. To open this scene, use the main drop-down menu and select the entry: **File** | **Open Scene**. This simulation is based on the `rosTopicPublisherAndSubscriber1.ttt` scene proposed in older V-REP versions.

After opening this scene, the simulation windows should appear, as in the following image:

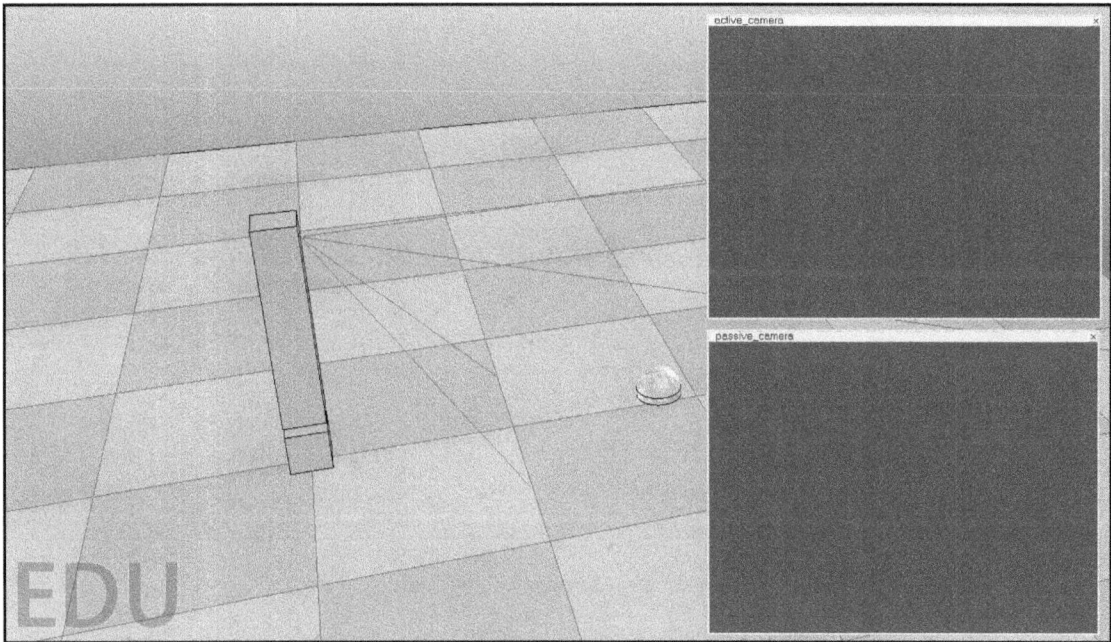

Figure 3: `plugin_publisher_subscriber.ttt` simulation scene

In this scene, a robot is equipped with two cameras: one active camera acquiring images from the environment, publishing the video stream on a specific topic, and a passive camera, that only acquires the video stream from the same topic. We can press the `play` button on the main bar of the V-REP interface.

After that the simulation starts; this is what will happen:

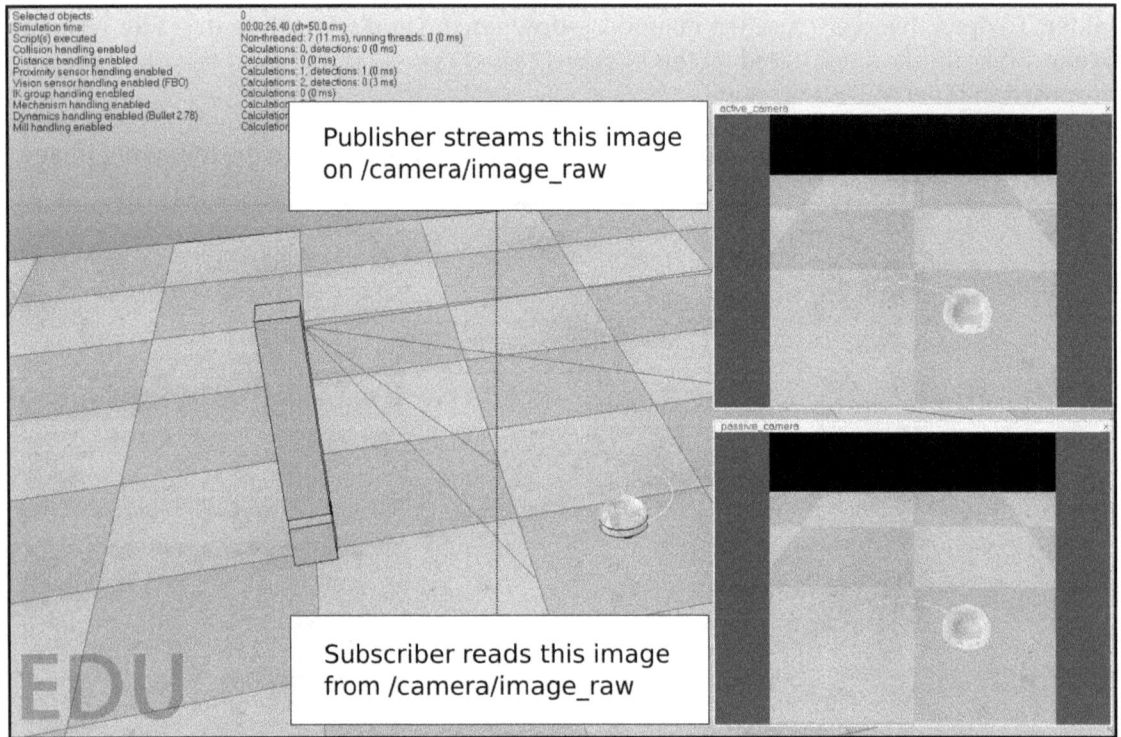

Figure 4: Image published and subscriber example

In this simulation, the passive camera displays the image published from the active one, receiving vision data directly from the ROS framework. We can also visualize the video stream published by V-REP using the image_view package:

```
$ rosrun image_view image_view image:=/camera/image_raw
```

Understanding the vrep_plugin

The vrep_plugin is part of the V-REP API framework. Even though the plugin is correctly installed in your system, the load operation will fail if the roscore was not running at that time. A pop-up error will inform users if the simulations scenes need the vrep_plugin because the roscore was not running before running the simulator, or it is not installed in the system:

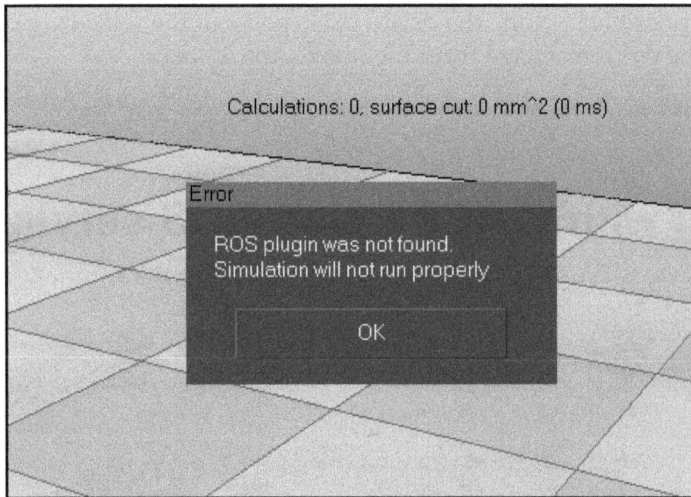

Figure 5: Error displayed when vrep_plugin is used without running the roscore

After starting up V-REP with the `vrep_plugin` correctly loaded, V-REP will act as a ROS node called `/vrep`. This can be shown using the following command:

```
$ rosnode list
```

Figure 6: List of active ROS nodes after running V-REP with vrep_plugin

Other ROS nodes can communicate with V-REP in the following ways:

- `vrep_plugin` offers ROS services. Different services are available after launching V-REP to control the simulation scene or its state.
- `vrep_plugin` can be enabled to subscribe or advertise topics. As a normal ROS node, simulation models can communicate via topics.

We can start interacting with V-REP using services. Let's create a ROS package with the following dependencies:

```
$ catkin_create_pkg vrep_demo_pkg roscpp vrep_common std_msgs geometry_msgs
```

Alternatively, it is possible to clone the entire package from the following GitHub repository or get the entire package from the book's source code:

```
$ git clone https://github.com/jocacace/vrep_demo_pkg.git
```

Interacting with V-REP using ROS services

As a first example, we will use ROS services to start and stop the simulation scene. To do this, we must call /vrep/simRosStartSimulation and the/vrep/simRosStopSimulation services respectively. We will discuss the source code of the start_stop_scene.cpp file located in the vrep_demo_pkg/src directory:

```
#include "ros/ros.h"
#include "vrep_common/simRosStartSimulation.h"
#include "vrep_common/simRosStopSimulation.h"

int main( int argc, char** argv ) {

ros::init( argc, argv, "start_stop_vrep_node");
    ros::NodeHandle n;
ros::ServiceClient start_vrep_client =
n.serviceClient<vrep_common::simRosStartSimulation>("/vrep/simRosStartSimul
ation");
    vrep_common::simRosStartSimulation start_srv;

ros::ServiceClient stop_vrep_client =
n.serviceClient<vrep_common::simRosStopSimulation>("/vrep/simRosStopSimulat
ion");
    vrep_common::simRosStopSimulation stop_srv;

    ROS_INFO("Starting Vrep simulation...");
    if( start_vrep_client.call( start_srv ) ) {
        if( start_srv.response.result == 1 ) {
            ROS_INFO("Simulation started, wait 5 seconds before stop
it!");
            sleep(5);
            if( stop_vrep_client.call( stop_srv ) ) {
                if( stop_srv.response.result == 1 ) {
                    ROS_INFO("Simulation stopped");
                }
            }
            else
                ROS_ERROR("Failed to call /vrep/simRosStopSimulation
service");
        }
```

```
    }
    else
        ROS_ERROR("Failed to call /vrep/simRosStartSimulation service");
}
```

Let's see the explanation of the code:

```
ros::ServiceClient start_vrep_client =
n.serviceClient<vrep_common::simRosStartSimulation>("/vrep/simRosStartSimul
ation");
vrep_common::simRosStartSimulation start_srv;

ros::ServiceClient stop_vrep_client =
n.serviceClient<vrep_common::simRosStopSimulation>("/vrep/simRosStopSimulat
ion");
vrep_common::simRosStopSimulation stop_srv;
```

Here, we declare the service client objects, as already seen in Chapter 1. These services communicate with the `vrep_common::simRosStartSimulation` and `vrep_common::simRosStartSimulation message` types respectively. These services do not require any input value, while returning the success or failure of the start/stop operation. If the start operation is executed without errors, we can stop the simulation after a certain time, as shown in the following code:

```
ROS_INFO("Starting Vrep simulation...");
if( start_vrep_client.call( start_srv ) ) {
if( start_srv.response.result != -1 ) {
ROS_INFO("Simulation started, wait 5 seconds before stop it!");
sleep(5);
        if( stop_vrep_client.call( stop_srv ) ) {
            if( stop_srv.response.result != -1 ) {
                ROS_INFO("Simulation stopped");
            }
        }
        else
            ROS_ERROR("Failed to call /vrep/simRosStopSimulation
service");
    }

}
else
ROS_ERROR("Failed to call /vrep/simRosStartSimulation service");
```

We can now use another service, `/vrep/simRosAddStatusbarMessage`, to publish messages to the status bar of V-REP. We can improve the previous code with the following lines, as reported in the `start_stop_scene_with_msg.cpp` file:

```
int cnt = 0;
while( cnt++ < 5 ) {
std::stringstream ss;
    ss << "Simulation while stop in " << 6-cnt << " seconds";
    msg_srv.request.message = ss.str();
    if( !msg_client.call( msg_srv ) ) {
            ROS_WARN("Failed to call /vrep/simRosAddStatusbarMessage
service");
    }
    sleep(1);
}
```

Here the `simRosAddStatusbarMessage` service is used to display how many seconds remain before stopping the simulation. We can test this behavior by compiling and running the `start_stop_scene_with_msg.cpp` node:

```
$ rosrun vrep_demo_pkg start_stop_scene_with_msg
```

The output of this node on the V-REP window is shown in the following screenshot:

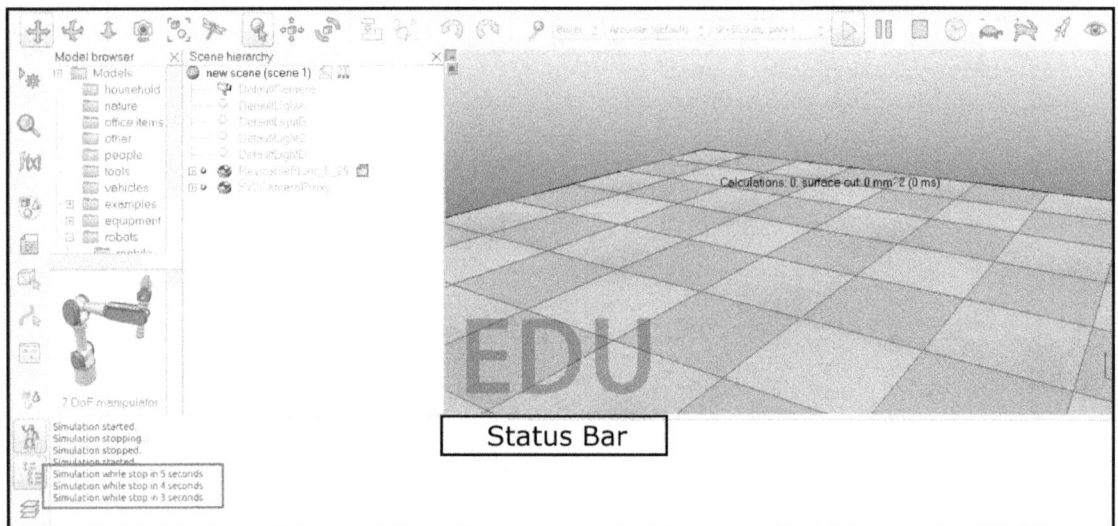

Figure 7: Messages sent to V-REP status bar via `vrep_plugin`

Interacting with V-REP using ROS topics

We will now discuss how to use topics to communicate with V-REP. This is useful when we want to send information to the objects of the simulation, or retrieve data generated by robots. While services are enabled when V-REP starts, topic communication happens only on demand, initializing publisher and subscriber variables in the simulation scene.

The most common way to program the simulation scene of V-REP is via *Lua* scripts. Every object of the scene can be associated to a script that is automatically invoked when a simulation starts and is cyclically executed during the simulation time.

In the next example, we will create a scene with two objects. One will be programmed to receive a float data from a specific topic, while the other one republishes the same data on another topic.

Use the drop-down menu on the *Scene hierarchy* panel, select the entry: **Add | Dummy**. We can create two objects, a `dummy_publisher` and a `dummy_subscriber`, and associate a script for each of them. Use the right mouse button on the created objects, and select the entry **Add | Associated child script | Non-threaded**, as shown in the following figure:

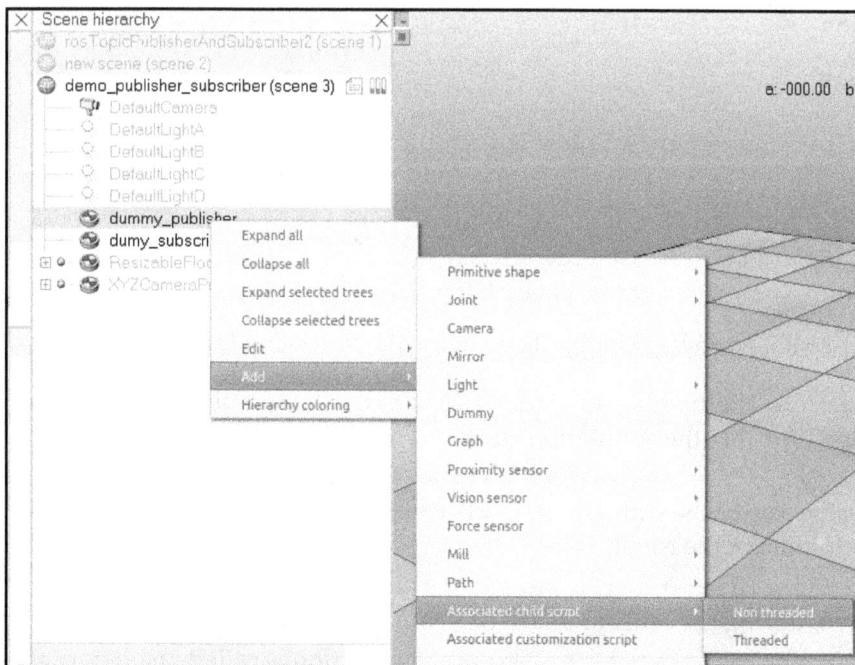

Figure 8: Associating a non-threaded script to V-REP object

Alternatively, we can directly load the simulation scene by opening the `demo_publisher_subscriber.ttt` file located in the `vrep_demo_pkg/scene` directory. Let's see the content of the script associated to the `dummy_subscriber` object:

```
if (sim_call_type==sim_childscriptcall_initialization) then
    local moduleName=0
    local moduleVersion=0
    local index=0
    local pluginNotFound=true
    while moduleName do
        moduleName,moduleVersion=simGetModuleName(index)
        if (moduleName=='Ros') then
            pluginNotFound=false
        end
        index=index+1
    end

    if (pluginNotFound) then
simDisplayDialog('Error','ROS plugin was not found.&&nSimulation will not
run properly', sim_dlgstyle_ok, false ,nil,{0.8,0,0,0,0,0},{0.5,0,0,1,1,1})
    else
--Enable subscriber to /vrep_demo/float_in topic
simExtROS_enableSubscriber("/vrep_demo/float_in",1,simros_strmcmd_set_float
_signal ,-1,-1,"in")
    end
end
if (sim_call_type==sim_childscriptcall_actuation) then
end
if (sim_call_type==sim_childscriptcall_sensing) then
end
if (sim_call_type==sim_childscriptcall_cleanup) then
end
```

Each Lua script linked to V-REP objects contains the following four sections:

- `sim_childscriptcall_initialization`: This section is executed only the first time that the simulation starts.
- `sim_childscriptcall_actuation`: This section is cyclically called at the same frame rate of the simulation. Users can put here the code that controls the actuation of the robot.
- `sim_childscriptcall_sensing`: This part will be executed in each simulation step, during the sensing phase of a simulation step.
- `sim_childscriptcall_cleanup`: This section is called just before the simulation ends.

Let's see the explanation of the preceding code:

```
if (sim_call_type==sim_childscriptcall_initialization) then
    local moduleName=0
    local moduleVersion=0
    local index=0
    local pluginNotFound=true
    while moduleName do
        moduleName,moduleVersion=simGetModuleName(index)
        if (moduleName=='Ros') then
            pluginNotFound=false
        end
        index=index+1
    end
```

In the initialization part, we check if the `vrep_plugin` is installed in the system, otherwise, an error is displayed:

```
simExtROS_enableSubscriber("/vrep_demo/float_in",1,simros_strmcmd_set_float
_signal ,-1,-1,"in")
```

This activates the subscriber of the input float value on the `/vrep_demo/float_in` topic. The `simExtROS_enableSubscriber` function expects as parameters the name of the topic, the desired queue size, the desired type to stream, and three enabling parameters. These parameters specify the item upon which the data should be applied. For example, if we want to set the position of a joint object, the first parameter will be the object handle, while the other parameters will not be used. In our case, we want to save the value received from the topic into the variable `"in"`.

Let's now see the content of the script associated to the `dummy_publisher` object:

```
if (sim_call_type==sim_childscriptcall_initialization) then
    -- Check if the required plugin is there (libv_repExtRos.so or
libv_repExtRos.dylib):
    local moduleName=0
    local moduleVersion=0
    local index=0
    local pluginNotFound=true
    while moduleName do
        moduleName,moduleVersion=simGetModuleName(index)
        if (moduleName=='Ros') then
            pluginNotFound=false
        end
        index=index+1
    end
    if (pluginNotFound) then
```

```
        simDisplayDialog('Error','ROS plugin was not found.&&nSimulation
will not run properly', sim_dlgstyle_ok, false, nil,
{0.8,0,0,0,0,0},{0.5,0,0,1,1,1})
    else
        simExtROS_enablePublisher("/vrep_demo/float_out",
1,simros_strmcmd_get_float_signal, -1,-1,"out")
        end
    end
end

if (sim_call_type==sim_childscriptcall_actuation) then
    --Get value of input signal and publish it on /vrep_demo/float_out topic
    data = simGetFloatSignal('in')
    if( data ) then
     simSetFloatSignal("out",data)
     simAddStatusbarMessage(data)
    end
end
if (sim_call_type==sim_childscriptcall_sensing) then
    -- Put your main SENSING code here
end
if (sim_call_type==sim_childscriptcall_cleanup) then
    -- Put some restoration code here
End
```

The code is explained here:

```
simExtROS_enablePublisher("/vrep_demo/float_out",
1,simros_strmcmd_get_float_signal, -1,-1,"out")
```

In this line, after checking the correct installation of the `vrep_plugin`, we will enable the publisher of the float value. After this line, the script publishes continuously the value of the variable `"out"`:

```
if (sim_call_type==sim_childscriptcall_actuation) then
    --Get value of input signal and publish it on /vrep_demo/float_out topic
    data = simGetFloatSignal('in')
    if( data ) then
     simSetFloatSignal("out",data)
     simAddStatusbarMessage(data)
    end
end
```

Finally, we set the value of the out variable with the one received from the `/vrep_demo/float_in topic`, stored in the in variable. Note that in and out are special global variables accessible from all scripts of the scene. These variables in V-REP are called *signals*.

After running the simulator, we can check that everything works correctly, publishing a desired number on the input topic and monitoring the output from the output topic, using the following commands:

```
$ rostopic pub /vrep_demo/float_in std_msgs/Float32 "data: 2.0" -r 12
$ rostopic echo /vrep_demo/float_out
```

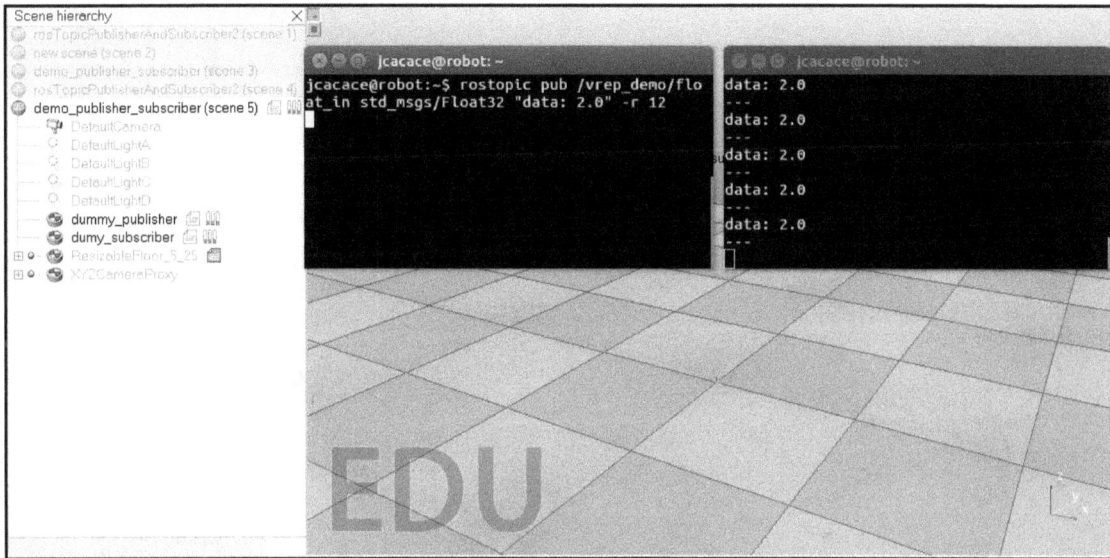

Figure 9: Running V-REP publisher and subscriber demo

Simulating the robotic arm using V-REP and ROS

In the previous chapter, we used Gazebo to import and simulate the seven-DOF arm designed in Chapter 3, *Working with 3D Robot Modeling in ROS*. Here, we will do the same thing using V-REP. The first step to simulate our seven-DOF arm is to import it in the simulation scene. V-REP allows you to import new robots using URDF files; for this reason, we must convert the xacro model of the arm in a URDF file, saving the generated URDF file in the URDF folder of the vrep_demo_pkg package:

```
$ rosrun xacro xacro seven_dof_arm.xacro -inorder >
/path/to/vrep_demo_pkg/urdf/seven_dof_arm.urdf
```

We can now import the robot model using the URDF import plugin. Select from the main drop-down menu the entry **Plugins | URDF import** and press the import button, choosing the default import options from the dialog window. Finally, select the desired file to import and the seven-DOF arm will appear in the scene:

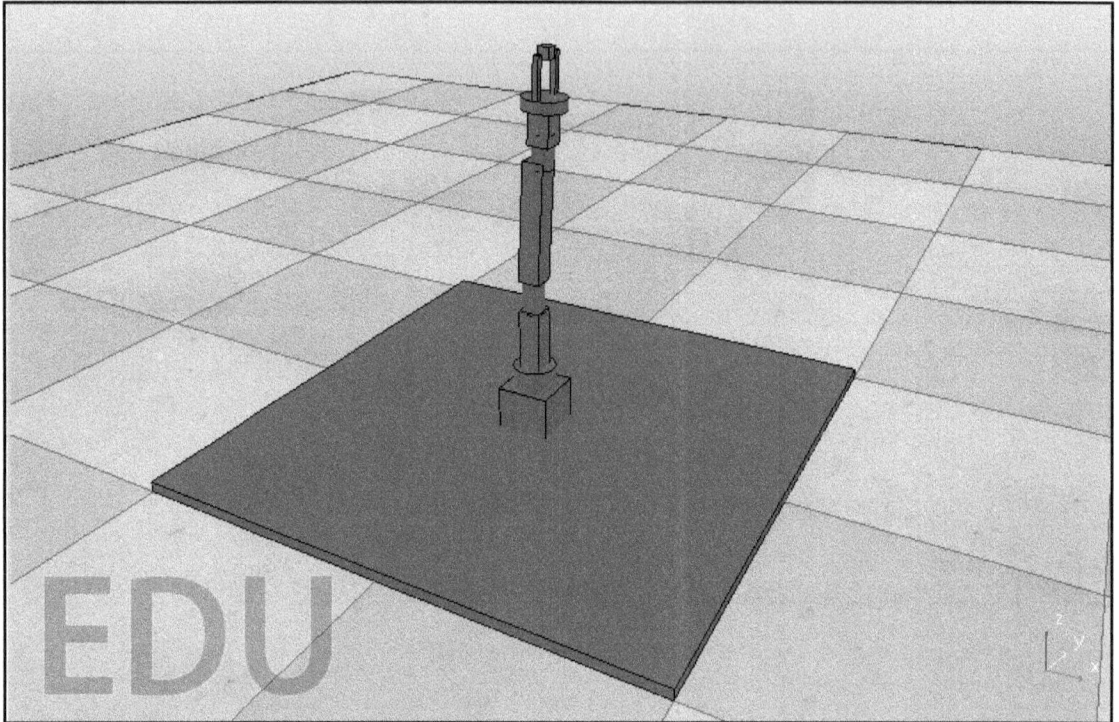

Figure 10: Simulation of seven-DOF arm in V-REP

All the components of the robot are now imported into the scene, as we can see from the *Scene hierarchy* panel, in which are reported the set of robot joints and links defined in the URDF file.

Even if the robot has been correctly imported, is not ready to be controlled yet. To actuate the robot, we need to enable all robot motors from the **Joint Dynamic Properties** panel. Until the motor is disabled, it is not possible to move it during the simulation. To enable the motor of a joint, open the **Scene object proprieties** panel, selecting its entry from the main drop-down menu: **Tools | Scene object proprieties**. You can also open this dialog with a double-click on an object icon in the `scene hierarchy`. From this new window, open the dynamic properties dialog and enable the motor and the control loop of the joint, selecting the controller type. By default, the motor is controlled via a PID, as shown in the following figure:

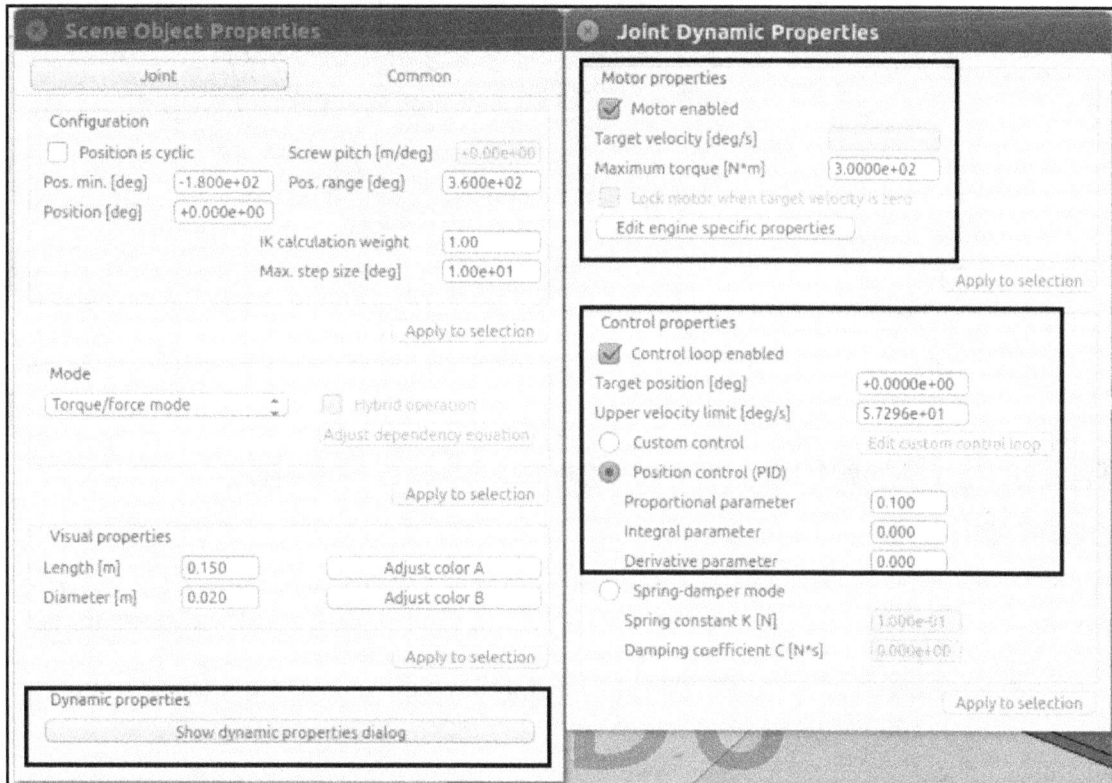

Figure 11: Scene Object Proprieties and Joint Dynamic Proprieties dialogs

To increase the performance of the control loop, PID gains should be properly tuned. After enabling motors and control loops for all robot joints, we can check that everything has been configured correctly. Run the simulation and set a target position from the **Scene Object Proprieties** panel.

Here is an example of moving the fourth joint to 1.0 radians:

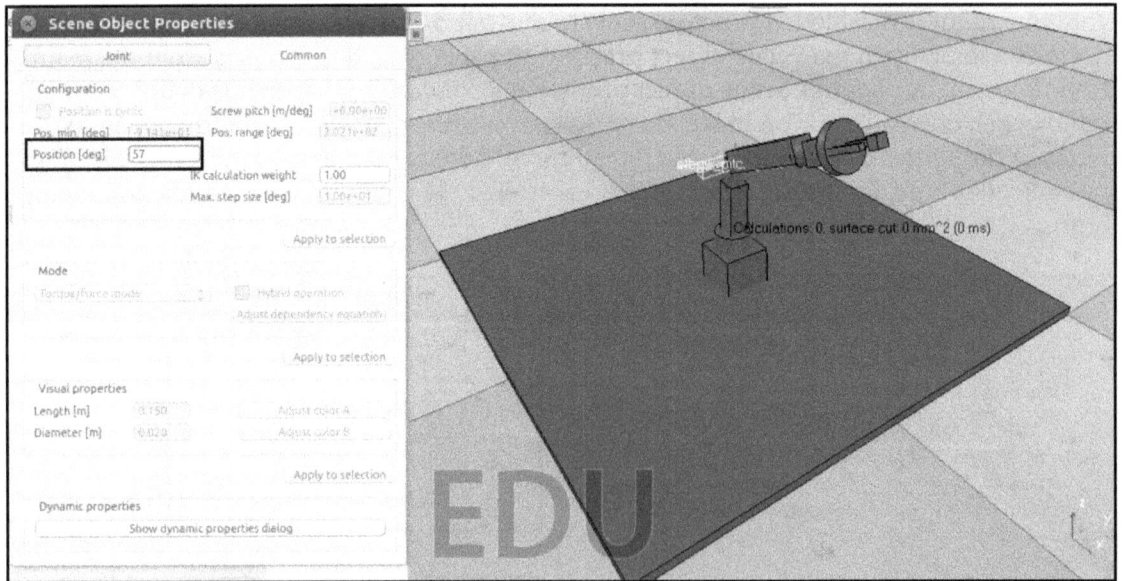

Figure 12: Moving a joint of the arm from V-REP Object Proprieties dialog.

Adding the ROS interface to V-REP joint controllers

In this section, we will learn how to interface the seven-DOF arm with the `vrep_plugin` to stream the state of its joints and receive the control input via topics. As already seen in the previous example, select a component of the robot (for example the `base_link_respondable`) and create a Lua script that will manage the communication between V-REP and ROS.

Here is the script source code:

```
if (sim_call_type==sim_childscriptcall_initialization) then
    -- Check if the required plugin is there (libv_repExtRos.so or
libv_repExtRos.dylib):
    local moduleName=0
    local moduleVersion=0
    local index=0
    local pluginNotFound=true
```

```
    while moduleName do
        moduleName,moduleVersion=simGetModuleName(index)
        if (moduleName=='Ros') then
            pluginNotFound=false
        end
        index=index+1
    end

    if (pluginNotFound) then
        -- Display an error message if the plugin was not found:
        simDisplayDialog('Error','ROS plugin was not found.&&nSimulation
will not run
properly',sim_dlgstyle_ok,false,nil,{0.8,0,0,0,0,0},{0.5,0,0,1,1,1})
    else
        -- Retrive the handle of all joints
        shoulder_pan_handle=simGetObjectHandle('shoulder_pan_joint')
        shoulder_pitch_handle=simGetObjectHandle('shoulder_pitch_joint')
        elbow_roll_handle=simGetObjectHandle('elbow_roll_joint')
        elbow_pitch_handle=simGetObjectHandle('elbow_pitch_joint')
        wrist_roll_handle=simGetObjectHandle('wrist_roll_joint')
        wrist_pitch_handle=simGetObjectHandle('wrist_pitch_joint')
        gripper_roll_handle=simGetObjectHandle('gripper_roll_joint')

        -- Enable joint publishing
simExtROS_enablePublisher('/vrep_demo/seve_dof_arm/shoulder_pan/state', 10,
simros_strmcmd_get_joint_state,shoulder_pan_handle,0,'')
simExtROS_enablePublisher('/vrep_demo/seven_dof_arm/shoulder_pitch/state',
10, simros_strmcmd_get_joint_state,shoulder_pitch_handle,0,'')
simExtRS_enablePublisher('/vrep_demo/seven_dof_arm/elbow_roll/state', 10,
simros_strmcmd_get_joint_state,elbow_roll_handle,0,'')
simExtROS_enablePublisher('/vrep_demo/seven_dof_arm/elbow_pitch/state', 10,
simros_strmcmd_get_joint_state,elbow_pitch_handle,0,'')
simExtROS_enablePublisher('/vrep_demo/seven_dof_arm/wrist_roll/state', 10,
simros_strmcmd_get_joint_state,wrist_roll_handle,0,'')
simExtROS_enablePublisher('/vrep_demo/seven_dof_arm/wrist_pitch/state', 10,
simros_strmcmd_get_joint_state,wrist_pitch_handle,0,'')
simExtROS_enablePublisher('/vrep_demo/seven_dof_arm/gripper_roll/state',
10, simros_strmcmd_get_joint_state,gripper_roll_handle,0,'')
--Enable joint subscriber
simExtROS_enableSubscriber('/vrep_demo/seven_dof_arm/shoulder_pan/ctrl',
10, simros_strmcmd_set_joint_target_position, shoulder_pan_handle, 0, '')
simExtROS_enableSubscriber('/vrep_demo/seven_dof_arm/shoulder_pitch/ctrl',
10, simros_strmcmd_set_joint_target_position, shoulder_pitch_handle, 0, '')
simExtROS_enableSubscriber('/vrep_demo/seven_dof_arm/elbow_roll/ctrl', 10,
simros_strmcmd_set_joint_target_position, elbow_roll_handle, 0, '')
simExtROS_enableSubscriber('/vrep_demo/seven_dof_arm/elbow_pitch/ctrl', 10,
simros_strmcmd_set_joint_target_position, elbow_pitch_handle, 0, '')
simExtROS_enableSubscriber('/vrep_demo/seven_dof_arm/wrist_roll/ctrl', 10,
```

```
    simros_strmcmd_set_joint_target_position, wrist_roll_handle, 0, '')
simExtROS_enableSubscriber('/vrep_demo/seven_dof_arm/wrist_pitch/ctrl', 10,
    simros_strmcmd_set_joint_target_position, wrist_pitch_handle, 0, '')
simExtROS_enableSubscriber('/vrep_demo/seven_dof_arm/gripper_roll/ctrl',
    10, simros_strmcmd_set_joint_target_position, gripper_roll_handle, 0, '')
        end
    end
    if (sim_call_type==sim_childscriptcall_cleanup) then
    end
    if (sim_call_type==sim_childscriptcall_sensing) then
    end
    if (sim_call_type==sim_childscriptcall_actuation) then
    end
```

Let's look at the following the explanation of the code. After we have checked the correct installation of `vrep_plugin`, we initialize an object handler for each joint of the arm:

```
shoulder_pan_handle=simGetObjectHandle('shoulder_pan_joint')
shoulder_pitch_handle=simGetObjectHandle('shoulder_pitch_joint')
elbow_roll_handle=simGetObjectHandle('elbow_roll_joint')
elbow_pitch_handle=simGetObjectHandle('elbow_pitch_joint')
wrist_roll_handle=simGetObjectHandle('wrist_roll_joint')
wrist_pitch_handle=simGetObjectHandle('wrist_pitch_joint')
gripper_roll_handle=simGetObjectHandle('gripper_roll_joint')
```

Here, we use the `simGetObjectHandle` function, whose argument is the name of the object as it appear in the scene hierarchy panel that we want to handle. We can now enable the joint state publishers:

```
simExtROS_enablePublisher('/vrep_demo/seven_dof_arm/shoulder_pan/state', 1,
    simros_strmcmd_get_joint_state,shoulder_pan_handle,0,'')
simExtROS_enablePublisher('/vrep_demo/seven_dof_arm/shoulder_pitch/state',
    1, simros_strmcmd_get_joint_state,shoulder_pitch_handle,0,')
simExtRS_enablePublisher('/vrep_demo/seven_dof_arm/elbow_roll/state', 1,
    simros_strmcmd_get_joint_state,elbow_roll_handle,0,'')
simExtROS_enablePublisher('/vrep_demo/seven_dof_arm/elbow_pitch/state', 1,
    simros_strmcmd_get_joint_state,elbow_pitch_handle,0,'')
simExtROS_enablePublisher('/vrep_demo/seven_dof_arm/wrist_roll/state', 1,
    simros_strmcmd_get_joint_state,wrist_roll_handle,0,'')
simExtROS_enablePublisher('/vrep_demo/seven_dof_arm/wrist_pitch/state', 1,
    simros_strmcmd_get_joint_state,wrist_pitch_handle,0,'')
simExtROS_enablePublisher('/vrep_demo/seven_dof_arm/gripper_roll/state', 1,
    simros_strmcmd_get_joint_state,gripper_roll_handle,0,'')
```

This code uses the `simExtROS_enablePublisher` function with the `simros_strmcmd_get_joint_state` argument, allowing V-REP to stream the state of the joint specified via its object handler (the fourth parameter in the function), using a `sensor_msgs::JointState` message type:

```
---
header:
  seq: 11900
  stamp:
    secs: 1504564905
    nsecs: 995165677
  frame_id: ''
name: ['elbow_roll_joint']
position: [-3.712777470354922e-06]
velocity: [-0.0002352813316974789]
effort: [-0.7412756085395813]
---
```

Figure 13: Joint state published by `vrep_plugin`

```
simExtROS_enableSubscriber('/vrep_demo/seven_dof_arm/shoulder_pan/ctrl',
10, simros_strmcmd_set_joint_target_position, shoulder_pan_handle, 0, '')
simExtROS_enableSubscriber('/vrep_demo/seven_dof_arm/shoulder_pitch/ctrl',
10, simros_strmcmd_set_joint_target_position, shoulder_pitch_handle, 0, '')
simExtROS_enableSubscriber('/vrep_demo/seven_dof_arm/elbow_roll/ctrl', 10,
simros_strmcmd_set_joint_target_position, elbow_roll_handle, 0, '')
simExtROS_enableSubscriber('/vrep_demo/seven_dof_arm/elbow_pitch/ctrl', 10,
simros_strmcmd_set_joint_target_position, elbow_pitch_handle, 0, '')
simExtROS_enableSubscriber('/vrep_demo/seven_dof_arm/wrist_roll/ctrl', 10,
simros_strmcmd_set_joint_target_position, wrist_roll_handle, 0, '')
simExtROS_enableSubscriber('/vrep_demo/seven_dof_arm/wrist_pitch/ctrl', 10,
simros_strmcmd_set_joint_target_position, wrist_pitch_handle, 0, '')
simExtROS_enableSubscriber('/vrep_demo/seven_dof_arm/gripper_roll/ctrl',
10, simros_strmcmd_set_joint_target_position, gripper_roll_handle, 0, '')
```

Finally, here we enable the arm to get the user control input. The `simExtROS_enableSubscriber` functions are called with the `simros_strmcmd_set_joint_target_position` command, enabling the arm to subscribe to a set of float streams. The received values will be automatically applied to the joints specified via the object handlers.

As usual, we can test that everything works fine by setting a target position to one of the joints of the robot:

```
$ rostopic pub /vrep_demo/seven_dof_arm/wrist_pitch/ctrl std_msgs/Float64
"data: 1.0"
```

Simulating a differential wheeled robot in V-REP

After simulating a robotic arm, we will now discuss how to set up a simulation scene to control a mobile robot. In this case, we will use one of the simulation models already implemented in V-REP. To import a model from the V-REP database, select the desired model class and object from the *Model Browser* panel and drag it into the scene.

For our simulation, we will simulate the *Pioneer 3dx*, one of the most popular differential wheeled mobile robots used as a research platform:

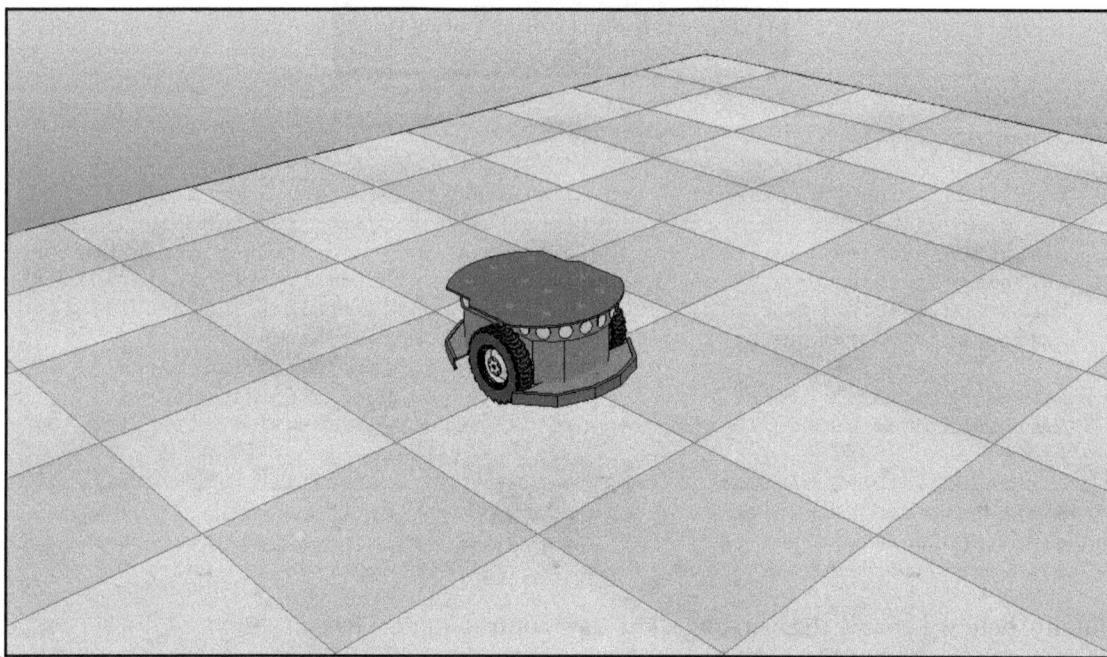

Figure 14: Pioneer 3dx in V-REP simulation scene

By default, the Pioneer robot is equipped with 16 sonar sensors, both forward and rear facing. In the next section, we will discuss how to equip the robot with other sensors.

To actuate the robot using ROS, we should add a script that receives the desired linear and angular velocity and convert it in wheel velocities. We can use the same script to enable sensor data streaming via a ROS topic.

Here is the complete code of the script associated to `Pioneer_p3dx` object in the Scene Hierarchy panel. Part of this code is released with the V-REP simulator and is already available when the `Pioneer_p3dx` is imported in the simulation scene:

```
if (sim_call_type==sim_childscriptcall_initialization) then
    usensors={-1,-1,-1,-1,-1,-1,-1,-1,-1,-1,-1,-1,-1,-1,-1,-1}
    sonarpublisher={-1,-1,-1,-1,-1,-1,-1,-1,-1,-1,-1,-1,-1,-1,-1,-1}
    for i=1,16,1 do
        usensors[i]=simGetObjectHandle("Pioneer_p3dx_ultrasonicSensor"..i)
sonarpublisher[i] = simExtROS_enablePublisher('/sonar'..i , 0,
simros_strmcmd_read_proximity_sensor, usensors[i], -1, '')
    end

    motorLeft=simGetObjectHandle("Pioneer_p3dx_leftMotor")
    motorRight=simGetObjectHandle("Pioneer_p3dx_rightMotor")

--Input
simExtROS_enableSubscriber('/linear_vel', 0,
simros_strmcmd_set_float_signal, -1, -1, 'vl')
simExtROS_enableSubscriber('/angular_vel', 0,
simros_strmcmd_set_float_signal, -1, -1, 'va')
--output
robotHandler=simGetObjectHandle('Pioneer_p3dx') -- body position
odomPublisher=simExtROS_enablePublisher('/odometry',1,simros_strmcmd_get_od
om_data,robotHandler,-1,'')
axes_length = 0.331;
    wheel_radius = 0.0970;
end

if (sim_call_type==sim_childscriptcall_cleanup) then
end

if (sim_call_type==sim_childscriptcall_actuation) then
    local v_l = simGetFloatSignal( 'vl' )
    local v_a = simGetFloatSignal( 'va' )

    if not v_l then
        v_l = 0.0
    end

    if not v_a then
        v_a = 0.0
    end
    local v_left = 0.0
    local v_right = 0.0
    v_left = ( 1/wheel_radius)*(v_l-axes_length/2*v_a)
    v_right = ( 1/wheel_radius)*(v_l+axes_length/2*v_a)
```

```
        simSetJointTargetVelocity(motorLeft,v_left)
        simSetJointTargetVelocity(motorRight, v_right)
    end
```

Here is the explanation of the code:

```
for i=1,16,1 do
usensors[i]=simGetObjectHandle("Pioneer_p3dx_ultrasonicSensor"..i)sonarpubl
isher[i] = simExtROS_enablePublisher('/sonar'..i , 0,
simros_strmcmd_read_proximity_sensor, usensors[i], -1, '')
  end
  motorLeft=simGetObjectHandle("Pioneer_p3dx_leftMotor")
  motorRight=simGetObjectHandle("Pioneer_p3dx_rightMotor")
```

Here, we stream the sonar data and initialize the handlers of the wheels to be controlled:

```
simExtROS_enableSubscriber('/linear_vel', 0,
simros_strmcmd_set_float_signal, -1, -1, 'vl')
simExtROS_enableSubscriber('/angular_vel', 0,
simros_strmcmd_set_float_signal, -1, -1, 'va')

robotHandler=simGetObjectHandle('Pioneer_p3dx') -- body position
odomPublisher=simExtROS_enablePublisher('/odometry',1,simros_strmcmd_get_od
om_data,robotHandler,-1,'')
```

This allows the robot to receive the desired cartesian velocities from the ROS topic and stream its odometry. The simros_strmcmd_set_float_signal command is used to read a float value from the /linear_vel and /angular_vel topics, while the simros_strmcmd_get_odom_data command enables the streaming of the odometry data of the robot via a nav_msgs::Odom message.

In the actuation part of the script, we can calculate the velocity of the wheels:

```
        local v_l = simGetFloatSignal( 'vl' )
        local v_a = simGetFloatSignal( 'va' )
```

This block of code retrieves the value of signals of the desired linear and angular velocities from the input topic:

```
if not v_l then
    v_l = 0.0
end
if not v_a then
    v_a = 0.0
end
```

Since, by default, signals are created with null values, it is recommended to check that they have been initialized before we use them:

```
v_left = ( 1/wheel_radius)*(v_l-axes_length/2*v_a)
v_right = ( 1/wheel_radius)*(v_l+axes_length/2*v_a)
simSetJointTargetVelocity(motorLeft,v_left)
simSetJointTargetVelocity(motorRight, v_right)
```

Finally, we can calculate and set the wheel velocities needed to actuate the robot with the desired control input. In our simulation, a wheel is represented by a simple joint. To move it, we can use `simSetJointTargetVelocity`, which sets the desired target velocity to the joint.

After running the simulation, the user should be able to read the sonar values and the position of the robot, calculated via the robot odometry, and set the linear and angular velocity:

```
$ rostopic pub /linear_vel std_msgs/Float32 "data: 0.2"
```

This will apply a linear velocity of 0.2 m/s to the robot.

Adding a laser sensor to V-REP

An important feature of robotic simulators is the possibility to simulate sensors as well as robots. We are now going to add a laser sensor to the `Pioneer_3dx`. V-REP offers different models of vision, inertial, and proximity sensors. These can be selected from the *Model Browser* panel in the **components | sensors** section.

To add a `laser` to the robot, select and drag and drop `Hokuyo_URG_04LX_UG01_ROS` into the scene. It's useful to put the sensor as a parent of the robot to be facilitated in its correct positioning on the robot frame. After importing the sensor, the `Scene Hierarchy` should appear, as show in the following figure:

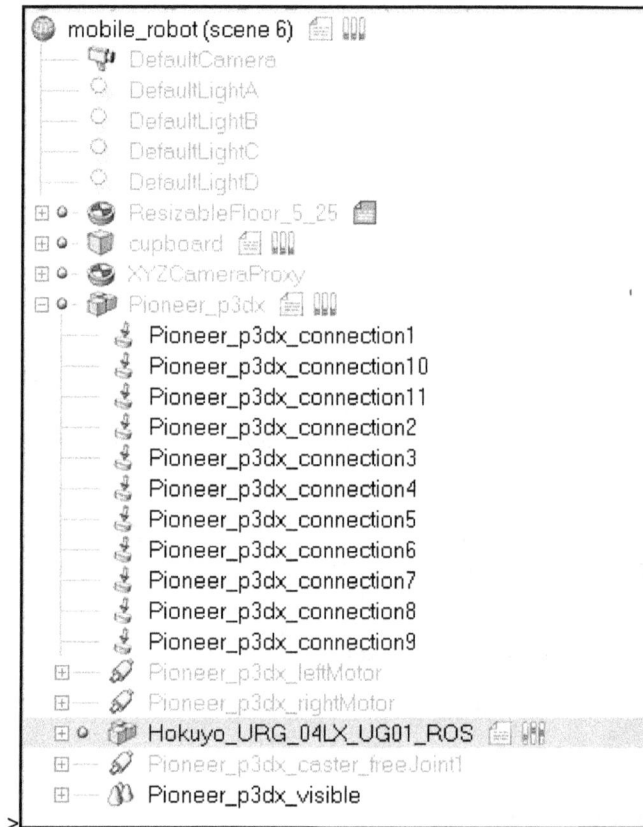

Figure 15: Scene Hierarchy panel with the Pioneer equipped with hokuyo laser

We can position the sensor on the robot frame using the `Object/Item position/orientation` window, accessible via the toolbar. This laser sensor is already suitable to stream laser data on the `/front_scan` topic, using a `sensor_msgs::LaserScan` message. After running the simulation, we can see the data generated by the laser scanner in RViz:

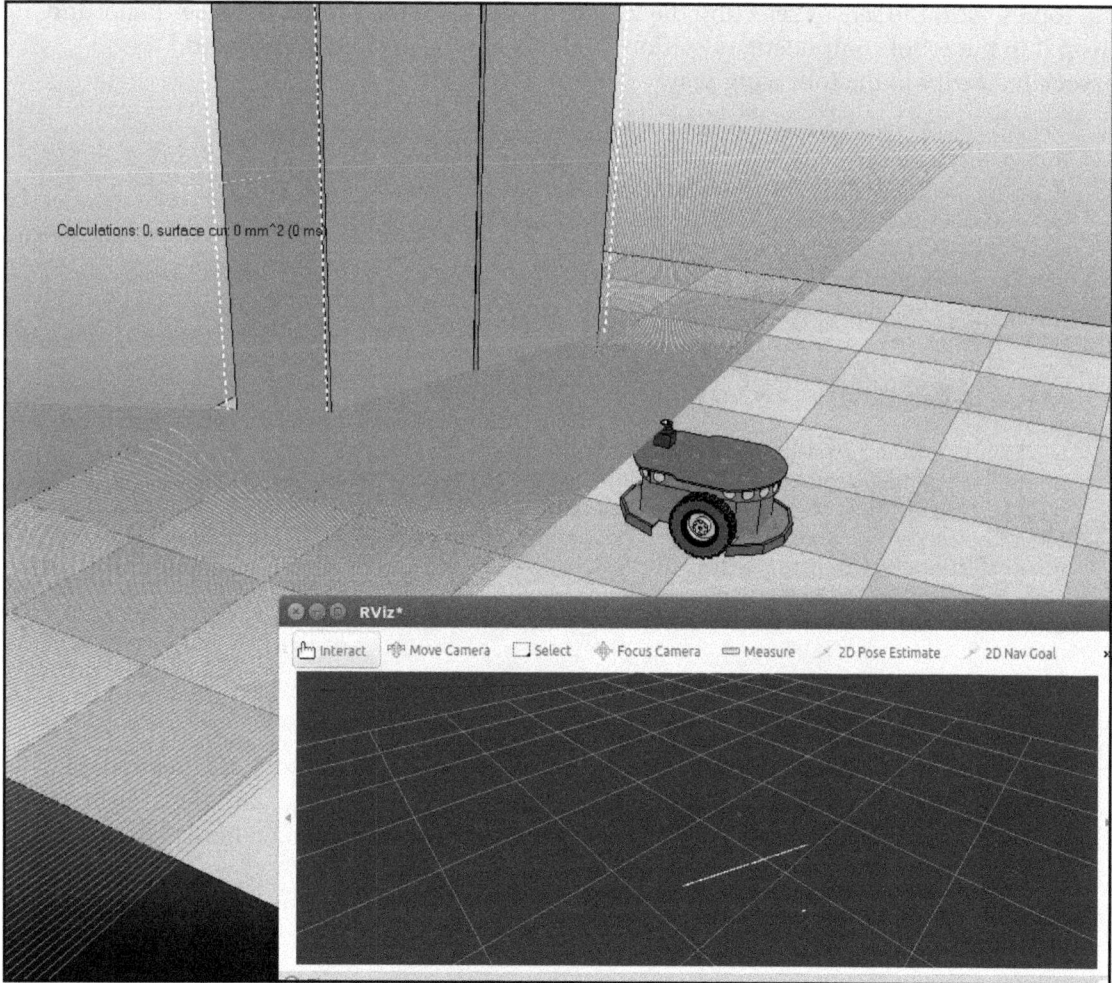

Figure 16: Laser scanner data visualized in V-REP and RViz

Adding a 3D vision sensor to V-REP

In this section, we will add another sensor to our mobile robot: an **rgb-d** sensor, like the one already used in `Chapter 4`, *Simulating Robots Using ROS and Gazebo*. V-REP already has a pre-built model for this sensor, but, unlike the laser scanner, it is not directly integrated with ROS. For this reason, let's modify the script associated to this sensor to stream its data via topics. Add the sensor selecting the **kinect** model from the **Model Browser** panel and drop it in the robot components. Position the kinect in the desired location and the associated script in the following way:

```
if (sim_call_type==sim_childscriptcall_initialization) then
depthCam=simGetObjectHandle('kinect_depth')
depthView=simFloatingViewAdd(0.9,0.9,0.2,0.2,0)
colorCam=simGetObjectHandle('kinect_rgb')
colorView=simFloatingViewAdd(0.69,0.9,0.2,0.2,0)
glass=simGetObjectHandle('kinect_glass')
kinect=simGetObjectHandle('kinect')
end

if(sim_call_type==sim_childscriptcall_sensing) then
rgbTopicName=simExtROS_enablePublisher('/rgb/image_raw',1,simros_strmcmd_ge
t_vision_sensor_image,colorCam,0,'')
DepthTopicName=simExtROS_enablePublisher('/depth/image_raw',1,simros_strmcm
d_get_vision_sensor_image,depthCam,0,'')
infoTopicName=simExtROS_enablePublisher('/cameraInfo',1,simros_strmcmd_get_
vision_sensor_info,colorCam,0,'')

end

if (sim_call_type==sim_childscriptcall_cleanup) then
end
```

Here, in the `sim_childscriptcall_sensing` section, we add the code to stream data generated by the *rgb-d* sensor: the colored image and the depth image, and the information concerning the camera calibration. We can run the simulation, as shown here:

```
$ rosrun image_view image_view image:=/rgb/image_raw
```

And we get the following image:

Figure 17: RGB and depth images streamed by kinect sensor in V-REP

We have now simulated a differential wheeled mobile robot equipped with different kinds of sensors fully integrated with ROS. This robot model is saved in the `mobile_robot.ttt` simulation scene provided with the `vrep_demo_pkg` package.

Questions

We should now be able to answer the following questions:

- How do V-REP and ROS communicate?
- In what way is it possible to control a V-REP simulation with ROS?
- How can we import new robot models in V-REP and integrate them with ROS?
- How can we integrate new V-REP model sensors with ROS?
- How can we move the mobile robot in a V-REP simulation?

Summary

In this chapter, we mainly replicated things already done in the previous chapter with Gazebo, using another simulator: V-REP. V-REP is a multi-platform simulation software that integrates different technologies and is very versatile. With respect to Gazebo, V-REP could appear easier to use for new users.

In this chapter, we simulated two robots, one imported using the URDF file of the seven-DOF arm designed in previous chapters, and the other was a popular differential wheeled robot provided by V-REP simulation models. We learned how to interface and control robot joints of our model with ROS and how to move a differential drive mobile robot using topics. In addition, we discussed how to add different type of sensors in our simulation scene, improving the equipment of the simulated mobile robot with a laser and a 3D vision sensor. Finally, we discussed how to connect a *rgb-d* sensor simulated in V-REP with the ROS framework.

In the next chapter, we will see how to interface the robotic arm with the ROS MoveIt package and the mobile robot with the Navigation stack.

6
Using the ROS MoveIt! and Navigation Stack

In the previous chapters, we have been discussing the design and simulation of a robotic arm and mobile robot. We controlled each joint of the robotic arm in Gazebo using the ROS controller and moved the mobile robot inside Gazebo using the teleop node.

In this chapter, we are going to address the *motion planning* problem. Moving a robot by directly controlling its joints manually might be a difficult task, especially if we want to add position or velocity constraints to the robot motion. Similarly, driving a mobile robot, avoiding obstacles, requires the planning of a path. For this reason, we will solve these problems using the ROS **MoveIt!** and **Navigation stack**.

MoveIt! is a set of packages and tools for doing mobile manipulation in ROS. The official web page (http://moveit.ros.org/) contains the documentations, the list of robots using MoveIt!, and various examples to demonstrate pick and place, grasping, simple motion planning using inverse kinematics, and so on.

MoveIt! contains state-of-the-art software for motion planning, manipulation, 3D perception, kinematics, collision checking, control, and navigation. Apart from the command line interface, MoveIt! has some good GUI to interface a new robot to MoveIt!. Also, there is a RViz plugin, which enables motion planning from RViz itself. We will also see how to motion plan our robot using MoveIt! C++ APIs.

Next is the Navigation stack, another set of powerful tools and libraries to work mainly for mobile robot navigation. The Navigation stack contains ready-to-use navigation algorithms which can be used in mobile robots, especially for differential wheeled robots. Using these stacks, we can make the robot autonomous, and that is the final concept that we are going to see in the Navigation stack.

The first section of this chapter will discuss more on the MoveIt! package, installation, and architecture. After discussing the main concepts of MoveIt!, we will see how to create a MoveIt! package for our robotic arm, which can provide collision-aware path planning to our robot. Using this package, we can perform motion planning (inverse kinematics) in RViz, and can interface to Gazebo or the real robot for executing the paths.

After discussing the interfacing, we will discuss more about the Navigation stack and see how to perform autonomous navigation using **SLAM** (**Simultaneous Localization And Mapping**) and **amcl** (**Adaptive Monte Carlo Localization**).

Installing MoveIt!

Let's start with installing MoveIt!. The installation procedure is very simple and is just a single command. Using the following commands, we install the MoveIt! core, a set of plugins ad planners for ROS Kinetic:

```
$ sudo apt-get install ros-kinetic-moveit ros-kinetic-moveit-plugins ros-
kinetic-moveit-planners
```

MoveIt! architecture

Let's start with MoveIt! and its architecture. Understanding the architecture of MoveIt! helps to program and interface the robot to MoveIt!. We will quickly go through the architecture and the important concepts of MoveIt!, and start interfacing and programming our robots.

Here is the MoveIt! architecture, included in their official web page, at
http://moveit.ros.org/documentation/concepts:

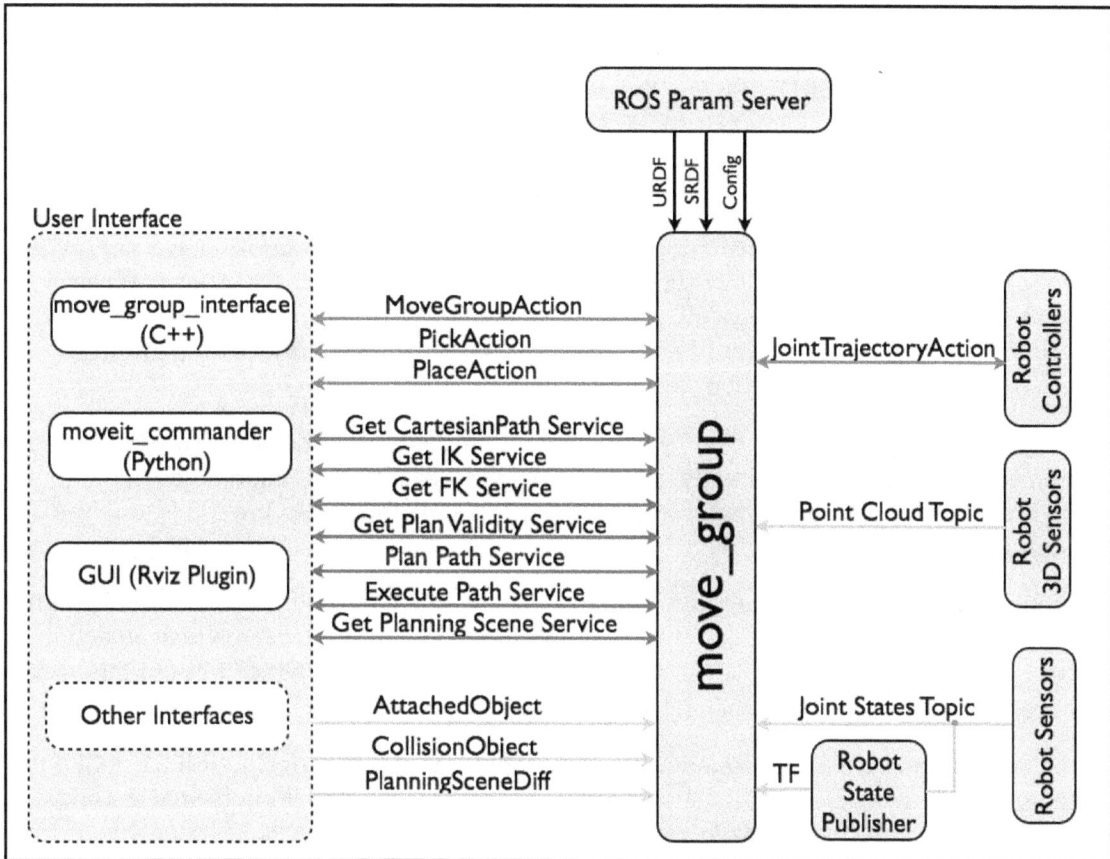

Figure 1: MoveIt! architecture diagram

The move_group node

We can say that `move_group` is the heart of MoveIt!, as this node acts as an integrator of the various components of the robot and delivers actions/services according to the user's needs.

From the architecture, it's clear that the `move_group` node collects robot information such as point cloud, joint state of the robot, and transform (TF) of the robot in the form of topics and services.

From the parameter server, it collects the robot kinematics data, such as `robot_description` (URDF), **Semantic Robot Description Format (SRDF)**, and the configuration files. The SRDF file and the configuration files are generated while we generate a MoveIt! package for our robot. The configuration files contains the parameter file for setting joint limits, perception, kinematics, end effector, and so on. We will see the files when we discuss generating the MoveIt! package for our robot.

When MoveIt! gets all this information about the robot and its configuration, we can say it is properly configured and we can start commanding the robot from the user interfaces. We can either use C++ or Python MoveIt! APIs to command the `move_group` node to perform actions such as pick/place, IK, and FK, among others. Using the RViz motion planning plugin, we can command the robot from the RViz GUI itself.

As we already discussed, the `move_group` node is an integrator; it does not run any kind of motion planning algorithms directly, but instead connects all the functionalities as plugins. There are plugins for kinematics solvers, motion planning, and so on. We can extend the capabilities through these plugins.

After motion planning, the generated trajectory talks to the controllers in the robot using the `FollowJointTrajectoryAction` interface. This is an action interface in which an action server is run on the robot, and `move_node` initiates an action client which talks to this server and executes the trajectory on the real robot/Gazebo simulator.

At the end of the MoveIt! discussion, we will see how to connect MoveIt! with RViz GUI to Gazebo. The following screenshot shows a robotic arm that is controlling from RViz and the trajectory is executed inside Gazebo:

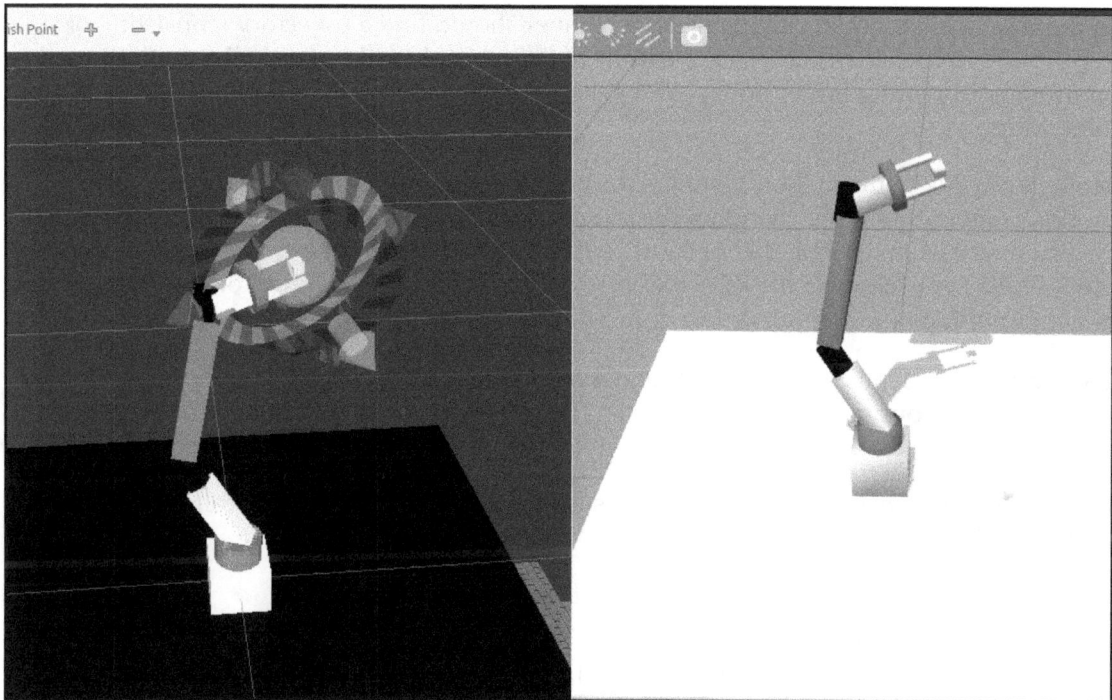

Figure 2: Trajectory from RViz GUI executing in Gazebo

Motion planning using MoveIt!

Assume that we know the starting pose of the robot, a desired goal pose of the robot, the geometrical description of the robot, and geometrical description of the world, then motion planning is the technique to find an optimum path that moves the robot gradually from the start pose to the goal pose, while never touching any obstacles in the world and without colliding with the robot links.

In this context, the robot geometry is described via the URDF file. We can also create a description file for the robot environment and use laser or vision sensors of the robot to map its operative space, in order to avoid static and dynamic obstacles during the execution of planned paths.

In the case of the robotic arm, the motion planner should find a trajectory (consisting of joint spaces of each joint) in which the links of the robot should never collide with the environment, avoid self-collision (collision between two robot links), and not violate the joint limits.

MoveIt! can talk to the motion planners through the plugin interface. We can use any motion planner by simply changing the plugin. This method is highly extensible so we can try our own custom motion planners using this interface. The move_group node talks to the motion planner plugin via the ROS action/services. The default planner for the `move_group` node is OMPL (`http://ompl.kavrakilab.org/`).

To start motion planning, we should send a motion planning request to the motion planner which specified our planning requirements. The planning requirement may be setting a new goal pose of the end-effector; for example, for a pick and place operation.

We can set additional kinematic constraints for the motion planners. The following are some inbuilt constraints in MoveIt!:

- **Position constraints**: These restrict the position of a link
- **Orientation constraints**: These restrict the orientation of a link
- **Visibility constraints**: These restrict a point on the link to be visible in an area (view of a sensor)
- **Joint constraints**: These restrict a joint within its joint limits
- **User-specified constraints**: Using these constraints, the user can define his own constraints using the callback functions

Using these constraints, we can send a motion planning request and the planner will generate a suitable trajectory according to the request. The `move_group` node will generate the suitable trajectory from the motion planner which obeys all the constraints. This can be sent to robot joint trajectory controllers.

Motion planning request adapters

The planning request adapters help to pre-process the motion planning request and post-process the motion planning response. One of the uses of pre-processing requests is that it helps to correct if there is a violation in the joint states and, for the post-processing, it can convert the path generated by the planner to a time-parameterized trajectory. The following are some of the default planning request adapters in MoveIt!:

- **FixStartStateBounds**: If a joint state is slightly outside the joint limits, then this adapter can fix the initial joint limits within the limits.
- **FixWorkspaceBounds**: This specifies a workspace for planning with a cube size of 10 m x 10 m x 10 m.
- **FixStartStateCollision**: This adapter samples a new collision free configuration if the existing joint configuration is in collision. It makes a new configuration by changing the current configuration by a small factor called `jiggle_factor`.
- **FixStartStatePathConstraints**: This adapter is used when the initial pose of the robot does not obey the path constraints. In this, it finds a near pose which satisfies the path constraints and uses that pose as the initial state.
- **AddTimeParameterization**: This adapter parameterizes the motion plan by applying the velocity and acceleration constraints.

MoveIt! planning scene

The term "planning scene" is used to represent the world around the robot and store the state of the robot itself. The planning scene monitor inside `move_group` maintains the planning scene representation. The `move_group` node consists of another section called the world geometry monitor, which builds the world geometry from the sensors of the robot and from the user input.

The planning scene monitor reads the joint_states topic from the robot, and the sensor information and world geometry from the world geometry monitor. The world scene monitor reads from the occupancy map monitor, which uses 3D perception to build a 3D representation of the environment, called **Octomap**. Octomaps can be generated from point clouds, which are handled by a point cloud occupancy map update plugin and depth images handled by a depth image occupancy map updater. The following image shows the representation of the planning scene from the MoveIt! official wiki (http://moveit.ros.org/documentation/concepts/):

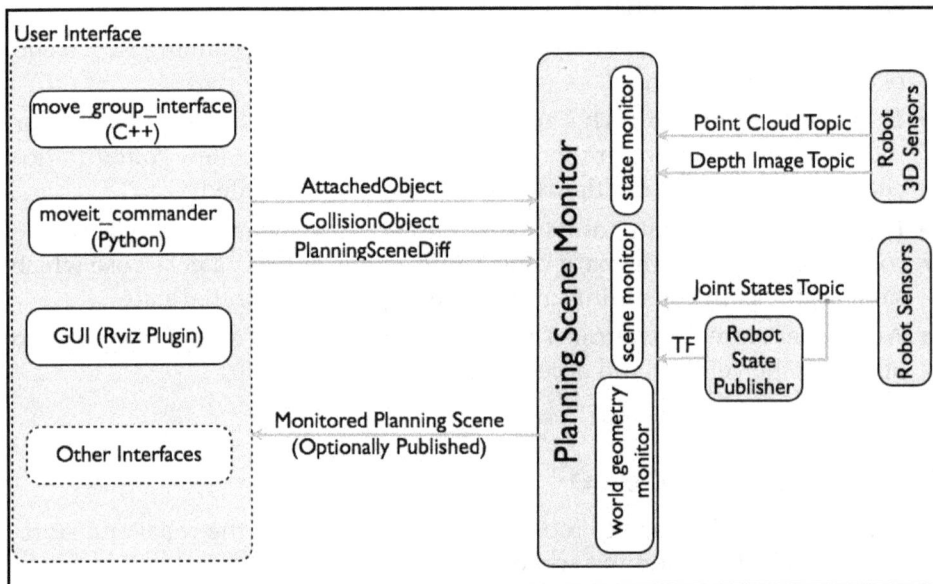

Figure 3: MoveIt! planning scene overview diagram.

MoveIt! kinematics handling

MoveIt! provides a great flexibility to switch the inverse kinematics algorithms using the robot plugins. Users can write their own IK solver as a MoveIt! plugin and switch from the default solver plugin whenever required. The default IK solver in MoveIt! is a numerical jacobian-based solver.

Compared to the analytic solvers, the numerical solver can take time to solve IK. The package called IKFast can be used to generate a C++ code for solving IK using analytical methods, which can be used for different kinds of robot manipulator and perform better if the DOF is less than 6. This C++ code can also be converted into the MoveIt! plugin by using some ROS tool. We will look at this procedure in the upcoming chapters.

Forward kinematics and finding jacobians are already integrated to the MoveIt! RobotState class, so we don't need to use plugins for solving FK.

MoveIt! collision checking

The CollisionWorld object inside MoveIt! is used to find collisions inside a planning scene which is using the **Flexible Collision Library** (**FCL**) package as a backend. MoveIt! supports collision checking for different types of objects, such as meshes, primitive shapes such as boxes, cylinders, cones, spheres, and Octomap.

Collision checking is one of the computationally expensive tasks during motion planning. To reduce this computation, MoveIt! provides a matrix called **ACM** (**Allowed Collision Matrix**). It contains a binary value corresponding to the need to check for a collision between two pairs of bodies. If the value of the matrix is 1, it means collision of the corresponding pair is not needed. We can set the value as 1 where the bodies are always so far that they would never collide with each other. Optimizing ACM can reduce the total computation needed for collision avoidance.

After discussing the basic concepts in MoveIt!, we can now discuss how to interface a robotic arm into MoveIt!. To interface a robot arm in MoveIt!, we need to satisfy the components that we saw in Figure 1. The `move_group` node essentially requires parameters, such as URDF, SRDF, config files, and joint states topics, along with TF from a robot to start with motion planning.

MoveIt! provides a GUI-based tool called Setup Assistant to generate all these elements. The following section describes the procedure to generate a MoveIt! configuration from the Setup Assistant tool.

Generating MoveIt! configuration package using the Setup Assistant tool

The MoveIt! Setup Assistant is a graphical user interface for configuring any robot to MoveIt!. Basically, this tool generates SRDF, configuration files, launch files, and scripts generating from the robot URDF model, which is required to configure the `move_group` node.

The SRDF file contains details about the arm joints, end-effector joints, virtual joints, and the collision link pairs, which are configured during the MoveIt! configuration process using the Setup Assistant tool.

The configuration file contains details about the kinematic solvers, joint limits, controllers, and so on, which are also configured and saved during the configuration process.

Using the generated configuration package of the robot, we can work with motion planning in RViz without the presence of a real robot or simulation interface.

Let's start the configuration wizard, and we can see the step-by-step procedure to build the configuration package of our robotic arm.

Step 1 – Launching the Setup Assistant tool

To start the MoveIt! Setup Assistant tool, we can use the following command:

```
$ roslaunch moveit_setup_assistant setup_assistant.launch
```

This will bring up a window with two choices: **Create New MoveIt! Configuration Package** or **Edit Existing MoveIt! Configuration Package**. Here we are creating a new package, so we need that option. If we have a MoveIt! package already, then we can select the second option.

Click on the **Create New MoveIt! Configuration Package button**, which will display a new screen, as shown next:

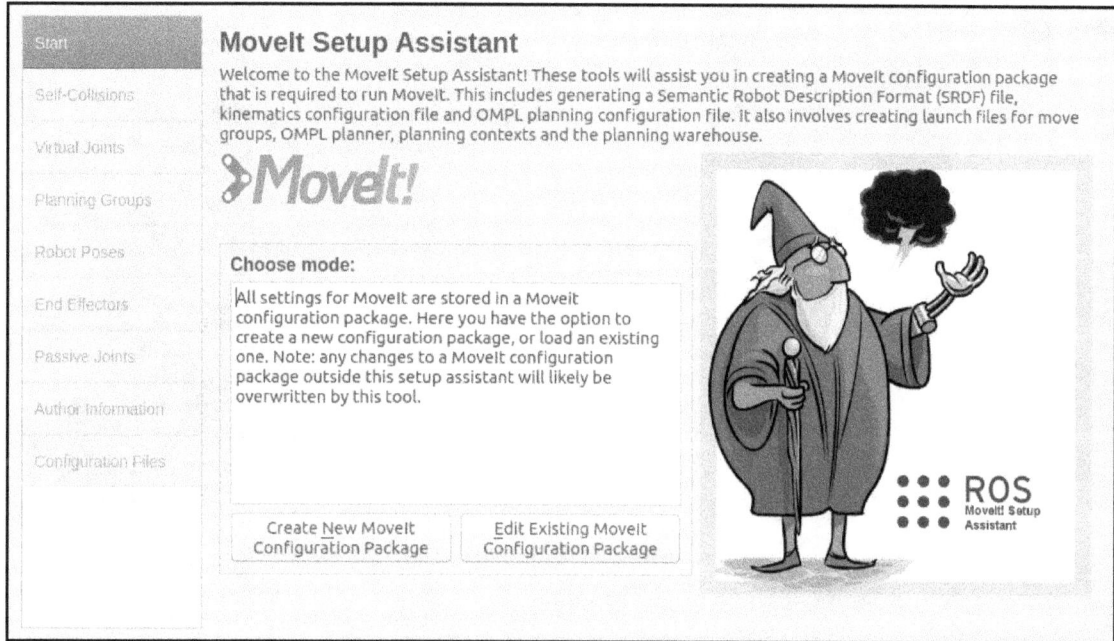

Figure 4: MoveIt! Setup Assistant

In this step, the wizard asks for the URDF model of the new robot. To give the URDF file, click on the **Browse** button and navigate to `mastering_ros_robot_description_pkg/urdf/ seven_dof_arm.urdf`. Choose this file and press the **Load** button to load the URDF. We can either give the robot model as pure URDF or xacro; if we give xacro, the tool will convert to RDF internally.

If the robot model is successfully parsed, we can see the robot model on the window, as shown in the following screenshot:

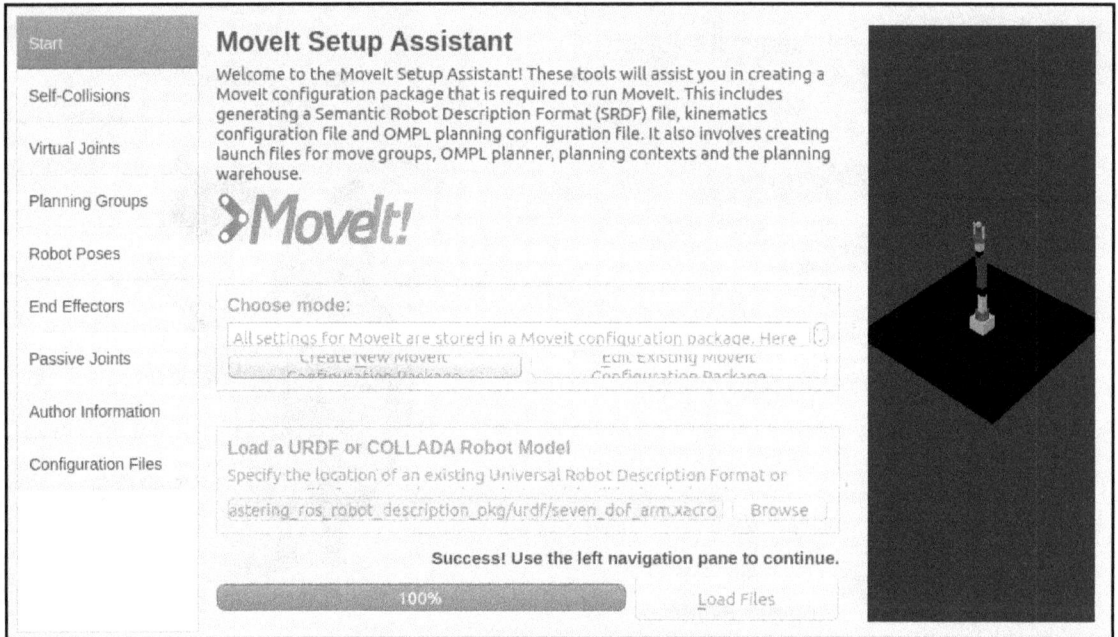

Figure 5: Successfully parsing the robot model in the Setup Assistant tool

Step 2 – Generating the Self-Collision matrix

We can now start to navigate all the panels of the window to properly configure our robot. In the **Self-Collisions** tab, MoveIt! searches for a pair of links on the robot which can be safely disabled from the collision checking. These can reduce the processing time. This tool analyzes each link pair and categorizes the links as always in collision, never in collision, default in collision, adjacent links disabled, and sometimes in collision, and it disables the pair of links which makes any kind of collision. The following image shows the **Self-Collisions** window:

Optimize Self-Collision Checking

The Default Self-Collision Matrix Generator will search for pairs of links on the robot that can safely be disabled from collision checking, decreasing motion planning processing time. These pairs of links are disabled when they are always in collision, never in collision, in collision in the robot's default position or when the links are adjacent to each other on the kinematic chain. Sampling density specifies how many random robot positions to check for self collision. Higher densities require more computation time.

Sampling Density: Low ⊖━━━━━━━━━━━━ High 10000

Min. collisions for "always"-colliding p 95% ⬍ [Generate Collision Matrix]

	Link A ▾	Link B	Disabled	ason to Disab
1	base_link	bottom_link	☑	Adjacent Li...
2	base_link	elbow_roll...	☑	Never in Co...
3	base_link	grasping_fr...	☑	Never in Co...
4	base_link	gripper_fin...	☑	Never in Co...
5	base_link	gripper_fin...	☑	Never in Co...
6	base_link	gripper_rol...	☑	Never in Co...
7	base_link	shoulder_p...	☑	Adjacent Li...
8	base_link	wrist_pitch...	☑	Never in Co...
9	base_link	wrist_roll_l...	☑	Never in Co...
10	bottom_link	elbow_roll...	☑	Never in Co...
11	bottom_link	shoulder_p...	☑	Never in Co...

[link n...] ☐ show enabled pairs ◉ linear view ○ matrix view [Revert]

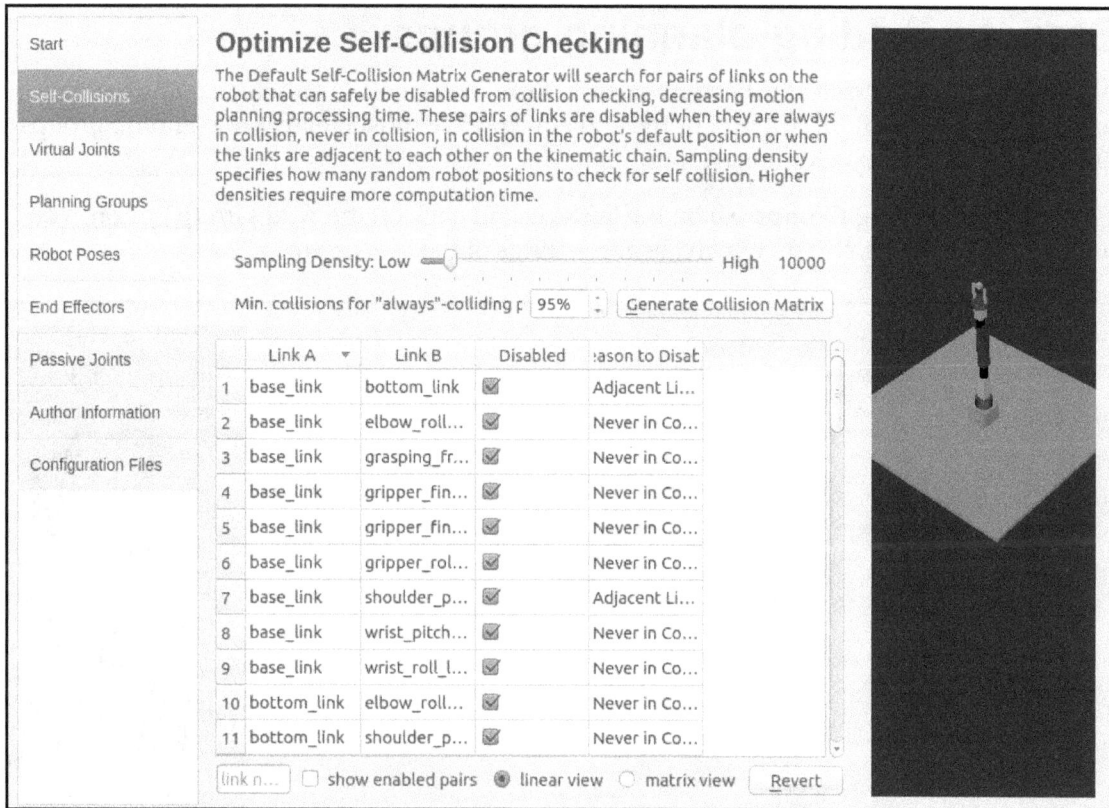

Figure 6: Regenerating the Self-Collision matrix

The sampling density is the number of random positions to check for self-collision. If the density is large, computation will be high but self-collision will be less. The default value is 10,000. We can see the disabled pair of links by pressing the **Regenerate Default Collision Matrix** button; it will take a few seconds to list out the disabled pair of links.

Step 3 – Adding virtual joints

Virtual joints attach the robot to the world. They are not mandatory for a static robot which does not move. We need virtual joints when the base position of the arm is not fixed. For example, if a robot arm is fixed on a mobile robot, we should define a virtual joint with respect to the odometry frame (odom).

In the case of our robot, we are not creating virtual joints.

Step 4 – Adding planning groups

A planning group is basically a group of joints/links in a robotic arm which plans together to achieve a goal position of a link or the end effector. We must create two planning groups, one for the arm and one for the gripper.

Click on the **Planning Groups** tab on the left side and click on the **Add Group** button. You will see the following screen, which has the settings of the `arm` group:

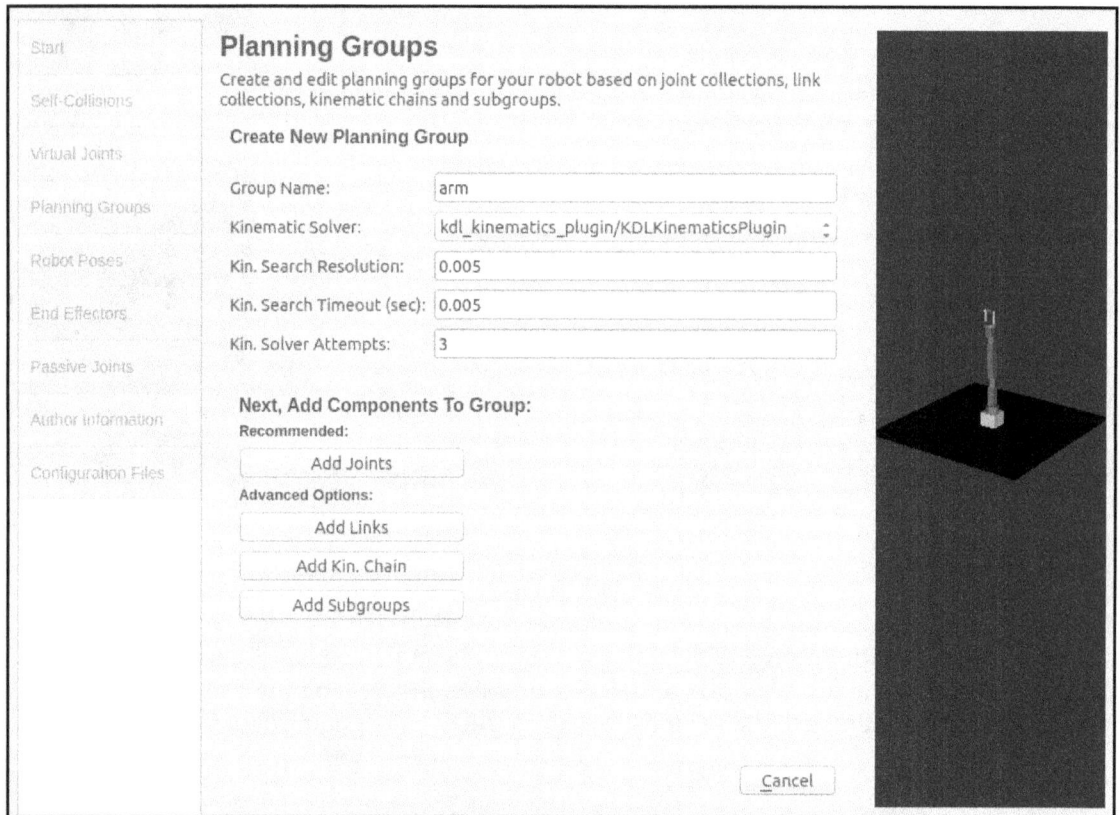

Figure 7: Adding the planning group of the arm

Here, we are giving **Group Name** as arm, and **Kinematic Solver** as `kdl_kinematics_plugin/KDLKinematicsPlugin`, which is the default numerical IK solver with MoveIt!. We can keep the other parameters as the default values. In addition, we can choose different ways to add elements in a planning group. For example, we could specify the joints of the group, add its links, or directly specify a kinematic chain.

Inside the arm group, first we have to add a kinematic chain, starting from `base_link` as the first link to the `grasping_frame`.

Add a group called `gripper` and we don't need to have a kinematic solver for the `gripper` group. Inside this group, we can add the joints and links of the gripper. These settings are shown next:

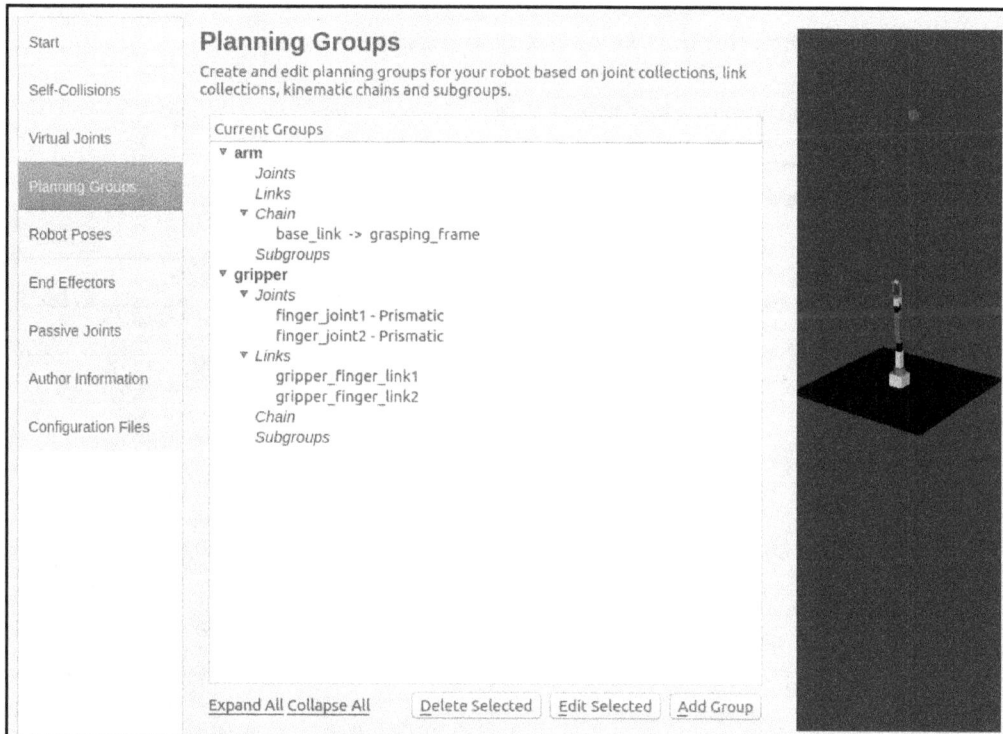

Figure 8: Adding the planning group of the arm and gripper

Step 5 – Adding the robot poses

In this step, we can add certain fixed poses in the robot configuration. For example, we can assign a home position or a pick/place position in this step. The advantage is that, while programming with MoveIt! APIs, we can directly call these poses, which are also called group states. These have many applications in the pick/place and grasping operation. The robot can switch to the fixed poses without any hassle.

Step 6 – Setting up the robot end effector

In this step, we name the robot end effector and assign the end-effector group, the parent link, and the parent group.

We can add any number of end effectors to this robot. In our case, it's a gripper designed for pick and place operations.

Click on the **Add End Effector** button and name the end effector as `robot_eef`, the planning group as gripper, which we have already created, the parent link as `grasping_frame`, and the parent group as `arm`:

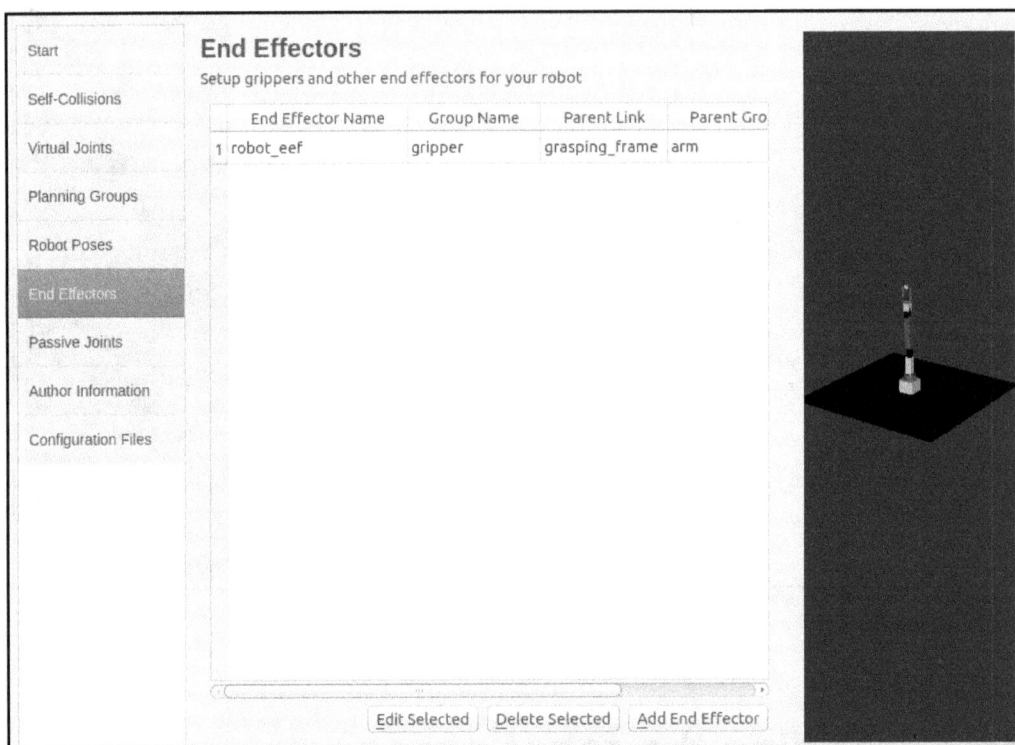

Figure 9: Adding end effectors

Step 7 – Adding passive joints

In this step, we can specify the passive joints in the robot. Passive joints mean that the joints do not have any actuators. Caster wheels are one of the examples of passive joints. The planner will ignore these kinds of joints during motion planning.

Step 8 – Author information

In this step, the author of the robotic model can add personal information, his name and email address, required by catkin to release the model to the ROS community.

Step 9 – Generating configuration files

We are almost done. We are in the final stage, that is, generating the configuration files. In this step, the tool will generate a configuration package which contains the file needed to interface MoveIt!.

Click on the **Browse** button to locate a folder to save the configuration file that is going to be generated by the Setup Assistant tool. Here we can see the files are generating inside a folder called `seven_dof_arm_config`. You can `add_config` or `_generated` along with the robot name for the configuration package.

Click on the **Generate Package** button, and it will generate the files to the given folder.

If the process is successful, we can click on **Exit Setup Assistant**, which will exit us from the tool.

The following screenshot shows the generation process:

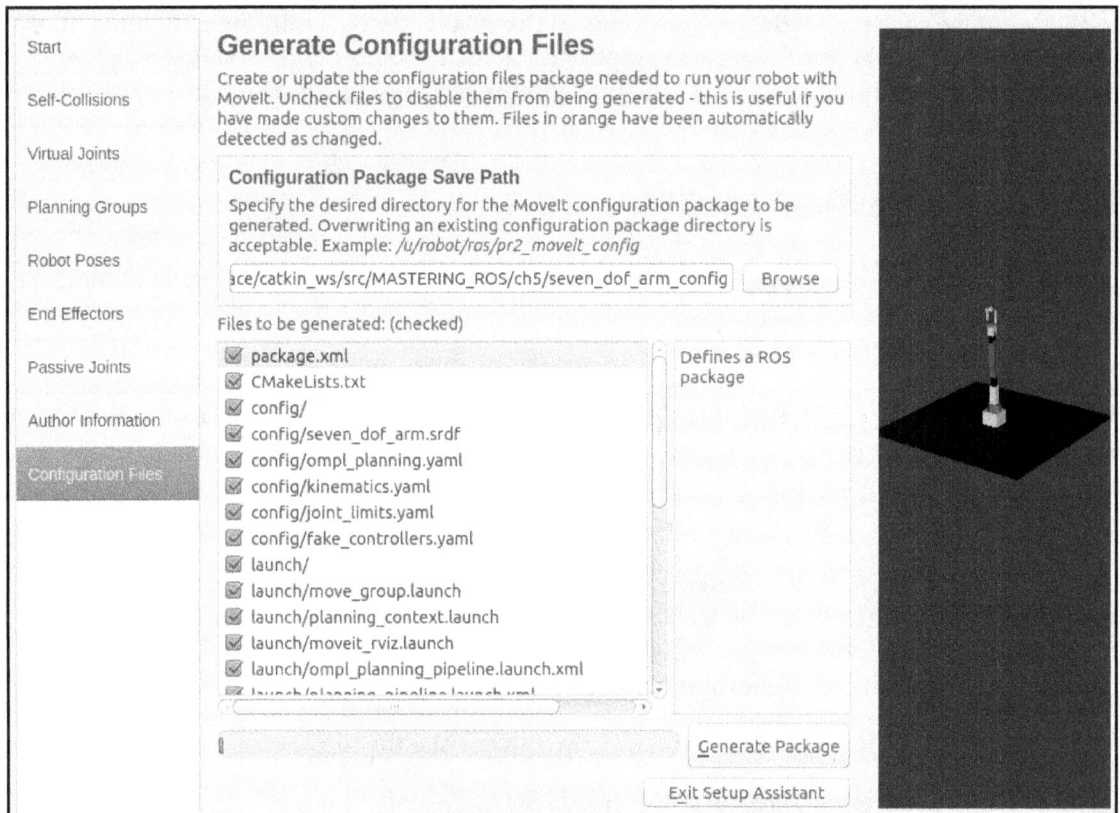

Figure 10: Generating the MoveIt! configuration package

After generating the MoveIt! configuration package, we can copy it into our `catkin` workspace. In the following section, we are going to work with this package. As usual, the model of the robot created can be downloaded from the following GitHub repository or can be obtained from the book's source code:

```
$ git clone https://github.com/jocacace/seven_dof_arm_config
```

Motion planning of robot in RViz using MoveIt! configuration package

MoveIt! provides a plugin for RViz, which allows it to create new planning scenes where **robot works**, **generate motion plans**, and **add new objects**, visualize the planning output and can directly interact with the visualized robot.

The MoveIt! configuration package consists of configuration files and launch files to start motion planning in RViz. There is a demo launch file in the package to explore all the functionalities of this package.

The following is the command to invoke the demo launch file:

```
$ roslaunch seven_dof_arm_config demo.launch
```

If everything works fine, we will get the following screen of RViz being loaded with the `MotionPlanning` plugin provided by MoveIt!:

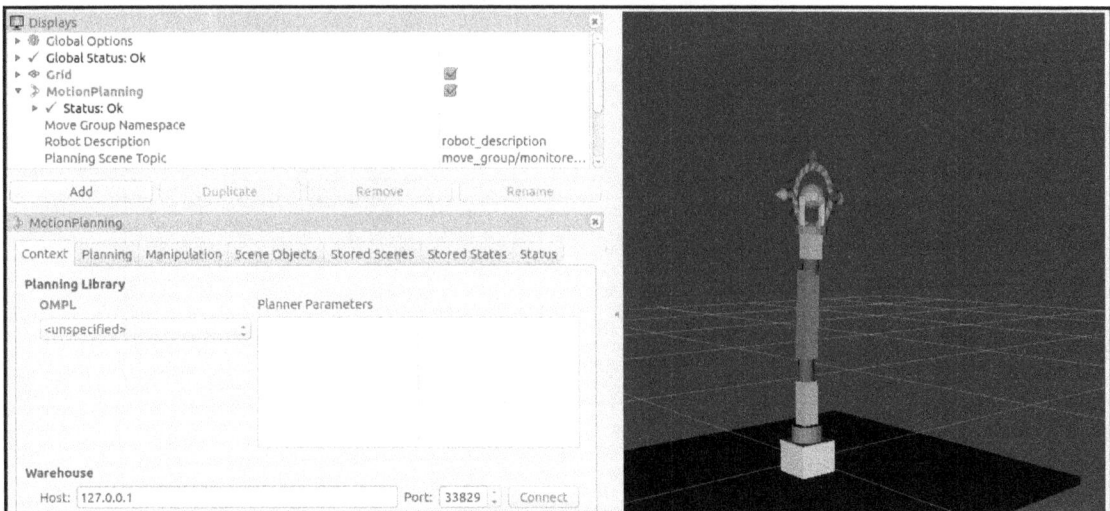

Figure 11: MoveIt! - RViz plugin

Using the RViz Motion Planning plugin

From the preceding figure , we can see that the RViz-Motion Planning plugin is loaded on the left side of the screen. There are several tabs on the **Motion Planning** window, such as **Context**, **Planning**, and so on. The default tab is the **Context** tab and we can see the default **Planning Library** as OMPL, which is shown in green. It indicates that MoveIt! successfully loaded the motion planning library. If it is not loaded, we can't perform motion planning.

Next is the **Planning** tab. This is one of the frequently used tabs used to assign the **Start State**, **Goal State**, **Plan** a path, and **Execute** the path. Shown next is the GUI of the **Planning** tab:

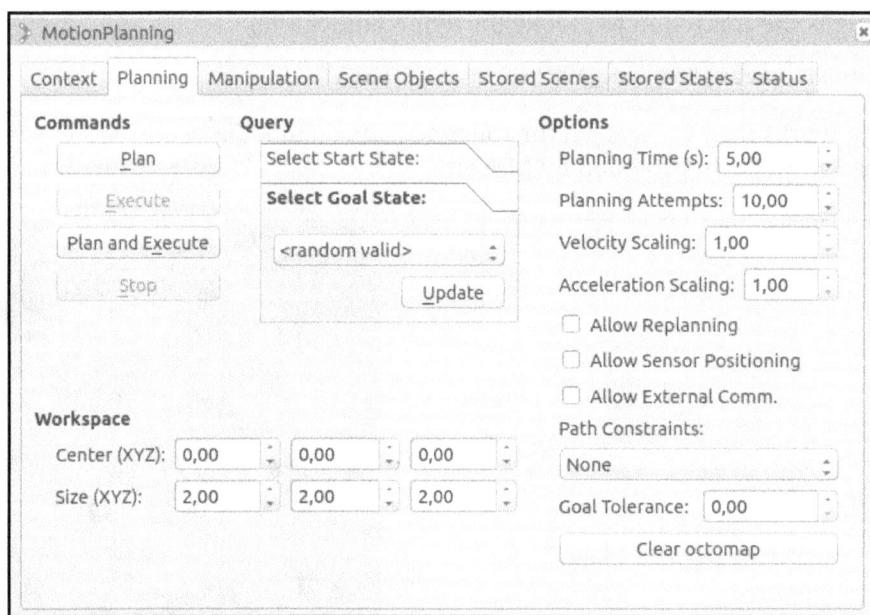

Figure 12: MoveIt! -RViz Planning tab

We can assign the start state and the goal state of the robot under the **Query** panel. Using the **Plan** button, we can plan the path from the start to the goal state, and if the planning is successful, we can execute it. By default, execution is done on fake controllers. We can change these controllers into trajectory controllers for executing the planned trajectory in Gazebo or the real robot.

We can set the starting and the goal position of the robot end effector by using the interactive marker attached on the arm gripper. We can translate and rotate the marker pose, and, if there is a planning solution, we can see an arm in orange color. In some situations, the arm will not move even the end-effector marker pose moves, and if the arm does not come to the marker position, we can assume that there is no IK solution in that pose. We may need more DOF to reach there or there might be some collision between the links.

The following screenshots show a valid goal pose and an invalid goal pose:

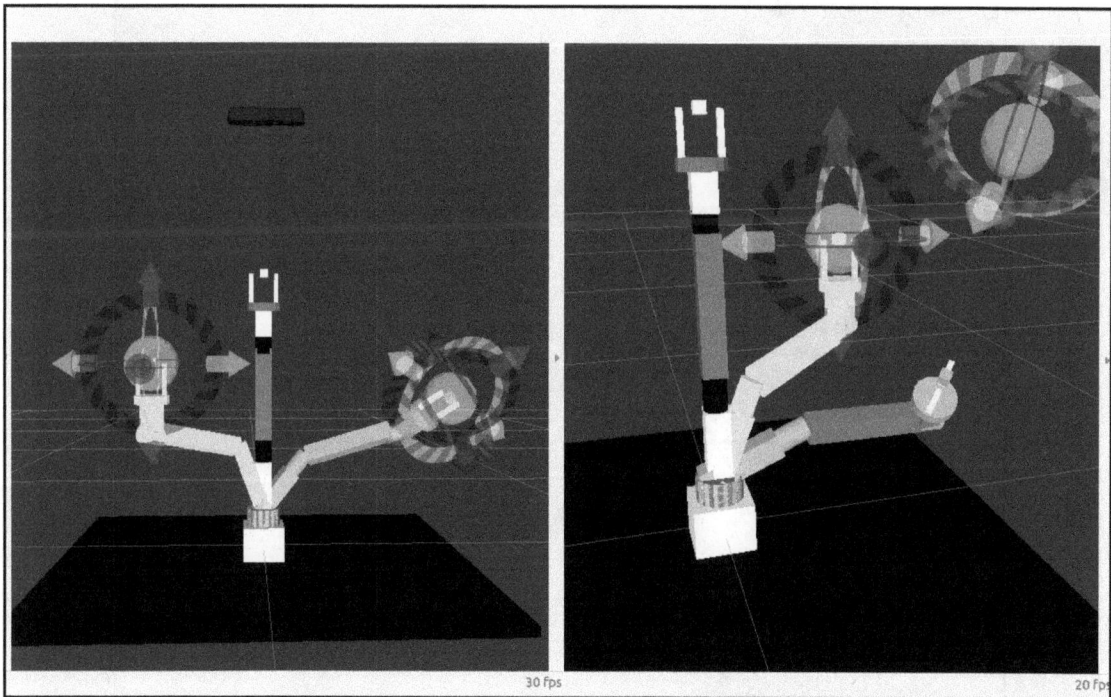

Figure 13: A valid pose and an invalid pose of the robot in RViz

The green colored arm represents the starting position of the arm, and the orange color represents the goal position. In the first figure, if we press the **Plan** button, MoveIt! plans a path from start to goal. In the second image, we can observe two things. First, one of the links of the orange arm is red, which means that the goal pose is in a self-collided state. Secondly, look at the end- effector marker; it is far from the actual end effector and it has also turned red.

We can also work with some quick motion planning using random valid options in the start state and the goal state. If we select the goal state as random valid and press the **Update** button, it will generate a random valid goal pose. Click on the **Plan** button and we can see the motion planning.

We can customize the RViz visualization using the various options in the `MotionPlanning` plugin. Shown next are some of the options of this plugin:

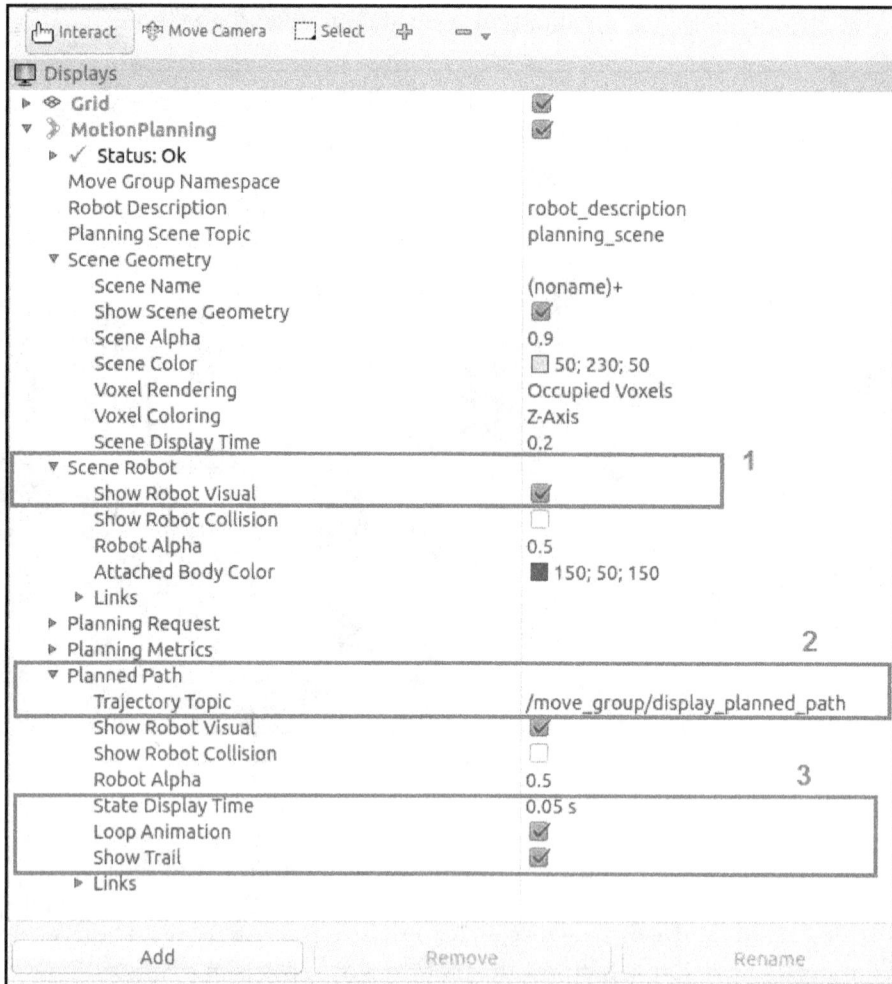

Figure 14: Settings of the MotionPlanning plugin on RViz

The first marked area is **Scene Robot**, which will show the robot model; if it is unchecked, we won't see any robot model. The second marked area is the **Trajectory Topic**, in which RViz gets the visualization trajectory. If we want to animate the motion planning and want to display the motion trails, we should enable this option.

One of the other sections in the plugin settings is shown in the following image:

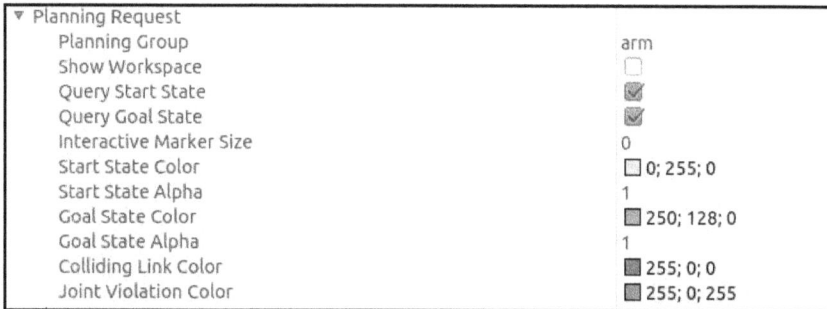

Figure 15: Planning Request setting in MotionPlanning plugin

In the preceding figure, we can see the **Query Start State** and the **Query Goal State** options. These options can visualize the start pose and the goal pose of the arm, which we saw in Figure 13. **Show Workspace** visualizes the cubic workspace (world geometry) around the robot. The visualization can help to debug our motion-planning algorithm and understand the robot motion behavior in detail.

In the next section, we will see how to interface the MoveIt! configuration package to Gazebo. This will execute the trajectory generated by MoveIt! in Gazebo.

Interfacing the MoveIt! configuration package to Gazebo

We have already worked with the Gazebo simulation of this arm and attached controllers to it. For interfacing the arm in MoveIt! to Gazebo, we need a trajectory controller which has the `FollowJointTrajectoryAction` interface, as we mentioned in the MoveIt! architecture.

The following is the procedure to interface MoveIt! to Gazebo.

Step 1 – Writing the controller configuration file for MoveIt!

The first step is to create a configuration file for talking with the trajectory controllers in Gazebo from MoveIt!. The controller configuration file called `controllers.yaml` has to be created inside the `config` folder of the `seven_dof_arm_config` package.

Given next is an example of the `controllers.yaml` definition:

```
controller_manager_ns: controller_manager
controller_list:
  - name: seven_dof_arm/seven_dof_arm_joint_controller
    action_ns: follow_joint_trajectory
    type: FollowJointTrajectory
    default: true
    joints:
      - shoulder_pan_joint
      - shoulder_pitch_joint
      - elbow_roll_joint
      - elbow_pitch_joint
      - wrist_roll_joint
      - wrist_pitch_joint
      - gripper_roll_joint

  - name: seven_dof_arm/gripper_controller
    action_ns: follow_joint_trajectory
    type: FollowJointTrajectory
    default: true
    joints:
      - finger_joint1
      - finger_joint2
```

The controller configuration file contains the definition of the two controller interfaces; one is for arm and the other is for gripper. The type of action used in the controllers is `FollowJointTrajectory`, and the action namespace is `follow_joint_trajectory`. We have to list out the joints under each group. The `default: true` indicates that it will use the default controller, which is the primary controller in MoveIt! for communicating with the set of joints.

Step 2 – Creating the controller launch files

Next, we have to create a new launch file called
`seven_dof_arm_moveit_controller_manager.launch`, which can start the trajectory
controllers. The name of the file starts with the robot name, which is added with
`_moveit_controller_manager`.

The following is the `seven_dof_arm_config/launch/`
`seven_dof_arm_moveit_controller_manager.launch` launch file definition:

```
<launch>
  <!-- Set the param that trajectory_execution_manager needs to find the
controller plugin -->
  <arg name="moveit_controller_manager"
default="moveit_simple_controller_manager/MoveItSimpleControllerManager" />
  <param name="moveit_controller_manager" value="$(arg
moveit_controller_manager)"/>

  <!-- load controller_list -->
  <arg name="use_controller_manager" default="true" />
  <param name="use_controller_manager" value="$(arg
use_controller_manager)" />

  <!-- Load joint controller configurations from YAML file to parameter
server -->
  <rosparam file="$(find seven_dof_arm_config)/config/controllers.yaml"/>
</launch>
```

This launch file starts the `MoveItSimpleControllerManager` and loads the joint
trajectory controllers defined inside `controllers.yaml`.

Step 3 – Creating the controller configuration file for Gazebo

After creating the MoveIt! files, we have to create the Gazebo controller configuration file
and the launch file.

Create a new file called `trajectory_control.yaml`, which contains the list of the Gazebo
ROS controllers that need to be loaded along with Gazebo.

You will get this file from the the `seven_dof_arm_gazebo` package created in Chapter 4, *Simulating Robots Using ROS and Gazebo* in the `/config` folder.

The following is the definition of this file:

```
seven_dof_arm:
  seven_dof_arm_joint_controller:
    type: "position_controllers/JointTrajectoryController"
    joints:
      - shoulder_pan_joint
      - shoulder_pitch_joint
      - elbow_roll_joint
      - elbow_pitch_joint
      - wrist_roll_joint
      - wrist_pitch_joint
      - gripper_roll_joint

    gains:
      shoulder_pan_joint:   {p: 1000.0, i: 0.0, d: 0.1, i_clamp: 0.0}
      shoulder_pitch_joint: {p: 1000.0, i: 0.0, d: 0.1, i_clamp: 0.0}
      elbow_roll_joint:   {p: 1000.0, i: 0.0, d: 0.1, i_clamp: 0.0}
      elbow_pitch_joint:     {p: 1000.0, i: 0.0, d: 0.1, i_clamp: 0.0}
      wrist_roll_joint:     {p: 1000.0, i: 0.0, d: 0.1, i_clamp: 0.0}
      wrist_pitch_joint:      {p: 1000.0, i: 0.0, d: 0.1, i_clamp: 0.0}
      gripper_roll_joint:     {p: 1000.0, i: 0.0, d: 0.1, i_clamp: 0.0}


  gripper_controller:
    type: "position_controllers/JointTrajectoryController"
    joints:
      - finger_joint1
      - finger_joint2
    gains:
      finger_joint1:  {p: 50.0, d: 1.0, i: 0.01, i_clamp: 1.0}
      finger_joint2:  {p: 50.0, d: 1.0, i: 0.01, i_clamp: 1.0}
```

Here, we created a `position_controllers/JointTrajectoryController`, which has an action interface of `FollowJointTrajectory` for both the `arm` and the `gripper`. We also defined the PID gain associated with each joint, which can provide a smooth motion.

Step 4 – Creating the launch file for Gazebo trajectory controllers

After creating the configuration file, we can load the controllers along with Gazebo. We have to create a launch file which launches Gazebo, the trajectory controllers, and the MoveIt! interface in a single command.

The launch file `seven_dof_arm_bringup_moveit.launch` contains the definition to launch all these commands:

```
<launch>
  <!-- Launch Gazebo  -->
  <include file="$(find
seven_dof_arm_gazebo)/launch/seven_dof_arm_world.launch" />

  <!-- ros_control seven dof arm launch file -->
  <include file="$(find
seven_dof_arm_gazebo)/launch/seven_dof_arm_gazebo_states.launch" />

  <!-- ros_control trajectory control dof arm launch file -->
  <include file="$(find
seven_dof_arm_gazebo)/launch/seven_dof_arm_trajectory_controller.launch" />

  <!-- moveit launch file -->
  <include file="$(find
seven_dof_arm_config)/launch/moveit_planning_execution.launch" />

   <node name="joint_state_publisher" pkg="joint_state_publisher"
type="joint_state_publisher">
        <param name="/use_gui" value="false"/>
        <rosparam
param="/source_list">[/move_group/fake_controller_joint_states]</rosparam>
   </node>
</launch>
```

This launch file spawns the robot model in Gazebo, publishes the joint states, attaches the position controller, attaches the trajectory controller, and, finally, launches `moveit_planning_execution.launch` inside the MoveIt! package for starting the MoveIt! nodes along with RViz. We may need to load the `MotionPlanning` plugin in RViz if it is not loaded by default.

We can start motion planning inside RViz and execute in Gazebo using the following single command:

```
$ roslaunch seven_dof_arm_gazebo seven_dof_arm_bringup_moveit.launch
```

Note that, before properly launching the planning scene, we should use the following command to install some packages needed by MoveIt! to use ROS controllers:

```
$ sudo apt-get install ros-kinetic-joint-state-controller ros-kinetic-
position-controllers ros-kinetic-joint-trajectory-controller
```

After we have installed the preceding packages, we can launch the planning scene. This will launch RViz and Gazebo, and we can do motion planning inside RViz. After motion planning, click on the **Execute** button to send the trajectory to the Gazebo controllers:

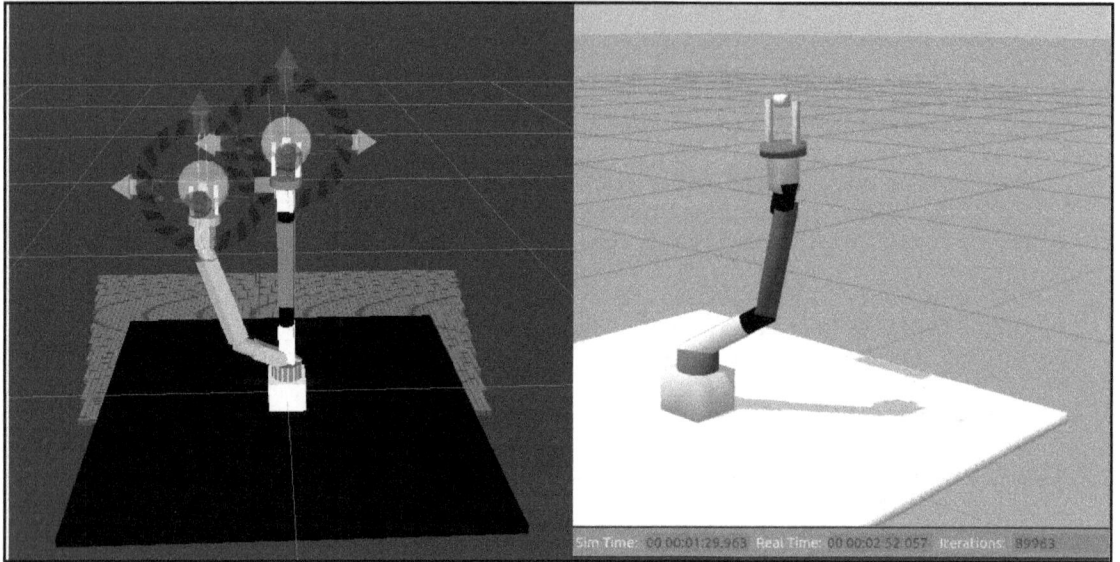

Figure 16: Gazebo trajectory controllers executing the trajectory from MoveIt!

Step 5 – Debugging the Gazebo- MoveIt! interface

In this section, we will discuss some of the common issues and debugging techniques in this interface.

If the trajectory is not executing on Gazebo, first list the topics:

```
$ rostopic list
```

If the Gazebo controllers are started properly, we will get the following joint trajectory topics in the list:

```
/seven_dof_arm/gripper_controller/command
/seven_dof_arm/gripper_controller/follow_joint_trajectory/cancel
/seven_dof_arm/gripper_controller/follow_joint_trajectory/feedback
/seven_dof_arm/gripper_controller/follow_joint_trajectory/goal
/seven_dof_arm/gripper_controller/follow_joint_trajectory/result
/seven_dof_arm/gripper_controller/follow_joint_trajectory/status
/seven_dof_arm/gripper_controller/state
/seven_dof_arm/joint_states
/seven_dof_arm/seven_dof_arm_joint_controller/command
/seven_dof_arm/seven_dof_arm_joint_controller/follow_joint_trajectory/cancel
/seven_dof_arm/seven_dof_arm_joint_controller/follow_joint_trajectory/feedback
/seven_dof_arm/seven_dof_arm_joint_controller/follow_joint_trajectory/goal
/seven_dof_arm/seven_dof_arm_joint_controller/follow_joint_trajectory/result
/seven_dof_arm/seven_dof_arm_joint_controller/follow_joint_trajectory/status
/seven_dof_arm/seven_dof_arm_joint_controller/state
/tf
/tf_static
/trajectory_execution_event
```

Figure 17: Topics from the Gazebo-ROS trajectory controllers

We can see `follow_joint_trajectory` for the gripper and the `arm` group. If the controllers are not ready, the trajectory will not execute in Gazebo.

Also, check the terminal message while starting the launch file:

```
[1505806707.153599116, 0.343000000]: Added FollowJointTrajectory controller for seven_dof_ar
ller
[1505806707.153740538, 0.343000000]: Returned 2 controllers in list
[1505806707.205783246, 0.347000000]: Trajectory execution is managing controllers
'move_group/ApplyPlanningSceneService'...
'move_group/ClearOctomapService'...
'move_group/MoveGroupCartesianPathService'...
'move_group/MoveGroupExecuteTrajectoryAction'...
'move_group/MoveGroupGetPlanningSceneService'...
'move_group/MoveGroupKinematicsService'...
'move_group/MoveGroupMoveAction'...
'move_group/MoveGroupPickPlaceAction'...
'move_group/MoveGroupPlanService'...
'move_group/MoveGroupQueryPlannersService'...
'move_group/MoveGroupStateValidationService'...                              1
[1505806835.903571251, 36.978000000]: arm[RRTkConfigDefault]: Starting planning with 1 state
astructure
[1505806835.994742622, 36.997000000]: arm[RRTkConfigDefault]: Created 21 states
[1505806836.036028021, 37.004000000]: arm[RRTkConfigDefault]: Created 38 states
[1505806836.038435520, 37.005000000]: ParallelPlan::solve(): Solution found by one or more t  2
41 seconds
```

Figure 18: The Terminal message showing successful trajectory execution

In the Figure 18, the first section shows that the `MoveItSimpleControllerManager` was able to connect with the Gazebo controller and if it couldn't connect to controller, it shows that it can't connect to the controller. The second section shows a successful motion planning. If the motion planning is not successful, MoveIt! will not send the trajectory to Gazebo.

In the next section, we will discuss the ROS Navigation stack and look at the requirements needed to interface the Navigation stack to the Gazebo simulation.

Understanding the ROS Navigation stack

The main aim of the ROS Navigation package is to move a robot from the start position to the goal position, without making any collision with the environment. The ROS Navigation package comes with an implementation of several navigation-related algorithms which can easily help implement autonomous navigation in the mobile robots.

The user only needs to feed the goal position of the robot and the robot odometry data from sensors such as wheel encoders, IMU, and GPS, along with other sensor data streams, such as laser scanner data or 3D point cloud from sensors such as **Kinect**. The output of the Navigation package will be the velocity commands that will drive the robot to the given goal position.

The Navigation stack contains the implementation of the standard algorithms, such as SLAM, A *(star), Dijkstra, amcl, and so on, which can directly be used in our application.

ROS Navigation hardware requirements

The ROS Navigation stack is designed as generic. There are some hardware requirements that should be satisfied by the robot. The following are the requirements:

- The Navigation package will work better in differential drive and holonomic (total DOF of robot equals to controllable DOF of robots). Also, the mobile robot should be controlled by sending velocity commands in the form of: `x: velocity`, `y: velocity` (linear velocity), and `theta: velocity` (angular velocity).
- The robot should be equipped with a vision (*rgb-d*) or laser sensor to build the map of the environment.
- The Navigation stack will perform better for square and circular shaped mobile bases. It will work on an arbitrary shape, but performance is not guaranteed.

The following are the basic building blocks of the Navigational stack taken from the ROS website (`http://wiki.ros.org/navigation/Tutorials/RobotSetup`). We can see the purposes of each block and how to configure the Navigation stack for a custom robot:

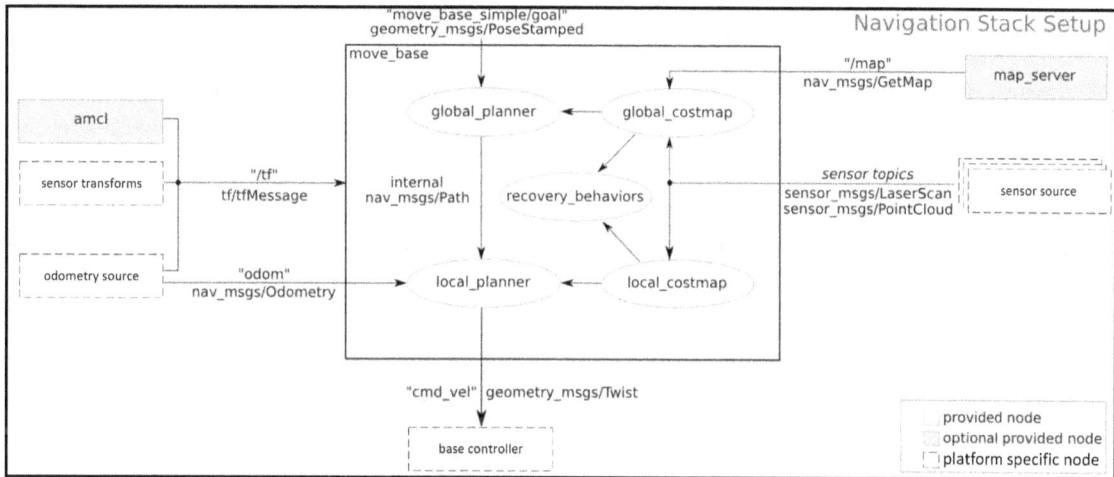

Figure 19: Navigation stack setup diagram

According to the Navigation setup diagram, for configuring the Navigation package for a custom robot, we must provide functional blocks that interface to the Navigation stack. The following are the explanations of all the blocks which are provided as input to the Navigational stack:

- **Odometry source**: Odometry data of a robot gives the robot position with respect to its starting position. The main odometry sources are wheel encoders, IMU, and 2D/3D cameras (visual odometry). The odom value should publish to the Navigation stack, which has a message type of `nav_msgs/Odometry`. The `odom` message can hold the position and the velocity of the robot. Odometry data is a mandatory input to the Navigational stack.

- **Sensor source**: We have to provide laser scan data or point cloud data to the Navigation stack for mapping the robot environment. This data, along with odometry, combines to build the global and local cost map of the robot. The main sensors used here are Laser Range finders or Kinect 3D sensors. The data should be of type `sensor_msgs/LaserScan` or `sensor_msgs/PointCloud`.

- **sensor transforms/tf**: The robot should publish the relationship between the robot coordinate frame using ROS tf.
- **base_controller**: The main function of the base controller is to convert the output of the Navigation stack, which is a twist (`geometry_msgs/Twist`) message, and convert it into corresponding motor velocities of the robot.

The optional nodes of the Navigation stack are `amcl` and map server, which allow localization of the robot and help to save/load the robot map.

Working with Navigation packages

Before working with the Navigation stack, we were discussing MoveIt! and the `move_group` node. In the Navigation stack, also, there is a node like the `move_group` node, called the `move_base` node. From Figure 19, it is clear that the `move_base` node takes input from sensors, joint states, TF, and odometry, which is very similar to the `move_group` node that we saw in MoveIt!.

Let's see more about the `move_base` node.

Understanding the move_base node

The `move_base` node is from a package called `move_base`. The main function of this package is to move a robot from its current position to a goal position with the help of other navigation nodes. The `move_base` node inside this package links the global-planner and the local-planner for the path planning, connecting to the rotate-recovery package if the robot is stuck in some obstacle and connecting global costmap and local costmap for getting the map.

The `move_base` node is basically an implementation of `SimpleActionServer`, which takes a goal pose with message type (`geometry_msgs/PoseStamped`). We can send a goal position to this node using a `SimpleActionClient` node.

The `move_base` node subscribes the goal from a topic called move_base_simple/goal, which is the input of the Navigation stack, as shown in the previous diagram.

When this node receives a goal pose, it links to components such as `global_planner`, `local_planner`, `recovery_behavior`, `global_costmap`, and `local_costmap`, generates the output, which is the command velocity (geometry_msgs/Twist), and sends it to the base controller for moving the robot for achieving the goal pose.

The following is the list of all the packages which are linked by the `move_base` node:

- **global-planner**: This package provides libraries and nodes for planning the optimum path from the current position of the robot to the goal position, with respect to the robot map. This package has the implementation of path-finding algorithms, such as A*, Dijkstra, and so on, for finding the shortest path from the current robot position to the goal position.
- **local-planner**: The main function of this package is to navigate the robot in a section of the global path planned using the global planner. The local planner will take the odometry and sensor reading, and send an appropriate velocity command to the robot controller for completing a segment of the global path plan. The base local planner package is the implementation of the trajectory rollout and dynamic window algorithms.
- **rotate-recovery**: This package helps the robot to recover from a local obstacle by performing a 360 degree rotation.
- **clear-costmap-recovery**: This package is also for recovering from a local obstacle by clearing the costmap by reverting the current costmap used by the Navigation stack to the static map.
- **costmap-2D**: The main use of this package is to map the robot environment. The robot can only plan a path with respect to a map. In ROS, we create 2D or 3D occupancy grid maps, which is a representation of the environment in a grid of cells. Each cell has a probability value that indicates whether the cell is occupied or not. The costmap-2D package can build the grid map of the environment by subscribing sensor values of the laser scan or point cloud and also the odometry values. There are global cost maps for global navigation and local cost maps for local navigation.

The following are the other packages which are interfaced to the `move_base` node:

- **map-server**: The map-server package allows us to save and load the map generated by the costmap-2D package.
- **AMCL**: AMCL (Adaptive Monte Carlo Localization) is a method to localize the robot in a map. This approach uses a particle filter to track the pose of the robot with respect to the map, with the help of probability theory. In the ROS system, AMCL accepts a `sensor_msgs/LaserScan` to create the map.
- **gmapping**: The gmapping package is an implementation of an algorithm called **Fast SLAM**, which takes the laser scan data and odometry to build a 2D occupancy grid map.

After discussing each functional block of the Navigation stack, let's see how it really works.

Working of Navigation stack

In the previous section, we saw the functionalities of each block in the ROS Navigation stack. Let's check how the entire system works. The robot should publish a proper odometry value, TF information, and sensor data from the laser, and have a base controller and map of the surroundings.

If all these requirements are satisfied, we can start working with the Navigation package.

Localizing on the map

The first step the robot is going to perform is localizing itself on the map. The AMCL package will help to localize the robot on the map.

Sending a goal and path planning

After getting the current position of the robot, we can send a goal position to the move_base node. The move_base node will send this goal position to a global planner, which will plan a path from the current robot position to the goal position.

This plan is with respect to the global costmap, which is feeding from the map server. The global planner will send this path to the local planner, which executes each segment of the global plan.

The local planner gets the odometry and the sensor value from the move_base node and finds a collision-free local plan for the robot. The local planner is associated with the local costmap, which can monitor the obstacle(s) around the robot.

Collision recovery behavior

The global and local costmap are tied with the laser scan data. If the robot is stuck somewhere, the Navigation package will trigger the recovery behavior nodes, such as the clear costmap recovery or rotate recovery nodes.

Sending the command velocity

The local planner generates the command velocity in the form of a twist message that contains linear and angular velocity (`geometry_msgs/Twist`), to the robot base controller. The robot base controller converts the twist message to the equivalent motor speed.

Installing the ROS Navigation stack

The ROS desktop full installation will not install the ROS Navigation stack. We must install the Navigation stack separately, using the following command:

```
$ sudo apt-get install ros-kinetic-navigation
```

After installing the Navigation package, let's start learning how to build a map of the robot environment. The robot we are using here is the differential wheeled robot that we discussed in the previous chapter. This robot satisfies all the three requirements of the Navigation stack.

Building a map using SLAM

The ROS Gmapping package is a wrapper of the open source implementation of SLAM, called OpenSLAM (https://www.openslam.org/gmapping.html). The package contains a node called slam_gmapping, which is the implementation of SLAM and helps to create a 2D occupancy grid map from the laser scan data and the mobile robot pose.

The basic hardware requirement for doing SLAM is a laser scanner which is horizontally mounted on the top of the robot, and the robot odometry data. In this robot, we have already satisfied these requirements. We can generate the 2D map of the environment, using the gmapping package through the following procedure.

Before operating with Gmapping, we need to install it using the following command:

```
$ sudo apt-get install ros-kinetic-gmapping
```

Creating a launch file for gmapping

The main task while creating a launch file for the gmapping process is to set the parameters for the slam_gmapping node and the move_base node. The slam_gmapping node is the core node inside the ROS Gmapping package. The slam_gmapping node subscribes the laser data (sensor_msgs/LaserScan) and the TF data, and publishes the occupancy grid map data as output (nav_msgs/OccupancyGrid). This node is highly configurable and we can fine tune the parameters to improve the mapping accuracy. The parameters are mentioned at http://wiki.ros.org/gmapping.

The next node we have to configure is the `move_base` node. The main parameters we need to configure are the global and local costmap parameters, the local planner, and the `move_base` parameters. The parameters list is very lengthy. We are representing these parameters in several YAML files. Each parameter is included in the `param` folder inside the `diff_wheeled_robot_gazebo` package.

The following is the `gmapping.launch` file used in this robot. The launch file is placed in the `diff_wheeled_robot_gazebo/launch` folder:

```
<launch>
  <arg name="scan_topic" default="scan" />

<!-- Defining parameters for slam_gmapping node -->

  <node pkg="gmapping" type="slam_gmapping" name="slam_gmapping"
output="screen">
    <param name="base_frame" value="base_footprint"/>
    <param name="odom_frame" value="odom"/>
    <param name="map_update_interval" value="5.0"/>
    <param name="maxUrange" value="6.0"/>
    <param name="maxRange" value="8.0"/>
    <param name="sigma" value="0.05"/>
    <param name="kernelSize" value="1"/>
    <param name="lstep" value="0.05"/>
    <param name="astep" value="0.05"/>
    <param name="iterations" value="5"/>
    <param name="lsigma" value="0.075"/>
    <param name="ogain" value="3.0"/>
    <param name="lskip" value="0"/>
    <param name="minimumScore" value="100"/>
    <param name="srr" value="0.01"/>
    <param name="srt" value="0.02"/>
    <param name="str" value="0.01"/>
    <param name="stt" value="0.02"/>
    <param name="linearUpdate" value="0.5"/>
    <param name="angularUpdate" value="0.436"/>
    <param name="temporalUpdate" value="-1.0"/>
    <param name="resampleThreshold" value="0.5"/>
    <param name="particles" value="80"/>
    <param name="xmin" value="-1.0"/>
    <param name="ymin" value="-1.0"/>
    <param name="xmax" value="1.0"/>
    <param name="ymax" value="1.0"/>

    <param name="delta" value="0.05"/>
    <param name="llsamplerange" value="0.01"/>
```

```xml
      <param name="llsamplestep" value="0.01"/>
      <param name="lasamplerange" value="0.005"/>
      <param name="lasamplestep" value="0.005"/>
      <remap from="scan" to="$(arg scan_topic)"/>
  </node>

<!-- Defining parameters for move_base node -->

  <node pkg="move_base" type="move_base" respawn="false" name="move_base"
output="screen">
    <rosparam file="$(find
diff_wheeled_robot_gazebo)/param/costmap_common_params.yaml" command="load"
ns="global_costmap" />
    <rosparam file="$(find
diff_wheeled_robot_gazebo)/param/costmap_common_params.yaml" command="load"
ns="local_costmap" />
    <rosparam file="$(find
diff_wheeled_robot_gazebo)/param/local_costmap_params.yaml" command="load"
/>
    <rosparam file="$(find
diff_wheeled_robot_gazebo)/param/global_costmap_params.yaml" command="load"
/>
    <rosparam file="$(find
diff_wheeled_robot_gazebo)/param/base_local_planner_params.yaml"
command="load" />
    <rosparam file="$(find
diff_wheeled_robot_gazebo)/param/dwa_local_planner_params.yaml"
command="load" />
    <rosparam file="$(find
diff_wheeled_robot_gazebo)/param/move_base_params.yaml" command="load" />

  </node>

</launch>
```

Running SLAM on the differential drive robot

We can build the ROS package called `diff_wheeled_robot_gazebo` and can run the `gmapping.launch` file for building the map. The following are the commands to start with the mapping procedure.

Start the robot simulation by using the Willow Garage world:

```
$ roslaunch diff_wheeled_robot_gazebo diff_wheeled_gazebo_full.launch
```

Start the `gmapping` launch file with the following command:

```
$ roslaunch diff_wheeled_robot_gazebo gmapping.launch
```

If the `gmapping` launch file is working fine, we will get the following kind of output on the Terminal:

```
[ INFO] [1505810240.049575967, 15.340000000]: Loading from pre-hydro parameter style
[ INFO] [1505810240.168699314, 15.381000000]: Using plugin "static_layer"
[ INFO] [1505810240.384469019, 15.449000000]: Requesting the map...
[ INFO] [1505810240.663457937, 15.552000000]: Resizing costmap to 288 X 608 at 0.050000 m/pix
[ INFO] [1505810240.871384865, 15.650000000]: Received a 288 X 608 map at 0.050000 m/pix
[ INFO] [1505810240.897210021, 15.656000000]: Using plugin "obstacle_layer"
[ INFO] [1505810240.913185546, 15.660000000]:     Subscribed to Topics: scan bump
[ INFO] [1505810241.183408917, 15.714000000]: Using plugin "inflation_layer"
[ INFO] [1505810241.592248141, 15.851000000]: Loading from pre-hydro parameter style
[ INFO] [1505810241.730240828, 15.900000000]: Using plugin "obstacle_layer"
[ INFO] [1505810241.978042290, 16.015000000]:     Subscribed to Topics: scan bump
[ INFO] [1505810242.124180243, 16.057000000]: Using plugin "inflation_layer"
[ INFO] [1505810242.504991688, 16.191000000]: Created local_planner dwa_local_planner/DWAPlannerROS
[ INFO] [1505810242.518319734, 16.198000000]: Sim period is set to 0.20
[ INFO] [1505810244.343111055, 16.967000000]: Recovery behavior will clear layer obstacles
[ INFO] [1505810244.546680028, 17.020000000]: Recovery behavior will clear layer obstacles
[ INFO] [1505810244.697982461, 17.046000000]: odom received!
```

Figure 20: Terminal messages during gmapping

Start the keyboard teleoperation for manually navigating the robot around the environment. The robot can map its environment only if it covers the entire area:

```
$ roslaunch diff_wheeled_robot_control keyboard_teleop.launch
```

The current Gazebo view of the robot and the robot environment is shown next. The environment is with obstacles around the robot:

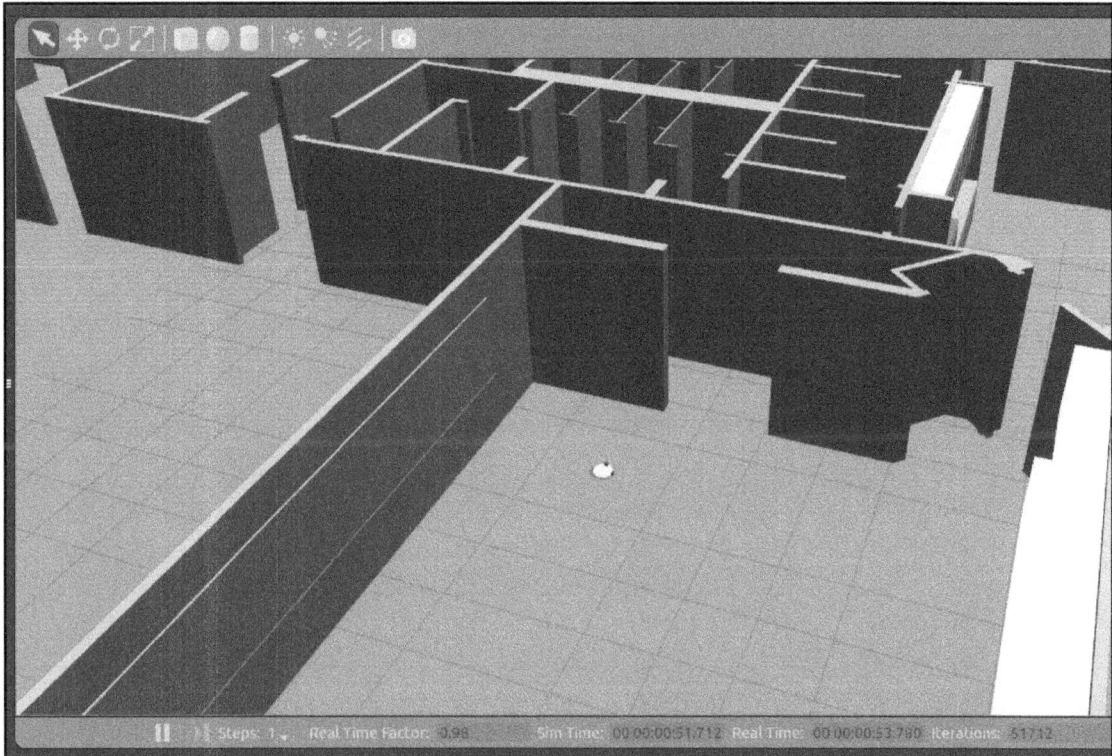

Figure 21: Simulation of the robot using the Willow Garage world

We can launch RViz and add a display type called **Map** and the topic name as /map.

We can start moving the robot inside the world by using key board teleoperation, and we can see a map building according to the environment. The following image shows the completed map of the environment shown in RViz:

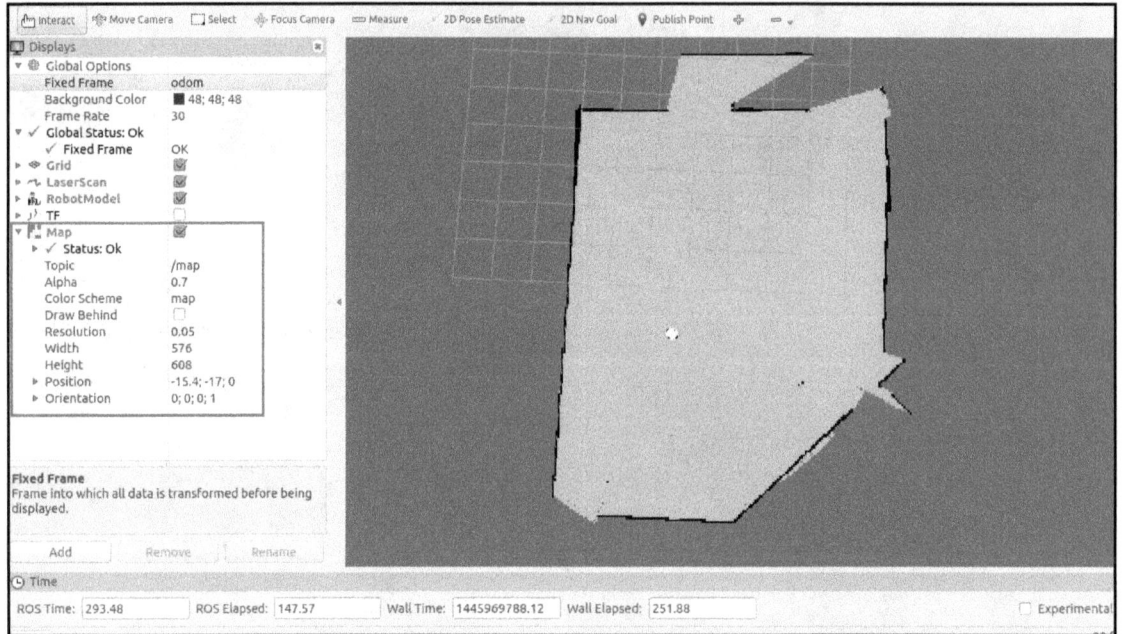

Figure 22: Completed map of the room in RViz

We can save the built map using the following command. This command will listen to the map topic and save into the image. The map server package does this operation:

```
$ rosrun map_server map_saver -f willo
```

Here `willo` is the name of the map file. The map file is stored as two files: one is the YAML file, which contains the map metadata and the image name, and second is the image, which has the encoded data of the occupancy grid map. The following is the screenshot of the preceding command, running without any errors:

```
jcacace@robot:~$ rosrun map_server map_saver -f willo
[ INFO] [1505810794.895750258]: Waiting for the map
[ INFO] [1505810795.117276658, 21.621000000]: Received a 288 X 608 map @ 0.050 m/pix
[ INFO] [1505810795.119888038, 21.621000000]: Writing map occupancy data to willo.pgm
[ INFO] [1505810795.138065942, 21.632000000]: Writing map occupancy data to willo.yaml
[ INFO] [1505810795.138632329, 21.632000000]: Done
```

Figure 23: Terminal screenshot while saving a map

The saved encoded image of the map is shown next. If the robot gives accurate robot odometry data, we will get this kind of precise map similar to the environment. The accurate map improves the navigation accuracy through efficient path planning:

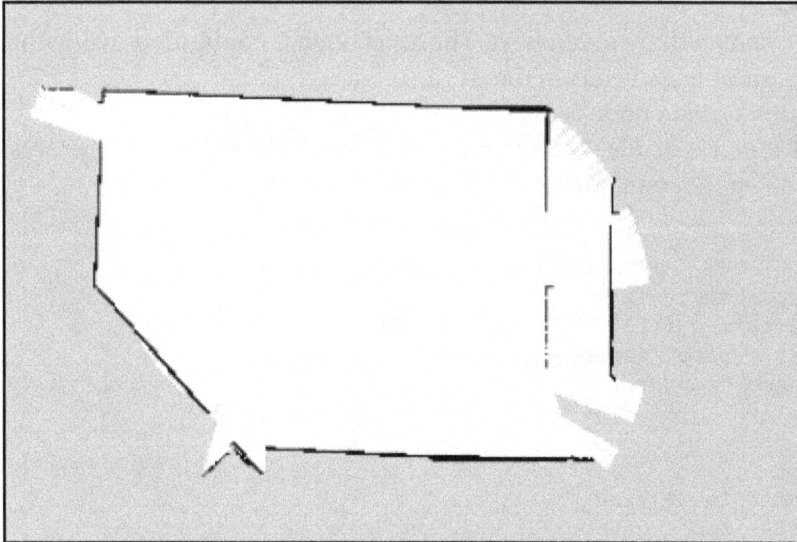

Figure 24: The saved map

The next procedure is to localize and navigate in this static map.

Implementing autonomous navigation using amcl and a static map

The ROS amcl package provides nodes for localizing the robot on a static map. The amcl node subscribes the laser scan data, laser scan based maps, and the TF information from the robot. The amcl node estimates the pose of the robot on the map and publishes its estimated position with respect to the map.

If we create a static map from the laser scan data, the robot can autonomously navigate from any pose of the map using amcl and the move_base nodes. The first step is to create a launch file for starting the amcl node. The amcl node is highly customizable; we can configure it with a lot of parameters. The list of parameters are available at the ROS package site (http://wiki.ros.org/amcl).

Creating an amcl launch file

A typical `amcl` launch file is given next. The amcl node is configured inside the `amcl.launch.xml` file, which is in the `diff_wheeled_robot_gazebo/launch/include` package. The `move_base` node is also configured separately in the `move_base.launch.xml` file. The map file we created in the `gmapping` process is loaded here, using the `map_server` node:

```
<launch>

  <!-- Map server -->
  <arg name="map_file" default="$(find
diff_wheeled_robot_gazebo)/maps/test1.yaml"/>
  <node name="map_server" pkg="map_server" type="map_server" args="$(arg
map_file)" />


  <include file="$(find
diff_wheeled_robot_gazebo)/launch/includes/amcl.launch.xml">

    <arg name="initial_pose_x" value="0"/>
    <arg name="initial_pose_y" value="0"/>
    <arg name="initial_pose_a" value="0"/>

  </include>

  <include file="$(find
diff_wheeled_robot_gazebo)/launch/includes/move_base.launch.xml"/>
```

```
</launch>
```

The following is the code snippet of `amcl.launch.xml`. This file is a bit lengthy, as we have to configure a lot of parameters for the `amcl` node:

```
<launch>
  <arg name="use_map_topic"  default="false"/>
  <arg name="scan_topic"     default="scan"/>
  <arg name="initial_pose_x" default="0.0"/>
  <arg name="initial_pose_y" default="0.0"/>
  <arg name="initial_pose_a" default="0.0"/>

  <node pkg="amcl" type="amcl" name="amcl">
    <param name="use_map_topic"               value="$(arg use_map_topic)"/>
    <!-- Publish scans from best pose at a max of 10 Hz -->
    <param name="odom_model_type"             value="diff"/>
    <param name="odom_alpha5"                 value="0.1"/>
    <param name="gui_publish_rate"            value="10.0"/>
    <param name="laser_max_beams"             value="60"/>
    <param name="laser_max_range"             value="12.0"/>
```

After creating this launch file, we can start the amcl node, using the following procedure:

Start the simulation of the robot in Gazebo:

```
$ roslaunch diff_wheeled_robot_gazebo diff_wheeled_gazebo_full.launch
```

Start the `amcl` launch file, using the following command:

```
$ roslaunch diff_wheeled_robot_gazebo amcl.launch
```

If the `amcl` launch file is correctly loaded, the Terminal shows the following message:

```
[ INFO] [1505821904.100025792, 139.365000000]: Using plugin "static_layer"
[ INFO] [1505821904.277281445, 139.434000000]: Requesting the map...
[ INFO] [1505821904.489128458, 139.541000000]: Resizing costmap to 512 X 480 at 0.050000 m/pix
[ INFO] [1505821904.667453907, 139.643000000]: Received a 512 X 480 map at 0.050000 m/pix
[ INFO] [1505821904.675176680, 139.648000000]: Using plugin "obstacle_layer"
[ INFO] [1505821904.681719452, 139.648000000]:     Subscribed to Topics: scan bump
[ INFO] [1505821904.813327088, 139.699000000]: Using plugin "inflation_layer"
[ INFO] [1505821905.081866940, 139.802000000]: Using plugin "obstacle_layer"
[ INFO] [1505821905.194340020, 139.871000000]:     Subscribed to Topics: scan bump
[ INFO] [1505821905.323469494, 139.903000000]: Using plugin "inflation_layer"
[ INFO] [1505821905.674954354, 140.036000000]: Created local_planner dwa_local_planner/DWAPlannerROS
[ INFO] [1505821905.689447045, 140.040000000]: Sim period is set to 0.20
[ INFO] [1505821907.560275254, 141.046000000]: Recovery behavior will clear layer obstacles
[ INFO] [1505821907.785016235, 141.138000000]: Recovery behavior will clear layer obstacles
[ INFO] [1505821907.949123108, 141.197000000]: odom received!
```

Figure 25: Terminal screenshot while executing amcl

If amcl is working fine, we can start commanding the robot to go into a position on the map using RViz, as shown in the following figure. In the figure, the arrow indicates the goal position. We have to enable LaserScan, Map, and Path visualizing plugins in RViz for viewing the laser scan, the global/local costmap, and the global/local paths. Using the **2D NavGoal** button in RViz, we can command the robot to go to a desired position.

The robot will plan a path to that point and give velocity commands to the robot controller to reach that point:

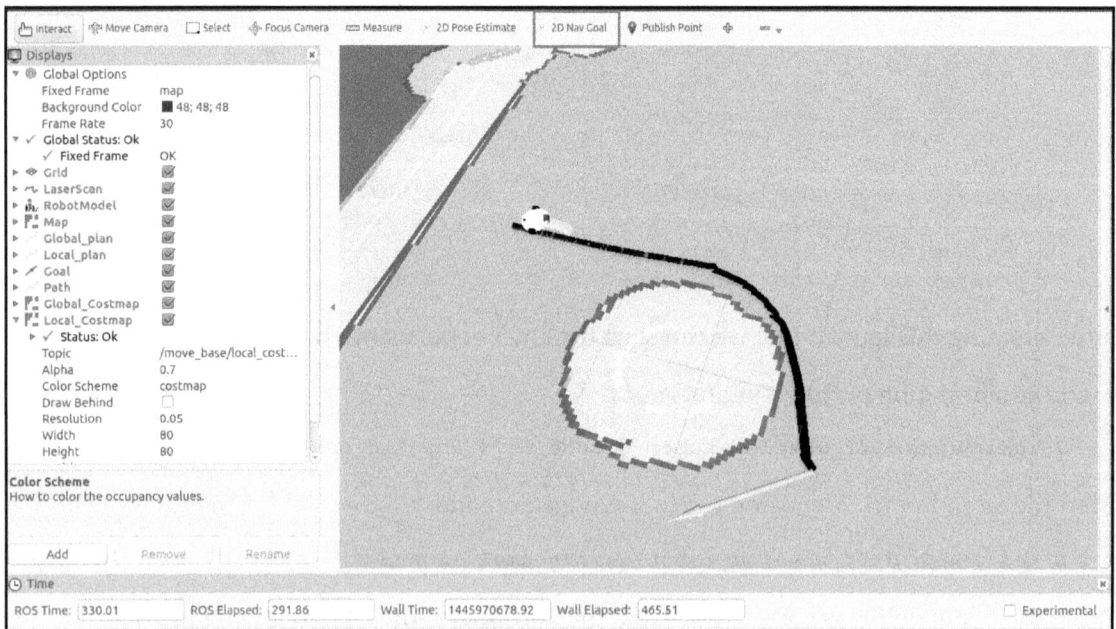

Figure 26: Autonomous navigation using amcl and the map

In the preceding image, we can see that we have placed a random obstacle in the robot's path, and that the robot has planned a path to avoid the obstacle.

We can view the amcl particle cloud around the robot by adding a **Pose Array** on RViz and the topic is /particle_cloud. The following image shows the amcl particle around the robot:

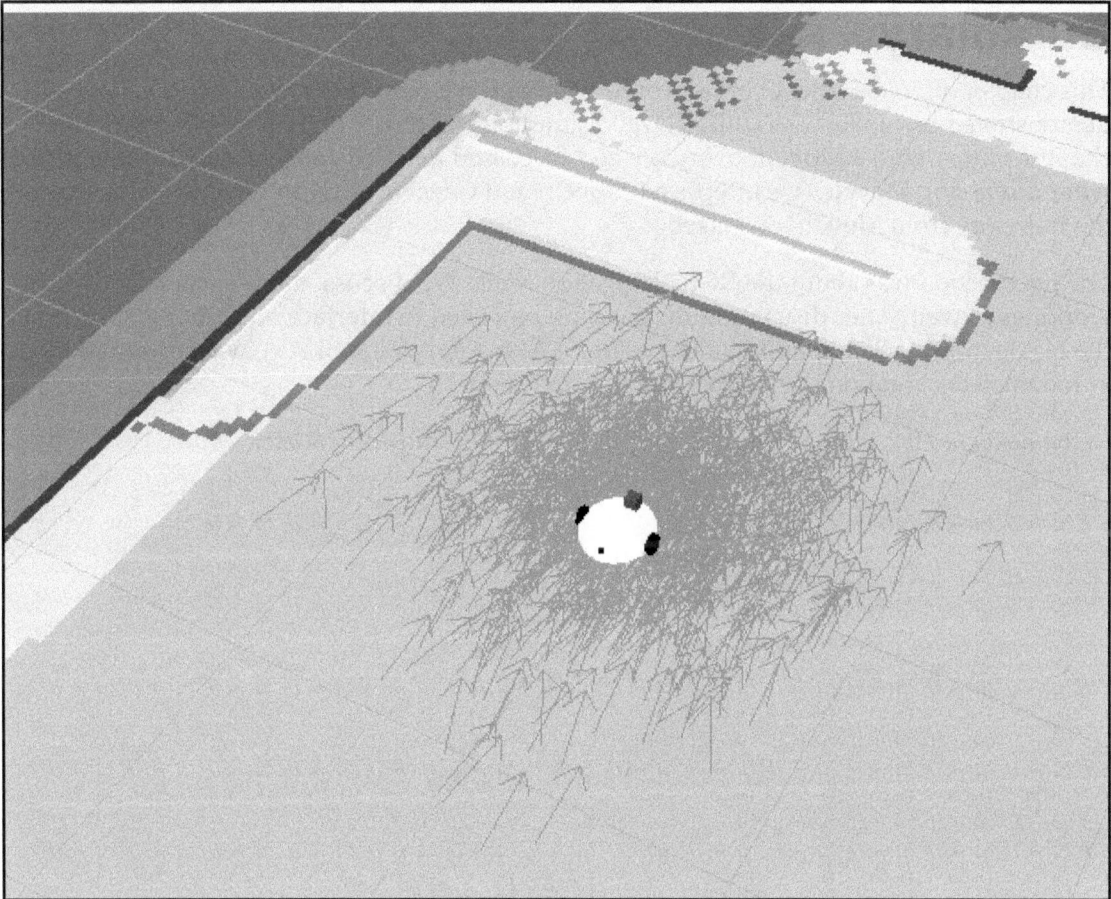

Figure 27: The amcl particle cloud and odometry

Questions

- What is the main purpose of MoveIt! packages?
- What is the importance of the `move_group` node in MoveIt!?
- What is the purpose of the move_base node in the Navigation stack?
- What are the functions of the SLAM and amcl packages?

Summary

This chapter offered a brief overview of MoveIt! and the Navigation stack of ROS, and demonstrated its capabilities using Gazebo simulation of a robotic arm mobile base. The chapter started with a MoveIt! overview and discussed detailed concepts about MoveIt!. After discussing MoveIt!, we interfaced MoveIt! and Gazebo. After interfacing, we executed the trajectory from MoveIt! on Gazebo.

The next section was about the ROS Navigation stack. We discussed its concepts and workings as well. After discussing the concepts, we tried to interface our robot in Gazebo to the Navigation stack and build a map using SLAM. After doing SLAM, we performed autonomous navigation using amcl and the static map.

In the next chapter, we will discuss pluginlib, nodelets, and controllers.

7
Working with pluginlib, Nodelets, and Gazebo Plugins

In the previous chapter, we discussed the interfacing and simulation of the robotic arm mobile robot to the ROS MoveIt! and Navigation stack. In this chapter, we will look at some of the advanced concepts in ROS, such as the ROS `pluginlib`, nodelets, and Gazebo plugins. We will discuss the functionalities and applications of each concept and will look at an example to demonstrate it's working. We have used Gazebo plugins in the previous chapters to get the sensor and robot behavior inside the Gazebo simulator. In this chapter, we are going to see how to create it. We will also discuss a modified form of ROS nodes called ROS nodelets. These features in ROS are implemented using a plugin architecture called `pluginlib`.

In this chapter, we will discuss the following topics:

- Understanding `pluginlib`
- Implementing a sample plugin using `pluginlib`
- Understanding ROS nodelets
- Implementing a sample nodelet
- Understanding and creating a Gazebo plugin

Understanding pluginlib

Plugins are a commonly used term in the computer world. They are modular pieces of software that can add a new feature to the existing software application. The advantage of plugins is that we don't need to write all the features in the main software; instead, we can make an infrastructure on the main software to accept new plugins to it. Using this method, we can extend the capabilities of the software to any level.

We need plugins for our robotics application too. When we are going to build a complex ROS-based application for a robot, plugins will be a good choice to extend the capabilities of the application.

The ROS system provides a plugin framework called `pluginlib` to dynamically load/unload plugins, which can be a library or class. `pluginlib` represents a set of a C++ library, which helps to write plugins and load/unload whenever we need to.

Plugin files are runtime libraries, such as **shared objects** (`.so`) or **dynamic link libraries** (`.DLL`), which are built without linking to the main application code. Plugins are separate entities that do not have any dependencies with the main software.

The main advantage of plugins is that we can expand the application capabilities without making many changes in the main application code.

We can create a simple plugin using `pluginlib` and can see all the procedures involved in creating a plugin using ROS pluginlib.

Here, we are going to create a simple calculator application using `pluginlib`. We are adding each functionality of the calculator using plugins.

Creating plugins for the calculator application using pluginlib

Creating a calculator application using plugins is a slightly tedious task compared to writing a single code. The aim of this example, however, is to show how to add new features to a calculator without modifying the main application code.

In this example, we will see a computer application that loads plugins to perform each operation. Here, we only implement the main operations ,such as addition, subtraction, multiplication, and division. We can expand to any level by writing individual plugins for each operation.

Before going on to create the plugin definition, we can access the calculator code from the `pluginlib_calculator` folder for reference.

We are going to create an ROS package called `pluginlib_calculator` to build these plugins and the main calculator application.

The following diagram shows how the calculator plugins and application are organized inside the `pluginlib_calculator` ROS package:

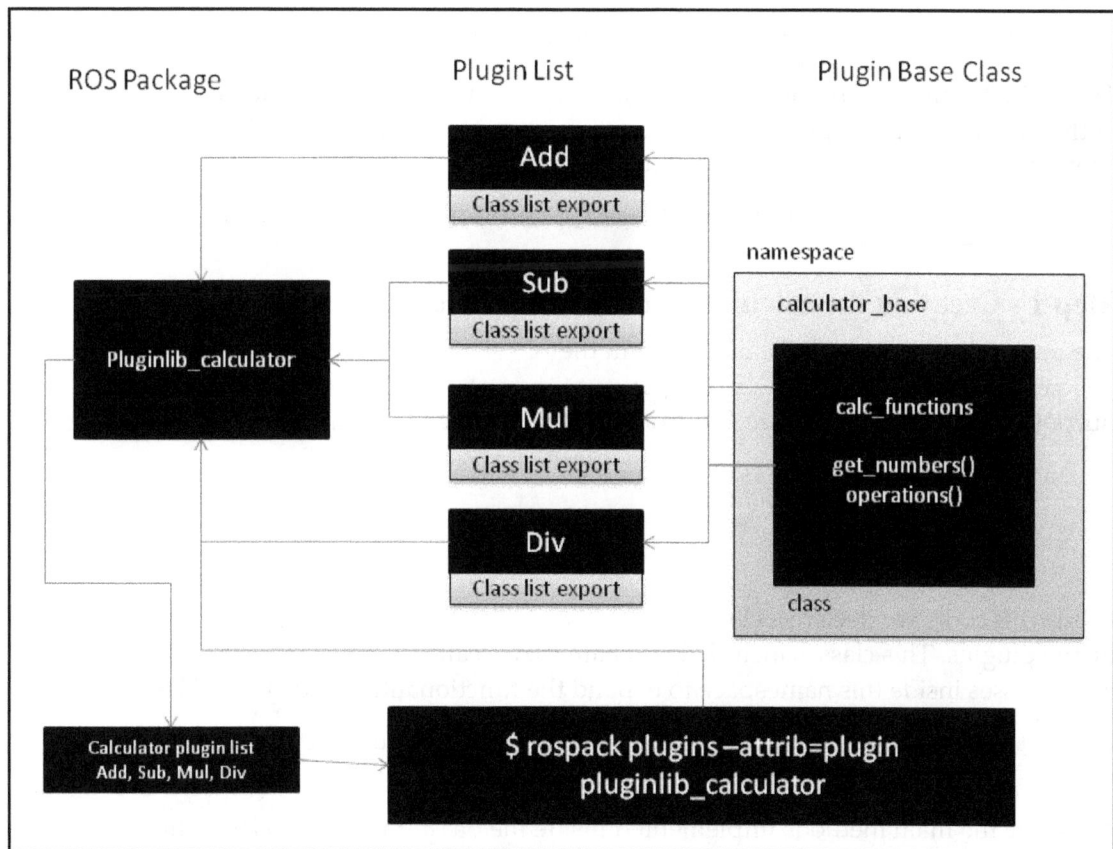

Figure 1: Organization of plugins in the calculator application

We can see the list of plugins of the calculator and a plugin base class called `calc_functions`. The plugin base class implements the common functionalities that are required by these plugins.

This is how, we can create the ROS package and start developing plugins for the main calculator application.

Working with the pluginlib_calculator package

For a quick start, we can use the existing ROS plugin package, `pluginlib_calculator`.

If we want to create this package from scratch, we can use the following command:

```
$ catkin_create_pkg pluginlib_calculator pluginlib roscpp std_msgs
```

The main dependency of this package is `pluginlib`. We can discuss the main source files in this package to build plugins. However, you can get the plugin code from the code provided with this book or download it at this link:

```
$ git clone https://github.com/jocacace/plugin_calculator
```

Step 1 - Creating the calculator_base header file

The `calculator_base.h` file is present in the `pluginlib_calculator/include/pluginlib_calculator` folder, and the main purpose of this file is to declare functions/methods that are commonly used by the plugins:

```
namespace calculator_base
{
class calc_functions
{
```

Inside this code, we declare a class called `calc_functions` that encapsulates methods used by the plugins. This class is included in a namespace called `calculator_base`. We can add more classes inside this namespace to expand the functionalities of this base class:

```
virtual void get_numbers(double number1, double number2) = 0;
virtual double operation() = 0;
```

These are the main methods implemented inside the `calc_function` class. The `get_number()` function can retrieve two numbers as input to the calculator, and the `operation()` function defines the mathematical operation we want to perform.

Step 2 - Creating the calculator_plugins header file

The `calculator_plugins.h` file is present in the
`pluginlib_calculator/include/pluginlib_calculator` folder, and the main
purpose of this file is to define complete functions of the calculator plugins, which are
named as `Add`, `Sub`, `Mul`, and `Div`. Here is the explanation of this code:

```
#include <pluginlib_calculator/calculator_base.h>
#include <cmath>

namespace calculator_plugins
{
  class Add : public calculator_base::calc_functions
  {
```

This header file includes the `calculator_base.h` for accessing the basic functionalities of
a calculator. Each plugin is defined as a class, and it inherits the `calc_functions` class
from the `calculator_base.h` class:

```
class Add : public calculator_base::calc_functions
  {
    public:
  Add()
  {
    number1_ = 0;
    number2_ = 0;
  }

  void get_numbers(double number1, double number2)
  {
    try{

      number1_ = number1;
      number2_ = number2;
        }

    catch(int e)
    {
    std::cerr<<"Exception while inputting numbers"<<std::endl;
    }

  }

  double operation()
  {
    return(number1_+number2_);
  }
```

```
    private:
      double number1_;
      double number2_;
};

};
```

In this code, we can see definitions of inherited `get_numbers()` and `operations()` functions. The `get_number()` retrieves two number inputs and `operations()` performs the desired operation. In this case, it performs additional operations. We can see all other plugin definitions inside this header file.

Step 3 - Exporting plugins using the calculator_plugins.cpp

To load the class of plugins dynamically, we must export each class using a special macro called `PLUGINLIB_EXPORT_CLASS`. This macro must be present in any CPP file that consists of plugin classes. We have already defined the plugin class, and, in this file, we are going to define the macro statement only.

Locate the `calculator_plugins.cpp` file from the `pluginlib_calculator/src` folder. Here is how we export each plugin:

```
#include <pluginlib/class_list_macros.h>
#include <pluginlib_calculator/calculator_base.h>
#include <pluginlib_calculator/calculator_plugins.h>

PLUGINLIB_EXPORT_CLASS(calculator_plugins::Add,
calculator_base::calc_functions);
```

Inside `PLUGINLIB_EXPORT_CLASS`, we need to provide the class name of the plugin and the base class.

Step 4 - Implementing the plugin loader using the calculator_loader.cpp

This plugin loader node loads each plugin and inputs the number to each plugin and fetches the result from the plugin. We can locate the `calculator_loader.cpp` file from the `pluginlib_calculator/src` folder.

Here is the explanation of this code:

```
#include <boost/shared_ptr.hpp>
#include <pluginlib/class_loader.h>
#include <pluginlib_calculator/calculator_base.h>
```

These are the necessary header files to load the plugins:

```
pluginlib::ClassLoader<calculator_base::calc_functions>
calc_loader("pluginlib_calculator", "calculator_base::calc_functions");
```

The `pluginlib` provides the `ClassLoader` class, which is inside `class_loader.h`, to load classes at runtime. We need to provide a name for the loader and the calculator base class as arguments:

```
boost::shared_ptr<calculator_base::calc_functions> add =
calc_loader.createInstance("pluginlib_calculator/Add");
```

This will create an instance of the `add` class using the `ClassLoader` object:

```
add->get_numbers(10.0,10.0);
double result = add->operation();
```

These lines give an input and perform the operations in the plugin instance.

Step 5 - Creating the plugin description file: calculator_plugins.xml

After creating the calculator loader code, next we must describe the list of plugins inside this package in an XML file called the `Plugin Description File`. The plugin description file contains all the information about the plugins inside a package, such as the name of the classes, types of classes, base class, and so on.

The plugin description is an important file for plugin-based packages, because it helps the ROS system to automatically discover, load, and reason about the plugin. It also holds information such as the description of the plugin.

The following code shows the plugin description file of our package called `calculator_plugins.xml`, which is stored along with the `CMakeLists.txt` and `package.xml` files. You can get this file from the package folder itself.

Here is the explanation of this file:

```
<library path="lib/libpluginlib_calculator">
    <class name="pluginlib_calculator/Add" type="calculator_plugins::Add"
base_class_type="calculator_base::calc_functions">
   <description>This is a add plugin.</description>
  </class>
```

This code is for the `Add` plugin and it defines the library path of the plugin, the class name, the class type, the base class, and the description.

Step 6 - Registering the plugin with the ROS package system

For `pluginlib` to find all plugin-based packages in the ROS system, we should export the plugin description file inside `package.xml`. If we do not include this plugin, the ROS system won't find the plugins inside the package.

Here, we add the export tag to `package.xml`, as follows:

```
<export>
  <pluginlib_calculator plugin="${prefix}/calculator_plugins.xml" />
</export>
```

To work this export command properly, we should insert the following lines in `package.xml`:

```
<build_depend>pluginlib_calculator</build_depend>
<run_depend>pluginlib_calculator</run_depend>
```

The current package should directly *depend* on itself, both at the time of building and also at runtime.

Step 7 - Editing the CMakeLists.txt file

Another difference with respect to a common ROS node regards the compilation directives included in the `CMakeLists.txt` file. To build the calculator plugins and loader nodes, we should add the following lines in `CMakeLists.txt`:

```
## pluginlib_tutorials library
add_library(pluginlib_calculator src/calculator_plugins.cpp)
target_link_libraries(pluginlib_calculator ${catkin_LIBRARIES})
## calculator_loader executable
add_executable(calculator_loader src/calculator_loader.cpp)
target_link_libraries(calculator_loader ${catkin_LIBRARIES})
```

We are almost done with all the settings, and now it's time to build the package using the `catkin_make` command.

Step 8 - Querying the list of plugins in a package

If the package is built properly, we can execute the loader. The following command will query the plugins inside a package:

```
$ rospack plugins --attrib=plugin pluginlib_calculator
```

We will get the following result if everything is built properly:

```
jcacace@robot:~$ rospack plugins --attrib=plugin pluginlib_calculator
pluginlib_calculator /home/jcacace/catkin_ws/src/MASTERING_ROS/ch6/pluginlib_calculator/calculator_
plugins.xml
```

Figure 2: The result of the plugin query

Step 9 - Running the plugin loader

After launched the roscore, we can execute the `calculator_loader` using the following command:

```
$ rosrun pluginlib_calculator calculator_loader
```

The following screenshot shows the output of this command, to check whether everything is working fine. The loader gives both inputs as `10.0` and we are getting the proper result, as shown, using plugins in the screenshot:

```
jcacace@robot:~$ rosrun pluginlib_calculator calculator_loader
[ INFO] [1506769896.353657043]: Triangle area: 20.00
[ INFO] [1506769896.353796789]: Substracted result: 0.00
[ INFO] [1506769896.353853201]: Multiplied result: 100.00
[ INFO] [1506769896.353886772]: Division result: 1.00
```

Figure 3: Result of the plugin loader node

In the next section, we will look at a new concept called **nodelets** and discuss how to implement them.

Understanding ROS nodelets

Nodelets are specific ROS nodes designed to run multiple algorithms within the same process in an efficient way, executing each process as threads. The threaded nodes can communicate with each other efficiently without overloading the network, with zero copy transport between two nodes. These threaded nodes can communicate with external nodes too.

As we did using pluginlib, in nodelets, we can also dynamically load each class as a plugin, which has a separate namespace. Each loaded class can act as separate nodes, which are on a single process called nodelet.

Nodelets are used when the volume of data transferred between nodes are very high; for example, in transferring data from 3D sensors or cameras.

Next, we will look at how to create a nodelet.

Creating a nodelet

In this section, we are going to create a basic nodelet that can subscribe a string topic called /msg_in and publish the same string (std_msgs/String) on the topic /msg_out.

Step 1 - Creating a package for a nodelet

We can create a package called nodelet_hello_world, using the following command to create our nodelet:

```
$ catkin_create_pkg nodelet_hello_world nodelet roscpp std_msgs
```

Otherwise, we can use the existing package from nodelet_hello_world, or download it from the following link:

```
$ git clone https://github.com/jocacace/nodelet_hello_world
```

Here, the main dependency of this package is the nodelet package, which provides APIs to build a ROS nodelet.

Step 2 - Creating the hello_world.cpp nodelet

Now, we are going to create the nodelet code. Create a folder called src inside the package and create a file called hello_world.cpp.

You will get the existing code from the nodelet_hello_world/src folder.

Step 3 - Explanation of hello_world.cpp

Here is the explanation of the code:

```
#include <pluginlib/class_list_macros.h>
#include <nodelet/nodelet.h>
#include <ros/ros.h>
#include <std_msgs/String.h>
#include <stdio.h>
```

These are the header files of this code. We should include `class_list_macro.h` and `nodelet.h` to access the `pluginlib` APIs and nodelets APIs:

```
namespace nodelet_hello_world
{
  class Hello : public nodelet::Nodelet
  {
```

Here, we create a nodelet class called `Hello`, which inherits a standard nodelet base class. All nodelet classes should inherit from the nodelet base class and be dynamically loadable using `pluginlib`. Here, the `Hello` class is going to be used for dynamic loading:

```
virtual void onInit()
{
  ros::NodeHandle& private_nh = getPrivateNodeHandle();
  NODELET_DEBUG("Initialized the Nodelet");
  pub = private_nh.advertise<std_msgs::String>("msg_out",5);
  sub = private_nh.subscribe("msg_in",5, &Hello::callback, this);
}
```

This is the initialization function of a nodelet. This function should not block or do significant work. Inside the function, we are creating a node handle object, topic publisher, and subscriber on the topic `msg_out` and `msg_in`, respectively. There are macros to print debug messages while executing a nodelet. Here, we use `NODELET_DEBUG` to print debug messages in the console. The subscriber is tied up with a callback function called `callback()`, which is inside the `Hello` class:

```
void callback(const std_msgs::StringConstPtr input)
{
  std_msgs::String output;
  output.data = input->data;
  NODELET_DEBUG("Message data = %s",output.data.c_str());
  ROS_INFO("Message data = %s",output.data.c_str());
  pub.publish(output);
}
```

In the `callback()` function, it will print the messages from the `/msg_in` topic and publish to the `/msg_out` topic:

```
PLUGINLIB_EXPORT_CLASS(nodelet_hello_world::Hello,nodelet::Nodelet);
```

Here, we are exporting `Hello` as a plugin for the dynamic loading.

Step 4 - Creating the plugin description file

Like the `pluginlib` example, we have to create a plugin description file inside the `nodelet_hello_world` package. The plugin description file, `hello_world.xml`, is as follows:

```
<library path="libnodelet_hello_world">
  <class name="nodelet_hello_world/Hello" type="nodelet_hello_world::Hello"
base_class_type="nodelet::Nodelet">
      <description>
      A node to republish a message
      </description>
  </class>
</library>
```

Step 5 - Adding the export tag in package.xml

We need to add the export tag in `package.xml` and add build and run dependencies:

```
<export>
    <nodelet plugin="${prefix}/hello_world.xml"/>
  </export>

  <build_depend>nodelet_hello_world</build_depend>
  <run_depend>nodelet_hello_world</run_depend>
```

Step 6 - Editing CMakeLists.txt

We need to add additional lines of code in `CMakeLists.txt` to build a nodelet package. Here are the extra lines. You will get the complete `CMakeLists.txt` file from the existing package itself:

```
## Declare a cpp library
 add_library(nodelet_hello_world
   src/hello_world.cpp
 )

## Specify libraries to link a library or executable target against
 target_link_libraries(nodelet_hello_world
   ${catkin_LIBRARIES}
 )
```

Step 7 - Building and running nodelets

After following this procedure, we can build the package using `catkin_make` and, if the build is successful, we can generate the shared object `libnodelet_hello_world.so` file, which represents the plugin.

The first step in running nodelets is to start the **nodelet manager**. A nodelet manager is a C++ executable program, which will listen to the ROS services and dynamically load nodelets. We can run a standalone manager or can embed it within a running node.

The following commands can start the nodelet manager:

Start `roscore`:

```
$ roscore
```

Start the nodelet manager, using the following command:

```
$ rosrun nodelet nodelet manager __name:=nodelet_manager
```

If the nodelet manager runs successfully, we will get a message, as shown here:

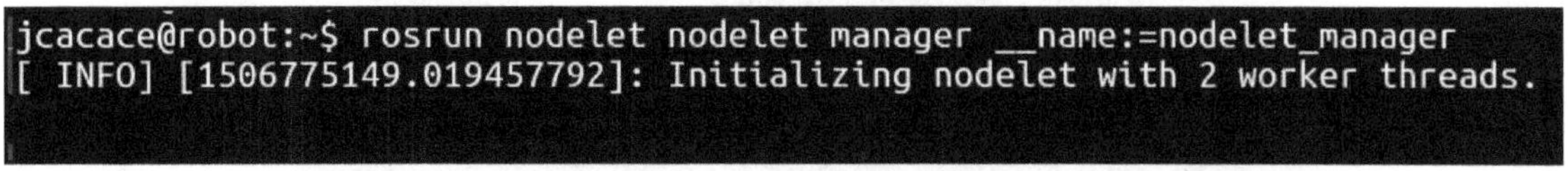

```
jcacace@robot:~$ rosrun nodelet nodelet manager __name:=nodelet_manager
[ INFO] [1506775149.019457792]: Initializing nodelet with 2 worker threads.
```

Figure 4: Running the nodelet manager

After launching the nodelet manager, we can start the nodelet by using the following command:

```
$ rosrun nodelet nodelet load nodelet_hello_world/Hello nodelet_manager
  __name:=nodelet1
```

When we execute the preceding command, the nodelet contacts the nodelet manager to instantiate an instance of the `nodelet_hello_world/Hello` nodelet with a name of `nodelet1`. The following screenshot shows the message when we load the nodelet:

```
jcacace@robot:~/catkin_ws$ rosrun nodelet nodelet load nodelet_hello_world/Hello
[ INFO] [1506776968.889742876]: Loading nodelet /nodelet1 of type nodelet_hello_
pings:
```

Figure 5: Running the nodelet

The topics generated after running this nodelet and the list of nodes are shown here:

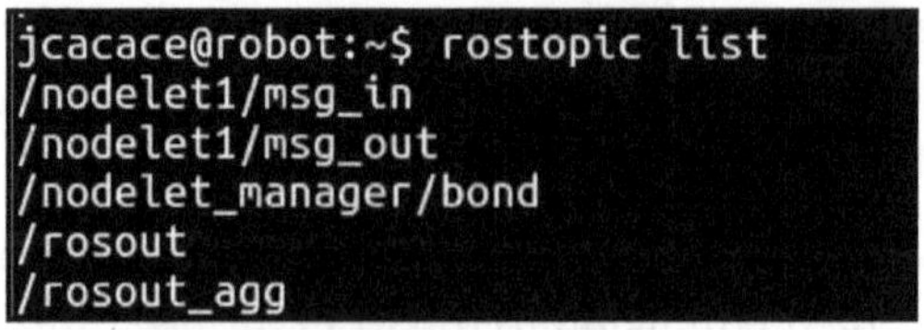

```
jcacace@robot:~$ rostopic list
/nodelet1/msg_in
/nodelet1/msg_out
/nodelet_manager/bond
/rosout
/rosout_agg
```

Figure 6: The list of topics of the nodelet

We can test the node by publishing a string to the `/nodelet1/msg_in` topic and check whether we receive the same message in `nodelet1/msg_out`.

The following command publishes a string to `/nodelet1/msg_in`:

```
$ rostopic pub /nodelet1/msg_in std_msgs/String "Hello"
```

```
jcacace@robot:~$ rostopic pub /nodelet1/msg_in std_msgs
/String "Hello"
publishing and latching message. Press ctrl-C to termin
ate
      jcacace@robot:~
jcacace@robot:~$ rostopic echo /nodelet1/msg_out
data: Hello
```

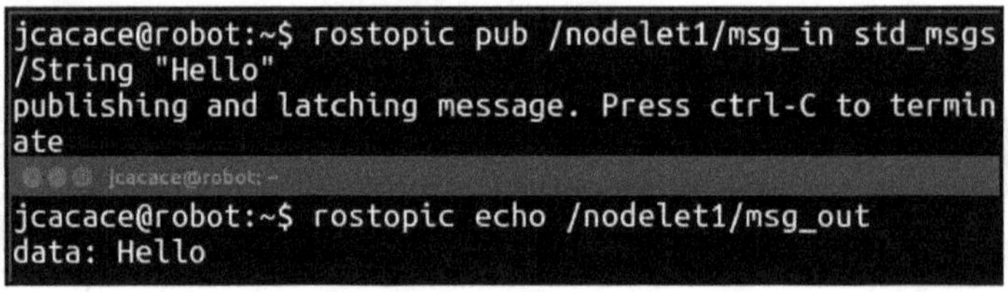

Figure 7: Publishing and subscribing using the nodelet

We can echo the `msg_out` topic and can confirm whether the code is working properly.

Here, we have seen that a single instance of the `Hello()` class is created as a node. We can create multiple instances of the `Hello()` class with different node names inside this nodelet.

Step 8 - Creating launch files for nodelets

We can also write launch files to load more than one instance of the nodelet class. The following launch file will load two nodelets, with the names `test1` and `test2`, and we can save it with the name `hello_world.launch`:

```
<launch>

<!-- Started nodelet manager -->

  <node pkg="nodelet" type="nodelet" name="standalone_nodelet"
args="manager" output="screen"/>

<!-- Starting first nodelet -->

  <node pkg="nodelet" type="nodelet" name="test1" args="load
nodelet_hello_world/Hello standalone_nodelet" output="screen">
  </node>

<!-- Starting second nodelet -->

  <node pkg="nodelet" type="nodelet" name="test2" args="load
nodelet_hello_world/Hello standalone_nodelet" output="screen">
  </node>

</launch>
```

The preceding launch can be launched with the following command:

```
$ roslaunch nodelet_hello_world hello_world.launch
```

The following message will show up on the Terminal if it is launched successfully:

```
[ INFO] [1506951118.603857605]: Loading nodelet /test2 of type nodelet_hello_world/Hello to manager
standalone_nodelet with the following remappings:
[ INFO] [1506951118.606768479]: Loading nodelet /test1 of type nodelet_hello_world/Hello to manager
standalone_nodelet with the following remappings:
[ INFO] [1506951118.610320371]: waitForService: Service [/standalone_nodelet/load_nodelet] has not
been advertised, waiting...
[ INFO] [1506951118.613444334]: waitForService: Service [/standalone_nodelet/load_nodelet] has not
been advertised, waiting...
[ INFO] [1506951118.627001318]: Initializing nodelet with 2 worker threads.
[ INFO] [1506951118.632595864]: waitForService: Service [/standalone_nodelet/load_nodelet] is now a
vailable.
[ INFO] [1506951118.634985422]: waitForService: Service [/standalone_nodelet/load_nodelet] is now a
vailable.
```

Figure 8: Launching multiple instances of the Hello() class.

The list of topics and nodes are shown here. We can see two nodelets instantiated and we can see their topics too:

```
jcacace@robot:~$ rostopic list
/rosout
/rosout_agg
/standalone_nodelet/bond
/test1/msg_in
/test1/msg_out
/test2/msg_in
/test2/msg_out
jcacace@robot:~$ rosnode list
/rosout
/standalone_nodelet
/test1
/test2
```

Figure 9: Topics generated by the multiple instances of Hello() class.

Topics are generated by the multiple instances of the `Hello()` class. We can see the interconnection between these nodelets using the `rqt_graph` tool. Open `rqt_gui`:

```
$ rosrun rqt_gui rqt_gui
```

Load the Node Graph plugin from the following option, **Plugins | Introspection | Node Graph** , and you will get the graph as shown in the following figure:

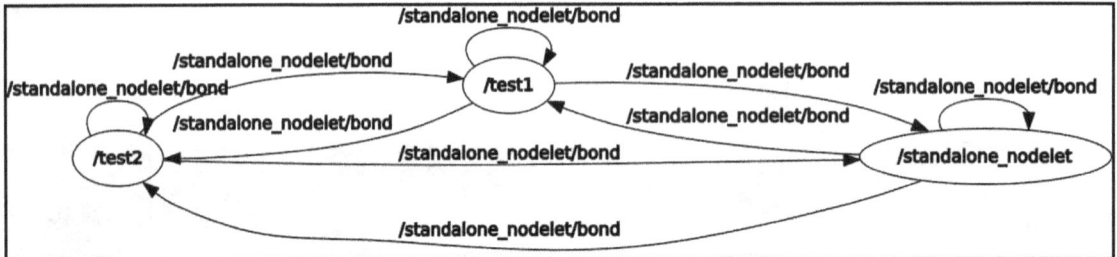

Figure 10: A two-node instance of a nodelet

Alternatively, you can directly load the `rqt_node` plugin:

```
$ rosrun rqt_graph rqt_graph
```

Understanding the Gazebo plugins

Gazebo plugins help us to control the robot models, sensors, world properties, and even the way Gazebo runs. Like pluginlib and nodelets, Gazebo plugins are a set of C++ code, which can be dynamically loaded/unloaded from the Gazebo simulator.

Using plugins, we can access all the components of Gazebo, and also it is independent of ROS, so that it can share with people who are not using ROS. We can mainly classify the plugins as follows:

- **The world plugin**: Using the world plugin, we can control the properties of a specific world in Gazebo. We can change the physics engine, the lighting, and other world properties using this plugin.
- **The model plugin**: The model plugin is attached to a specific model in Gazebo and controls its properties. The parameters, such as the joint state of the model, control of the joints, and so on, can be controlled using this plugin.
- **The sensor plugin**: The sensor plugins are for modeling sensors, such as camera, IMU, and so on, in Gazebo.
- **The system plugin**: The system plugin is started along with the Gazebo startup. A user can control a system-related function in Gazebo using this plugin.
- **The visual plugin**: The visual property of any Gazebo component can be accessed and controlled using the visual plugin.

Before starting development with Gazebo plugins, we might need to install some packages. The Gazebo version installed along with ROS Kinetic is 7.0, so you might need to install its development package in Ubuntu using the following command:

```
$ sudo apt-get install libgazebo7-dev
```

The Gazebo plugins are independent of ROS and we don't need ROS libraries to build a plugin.

Creating a basic world plugin

We will look at a basic Gazebo world plugin and try to build and load it in Gazebo.

Create a folder called gazebo_basic_world_plugin in a desired folder and create a CPP file called hello_world.cc:

```
$ mkdir gazebo_basic_world_plugin && cd gazebo_basic_world_plugin
$ nano hello_world.cc
```

The definition of `hello_world.cc` is as follows:

```
//Gazebo header for getting core gazebo functions
#include <gazebo/gazebo.hh>

//All gazebo plugins should have gazebo namespace

namespace gazebo
{

  //The custom WorldpluginTutorials is inheriting from standard
worldPlugin. Each world plugin has to inheriting from standard plugin type.

  class WorldPluginTutorial : public WorldPlugin
  {

    public: WorldPluginTutorial() : WorldPlugin()
            {
              printf("Hello World!\n");
            }


  //The Load function can receive the SDF elements
    public: void Load(physics::WorldPtr _world, sdf::ElementPtr _sdf)
            {
            }
  };

//Registering World Plugin with Simulator
  GZ_REGISTER_WORLD_PLUGIN(WorldPluginTutorial)
}
```

The header file used in this code is `<gazebo/gazebo.hh>;` . The header contains core functionalities of Gazebo. Other headers are as follows:

- `gazebo/physics/physics.hh`: This is the Gazebo header for accessing the physics engine parameters
- `gazebo/rendering/rendering.hh`: This is the Gazebo header for handling rendering parameters
- `gazebo/sensors/sensors.hh`: This is the header for handling sensors

At the end of the code, we must export the plugin using the following statements.

The GZ_REGISTER_WORLD_PLUGIN(WorldPluginTutorial) macro will register and export the plugin as a world plugin. The following macros are used to register for sensors, models, and so on:

- GZ_REGISTER_MODEL_PLUGIN: This is the export macro for the Gazebo robot model
- GZ_REGISTER_SENSOR_PLUGIN: This is the export macro for the Gazebo sensor model
- GZ_REGISTER_SYSTEM_PLUGIN: This is the export macro for the Gazebo system
- GZ_REGISTER_VISUAL_PLUGIN: This is the export macro for Gazebo visuals

After setting the code, we can make the CMakeLists.txt for compiling the source. The following is the source of CMakeLists.txt:

```
$ nano gazebo_basic_world_plugin/CMakeLists.txt

cmake_minimum_required(VERSION 2.8 FATAL_ERROR)

set(CMAKE_CXX_FLAGS "-std=c++0x ${CMAKE_CXX_FLAGS}")

find_package(Boost REQUIRED COMPONENTS system)
include_directories(${Boost_INCLUDE_DIRS})
link_directories(${Boost_LIBRARY_DIRS})

include (FindPkgConfig)
if (PKG_CONFIG_FOUND)
  pkg_check_modules(GAZEBO gazebo)
endif()
include_directories(${GAZEBO_INCLUDE_DIRS})
link_directories(${GAZEBO_LIBRARY_DIRS})

add_library(hello_world SHARED hello_world.cc)
target_link_libraries(hello_world ${GAZEBO_LIBRARIES} ${Boost_LIBRARIES})
```

Create a build folder for storing the shared object:

```
$ mkdir build && cd build
```

After switching to the build folder, execute the following command to compile and build the source code:

```
$ cmake ../
$ make
```

After building the code, we will get a shared object called `libhello_world.so` and we have to export the path of this shared object in `GAZEBO_PLUGIN_PATH` and add it to the `.bashrc` file:

```
export
GAZEBO_PLUGIN_PATH=${GAZEBO_PLUGIN_PATH}:/path/to/gazebo_basic_world_plugin
/build
```

After setting the Gazebo plugin path and reloading the `bashrc` file, we can use it inside the URDF file or the SRDF file. The following is a sample world file called `hello.world`, which includes this plugin:

```
$ nano gazebo_basic_world_plugin/hello.world

<?xml version="1.0"?>
<sdf version="1.4">
  <world name="default">
    <plugin name="hello_world" filename="libhello_world.so"/>
  </world>
</sdf>
```

This file is also contained in the code provided with this book and in the following Git repository:

```
$ git clone https://github.com/jocacace/gazebo_basic_world_plugin
```

Run the Gazebo server and load this world file:

```
$ cd gazebo_basic_world_plugin
$ gzserver hello.world --verbose
```

```
jcacace@robot:~/catkin_ws/src/MASTERING_ROS/ch6/gazebo_basic_world_plugin$ gzserver hello.world  --verbose
Gazebo multi-robot simulator, version 7.0.0
Copyright (C) 2012-2016 Open Source Robotics Foundation.
Released under the Apache 2 License.
http://gazebosim.org

[Msg] Waiting for master.
[Msg] Connected to gazebo master @ http://127.0.0.1:11345
[Msg] Publicized address: 10.0.2.15
Hello World!
```

Figure 11: The Gazebo world plugin printing "Hello World"

The Gazebo world plugin prints `Hello World!`. We will source the code for various Gazebo plugins from the Gazebo repository.

We can check `https://bitbucket.org/osrf/gazebo,` browse for the source code., take the examples folder and then the plugins, as shown in the following figure:

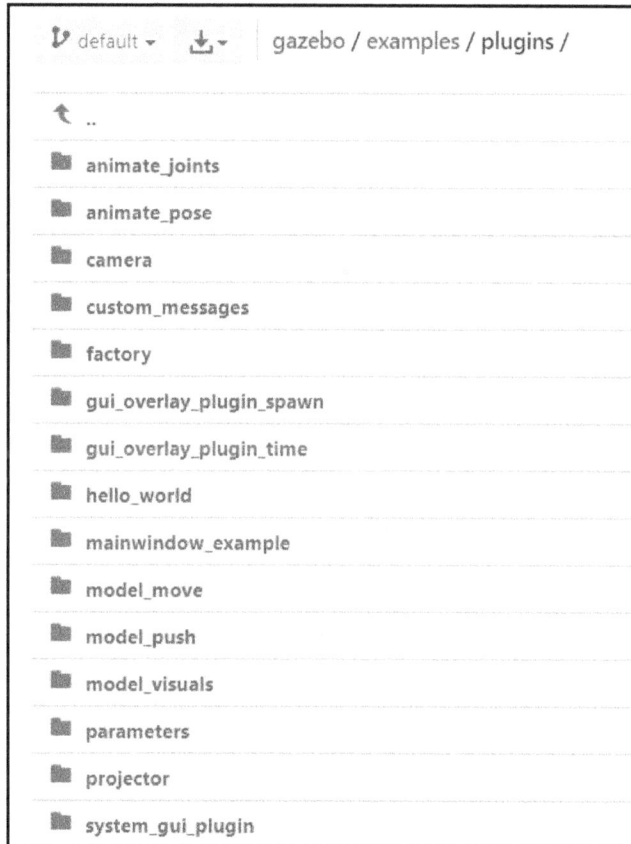

Figure 12: The list of Gazebo plugins in the repository

Questions

- What is `pluginlib` and what are its main applications?
- What is the main application of nodelets?
- What are the different types of Gazebo plugins?
- What is the function of the model plugin in Gazebo?

Summary

In this chapter, we covered some advanced concepts, such as the `pluginlib`, `nodelets`, and Gazebo plugins, which can be used to add more functionalities to a complex ROS application. We discussed the basics of `pluginlib` and saw an example using it. After covering `pluginlib`, we looked at the ROS nodelets, which are widely used in high-performance applications. Also, we looked at an example using the ROS nodelets. Finally, we came to the Gazebo plugins that are used to add functionalities to Gazebo simulators.

In the next chapter, we will discuss more on the RViz plugin and the ROS controllers.

8
Writing ROS Controllers and Visualization Plugins

In the last chapter, we discussed pluginlib, nodelets, and Gazebo plugins. The base library for making plugins in ROS is pluginlib, and the same library can be used in nodelets and Gazebo plugins. In this chapter, we will continue with pluginlib-based concepts, such as ROS controllers and RViz plugins. We have already worked with ROS controllers and have reused some standard controllers, such as joint state, position, and trajectory controllers in Chapter 4: *Simulating Robots Using ROS and Gazebo*.

In this chapter, we will see how to write a basic ROS controller for a generic robot. We will implement a desired controller for our `seven_dof_arm` robot, developed in previous chapters, executing it in the Gazebo simulator. The RViz plugins can add more functionality to RViz, and in this chapter we will look at how to create a basic RViz plugin. The detailed topics that we are going to discuss in this chapter are as follows:

- Understanding packages required for ROS controller development
- Setting the ROS controller development environment
- Understanding `ros_control` packages
- Writing and running a basic ROS controller
- Writing and running an RViz plugin

Let us see how to develop an ROS controller; the first step is to understand the dependency packages required to start building custom controllers.

The main set of packages used to develop a controller generic to all robots is contained in the `ros_control` stack. This is a rewritten version of the `pr2_mechanism`, containing useful libraries to write low-level controllers for PR2 robots (https://www.willowgarage.com/pages/pr2/overview) used in the past version of ROS. In ROS Kinetic, `pr2_mechanism` has been substituted by the `ros_control` stack. The following is the description of some useful packages that help us to write robot controllers:

- `ros_control`: This package takes as input the joint state data directly from the robot's actuators and a desired set point, generating the output to send to its motors. The output is usually represented by the join position, velocity, or effort.
- `controller_manager`: The controller manager can load and manage multiple controllers and can work them in a real-time compatible loop.
- `controller_interface`: This is the controller base class package from which all custom controllers should inherit the controller base class. The controller manager will only load the controller if it inherits from this package.
- `hardware_interface`: This package represents the interface between the implemented controller and hardware of the robot. Using this interface, controllers can directly access cyclically the hardware components.
- `joint_limits_interface`: This package allows us to set joint limits to safely work with our robot. Joint limits are also included in the URDF of the robot. This package is different than the URDF, because it allows us to additionally specify acceleration and jerk limits. In addition, the position, velocity, and effort values contained within the URDF model can be overridden using this package. Commands sent to the hardware are filtered according to the specified joint limits.
- `realtime_tools`: This contains a set of tools that can be used from a hard real-time thread, if the operating system supports real-time behavior. The tools currently only provide the real-time publisher, which makes it possible to publish messages to an ROS topic in real time.

Because we have already worked with `ros_control` in Chapter 4, *Simulating Robots Using ROS and Gazebo*, everything should be already installed on to our system. Otherwise, to operate this package, we should install the following ROS packages from the Ubuntu/Debian repositories:

```
$ sudo apt-get install ros-kinetic-ros-control ros-kinetic-ros-controllers
```

Before writing the ROS controller, it will be good to understand the use of each package of the `ros_control` stack.

Understanding ros_control packages

The `ros_control` stack contains packages for writing ROS low-level controllers. The first package that we are going to discuss is the controller interface package.

The controller_interface package

The basic ROS low-level controller that we want to implement must inherit a base class called `controller_interface::Controller` from this package. This represents a base class containing four fundamental functions: `init()`, `start()`, `update()`, and `stop()`. The basic structure of the `Controller` class is given as follows:

```
namespace controller_interface
{
  class Controller
  {
  public:
    virtual bool init(hardware_interface *robotHW,
                      ros::NodeHandle &nh);
    virtual void starting();
    virtual void update();
    virtual void stopping();
  };
}
```

The workflow of the controller class is shown as follows:

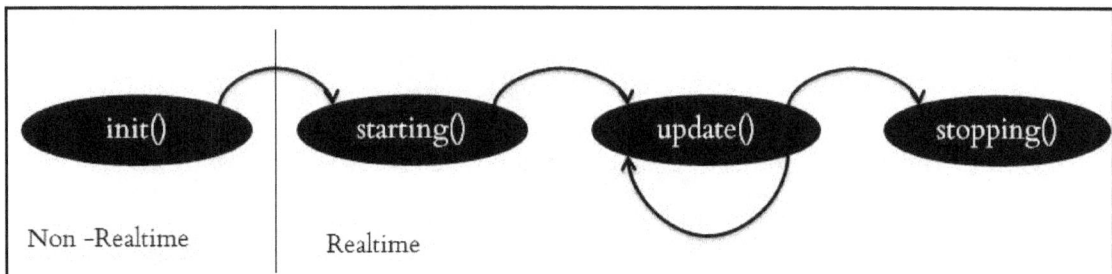

Initializating the controller

The first function executing when a controller is loaded is `init()`. The `init()` function will not start running the controller, it will just initialize it. The initialization can take any amount of time before starting the controllers. The declaration of the `init` function is given as follows:

```
virtual bool init(harware_interface *robotHW, ros::NodeHandle &nh);
```

The function arguments are given as follows:

- `hardware_interface *robotHW`: This variable represents the specific hardware interface used by the controller to develop. ROS contains a list of already-implemented hardware interfaces, such as:
    - Joint Command Interfaces (effort, velocity, and position)
    - Joint State Interfaces
    - Actuator State Interfaces
- We can even create our own hardware interface. In the next example, a Position Joint Interface will be used.
- `ros::NodeHandle &nh`: The controller can read the robot configuration and even advertise topics using this `Nodehandle`.
- The `init()` method only executes once while the controller is loaded by the controller manager. If the `init()` method is not successful, it will unload from the controller manager. We can write a custom message if any error occurs inside the `init()` method.

Starting the ROS controller

The `starting()` method executes once just before running the controller. This method will only execute once before updating and running the controller. The `starting()` method declaration is given as follows:

```
virtual void starting();
```

The controller can also call the `starting()` method when it restarts the controller without unloading it.

Updating the ROS controller

The update() function is the most important method that makes the controller alive. The update method, by default, executes the code inside it at a rate of 1,000 Hz. It means the controller completes one execution within 1 millisecond.

```
virtual void update();
```

Stopping the controller

This method will call when a controller is stopped. The stopping() method will execute as the last update() call and only executes once. The stopping() method will not fail and return nothing too. The following is the declaration of the stopping() method:

```
virtual void stopping();
```

The controller_manager

The controller_manager package can load and unload the desired controller. The controller manager also ensures that the controller will not set a goal value that is less than or greater than the safety limits of the joint. The controller manager also publishes the states of the joint in the /joint_state (sensor_msgs/JointState) topic at a default rate of 100 Hz. The following figure shows the basic workflow of a controller manager:

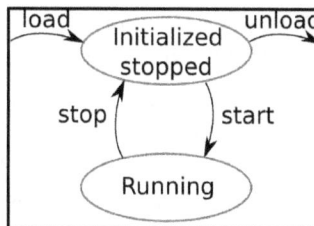

The controller manager can load and unload a plugin. When a controller is loaded by the controller manager, it will first initialize it, but it will not start running.

After loading the controller, we can start and stop the controller. When we start the controller, it will run the controller, and when we stop it, it will simply stop. Stopping doesn't mean it is unloaded. But if the controller is unloaded from the controller manager, we can't access the controller.

Writing a basic joint controller in ROS

The basic prerequisites for writing an ROS controller are already installed. We have discussed the underlying concepts of controllers. Now we can start creating a package for our own controller.

We are going to develop a controller that can access a joint of the robot and move the robot in a sinusoidal fashion. In particular, the first joint of the `seven_dof_arm` will follow a sinusoidal motion.

The procedure of building a controller is similar to other plugins development that we have seen earlier. The list of procedures to create an ROS controller is given as follows:

1. Create an ROS package with the necessary dependencies.
2. Write controller code in C++.
3. Register or export the C++ class as a plugin.
4. Define the plugin definition in an XML file.
5. Edit the `CMakeLists.txt` and `package.xml` files for exporting the plugin.
6. Write the configuration for our controller.
7. Load the controller using the controller manager.

Step 1 - Creating the controller package

The first step is to create the controller package with all its dependencies. The following command can create a package for the controller called `my_controller`:

```
$ catkin_create_pkg my_controller roscpp pluginlib controller_interface
```

We will get the existing package from the `my_controller` folder of the code provided with this book or clone the package from the following Git repository:

```
$ git clone https://github.com/jocacace/my_controller.git
```

Step 2 – Creating the controller header file

We will get the header file `my_controller.h` from the `my_controller/src/` folder. Given in the following is the header file definition of `my_controller.h`. As already stated, in this header we are going to implement the functions contained in the `controller_interface::Controller` class:

```
#include <controller_interface/controller.h>
#include <hardware_interface/joint_command_interface.h>
#include <pluginlib/class_list_macros.h>


namespace my_controller_ns {

    class MyControllerClass: public
controller_interface::Controller<hardware_interface::PositionJointInterface
>
    {
    public:
        bool init(hardware_interface::PositionJointInterface* hw,
ros::NodeHandle &n);
        void update(const ros::Time& time, const ros::Duration& period);
        void starting(const ros::Time& time);
        void stopping(const ros::Time& time);

    private:
        hardware_interface::JointHandle joint_;
        double init_pos_;
    };
}
```

In the preceding code, we can see the controller class, `MyControllerClass`, and we are inheriting the base class, `controller_interface::Controller`. We can see that each function inside the `Controller` class is overriding in our class.

Step 3 – Creating the controller source file

Create a folder called `src` inside the package and create a C++ file called `my_controller_file.cpp`, which is the class definition of the preceding header.

Given in the following is the definition of `my_controller_file.cpp`, which has to be saved inside the `src` folder:

```
#include "my_controller.h"
```

```
namespace my_controller_ns {
//Controller initialization
bool MyControllerClass::init(hardware_interface::PositionJointInterface*
hw, ros::NodeHandle &n)
{
//Retrieve the joint object to control
      std::string joint_name;
      if( !nh.getParam( "joint_name", joint_name ) ) {
            ROS_ERROR("No joint_name specified");
            return false;
      }
      joint_ = hw->getHandle("shoulder_pan_joint");
      return true;
}
//Controller startup
void MyControllerClass::starting(const ros::Time& time) {
        //Get initial position to use in the control procedure
        init_pos_ = joint_.getPosition();
  }

//Controller running
void MyControllerClass::update(const ros::Time& time, const ros::Duration&
period)
{
//---Perform a sinusoidal motion for joint shoulder_pan_joint
double dpos = init_pos_ + 10 * sin(ros::Time::now().toSec());
        double cpos = joint_.getPosition();
      joint_.setCommand( -10*(cpos-dpos)); //Apply command to the selected
joint
        //---
}

//Controller exiting
void MyControllerClass::stopping(const ros::Time& time) { }
}

//Register the plugin: PLUGINLIB_EXPORT_CLASS(my_namespace::MyPlugin,
base_class_namespace::PluginBaseClass)
PLUGINLIB_EXPORT_CLASS(my_controller_ns::MyControllerClass,
controller_interface::ControllerBase);
```

Step 4 – Explaining the controller source file

In this section, we can see the explanation of each section of the code:

```
/// Controller initialization in non-real-time
```

```
bool MyControllerClass::init(hardware_interface::PositionJointInterface*
hw, ros::NodeHandle &n)
{
```

The preceding is the `init()` function definition of the controller. This will be called when a controller is loaded by the controller manager. Inside the `init()` function, we are creating an instance of the state of the robot (`hw`) and `NodeHandle`, and we also get the manager of the joint interacting with the controller. In our example, we defined the joint to control in the `my_contoller.yaml` file, loading the joint name into the ROS parameter server. This function returns the success or the failure in the controller initialization:

```
if( !nh.getParam( "joint_name", joint_name ) ) {
ROS_ERROR("No joint_name specified");
    return false;
}
```

This code will create a joint state object for a desired joint. Here is an instance of the `hardware_interface` class. `joint_name` is the desired joint in which we are attaching the controller:

```
/// Controller startup in realtime
void MyControllerClass::starting(const ros::Time& time)
{
init_pos_ = joint_.getPosition();
}
```

After the controller is loaded, the next step is to start it. The preceding function will execute when we start a controller. In this function, it will retrieve the current position of the joint, storing its value into the `init_pos_` variable:

```
/// Controller update loop in real-time
void MyControllerClass::update(const ros::Time& time, const ros::Duration&
period)
{
//---Perform a sinusoidal motion for joint shoulder_pan_joint
double dpos = init_pos_ + 10 * sin(ros::Time::now().toSec());
          double cpos = joint_.getPosition();
      joint_.setCommand( -10*(cpos-dpos)); //Apply command to the selected
joint
      //---
}
```

This is the `update` function of the controller, which will continuously move the joint in a sinusoidal fashion.

Step 5 – Creating the plugin description file

We can define the plugin definition file, which is given in the following code. The plugin file is being saved inside the package folder under the name of `controller_plugins.xml`:

```
<library path="lib/libmy_controller_lib">
   <class name="my_controller_ns/MyControllerClass"
                     type="my_controller_ns::MyControllerClass"
base_class_type="controller_interface::ControllerBase" />
</library>
```

Step 6 – Updating package.xml

We need to update `package.xml` for pointing the `controller_plugins.xml` file:

```
  <export>
   <controller_interface plugin="${prefix}/controller_plugins.xml" />
  </export>
```

Step 7 – Updating CMakeLists.txt

After doing all these things, we can compose `CMakeLists.txt` of the package:

```
## my_controller_file library
add_library(my_controller_lib src/my_controller.cpp)
target_link_libraries(my_controller_lib ${catkin_LIBRARIES})
```

Step 8 – Building the controller

After completing `CMakeLists.txt`, we can build our controller using the `catkin_make` command. After building, check that the controller is configured as a plugin using the `rospack` command, as shown here:

```
$ rospack plugins --attrib=plugin controller_interface
```

With this command, all the controllers related to `controller_interface` will be listed.

If everything has been performed correctly, the output may look like the following:

```
jcacace@robot:~$ rospack plugins --attrib=plugin controller_interface
my_controller /home/jcacace/catkin_ws/src/MASTERING_ROS/ch7/my_controller/controller_plugins.xml
joint_trajectory_controller /opt/ros/kinetic/share/joint_trajectory_controller/ros_control_plugins.xml
position_controllers /opt/ros/kinetic/share/position_controllers/position_controllers_plugins.xml
effort_controllers /opt/ros/kinetic/share/effort_controllers/effort_controllers_plugins.xml
diff_drive_controller /opt/ros/kinetic/share/diff_drive_controller/diff_drive_controller_plugins.xml
joint_state_controller /opt/ros/kinetic/share/joint_state_controller/joint_state_plugin.xml
```

Step 9 – Writing the controller configuration file

After proper installation of the controller, we can configure it and run it. The first procedure is to create the configuration file of the controller that consists of the controller type, joint name, joint limits, and so on. The configuration file is saved as a YAML file that must be saved inside the package. We are creating a YAML file with the name of my_controller.yaml, and the definition is given as follows:

```
#File loaded during Gazebo startup
my_controller_name:
   type: my_controller_ns/MyControllerClass
   joint_name: elbow_pitch_joint
```

This file is the configuration of the controller. In particular, this file contains the type of the controller represented by the name of the class compiled with the controller source code and the set of parameters to pass to the controller. In our case, this is the name of the joint to control.

Step 10 – Writing the launch file for the controller

The joint assigned for showing the working of this controller is shoulder_pan_joint of the robot seven_dof_arm. After creating the YAML file, we can create a launch file inside the launch folder, which can load the controller configuration file and run the controller. The launch file is called my_controller.launch, which is given as follows:

```
<?xml version="1.0" ?>
<launch>
  <include file="$(find my_controller)/launch/seven_dof_arm_world.launch"
/>
  <rosparam file="$(find my_controller)/my_controller.yaml"
command="load"/>
  <node name="my_controller_spawner" pkg="controller_manager"
type="spawner" respawn="false"
```

```
     output="screen" args="my_controller_name"/>
  </launch>
```

In the following code, we explain the launch file:

```
<launch>
  <include file="$(find my_controller)/launch/seven_dof_arm_world.launch"
/>
```

Here we run the Gazebo simulator, launching a modified version of `seven_dof_arm`:

```
<rosparam file="$(find my_controller)/my_controller.yaml" command="load"/>
```

Then, we load the developed controller.

Finally, we spawn the controller:

```
     <node name="my_controller_spawner" pkg="controller_manager"
type="spawner" respawn="false"
       output="screen" args="my_controller_name"/>
```

In this way, the `controller_manager` will run the controller specified in the `"args"` list. In our case, only the `my_controller_name` is executed through the `init()`, the `start()`, and the `update()` functions implemented by the controller.

Step 11 – Running the controller along with the seven dof arm in Gazebo

After creating the controller launch files, we should test it on our robot. We can launch the Gazebo simulation using the following command:

```
$ roslaunch my_controller my_controller.launch
```

When we launch the simulation, all of the controllers associated with the robot also get started. The purpose of our controller is to move the `elbow_pitch_joint` of the `seven_dof_arm`, as defined in the controller. If everything is properly working, the elbow of the robot should start to move in a sinusoidal way:

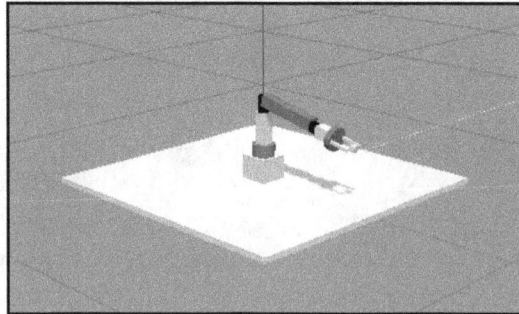

If there are existing controllers handling this same joint, our controller can't work properly. To avoid this situation, we need to stop the controller that is handling the same joint of the robot. A set of services are exposed by the `controller_manager` to manage the controllers of the robot. For example, we can use the following command to check the state of the controllers loaded in the system:

```
$ rosservice call /controller_manager/list_controllers
```

The output of this command is shown in the following screenshot:

```
jcacace@robot:~$ rosservice call /controller_manager/list_controllers
controller:
  -
    name: my_controller_name
    state: running
    type: my_controller_ns/MyControllerClass
    claimed_resources:
      -
        hardware_interface: hardware_interface::PositionJointInterface
        resources: ['elbow_pitch_joint']
```

In the previous screenshot, you can see that our controller (`my_controller_name`) is running. We can stop it using the `/controller_manager/switch_controller` service, as shown in the following screenshot:

```
jcacace@robot:~$ rosservice call /controller_manager/switch_controller "start_controllers:
- ''
stop_controllers:
- 'my_controller_name'
strictness: 0"
ok: True
jcacace@robot:~$ rosservice call /controller_manager/list_controllers
controller:
  -
    name: my_controller_name
    state: stopped
    type: my_controller_ns/MyControllerClass
    claimed_resources:
      -
        hardware_interface: hardware_interface::PositionJointInterface
        resources: ['elbow_pitch_joint']
```

Consider that in this example we are exploiting the `gazebo_ros_control` plugin to run our controller. This plugin represents the hardware interface of our robot in the simulated scene. In the case of a real robot, we should write our own hardware interface to apply control data to robot actuators.

In conclusion, `ros_control` implements a standard set of generic controllers, such as `effort_controllers`, `joint_state_controllers`, `position_controllers`, and velocity controllers for any kind of robots. We have already used these ROS controllers from `ros_control` in Chapter 3, *Working with 3D Robot Modeling in ROS*. `ros_control` is still in development. Here we used `ros_control` to develop a simple dedicated position controller for our `seven_dof_arm` robot. You can check the availability of new controllers through the wiki page of `ros_control` at `https://github.com/ros-controls/ros_control/wiki`.

Understanding the ROS visualization tool (RViz) and its plugins

The RViz tool is an official 3D visualization tool of ROS. Almost all kinds of data from sensors can be viewed through this tool. RViz will be installed along with the ROS desktop full installation. Let's launch RViz and see the basic components present in RViz.

Start `roscore`:

```
$ roscore
```

Start `rviz`:

```
$ rviz
```

The important sections of the RViz GUI are marked, and the uses of each section are shown in the following screenshot:

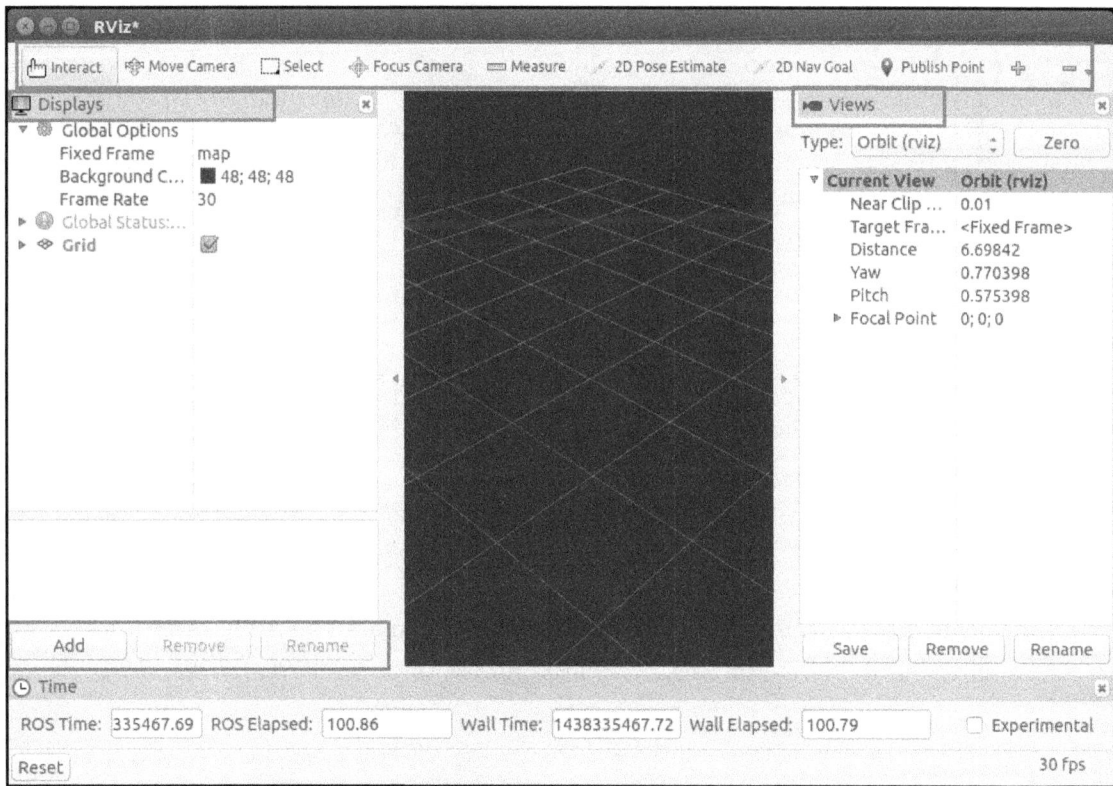

Displays panel

The panel on the left side of the RViz is called the **Displays** panel. The **Displays** panel contains a list of the display plugins of RViz and its properties. The main use of display plugins is to visualize different types of ROS messages, mainly sensor data in the RViz 3D viewport. There are lots of display plugins already present in RViz for viewing images from the camera, and for viewing the 3D point cloud, LaserScan, robot model, TF, and so on. Plugins can be added by pressing the **Add** button on the left panel. We can also write our own display plugin and add it there.

RViz toolbar

There are set of tools present in the RViz toolbar for manipulating the 3D viewport. The toolbar is present at the top of RViz. There are tools present for interacting with the robot model, modifying the camera view, giving navigation goals, and giving robot 2D pose estimations. We can add our own custom tools to the toolbar in the form of plugins.

Views

The **Views** panel is placed on the right side of RViz. Using the **Views** panel, we can save different views of the 3D viewport and switch to each view by loading the saved configuration.

Time panel

The **Time** panel displays the simulator time elapsed and is mainly useful if there is a simulator running along with RViz. We can also reset to the RViz initial setting using this panel.

Dockable panels

The preceding toolbar and panels belong to dockable panels. We can create our own dockable panels as an RViz plugin. We are going to create a dockable panel that has an RViz plugin for robot teleoperation.

Writing an RViz plugin for teleoperation

In this chapter, we design a teleoperation commander in which we can manually enter the teleoperation topic, linear velocity, and angular velocity, as shown in the following screenshot:

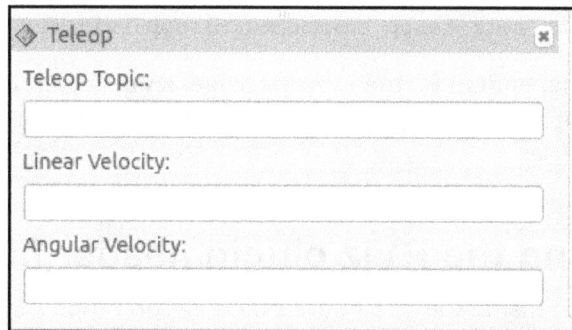

The following is a detailed procedure on how to build this plugin.

Methodology of building the RViz plugin

Before starting to build this plugin, we should know how to do it. The standard method to build an ROS plugin is applicable for this plugin too. The difference is that the RViz plugin is GUI based. The RViz is written using a GUI framework called **Qt**, so we need to create a GUI in Qt and, using Qt APIs, we have to get the GUI values and send them to the ROS system.

The following steps describe how this teleoperation RViz plugin is going to work:

1. The dockable panel will have a Qt GUI interface, and the user can input the topic, linear velocity, and angular velocity of teleoperation from the GUI.
2. Collect the user input from GUI using Qt signals and slots, and publish the values using the ROS subscribe-and-publish method. (The Qt signals and slots are a trigger-invoke technique available in Qt. When a signal/trigger is generated by a GUI field, it can invoke a slot or function, such as a callback mechanism.)
3. Here, also, we can use the same procedure to build a plugin as we discussed earlier.

Now we can see the step-by-step procedure to build this plugin.

Step 1 – Creating the RViz plugin package

Let's create a new package for creating the teleop plugin:

```
$ catkin_create_pkg rviz_telop_commander roscpp rviz std_msgs
```

The package is mainly dependent on the `rviz` package. RViz is built using Qt libraries, so we don't need to include additional Qt libraries in the package. In the Ubuntu 16.04 version, we need to use Qt5 libraries.

Step 2 – Creating the RViz plugin header file

Let's create a new header inside the `src` folder called `teleop_pad.h`. You will get this source code from the existing package. This header file consists of the class and methods declaration for the plugin.

The following is the explanation of this header file:

```
#include <ros/ros.h>
#include <ros/console.h>
#include <rviz/panel.h>
```

The preceding code is the header file required to build this plugin; we need ROS headers for publishing the `teleop` topic and `<rviz/panel.h>` for getting the base class of the RViz panel for creating a new panel:

```
class TeleopPanel: public rviz::Panel
{
```

This is a plugin class and it is inherited from the `rviz::Panel` base class:

```
Q_OBJECT
public:
```

This class is using the Qt signal and slots, and it's also a subclass of QObject in Qt. In that case, we should use the `Q_OBJECT` macro:

```
TeleopPanel( QWidget* parent = 0 );
```

This is the constructor of the `TeleopPanel()` class, and we are initializing a `QWidget` class to 0. We are using the `QWidget` instance inside the `TeleopPanel` class for implementing the GUI of the `teleop` plugin:

```
virtual void load( const rviz::Config& config );
virtual void save( rviz::Config config ) const;
```

The following shows how to override the `rviz::Panel` functions for saving and loading the RViz config file:

```
public Q_SLOTS:
```

After this line, we can define some public Qt slots:

```
void setTopic( const QString& topic );
```

When we enter the topic name in the GUI and press `Enter`, this slot will be called and will create the topic publisher in the given name:

```
protected Q_SLOTS:
    void sendVel();
    void update_Linear_Velocity();
    void update_Angular_Velocity();
    void updateTopic();
```

These are the protected slots for sending velocity, updating linear velocity and angular velocity, and updating the topic name, when we change the name of the existing topic:

```
QLineEdit* output_topic_editor_;
QLineEdit* output_topic_editor_1;
QLineEdit* output_topic_editor_2;
```

We are creating the Qt `LineEdit` object to create three text fields in the plugin to receive the topic name, linear velocity, and angular velocity:

```
ros::Publisher velocity_publisher_;
ros::NodeHandle nh_;
```

These are the publisher object and the `Nodehandle` object for publishing topics and handling an ROS node.

Step 3 – Creating the RViz plugin definition

In this step, we will create the main C++ file that contains the definition of the plugin. The file is `teleop_pad.cpp`, and you will get it from the `src` package folder.

The main responsibilities of this file are as follows:

- It acts as a container for a Qt GUI element, such as `QLineEdit`, to accept text entries
- It publishes the command velocity using the ROS publisher
- It saves and restores the RViz config files

The following is the explanation for each section of the code:

```
TeleopPanel::TeleopPanel( QWidget* parent )
  : rviz::Panel( parent )
  , linear_velocity_( 0 )
  , angular_velocity_( 0 ) {
```

This is the constructor and initialize `rviz::Panel` with `QWidget`, setting linear and angular velocity as 0:

```
QVBoxLayout* topic_layout = new QVBoxLayout;
topic_layout->addWidget( new QLabel( "Teleop Topic:" ));
output_topic_editor_ = new QLineEdit;
topic_layout->addWidget( output_topic_editor_ );
```

This will add a new `QLineEdit` widget on the panel for handling the topic name. Similarly, two other `QLineEdit` widgets handle linear velocity and angular velocity.

```
QTimer* output_timer = new QTimer( this );
```

This will create a Qt `timer` object for updating a function that is publishing the velocity topic:

```
connect( output_topic_editor_, SIGNAL( editingFinished() ), this, SLOT(
updateTopic() ));
connect( output_topic_editor_, SIGNAL( editingFinished() ), this, SLOT(
updateTopic() ));
connect( output_topic_editor_1, SIGNAL( editingFinished() ), this, SLOT(
update_Linear_Velocity() ));
connect( output_topic_editor_2, SIGNAL( editingFinished() ), this, SLOT(
update_Angular_Velocity() ));
```

This will connect a Qt signal to the slots. Here, the signal is triggered when
`editingFinished()` returns `true`, and the `Slot` here is `updateTopic()`. When the
editing inside a Qt `LineEdit` is finished by pressing the *Enter* key, the signal will trigger,
and the corresponding slot will execute. Here, this slot will set the topic name, angular
velocity, and linear velocity value from the text field of the plugin:

```
connect( output_timer, SIGNAL( timeout() ), this, SLOT( sendVel() ));
output_timer->start( 100 );
```

These lines generate a signal when the Qt `timer` times out. The timer will time out in each
100 ms and execute a slot called `sendVel()`, which will publish the velocity topic.

We can see the definition of each slot after this section. This code is self-explanatory and,
finally, we can see the following code to export it as a plugin:

```
#include <pluginlib/class_list_macros.h>
PLUGINLIB_EXPORT_CLASS(rviz_telop_commander::TeleopPanel, rviz::Panel )
```

Step 4 – Creating the plugin description file

The definition of `plugin_description.xml` is given as follows:

```
<library path="lib/librviz_telop_commander">
  <class name="rviz_telop_commander/Teleop"
         type="rviz_telop_commander::TeleopPanel"
         base_class_type="rviz::Panel">
    <description>
      A panel widget allowing simple diff-drive style robot base control.
    </description>
  </class>
</library>
```

Step 5 – Adding the export tags in package.xml

We have to update the `package.xml` file to include the plugin description. The following is
the update of `package.xml`:

```
<export>
    <rviz plugin="${prefix}/plugin_description.xml"/>
</export>
```

Step 6 – Editing CMakeLists.txt

We need to add extra lines to the CMakeLists.txt definition, as given in the following code:

```
find_package(Qt5 COMPONENTS Core Widgets REQUIRED)
set(QT_LIBRARIES Qt5::Widgets)
catkin_package(
    LIBRARIES ${PROJECT_NAME}
    CATKIN_DEPENDS roscpp
                   rviz
)

include_directories(include
    ${catkin_INCLUDE_DIRS}
    ${Boost_INCLUDE_DIRS}
)

link_directories(
    ${catkin_LIBRARY_DIRS}
    ${Boost_LIBRARY_DIRS}
)

add_definitions(-DQT_NO_KEYWORDS)

QT5_WRAP_CPP(MOC_FILES
  src/teleop_pad.h
  OPTIONS -DBOOST_TT_HAS_OPERATOR_HPP_INCLUDED -
DBOOST_LEXICAL_CAST_INCLUDED
  )

set(SOURCE_FILES
  src/teleop_pad.cpp
  ${MOC_FILES}
)
add_library(${PROJECT_NAME} ${SOURCE_FILES})
target_link_libraries(${PROJECT_NAME} ${QT_LIBRARIES}
${catkin_LIBRARIES})
```

You will get the complete CMakeLists.txt from the rviz_telop_commander package released with the code book, or you can clone the entire package from the following Git repositories:

```
$ git clone https://github.com/jocacace/rviz_teleop_commander.git
```

Step 7 – Building and loading plugins

After creating these files, build a package using `catkin_make`. If the build is successful, we can load the plugin in RViz itself. Take the RViz and load the panel by going to **Menu Panel | Add New Panel.** We will get a panel such as the following:

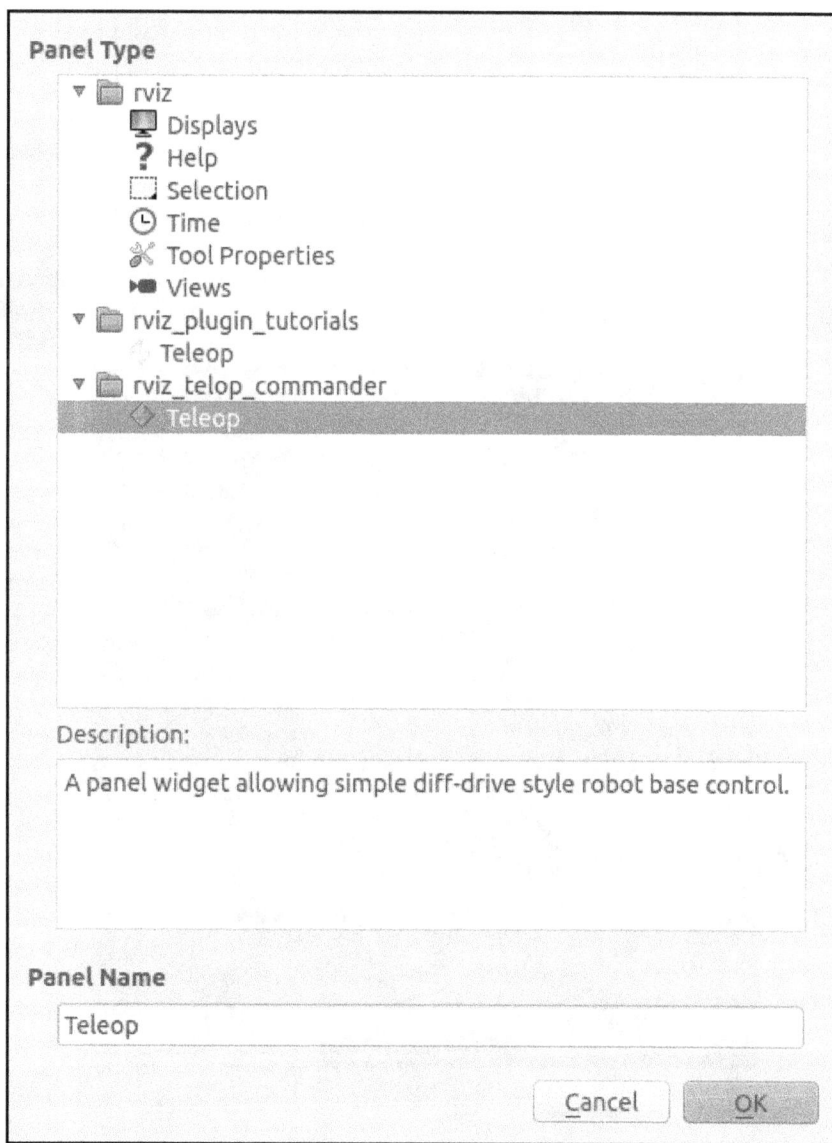

If we load the **Teleop** plugin from the list, we will get a panel such as the following:

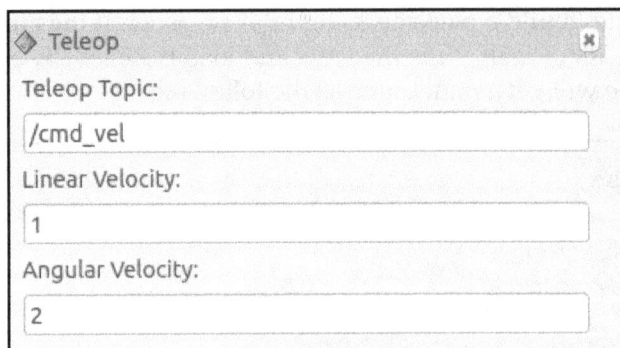

We can put the **Teleop Topic** name and values inside the **Linear Velocity** and **Angular Velocity**, and we can echo the **Teleop Topic** and get the topic values such as the following:

```
jcacace@robot:~/catkin_ws$ rostopic echo /cmd_vel
linear:
  x: 1.0
  y: 0.0
  z: 0.0
angular:
  x: 0.0
  y: 0.0
  z: 2.0
---
linear:
  x: 1.0
  y: 0.0
  z: 0.0
angular:
  x: 0.0
  y: 0.0
  z: 2.0
---
linear:
  x: 1.0
  y: 0.0
  z: 0.0
angular:
  x: 0.0
  y: 0.0
  z: 2.0
```

Questions

- What are the list of packages needed for writing a low-level controller in ROS?
- What are the different processes happening inside an ROS controller?
- What are the main packages of the `ros_control` stack?
- What are the different types of RViz plugins?

Summary

In this chapter, we discussed creating plugins for the ROS visualization tool (RViz) and writing basic ROS controllers. We have already worked with default controllers in ROS, and, in this chapter, we developed a custom controller for moving joints. After building and testing the controller, we looked at RViz plugins. We created a new RViz panel for teleoperation. We can manually enter the topic name; we need the twist messages and to enter the linear and angular velocity in the panel. This panel is useful for controlling robots without starting another teleoperation node. In the next chapter, we will discuss interfacing I/O boards and running ROS in embedded systems.

9
Interfacing I/O Boards, Sensors, and Actuators to ROS

In the previous chapters, we discussed different kinds of plugin frameworks that are used in ROS. In this chapter, we are going to discuss the interfacing of some hardware components, such as sensors and actuators, to ROS. We will look at the interfacing of sensors using I/O boards, such as Arduino, Raspberry Pi, and Odroid-XU4 to ROS, and we will discuss interfacing smart actuators, such as DYNAMIXEL, to ROS. The following is the detailed list of topics that we are going to cover in this chapter:

- Understanding the Arduino-ROS interface
- Setting up the Arduino-ROS interface packages
- Arduino-ROS examples: Chatter and Talker, blink LED and push button, Accelerometer ADXL 335, ultrasonic distance sensors, and Odometry Publisher
- Interfacing a non-Arduino board to ROS
- Setting ROS on Odroid-XU4 and Raspberry Pi 2
- Working with Raspberry Pi and Odroid GPIOs using ROS
- Interfacing DYNAMIXEL actuators to ROS

Understanding the Arduino-ROS interface

Let's see what Arduino is first. Arduino is one of the most popular open source development boards in the market. The ease of programming and the cost effectiveness of the hardware have made Arduino a big success. Most of the Arduino boards are powered by Atmel microcontrollers, which are available from 8-bit to 32-bit, with clock speeds from 8 MHz to 84 MHz. Arduino can be used for the quick prototyping of robots. The main applications of Arduino in robotics are interfacing sensors and actuators, used for communicating with PCs for receiving high-level commands and sending sensor values to PCs using the UART protocol.

There are different varieties of Arduino available in the market. Selecting one board for our purpose will be dependent on the nature of our robotic application. Let's see some boards which we can use for beginners, intermediate, and high-end users:

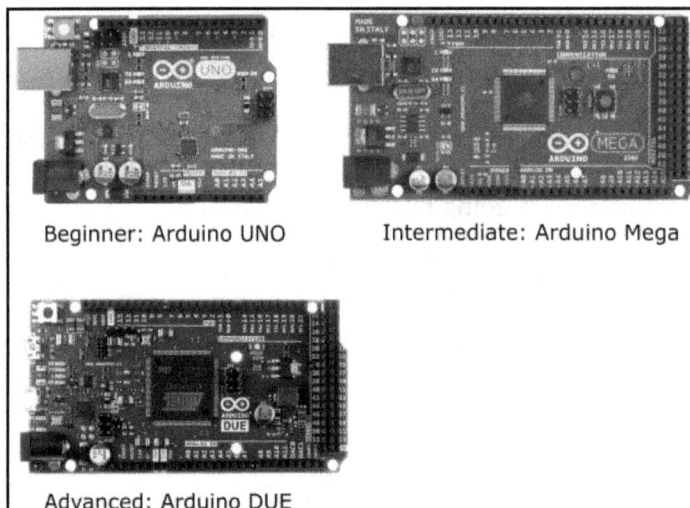

Beginner: Arduino UNO   Intermediate: Arduino Mega

Advanced: Arduino DUE

Figure 1: Different versions of the Arduino board

In the following table, we will look at each Arduino board specification in brief and see where it can be deployed:

Boards	Arduino UNO	Arduino Mega 2560	Arduino Due
Processor	ATmega328P	ATmega2560	ATSAM3X8E
Operating/Input Voltage	5V / 7-12 V	5V/ 7-12V	3.3V / 7 - 12 V

CPU Speed	16 MHz	16 MHz	84 MHz
Analog In/Out	6/0	16/0	12/2
Digital IO/PWM	14/6	54/15	54/12
EEPROM[KB]	1	4	-
SRAM [KB]	2	8	96
Flash [KB]	32	256	512
USB	Regular	Regular	2 Micro
UART	1	4	4
Application	Basic robotics and sensor interfacing	Intermediate robotic application-level application	High-end robotics application

Let's look at how to interface Arduino to ROS.

What is the Arduino-ROS interface?

Most of the communication between PCs and I/O boards in robots will be through the UART protocol. When both the devices communicate with each other, there should be some program in both the sides that can translate the serial commands from each of these devices. We can implement our own logic to receive and transmit the data from board to PC and vice versa. The interfacing code can be different in each I/O board because there are no standard libraries to do this communication.

The Arduino-ROS interface is a standard way of communication between the Arduino boards and the PC. Currently, this interface is exclusive for Arduino. We may need to write custom nodes to interface with other I/O boards.

We can use the similar C++ APIs of ROS used in the PC in the Arduino IDE also for programming the Arduino board. Detailed information about the interfacing package follows.

Understanding the rosserial package in ROS

The `rosserial` package is a set of standardized communication protocols implemented for communicating from ROS to character devices, such as serial ports, and sockets, and vice versa. The `rosserial` protocol can convert the standard ROS messages and services data types to embedded device equivalent data types. It also implements multi-topic support by multiplexing the serial data from a character device. The serial data is sent as data packets by adding header and tail bytes on the packet. The packet representation is shown next:

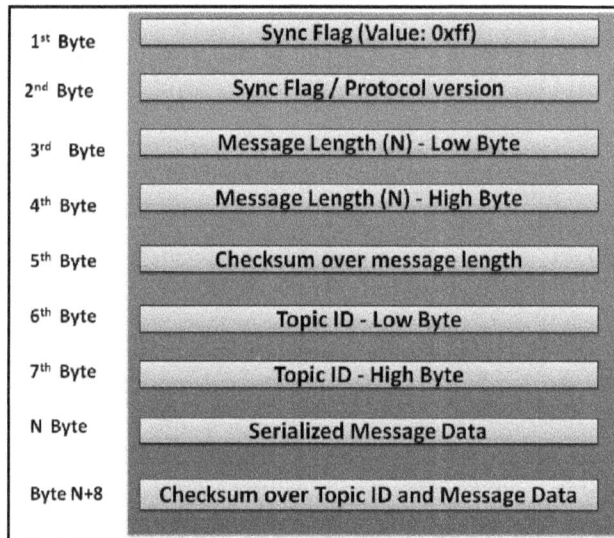

1st Byte	Sync Flag (Value: 0xff)
2nd Byte	Sync Flag / Protocol version
3rd Byte	Message Length (N) - Low Byte
4th Byte	Message Length (N) - High Byte
5th Byte	Checksum over message length
6th Byte	Topic ID - Low Byte
7th Byte	Topic ID - High Byte
N Byte	Serialized Message Data
Byte N+8	Checksum over Topic ID and Message Data

Figure 2: rosserial packet representation

The function of each byte follows:

- **Sync Flag**: This is the first byte of the packet, which is always `0xff`
- **Sync Flag/Protocol version**: This byte was `0xff` on ROS Groovy and after that it is set to `0xfe`
- **Message Length**: This is the length of the packet
- **Checksum Over Message Length**: This is the checksum of length for finding packet corruption
- **Topic ID**: This is the ID allocated for each topic; the range `0-100` is allocated for the system-related functionalities

- **Serialized Message data**: This is the data associated with each topic
- **Checksum of Topic ID and Message data**: This is the checksum for the topic and its serial data for finding the packet, `corruption`

The checksum of length is computed using the following equation:

Checksum = 255 - ((Topic ID Low Byte + Topic ID High Byte + ... data byte values) % 256)

The ROS client libraries, such as `roscpp`, `rospy`, and `roslisp`, enable us to develop ROS nodes that can run from various devices. One of the ports of the ROS clients that enables us to run a ROS node from the embedded devices, such as Arduino and embedded Linux based boards, is called the `rosserial_client` library. Using the `rosserial_client` libraries, we can develop the ROS nodes from Arduino, embedded Linux platforms, and Windows. The following is the list of `rosserial_client` libraries for each of these platforms:

- `rosserial_arduino`: This `rosserial_client` works on Arduino platforms, such as Arduino UNO, Leonardo, Mega, and Due series for advance robotic projects
- `rosserial_embeddedlinux`: This client supports embedded Linux platforms, such as VEXPro, Chumby alarm clock, WRT54GL router, and so on
- `rosserial_windows`: This is a client for the Windows platform

In the PC side, we need some other packages to decode the serial message and convert to exact topics from the `rosserial_client` libraries. The following packages help in decoding the serial data:

- `rosserial_python`: This is the recommended PC-side node for handling serial data from a device. The receiving node is completely written in Python.
- `rosserial_server`: This is a C++ implementation of `rosserial` in the PC side. The inbuilt functionalities are less compared to `rosserial_python`, but it can be used for high-performance applications.

We are mainly focusing on running the ROS nodes from Arduino. First, we will see how to set up the `rosserial` packages, and then discuss how to set up the `rosserial_arduino` client in the Arduino IDE.

Installing rosserial packages on Ubuntu 16.04

To operate with Arduino on Ubuntu 16.04, we must install `rosserial` ROS packages and then set up the Arduino client, installing the libraries needed to communicate with ROS. We can install the `rosserial` packages on Ubuntu using the following commands:

1. Install the `rosserial` package binaries, using `apt-get`:

   ```
   $ sudo apt-get install ros-kinetic-rosserial-arduino ros-kinetic-
   rosserial-embeddedlinux ros-kinetic-rosserial-windows ros-kinetic-
   rosserial-server ros-kinetic-rosserial-python
   ```

2. For installing the `rosserial_client` library called `ros_lib` in Arduino, we must download the latest Arduino IDE for Linux 32/64 bit. The following is the link for downloading the Arduino IDE: `https://www.arduino.cc/en/main/software`. Here we download the Linux 64-bit version and copy the Arduino IDE folder to the Ubuntu desktop. Arduino requires Java runtime support to run it. If it is not installed, we can install it using the following command:

   ```
   $ sudo apt-get install java-common
   ```

3. After installing Java runtime, we can switch the `arduino` folder using the following command:

   ```
   $ cd ~/Desktop/arduino-1.8.5
   ```

4. Start Arduino, using the following command:

   ```
   $ ./arduino
   ```

Shown next is the Arduino IDE window:

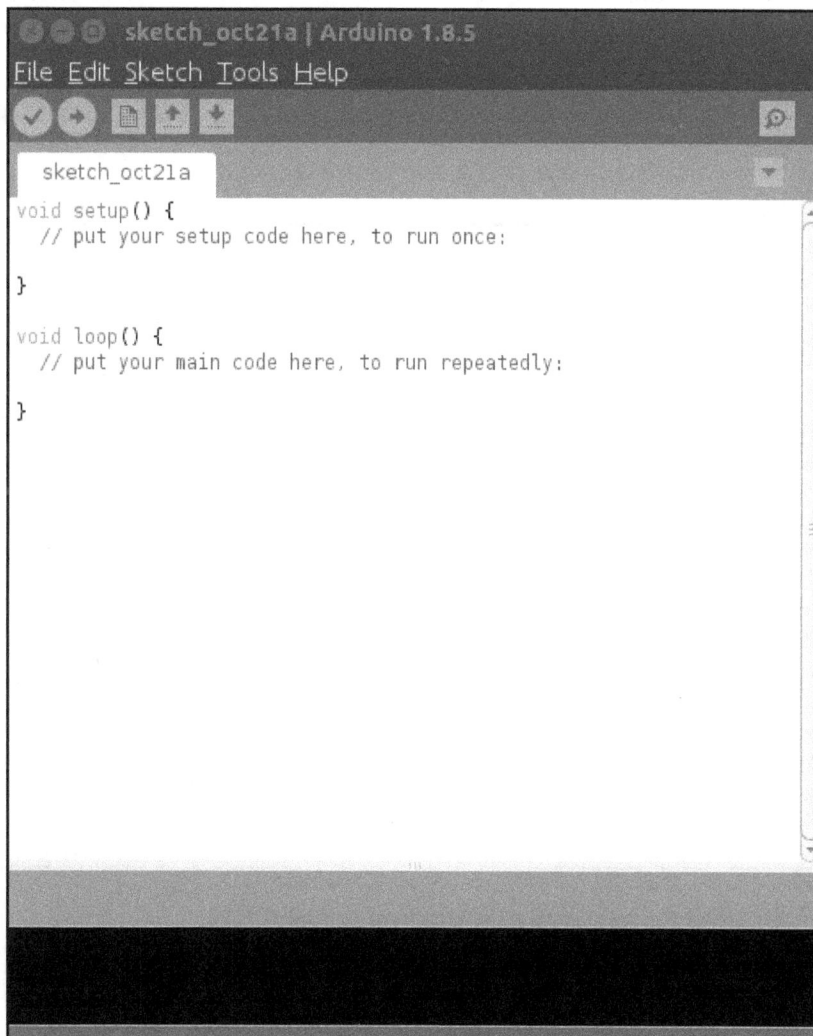

Figure 3: Arduino IDE

5. Go to **File** | **Preference** for configuring the sketchbook folder of Arduino. The Arduino IDE stores the sketches to this location. We created a folder called `Arduino1` in the user `home` folder and set this folder as the **Sketchbook location**:

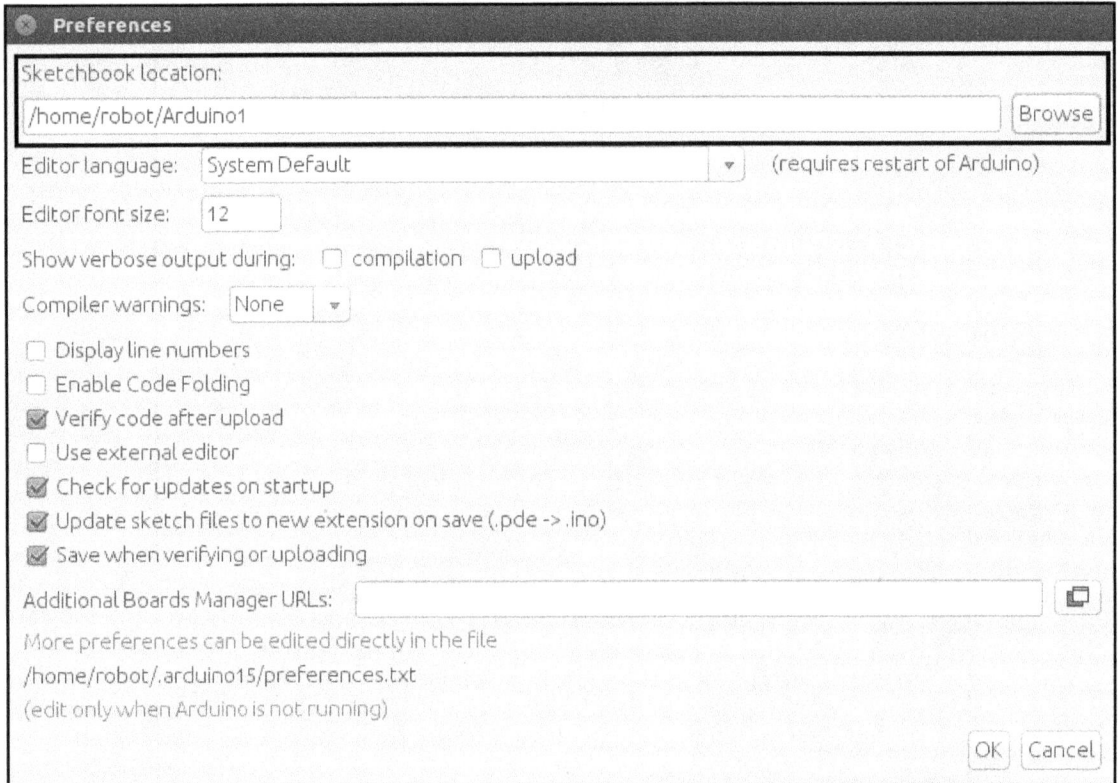

Figure 4: Preferences of Arduino IDE

We can see a folder called `libraries` inside the `Arduino1` folder. Switch to this folder, using the following command:

$ cd ~/Arduino1/libraries/

If there is no `libraries` folder, we can create a new one. After switching into this folder, we can generate `ros_lib` , using a script called `make_libraries.py`, which is present inside the `rosserial_arduino` package. `ros_lib` is the `rosserial_client` for Arduino, which provides the ROS client APIs inside an Arduino IDE environment:

$ rosrun rosserial_arduino make_libraries.py

`rosserial_arduino` is the ROS client for `arduino` , which can communicate using UART, and can publish topics, services, TF, and so on, like a ROS node. The `make_libraries.py` script will generate a wrapper of the ROS messages and services which are optimized for Arduino data types. These ROS messages and services will convert into Arduino C/C++ code equivalent, as shown next:

- Conversion of ROS messages:

    ros_package_name/msg/Test.msg --> ros_package_name::Test

- Conversion of ROS services:

    ros_package_name/srv/Foo.srv --> ros_package_name::Foo

For example, if we include `#include <std_msgs/UInt16.h>`, we can instantiate the `std_msgs::UInt16` number.

If the `make_libraries.py` script works fine, a folder called `ros_lib` will generate inside the `libraries` folder. Restart the Arduino IDE and we will see `ros_lib` examples as follows:

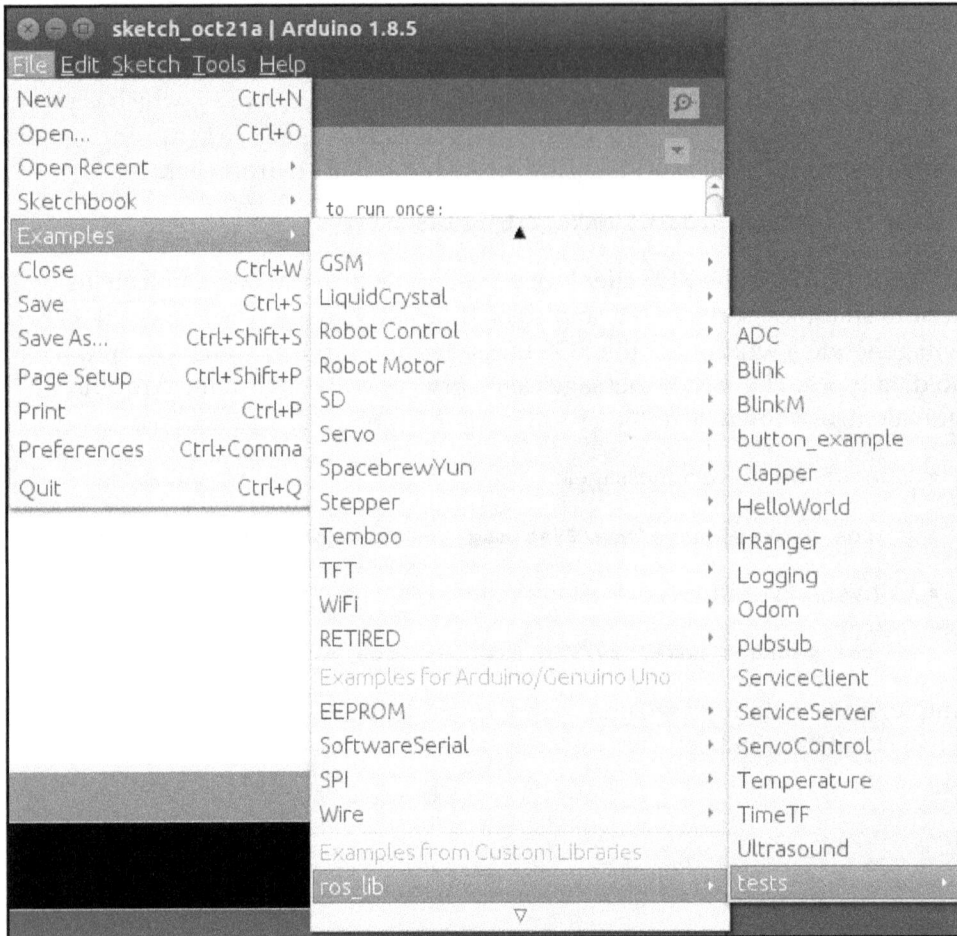

Figure 5: List of Arduino - ros_lib examples

We can take any example and make sure that it is building properly to ensure that the `ros_lib` APIs are working fine. The necessary APIs required for building ROS Arduino nodes are discussed next.

Understanding ROS node APIs in Arduino

The following is a basic structure of the ROS Arduino node. We can see the function of each line of code:

```
#include <ros.h>

ros::NodeHandle nh;

void setup() {
  nh.initNode();
}

void loop() {
  nh.spinOnce();
}
```

The creation of `NodeHandle` in Arduino is done using the following line of code:

```
ros::NodeHandle nh;
```

Note that `Nodehandle` should be declared before the `setup()` function, which will give a global scope to the `NodeHandle` instance called `nh`. The initialization of this node is done inside the `setup()` function:

```
nh.initNode();
```

The Arduino `setup()` function will execute only once when the device starts. Note that we can only create one node from a serial device.

Inside the `loop()` function, we have to use the following line of code to execute the ROS callback once:

```
nh.spinOnce();
```

We can create the `Subscriber` and `Publisher` objects in Arduino, like the other ROS client libraries. The following are the procedures for defining the subscriber and the publisher.

Here is how we define a subscriber object in Arduino:

```
ros::Subscriber<std_msgs::String> sub("talker", callback);
```

Here we define a subscriber which is subscribing a `String` message, where the callback is the callback function executing when a `String` message arrives on the talker topic. Given next is an example callback for handling the string data:

```
std_msgs::String str_msg;

ros::Publisher chatter("chatter", &str_msg);

void callback ( const std_msgs::String& msg){
  str_msg.data = msg.data;

  chatter.publish( &str_msg );

}
```

Note that the `callback()`, `Subscriber`, and `Publisher` definitions will be above the `setup()` function for getting the global scope. Here we are receiving `String` data, using `const std_msgs::String& msg`.

The following code shows how to define a publisher object in Arduino:

```
ros::Publisher chatter("chatter", &str_msg);
```

This next code shows how we publish the string message:

```
chatter.publish( &str_msg );
```

After defining the publisher and the subscriber, we have to initiate this inside the `setup()` function, using the following lines of code:

```
nh.advertise(chatter);
nh.subscribe(sub);
```

There are ROS APIs for logging from Arduino. The following are the different logging APIs supported:

```
nh.logdebug("Debug Statement");
nh.loginfo("Program info");
nh.logwarn("Warnings.);
nh.logerror("Errors..");
nh.logfatal("Fatalities!");
```

We can retrieve the current ROS time in Arduino using ROS built-in functions, such as time and duration.

- Current ROS time:

```
ros::Time begin = nh.now();
```

- Converting ROS time in seconds:

```
double secs = nh.now().toSec();
```

- Creating a duration in seconds:

```
ros::Duration ten_seconds(10, 0);
```

ROS - Arduino Publisher and Subscriber example

The first example using the Arduino and ROS interface is a chatter and talker interface. Users can send a String message to the talker topic and Arduino will publish the same message in a chatter topic. The following ROS node is implemented for Arduino, and we will discuss this example in detail:

```
#include <ros.h>
#include <std_msgs/String.h>

//Creating Nodehandle
ros::NodeHandle   nh;

//Declaring String variable
std_msgs::String str_msg;

//Defining Publisher
ros::Publisher chatter("chatter", &amp;str_msg);
//Defining callback
void callback ( const std_msgs::String&amp; msg){

  str_msg.data = msg.data;
  chatter.publish( &amp;str_msg );
}

//Defining Subscriber
ros::Subscriber<std_msgs::String> sub("talker", callback);


void setup()
```

```
{
  //Initializing node
  nh.initNode();
  //Start advertising and subscribing
  nh.advertise(chatter);
  nh.subscribe(sub);
}

void loop()
{
  nh.spinOnce();
  delay(3);
}
```

We can compile the preceding code and upload to the Arduino board. After uploading the code, select the desired Arduino board that we are using for this example and the device serial port of the Arduino IDE.

Go to **Tools** I **Boards** to select the board and **Tools** I **Port** to select the device port name of the board. We are using Arduino Mega for these examples.

After compiling and uploading the code, we can start the ROS bridge nodes in the PC that connects Arduino and the PC, using the following command. Ensure that Arduino is already connected to the PC before executing this command:

```
$ rosrun rosserial_python serial_node.py /dev/ttyACM0
```

In this case, we are running the `serial_node.py` on the port `/dev/ttyACM0`. We can search for the port name listing the contents of the `/dev` directory. Note that, to use this port, root permissions are needed. In this case, we could change the permissions using the following command in order to read and write data on the desired port:

```
$ sudo chmod 666 /dev/ttyACM0
```

We are using the `rosserial_python` node here as the ROS bridging node. We have to mention the device name and baud-rate as arguments. The default baud-rate of this communication is 57600. We can change the baud-rate according to our application and the usage of `serial_node.py` inside the `rosserial_python` package is given at `http://wiki.ros.org/rosserial_python`. If the communication between the ROS node and the Arduino node is correct, we will get the following message:

```
[INFO] [WallTime: 1438880620.972231] ROS Serial Python Node
[INFO] [WallTime: 1438880620.982245] Connecting to /dev/ttyACM0 at 57600 baud
[INFO] [WallTime: 1438880623.117417] Note: publish buffer size is 512 bytes
[INFO] [WallTime: 1438880623.118587] Setup publisher on chatter [std_msgs/String
]
[INFO] [WallTime: 1438880623.132048] Note: subscribe buffer size is 512 bytes
[INFO] [WallTime: 1438880623.132745] Setup subscriber on talker [std_msgs/String
```

Figure 6: Running the `rosserial_python` node

When `serial_node.py` starts running from the PC, it will send some serial data packets called query packets to get the number of topics, the topic names, and the types of topics which are received from the Arduino node. We have already seen the structure of serial packets that are being used for Arduino ROS communication. Given next is the structure of a query packet which is sent from `serial_node.py` to Arduino:

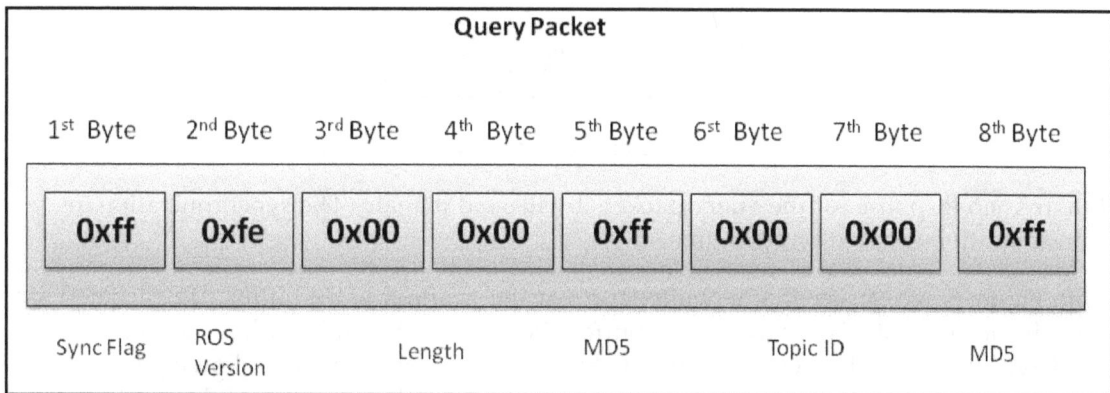

Query Packet							
1st Byte	2nd Byte	3rd Byte	4th Byte	5th Byte	6st Byte	7th Byte	8th Byte
0xff	0xfe	0x00	0x00	0xff	0x00	0x00	0xff
Sync Flag	ROS Version	Length		MD5	Topic ID		MD5

Figure 7: Structure of the query packet

The query topic contains fields such as Sync Flag, ROS version, length of the message, MD5 sum, Topic ID, and so on. When the query packet is received on the Arduino, it will reply with a topic info message that contains the topic name, type, length, topic data, and so on. The following is a typical response packet from Arduino:

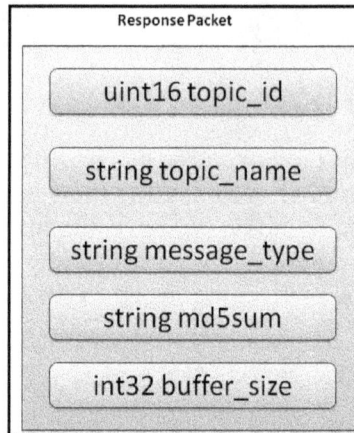

Figure 8: Structure of response packet

If there is no response for the query packet, it will send it again. The synchronization in communication is based on ROS time.

From Figure 6, we can see that when we run `serial_node.py`, the buffer size allocated for publish and subscribe is 512 bytes. The buffer allocation is dependent on the amount of RAM available on each microcontroller that we are working with. The following is a table showing the buffer allocation of each Arduino controller. We can override these settings by changing the `BUFFER_SIZE` macro inside `ros.h`.

AVR model	Buffer size	Publishers/Subscribers
ATMEGA 168	150 bytes	6/6
ATMEGA 328P	280 bytes	25/25
All others	512 bytes	25/25

There are also some limitations in the *float64* data type of ROS in Arduino. It will truncate to 32-bit. Also, when we use string data types, use the unsigned char pointer for saving memory.

After running `serial_node.py`, we will get the list of topics, using the following command:

```
$ rostopic list
```

We can see that topics such as `chatter` and `talker` are being generated. We can simply publish a message to the `talker` topic, using the following command:

```
$ rostopic pub -r 5 talker std_msgs/String "Hello World"
```

It will publish the `"Hello World"` message with a rate of 5.

We can echo the `chatter` topic, and we will get the same message as we published:

```
$ rostopic echo /chatter
```

Arduino-ROS, example - blink LED and push button

In this example, we can interface the LED and push button to Arduino and control using ROS. When the push button is pressed, the Arduino node sends a `True` value to a topic called pushed, and at the same time, it switches on the LED which is on the Arduino board.

The following shows the circuit for doing this example:

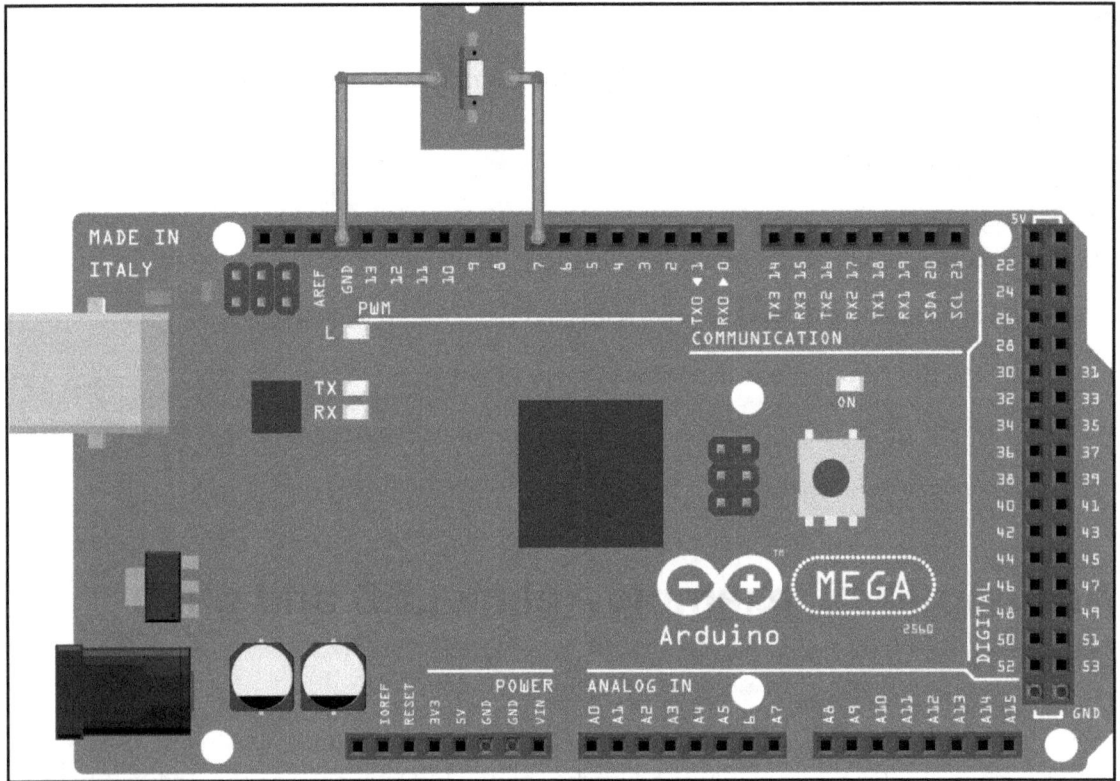

Figure 9: Interfacing the push button to Arduino

```
/*
 * Button Example for Rosserial
 */

#include <ros.h>
#include <std_msgs/Bool.h>

//Nodehandle
ros::NodeHandle nh;

//Boolean message for Push button
std_msgs::Bool pushed_msg;

//Defining Publisher in a topic called pushed
ros::Publisher pub_button("pushed", &pushed_msg);
```

```
//LED and Push button pin definitions
const int button_pin = 7;
const int led_pin = 13;

//Variables to handle debouncing
//https://www.arduino.cc/en/Tutorial/Debounce

bool last_reading;
long last_debounce_time=0;
long debounce_delay=50;
bool published = true;

void setup()
{
  nh.initNode();
  nh.advertise(pub_button);
  //initialize an LED output pin
  //and a input pin for our push button
  pinMode(led_pin, OUTPUT);
  pinMode(button_pin, INPUT);
  //Enable the pullup resistor on the button
  digitalWrite(button_pin, HIGH);
  //The button is a normally button
  last_reading = ! digitalRead(button_pin);
}

void loop()
{
  bool reading = ! digitalRead(button_pin);
  if (last_reading!= reading){
      last_debounce_time = millis();
      published = false;
  }
  //if the button value has not changed for the debounce delay, we know its
stable

  if ( !published &amp;&amp; (millis() - last_debounce_time)  >
debounce_delay) {
    digitalWrite(led_pin, reading);
    pushed_msg.data = reading;
    pub_button.publish(&amp;pushed_msg);
    published = true;
  }

  last_reading = reading;
  nh.spinOnce();
}
```

The preceding code handles the key debouncing and changes the button state only after the button release. The preceding code can upload to Arduino and can interface to ROS, using the following commands:

- Start `roscore`:

  ```
  $ roscore
  ```

- Start `serial_node.py`:

  ```
  $ rosrun roserial_python serial_node.py /dev/ttyACM0
  ```

We can see the button press event by echoing the topic pushed:

```
$ rostopic echo pushed
```

We will get following values when a button is pressed:

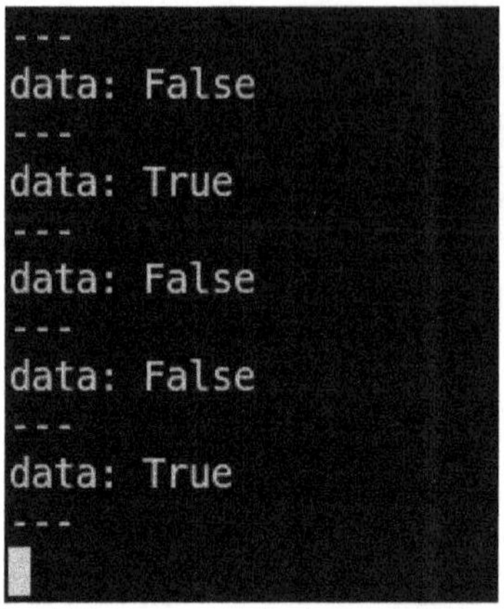

Figure 10: Output of Arduino pushing button

Arduino-ROS, example - Accelerometer ADXL 335

In this example, we are interfacing Accelerometer ADXL 335 to Arduino Mega through ADC pins and plotting the values using the ROS tool called `rqt_plot`.

The following image shows the circuit of the connection between ADLX 335 and Arduino:

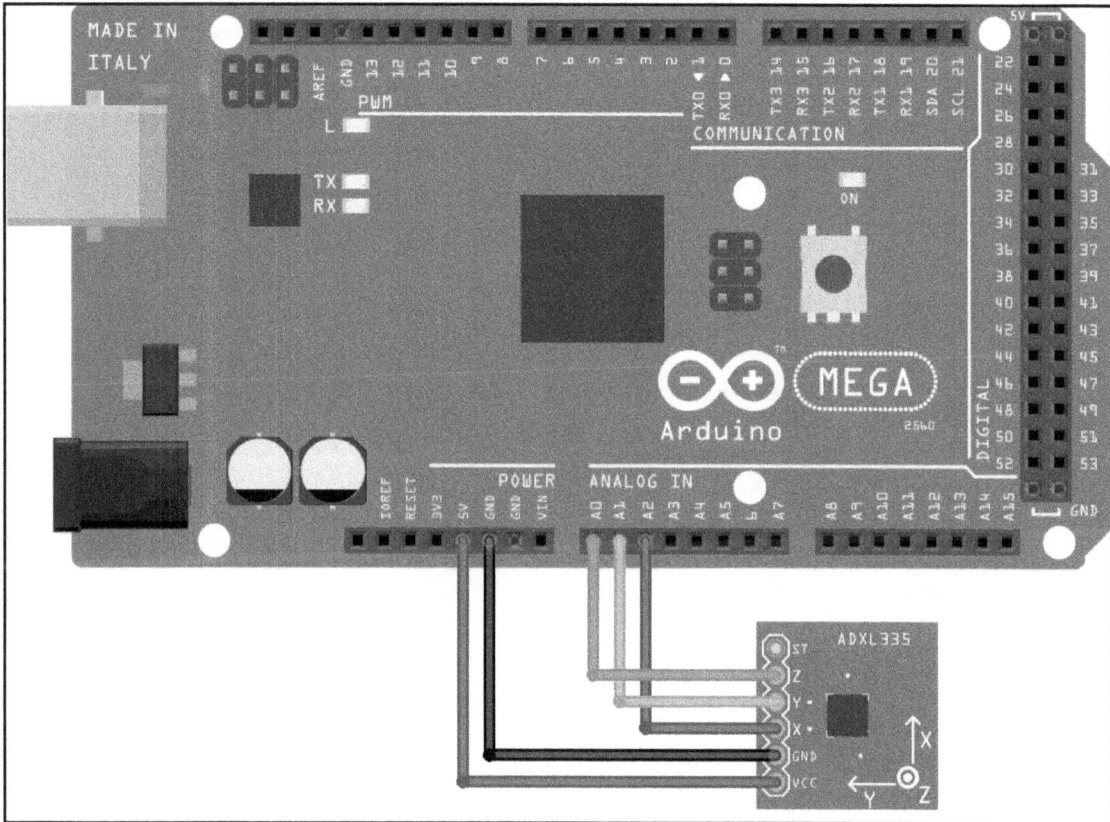

Figure 11: Interfacing Arduino - ADXL 335

ADLX 335 is an analog accelerometer. We can simply connect to the ADC port and read the digital value. The following is the embedded code to interface ADLX 335 via Arduino ADC:

```
#if (ARDUINO >= 100)
 #include <Arduino.h>
#else
 #include <WProgram.h>
#endif
#include <ros.h>
#include <rosserial_arduino/Adc.h>

const int xpin = A2;                    // x-axis of the accelerometer
const int ypin = A1;                    // y-axis
const int zpin = A0;                    // z-axis (only on 3-axis models)
```

```
ros::NodeHandle nh;

//Creating an adc message
rosserial_arduino::Adc adc_msg;

ros::Publisher pub("adc", &amp;adc_msg);

void setup()
{

  nh.initNode();

  nh.advertise(pub);

}

//We average the analog reading to eliminate some of the noise
int averageAnalog(int pin){
  int v=0;
  for(int i=0; i<4; i++) v+= analogRead(pin);
  return v/4;
}


void loop()
{

//Inserting ADC values to ADC message
  adc_msg.adc0 = averageAnalog(xpin);
  adc_msg.adc1 = averageAnalog(ypin);
  adc_msg.adc2 = averageAnalog(zpin);

  pub.publish(&amp;adc_msg);

  nh.spinOnce();

  delay(10);

}
```

The preceding code will publish the ADC values of *X*, *Y*, and *Z* axes in a topic called /adc. The code uses the rosserial_arduino::Adc message to handle the ADC value. We can plot the values using the rqt_plot tool.

The following is the command to plot the three axes values in a single plot:

```
$ rqt_plot adc/adc0 adc/adc1 adc/adc2
```

Next is a screenshot of the plot of the three channels of ADC:

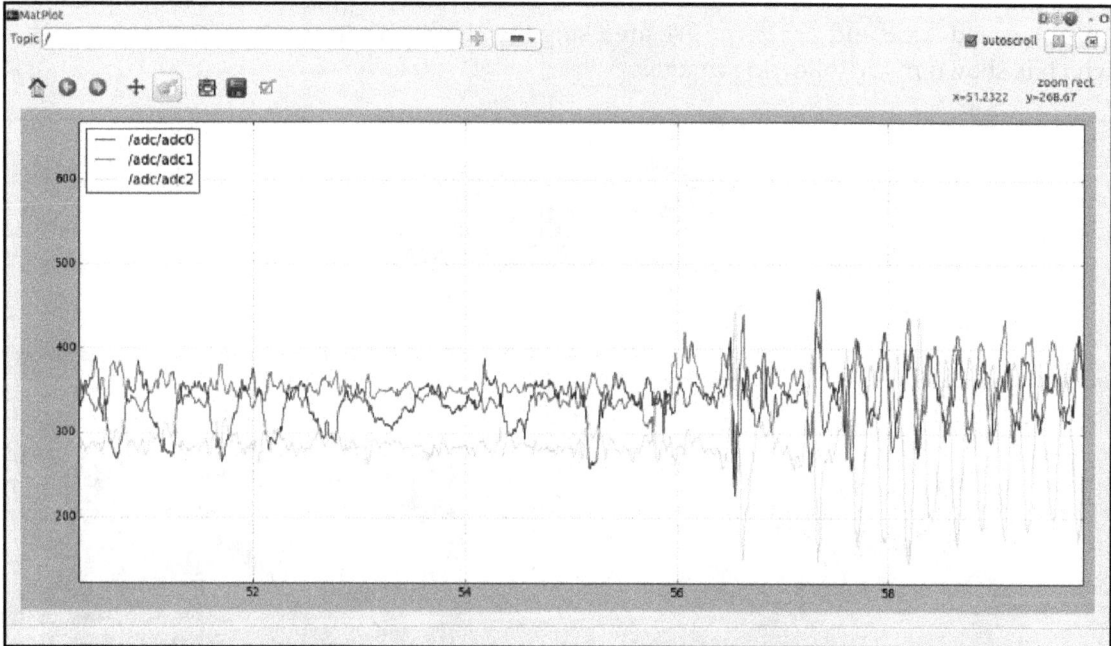

Figure 12: Plotting ADXL 335 values using rqt_plot

Arduino-ROS, example - ultrasonic distance sensor

One of the useful sensors in robots are the range sensors. One of the cheapest range sensors is the ultrasonic distance sensor. The ultrasonic sensor has two pins for handling input and output, called `Echo` and `Trigger`. We are using the HC-SR04 ultrasonic distance sensor, which is shown in the following image:

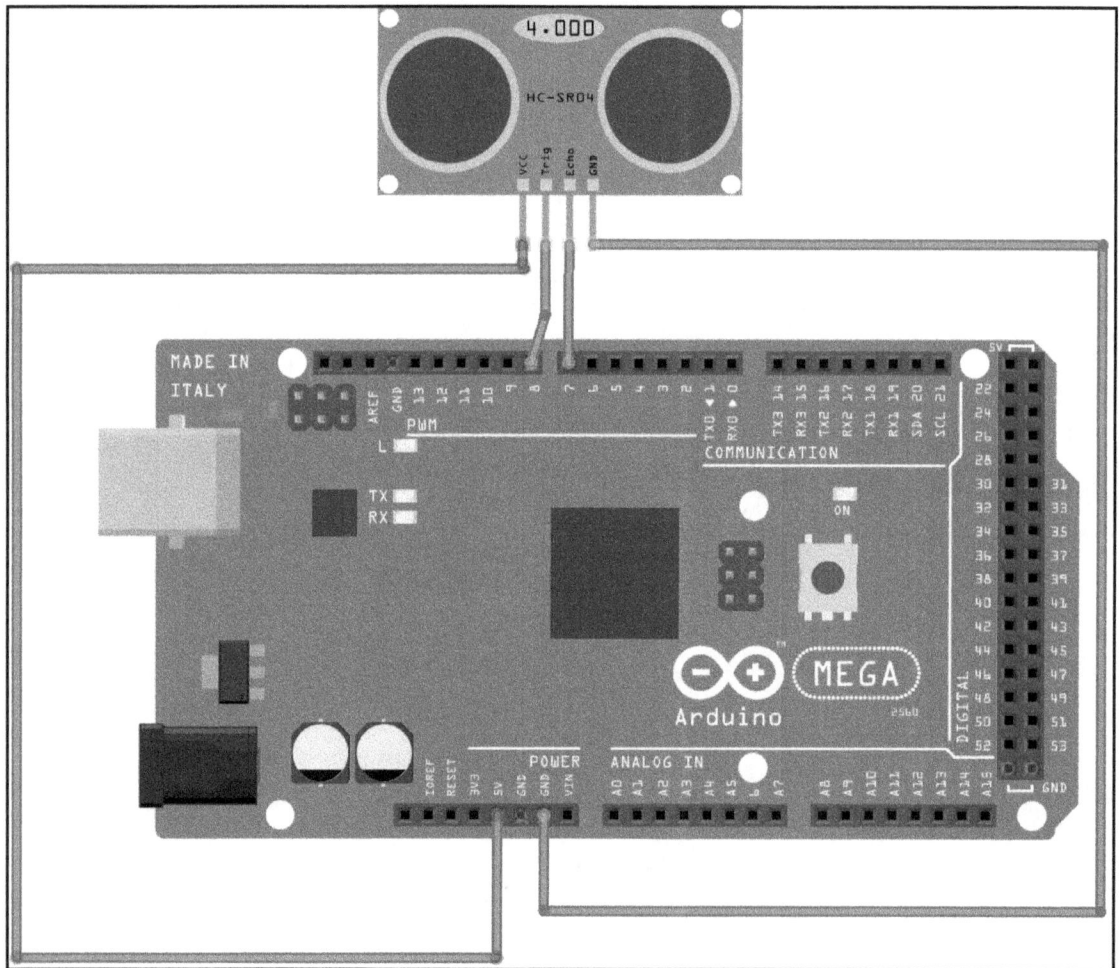

Figure 13: Plotting ADXL 335 values using rqt_plot

The ultrasonic sound sensor contains two sections: one is the transmitter and the other is the receiver. The ultrasonic distance sensor works like this: when a trigger pulse of a short duration is applied to the trigger pin of the ultrasonic sensors, the ultrasonic transmitter sends the sound signals to the robot environment. The sound signal sent from the transmitter hits on some obstacles and is reflected to the sensor. The reflected sound waves are collected by the ultrasonic receiver, generating an output signal which has a relation to the time required to receive the reflected sound signals.

Equations to find distance using the ultrasonic range sensor

The following are the equations used to compute the distance from an ultrasonic range sensor to an obstacle:

*Distance = Speed * Time/2*

Speed of sound at sea level = 343 m/s or 34,300 cm/s

*Thus, Distance = 17,150 * Time (unit cm)*

We can compute the distance to the obstacle using the pulse duration of the output. The following is the code to work with the ultrasonic sound sensor and send a value through the ultrasound topic using the range message definition in ROS:

```
#include <ros.h>
#include <ros/time.h>
#include <sensor_msgs/Range.h>

ros::NodeHandle   nh;

#define echoPin 7 // Echo Pin
#define trigPin 8 // Trigger Pin

int maximumRange = 200; // Maximum range needed
int minimumRange = 0; // Minimum range needed
long duration, distance; // Duration used to calculate distance

sensor_msgs::Range range_msg;
ros::Publisher pub_range( "/ultrasound", &amp;range_msg);


char frameid[] = "/ultrasound";
```

```
void setup() {
  nh.initNode();
  nh.advertise(pub_range);
  range_msg.radiation_type = sensor_msgs::Range::ULTRASOUND;
  range_msg.header.frame_id =  frameid;
  range_msg.field_of_view = 0.1;   // fake
  range_msg.min_range = 0.0;
  range_msg.max_range = 60;
  pinMode(trigPin, OUTPUT);
  pinMode(echoPin, INPUT);
}

float getRange_Ultrasound(){

  int val = 0;

 for(int i=0; i<4; i++) {
 digitalWrite(trigPin, LOW);
 delayMicroseconds(2);

 digitalWrite(trigPin, HIGH);
 delayMicroseconds(10);
 digitalWrite(trigPin, LOW);
 duration = pulseIn(echoPin, HIGH);
 //Calculate the distance (in cm) based on the speed of sound.
  val += duration;
 }
 return val / 232.8 ;
}
long range_time;

void loop() {
/* The following trigPin/echoPin cycle is used to determine the
 distance of the nearest object by bouncing soundwaves off of it. */

   if ( millis() >= range_time ){
    int r =0;

    range_msg.range = getRange_Ultrasound();
    range_msg.header.stamp = nh.now();
    pub_range.publish(&amp;range_msg);
    range_time =  millis() + 50;
  }
  nh.spinOnce();
 delay(50);
}
```

We can plot the distance value, using the following commands:

- Start `roscore`:

  $ roscore

- Start `serial_node.py`:

  $ rosrun rosserial_python serial_node.py /dev/ttyACM0

- Plot values using `rqt_plot`:

  $ rqt_plot /ultrasound

As seen in the screenshot below, the center line indicates the current distance (`range`) from the sensor. The upper line is the `max_range` and line below is the `min_range`.

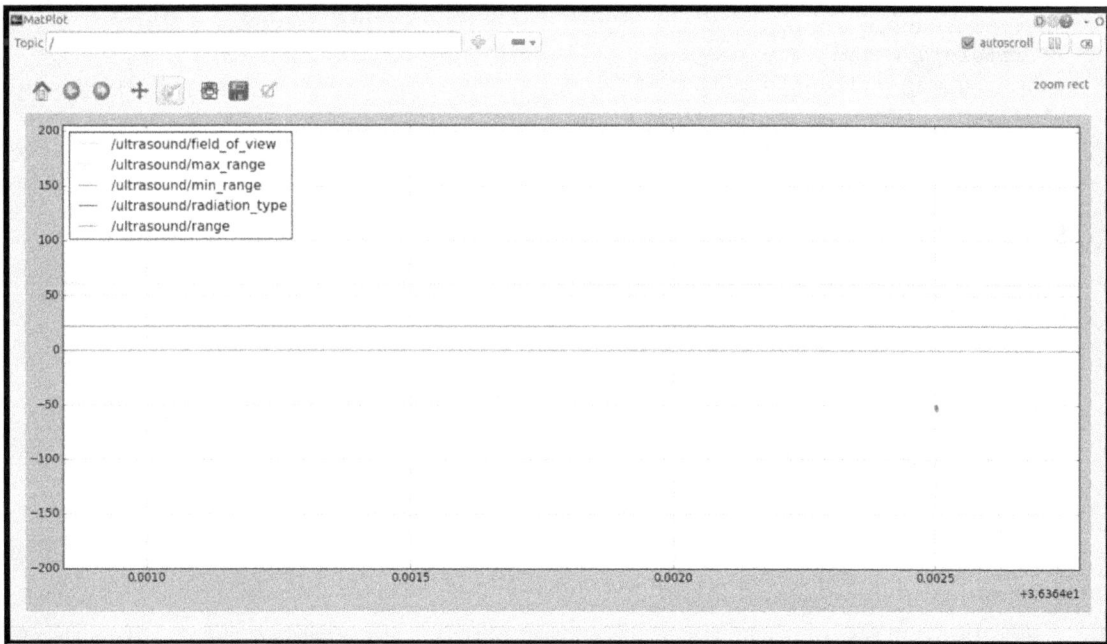

Figure 14: Plotting ultrasonic sound sensor distance value

Arduino-ROS example - Odometry Publisher

In this example, we will see how to send an odom message from an Arduino node to a PC. This example can be used in a robot for computing odom and sending to the ROS Navigation stack as the input. The motor encoders can be used for computing odom and can transmit to a PC. In this example, we will see how to send odom for a robot which is moving in a circle, without taking the motor encoder values:

```
/*
 * rosserial Planar Odometry Example
 */

#include <ros.h>
#include <ros/time.h>
#include <tf/tf.h>
#include <tf/transform_broadcaster.h>

ros::NodeHandle  nh;
//Transform broadcaster object
geometry_msgs::TransformStamped t;
tf::TransformBroadcaster broadcaster;

double x = 1.0;
double y = 0.0;
double theta = 1.57;

char base_link[] = "/base_link";
char odom[] = "/odom";

void setup()
{
  nh.initNode();
  broadcaster.init(nh);
}

void loop()
{
  // drive in a circle
  double dx = 0.2;
  double dtheta = 0.18;

  x += cos(theta)*dx*0.1;
  y += sin(theta)*dx*0.1;
  theta += dtheta*0.1;

  if(theta > 3.14)
```

```
    theta=-3.14;
// tf odom->base_link
t.header.frame_id = odom;
t.child_frame_id = base_link;
t.transform.translation.x = x;
t.transform.translation.y = y;
t.transform.rotation = tf::createQuaternionFromYaw(theta);
t.header.stamp = nh.now();
broadcaster.sendTransform(t);
nh.spinOnce();
delay(10);
}
```

After uploading the code, run `roscore` and `rosserial_node.py`. We can view `tf` and `odom` in RViz. Open RViz and view `tf`, as shown next. We will see the `odom` pointer moving in a circle on RViz, as follows:

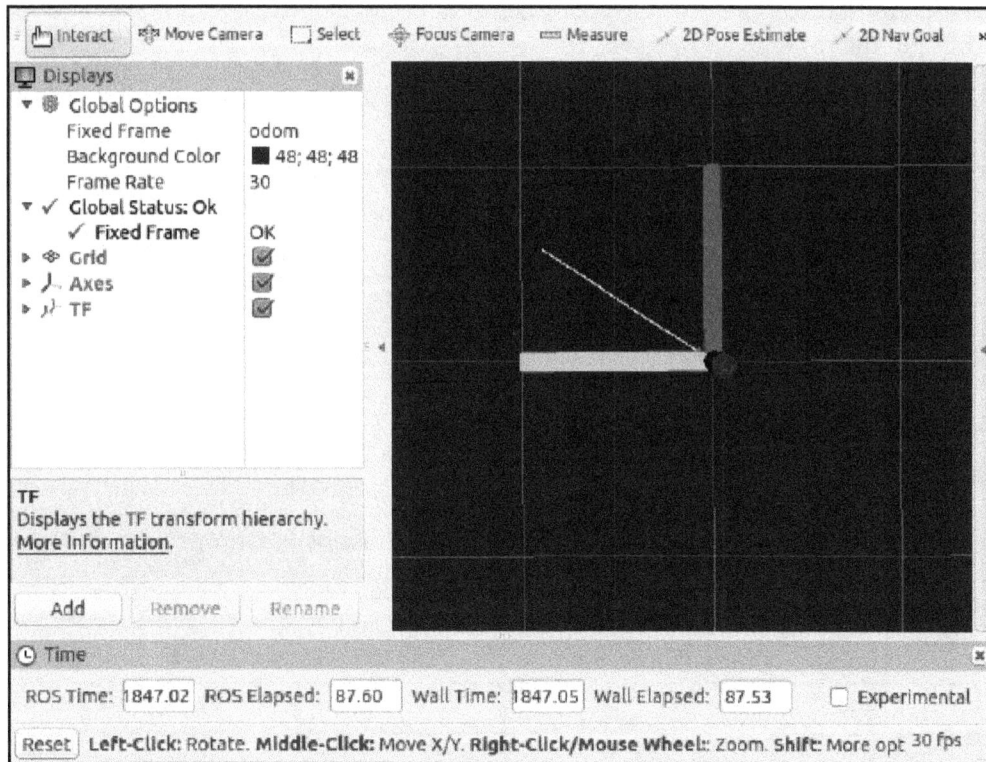

Figure 15: Visualizing odom data from Arduino

Interfacing non-Arduino boards to ROS

Arduino boards are commonly used boards in robots, but what happens if we want a board that is more powerful than Arduino? In such a case, we may want to write our own driver for the board, which can convert the serial messages into topics.

We will look at the interfacing of a non-Arduino board called *Tiva C Launchpad* to ROS, using a Python driver node, in Chapter 11: *Building and Interfacing Differential Drive Mobile Robot Hardware in ROS*. This chapter is about interfacing a real mobile robot to ROS, and the robot using the *Tiva C* Launchpad board for its operation.

Setting ROS on Odroid-XU4 and Raspberry Pi 2

Odroid-XU4 and Raspberry Pi2 are single board computers which have a low form factor the size of a credit card. These single board computers can be installed in robots and we can install ROS on them.

The main specifications comparison of Odroid-XU4 and Raspberry Pi2 is shown next:

Device	Odroid-XU4	Raspberry Pi 2
CPU	2.0 GHz Quad core ARM Cortex-A15 CPU from Samsung	900 MHz quad core ARM Cortex A7 CPU from Broadcom
GPU	Mali-T628 MP6 GPU	VideoCore IV
Memory	2 GB	1 GB
Storage	SD card slot or eMMC module	SD card slot
Connectivity	2 x USB 3.0, 1 x USB 2.0, micro HDMI, Gigabit Ethernet	4 x USB, HDMI, Ethernet, 3.5 mm audio jack
OS	Android, Ubuntu/Linux	Raspbian, Ubuntu/Linux, Windows 10
Connectors	GPIO, SPI, I2C, RTC (Real Time Clock) backup battery connector	Camera interface (CSI), GPIO, SPI, I2C, JTAG
Price	$59	$35

The following is an image of the Odroid-XU4 board:

Figure 16: Odroid-XU4 board

The Odroid board is manufactured by a company called **Hard Kernel**. The official web page of the Odroid-XU4 board is at `http://www.hardkernel.com/main/products/prdt_info.php?g_code=G143452239825`.

Odroid-XU4 is the most powerful board of the Odroid family. There are cheaper and lower performance boards as well, such as Odroid-C1+ and C2. All these boards support ROS. One of the popular single board computers is Raspberry Pi. The Raspberry Pi boards are manufactured by the Raspberry Pi Foundation, which is based in the UK (visit `https://www.raspberrypi.org`).

The following is an image of the Raspberry Pi 2 board:

Figure 17: The Raspberry Pi 2 board

We can install Ubuntu and Android on Odroid. There are also unofficial distributions of Linux, such as Debian mini, Kali Linux, Arch Linux, and Fedora, and support libraries, such as ROS, OpenCV, PCL, and so on. For getting ROS on Odroid, we can either install a fresh Ubuntu and install ROS manually like a standard desktop PC, or directly download the unofficial Ubuntu distribution for Odroid with ROS already installed.

The image for Ubuntu 16.04 for Odroid boards can be downloaded from `http://de.eu.odroid.in/ubuntu_16.04lts/`. You can download the desired kernel version for the Odroid-XU4 board (for example, ubuntu-16.04-mate-odroid-xu4-20170731.img.xz). This file contains pre-installed images of Ubuntu.

The list of the other operating systems supported on Odroid-XU4 is given on the wiki page at `http://odroid.com/dokuwiki/doku.php?id=en:odroid-xu4`, while the Raspberry Pi 2 official OS images are given at `https://www.raspberrypi.org/downloads/`.

The official OSes supported by the Raspberry Pi Foundation are Raspbian and Ubuntu. There are unofficial images based on these OSes which have ROS pre-installed on them. In this book, we are using the Raspbian Jessie images (`https://www.raspberrypi.org/downloads/`) with ROS installed, following the ROS wiki page for the installation: `http://wiki.ros.org/ROSberryPi/Installing%20ROS%20Kinetic%20on%20the%20Raspberry%20Pi`.

How to install an OS image to Odroid-XU4 and Raspberry Pi 2

We can download the Ubuntu image for Odroid and Raspbian Jessie image for Raspberry Pi 2 and can install to a micro SD card, preferably 16 GB. Format the micro SD card in the FAT32 filesystem, or we can use the SD card adapter or the USB-memory card reader for connecting to a PC.

We can either install the OS in Windows or in Linux. The procedure for installing the OS on these boards follows.

Installation in Windows

In Windows, there is a tool called **Win32diskimage** which is designed specifically for Odroid. You can download the tool from `http://dn.odroid.com/DiskImager_ODROID/Win32DiskImager-odroid-v1.3.zip`.

Run **Win32 Disk Imager** with the Administrator privilege. Select the downloaded image, select the memory card drive, and write the image to the drive.

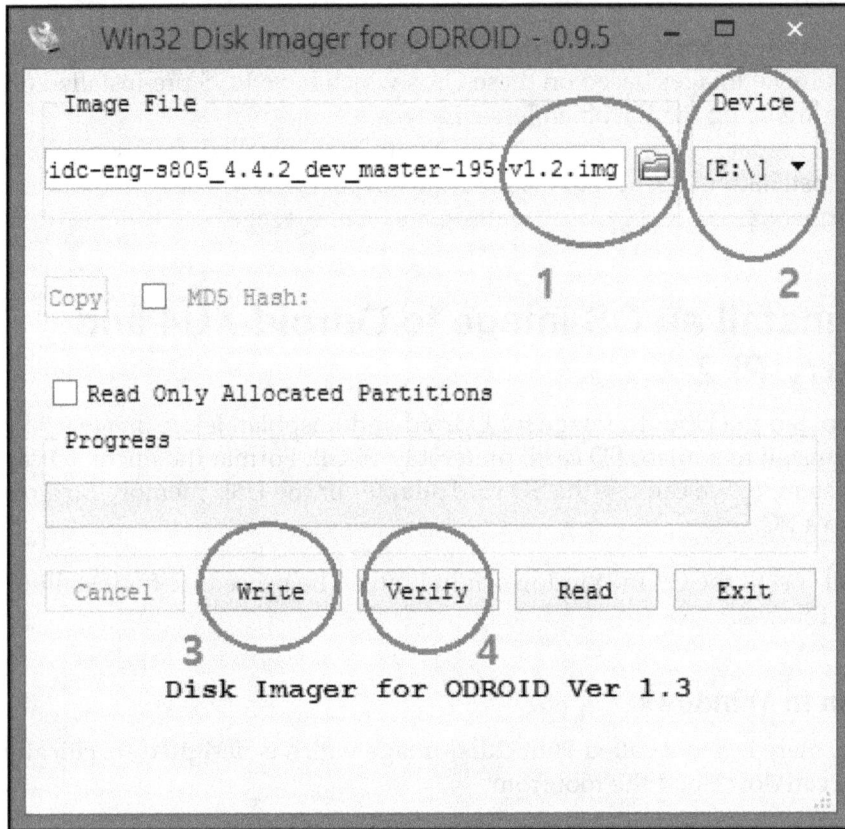

Figure 18: Win32 Disk Imager for Odroid

After completing this wizard, we can put the micro SD card in Odroid and boot up the OS with ROS support. The same tool can be used for Raspbian installation in Raspberry Pi 2. We can use the actual version of Win32 Disk Imager for writing Raspbian to a micro SD card from the following link:

http://sourceforge.net/projects/win32diskimager/.

Installation in Linux

In Linux, there is a tool called **disk dump** (**dd**). This tool helps to copy the content of the image to the SD card. *dd* is a command line tool which is available in all the Ubuntu/Linux-based OSes. Insert the micro SD card, format to the FAT32 filesystem, and use the command mentioned later to write an image to the micro SD card.

In the *dd* tool, there is no progress bar to indicate the copy progress. To get the progress bar, we can install a pipe viewer tool called *pv*:

```
$ sudo apt-get install pv
```

After installing *pv*, we can use the following command to install the image file to the micro SD card. Note that you should have the OS image in the same path of the Terminal, and note the micro SD card device name; for example, mmcblk0, sdb, sdd, and so on. You will get the device name using the dmesg command:

```
$ dd bs=4M if=image_name.img | pv | sudo dd of=/dev/mmcblk0
```

image_name.img is the image name and the device name is /dev/mmcblk0. bs=4M indicates the block size. If the block size is 4M, *dd* will read 4 megabytes from the image and write 4 megabytes to the device. After completing the operation, we can send it to Odroid and Raspberry Pi and boot the OS.

Connecting to Odroid-XU4 and Raspberry Pi 2 from a PC

We can work with Odroid-XU4 and Raspberry Pi 2 by connecting to the HDMI display port and connecting the keyboard and mouse to the USB like a normal PC. This is the simplest way of working with Odroid and Raspberry Pi.

In most of the projects, the boards will be placed on the robot, so we can't connect the display and the keyboards to it. There are several methods for connecting these boards to the PC. It will be good if we can connect the internet to these boards too. The following methods can connect the internet to these boards, and, at the same time, we can remotely connect via the SSH protocol:

- **Remote connection using Wi-Fi router and Wi-Fi dongle through SSH**: In this method, we need a Wi-Fi router with internet connectivity and a Wi-Fi dongle in the board for getting the Wi-Fi support. Both the PC and board will connect to the same network, so each will have an IP address and can communicate using that address.

- **Direct connection using an Ethernet hotspot**: We can share the internet connection and communicate using SSH via Dnsmasq, a free software DNS forwarder and DHCP server using low system resources. Using this tool, we can tether the Wi-Fi internet connection of the laptop to the Ethernet and we can connect the board to the Ethernet port of the PC. This kind of communication can be used for robots which are static in operation.

The first method is very easy to configure; it's like connecting two PCs on the same network. The second method is a direct connection of the board to the laptop through the Ethernet. This method can be used when the robot is not moving. In this method, the board and the laptop can communicate via SSH at the same time and can share Internet access too. We are using this method in this chapter for working with ROS.

Configuring an Ethernet hotspot for Odroid-XU4 and Raspberry Pi 2

The procedure for creating an Ethernet hotspot in Ubuntu and sharing Wi-Fi internet through this connection follows.

Go to **Edit Connections...** from the network settings and click on **Add** to add a new connection, as shown next:

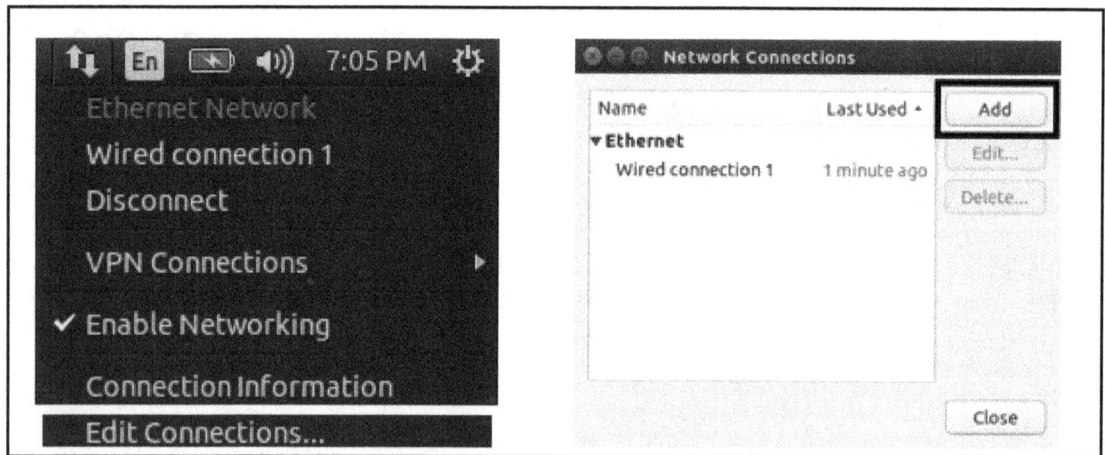

Figure 19: Configuring a network connection in Ubuntu

Create an **Ethernet** connection and in the **IPv4** setting, change the method to **Shared to Other computers** , and give the connection name as **Share**, as shown next:

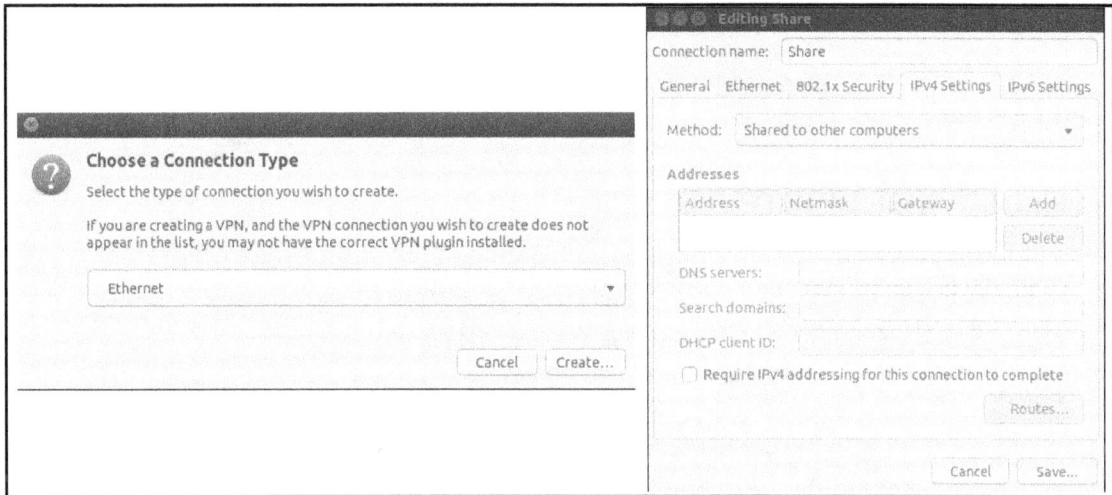

Figure 20: Creating a new connection for sharing through the Ethernet

Plug in the micro SD card, power up the Odroid or Raspberry Pi, and connect the Ethernet port from the board to the PC. When the board boots up, we will see that the shared network is automatically connected to the board.

We can communicate with the board using the following commands:

- In Odroid:

```
$ ssh odroid@ip_address
password is odroid
```

- In Raspberry Pi 2:

```
$ ssh pi@ip_adress
password is raspberry
```

After doing SSH into the board, we can launch `roscore` and most of the ROS commands on the board like our PC. We will look at two examples using these boards. One is for blinking an LED, and the other is for handling a push button. The library we are using for handling the GPIO pins of Odroid and Raspberry is called **Wiring Pi**.

Odroid and Raspberry Pi have the same pin layout and most of the Raspberry Pi GPIO libraries are ported to Odroid, which will make the programming easier. One of the libraries we are using in this chapter for GPIO programming is Wiring Pi. Wiring Pi is based on C++ APIs, which can access the board GPIO using C++ APIs.

In the following sections, we will look at the instructions for installing Wiring Pi on Odroid and Raspberry 2.

Installing Wiring Pi on Odroid-XU4

The following procedure can be used to install Wiring Pi on Odroid-XU4. This is a customized version of Wiring Pi, which is used in Raspberry Pi 2:

```
$ git clone https://github.com/hardkernel/wiringPi.git
$ cd wiringPi
$ sudo ./build
```

Odroid-XU4 has 42 pins placed on two different connectors, CON10 and CON11 respectively, as show in the following image:

Figure 21: The CON10 and CON11 headers on Odroid-XU4

The Wiring Pi pin out of Odroid-XU4 (CON10) for bot connectors is given next:

ODROID XU4 Pin Layout (CON10)

WiringPi GPIO#	Name(GPIO#)	Label	HEADER		Label	Name(GPIO#)	WiringPi GPIO#
		5V0	1	2	GND		
	ADC_0.AIN0	AIN0	3	4	#173	UART0_RTS	1
0	UART_CTS	#174	5	6	#171	UART0_RxD	16
12	MOSI_SPI1	#192	7	8	#172	UART0_TxD	15
13	MISO_SPI1	#191	9	10	#189	CLK_SPI1	14
10	CSN_SPI1	#190	11	12	PRWON		
2	GPIO	#21	13	14	#210	SCL.i2c	9
7	GPIO	#18	15	16	#209	SDA.i2c	8
3	GPIO	#22	17	18	#19	GPIO	4
22	GPIO	#30	19	20	#28	GPIO	21
26	GPIO	#29	21	22	#31	GPIO	23
	ADC_0.AIN3	AIN3	23	24	#25	GPIO	11
5	SCL_i2c	#23	25	26	#24	GPIO	6
27	SDA_i2c	#33	27	28	GND	GND	
		1V8	29	30	GND	GND	

Figure 22: Pin out of Odroid-XU4, CON10

The Wiring Pi pin out of Odroid-XU4 (CON11) for bot connectors is given next:

ODROID XU4 Pin Layout (CON11)

WiringPi GPIO#	Name(GPIO#)	Label	HEADER		Label	Name(GPIO#)	WiringPi GPIO#
		5V0	1	2	GND		
		1V8	3	4	#173	SDA_i2c_5	30
	GPIO	#34	5	6	#171	SCL_i2c_5	31
	SCLK_i2s_0	#225	7	8	#172	GND	
	CDCLK_i2s_0	#226	9	10	#189	SDO_i2s_0	
	LRCK_i2s_0	#227	11	12	PRWON	SDI_i2s_0	

Figure 23: Pin out of Odroid-XU4, CON11

Installing Wiring Pi on Raspberry Pi 2

The following procedure can be used to install Wiring Pi on Raspberry Pi 2:

```
$ git clone git clone git://git.drogon.net/wiringPi
$ cd wiringPi
$ sudo ./build
```

The pin out of Raspberry Pi 2 and Wiring Pi is shown next:

P1: The Main GPIO connector						
WiringPi Pin	BCM GPIO	Name	Header		Name	BCM GPIO	WiringPi Pin
		3.3v	1	2	5v		
8	Rv1:0 - Rv2:2	SDA	3	4	5v		
9	Rv1:1 - Rv2:3	SCL	5	6	0v		
7	4	GPIO7	7	8	TXD	14	15
		0v	9	10	RXD	15	16
0	17	GPIO0	11	12	GPIO1	18	1
2	Rv1:21 - Rv2:27	GPIO2	13	14	0v		
3	22	GPIO3	15	16	GPIO4	23	4
		3.3v	17	18	GPIO5	24	5
12	10	MOSI	19	20	0v		
13	9	MISO	21	22	GPIO6	25	6
14	11	SCLK	23	24	CE0	8	10
		0v	25	26	CE1	7	11
WiringPi Pin	BCM GPIO	Name	Header		Name	BCM GPIO	WiringPi Pin

P5: Secondary GPIO connector (Rev. 2 Pi only)						
WiringPi Pin	BCM GPIO	Name	Header		Name	BCM GPIO	WiringPi Pin
		5v	1	2	3.3v		
17	28	GPIO8	3	4	GPIO9	29	18
19	30	GPIO10	5	6	GPIO11	31	20
		0v	7	8	0v		
WiringPi Pin	BCM GPIO	Name	Header		Name	BCM GPIO	WiringPi Pin

Figure 24: Pin out of Raspberry Pi 2

The following are the ROS examples for Raspberry Pi 2.

Blinking LED using ROS on Raspberry Pi 2

This is a basic LED example which can blink the LED connected to the first pin of Wiring Pi, that is the 12th pin on the board. The LED cathode is connected to the GND pin and 12th pin as an anode. The following image shows the circuit of Raspberry Pi with an LED:

Figure 25: Blinking an LED using Raspberry Pi 2

We can create the example ROS package, using the following command:

```
$ catkin_create_pkg ros_wiring_example roscpp std_msgs
```

You will get the existing package from the `ros_wiring_examples` folder.

Create a `src` folder and create the following code called `blink.cpp` inside the `src` folder:

```
#include "ros/ros.h"
#include "std_msgs/Bool.h"
#include <iostream>

//Wiring Pi header
#include "wiringPi.h"

//Wiring PI first pin

#define LED 1

//Callback to blink the LED according to the topic value
void blink_callback(const std_msgs::Bool::ConstPtr&amp; msg)
{

 if(msg->data == 1){
  digitalWrite (LED, HIGH) ;
  ROS_INFO("LED ON");
  }
 if(msg->data == 0){
   digitalWrite (LED, LOW) ;
  ROS_INFO("LED OFF");
    }
}
int main(int argc, char** argv)
{
  ros::init(argc, argv,"blink_led");
  ROS_INFO("Started Raspberry Blink Node");
   //Setting WiringPi
  wiringPiSetup ();  //Setting LED pin as output
  pinMode(LED, OUTPUT);
  ros::NodeHandle n;
  ros::Subscriber sub = n.subscribe("led_blink",10,blink_callback);
  ros::spin();
}
```

This code will subscribe a topic called `led_blink`, which is a `Boolean` type. If we publish 1 to this topic, it will switch on the LED. If we publish 0, the LED will turn off.

Push button + blink LED using ROS on Raspberry Pi 2

The next example is handling input from a button. When we press the button, the code will publish to the `led_blink` topic and blink the LED. When the switch is off, the LED will also be `OFF`. The LED is connected to the 12th pin and GND, and the button is connected to the 11th pin and GND. The following image shows the circuit of this example. The circuit is also the same for Odroid:

Figure 26: LED + button in Raspberry Pi 2

The code for interfacing the LED and button is given next. The code can be saved with the name button.cpp inside the src folder:

```cpp
#include "ros/ros.h"
#include "std_msgs/Bool.h"

#include <iostream>
#include "wiringPi.h"

//Wiring PI 1
#define BUTTON 0
#define LED 1


void blink_callback(const std_msgs::Bool::ConstPtr&amp; msg)
{
 if(msg->data == 1){

   digitalWrite (LED, HIGH) ;
  ROS_INFO("LED ON");
  }

 if(msg->data == 0){
   digitalWrite (LED, LOW) ;
  ROS_INFO("LED OFF");
  }

}

int main(int argc, char** argv)
{

  ros::init(argc, argv,"button_led");
  ROS_INFO("Started Raspberry Button Blink Node");


  wiringPiSetup ();

  pinMode(LED, OUTPUT);
  pinMode(BUTTON, INPUT);
    pullUpDnControl(BUTTON, PUD_UP); // Enable pull-up resistor on button


  ros::NodeHandle n;
  ros::Rate loop_rate(10);

  ros::Subscriber sub = n.subscribe("led_blink",10,blink_callback);
```

```
    ros::Publisher chatter_pub = n.advertise<std_msgs::Bool>("led_blink",
10);


  std_msgs::Bool button_press;
  button_press.data = 1;

  std_msgs::Bool button_release;
  button_release.data = 0;

   while (ros::ok())
    {

         if (!digitalRead(BUTTON)) // Return True if button pressed
    {
      ROS_INFO("Button Pressed");
      chatter_pub.publish(button_press);

    }
    else
    {

      ROS_INFO("Button Released");
      chatter_pub.publish(button_release);

    }

    ros::spinOnce();
        loop_rate.sleep();

   }
 }
```

CMakeLists.txt for building these two examples is given next. The Wiring Pi code needs to link with the Wiring Pi library. We have added this in the CMakeLists.txt file:

```
cmake_minimum_required(VERSION 2.8.3)
project(ros_wiring_examples)

find_package(catkin REQUIRED COMPONENTS
  roscpp
  std_msgs
)

find_package(Boost REQUIRED COMPONENTS system)

//Include directory of wiring Pi
```

```
set(wiringPi_include "/usr/local/include")


include_directories(
  ${catkin_INCLUDE_DIRS}
  ${wiringPi_include}
)

//Link directory of wiring Pi
LINK_DIRECTORIES("/usr/local/lib")


add_executable(blink_led src/blink.cpp)

add_executable(button_led src/button.cpp)

target_link_libraries(blink_led
   ${catkin_LIBRARIES} wiringPi
 )

target_link_libraries(button_led
   ${catkin_LIBRARIES} wiringPi
 )
```

Build the project using `catkin_make` and we can run each example. For executing the Wiring Pi based code, we need a root permission.

Running examples in Raspberry Pi 2

Now that we have built the project, before running the examples, we should do the following setup in Raspberry Pi. You can do this setup by logging in to Raspberry Pi through SSH.

We need to add the following lines to the `.bashrc` file of the root user. Take the `.bashrc` file of the root user:

```
$ sudo -i
$ nano .bashrc
```

Add the following lines to the end of this file:

```
source /opt/ros/indigo/setup.sh
source /home/pi/catkin_ws/devel/setup.bash
export ROS_MASTER_URI=http://localhost:11311
```

We can now log in with a different Terminal in our Raspberry Pi 2, and run the following commands to execute the blink_demo program:

Start roscore in one Terminal:

```
$ roscore
```

Run the executable as the root in another Terminal:

```
$ sudo -s
# cd  /home/odroid/catkin_ws/build/ros_wiring_examples
#./blink_led
```

After starting the `blink_led` node, publish 1 to the `led_blink` topic in another Terminal:

- For setting the LED to the ON state:

  ```
  $ rostopic pub /led_blink std_msgs/Bool 1
  ```

- For setting the LED to the OFF state:

  ```
  $ rostopic pub /led_blink std_msgs/Bool 0
  ```

- Run the button LED node in another Terminal:

  ```
  $ sudo -s
  # cd  /home/odroid/catkin_ws/build/ros_wiring_examples
  #./button_led
  ```

Press the button and we can see the LED blinking. We can also check the button state by echoing the topic `led_blink`:

```
$ rostopic echo /led_blink
```

Interfacing DYNAMIXEL actuators to ROS

One of the latest smart actuators available on the market is DYNAMIXEL, which is manufactured by a company called Robotis. The DYNAMIXEL servos are available in various versions, some of which are shown in the following image:

Figure 27: Different types of DYNAMIXEL servos

These smart actuators have complete support in ROS, and clear documentation is also available for them.

The official ROS wiki page of DYNAMIXEL is at `http://wiki.ros.org/dynamixel_controllers/Tutorials`.

Questions

- What are the different rosserial packages?
- What is the main function of `rosserial_arduino`?
- How does rosserial protocol work?
- What are the main differences between Odroid and Raspberry Pi boards?

Summary

This chapter was about interfacing I/O boards to ROS and adding sensors on it. We have discussed the interfacing of the popular I/O board called Arduino to ROS, and interface's basic components, such as LEDs, buttons, accelerometers, ultrasonic sound sensors, and so on. After looking at the interfacing of Arduino, we discussed how to set up ROS on Raspberry Pi 2 and Odroid-XU4. We also presented a few basic examples in Odroid and Raspberry Pi based on ROS and Wiring Pi. Finally, we looked at the interfacing of smart actuators called DYNAMIXEL in ROS.

10
Programming Vision Sensors Using ROS, Open CV, and PCL

In the last chapter, we discussed the interfacing of sensors and actuators using I/O boards in ROS. In this chapter, we are going to discuss how to interface various vision sensors in ROS and program them using libraries such as **Open Source Computer Vision** (**OpenCV**) and **Point Cloud Library** (**PCL**). The vision of a robot is an important aspect of the robot for manipulating objects and navigation. There are lots of 2D/3D vision sensors available on the market, and most of the sensors have an interface driver package in ROS. We will discuss the interfacing of new vision sensors to ROS and programming them using OpenCV and PCL. Finally, we will discuss the use of fiducial marker libraries to develop vision-based robotic applications.

We will cover the following topics in this chapter:

- Integrating ROS, PCL, and OpenCV
- Using a USB webcam in ROS
- Learning how to calibrate a camera
- Using RGB-D sensors in ROS
- Using laser scanners in ROS
- Working with augmented-reality markers in ROS

Understanding ROS – OpenCV interfacing packages

OpenCV is one of the popular open source real-time computer vision libraries, which is mainly written in C/C++. OpenCV comes with a BSD license, and is free both for academic and commercial applications. OpenCV can be programmed using C/C++, Python, and Java, and it has multi-platform support, such as Windows, Linux, macOS X, Android, and iOS. OpenCV has tons of computer vision APIs that can be used for implementing computer vision applications. The web page of OpenCV library can be found at `http://opencv.org/`.

The OpenCV library is interfaced to ROS via a ROS stack, called `vision_opencv`. `vision_opencv` consists of two important packages for interfacing OpenCV to ROS. They are:

- `cv_bridge`: The `cv_bridge` package contains a library that provides APIs for converting the OpenCV image data type, `cv::Mat`, to the ROS image message called `sensor_msgs/Image` and vice versa. In short, it can act as a bridge between OpenCV and ROS. We can use OpenCV APIs to process the image and convert to ROS image messages whenever we want to send to another node. We will discuss how to do this conversion in the upcoming sections.
- `image_geometry`: One of the first processes that we should do before working with cameras is calibration. The `image_geometry` package contains libraries written in C++ and Python, which helps to correct the geometry of the image using calibration parameters. The package uses a message type called `sensor_msgs/CameraInfo` for handling the calibration parameters and feeding to the OpenCV image rectification function.

Understanding ROS - PCL interfacing packages

The point cloud data can be defined as a group of data points in some coordinate system. In 3D, it has x, y, and z coordinates. The PCL library is an open source project for handling 2D/3D images and point cloud processing.

Like OpenCV, it is under BSD license, and free for academic and commercial purposes. It is also a cross-platform packages that has support in Linux, Windows, macOS, and Android/iOS.

The library consists of standard algorithms for filtering, segmentation, feature estimation, and so on, which are required to implement different point cloud applications. The main web page of the point cloud library can be found at http://pointclouds.org/.

The point cloud data can be acquired by sensors such as Kinect, Asus Xtion Pro, Intel Real Sense, and others. We can use this data for robotic applications, such as robot object manipulation and grasping. PCL is tightly integrated into ROS for handling point cloud data from various sensors. The perception_pcl stack is the ROS interface for the PCL library. It consists of packages for pumping the point cloud data from ROS to PCL data types and vice versa. perception_pcl consists of the following packages:

- pcl_conversions: This package provides APIs to convert PCL data types to ROS messages and vice versa.
- pcl_msgs: This package contains the definition of PCL-related messages in ROS. The PCL messages are:
  - ModelCoefficients
  - PointIndices
  - PolygonMesh
  - Vertices
- pcl_ros: This is the PCL bridge of ROS. This package contains tools and nodes to bridge ROS messages to PCL data types and vice versa.
- pointcloud_to_laserscan: The main function of this package is to convert the 3D point cloud into a 2D laser scan. This package is useful for converting an inexpensive 3D vision sensor, such as Kinect and Asus Xtion Pro, to a laser scanner. The laser scanner data is mainly used for 2D-SLAM, for the purpose of robot navigation.

Installing ROS perception

We are going to install a single package called perception, which is a metapackage of ROS containing all the perception-related packages, such as OpenCV, PCL, and so on:

```
$ sudo apt-get install ros-kinetic-perception
```

The ROS perception stack contains the following ROS packages:

- `image_common`: This metapackage contains common functionalities to handle an image in ROS. The metapackage consists of the following list of packages (http://wiki.ros.org/image_common):
    - `image_transport`: This package helps to compress the image during publishing and subscribes the images to save the band width (http://wiki.ros.org/image_transport). The various compression methods are JPEG/PNG compression and Theora for streaming videos. We can also add custom compression methods to `image_transport`.
    - `camera_calibration_parsers`: This package contains a routine to read/write camera calibration parameters from an XML file. This package is mainly used by camera drivers for accessing calibration parameters.
    - `camera_info_manager`: This package consists of a routine to save, restore, and load the calibration information. This is mainly used by camera drivers.
    - `polled_camera`: This package contains the interface for requesting images from a polling camera driver (for example, `prosilica_camera`).
    - `Image_pipeline`: This metapackage contains packages to process the raw image from the camera driver. The various processing done by this metapackage include calibration, distortion removal, stereo vision processing, depth-image processing, and so on. The following packages are present in this metapackage for this processing (http://wiki.ros.org/image_pipeline).
- `camera_calibration`: One of the important tools for relating the 3D world to the 2D camera image is calibration. This package provides tools for doing monocular and stereo image calibration in ROS.
- `image_proc`: The nodes in this package act between the camera driver and the vision processing nodes. It can handle the calibration parameters, correct image distortion from the raw image, and convert to color images.
- `depth_image_proc`: This package contains nodes and `nodelets` for handling depth images from Kinect and 3D vision sensors. The depth image can be processed by these `nodelets` to produce point cloud data.

- `stereo_image_proc`: This package has nodes to perform distortion removal for a pair of cameras. It is the same as the `image_proc` package, except that it handles two cameras for stereo vision and for developing point cloud and disparity images.
- `image_rotate`: This package contains nodes to rotate the input image.
- `image_view`: This is a simple ROS tool for viewing ROS message topics. It can also view stereo and disparity images.
- `Image_transport_plugins`: These are the plugins of ROS image transport for publishing and subscribing the ROS images in different compression levels or different video codec to reduce the bandwidth and latency.
- `Laser_pipeline`: This is a set of packages that can process laser data, such as filtering and converting into 3D Cartesian points and assembling points to form a cloud. The `laser-pipeline` stack contains the following packages:
  - `laser_filters`: This package contains nodes to filter the noise in the raw laser data, remove the laser points inside the robot footprint, and remove spurious values inside the laser data.
  - `laser_geometry`: After filtering the laser data, we have to transform the laser ranges and angles into 3D Cartesian coordinates efficiently by taking into account the tilt and skew angle of laser scanner
  - `laser_assembler`: This package can assemble the laser scan into a 3D point cloud or 2.5D scan.
- `perception_pcl`: This is the stack of the PCL-ROS interface.
- `vision_opencv`: This is the stack of the OpenCV-ROS interface.

Interfacing USB webcams in ROS

We can start interfacing with an ordinary webcam or a laptop cam in ROS. Overall, there are no ROS-specific packages to install and use web cameras. If the camera is working in Ubuntu/Linux, it may be supported by the ROS driver too. After plugging in the camera, check whether a `/dev/videoX` device file has been created, or check with some application such as Cheese, VLC, or similar others. The guide to check whether the webcam is supported on Ubuntu is available at `https://help.ubuntu.com/community/Webcam`.

We can find the video devices present on the system using the following command:

```
$ ls /dev/ | grep video
```

If you get an output of `video`, you can confirm a USB cam is available for use.

After ensuring the webcam support in Ubuntu, we can install a ROS webcam driver called `usb_cam` using the following command:

```
$ sudo apt-get install ros-kinetic-usb-cam
```

We can install the latest package of `usb_cam` from the source code. The driver is available on GitHub, at `https://github.com/bosch-ros-pkg/usb_cam`.

The `usb_cam` package contains a node called `usb_cam_node`, which is the driver of USB cams. There are some parameters that need to be set before running this node. We can run the ROS node along with its parameters. The `usb_cam-test.launch` file can launch the USB cam driver with the necessary parameters:

```xml
<launch>
  <node name="usb_cam" pkg="usb_cam" type="usb_cam_node" output="screen" >
    <param name="video_device" value="/dev/video0" />
    <param name="image_width" value="640" />
    <param name="image_height" value="480" />
    <param name="pixel_format" value="yuyv" />
    <param name="camera_frame_id" value="usb_cam" />
    <param name="io_method" value="mmap"/>
  </node>
  <node name="image_view" pkg="image_view" type="image_view"
respawn="false" output="screen">
    <remap from="image" to="/usb_cam/image_raw"/>
    <param name="autosize" value="true" />
  </node>
</launch>
```

This launch file will start `usb_cam_node` with the video device `/dev/video0`, with a resolution of 640 x 480. The pixel format here is YUV (`https://en.wikipedia.org/wiki/YUV`). After initiating `usb_cam_node`, it will start an `image_view` node for displaying the raw image from the driver. We can launch the previous file by using the following command:

```
$ roslaunch usb_cam usb_cam-test.launch
```

We will get the following message with an image view, as shown next:

```
[ INFO] [1509310151.685693448]: Using transport "raw"
[ INFO] [1509310151.851576979]: using default calibration URL
[ INFO] [1509310151.851731568]: camera calibration URL: file:///home/jcaca
ce/.ros/camera_info/head_camera.yaml
[ INFO] [1509310151.851937275]: Unable to open camera calibration file [/h
ome/jcacace/.ros/camera_info/head_camera.yaml]
[ WARN] [1509310151.852013709]: Camera calibration file /home/jcacace/.ros
/camera_info/head_camera.yaml not found.
[ INFO] [1509310151.852111773]: Starting 'head_camera' (/dev/video0) at 64
0x480 via mmap (yuyv) at 30 FPS
[ WARN] [1509310152.108112434]: unknown control 'focus_auto'
```

Figure 1: USB camera view using the image view tool

The topics generated by the driver are shown next. There are raw, compressed, and Theora codec topics generated by the driver:

```
/image_view/output
/image_view/parameter_descriptions
/image_view/parameter_updates
/rosout
/rosout_agg
/usb_cam/camera_info
/usb_cam/image_raw
/usb_cam/image_raw/compressed
/usb_cam/image_raw/compressed/parameter_descriptions
/usb_cam/image_raw/compressed/parameter_updates
/usb_cam/image_raw/compressedDepth
/usb_cam/image_raw/compressedDepth/parameter_descriptions
/usb_cam/image_raw/compressedDepth/parameter_updates
/usb_cam/image_raw/theora
/usb_cam/image_raw/theora/parameter_descriptions
/usb_cam/image_raw/theora/parameter_updates
```

Figure 2: List of topics generated by the USB camera driver

We can visualize the image in another window by using the following command:

```
$ rosrun image_view image_view image:=/usb_cam/image_raw
```

As you can see from the topic list, due to the installation of the image_trasport package, images are published in multiple ways, compressed and uncompressed. The latter format is useful to send images to other ROS nodes over the network or store video data of the topic into bagfiles, occupying little space on the hard disk. In order to use the compressed image from a bagfiles on a remote machine or from a bagfile , we need to republish it in an uncompressed format, using the republish node of the image_transport package:

```
$ rosrun image_transport republish [input format] in:=<in_topic_base>
[output format] out:=<out_topic>
```

For example:

```
$ rosrun image_transport republish compressed in:=/usb_cam/image_raw
[output format] out:=/usb_cam/image_raw/republished
```

> Note that in the previous example, we have used the topic base name as input (/usb_cam/img_raw), and not its compressed version (/usb_cam/image_raw/compressed).

Now that we have learned how to acquire images from the camera, we have to work with the camera calibration.

Working with ROS camera calibration

Like all sensors, cameras also need calibration for correcting the distortions in the camera images due to the camera's internal parameters, and for finding the world coordinates from the camera coordinates.

The primary parameters that cause image distortions are radial distortions and tangential distortions. Using the camera calibration algorithm, we can model these parameters and also calculate the real-world coordinates from the camera coordinates by computing the camera calibration matrix, which contains the focal distance and the principle points.

Camera calibration can be done using a classic black-white chessboard, symmetrical circle pattern, or an asymmetrical circle pattern. According to each different pattern, we use different equations to get the calibration parameters. Using the calibration tools, we detect the patterns, and each detected pattern is taken as a new equation. When the calibration tool gets enough detected patterns it can compute the final parameters for the camera.

ROS provides a package named `camera_calibration`
(`http://wiki.ros.org/camera_calibration/Tutorials/MonocularCalibration`) to do camera calibration, which is a part of the image pipeline stack. We can calibrate monocular, stereo, and even 3D sensors, such as Kinect and Asus Xtion pro.

The first thing we have to do before calibration is to download the chessboard pattern mentioned in the ROS Wiki page, and print it and paste it onto a card board. This is the pattern we are going to use for calibration. This check board has 8x6 with 108 mm squares.

Run the `usb_cam` launch file to start the camera driver. We are going to run the camera calibration node of ROS using the raw image from the `/usb_cam/image_raw` topic. The following command will run the calibration node with the necessary parameters:

```
$ rosrun camera_calibration cameracalibrator.py --size 8x6 --square 0.108
image:=/usb_cam/image_raw camera:=/usb_cam
```

A calibration window will pop up, and when we show the calibration pattern to the camera, and the detection is made, we will see the following screenshot:

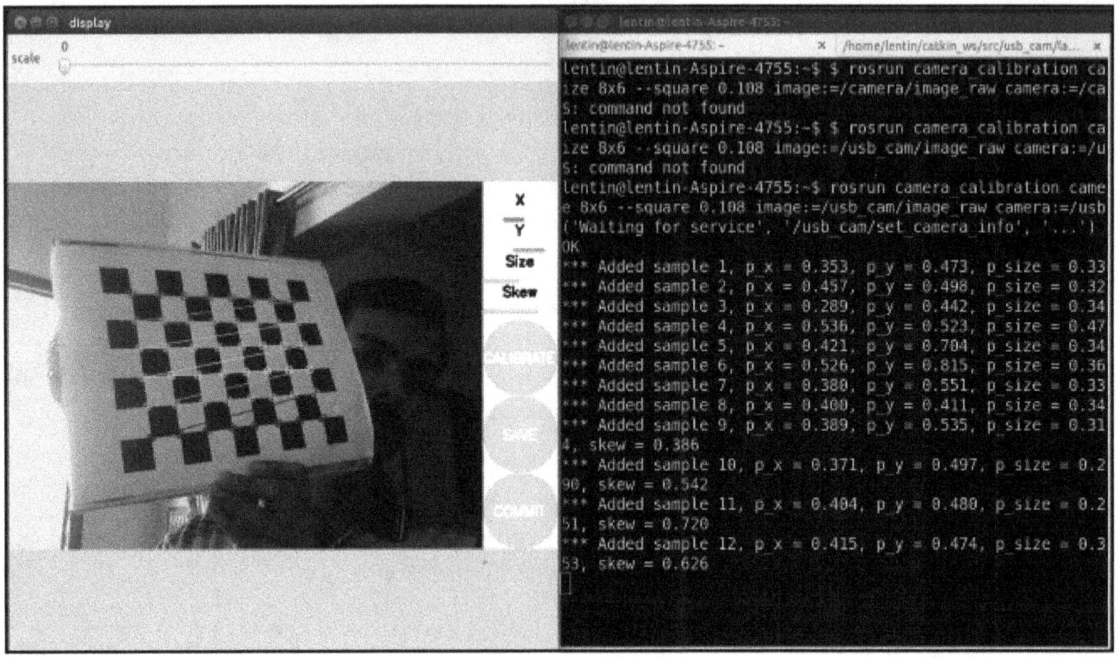

Figure 3: ROS camera calibration

Move the calibration pattern in the *X* direction and *Y* direction. If the calibrator node gets a sufficient amount of samples, a **CALIBRATE** button will become active on the window. When we press the **CALIBRATE** button, it will compute the camera parameters using these samples. It will take some time for the calculation. After computation, two buttons, **SAVE** and **COMMIT**, will become active inside the window, as shown in the following image. If we press the **SAVE** button, it will save the calibration parameters to a file in the /tmp folder. If we press the **COMMIT** button, it will save them to
./ros/camera_info/head_camera.yaml:

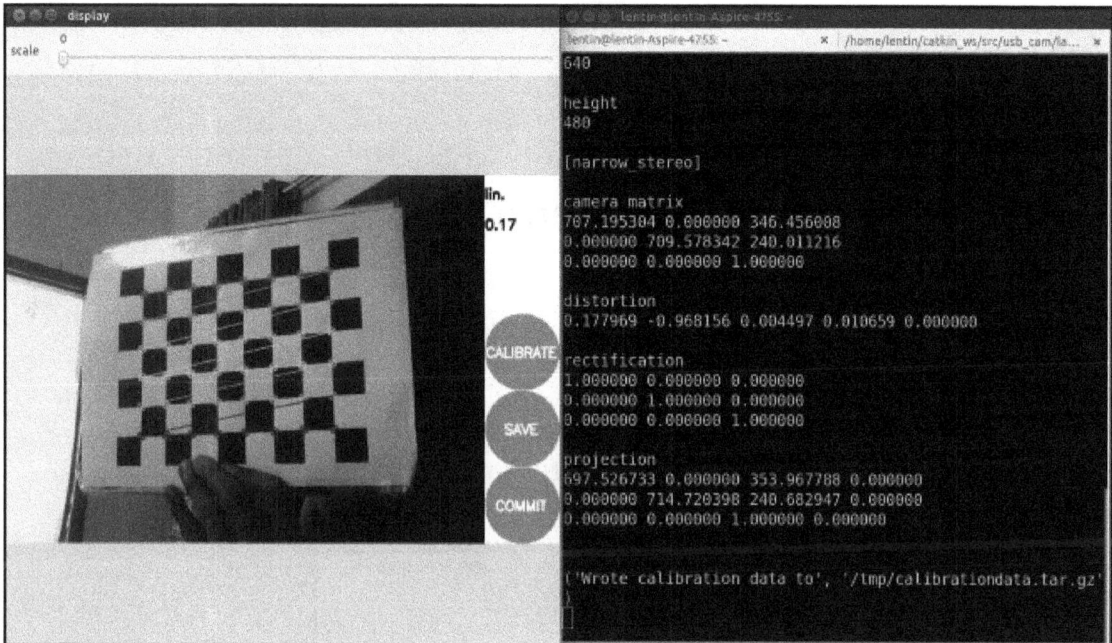

Figure 4: Generating the camera calibration file

Restart the camera driver, and we will see the YAML calibration file loaded along with the driver. The calibration file that we generated will look as follows:

```
image_width: 640
image_height: 480
camera_name: head_camera
camera_matrix:
rows: 3
cols: 3
data: [707.1953043273086, 0, 346.4560078627374, 0, 709.5783421541863,
240.0112155124814, 0, 0, 1]
distortion_model: plumb_bob
distortion_coefficients:
rows: 1
cols: 5
data: [0.1779688561999974, -0.9681558538432319, 0.004497434720139909,
0.0106588921249554, 0]
rectification_matrix:
rows: 3
cols: 3
data: [1, 0, 0, 0, 1, 0, 0, 0, 1]
projection_matrix:
```

```
rows: 3
cols: 4
data: [697.5267333984375, 0, 353.9677879190494, 0, 0, 714.7203979492188,
240.6829465337159, 0, 0, 0, 1, 0]
```

Converting images between ROS and OpenCV using cv_bridge

In this section, we will see how to convert between the ROS image message (sensor_msgs/Image) and the OpenCV image data type (cv::Mat). The main ROS package used for this conversion is cv_bridge, which is part of the vision_opencv stack. The ROS library inside cv_bridge, called CvBridge, helps to perform this conversion. We can use the CvBridge library inside our code and perform the conversion. The following figure shows how the conversion is performed between ROS and OpenCV:

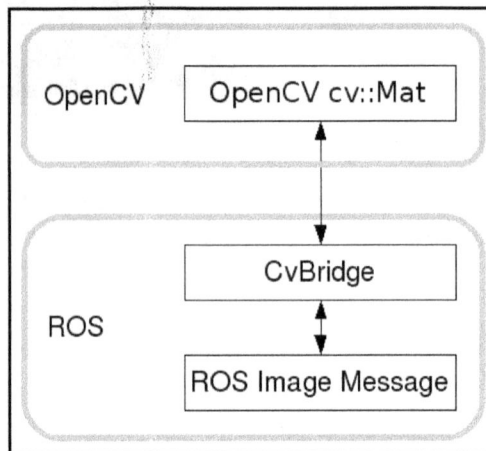

Figure 5: Converting images using CvBridge

Here, the CvBridge library acts as a bridge for converting the ROS messages to OpenCV images and vice versa. We will see how the conversion between ROS and OpenCV is performed in the following example.

Image processing using ROS and OpenCV

In this section, we will see an example of using `cv_bridge` for acquiring images from a camera driver, and converting and processing the images using OpenCV APIs. The following is how the example works:

1. Subscribe the images from the camera driver from the topic `/usb_cam/image_raw` (`sensor_msgs/Image`)
2. Convert the ROS images to the OpenCV image type using `CvBridge`
3. Process the OpenCV image using its APIs and find the edges on the image
4. Convert the OpenCV image type of the edge detection to the ROS image messages and publish into the topic `/edge_detector/processed_image`

The step-by-step procedure to build this example follows:

Step 1 – Creating a ROS package for the experiment

You can get the existing package `cv_bridge_tutorial_pkg` provided with this book, or you can create a new package, using the following command:

```
$ catkin_create_pkg cv_bridge_tutorial_pkg cv_bridge image_transport roscpp
sensor_msgs std_msgs
```

This package is mainly dependent on `cv_bridge`, `image_transport`, and `sensor_msgs`.

Step 2 – Creating source files

You can get the source code of the example `sample_cv_bridge_node.cpp` from the `cv_bridge_tutorial_pkg/src` folder.

Step 3 – Explanation of the code

The following is the explanation of the complete code:

```
#include <image_transport/image_transport.h>
```

We are using the `image_transport` package in this code for publishing and subscribing to an image in ROS:

```
#include <cv_bridge/cv_bridge.h>
#include <sensor_msgs/image_encodings.h>
```

This header includes the `CvBridge` class and image encoding related functions in the code:

```
#include <opencv2/imgproc/imgproc.hpp>
#include <opencv2/highgui/highgui.hpp>
```

These are main OpenCV image processing modules and GUI modules which provide image processing and GUI APIs in our code:

```
    image_transport::ImageTransport it_;
  public:
    Edge_Detector()
      : it_(nh_)
    {
      // Subscribe to input video feed and publish output video feed
      image_sub_ = it_.subscribe("/usb_cam/image_raw", 1,
        &ImageConverter::imageCb, this);

      image_pub_ = it_.advertise("/edge_detector/processed_image", 1);
```

We will look in more detail at the line `image_transport::ImageTransport it_`. This line creates an instance of `ImageTransport`, which is used to publish and subscribe the ROS image messages. More information about the `ImageTransport` API is given next.

Publishing and subscribing images using image_transport

ROS image transport is very similar to ROS publishers and subscribers, and it is used to publish or subscribe the images along with the camera information. We can publish the image data using `ros::Publisher`, but image transport is a more efficient way of sending the image data.

The image transport APIs are provided by the `image_transport` package. Using these APIs, we can transport an image in different compression formats; for example, we can transport it as an uncompressed image, JPEG/PNG compression, or Theora compression in separate topics. We can also add different transport formats by adding plugins. By default, we can see the compressed and Theora transports:

```
    image_transport::ImageTransport it_;
```

In the following line, we are creating an instance of the `ImageTransport` class:

```
image_transport::Subscriber image_sub_;
image_transport::Publisher image_pub_;
```

After that, we declare the subscriber and publisher objects for subscribing and publishing the images, using the `image_transport` object:

```
image_sub_ = it_.subscribe("/usb_cam/image_raw", 1,
    &ImageConverter::imageCb, this);
image_pub_ = it_.advertise("/edge_detector/processed_image", 1);
```

The following is how we subscribe and publish an image:

```
    cv::namedWindow(OPENCV_WINDOW);
}
~Edge_Detector()
{
  cv::destroyWindow(OPENCV_WINDOW);
}
```

This is how we subscribe and publish an `image.cv::namedWindow()`, which is an OpenCV function to create a GUI for displaying an image. The argument inside this function is the window name. Inside the class destructor, we are destroying the named window.

Converting OpenCV to ROS images using cv_bridge

This is an image callback function, and it basically converts the ROS image messages into the OpenCV `cv::Mat` type using the `CvBridge` APIs. The following is how we can convert ROS to OpenCV, and vice versa:

```
void imageCb(const sensor_msgs::ImageConstPtr& msg)
{

  cv_bridge::CvImagePtr cv_ptr;
  namespace enc = sensor_msgs::image_encodings;

  try
  {
    cv_ptr = cv_bridge::toCvCopy(msg,
sensor_msgs::image_encodings::BGR8);
  }
  catch (cv_bridge::Exception& e)
  {
    ROS_ERROR("cv_bridge exception: %s", e.what());
```

```
        return;
    }
```

To start with CvBridge, we should start with creating an instance of a CvImage. Given next is the creation of the CvImage pointer:

```
    cv_bridge::CvImagePtr cv_ptr;
```

The CvImage type is a class provided by cv_bridge, which consists of information such as an OpenCV image, its encoding, ROS header, and so on. Using this type, we can easily convert an ROS image to OpenCV, and vice versa:

```
    cv_ptr = cv_bridge::toCvCopy(msg, sensor_msgs::image_encodings::BGR8);
```

We can handle the ROS image message in two ways: either we can make a copy of the image or we can share the image data. When we copy the image, we can process the image, but if we use a shared pointer, we can't modify the data. We use toCvCopy() for creating a copy of the ROS image, and the toCvShare() function is used to get the pointer of the image. Inside these functions, we should mention the ROS message and the type of encoding:

```
    if (cv_ptr->image.rows > 400 && cv_ptr->image.cols > 600){
    detect_edges(cv_ptr->image);
        image_pub_.publish(cv_ptr->toImageMsg());
    }
```

In this section, we are extracting the image and its properties from the CvImage instance, and accessing the cv::Mat object from this instance. This code simply checks whether the rows and columns of the image are in a particular range, and, if it is true, it will call another method called detect_edges(cv::Mat), which will process the image given as an argument and display the edge-detected-image:

```
    image_pub_.publish(cv_ptr->toImageMsg());
```

The preceding line will publish the edge-detected-image after converting to the ROS image message. Here we are using the toImageMsg() function for converting the CvImage instance to a ROS image message.

Finding edges on the image

After converting the ROS images to OpenCV type, the `detect_edges(cv::Mat)` function will be called for finding the edges on the image, using the following inbuilt OpenCV functions:

```
cv::cvtColor( img, src_gray, CV_BGR2GRAY );
cv::blur( src_gray, detected_edges, cv::Size(3,3) );
cv::Canny( detected_edges, detected_edges, lowThreshold,
lowThreshold*ratio, kernel_size );
```

Here, the `cvtColor()` function will convert an RGB image to a gray color space and `cv::blur()` will add blurring to the image. After that, using the Canny edge detector, we extract the edges of the image.

Visualizing raw and edge-detected-images

Here we are displaying the image data using the OpenCV function called `imshow()`, which consists of the window name and the image name:

```
cv::imshow(OPENCV_WINDOW, img);
cv::imshow(OPENCV_WINDOW_1, dst);
cv::waitKey(3);
```

Step 4 – Editing the CMakeLists.txt file

The definition of the `CMakeLists.txt` file is given next. In this example, we need OpenCV support, so we should include the OpenCV header path and also link the source code against the OpenCV library path:

```
include_directories(
  ${catkin_INCLUDE_DIRS}
  ${OpenCV_INCLUDE_DIRS}
)

add_executable(sample_cv_bridge_node src/sample_cv_bridge_node.cpp)

## Specify libraries to link a library or executable target against
 target_link_libraries(sample_cv_bridge_node
   ${catkin_LIBRARIES}
   ${OpenCV_LIBRARIES}
  )
```

Step 5 – Building and running an example

After building the package using `catkin_make`, we can run the node using the following command:

1. Launch the webcam driver:

   ```
   $ roslaunch usb_cam usb_cam-test.launch
   ```

2. Run the `cv_bridge` sample node:

   ```
   $ rosrun cv_bridge_tutorial_pkg sample_cv_bridge_node
   ```

3. If everything works fine, we will get two windows, as shown in the following image. The first window shows the raw image and the second is the processed edge-detected-image:

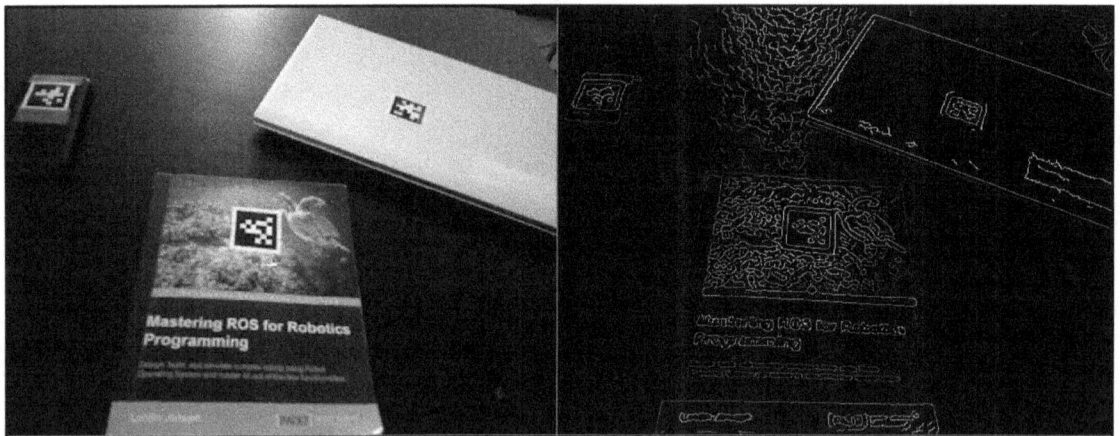

Figure 6: Raw image and edge-detected-image

Interfacing Kinect and Asus Xtion Pro in ROS

The webcams that we have worked with until now can only provide 2D visual information of the surroundings. For getting 3D information about the surroundings, we have to use 3D vision sensors or range finders, such as laser finders. Some of the 3D vision sensors that we are discussing in this chapter are Kinect, Asus Xtion Pro, Intel Real sense, and Hokuyo laser scanner:

Figure 7: Top: Kinect; bottom: Asus Xtion Pro.

The first two sensors we are going to discuss are Kinect and Asus Xtion Pro. Both of these devices need the **OpenNI** (**Open source Natural Interaction**) driver library for operating in the Linux system. OpenNI acts as a middleware between the 3D vision devices and the application software. The OpenNI driver is integrated to ROS and we can install these drivers by using the following commands. These packages help to interface the OpenNI supported devices, such as Kinect and Asus Xtion Pro:

```
$ sudo apt-get install ros-kinetic-openni-launch ros-kinetic-openni2-launch
```

The preceding command will install OpenNI drivers and launch files for starting the RGB/depth streams. After successful installation of these packages, we can launch the driver by using the following command:

```
$ roslaunch openni2_launch openni2.launch
```

This launch file will convert the raw data from the devices into useful data, such as 3D point clouds, disparity images, and depth, and the RGB images using ROS nodelets.

Other than the OpenNI drivers, there is another driver available called `lib-freenect`. The common launch files of the drivers are organized into a package called `rgbd_launch`. This package consists of common launch files that are used for the freenect and openni drivers.

We can visualize the point cloud generated by the OpenNI ROS driver by using RViz.

Run RViz, using the following command:

```
$ rosrun rviz rviz
```

Set the fixed frame to `/camera_depth_optical_frame`, add a **PointCloud2** display, and set the topic as `/camera/depth/points`. This is the unregistered point cloud from the IR camera, that is, it may have a complete match with the RGB camera and it only uses the depth camera for generating the point cloud:

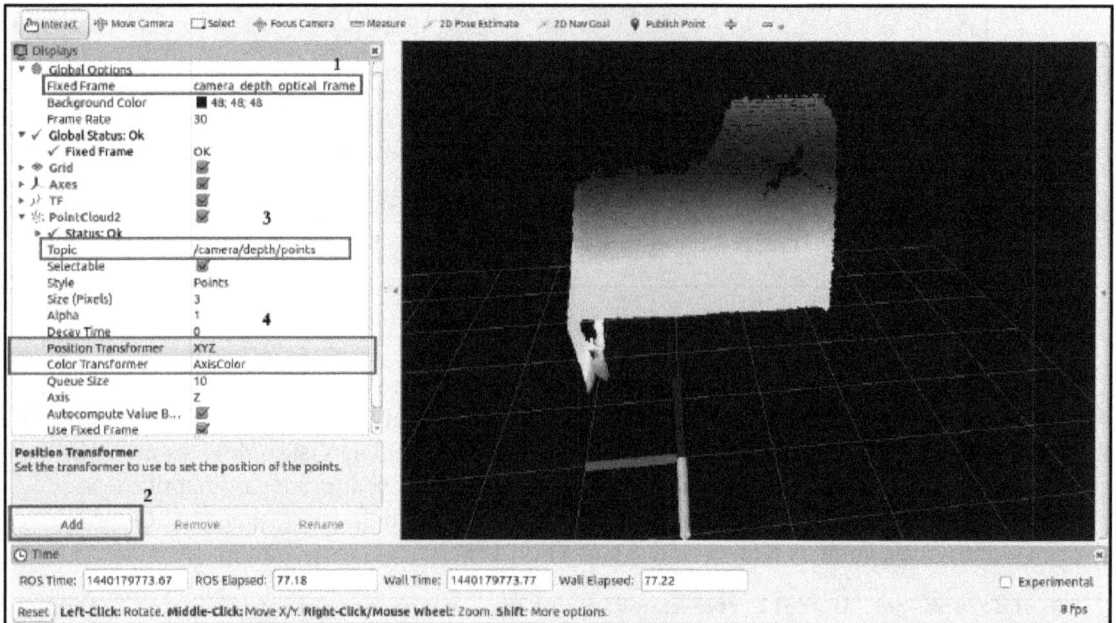

Figure 8: Unregistered point cloud view in RViz

We can enable the registered point cloud by using the **Dynamic Reconfigure** GUI, by using the following command:

```
$ rosrun rqt_reconfigure rqt_reconfigure
```

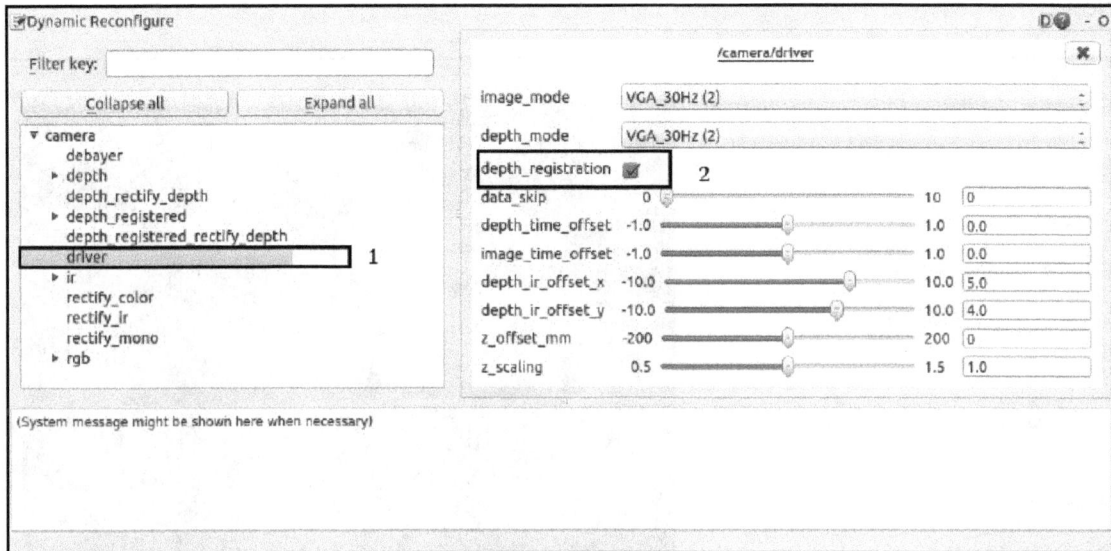

Figure 9: Dynamic Reconfigure GUI

Click on **camera** | **driver** and tick `depth_registration`. Change the point cloud to `/camera/depth_registered/points` and **Color Transformer** to `RGB8` in RViz. We will see the registered point cloud in RViz as it appears in the following image. The registered point cloud takes information from the depth and the RGB camera to generate the point cloud:

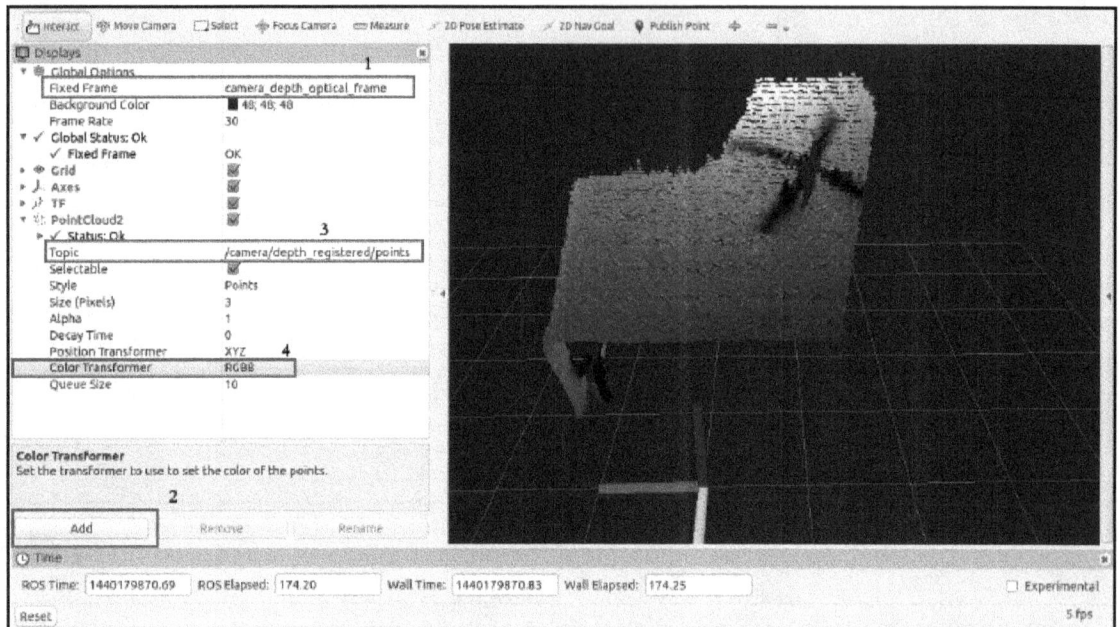

Figure 10: The registered point cloud

Interfacing Intel Real Sense camera with ROS

One of the new 3D depth sensors from Intel is Real Sense. Until now, different versions of this sensor have been released (F200, R200, SR30, ...). To interface Real Sense sensors with ROS, we first have to install the `librealsense` library.

Download the Real Sense library from the following link: `https://github.com/IntelRealSense/librealsense`, using the following code:

```
$ git clone https://github.com/IntelRealSense/librealsense.git
```

Then follow these steps:

1. Install `libudev-dev`, `pkg-config`, and `libgtk-3`:

```
$ sudo apt-get install libudev-dev pkg-config libgtk-3-dev
```

2. Install `glfw3`:

```
$ sudo apt-get install libglfw3-dev
```

3. Navigate to the `librealsense` root directory and run:

```
$ mkdir build && cd build
$ cmake ..
$ make
$ sudo make install
```

After installing the Real Sense library, we can install the ROS package to start sensor data streaming. We can install from the Ubuntu/Debian package manager by using the following command:

```
$ sudo make install ros-kinetic-realsense
```

Or we can directly clone the package from the Git repository and compile the workspace:

```
$ git clone https://github.com/intel-ros/realsense.git
```

Now we can start the sensor using the example launch file and open Rviz to visualize the color and depth data streamed by `realsense`:

```
roslaunch realsense_camera sr300_nodelet_rgbd.launch
```

Figure 12: Intel Real Sense view in RViz

The following are the topics generated by the Real Sense driver:

```
sensor_msgs::PointCloud2
/camera/depth/points              point cloud without RGB
/camera/depth_registered/points   point cloud with RGB

sensor_msgs::Image
/camera/image/rgb_raw                raw image for RGB sensor
/camera/image/depth_raw           raw image for depth sensor
/camera/image/ir_raw              raw image for infrared sensor
```

Working with a point cloud to a laser scan package

One of the important applications of 3D vision sensors is mimicking the functionalities of a laser scanner. We need the laser scanner data for working with autonomous navigation algorithms, such as SLAM. We can make a fake laser scanner using a 3D vision sensor. We can take a slice of the point cloud data/depth image and convert it to laser range data. In ROS, we have a set of packages to convert the point cloud to laser scans:

- `depthimage_to_laserscan`: This package contains nodes that take the depth image from the vision sensor and generate a 2D laser scan based on the provided parameters. The inputs of the node are depth image and camera info parameters, which include calibration parameters. After conversion to the laser scan data, it will publish laser scanner data in the `/scan` topic. The node parameters are `scan_height, scan_time, range_min, range_max,` and the output frame ID. The official ROS Wiki page of this package can be found at http://wiki.ros.org/depthimage_to_laserscan.

- `pointcloud_to_laserscan`: This package converts the real point cloud data into 2D laser scan, instead of taking a depth image as in the previous package. The official Wiki page of this package can be found at http://wiki.ros.org/pointcloud_to_laserscan.

The first package is suitable for normal applications; however, if the sensor is placed on an angle, it is better to use the second package. Also, the first package takes less processing than the second one. Here we are using the `depthimage_to_laserscan` package to convert a laser scan. We can install `depthimage_to_laserscan` and `pointcloud_to_laserscan` by using the following command:

```
$ sudo apt-get install ros-kinetic-depthimage-to-laserscan ros- kinetic-
pointcloud-to-laserscan
```

We can start converting from the depth image of the OpenNI device to the 2D laser scanner by using the following package.

Create a package for performing the conversion:

```
$ catkin_create_pkg fake_laser_pkg depthimage_to_laserscan nodelet roscpp
```

Create a folder called `launch`, and inside this folder create the following launch file called `start_laser.launch`. You will get this package and file from the `fake_laser_pkg/launch` folder:

```
<launch>
  <!-- "camera" should uniquely identify the device. All topics   are
pushed down
       into the "camera" namespace, and it is prepended to tf        frame
ids. -->
  <arg name="camera"      default="camera"/>
  <arg name="publish_tf"  default="true"/>


  . . .

  . . .

  <group if="$(arg scan_processing)">
    <node pkg="nodelet" type="nodelet"     name="depthimage_to_laserscan"
args="load     depthimage_to_laserscan/DepthImageToLaserScanNodelet $(arg
camera)/$(arg camera)_nodelet_manager">
      <!-- Pixel rows to use to generate the laserscan. For each
column, the scan willreturn the minimum value for those        pixels
centered vertically in the image. -->
      <param name="scan_height" value="10"/>
      <param name="output_frame_id" value="/$(arg
camera)_depth_frame"/>
      <param name="range_min" value="0.45"/>
      <remap from="image" to="$(arg camera)/$(arg        depth)/image_raw"/>
      <remap from="scan" to="$(arg scan_topic)"/>


  . . .

  . . .
</launch>
```

The following code snippet will launch the nodelet for converting the depth image to laser scanner:

```
<node pkg="nodelet" type="nodelet" name="depthimage_to_laserscan"
args="load depthimage_to_laserscan/DepthImageToLaserScanNodelet $(arg
camera)/$(arg camera)_nodelet_manager">
```

Launch this file and we can view the laser scanner in RViz.

Launch this file using the following command:

```
$ roslaunch fake_laser_pkg start_laser.launch
```

We will see the data in RViz, as shown in the following image:

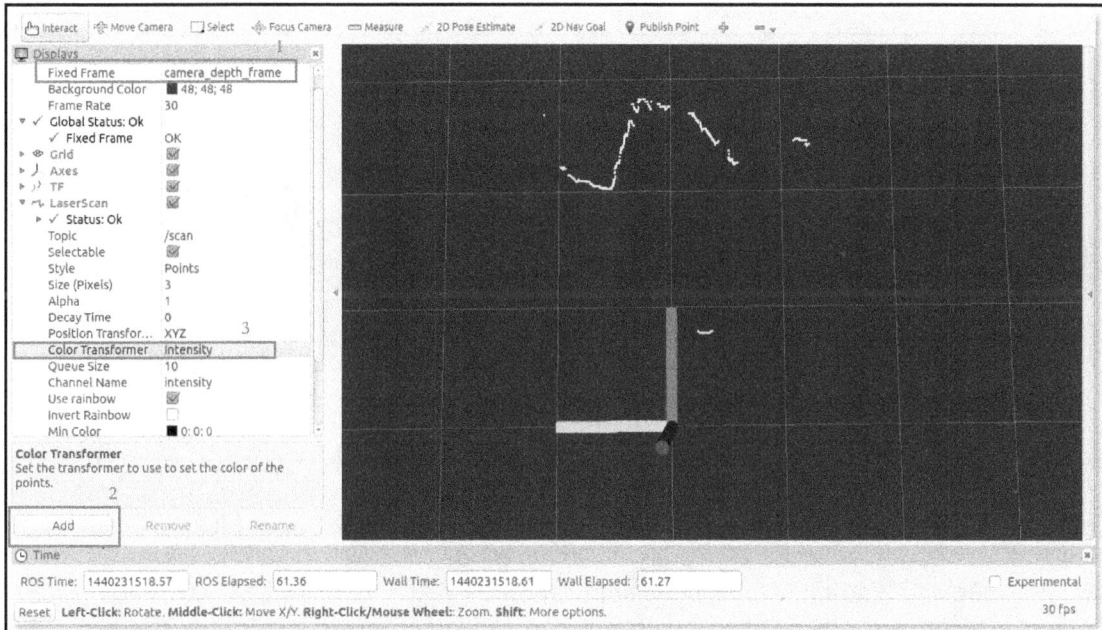

Figure 13: Laser scan in RViz

Set **Fixed Frame** as camera_depth_frame and **Add LaserScan** in the topic /scan. We can see the laser data in the view port.

Interfacing Hokuyo Laser in ROS

We can interface different ranges of laser scanners in ROS. One of the popular laser scanners available in the market is Hokuyo Laser scanner (http://www.robotshop.com/en/hokuyo-utm-031x-laser-scanning-rangefinder.html):

Figure 14: Different series of Hokuyo laser scanners

One of the commonly used Hokuyo laser scanner models is UTM-30LX. This sensor is fast and accurate and is suitable for robotic applications. The device has a USB 2.0 interface for communication, and has up to a 30 meters range with a millimeter resolution. The arc range of the scan is about 270 degrees:

Figure 15: Hokuyo UTM-30LX

There is already a driver available in ROS for interfacing these scanners. One of the interfaces is called urg_node (http://wiki.ros.org/urg_node).

We can install this package by using the following command:

```
$ sudo apt-get install ros-kinetic-urg-node
```

When the device connects to the Ubuntu system, it will create a device called ttyACMx. Check the device name by entering the dmesg command in the Terminal. Change the USB device permission by using the following command:

```
$ sudo chmod a+rw /dev/ttyACMx
```

Start the laser scan device, using the following launch file called hokuyo_start.launch:

```
<launch>
 <node name="urg_node" pkg="urg_node" type="urg_node" output="screen">
        <param name="serial_port" value="/dev/ttyACM0"/>
    <param name="frame_id" value="laser"/>
    <param name="angle_min" value="-1.5707963"/>
        <param name="angle_max" value="1.5707963"/>
  </node>
  name="rviz" pkg="rviz" type="rviz" respawn="false" output="screen"
args="-d $(find hokuyo_node)/hokuyo_test.vcg"/>
</launch>
```

This launch file starts the node to get the laser data from the device `/dev/ttyACM0`. The laser data can be viewed inside the RViz window, as shown in the following image:

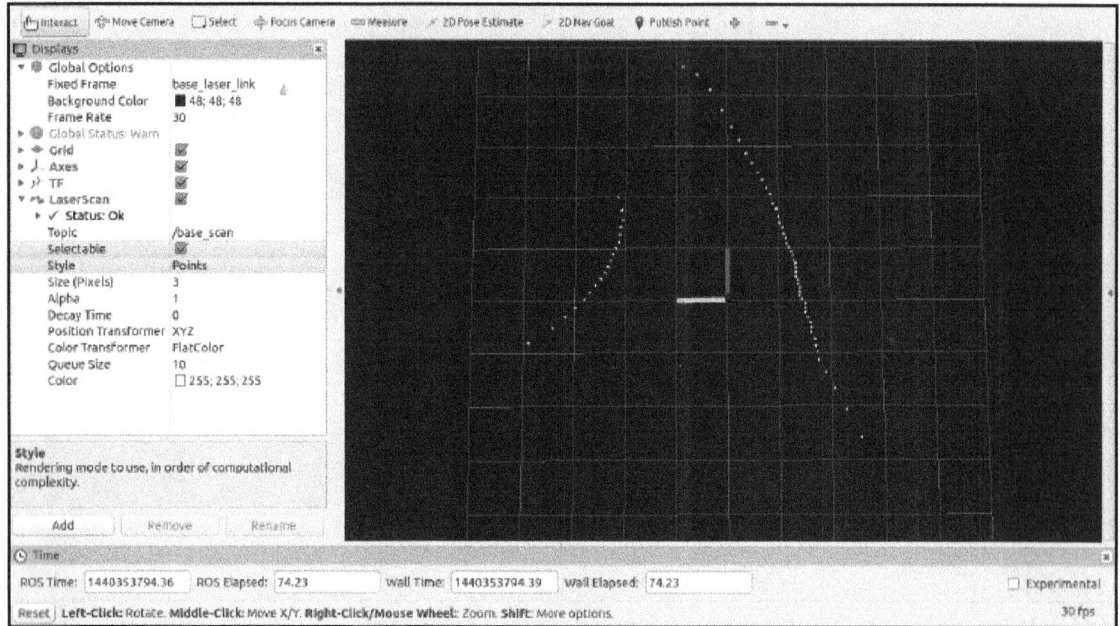

Figure 16: Hokuyo Laser scan data in RViz

Working with point cloud data

We can handle the point cloud data from Kinect or the other 3D sensors for performing a wide variety of tasks, such as 3D object detection and recognition, obstacle avoidance, 3D modeling, and so on. In this section, we will see some basic functionalities: using the PCL library and its ROS interface. We will discuss the following examples:

- How to publish a point cloud in ROS
- How to subscribe and process a point cloud
- How to write point cloud data to a PCD file
- How to read and publish a point cloud from a PCD file

How to publish a point cloud

In this example, we will see how to publish a point cloud data using the sensor_msgs/PointCloud2 message. The code will use PCL APIs for handling and creating the point cloud, and converting the PCL cloud data to the PointCloud2 message type.

You will get the example code pcl_publisher.cpp from the pcl_ros_tutorial/src folder:

```cpp
#include <ros/ros.h>

// point cloud headers
#include <pcl/point_cloud.h>
//Header which contain PCL to ROS and ROS to PCL conversion functions
#include <pcl_conversions/pcl_conversions.h>

//sensor_msgs header for point cloud2
#include <sensor_msgs/PointCloud2.h>

main (int argc, char **argv)
{
    ros::init (argc, argv, "pcl_create");


    ROS_INFO("Started PCL publishing node");

    ros::NodeHandle nh;

//Creating publisher object for point cloud

    ros::Publisher pcl_pub = nh.advertise<sensor_msgs::PointCloud2>
("pcl_output", 1);

//Creating a cloud object
    pcl::PointCloud<pcl::PointXYZ> cloud;

//Creating a sensor_msg of point cloud

    sensor_msgs::PointCloud2 output;

    //Insert cloud data
    cloud.width  = 50000;
    cloud.height = 2;
    cloud.points.resize(cloud.width * cloud.height);
```

```
//Insert random points on the clouds

    for (size_t i = 0; i < cloud.points.size (); ++i)
    {
        cloud.points[i].x = 512 * rand () / (RAND_MAX + 1.0f);
        cloud.points[i].y = 512 * rand () / (RAND_MAX + 1.0f);
        cloud.points[i].z = 512 * rand () / (RAND_MAX + 1.0f);
    }

    //Convert the cloud to ROS message
    pcl::toROSMsg(cloud, output);
    output.header.frame_id = "point_cloud";

    ros::Rate loop_rate(1);
    while (ros::ok())
    {
        //publishing point cloud data
      pcl_pub.publish(output);
        ros::spinOnce();
        loop_rate.sleep();
    }

    return 0;
}
```

The creation of the PCL cloud is done as follows:

```
//Creating a cloud object
pcl::PointCloud<pcl::PointXYZ> cloud;
```

After creating this cloud, we insert random points to the clouds. We convert the PCL cloud to a ROS message by using the following function:

```
//Convert the cloud to ROS message
pcl::toROSMsg(cloud, output);
```

After converting to ROS messages, we can simply publish the data on the topic `/pcl_output`.

How to subscribe and process the point cloud

In this example, we will see how to subscribe the generated point cloud on the topic /pcl_output. After subscribing the point cloud, we apply a filter called the VoxelGrid class in PCL to down-sample the input cloud by keeping the same centroid of the input cloud. You will get the example code pcl_filter.cpp from the src folder of the package:

```cpp
#include <ros/ros.h>
#include <pcl/point_cloud.h>
#include <pcl_conversions/pcl_conversions.h>
#include <sensor_msgs/PointCloud2.h>
//Vortex filter header
#include <pcl/filters/voxel_grid.h>

//Creating a class for handling cloud data
class cloudHandler
{
public:
    cloudHandler()
    {
//Subscribing pcl_output topics from the publisher
//This topic can change according to the source of point cloud

    pcl_sub = nh.subscribe("pcl_output", 10, &cloudHandler::cloudCB, this);
//Creating publisher for filtered cloud data
        pcl_pub = nh.advertise<sensor_msgs::PointCloud2>("pcl_filtered",
1);
    }
//Creating cloud callback
    void cloudCB(const sensor_msgs::PointCloud2& input)
    {
        pcl::PointCloud<pcl::PointXYZ> cloud;
        pcl::PointCloud<pcl::PointXYZ> cloud_filtered;

        sensor_msgs::PointCloud2 output;
        pcl::fromROSMsg(input, cloud);

     //Creating VoxelGrid object
      pcl::VoxelGrid<pcl::PointXYZ> vox_obj;
      //Set input to voxel object
     vox_obj.setInputCloud (cloud.makeShared());
      //Setting parameters of filter such as leaf size
     vox_obj.setLeafSize (0.1f, 0.1f, 0.1f);
     //Performing filtering and copy to cloud_filtered variable
     vox_obj.filter(cloud_filtered);
       pcl::toROSMsg(cloud_filtered, output);
       output.header.frame_id = "point_cloud";
```

```
        pcl_pub.publish(output);
    }

protected:
    ros::NodeHandle nh;
    ros::Subscriber pcl_sub;
    ros::Publisher pcl_pub;
};
main(int argc, char** argv)
{
    ros::init(argc, argv, "pcl_filter");
    ROS_INFO("Started Filter Node");
    cloudHandler handler;
    ros::spin();
    return 0;
}
```

This code subscribes the point cloud topic called /pcl_output, filters, using VoxelGrid, and publishes the filtered cloud through the /cloud_filtered topic.

Writing data to a Point Cloud Data (PCD) file

We can save the point cloud to a PCD file by using the following code. The filename is pcl_write.cpp inside the src folder:

```
#include <ros/ros.h>
#include <pcl/point_cloud.h>
#include <pcl_conversions/pcl_conversions.h>
#include <sensor_msgs/PointCloud2.h>
//Header file for writing PCD file
#include <pcl/io/pcd_io.h>

void cloudCB(const sensor_msgs::PointCloud2 &input)
{
    pcl::PointCloud<pcl::PointXYZ> cloud;
    pcl::fromROSMsg(input, cloud);

//Save data as test.pcd file
    pcl::io::savePCDFileASCII ("test.pcd", cloud);
}

main (int argc, char **argv)
{
    ros::init (argc, argv, "pcl_write");
```

```
    ROS_INFO("Started PCL write node");

    ros::NodeHandle nh;
    ros::Subscriber bat_sub = nh.subscribe("pcl_output", 10, cloudCB);

    ros::spin();

    return 0;
}
```

Reading and publishing a point cloud from a PCD file

This code can read a PCD file and publish the point cloud in the /pcl_output topic. The code pcl_read.cpp is available in the src folder:

```
#include <ros/ros.h>
#include <pcl/point_cloud.h>
#include <pcl_conversions/pcl_conversions.h>
#include <sensor_msgs/PointCloud2.h>
#include <pcl/io/pcd_io.h>

main(int argc, char **argv)
{
    ros::init (argc, argv, "pcl_read");

    ROS_INFO("Started PCL read node");

    ros::NodeHandle nh;
    ros::Publisher pcl_pub = nh.advertise<sensor_msgs::PointCloud2>
("pcl_output", 1);

    sensor_msgs::PointCloud2 output;
    pcl::PointCloud<pcl::PointXYZ> cloud;

//Load test.pcd file
    pcl::io::loadPCDFile ("test.pcd", cloud);

    pcl::toROSMsg(cloud, output);
    output.header.frame_id = "point_cloud";

    ros::Rate loop_rate(1);
    while (ros::ok())
    {
//Publishing the cloud inside pcd file
```

```
        pcl_pub.publish(output);
        ros::spinOnce();
        loop_rate.sleep();
    }

    return 0;
}
```

We can create a ROS package called `pcl_ros_tutorial` for compiling these examples:

```
$ catkin_create_pkg pcl_ros_tutorial pcl pcl_ros roscpp sensor_msgs
```

Otherwise, we can use the existing package.

Create the preceding examples inside `src` as `pcl_publisher.cpp`, `pcl_filter.cpp`, `pcl_write.cpp`, and `pcl_read.cpp`.

Create `CMakeLists.txt` for compiling all the sources:

```
## Declare a cpp executable
add_executable(pcl_publisher_node src/pcl_publisher.cpp)
add_executable(pcl_filter src/pcl_filter.cpp)
add_executable(pcl_write src/pcl_write.cpp)
add_executable(pcl_read src/pcl_read.cpp)

target_link_libraries(pcl_publisher_node
   ${catkin_LIBRARIES}
 )
target_link_libraries(pcl_filter
   ${catkin_LIBRARIES}
 )
target_link_libraries(pcl_write
   ${catkin_LIBRARIES}
 )
target_link_libraries(pcl_read
   ${catkin_LIBRARIES}
 )
```

Build this package using `catkin_make`, and we can run `pcl_publisher_node` and the view point cloud inside RViz by using the following command:

```
$ rosrun rviz rviz -f point_cloud
```

A screenshot of the point cloud from `pcl_output` is shown in the following image:

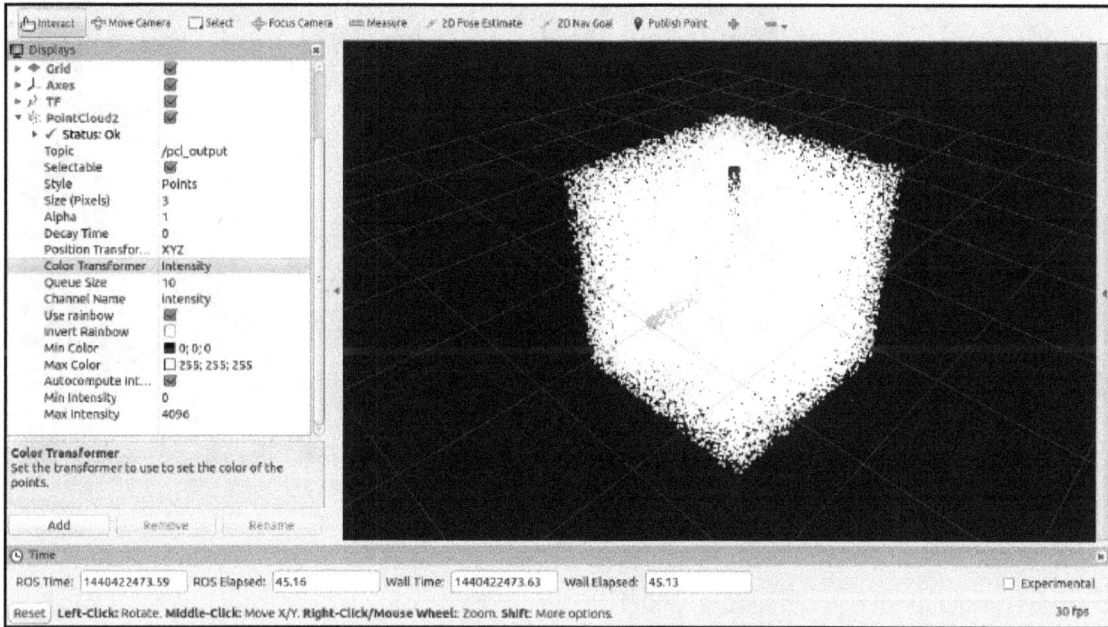

Figure 17: PCL cloud in RViz

We can run the `pcl_filter` node to subscribe this same cloud and do voxel grid filtering. The following screenshot shows the output from the `/pcl_filtered` topic, which is the resultant down-sampled cloud:

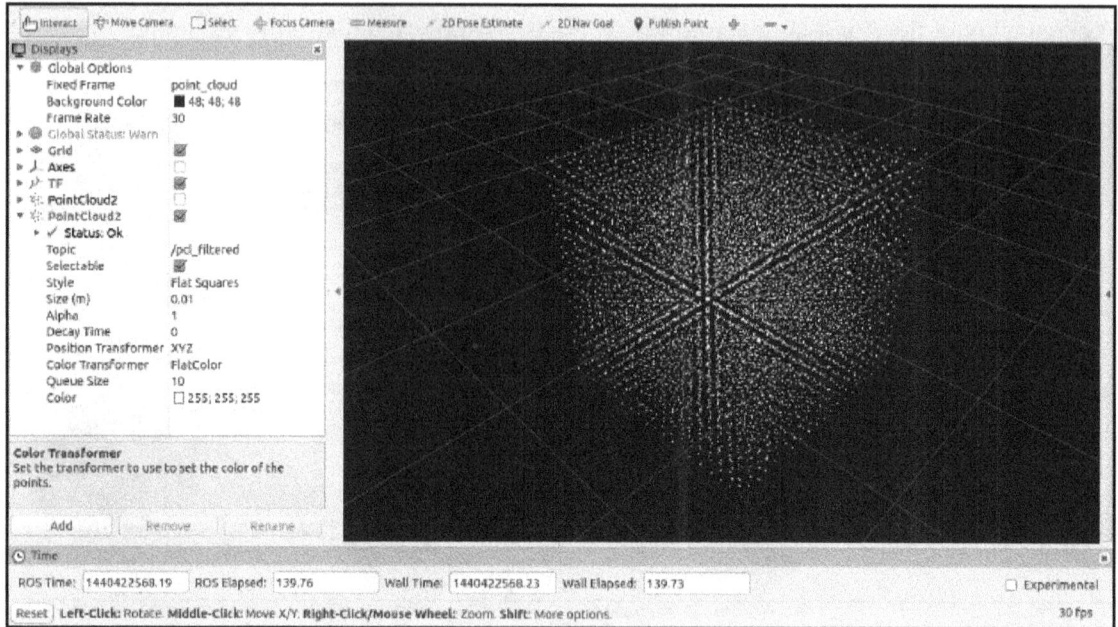

Figure 18: Filtered PCL cloud in RViz

We can write the `pcl_output` cloud by using the `pcl_write` node and read or publish by using the `pcl_read` nodes.

Working with AR Marker detection for object pose estimation

In this section, we will see how to use fiducial markers in order to enable a robot to easily interact with its environment. To interact with arbitrary objects, a robot should be able to recognize and localize them by relying on its vision sensors. Estimating the pose of an object represents an important feature of all robotic and computer-vision applications. However, efficient algorithms to perform object recognition and pose estimation working in real-world environments are difficult to implement, and in many cases one camera is not enough to retrieve the three-dimensional pose of an object.

More precisely, with the use of only one fixed camera, it is not possible to get spatial information about the depth of a framed scene. For this reason, object pose estimation is often simplified by exploiting AR markers. An AR marker is typically represented by a synthetic square image composed by a wide black border and an inner binary matrix which determines its unique identifier, as shown in Figure 19. The presence of a black border facilitates its fast detection in the image, and the binary codification allows its identification and the application of error detection and correction techniques:

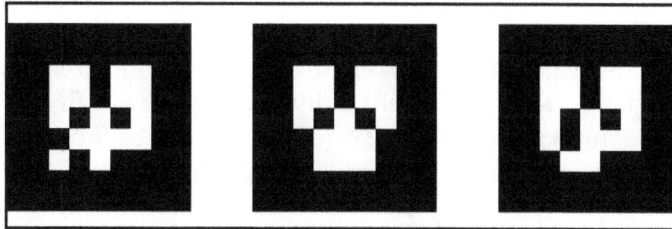

Figure 19: Augmented reality markers

The main benefit of these markers is that every fiducial image can be uniquely detected by our program, starting from a dictionary of markers, allowing the robot to identify and interact with a high number of objects. In addition, by configuring the size of the markers to detect, it is possible to estimate the distance of a given object with respect to the visual sensor. These markers are commonly called Augmented Reality markers because they have been widely used in augmented reality applications to display artificial information or artificial objects upon video frames. Different programs working with AR markers have been developed and many of these have been interfaced with ROS, such as, for example, ARToolKit (https://github.com/ar-tools/ar_tools) or ArUco: a minimal library for Augmented Reality applications (https://www.uco.es/investiga/grupos/ava/node/26). In the following section, we will discuss how to use the AprilTag visual fiducial system to detect and localize markers, interfacing it with ROS, and estimating the three-dimensional position and orientation of different objects.

Using AprilTag with ROS

AprilTag (https://april.eecs.umich.edu/software/apriltag.html) is a fiducial system particularly designed for robotics applications, thanks to its high level of precision computing the pose of AR markers, AprtilTag is particularly designed for robotics applications, you should clone the following repository:

```
$ git clone https://github.com/RIVeR-Lab/apriltags_ros.git
```

Now you can compile the ROS workspace in order to build the `apriltags` package and its ROS porting `apriltags_ros`. To use AprilTag, the following things are needed:

- **Video stream**: The video data received via `sensor_msgs/Image` is elaborated by searching for a list.
- **Camera calibration**: The calibration data received via `sensor_msgs/CameraInfo`, as shown in the previous sections.
- **Tag description**: The configuration of the marker to detect. In particular its ID, the size of the markers, and the frames associated with its pose must be specified.
- **Tags**: A printed copy of the markers to detect. ApriTag already provides a complete set of `png` ready-to-print individual markers of five different encodings: 16h5, 25h7, 25h9, 36h9, or 36h11. These markers can be found in the `apriltags/tags` directory of `apriltags` package.

After it has been configured and launched, `apriltags_ros` will publish the pose of all the markers detected in the framed scene and configured in the launch file. In particular, the following topics will be published by the `apriltags` node:

```
/tag_detections
/tag_detections_image
/tag_detections_image/compressed
/tag_detections_image/compressed/parameter_descriptions
/tag_detections_image/compressed/parameter_updates
/tag_detections_image/compressedDepth
/tag_detections_image/compressedDepth/parameter_descriptions
/tag_detections_image/compressedDepth/parameter_updates
/tag_detections_image/theora
/tag_detections_image/theora/parameter_descriptions
/tag_detections_image/theora/parameter_updates
/tag_detections_pose
/tf
```

Figure 20: ROS topics published by AprilTag

The image elaboration process and the detected markers can be graphically seen displaying the image published on `/tag_detections_image`, where each fiducial marker is enlightened and labelled with its ID:

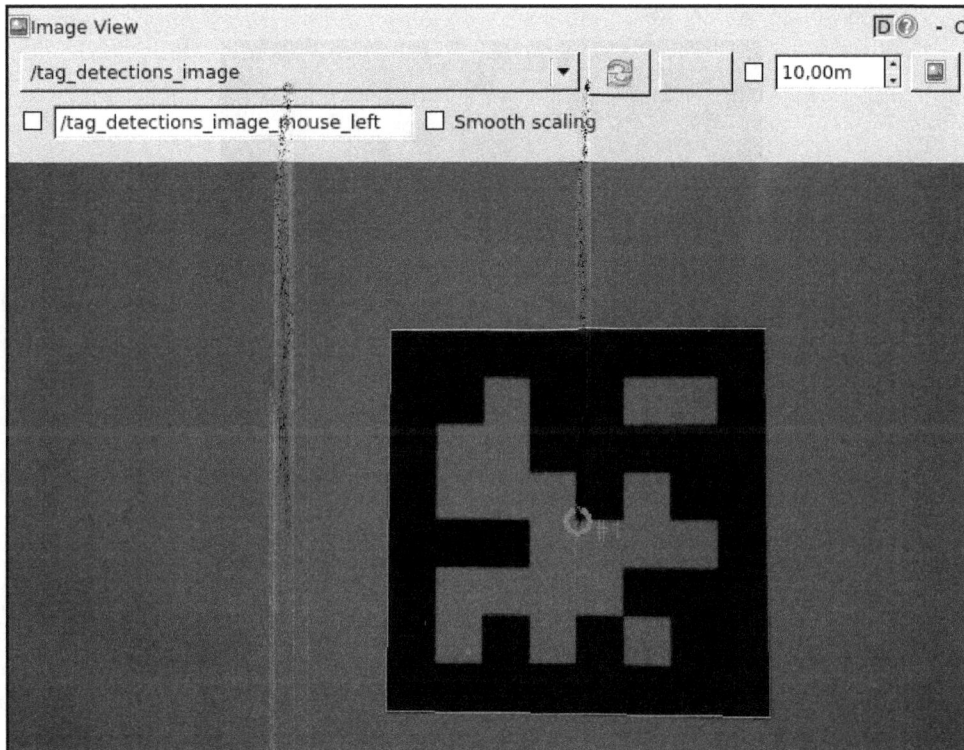

Figure 21: Graphical output of ROS AprilTag

Pose information about detected markers is published on `/tag_detections` of the `apriltags_ros/AprilTagDetectionArray` type. In this topic, the IDs and the poses of all detected markers are published. The content of this topic, associated to the frame of the previous figure, is shown following:

```
detections:
  -
    id: 1
    size: 0.08
    pose:
      header:
        seq: 55709
        stamp:
          secs: 1510415864
          nsecs: 148304216
        frame_id: camera_rgb_optical_frame
      pose:
        position:
          x: 0.0201272971812
          y: -0.02393358631
          z: 0.383437954847
        orientation:
          x: 0.713140734773
          y: -0.681737860948
          z: 0.153311144456
          w: 0.0562092015923
---
```

Figure 22: Position and orientation of markers detected by ROS AprilTag

Let's now discuss how to use `apriltags` to get the position of three objects. After calibrating our vision system, as shown in previous sections, we could configure and launch the `apriltags_ros` node. However, you could run this demo using the files of the `apriltags_ros_demo` ROS packages provided with the code of this book, or directly downloaded from the following Git repository:

```
$ git clone https://github.com/jocacace/apriltags_ros_demo
```

This package contains useful files to launch `apriltags` properly configured. In particular, you can find two main files:

- `bags`: This contains the `object.bag` bagfile, in which a video data and camera calibration information are streamed via ROS topics
- `launch`: This contains the launch file `apriltags_ros_objects.launch` that plays the `objects.bag` bagfile, and launches the `apriltags_ros` node configured to recognize three different markers

To configure the `apriltags_ros` node, we have to modify the launch file in the following way:

```
<node pkg="apriltags_ros" type="apriltag_detector_node"
name="apriltag_detector" output="screen">

    <remap from="image_rect" to="/camera/rgb/image_raw" />
    <remap from="camera_info" to="/camera/rgb/camera_info" />

    <param name="image_transport" type="str" value="compressed" />

    <param name="tag_family" type="str" value="36h11" />

    <rosparam param="tag_descriptions">[
      {id: 6, size: 0.035, frame_id: mastering_ros},
      {id: 1, size: 0.035, frame_id: laptop},
      {id: 7, size: 0.035, frame_id: smartphone}
      ]
    </rosparam>
</node>
```

In this launch file, we could set the topic used by the camera to stream the video stream and its image, using the `remap` command:

```
<remap from="image_rect" to="/camera/rgb/image_raw" />
<remap from="camera_info" to="/camera/rgb/camera_info" />
```

In addition, we must inform `apriltags_ros` about which markers must be detected. First, we should specify the family name:

```
<param name="tag_family" type="str" value="36h11" />
```

Finally, the ID of the markers, their size expressed in meters, and the frame attached to each tag, should be specified in the following way:

```
    <rosparam param="tag_descriptions">[
      {id: 6, size: 0.035, frame_id: mastering_ros},
      {id: 1, size: 0.035, frame_id: laptop},
      {id: 7, size: 0.035, frame_id: smartphone}
      ]
    </rosparam>
```

Note that the size of the marker is represented by the length of one of the sides of its black border. This information allows AR marker detectors to estimate the distance of the tag from the camera. For this reason, you should pay attention when providing this measure to get a precise pose estimation.

In this case, we want to detect three different markers, with IDs 6, 1, and 7 respectively, and with a size of 3.5 centimetres. Each marker is linked to a different frame, which will be even displayed on Rviz using `tf`. The complete launch file can be found in the `apriltags_ros_demo/launch` directory.

We can launch this example directly using the provided launch file, which firstly reproduces a `bagfile` containing the video of a scene composed by three objects or markers and the calibration of the camera:

```
$ roslaunch apriltag_ros_demo apriltags_ros_objects.launch
```

Now you can read the poses of these objects via the `apriltags_ros` topic output, or visualize them using Rviz, as show in the next image:

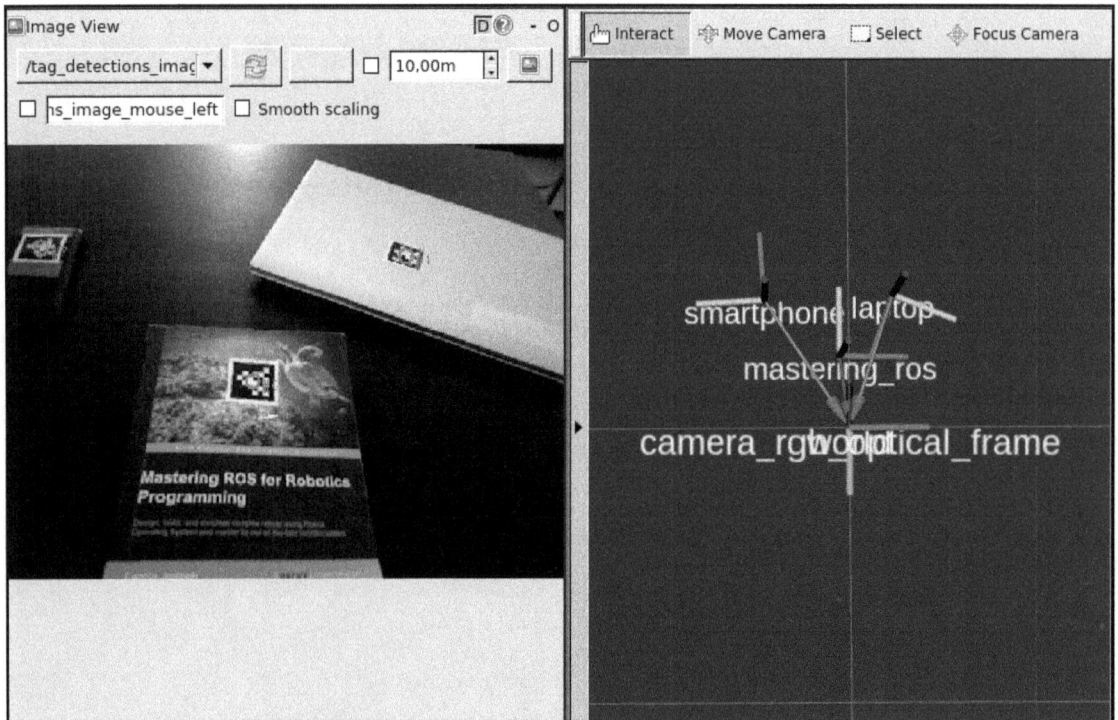

Figure 23: Tracking multiple objects using AR markers and ROS

Questions

- What are the packages in the `vision_opencv` stack?
- What are the packages in the `perception_pcl` stack?
- What are the functions of `cv_bridge`?
- How do we convert a PCL cloud to a ROS message?
- How do we do distributive computing using ROS?
- What is the main benefit of the AR markers?

Summary

This chapter was about vision sensors and their programming in ROS. We saw the interfacing packages used to interface the cameras and 3D vision sensors, such as `vision_opencv` and `perception_pcl`. We looked at each package and its functions on these stacks. We looked at the interfacing of a basic webcam and processing image, using ROS `cv_bridge`. After discussing `cv_bridge`, we looked at the interfacing of various 3D vision sensors and laser scanners with ROS. After interfacing, we learned how to process the data from these sensors, using the PCL library and ROS. Finally, in the last part of the chapter, we showed how to use fiducial markers to easily perform object pose estimation and localization. In the next chapter, we will look at the interfacing of robotic hardware in ROS.

11
Building and Interfacing Differential Drive Mobile Robot Hardware in ROS

In the previous chapter, we discussed robotic vision using ROS. In this chapter, we will see how to build autonomous mobile robot hardware with a differential drive configuration and how to interface it into ROS. We will see how to configure the ROS Navigation stack for this robot and perform SLAM and AMCL to move the robot autonomously. This chapter aims to give you an idea about building a custom mobile robot and interfacing it on ROS. We will cover the following topics in this chapter:

- Introduction to Chefbot a DIY autonomous mobile robot
- Developing base controller and odometry nodes for Chefbot in ROS
- Configuring the Navigation stack for Chefbot and understanding AMCL
- Working with the Chefbot simulation
- Interacting with the Navigation stack with a ROS node

The first topic we are going to discuss in this chapter is how to build a **DIY (Do It Yourself)** autonomous mobile robot, develop its firmware, and interface it to the ROS Navigation stack. The robot, called Chefbot, was built as part of a book called *Learning Robotics using Python* by Josep Lentin and published by Packt Publishing (http://learn-robotics.com). The step-by-step procedure to build this robot is discussed in that book. In this chapter, we will cover abstract information about this robot hardware, and we will learn more about configuring the ROS Navigation stack and its fine tuning for performing autonomous navigation using SLAM and AMCL. We have already discussed the ROS Navigation stack in Chapter 6, *Using the ROS MoveIt! and Navigation Stack,* and we have simulated a differential robot using Gazebo and performed SLAM and AMCL. In the first part of the chapter, the Chefbot hardware is required to follow the tutorials. However, the concepts discussed in the first part of the chapter are then applied to a simulated robot in the second part of the chapter.

Introducing to Chefbot – a DIY mobile robot and its hardware configuration

In Chapter 6, *Using the ROS MoveIt! and Navigation Stack,* we have discussed some mandatory requirements for interfacing a mobile robot with the ROS Navigation package. These requirements are recalled in the following:

- **Odometry source**: The robot should publish its odometry/position data with respect to the starting position. The necessary hardware components that provide odometry information are wheel encoders, IMU, or 2D/3D cameras (visual odometry).
- **Sensor source**: There should be a laser scanner, or a vision sensor that can act as a laser scanner. The laser scanner data is essential for the map-building process using SLAM.
- **Sensor transform using tf**: The robot should publish the transform of the sensors and other robot components using ROS transform.
- **Base controller**: The base controller is an ROS node, which can convert a twist message from the Navigation stack to corresponding motor velocities:

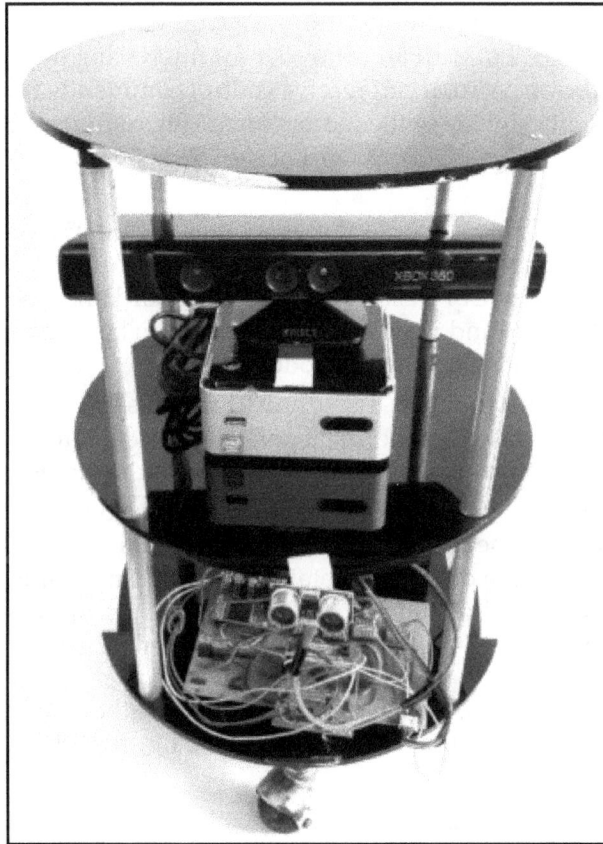

Figure 1: Chefbot prototype

We can check the components present in the robot and determine whether they satisfy the Navigation stack requirements. The following components are present in the robot:

- **Pololu DC Gear motor with Quadrature encoder** (https://www.pololu.com/product/1447): The motor is operated in 12V, 80 RPM, and an 18 kg-cm torque. It takes a current of 300 mA in free run and a 5 A in-stall condition. The motor shaft is attached to a quadrature encoder, which can deliver a maximum count of 8,400 counts per revolution of the gearbox's output shaft. Motor encoders are one source of odometry of robot.
- **Pololu motor drivers** (https://www.pololu.com/product/708): These are dual motor controllers for Pololu motors that can support up to 30 A and motor voltage from 5.5V to 16V.

- **Tiva C Launchpad Controller** (http://www.ti.com/tool/ek-tm4c123gxl): This robot has a Tiva C LaunchPad controller for interfacing motors, encoders, sensors, and so on. Also, it can receive control commands from the PC and can send appropriate signals to the motors according to the command. This board can act as an embedded controller board of the robot. Tiva C LaunchPad board runs on 80 MHz.

- **MPU 6050 IMU**: The IMU used in this robot is **MPU 6050**, which is a combination of accelerometer, gyroscope, and **Digital Motion Processer** (**DMP**). This motion processor can run sensor fusion algorithms onboard and can provide accurate results of roll, pitch, and yaw. The IMU values can be taken to calculate the odometry along with the wheel encoders.

- **Xbox Kinect/Asus Xtion Pro**: These are 3D vision sensors and we can use these sensors to mock a laser scanner. The point cloud generated from these sensors can be converted into laser scan data and used in the Navigation stack.

- **Intel NUC PC**: This is a mini PC from Intel, and we have to load this with Ubuntu and ROS. The PC is connected to Kinect and LaunchPad to retrieve the sensor values and the odometry details. The program running on the PC can compute **TF** of the robot and run the Navigation stack and associated packages, such as SLAM and AMCL. This PC is placed within the robot itself.

We can check from the aforementioned hardware list that all the requirements needed by the ROS Navigation package are satisfied. The following figure shows the block diagram of this robot:

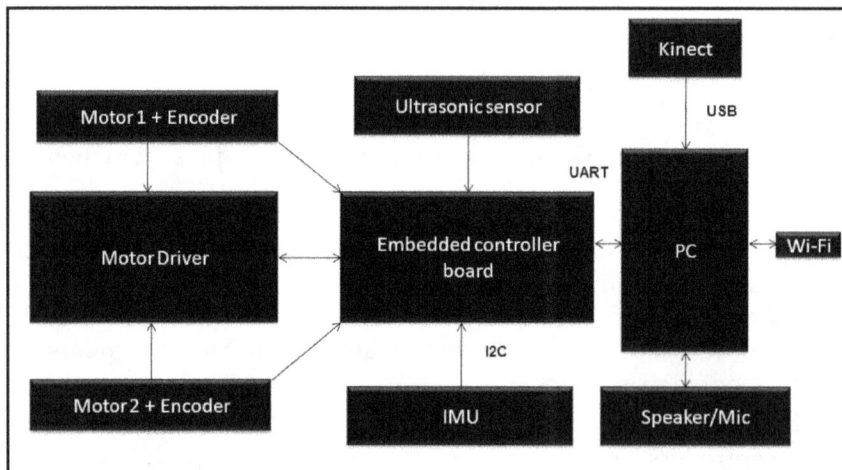

Figure 2: Block diagram of Chefbot

In this robot, the embedded controller board is the Tiva C LaunchPad. All the sensors and actuators are connected to the controller board, and it is connected to the Intel NUC PC for receiving higher-level commands. The board and the PC communicate in the UART protocol, IMU, and the board communicates using I2C. Kinect is interfaced to the PC via USB, and all the other sensors are interfaced through GPIO pins. A detailed connection diagram of the robot components follows:

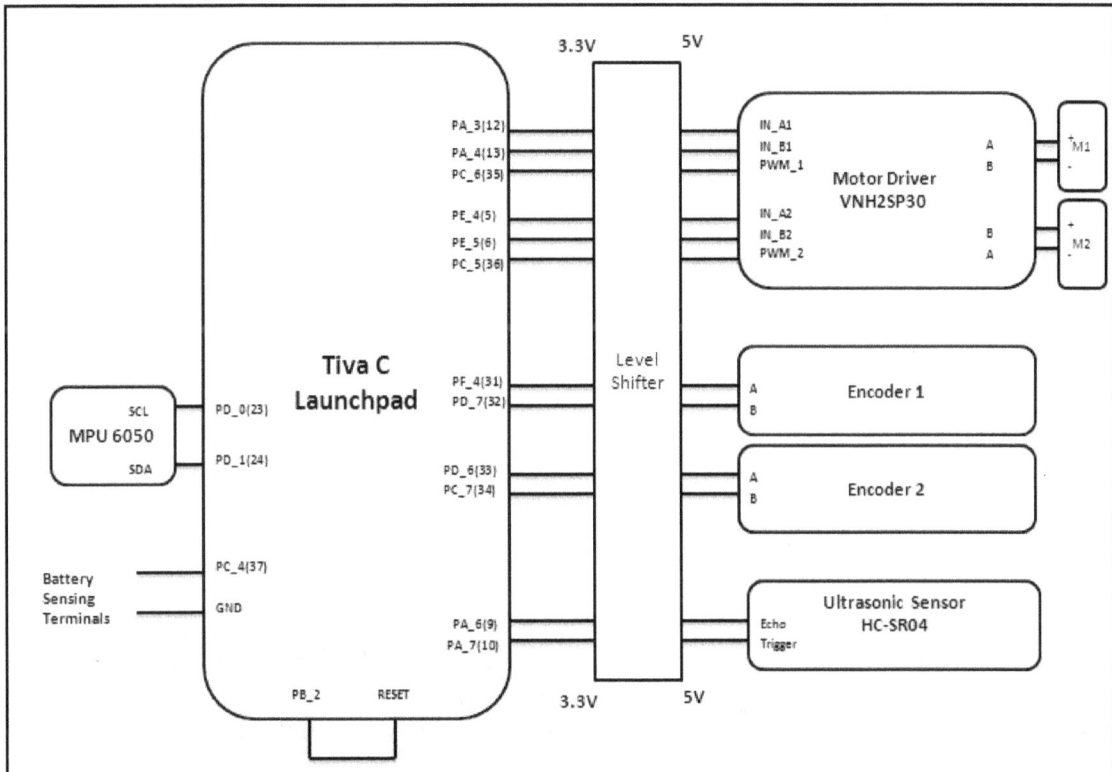

Figure 3: Connection diagram of Chefbot

Flashing Chefbot firmware using Energia IDE

After developing the preceding connections, we can program the Launchpad using the Energia IDE (http://energia.nu/). After setting Energia IDE on the PC (Ubuntu is preferred), we can flash the robot firmware to the board. We will get the firmware code and the ROS interface package by using the following command:

```
$ git clone https://github.com/qboticslabs/Chefbot_ROS_pkg
```

The folder contains a folder called `tiva_c_energia_code`, which has the firmware code that flashes to the board after compilation in Energia IDE. The firmware can read the encoder, ultrasonic sensor, and IMU values, and can receive values of the motor velocity command. The important section of the firmware is discussed here. The programming language in the LaunchPad is the same as Arduino. Here we are using Energia IDE to program the controller, which is built using the Arduino IDE. The following code snippet is the `setup()` function definition of the code. This function starts serial communication with a baud rate of 115,200. It also configures the pins of the motor encoder, motor driver pins, ultrasonic distance sensor, and the IMU. Also, through this code, we are configuring a pin to reset the LaunchPad:

```
void setup()
{
  //Init Serial port with 115200 baud rate
  Serial.begin(115200);
  //Setup Encoders
  SetupEncoders();
  //Setup Motors
  SetupMotors();
  //Setup Ultrasonic
  SetupUltrasonic();
  //Setup MPU 6050
  Setup_MPU6050();
  //Setup Reset pins
  SetupReset();
  //Set up Messenger
  Messenger_Handler.attach(OnMssageCompleted);
}
```

In the `loop()` function, the sensor values are continuously polled and the data is sent through a serial port and incoming serial data is continuously polled for getting the robot commands. The following convention protocols are used to send each sensor value from the LaunchPad to the PC using serial communication (UART):

Serial data sending protocol from LaunchPad to PC

For the encoder, the protocol will be as follows:

```
e<space><left_encoder_ticks><space><right_encoder_ticks>
```

For the ultrasonic sensor, the protocol will be as follows:

```
u<space><distance_in_centimeter>
```

For IMU, the protocol will be as follows:

```
i<space><value_of_x_quaternion><space><value_of_y_quaternion>
<space><value_of_z_quaternion><space><value_of_w_quaternion>
```

Serial data sending protocol from PC to Launchpad

For the motor, the protocol will be as follows:

```
s<space><pwm_value_of_motor_1><space><pwm_value_of_motor_2>
```

For resetting the device, the protocol will be as follows:

```
r<space>
```

We can check the serial values from the LaunchPad using a command-line tool called `miniterm.py`. This tool can view the serial data coming from a device. This script is already installed with the `python-serial` package, which is installed along with the `rosserial-python` Debian package. The following command will display the serial values from the robot controller:

```
$ miniterm.py /dev/ttyACM0 115200
```

We will get values such as these shown in the following screenshot:

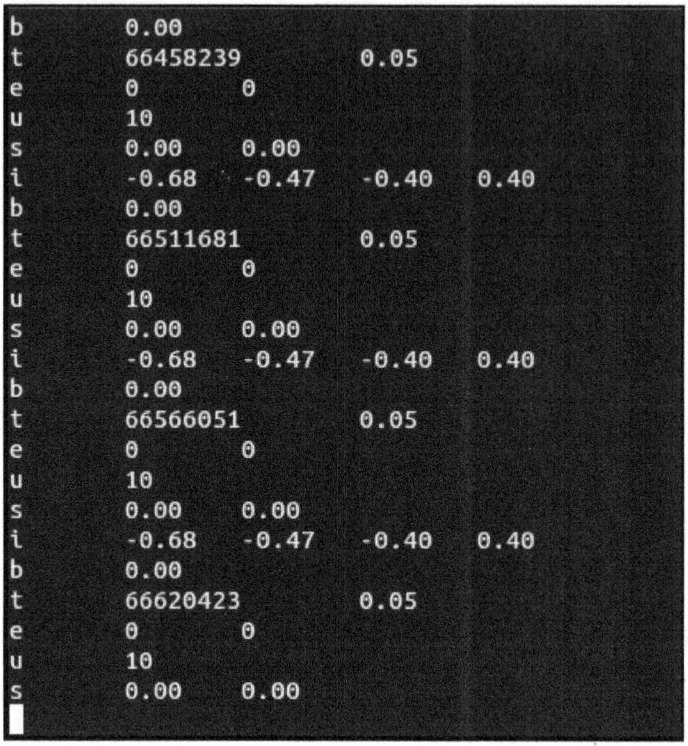

Figure 4: Checking serial data using `miniterm.py`

Discussing Chefbot interface packages on ROS

After confirming the serial values from the board, we can install the Chefbot ROS package. The Chefbot package contains the following files and folders:

- `chefbot_bringup`: This package contains Python scripts, C++ nodes, and launch files to start publishing robot odometry and `tf`, and performing gmapping and AMCL. It contains the Python/C++ nodes to read/write values from the LaunchPad, convert the encoder ticks to `tf`, and twist messages to motor commands. It also has the PID node for handling velocity commands from the motor commands.
- `chefbot_description`: This package contains the Chefbot URDF model.

- chefbot_simulator: This package contains launch files to simulate the robot in Gazebo.
- chefbot_navig_cpp: This package contains the C++ implementation of a few nodes that are already implemented in chefbot_bringup as the Python node.

After cloning the Chefbot main directory from the previous GitHub repository, we could compile the workspace. To successfully compile the packages of the repository, some dependencies must be installed using the following command:

```
$ sudo apt-get install ros-kinetic-depthimage-to-laserscan ros-kinetic-
kobuki-gazebo-plugins ros-kinetic-robot-pose-ekf ros-kinetic-yocs-cmd-vel-
mux ros-kinetic-move-base-msgs ros-kinetic-openni-launch ros-kinetic-
kobuki-description ros-kinetic-gmapping ros-kinetic-amcl ros-kinetic-map-
server
```

The following launch file will start the robot odometry and the tf publishing nodes:

```
$ roslaunch chefbot_bringup robot_standalone.launch
```

In the next figure, the nodes started by this launch file and how they are interconnected are shown:

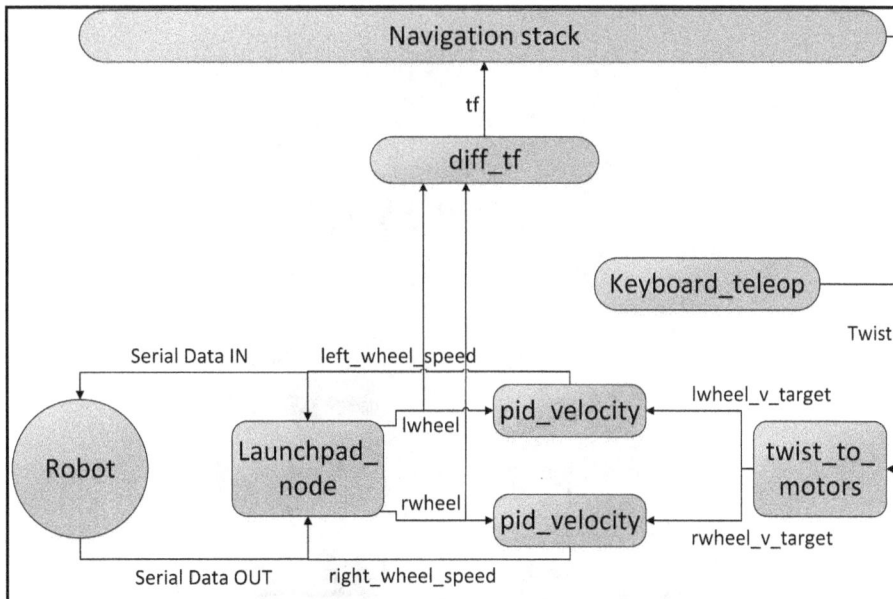

Figure 5: Interconnection of each node in Chefbot

The nodes run by this launch file and their workings are described next:

- `launchpad_node.py`: We know that this robot uses the Tiva C LaunchPad board as its controller. This node acts as a bridge between the robot controller and the ROS. The basic functionality of this node is to receive serial values from the LaunchPad and convert each sensor data into ROS topics. This acts as the ROS driver for the LaunchPad board.

- `twist_to_motors.py`: This node converts the `geometry_msgs/Twist` message to motor velocity targets. It subscribes the command velocity, which is either from a teleop node or from an ROS Navigation stack, and publishes `lwheel_vtarget` and `rwheel_vtarget`.

- `pid_velocity.py`: This node subscribes `wheel_vtarget` from the `twist_to_motors` node and the wheel topic, which is the encoder tick from the `launchpad_node`. We have to start two PID nodes for each wheel of the robot, as shown in the previous figure. This node finally generates the motor speed commands for each motor.

- `diff_tf.py`: This node subscribes the encoder ticks from the two motors, and computes odometry, and publishes `tf` for the Navigation stack.

- The list of topics generated after running `robot_standalone.launch` are shown in the following image:

```
lentin@lentin-Aspire-4755:~$ rostopic list
/battery_level
/cmd_vel_mux/input/teleop
/imu/data
/joint_states
/left_wheel_speed
/lwheel
/lwheel_vel
/lwheel_vtarget
/odom
/qw
/qx
/qy
/qz
/right_wheel_speed
/rosout
/rosout_agg
/rwheel
/rwheel_vel
/rwheel_vtarget
/serial
/tf
/ultrasonic_distance
```

Figure 6: List of topics generated when executing `robot_standalone.launch`.

The following is the content of the `robot_standalone.launch` file:

```
<launch>
 <arg name="simulation" default="$(optenv TURTLEBOT_SIMULATION false)"/>
 <param name="/use_sim_time" value="$(arg simulation)"/>

<!-- URDF robot model -->
  <arg name="urdf_file" default="$(find xacro)/xacro.py '$(find
chefbot_description)/urdf/chefbot_base.xacro'" />
  <param name="robot_description" command="$(arg urdf_file)" />

  <!-- important generally, but specifically utilised by the current app
manager -->
  <param name="robot/name" value="$(optenv ROBOT turtlebot)"/>
  <param name="robot/type" value="turtlebot"/>

<!-- Starting robot state publisher -->
  <node pkg="robot_state_publisher" type="robot_state_publisher"
name="robot_state_publisher">
    <param name="publish_frequency" type="double" value="5.0" />
  </node>

<!-- Robot parameters -->
  <rosparam param="base_width">0.3</rosparam>
  <rosparam param="ticks_meter">14865</rosparam>

<!-- Starting launchpad_node -->
  <node name="launchpad_node" pkg="chefbot_bringup"
type="launchpad_node.py">
    <rosparam file="$(find chefbot_bringup)/param/serial.yaml"
command="load" />
  </node>

<!-- PID node for left motor , setting PID parameters -->
  <node name="lpid_velocity" pkg="chefbot_bringup" type="pid_velocity.py"
output="screen">
      <remap from="wheel" to="lwheel"/>
      <remap from="motor_cmd" to="left_wheel_speed"/>
      <remap from="wheel_vtarget" to="lwheel_vtarget"/>
      <remap from="wheel_vel" to="lwheel_vel"/>
      <rosparam param="Kp">400</rosparam>
      <rosparam param="Ki">100</rosparam>
      <rosparam param="Kd">0</rosparam>
      <rosparam param="out_min">-1023</rosparam>
      <rosparam param="out_max">1023</rosparam>
      <rosparam param="rate">30</rosparam>
      <rosparam param="timeout_ticks">4</rosparam>
```

```
        <rosparam param="rolling_pts">5</rosparam>
    </node>

  <!-- PID node for right motor, setting PID parameters -->
    <node name="rpid_velocity" pkg="chefbot_bringup" type="pid_velocity.py"
output="screen">
        <remap from="wheel" to="rwheel"/>
        <remap from="motor_cmd" to="right_wheel_speed"/>
        <remap from="wheel_vtarget" to="rwheel_vtarget"/>
        <remap from="wheel_vel" to="rwheel_vel"/>
        <rosparam param="Kp">400</rosparam>
        <rosparam param="Ki">100</rosparam>
        <rosparam param="Kd">0</rosparam>
        <rosparam param="out_min">-1023</rosparam>
        <rosparam param="out_max">1023</rosparam>
        <rosparam param="rate">30</rosparam>
        <rosparam param="timeout_ticks">4</rosparam>
        <rosparam param="rolling_pts">5</rosparam>
    </node>

  <!-- Starting twist to motor and diff_tf nodes -->

    <node pkg="chefbot_bringup" type="twist_to_motors.py"
name="twist_to_motors" output="screen"/>
    <node pkg="chefbot_bringup" type="diff_tf.py" name="diff_tf"
output="screen"/>

</launch>
```

After running `robot_standalone.launch`, we can visualize the robot in RViz, using the following command:

```
$ roslaunch chefbot_bringup view_robot.launch
```

We will see the robot model, as shown in this next screenshot:

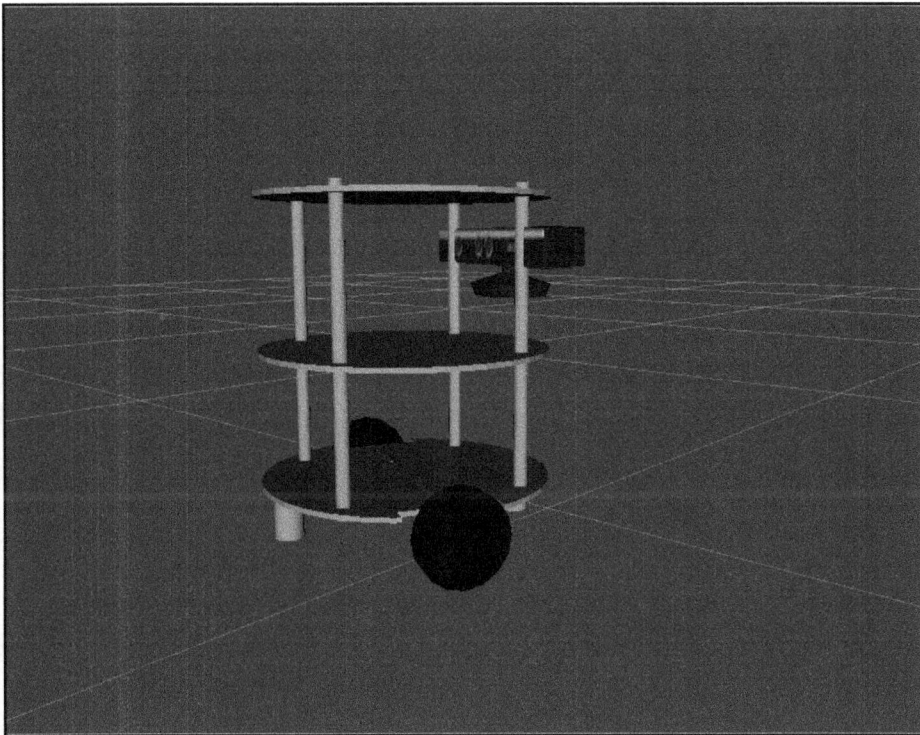

Figure 7: Visualization of robot model using real robot values

Launch the keyboard `teleop` node and we can start moving the robot:

```
$ roslaunch chefbot_bringup keyboard_teleop.launch
```

Move the robot using the keys and we will see that the robot is moving around. If we enable `tf` of the robot in RViz, we can view the odometry, as shown in the following screenshot:

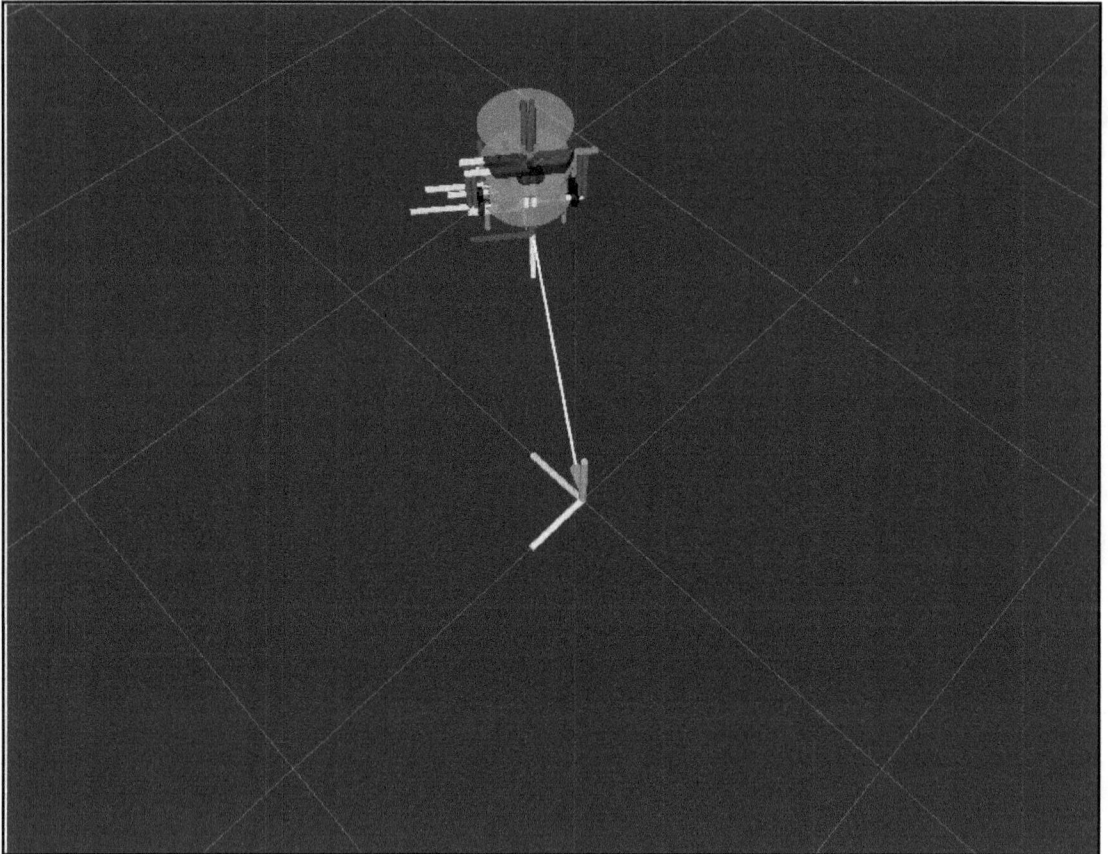

Figure 8: Visualizing robot odometry

The graph of the connections between each node can be viewed, using the `rqt_graph` tool:

```
$ rqt_graph
```

Until now we have discussed the Chefbot interfacing on ROS. The coding of Chefbot is completely done in Python. There are some nodes implemented in C++ for computing odometry from the encoder ticks and generating motor speed commands from the twist messages.

Computing odometry from encoder ticks

In this section, we will see the C++ interpretation of the `diff_tf.py` node, which subscribes the encoder data and computes the odometry, and publishes the odometry and `tf` of the robot. We can see the C++ interpretation of this node, called `diff_tf.cpp`, which can be found in the `src` folder of a package named `chefbot_navig_cpp`.

Discussed next are the important code snippets of this code and their explanations. The following code snippet is the constructor of the `Odometry_calc` class. This class contains the definition of computing odometry. The following code declares the subscriber for the left and right wheel encoders along with the publisher for the `odom` value:

```
Odometry_calc::Odometry_calc(){

  //Initialize variables used in the node
   init_variables();

  ROS_INFO("Started odometry computing node");

  //Subscribing left and right wheel encoder values
   l_wheel_sub = n.subscribe("/lwheel",10, &Odometry_calc::leftencoderCb,
this);
   r_wheel_sub = n.subscribe("/rwheel",10, &Odometry_calc::rightencoderCb,
this);

   //Creating a publisher for odom
    odom_pub = n.advertise<nav_msgs::Odometry>("odom", 50);

  //Retrieving parameters of this node
   get_node_params();
}
```

The following code is the update loop of computing odometry. It computes the delta distance moved and the angle rotated by the robot using the encoder values, base width of the robot, and ticks per meter of the encoder. After calculating the delta distance and the delta theta, we can compute the final x, y, and theta using the standard differential drive robot equations:

```
if ( now > t_next) {

  elapsed = now.toSec() - then.toSec();

  if(enc_left == 0){
    d_left = 0;
    d_right = 0;
```

```
    }
    else{
      d_left = (left - enc_left) / ( ticks_meter);
      d_right = (right - enc_right) / ( ticks_meter);
    }
    enc_left = left;
    enc_right = right;

    d = (d_left + d_right ) / 2.0;

    th = ( d_right - d_left ) / base_width;
    dx = d /elapsed;

    dr = th / elapsed;

    if ( d != 0){

                    x = cos( th ) * d;
                    y = -sin( th ) * d;

                    // calculate the final position of the robot
                    x_final = x_final + ( cos( theta_final ) * x - sin(
theta_final ) * y );
                    y_final = y_final + ( sin( theta_final ) * x + cos(
theta_final ) * y );

      }
      if( th != 0)
            theta_final = theta_final + th;
```

After computing the robot position and the orientation from the preceding code snippet, we can feed the odom values to the odom message header and the tf header, which will publish the topics in /odom and /tf:

```
    geometry_msgs::Quaternion odom_quat ;

    odom_quat.x = 0.0;
    odom_quat.y = 0.0;
    odom_quat.z = 0.0;

        odom_quat.z = sin( theta_final / 2 );
        odom_quat.w = cos( theta_final / 2 );

    //first, we'll publish the transform over tf
    geometry_msgs::TransformStamped odom_trans;
    odom_trans.header.stamp = now;
    odom_trans.header.frame_id = "odom";
```

```
odom_trans.child_frame_id = "base_footprint";

odom_trans.transform.translation.x = x_final;
odom_trans.transform.translation.y = y_final;
odom_trans.transform.translation.z = 0.0;
odom_trans.transform.rotation = odom_quat;

//send the transform
odom_broadcaster.sendTransform(odom_trans);

//next, we'll publish the odometry message over ROS
nav_msgs::Odometry odom;
odom.header.stamp = now;
odom.header.frame_id = "odom";

//set the position
odom.pose.pose.position.x = x_final;
odom.pose.pose.position.y = y_final;
odom.pose.pose.position.z = 0.0;
odom.pose.pose.orientation = odom_quat;

//set the velocity
odom.child_frame_id = "base_footprint";
odom.twist.twist.linear.x = dx;
odom.twist.twist.linear.y = 0;
odom.twist.twist.angular.z = dr;

//publish the message
odom_pub.publish(odom);
```

Computing motor velocities from ROS twist message

The C++ implementation of `twist_to_motor.py` is discussed in this section. This node will convert the twist message (`geometry_msgs/Twist`) to motor target velocities. The topic subscribed by this node is the twist message from the `teleop` node or Navigation stack and it publishes the target velocities for the two motors. The target velocities are fed into the PID nodes, which will send appropriate commands to each motor. The CPP filename is `twist_to_motor.cpp`, and you can get it from the `chefbot_navig_cpp/src` folder:

```
TwistToMotors::TwistToMotors()
{
    init_variables();
    get_parameters();
```

```
    ROS_INFO("Started Twist to Motor node");
    cmd_vel_sub = n.subscribe("cmd_vel_mux/input/teleop",10,
&TwistToMotors::twistCallback, this);
    pub_lmotor = n.advertise<std_msgs::Float32>("lwheel_vtarget", 50);

    pub_rmotor = n.advertise<std_msgs::Float32>("rwheel_vtarget", 50);
}
```

The following code snippet is the callback function of the twist message. The linear velocity X is assigned as dx, Y as dy, and angular velocity Z as dr:

```
void TwistToMotors::twistCallback(const geometry_msgs::Twist &msg)
{

    ticks_since_target = 0;
    dx = msg.linear.x;
    dy = msg.linear.y;
    dr = msg.angular.z;


}
```

After getting dx, dy, and dr, we can compute the motor velocities using the following equations:

```
dx = (l + r) / 2
dr = (r - l) / w
```

Here, *r* and *l* are the right and left wheel velocities, and *w* is the base width. The preceding equations are implemented in the following code snippet. After computing the wheel velocities, they are published to the lwheel_vtarget and rwheel_vtarget topics:

```
    right = ( 1.0 * dx ) + (dr * w /2);
    left = ( 1.0 * dx ) - (dr * w /2);
    std_msgs::Float32 left_;
    std_msgs::Float32 right_;

    left_.data = left;
    right_.data = right;


    pub_lmotor.publish(left_);
    pub_rmotor.publish(right_);

    ticks_since_target += 1;

    ros::spinOnce();
```

Running the robot standalone launch file using C++ nodes

The following command can launch `robot_stand_alone.launch`, which uses the C++ nodes:

```
$ roslaunch chefbot_navig_cpp robot_standalone.launch
```

Configuring the Navigation stack for Chefbot

After setting the odometry nodes, the base controller node, and the PID nodes, we need to configure the Navigation stack to perform SLAM and **Adaptive Monte Carlo Localization** (**AMCL**) for building the map, localizing the robot, and performing autonomous navigation. In `Chapter 6`, *Using the ROS MoveIt! and Navigation Stack*, we have seen the basic packages in the Navigation stack. To build the map of the environment, we need to configure mainly two nodes: the `gmapping` node for performing SLAM and the `move_base` node. We also need to configure the global planner, the local planner, the global cost map, and the local cost map inside the Navigation stack. Let's look at the configuration of the `gmapping` node first.

Configuring the gmapping node

The gmapping node is the package to perform SLAM (`http://wiki.ros.org/gmapping`).

The `gmapping` node inside this package mainly subscribes and publishes the following topics.

The following are the subscribed topics:

- `tf` (`tf/tfMessage`): The robot transform that relates to Kinect, robot base, and odometry
- `scan` (`sensor_msgs/LaserScan`): The laser scan data that is required to create the map

The following are the published topics:

- `map` (`nav_msgs/OccupancyGrid`): Publishes the occupancy grid map data
- `map_metadata` (`nav_msgs/MapMetaData`): Basic information about the occupancy grid

The `gmapping` node is highly configurable, using various parameters. The `gmapping` node parameters are defined inside the `chefbot_bringup/launch/include/gmapping.launch.xml` file. The following is a code snippet of this file and its uses:

```
<launch>
  <arg name="scan_topic" default="scan" />

<!-- Starting gmapping node -->
  <node pkg="gmapping" type="slam_gmapping" name="slam_gmapping"
output="screen">

<!-- Frame of mobile base -->
    <param name="base_frame" value="base_footprint"/>
    <param name="odom_frame" value="odom"/>
<!-- The interval of map updation, reducing this value will speed of map
generation but increase computation load -->
    <param name="map_update_interval" value="5.0"/>
<!-- Maximum usable range of laser/kinect -->
    <param name="maxUrange" value="6.0"/>
<!-- Maximum range of sensor, max range should be > maxUrange -->
    <param name="maxRange" value="8.0"/>
    <param name="sigma" value="0.05"/>
    <param name="kernelSize" value="1"/>
  </node>
</launch>
```

By fine tuning these parameters, we improve the accuracy of the gmapping node.

The main `gmapping` launch file is given next. It is placed in `chefbot_bringup/launch/includes/gmapping_demo.launch`. This launch file launches the `openni_launch` file and the `depth_to_laserscan` node to convert the depth image to the laser scan. After launching the Kinect nodes, it launches the `gmapping` node and the `move_base` configurations:

```
<launch>
<!-- Launches 3D sensor nodes -->
  <include file="$(find chefbot_bringup)/launch/3dsensor.launch">
    <arg name="rgb_processing" value="false" />
    <arg name="depth_registration" value="false" />
    <arg name="depth_processing" value="false" />
    <arg name="scan_topic" value="/scan" />
  </include>

<!-- Start gmapping nodes and its configurations -->
  <include file="$(find
```

```
chefbot_bringup)/launch/includes/gmapping.launch.xml"/>

<!-- Start move_base node and its configuration -->
  <include file="$(find
chefbot_bringup)/launch/includes/move_base.launch.xml"/>
</launch>
```

Configuring the Navigation stack packages

The next node we need to configure is move_base. Along with the move_base node, we need to configure the global and the local planners, and also the global and the local cost maps. We will first look at the launch file to load all these configuration files. The following launch file, chefbot_bringup/launch/includes/move_base.launch.xml, will load all the parameters of move_base, planner, and costmap:

```
<launch>
  <arg name="odom_topic" default="odom" />
<!-- Starting move_base node -->
  <node pkg="move_base" type="move_base" respawn="false" name="move_base"
output="screen">

<!-- common parameters of global costmap -->
    <rosparam file="$(find
chefbot_bringup)/param/costmap_common_params.yaml" command="load"
ns="global_costmap" />

<!-- common parameters of local costmap -->
    <rosparam file="$(find
chefbot_bringup)/param/costmap_common_params.yaml" command="load"
ns="local_costmap" />

<!-- local cost map parameters -->
    <rosparam file="$(find
chefbot_bringup)/param/local_costmap_params.yaml" command="load" />

<!-- global cost map parameters -->
    <rosparam file="$(find
chefbot_bringup)/param/global_costmap_params.yaml" command="load" />

<!-- base local planner parameters -->
    <rosparam file="$(find
chefbot_bringup)/param/base_local_planner_params.yaml" command="load" />

<!-- dwa local planner parameters -->
    <rosparam file="$(find
```

```
chefbot_bringup)/param/dwa_local_planner_params.yaml" command="load" />

<!-- move_base node parameters -->
    <rosparam file="$(find chefbot_bringup)/param/move_base_params.yaml"
command="load" />

    <remap from="cmd_vel" to="/cmd_vel_mux/input/navi"/>
    <remap from="odom" to="$(arg odom_topic)"/>
  </node>
</launch>
```

We will now take a look at each configuration file and its parameters.

Common configuration local_costmap and global_costmap

The common parameters of the local and the global costmap are discussed in this section. The costmap is created using the obstacles present around the robot. Fine tuning the parameters of the costmap can increase the accuracy of map generation. The customized file costmap_common_params.yaml of Chefbot follows. This configuration file contains the common parameters of both the global and the local cost maps. It is present in the chefbot_bringup/param folder. For more about costmap common parameters, check http://wiki.ros.org/costmap_2d/flat:

```
#The maximum value of height which has to be taken as an obstacle
max_obstacle_height: 0.60
#This parameters set the maximum obstacle range. In this case, the robot
will only look at obstacles within 2.5 meters in front of robot
obstacle_range: 2.5
#This parameter helps robot to clear out space in front of it upto 3.0
meters away given a sensor reading
raytrace_range: 3.0
#If the robot is circular, we can define the robot radius, otherwise we
need to mention the robot
footprint
robot_radius: 0.45
#footprint: [[-0.,-0.1],[-0.1,0.1], [0.1, 0.1], [0.1,-0.1]]
#This parameter will actually inflate the obstacle up to this distance from
the actual obstacle. This can be taken as a tolerance value of obstacle.
The cost of map will be same as the actual obstacle up to the inflated
value.
inflation_radius: 0.50
#This factor is used for computing cost during inflation
cost_scaling_factor: 5
```

```
#We can either choose map type as voxel which will give a 3D view of the
world, or the other type, costmap which is a 2D view of the map. Here we
are opting voxel.
map_type: voxel
#This is the z_origin of the map if it voxel
origin_z: 0.0
#z resolution of map in meters
z_resolution: 0.2
#No of voxel in a vertical column
z_voxels: 2
#This flag set whether we need map for visualization purpose
publish_voxel_map: false
#A list of observation source in which we get scan data and its parameters
observation_sources: scan
#The list of scan, which mention, data type of scan as LaserScan, marking
and clearing indicate whether the laser data is used for marking and
clearing costmap.
scan: {data_type: LaserScan, topic: scan, marking: true, clearing: true,
min_obstacle_height: 0.0, max_obstacle_height: 3}
```

After discussing the common parameters, we will now look at the global_costmap configuration.

Configuring global costmap parameters

The following are the main configurations required for building a global costmap. The definition of the costmap parameters is dumped in chefbot_bringup/param/ global_costmap_params.yaml. The following is the definition of this file and its uses:

```
global_costmap
global_frame: /map
robot_base_frame: /base_footprint
update_frequency: 1.0
publish_frequency: 0.5
static_map: true
transform_tolerance: 0.5
```

The `global_frame` here is `/map`, which is the coordinate frame of the `costmap`. The `robot_base_frame` parameter is `/base_footprint`; it is the coordinate frame in which the `costmap` should reference as the robot base. The `update_frequency` is the frequency at which the `costmap` runs its main update loop. The `publishing_frequency` of the costmap is given as `publish_frequency`, which is `0.5`. If we are using an existing map, we have to set `static_map` as `true`, otherwise we set it as `false`. The `transform_tolerance` is the rate at which the transform has to perform. The robot would stop if the transforms are not updated at this rate.

Configuring local costmap parameters

The following is the local `costmap` configuration of this robot. The configuration of this file is located in `chefbot_bringup/param/local_costmap_params.yaml`:

```
local_costmap:
global_frame: odom
robot_base_frame: /base_footprint
update_frequency: 5.0
publish_frequency: 2.0
static_map: false
rolling_window: true
width: 4.0
height: 4.0
resolution: 0.05
transform_tolerance: 0.5
```

The `global_frame`, `robot_base_frame`, `publish_frequency`, and `static_map` are the same as the global `costmap`. The `rolling_window` parameter makes the `costmap` centered around the robot. If we set this parameter to `true`, we will get a `costmap` that is built centered around the robot. The width , height, and resolution parameters are the width, height, and resolution of the `costmap`. The next step will be to configure the base local planner.

Configuring base local planner parameters

The main function of the base local planner is to compute the velocity commands from the goal sent from the ROS nodes. This file mainly contains the configurations related to velocity, acceleration, and so on. The base local planner configuration file of this robot is in `chefbot_bringup/param/base_local_planner_params.yaml`. The definition of this file is as follows:

```
TrajectoryPlannerROS
# Robot Configuration Parameters, these are the velocity limit of the robot
max_vel_x: 0.3
min_vel_x: 0.1
#Angular velocity limit
max_vel_theta: 1.0
min_vel_theta: -1.0
min_in_place_vel_theta: 0.6
#These are the acceleration limits of the robot
acc_lim_x: 0.5
acc_lim_theta: 1.0
# Goal Tolerance Parameters: The tolerance of robot when it reach the goal
position
yaw_goal_tolerance: 0.3
xy_goal_tolerance: 0.15
# Forward Simulation Parameters
sim_time: 3.0
vx_samples: 6
vtheta_samples: 20
# Trajectory Scoring Parameters
meter_scoring: true
pdist_scale: 0.6
gdist_scale: 0.8
occdist_scale: 0.01
heading_lookahead: 0.325
dwa: true
# Oscillation Prevention Parameters
oscillation_reset_dist: 0.05
# Differential-drive robot configuration : If the robot is holonomic
configuration, set to true other vice set to false. Chefbot is a non
holonomic robot.
holonomic_robot: false
max_vel_y: 0.0
min_vel_y: 0.0
acc_lim_y: 0.0
vy_samples: 1
```

Configuring DWA local planner parameters

The DWA planner is another local planner in ROS. Its configuration is almost the same as the base local planner. It is located in `chefbot_bringup/param/dwa_local_planner_params.yaml`. We can either use the base local planner or the DWA local planner for our robot.

Configuring move_base node parameters

There are some configurations to the `move_base` node too. The `move_base` node configuration is placed in the `param` folder. The following is the definition of `move_base_params.yaml`:

```
#This parameter determine whether the cost map need to shutdown when
move_base in inactive state
  shutdown_costmaps: false
#The rate at which move base run the update loop and send the velocity
commands
  controller_frequency: 5.0
#Controller wait time for a valid command before a space-clearing
operations
  controller_patience: 3.0
#The rate at which the global planning loop is running, if it is 0, planner
only plan when a new goal is received
  planner_frequency: 1.0
#Planner wait time for finding a valid path befire the space-clearing
operations
  planner_patience: 5.0
#Time allowed for oscillation before starting robot recovery operations
  oscillation_timeout: 10.0
#Distance that robot should move to be considered which not be oscillating.
Moving above this distance will reset the oscillation_timeout
  oscillation_distance: 0.2
# local planner - default is trajectory rollout
  base_local_planner: "dwa_local_planner/DWAPlannerROS"
```

We have discussed most of the parameters used in the Navigation stack, the `gmapping` node, and the `move_base` node. Now we can start running a `gmapping` demo for building the map.

Start the robot's `tf` nodes and base controller nodes:

```
$ roslaunch chefbot_bringup robot_standalone.launch
```

Start the `gmapping` node by using the following command:

```
$ roslaunch chefbot_bringup gmapping_demo.launch
```

The `gmapping_demo.launch` launches the OpenNI driver and the depth to laser scan nodes in order to stream the 3D sensor data, and launches the `gmapping` node and the `movebase` node with the necessary parameters. We can now launch a `teleop` node for moving the robot to build the map of the environment. The following command will launch the `teleop` node for moving the robot:

```
$ roslaunch chefbot_bringup keyboard_teleop.launch
```

We can see the map building in RViz, which can be invoked by using the following command:

```
$ roslaunch chefbot_bringup view_navigation.launch
```

We are testing this robot in a plain room; we can move robot in all areas inside the room. If we move the robot in all the areas, we will get a map, as shown in the following screenshot:

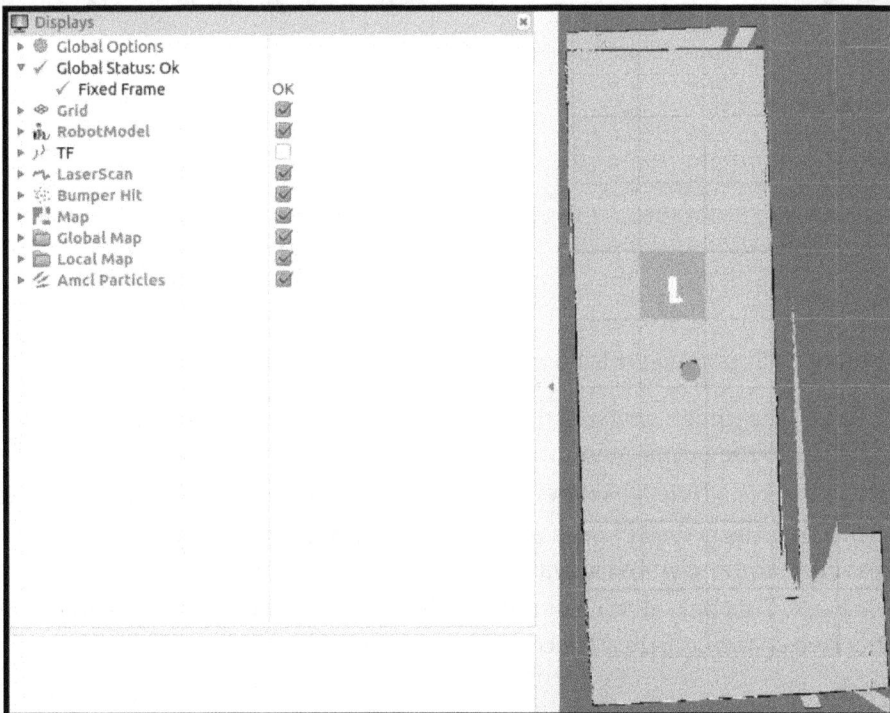

Figure 9: Creating a map using gmapping is shown in RViz

After completing the mapping process, we can save the map by using the following command:

```
$ rosrun map_server map_saver -f /home/lentin/room
```

The `map_server` package in ROS contains the `map_server` node, which provides the current map data as an ROS service. It provides a command utility called `map_saver`, which helps to save the map.

It will save the current map as two files: `room.pgm` and `room.yaml`. The first one is the map data and the next is its metadata, which contains the map file's name and its parameters. The following screenshot shows map generation using the `map_server` tool, which is saved in the home folder:

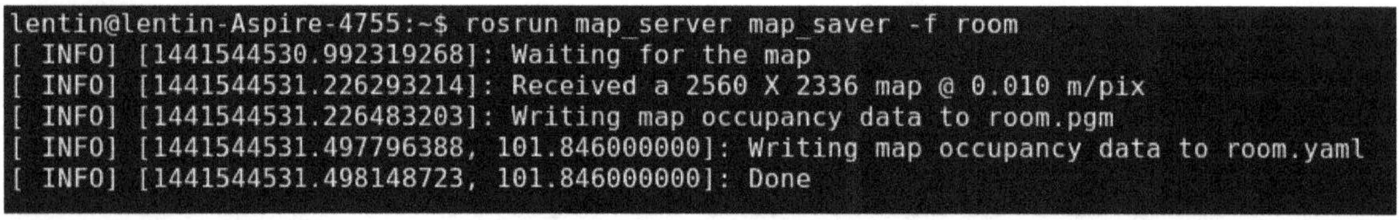

```
lentin@lentin-Aspire-4755:~$ rosrun map_server map_saver -f room
[ INFO] [1441544530.992319268]: Waiting for the map
[ INFO] [1441544531.226293214]: Received a 2560 X 2336 map @ 0.010 m/pix
[ INFO] [1441544531.226483203]: Writing map occupancy data to room.pgm
[ INFO] [1441544531.497796388, 101.846000000]: Writing map occupancy data to room.yaml
[ INFO] [1441544531.498148723, 101.846000000]: Done
```

Figure 10: Terminal messages while saving a map

The following is the `room.yaml`:

```
image: room.pgm
resolution: 0.010000
origin: [-11.560000, -11.240000, 0.000000]
negate: 0
occupied_thresh: 0.65
free_thresh: 0.196
```

The definition of each parameter follows:

- `image`: The image contains the occupancy data. The data can be absolute or relative to the origin mentioned in the YAML file.
- `resolution`: This parameter is the resolution of the map, which is meters/pixels.
- `origin`: This is the 2D pose of the lower left pixel in the map (*x*, *y*, *yaw*), where yaw is counter-clockwise (yaw = 0 means no rotation).
- `negate`: This parameter can reverse the semantics of white/black in the map and the free space/occupied space representation.

- `occupied_thresh`: This is the threshold deciding whether the pixel is occupied or not. If the occupancy probability is greater than this threshold, it is considered free space.
- `free_thresh`: The map pixel with occupancy probability less than this threshold is considered completely occupied. After mapping the environment, we can quit all the terminals and rerun the following commands to start AMCL.

Before starting the AMCL nodes, we will look at the configuration and the main application of AMCL.

Understanding AMCL

After building a map of the environment, the next thing we need to implement is localization. The robot should localize itself on the generated map. We have worked with AMCL in Chapter 6, *Using the ROS MoveIt! and Navigation Stack*. In this section, we will see a detailed study of the `amcl` package and the `amcl` launch files used in Chefbot. AMCL implements the probabilistic localization technique for robot working in 2D. This algorithm uses particle filters for tracking the pose of the robot with respect to the known map. To know more about this localization technique, you can refer to a book called *Probabilistic Robotics* by Thrun (http://www.probabilistic-robotics.org/). The AMCL algorithm is implemented in the AMCL ROS package (http://wiki.ros.org/amcl), which has an AMCL node that subscribes the scan (`sensor_msgs/LaserScan`), the tf (`tf/tfMessage`), the initial pose (`geometry_msgs/PoseWithCovarianceStamped`), and the map (`nav_msgs/OccupancyGrid`).

After processing the sensor data, it publishes amcl_pose (`geometry_msgs/PoseWithCovarianceStamped`), `particlecloud`(`geometry_msgs/PoseArray`) and `tf` (`tf/Message`).

`amcl_pose` is the estimated pose of the robot after processing, where the particle cloud is the set of pose estimates maintained by the filter.

If the initial pose of the robot is not mentioned, the particle will be around the origin. We can set the initial pose of the robot in RViz by using the **2D Pose estimate** button. We can see the `amcl` launch file used in this robot. The following is the main launch file for starting `amcl`, called `amcl_demo.launch`:

```
<launch>
  <rosparam command="delete" ns="move_base" />
  <include file="$(find chefbot_bringup)/launch/3dsensor.launch">
    <arg name="rgb_processing" value="false" />
```

```
        <arg name="depth_registration" value="false" />
        <arg name="depth_processing" value="false" />
        <!-- We must specify an absolute topic name because if not it will be
prefixed by "$(arg camera)".
        <arg name="scan_topic" value="/scan" />
    </include>

    <!-- Map server -->
    <arg name="map_file" default="$(find
turtlebot_navigation)/maps/willow-2010-02-18-0.10.yaml"/>
    <node name="map_server" pkg="map_server" type="map_server" args="$(arg
map_file)" />

    <arg name="initial_pose_x" default="0.0"/> <!-- Use 17.0 for willow's map
in simulation -->
    <arg name="initial_pose_y" default="0.0"/> <!-- Use 17.0 for willow's map
in simulation -->
    <arg name="initial_pose_a" default="0.0"/>

    <include file="$(find chefbot_bringup)/launch/includes/amcl.launch.xml">
       <arg name="initial_pose_x" value="$(arg initial_pose_x)"/>
       <arg name="initial_pose_y" value="$(arg initial_pose_y)"/>
       <arg name="initial_pose_a" value="$(arg initial_pose_a)"/>
    </include>

    <include file="$(find
chefbot_bringup)/launch/includes/move_base.launch.xml"/>

</launch>
```

The preceding launch file starts the 3D sensor-related nodes, the map server for providing the map data, the amcl node for performing localization, and the move_base node to move the robot from the commands received from the higher level.

The complete amcl launch parameters are mentioned inside another sub-file called amcl.launch.xml. It is placed in chefbot_bringup/launch/include. The following is the definition of this file:

```
<launch>
  <arg name="use_map_topic"   default="false"/>
  <arg name="scan_topic"      default="scan"/>
  <arg name="initial_pose_x"  default="0.0"/>
  <arg name="initial_pose_y"  default="0.0"/>
  <arg name="initial_pose_a"  default="0.0"/>

  <node pkg="amcl" type="amcl" name="amcl">
    <param name="use_map_topic"                    value="$(arg use_map_topic)"/>
```

```
.....................
.....................

    <!-- Increase tolerance because the computer can get quite busy -->
    <param name="transform_tolerance"    value="1.0"/>
    <param name="recovery_alpha_slow"    value="0.0"/>
    <param name="recovery_alpha_fast"    value="0.0"/>
    <param name="initial_pose_x"          value="$(arg initial_pose_x)"/>
    <param name="initial_pose_y"          value="$(arg initial_pose_y)"/>
    <param name="initial_pose_a"          value="$(arg initial_pose_a)"/>
    <remap from="scan"                    to="$(arg scan_topic)"/>
  </node>
</launch>
```

We can refer to the ROS `amcl` package wiki for getting more details about each parameter. We will see how to localize and path plan the robot using the existing map. Launch the robot hardware nodes by using the following command:

```
$ roslaunch chefbot_bringup robot_standalone.launch
```

Run the `amcl` launch file by using the following command:

```
$ roslaunch chefbot_bringup amcl_demo.launch
map_file:=/home/lentin/room.yaml
```

We can launch RViz for commanding the robot to move to a particular pose on the map by using the following command:

```
$ roslaunch chefbot_bringup view_navigation.launch
```

The following is the screenshot of RViz:

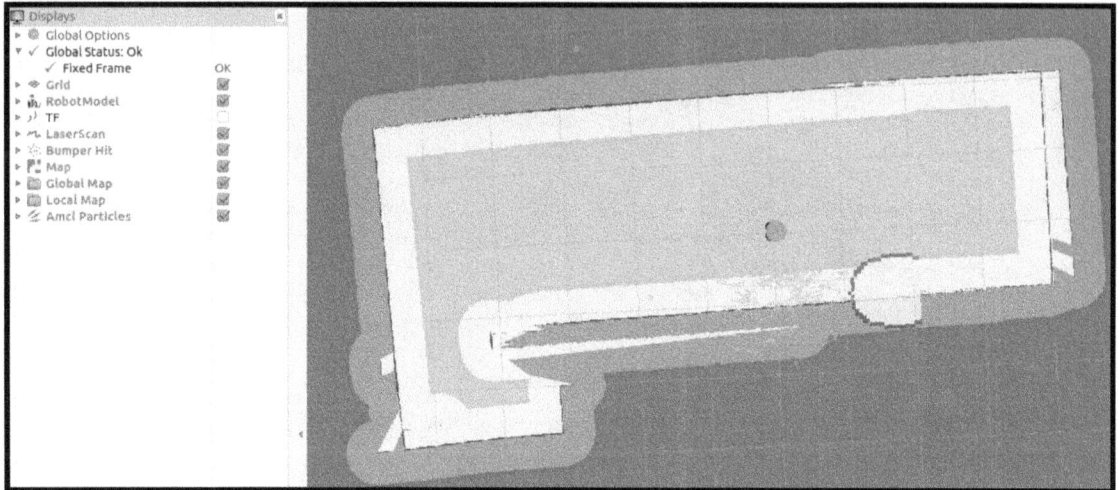

Figure 11: Robot autonomous navigation using AMCL.

We will see more about each option in RViz and how to command the robot in the map in the following section.

Understanding RViz for working with the Navigation stack

We will explore various GUI options inside RViz to visualize each parameter in the Navigation stack.

2D Pose Estimate button

The first step in RViz is to set the initial position of the robot on the map. If the robot is able to localize on the map by itself, there is no need to set the initial position. Otherwise, we have to set the initial position using the **2D Pose Estimate** button in RViz, as shown in the following screenshot:

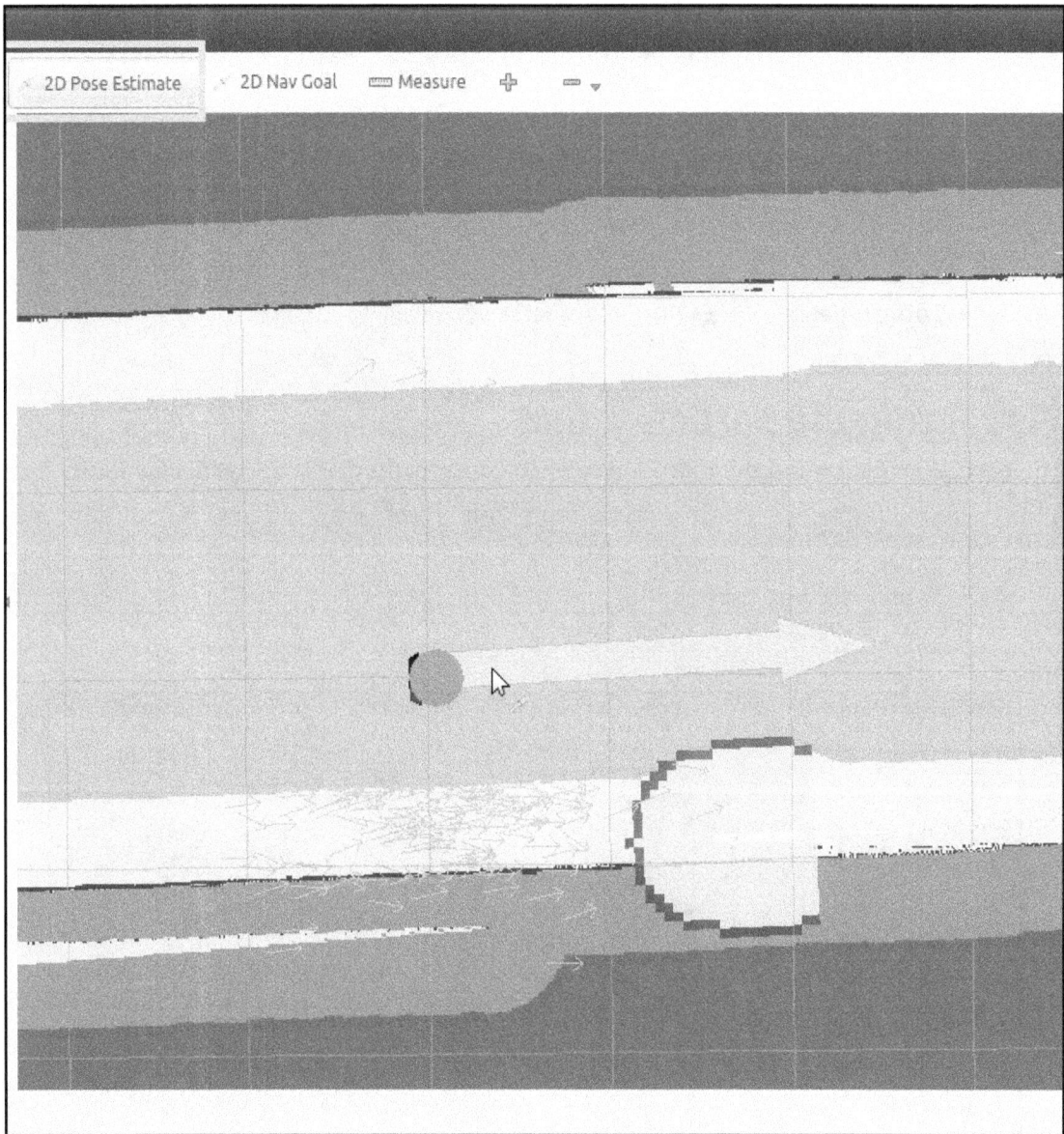

Figure 12: RViz 2D Pose Estimate button

Press the **2D Pose Estimate** button and select a pose of the robot by using the left mouse button, as shown in the preceding figure. Check if the actual pose of the robot and the robot model in RViz are the same. After setting the pose, we can start the path plan to the robot. The green color cloud around the robot is the particle cloud of `amcl`. If the particle amount is high, it means the uncertainty in the robot position is high, and if the cloud is less, it means that the uncertainty is low and the robot is almost sure about its position. The topic handling the robot's initial pose is:

- **Topic name:** `initialpose`
- **Topic type:** `geometry_msgs/PoseWithCovarianceStamped`

Visualizing the particle cloud

The particle cloud around the robot can be enabled using the `PoseArray` display topic. Here the `PoseArray` topic is `/particlecloud` displayed in RViz. The `PoseArray` type is renamed as `Amcl` particles:

- **Topic:** `/particlecloud`
- **Type:** `geometry_msgs/PoseArray`

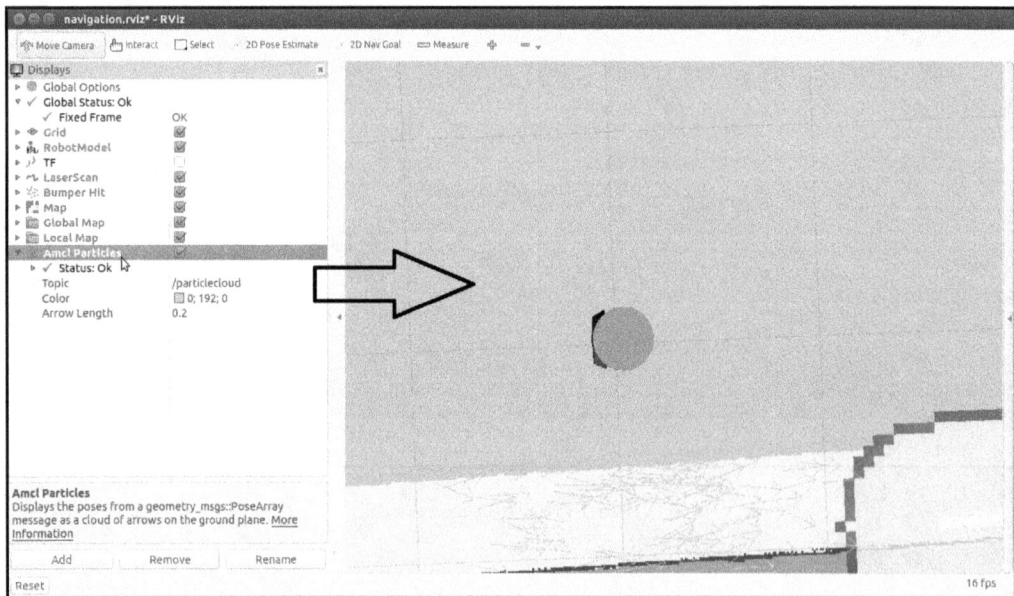

Figure 13: Visualizing AMCL particles

The 2D Nav Goal button

The **2D Nav Goal** button is used to give a goal position to the move_base node in the ROS Navigation stack through RViz. We can select this button from the top panel of RViz and can give the goal position inside the map by left clicking the map using the mouse. The goal position will send to the move_base node for moving the robot to that location:

- **Topic**: move_base_simple/goal
- **Topic type**: geometry_msgs/PoseStamped

Figure 14: Setting the robot's goal position in RViz using 2D Nav Goal

Displaying the static map

The static map is the map that we feed into the `map_server` node. The `map_server` node serves the static map in the `/map` topic:

- **Topic**: `/map`
- **Type**: `nav_msgs/GetMap`

The following is the static map in RViz:

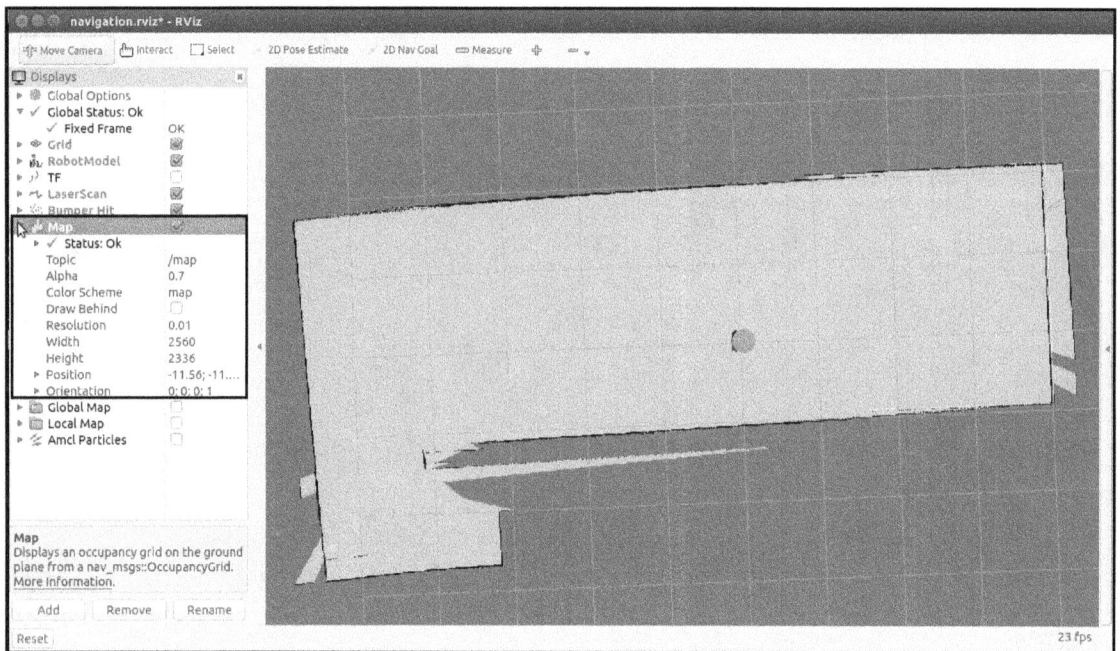

Figure 15: Visualizing static map in RViz

Displaying the robot footprint

We have defined the robot footprint in the configuration file called
`costmap_common_params.yaml`. This robot has a circular shape, and we have given the
radius as 0.45 meters. It can visualize using the **Polygon** display type in RViz. The following
is the circular footprint of the robot around the robot model and its topics:

- **Topic**:
  `/move_base/global_costmap/obstacle_layer_footprint/footprint_st`
  `amped`
- **Topic**:
  `/move_base/local_costmap/obstacle_layer_footprint/footprint_sta`
  `mped`
- **Type:** `geometry_msgs/Polygon`

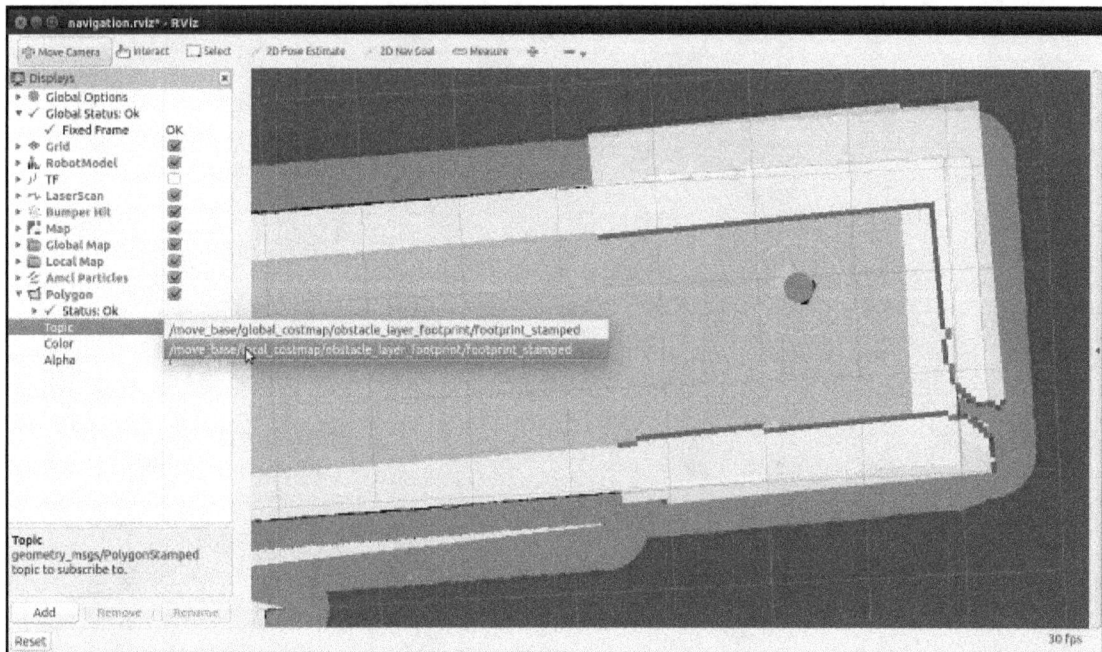

Figure 16: Global and local robot footprint in RViz

Displaying the global and local cost map

The following RViz screenshot shows the local cost map, the global cost map, the real obstacles, and the inflated obstacles. The display type of each of these maps is the map itself:

- **Local cost map topic**: `/move_base/local_costmap/costmap`
- **Local cost map topic type**: `nav_msgs/OccupancyGrid`
- **Global cost map topic**: `/move_base/global_costmap/costmap`
- **Global cost map topic type**: `nav_msgs/OccupancyGrid`

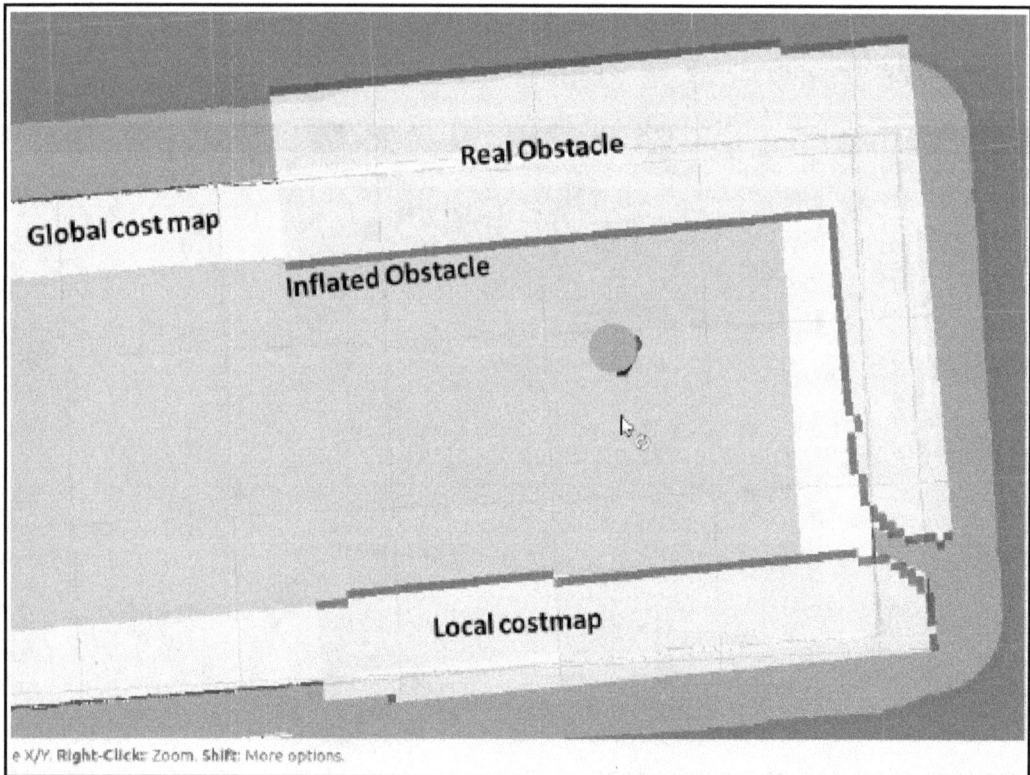

Figure 17: Visualizing the global and local map, and real and inflated obstacle in RViz

To avoid collision with the real obstacles, it is inflated to some distance from the real obstacles, called inflated obstacles, as per the values in the configuration files. The robot only plans a path beyond the inflated obstacle; inflation is a technique to avoid collision with the real obstacles.

Displaying the global plan, the local plan, and the planner plan

In the next figure, the global, local, and planner plans are shown. In this context, the planner and the global plans represent the complete plan to reach the goal. The local plan represents a short-term plan to follow the global planning. The global plan and the planner plan can be changed if there are any obstacles. The plans can be displayed using the Path display type in RViz:

- **Global plan topic**: /move_base/DWAPlannerROS/global_plan
- **Global plan topic type**: nav_msgs/Path
- **Local plan topic**: /move_base/DWAPlannerROS/local_plan
- **Local plan topic type**: nav_msgs/Path
- **Planner plan topic**: /move_base/NavfnROS/plan
- **Planner plan topic type**: nav_msgs/Path

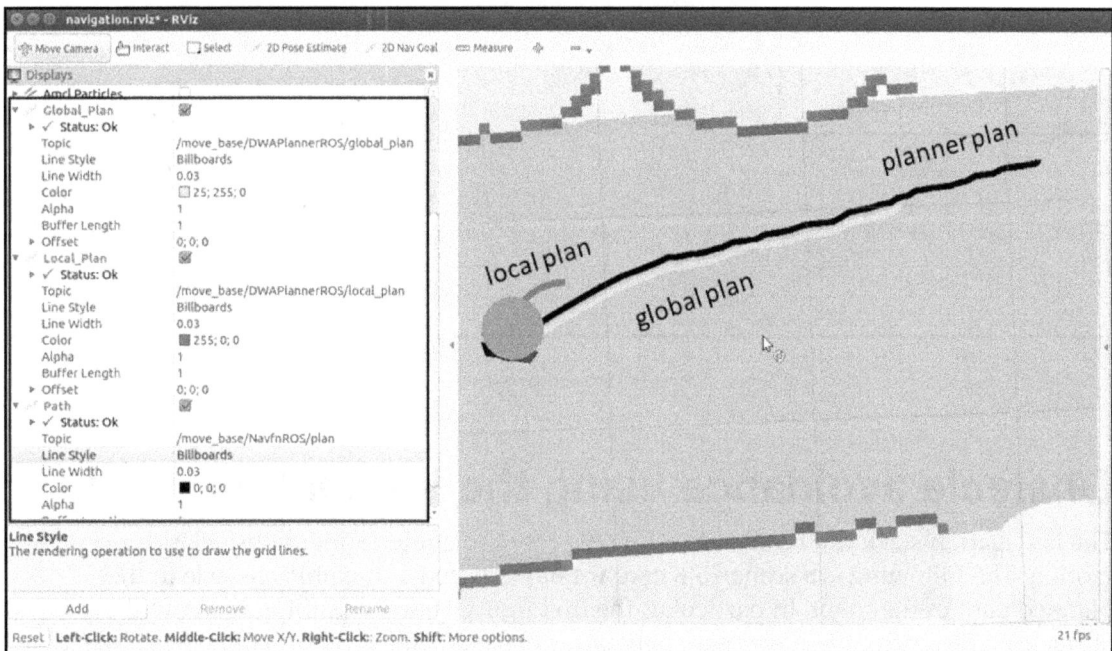

Figure 19: Visualizing the global, local, and planner plan in RViz

The current goal

The current goal is the commanded position of the robot using the **2D Nav Goal** button or using the ROS client nodes. The red arrow indicates the current goal of the robot:

- **Topic**: `/move_base/current_goal`
- **Topic type**: `geometry_msgs/PoseStamped`

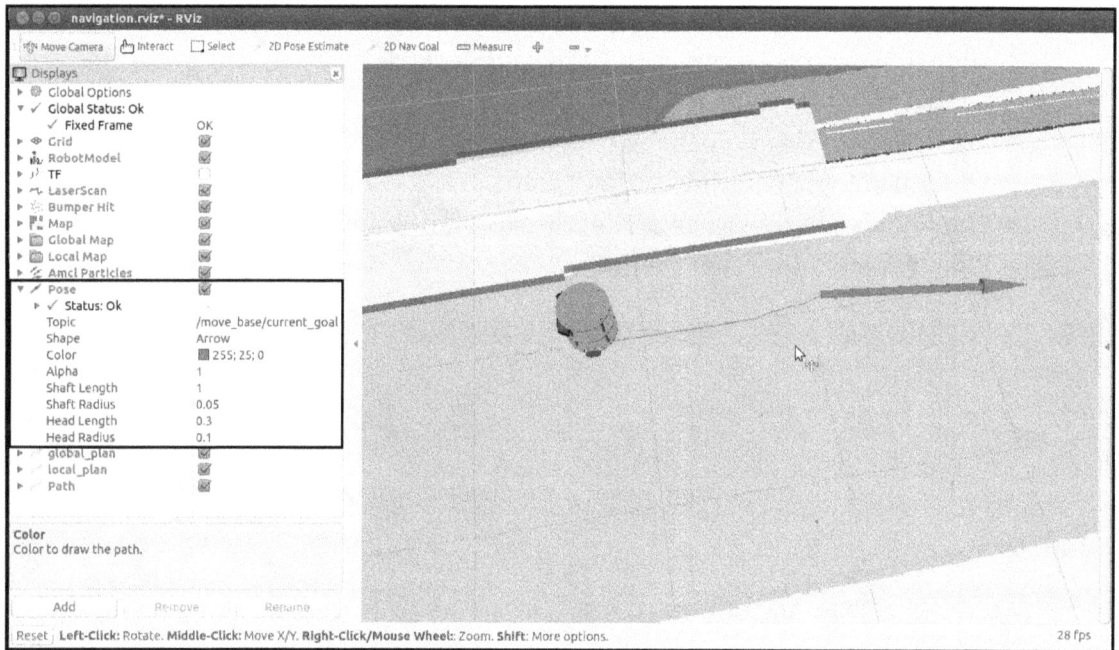

Figure 19: Visualizing robot goal position

Obstacle avoidance using the Navigation stack

The Navigation stack can be used to allow the robot to avoid random obstacles during its motion. The following is a scenario where we have placed a dynamic obstacle in the planned path of the robot. In particular, the first figure shows a path planning without any obstacle on the path. When we place a dynamic obstacle on the robot path, we can see it planning a path by avoiding the obstacle:

No obstacle

With obstacle

Figure 20: Visualizing obstacle avoidance capabilities in RViz

Working with Chefbot simulation

The `chefbot_gazebo` simulator package is available along with the `chefbot_bringup` package, and we can simulate the robot in Gazebo. We will see how to build a room similar to the room we tested with the hardware. First, we will check how to build a virtual room in Gazebo.

Building a room in Gazebo

We will start building the room in Gazebo, save into **Semantic Description Format (SDF)**, and insert in the Gazebo environment.

Launch Gazebo with the Chefbot robot in an empty world:

```
$ roslaunch chefbot_gazebo chefbot_empty_world.launch
```

It will open the Chefbot model in an empty world on Gazebo. We can build the room using walls, windows, doors, and stairs.

There is a **Building Editor** in Gazebo. We can take this editor from the menu **Edit | Building Editor**. We will get an editor in the Gazebo viewport:

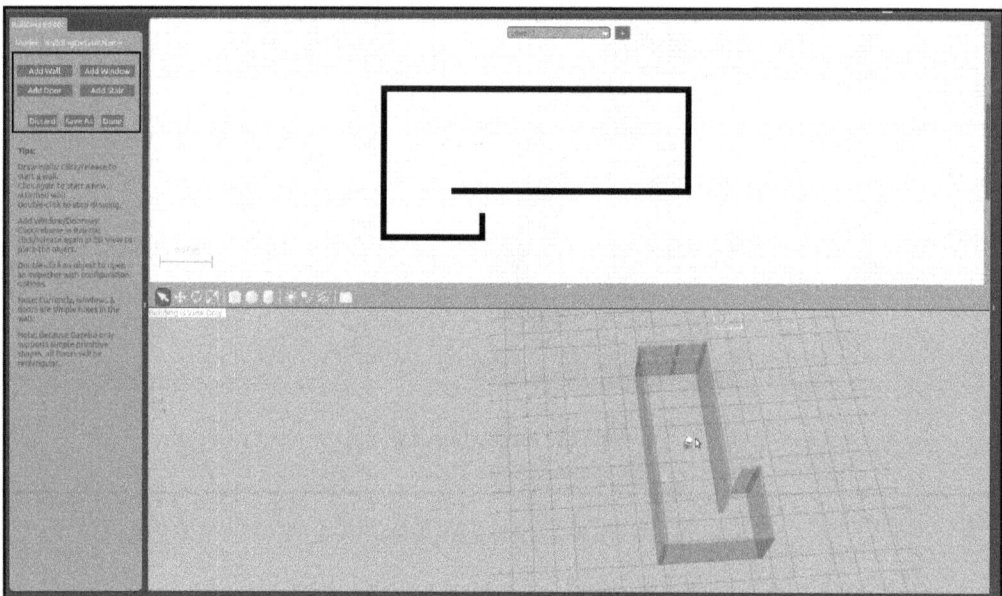

Figure 21: Building walls in Gazebo

We can add walls by clicking the **Add Wall** option on the left-side pane of Gazebo. In the **Building Editor**, we can draw the walls by clicking the left mouse button. We can see that adding walls in the editor will build real 3D walls in Gazebo. We are building a similar layout of the room that we tested for the real robot. Save the room through the **Save As** option, or press the **Done** button; a box will pop up to save the file. The file will get saved in the .sdf format. We can save this example as final_room.

After saving the room file, we can add the model of this room to the gazebo model folder, so that we can access the model in any simulation.

Adding model files to the Gazebo model folder

The following is the procedure to add a model to the Gazebo folder.

Locate the default model folder of Gazebo, which is located in the ~/.gazebo/models folder. Create a folder called final_room and copy final_room.sdf inside this folder. Also, create a file called model.config, which contains the details of the model file. The definition of this file follows:

```
<?xml version="1.0"?>
<model>
    <!-- Name of model which is displaying in Gazebo -->
<name>Test Room</name>
<version>1.0</version>
<!-- Model file name -->
<sdf version="1.2">final_room.sdf</sdf>

<author>
    <name>Lentin Joseph</name>
    <email>qboticslabs@gmail.com</email>
</author>

<description>
    A test room for performing SLAM
</description>
</model>
```

After adding this model to the model folder, restart Gazebo, and we can see the model named `Test Room` in the entry in the **Insert** tab, as shown in the next screenshot. We have named this model as `Test Room` in the `model.config` file; that name will show on this list. We can select this file and add it to the viewport, as shown next:

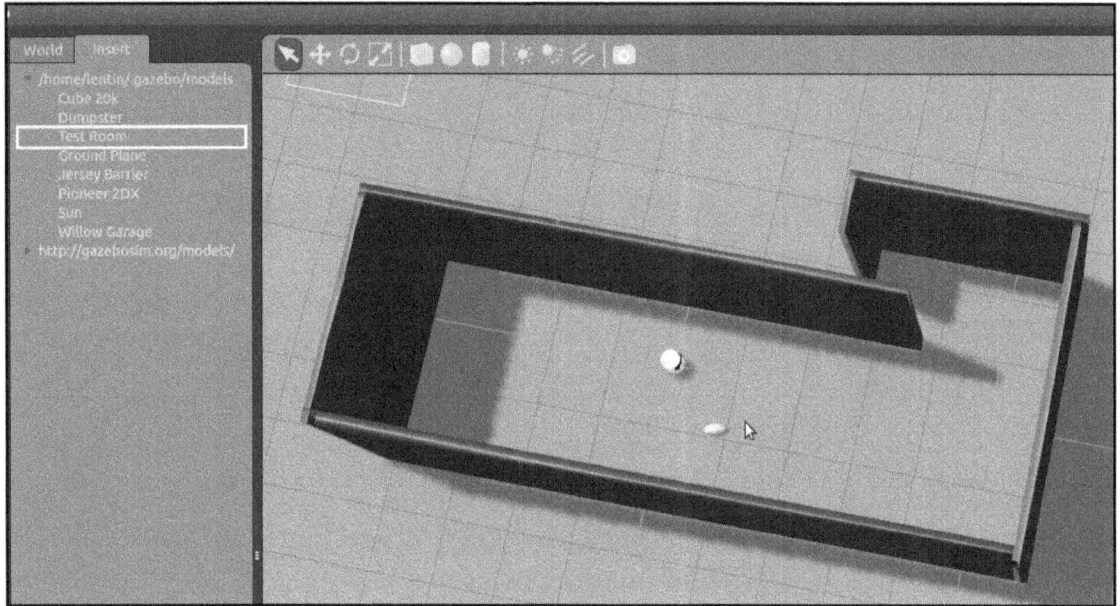

Figure 22: Inserting the walls in Chefbot simulation

After adding to the viewport, we can save the current world configuration. Select `File` from the `Gazebo` menu and the `Save world as` option. Save the file as `test_room.sdf` in the `worlds` folder of the `chefbot_gazebo` ROS package, then add it to the `chefbot_empty_world.launch` file, and save this launch file as the `chefbot_room_world.launch` file, which is shown next:

```
<include file="$(find gazebo_ros)/launch/empty_world.launch">
  <arg name="use_sim_time" value="true"/>
  <arg name="debug" value="false"/>

<!-- Adding world test_room.sdf as argument -->
  <arg name="world_name" value="$(find
chefbot_gazebo)/worlds/test_room.sdf"/>
  </include>
```

After saving this launch file, we can start the launch file `chefbot_room_world.launch` for simulating the same environment as the hardware robot. We can add obstacles in Gazebo, using the primitive shapes available in it.

Instead of launching the `robot_standalone.launch` file from `chefbot_bringup` for the hardware, we can start `chefbot_hotel_world.launch` for getting a more complex environment of the robot, and the `odom` and tf data in simulation:

```
$ roslaunch chefbot_gazebo chefbot_hotel_world.launch
```

Other operations, such as SLAM and AMCL, have the same procedure that we followed for the hardware. The following launch files are used to perform SLAM and AMCL in the simulation. To use `gmapping` and the AMCL program to perform localization and mapping, we should install it by using the following commands:

Run SLAM in the simulation:

```
$ roslaunch chefbot_gazebo gmapping_demo.launch
```

Run the Teleop node:

```
$ roslaunch chefbot_bringup keyboard_teleop.launch
```

Run AMCL in the simulation:

```
$ roslaunch chefbot_gazebo amcl_demo.launch
```

After moving the robot into its environment, we can save the generated map as already seen:

```
$ rosrun map_server map_saver -f /tmp/hotel
```

Sending a goal to the Navigation stack from a ROS node

We have seen how to send a goal position to a robot for moving it from point A to B using the RViz `2D Nav Goal` button. Now we will see how to command the robot using the actionlib client and the ROS C++ APIs. The following is a sample package and node for communicating with the Navigation stack `move_base` node.

The `move_base` node is `SimpleActionServer`. We can send and cancel the goals to the robot if the task takes a lot of time to complete.

The following code is `SimpleActionClient` for the `move_base` node, which can send the x, y, and theta from the command-line arguments. The following code is in the `chefbot_bringup/src` folder with the name of `send_robot_goal.cpp`:

```cpp
#include <ros/ros.h>
#include <move_base_msgs/MoveBaseAction.h>
#include <actionlib/client/simple_action_client.h>
#include <tf/transform_broadcaster.h>
#include <sstream>
#include <iostream>
//Declaring a new SimpleActionClient with action of
move_base_msgs::MoveBaseAction
typedef
actionlib::SimpleActionClient<move_base_msgs::MoveBaseAction>
MoveBaseClient;

int main(int argc, char** argv){
  ros::init(argc, argv, "navigation_goals");
//Initiating move_base client
  MoveBaseClient ac("move_base", true);
//Waiting for server to start
  while(!ac.waitForServer(ros::Duration(5.0))){
    ROS_INFO("Waiting for the move_base action server");
  }
//Declaring move base goal
  move_base_msgs::MoveBaseGoal goal;

//Setting target frame id and time in the goal action
  goal.target_pose.header.frame_id = "map";
  goal.target_pose.header.stamp = ros::Time::now();

//Retrieving pose from command line other vice execute a default value
  try{
    goal.target_pose.pose.position.x = atof(argv[1]);
    goal.target_pose.pose.position.y = atof(argv[2]);
    goal.target_pose.pose.orientation.w = atof(argv[3]);
    }
  catch(int e){
    goal.target_pose.pose.position.x = 1.0;
    goal.target_pose.pose.position.y = 1.0;
    goal.target_pose.pose.orientation.w = 1.0;
  }
  ROS_INFO("Sending move base goal");

//Sending goal
  ac.sendGoal(goal);
```

```
    ac.waitForResult();

    if(ac.getState() == actionlib::SimpleClientGoalState::SUCCEEDED)
        ROS_INFO("Robot has arrived to the goal position");
    else{
        ROS_INFO("The base failed for some reason");
    }
    return 0;
}
```

The following lines are added to `CMakeLists.txt` for building this node:

```
add_executable(send_goal src/send_robot_goal.cpp)
target_link_libraries(send_goal  ${catkin_LIBRARIES})
```

Build the package using `catkin_make` and test the working of the client using the following set of commands using Gazebo.

Start the Gazebo simulation in a room:

```
$ roslaunch chefbot_gazebo chefbot_room_world.launch
```

Start the `amcl` node with the generated map:

```
$ roslaunch chefbot_gazebo amcl_demo.launch map_file:=/tmp/hotel.yaml
```

Start RViz for the navigation:

```
$ roslaunch chefbot_bringup view_navigation.launch
```

Run the send `goal` node for sending the move base goal:

```
$ rosrun chefbot_bringup send_goal 1 0 1
```

We will get the desired pose of the robot in the map by using the RViz **2D Nav goal** button. Simply echoing the topic `/move_base/goal` will print the pose that we commanded through RViz. We can use these values as command-line arguments in the `send_goal` node.

Questions

- What are the basic requirements for working with the ROS Navigation stack?
- What are the main configuration files for working with the ROS Navigation stack?
- How does the AMCL package in ROS work?
- What are the methods to send a goal pose to the Navigation stack?

Summary

In this chapter, we mainly covered interfacing a DIY autonomous mobile robot to ROS and the Navigation package. We looked at an introduction to this robot and the necessary components and connection diagrams. We looked at the robot firmware and saw how to flash it into the real robot. After flashing the firmware, we learned how to interface it to the ROS and saw the Python nodes for interfacing the LaunchPad controller in the robot and the nodes for converting twist messages to motor velocities and encoder ticks to odom and tf.

After discussing the interconnection of the Chefbot nodes, we covered the C++ port of some important nodes for odometry calculation and the base controller node. After discussing these nodes, we looked at detailed configurations of the ROS Navigation stack. We also did `gmapping` and AMCL and looked at a detailed description of each option in RViz for working with the Navigation stack. We also covered obstacle avoidance using the Navigation stack and worked with the Chefbot simulation. We set up a similar environment in Gazebo to the environment of the real robot and went through the steps to perform SLAM and AMCL. At the end of this chapter, we saw how we can send a goal pose to the Navigation stack using `actionlib`.

12
Exploring the Advanced Capabilities of ROS-MoveIt!

In the previous chapter, we covered ROS navigation and interfacing with mobile robotic hardware. Similarly, in this chapter, we are going to cover the advanced capabilities of ROS-MoveIt!, such as collision avoidance, perception with 3D sensors, grasping, picking, and placing. After this, we will see how to interface robotic manipulator hardware with MoveIt!.

The following are the main topics discussed in this chapter:

- Motion planning collision checking of a robotic arm, using MoveIt! C++ APIs
- Working with perception in MoveIt! and Gazebo
- Performing object manipulation with MoveIt!
- Understanding DYNAMIXEL ROS servo controllers for robot hardware interfacing
- Interfacing 7-DOF DYNAMIXEL-based robotic arm to ROS MoveIt!

In Chapter 4, *Simulating Robots Using ROS and Gazebo*, and Chapter 6, *Using the ROS MoveIt! and Navigation Stack*, we discussed MoveIt! and how to simulate an arm in Gazebo, and motion plan using MoveIt!. In this chapter, we are going to see some of the advanced capabilities of MoveIt! and how to interface a real robotic manipulator to ROS MoveIt!.

The first topic that we are going to discuss is how to motion plan our robot using MoveIt! C++ APIs.

Motion planning using the move_group C++ interface

In Chapter 6, *Using the ROS MoveIt! and Navigation Stack*, we discussed how to interact with a robot arm, and how to plan its path using the **MoveIt! RViz motion planning** plugin. In this section, we will see how to program the robot motion using the move_group C++ APIs. Motion planning using RViz can also be done programmatically through the move_group C++ APIs.

The first step to start working with C++ APIs is to create another ROS package that has the MoveIt! packages as dependencies. You can get an existing seven_dof_arm_test package from the code provided with this book, or you can download it from the following repository:

```
$ git clone https://github.com/jocacace/seven_dof_arm_test.git
```

We can create this same package using the following command:

```
$ catkin_create_pkg seven_dof_arm_test catkin cmake_modules
interactive_markers moveit_core moveit_ros_perception
moveit_ros_planning_interface pluginlib roscpp std_msgs
```

Motion planning a random path using MoveIt! C++ APIs

The first example that we are going to see is a random motion plan using MoveIt! C++ APIs. You will get the code named test_random.cpp from the src folder. The code and the description of each line follows. When we execute this node, it will plan a random path and execute it:

```
#include <moveit/move_group_interface/move_group_interface.h>
int main(int argc, char **argv)
{
ros::init(argc, argv, "move_group_interface_demo",
ros::init_options::AnonymousName);
  // start a ROS spinning thread
  ros::AsyncSpinner spinner(1);
  spinner.start();
  // this connects to a running instance of the move_group node
  //move_group_interface::MoveGroup group("arm");
  moveit::planning_interface::MoveGroupInterface group("arm");
```

```
// specify that our target will be a random one
group.setRandomTarget();
// plan the motion and then move the group to the sampled target
group.move();
ros::waitForShutdown();
}
```

To build the source code, we should add the following lines of code to CMakeLists.txt. You will get the complete CMakeLists.txt file from the existing package itself:

```
add_executable(test_random_node src/test_random.cpp)
add_dependencies(test_random_node seven_dof_arm_test_generate_messages_cpp)
target_link_libraries(test_random_node
${catkin_LIBRARIES})
```

We can build the package using the catkin_make command. First, check whether test_random.cpp is built properly or not. If the code is built properly, we can start testing the code.

The following command will start the RViz with 7-DOF arm with the motion planning plugin:

$ roslaunch seven_dof_arm_config demo.launch

Move the end effector to check whether everything is working properly in RViz.

Run the C++ node for planning to a random position using the following command:

$ rosrun seven_dof_arm_test test_random_node

The output of the RViz is shown next. The arm will select a random position that has a valid IK and motion plan from the current position:

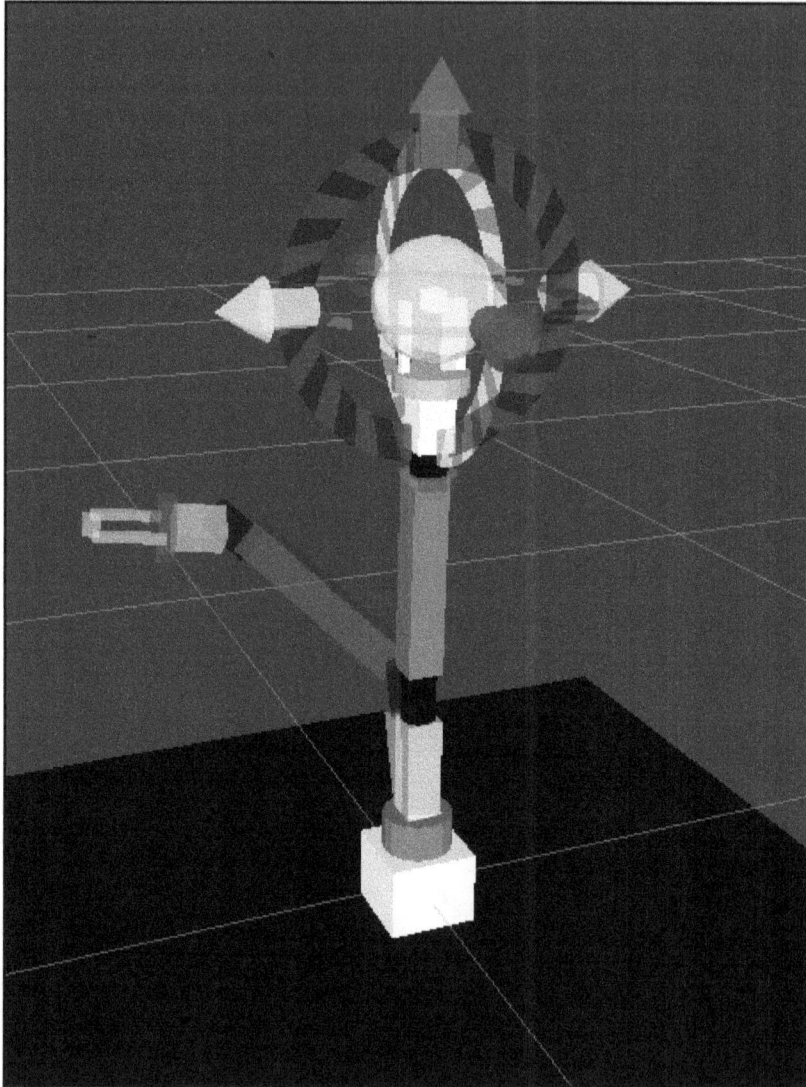

Figure 1: Random motion planning using move_group APIs.

Motion planning a custom path using MoveIt! C++ APIs

We saw random motion planning in the preceding example. In this section, we will check how to command the robot end effector to move to a custom goal position. The following example, `test_custom.cpp`, will do that job:

```cpp
#include <moveit/move_group_interface/move_group_interface.h>
#include <moveit/planning_scene_interface/planning_scene_interface.h>
#include <moveit/move_group_interface/move_group_interface.h>
#include <moveit_msgs/DisplayRobotState.h>
#include <moveit_msgs/DisplayTrajectory.h>
#include <moveit_msgs/AttachedCollisionObject.h>
#include <moveit_msgs/CollisionObject.h>

int main(int argc, char **argv)
{
  //ROS initialization
  ros::init(argc, argv, "move_group_interface_tutorial");
  ros::NodeHandle node_handle;
  ros::AsyncSpinner spinner(1);
  spinner.start();
  sleep(2.0);
  //Move group setup
  moveit::planning_interface::MoveGroupInterface group("arm");
  moveit::planning_interface::PlanningSceneInterface
planning_scene_interface;
  ros::Publisher display_publisher =
node_handle.advertise<moveit_msgs::DisplayTrajectory>("/move_group/display_
planned_path", 1, true);
  moveit_msgs::DisplayTrajectory display_trajectory;
  ROS_INFO("Reference frame: %s",    group.getEndEffectorLink().c_str());
  //Target pose setup
  geometry_msgs::Pose target_pose1;
  target_pose1.orientation.w = 0.726282;
  target_pose1.orientation.x= 4.04423e-07;
  target_pose1.orientation.y = -0.687396;
  target_pose1.orientation.z = 4.81813e-07;
  target_pose1.position.x = 0.0261186;
  target_pose1.position.y = 4.50972e-07;
  target_pose1.position.z = 0.573659;
  group.setPoseTarget(target_pose1);
  //Motion planning
  moveit::planning_interface::MoveGroupInterface::Plan my_plan;
  moveit::planning_interface::MoveItErrorCode success =
group.plan(my_plan);
```

```
    ROS_INFO("Visualizing plan 1 (pose goal) %s", success.val ? "":"FAILED");
    // Sleep to give Rviz time to visualize the plan.
    sleep(5.0);
    ros::shutdown();
}
```

The following are the extra lines of code added on for building the source code:

```
add_executable(test_custom_node src/test_custom.cpp)
add_dependencies(test_custom_node seven_dof_arm_test_generate_messages_cpp)
target_link_libraries(test_custom_node
${catkin_LIBRARIES})
```

Following is the command to execute the custom node:

```
$ rosrun seven_dof_arm_test test_custom_node
```

The following screenshot shows the result of the `test_custom_node`:

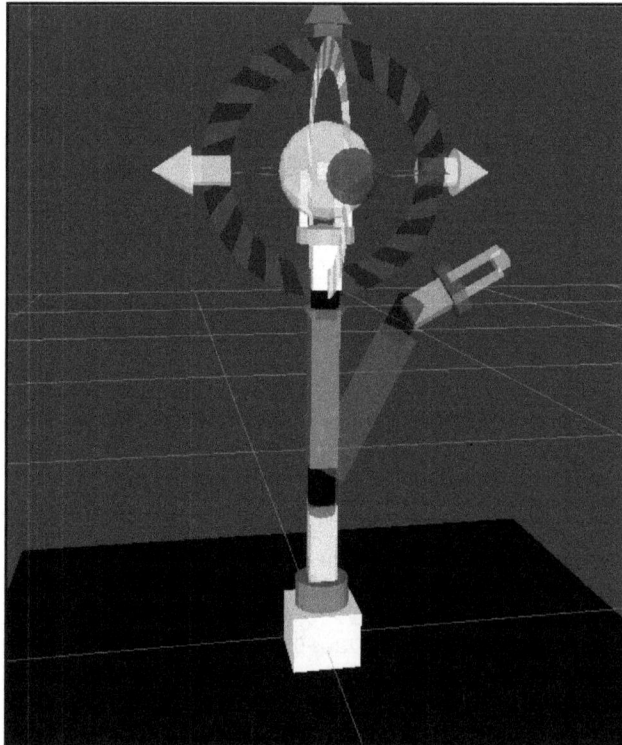

Figure 2: Custom motion planning using MoveIt! C++ APIs.

Collision checking with a robot arm using MoveIt!

Along with motion planning and the IK solving algorithm, one of the most important tasks that is done in parallel in MoveIt! is collision checking, and its avoidance. MoveIt! can handle both self-collisions and environmental collisions exploiting the built-in **Flexible Collision Library (FCL)** (`http://gamma.cs.unc.edu/FCL/fcl_docs/webpage/generated/index.html`), an open source project that implements various collision-detection and-avoidance algorithms. MoveIt! takes the power of FCL and handles the collision inside the planning scene using a `collision_detection::CollisionWorld` class. The MoveIt! collision checking includes objects, such as meshes; primitive shapes, such as boxes and cylinders, and OctoMap. The **OctoMap** (`http://octomap.github.io/`) library implements a 3D occupancy grid, called an **octree**, which consists of probabilistic information regarding obstacles in the environment. The MoveIt! package can build an OctoMap using 3D point cloud information, and can directly feed the OctoMap to FCL for collision checking.

Like motion planning, collision checking is also very computationally intensive. We can fine-tune the collision checking between two bodies—say, a robot link, or with the environment - using a parameter called **Allowed Collision Matrix (ACM)**. If the value of a collision between two links is set to 1 in ACM, there will not be any collision checks. We may set this for links that are far from each other. We can optimize the collision-checking process by optimizing this matrix.

Adding a collision object to MoveIt!

We can add a collision object to the MoveIt! planning scene, and we can see how the motion-planning works. For adding a collision object, we can use mesh files, which can directly be imported from the MoveIt! interface, and can be added by writing a ROS node using MoveIt! APIs.

We will first discuss how to add a collision object using the ROS node:

1. In the node `add_collision_object.cpp`, which is inside the `seven_dof_arm_test/src` folder, we are starting a ROS node and creating an object of `moveit::planning_interface::PlanningSceneInterface`, which can access the planning scene of MoveIt! and perform any action on the current scene. We will now add a sleep of 5 seconds to wait for the `planningSceneInterface` object instantiation:

   ```
   moveit::planning_interface::PlanningSceneInterface
   current_scene;
   sleep(5.0);
   ```

2. In the next step, we need to create an instance of the collision object message `moveit_msgs::CollisionObject`. This message is going to be sent to the current planning scene. Here, we are making a collision object message for a cylinder shape, and the message is given as `seven_dof_arm_cylinder`. When we add this object to the planning scene, the name of the object is its ID:

   ```
   moveit_msgs::CollisionObject cylinder;
   cylinder.id = "seven_dof_arm_cylinder";
   ```

3. After making the collision object message, we have to define another message of type `shape_msgs::SolidPrimitive`, which is used to define what kind of primitive shape we are using and its properties. In this example, we are creating a cylinder object, as shown in the following code. We have to define the type of shape, the resizing factor, the width, and the height of the cylinder:

   ```
   shape_msgs::SolidPrimitive primitive;
   primitive.type = primitive.CYLINDER;
   primitive.dimensions.resize(3);
   primitive.dimensions[0] = 0.6;
   primitive.dimensions[1] = 0.2;
   primitive.dimensions[2] = 0.2;
   ```

4. After creating the shape message, we have to create a `geometry_msgs::Pose` message to define the pose of this object. We define a pose that may be closer to robot. We can change the pose after the creation of the object in the planning scene:

```
geometry_msgs::Pose pose;
pose.orientation.w = 1.0;
pose.position.x =   0.0;
pose.position.y = -0.4;
pose.position.z =   -0.4;
```

5. After defining the pose of the collision object, we need to add the defined primitive object, and the pose to the cylinder collision object. The operation we need to perform is adding the planning scene:

```
cylinder.primitives.push_back(primitive);
cylinder.primitive_poses.push_back(pose);
cylinder.operation = cylinder.ADD;
```

6. In the next step, we create a vector called `collision_objects` of type `moveit_msgs::CollisionObject`, inserting the collision object to this vector:

```
std::vector<moveit_msgs::CollisionObject> collision_objects;
collision_objects.push_back(cylinder);
```

7. We will add the collision objects vector to the current planning scene by using the following line of code. `addCollisionObjects()` inside the `PlanningSceneInterface` class is used to add the object to the planning scene:

```
current_scene.addCollisionObjects(collision_objects);
```

8. The following are the compile and build lines of the code in `CMakeLists.txt`:

```
add_executable(add_collision_object
src/add_collision_object.cpp)
add_dependencies(add_collision_object
seven_dof_arm_test_generate_messages_cpp)
target_link_libraries(add_collision_object
${catkin_LIBRARIES})
```

Let's see how this node works in RViz with the MoveIt! motion-planning Plugin:

- We will start the `demo.launch` inside the `seven_dof_arm_config` package for testing this node:

```
$ roslaunch seven_dof_arm_config demo.launch
```

- Then we, add the following collision object:

```
$ rosrun seven_dof_arm_test add_collision_object
```

When we run the `add_collision_object` node, a green cylinder will pop up, and we can move the collision object as shown in the following screenshot. When the collision object is successfully added to the planning scene, it will list out in the **Scene Objects** tab. We can click on the object and modify its pose. We can also attach the new model in any links of robots too. There is a **Scale** option to scale down the collision model:

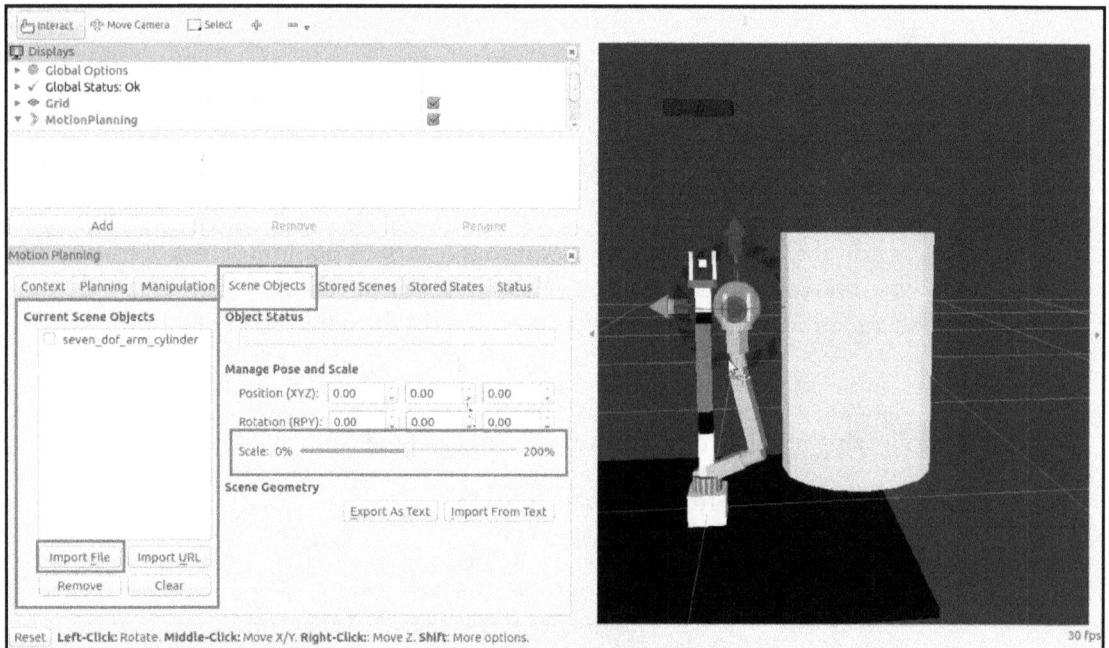

Figure 3: Adding collision objects to RViz using MoveIt!! C++ APIs.

The RViz Motion-Planning plugin also gives an option to import a 3D mesh to the planning scene. Click the **Import File** button for importing the meshes. The following image shows our importing of a cube mesh DAE file, which is imported along with the cylinder in the planning scene. We can scale up the collision object using the **Scale** slider, and set the desired pose using the **Manage Pose** option. When we move the arm end effector to any of these collision objects, MoveIt! detects it as a collision. The MoveIt! collision detection can detect environment collision as well as self-collision. The following is a snapshot of a collision with the environment:

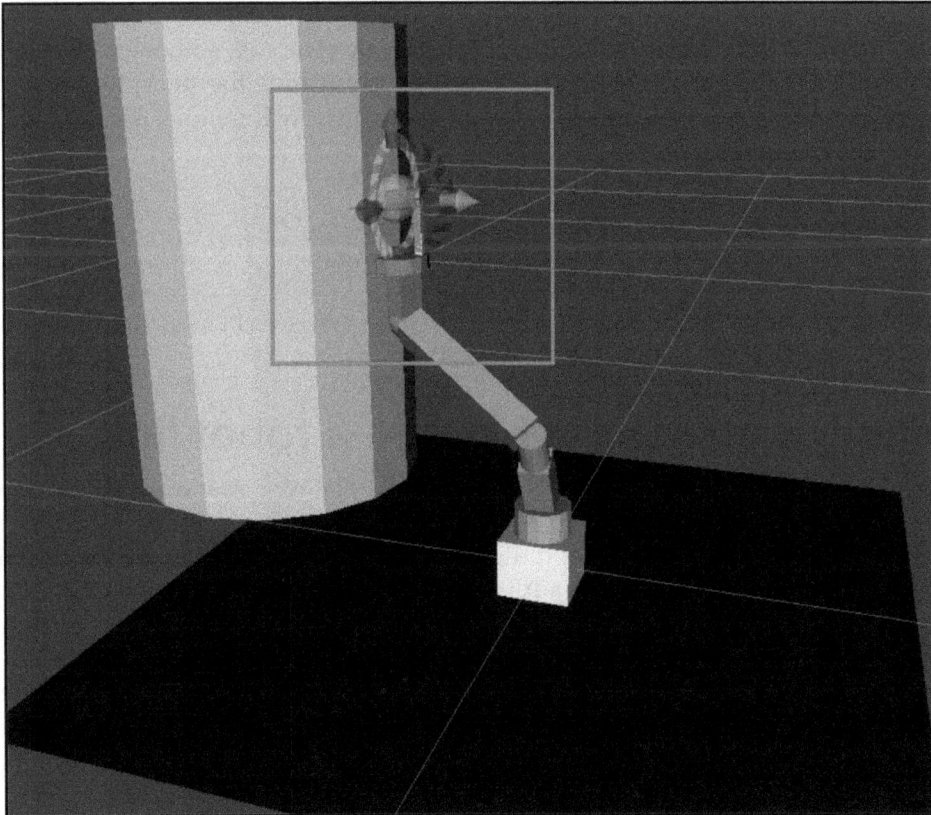

Figure 4: Visualizing collided link.

The collided link will turn red when the arm touches the object. In self-collision also, the collided link will turn red. We can change the color setting of the collision in the Motion Planning plugin settings.

Removing a collision object from the planning scene

Removing the collision object from the planning scene is easy. We have to create an object of `moveit::planning_interface::PlanningSceneInterface`, as we did in the previous example, along with some delay:

```
moveit::planning_interface::PlanningSceneInterface current_scene;
sleep(5.0);
```

Next, we need to create a vector of the string that contains the collision object IDs. Here, our collision object ID is `seven_dof_arm_cylinder`. After pushing the string to this vector, we will call `removeCollisionObjects(object_ids)`, which will remove the collision objects from the planning scene:

```
std::vector<std::string> object_ids;
object_ids.push_back("seven_dof_arm_cylinder");
current_scene.removeCollisionObjects(object_ids);
```

This code is placed in `seven_dof_arm_test/src/remove_collision_object.cpp`.

Attaching a collision object to a robot link

After seeing how to insert and remove objects from the planning scene, we are now going to discuss how to attach and detach objects to the robot's body. This important feature of ROS MoveIt! allow us to perform object manipulation. In fact, after attaching an object to the robot's body, the obstacle avoidance is additionally extended to the grasped object. In this way, the robot will be free to move into its workspace, avoiding obstacles and carrying the object to manipulate. The code we are going to discuss in place is the `seven_dof_arm_test/src/attach_detach_objs.cpp` source code. After creating a `moveit::planning_interface::PlanningSceneInterface`, as shown in the previous examples, we must initialize a `moveit_msgs::AttachedCollisionObject`, filling information about which scene object will be attached to a specific link of the robot's body:

```
moveit_msgs::AttachedCollisionObject attacched_object;
attacched_object.link_name = "grasping_frame";
attacched_object.object = grasping_object;
current_scene.applyAttachedCollisionObject( attacched_object );
```

In this example, the `grasping_object` attached to the robot link is the one already used in the `add_collision_object.cpp` example. When an object is successfully attached to a robot, its color in the Moveit! visualization will change from green to purple, and will move along with the robot motion. To detach an object from the robot's body, we should invoke the `applyAttachedCollisionObject` function on the desired object to detach modifying its operation from `ADD` to `REMOVE`:

```
grasping_object.operation = grasping_object.REMOVE;
attacched_object.link_name = "grasping_frame";
attacched_object.object = grasping_object;
```

Checking self-collisions using Movelt! APIs

We have seen how to detect collision in RViz, but what do we have to do if we want to get collision information in our ROS node? In this section, we will discuss how to get the collision information of our robot in a ROS code. This example can check self collisions and environment collisions, and also tell which links were collided. The example called X is placed in the `seven_dof_arm_test/src` folder. This code is a modified version of the collision-checking example of PR2 Movelt! robot tutorials. In this code, the following snippet loads the kinematic model of the robot to the planning scene:

```
robot_model_loader::RobotModelLoader
robot_model_loader("robot_description");
robot_model::RobotModelPtr kinematic_model = robot_model_loader.getModel();
planning_scene::PlanningScene planning_scene(kinematic_model);
```

To test self-collision in the robot's current state, we can create two instances of class `collision_detection::CollisionRequest` and `collision_detection::CollisionResult`, which have the name of `collision_request` and `collision_result`. After creating these objects, pass it Movelt! collision-checking function, `planning_scene.checkSelfCollision()`, which can give the collision result in the `collision_result` object, and we can print the details, which are shown in the following code:

```
planning_scene.checkSelfCollision(collision_request, collision_result);
ROS_INFO_STREAM("1. Self collision Test: "<< (collision_result.collision ?
"in" : "not in")
<< " self collision");
```

If we want to test collision in a particular group, we can do that by mentioning group_name, as shown in the following code. Here, the group_name is arm:

```
collision_request.group_name = "arm";
current_state.setToRandomPositions();
//Previous results should be cleared
collision_result.clear();
planning_scene.checkSelfCollision(collision_request, collision_result);
ROS_INFO_STREAM("3. Self collision Test(In a group): "<<
(collision_result.collision ? "in" : "not in"));
```

For performing a full collision check, we have to use the following function, called planning_scene.checkCollision(). We need to mention the current robot state and the ACM matrix in this function.

The following is the code snippet to perform full collision checking using this function:

```
collision_detection::AllowedCollisionMatrix acm =
planning_scene.getAllowedCollisionMatrix();
robot_state::RobotState copied_state = planning_scene.getCurrentState();
planning_scene.checkCollision(collision_request, collision_result,
copied_state, acm);
ROS_INFO_STREAM("6. Full collision Test: "<< (collision_result.collision ?
"in" : "not in")
<< " collision");
```

We can launch the demo of motion planning and run this node using the following command:

```
$ roslaunch seven_dof_arm_config demo.launch
```

Run the collision-checking node:

```
$ rosrun seven_dof_arm_test check_collision
```

You will get a report, such as the one shown in the following image. The robot is now not in collision; if it is in collision, it will send a report of it:

```
[ INFO] [1512837566.744018279]: 1. Self collision Test: not in self collision
[ INFO] [1512837566.744073739]: 2. Self collision Test(Change the state): in
[ INFO] [1512837566.744108096]: 3. Self collision Test(In a group): in
[ INFO] [1512837566.744122925]: 4. Collision points valid
[ INFO] [1512837566.744167799]: 5. Self collision Test: in self collision
[ INFO] [1512837566.744179527]: 6 . Contact between: elbow_pitch_link and wrist_pitch_link
[ INFO] [1512837566.744227589]: 6. Self collision Test after modified ACM: not in self collision
[ INFO] [1512837566.744262790]: 6. Full collision Test: not in collision
```

Figure 5: Collision checking information messages.

Working with perception using MoveIt! and Gazebo

Until now, in MoveIt!, we have worked with an arm only. In this section, we will see how to interface a 3D vision sensor data to MoveIt!. The sensor can be either simulated using Gazebo, or you can directly interface an RGB-D sensor, such as Kinect or Xtion Pro, using the `openni_launch` package. Here, we will work using Gazebo simulation. We will add sensors to MoveIt! for vision-assisted pick-and-place. We will create a grasp table and a grasp object in Gazebo for the pick-and-place operation. We will add two custom models called `Grasp_Object` and `Grasp_Table`. The sample models are placed into the `seven_dof_arm_test` package in the model directory, and should be copied to the `~/.gazebo/models` folder for accessing the models from Gazebo. The following command will launch the robot arm and the Asus Xtion pro simulation in Gazebo:

```
$ roslaunch seven_dof_arm_gazebo seven_dof_arm_bringup_grasping.launch
```

This command will open up Gazebo with arm joint controllers and the Gazebo plugin for 3D vision sensor. We can add a grasp table and grasp objects to the simulation, as shown in the following image, by simply clicking and dragging them to the workspace. We can create any kind of table or object. The objects shown in the following image are only for demonstration purposes. We can edit the model SDF file to change the size and shape of the model:

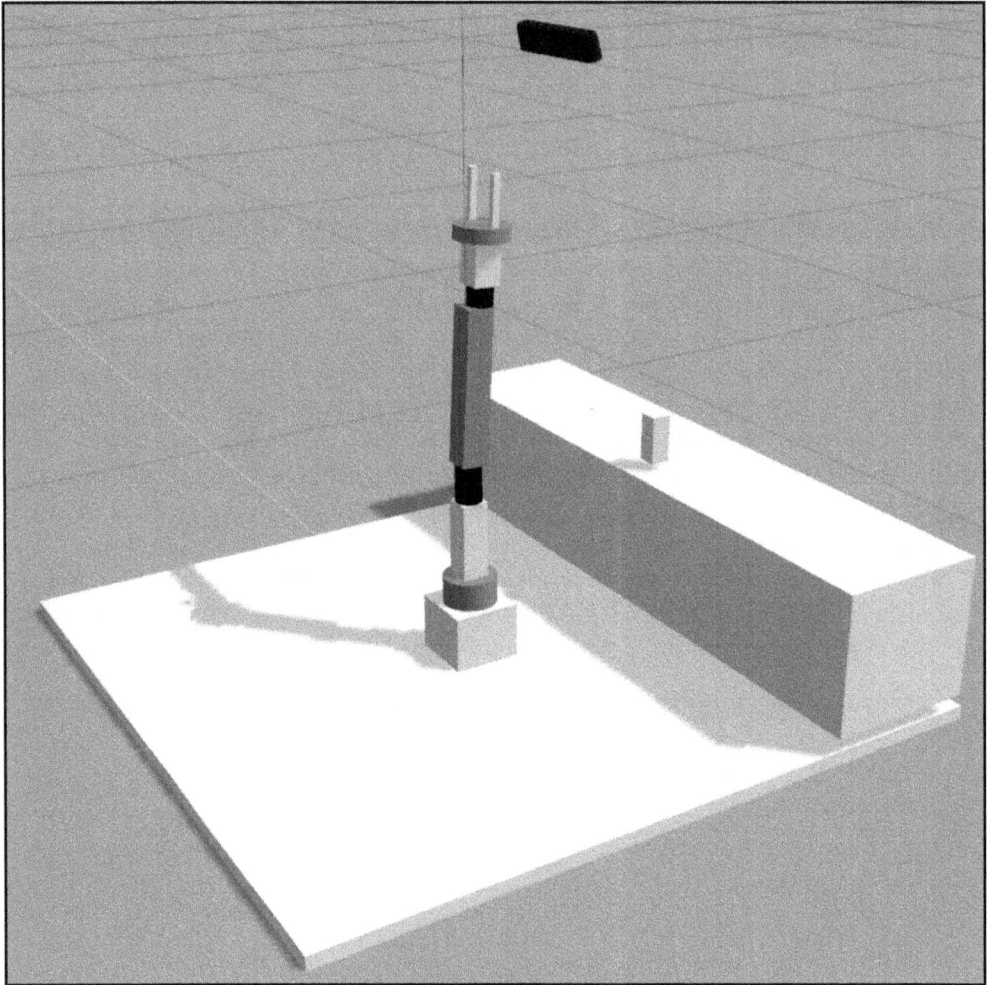

Figure 6: Robot arm with grasp table and object in Gazebo.

Check the topics generated after starting the simulation:

```
$ rostopic list
```

Make sure that we are getting the RGB-D camera topics, as shown in the following code snippet:

```
/rgbd_camera/depth/camera_info
/rgbd_camera/depth/image_raw
/rgbd_camera/depth/points
/rgbd_camera/ir/camera_info
/rgbd_camera/ir/image_raw
/rgbd_camera/ir/image_raw/compressed
/rgbd_camera/ir/image_raw/compressed/parameter_descriptions
/rgbd_camera/ir/image_raw/compressed/parameter_updates
/rgbd_camera/ir/image_raw/compressedDepth
/rgbd_camera/ir/image_raw/compressedDepth/parameter_descriptions
/rgbd_camera/ir/image_raw/compressedDepth/parameter_updates
/rgbd_camera/ir/image_raw/theora
/rgbd_camera/ir/image_raw/theora/parameter_descriptions
/rgbd_camera/ir/image_raw/theora/parameter_updates
/rgbd_camera/parameter_descriptions
/rgbd_camera/parameter_updates
/rgbd_camera/rgb/camera_info
/rgbd_camera/rgb/image_raw
/rgbd_camera/rgb/image_raw/compressed
/rgbd_camera/rgb/image_raw/compressed/parameter_descriptions
/rgbd_camera/rgb/image_raw/compressed/parameter_updates
/rgbd_camera/rgb/image_raw/compressedDepth
/rgbd_camera/rgb/image_raw/compressedDepth/parameter_descriptions
/rgbd_camera/rgb/image_raw/compressedDepth/parameter_updates
/rgbd_camera/rgb/image_raw/theora
/rgbd_camera/rgb/image_raw/theora/parameter_descriptions
/rgbd_camera/rgb/image_raw/theora/parameter_updates
/rgbd_camera/rgb/points
```

Figure 7: Listing RGB-D sensor topics.

We can view the point cloud in RViz using the following command:

```
$ rosrun rviz rviz -f base_link
```

The following is the output generated:

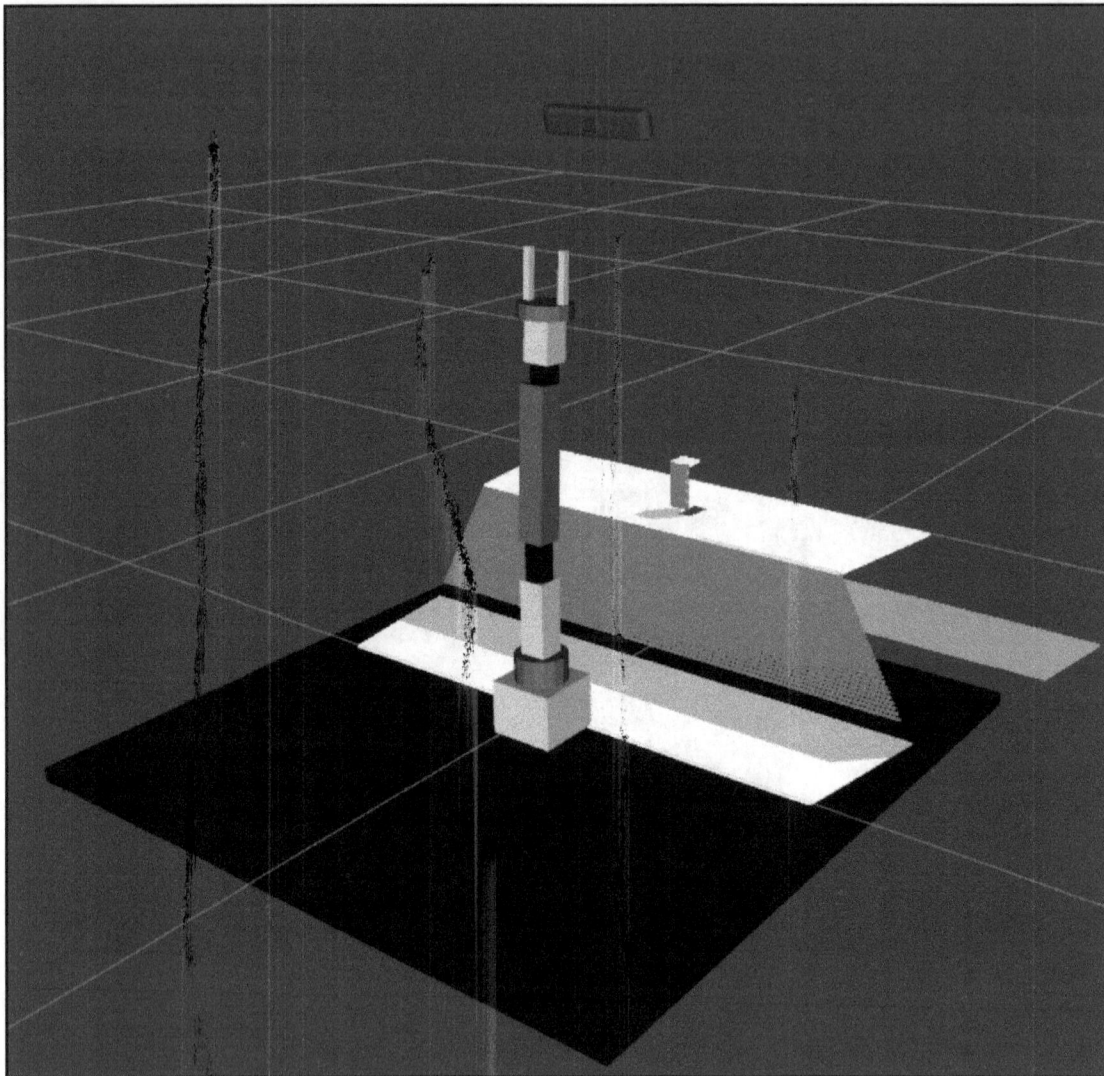

Figure 8: Visualizing point cloud data in RViz.

After confirming the point cloud data from the Gazebo plugins, we have to add some files to the MoveIt! configuration package of this arm, that is, the `seven_dof_arm_config`, for bringing the point cloud data from Gazebo to the MoveIt! planning scene.

The robot environment is mapped as octree representation
(https://en.wikipedia.org/wiki/Octree), which can be built using a library called
OctoMap, which we have already seen in the previous section. The OctoMap is
incorporated as a plugin in MoveIt!, called the **Occupany Map Updator** plugin, which can
update octree from different kinds of sensor inputs, such as point cloud and depth images
from 3D vision sensors. Currently, there are the following plugins for handling 3D data:

- PointCloudOccupancymap Updater: This plugin can take input in the form of
  point clouds (sensor_msgs/PointCloud2)
- DepthImageOccupancymapUpdater: This plugin can take input in the form of
  input depth images (sensor_msgs/Image)

The first step is to write a configuration file for these plugins. This file contains information
about which plugin we are using in this robot, and what its properties are. The file
exploiting the first plugin is found in the seven_dof_arm_config/config folder, called
sensor_kinect_pointcloud.yaml.

The definition of this file is as follows:

```
sensors:
- sensor_plugin: occupancy_map_monitor/PointCloudOctomapUpdater
  point_cloud_topic: /rgbd_camera/depth/points
  max_range: 10
  padding_offset: 0.01
  padding_scale: 1.0
  point_subsample: 1
  filtered_cloud_topic: output_cloud
```

The explanation of a general parameter is:

- sensor_plugin: This parameter specifies the name of the plugin we are using in
  the robot

The following are the parameters of the given sensor_plugin:

- point_cloud_topic: The plugin will listen to this topic for point cloud data
- max_range: This is the distance limit in meters in which points above the range
  will not be used for processing
- padding_offset: This value will be taken into account for robot links and
  attached objects when filtering clouds containing the robot links (self-filtering)

- `padding_scale`: This value will also be taken into account while self-filtering
- `point_subsample`: If the update process is slow, points can be subsampled. If we make this value greater than 1, the points will be skipped instead of processed
- `filtered_cloud_topic`: This is the final filtered cloud topic. We will get the processed point cloud through this topic. It can be used mainly for debugging

If we are using the `DepthImageOctomapUpdater` plugin, we can have a different configuration file. We are not using this plugin in our example robot, but we can see its usage and properties:

```
sensors:
  - sensor_plugin: occupancy_map_monitor/DepthImageOctomapUpdater
    image_topic: /head_mount_kinect/depth_registered/image_raw
    queue_size: 5
    near_clipping_plane_distance: 0.3
    far_clipping_plane_distance: 5.0
    skip_vertical_pixels: 1
    skip_horizontal_pixels: 1
    shadow_threshold: 0.2
    padding_scale: 4.0
    padding_offset: 0.03
    filtered_cloud_topic: output_cloud
```

The explanation of a general parameter is:

- `sensor_plugin`: This parameter specifies the name of the plugin we are using in the robot.

The following are the parameters of the given `sensor_plugin`:

- `image_topic`: The topic that streams the image.
- `queue_size`: This is the queue size for the depth image transport subscriber.
- `near_clipping_plane_distance`: This is the minimum valid distance from the sensor.
- `far_clipping_plane_distance`: This is the maximum valid distance from the sensor.
- `skip_vertical_pixels`: This is the number of pixels we have to skip from the top and bottom of the image. If we give a value of 5, it will skip five columns from first and last of the image.

- `skip_horizontal_pixels`: Skipping pixels in horizontal direction.
- `shadow_threshold`: In some situations, points can appear below the robot links. This happens because of padding. `shadow_threshold` removes the points with a distance that is greater than the `shadow_threshold`.

After discussing the OctoMap update plugin and its properties, we can switch to the launch files necessary to initiate this plugin and its parameters. The first file we need to create is inside the `seven_dof_arm_config/launch` folder with the name `seven_dof_arm_moveit_sensor_manager.launch`. The following is the definition of this file. This launch file basically loads the plugin parameters:

```
<launch>
  <rosparam command="load" file="$(find
seven_dof_arm_config)/config/sensors_kinect_pointcloud.yaml" />
</launch>
```

The next file that we need to edit is the `sensor_manager.launch`, which is located inside the `launch` folder. The definition of this file is as follows:

```
<launch>
  <!-- This file makes it easy to include the settings for sensor managers
-->

  <!-- Params for the octomap monitor -->
  <!--  <param name="octomap_frame" type="string" value="some frame in
which the robot moves" /> -->
  <param name="octomap_resolution" type="double" value="0.015" />
  <param name="max_range" type="double" value="5.0" />

  <!-- Load the robot specific sensor manager; this sets the
moveit_sensor_manager ROS parameter -->

  <arg name="moveit_sensor_manager" default="seven_dof_arm" />
  <include file="$(find seven_dof_arm_config)/launch/$(arg
moveit_sensor_manager)_moveit_sensor_manager.launch.xml" />

</launch>
```

The following line is commented because it can be used if the robot is mobile. In our case, our robot is static. If it is fixed on a mobile robot, we can give the frame value as odom, or odom_combined of the robot:

```
<param name="octomap_frame" type="string" value="some frame in which the
robot moves" />
```

The following parameter is the resolution of OctoMap, which is visualizing in RViz measured in meters. The rays beyond the max_range value will be truncated:

```
<param name="octomap_resolution" type="double" value="0.015" />
<param name="max_range" type="double" value="5.0" />
```

The interfacing is now complete. We can test the MoveIt! interface using the following command. Launch Gazebo for perception using the following command, and add the desired grasp table and grasp object model:

```
$ roslaunch seven_dof_arm_gazebo seven_dof_arm_bringup_grasping.launch
```

Start the MoveIt! planner with sensor support:

```
$ roslaunch seven_dof_arm_config moveit_planning_execution.launch
```

Now RViz has sensor support. We can see the OctoMap in front of the robot in the following screenshot:

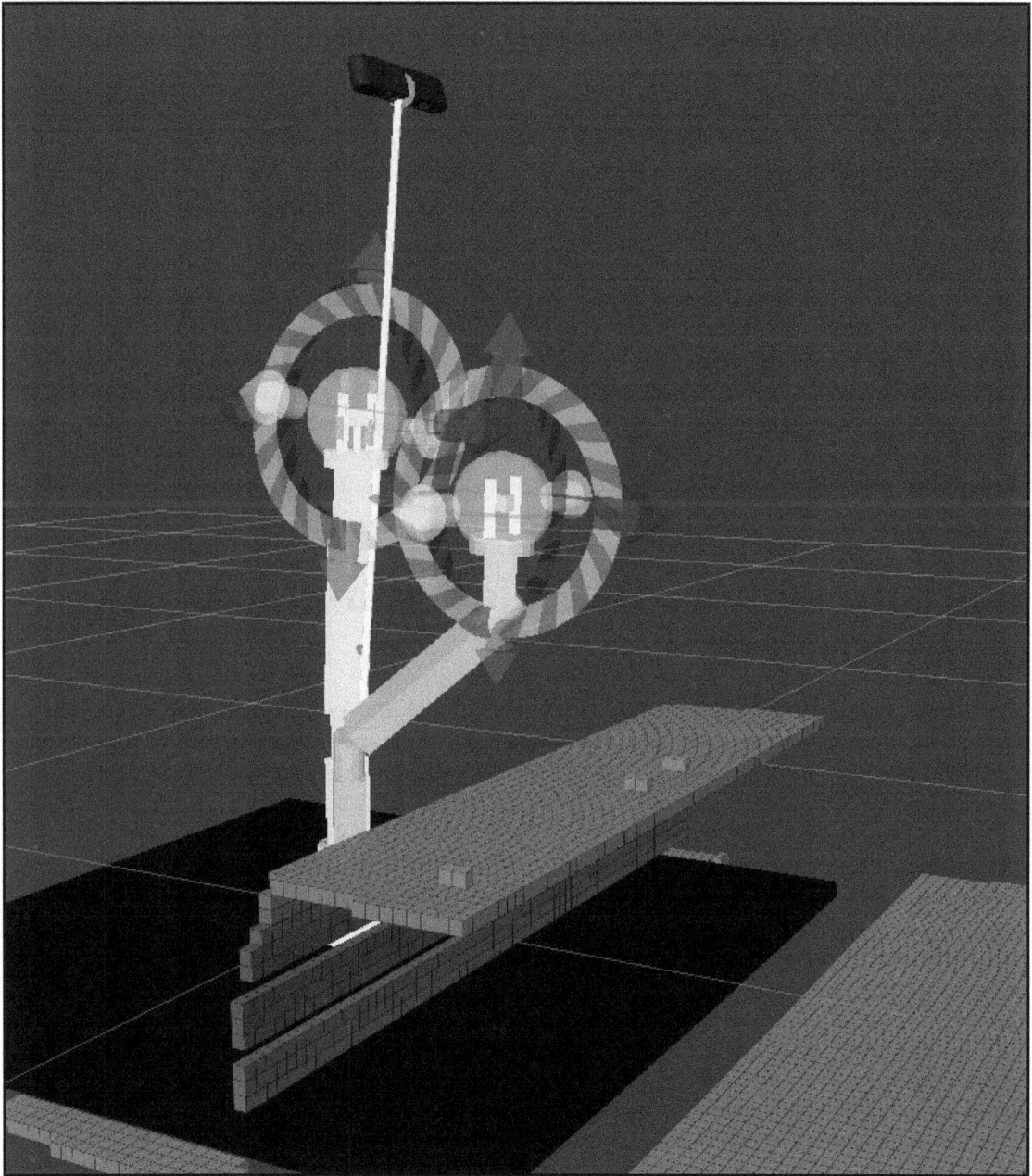

Figure 9: Visualizing octomap in RViz.

Manipulating objects with MoveIt!

Manipulating objects is one of main usages of robotic arms. The capacity to pick up objects and place them in a different location of the robot's workspace is extremely useful both in industry and research applications. The picking process is also known as *grasping*, and represents a complex task because a lot of constraints are required to pick an object up in a proper way. Humans handle grasping operations using their intelligence, but robots need rules for it. One of the constraints in grasping is the approaching force; the end effector should adjust the grasping force for picking the object, but not make any deformation on the object while grasping. In addition, a grasping pose is needed to pick an object in the best way, and should be calculated considering its shape and its pose. MoveIt! doesn't provide any built-in functionality to find the best approaching or grasping pose to pick objects. For this reason, in this section, we will first discuss how to pick-and-place an object placed into the planning scene considering a known grasping pose. Later, we will present the **Grasping Pose Detector** (**GPD**) package, a ROS package able to detect 6-DOF grasp poses based on the point clouds.

Working with a robot pick-and-place task using MoveIt!

We can do pick and place in various ways. One is by using pre-defined sequences of joint values; in this case, we put the object in a known position, and move the robot into towards that by providing direct joint values or forward kinematics. Another method of pick and place is by using inverse kinematics without any visual feedback. In this case, we command the robot to move in a cartesian position with respect to the robot base frame, and by solving IK. In this way, the robot can reach that position and pick up that object. One more method is to use external sensors, such as the vision ones, to calculate the pick-and-place positions; in this case, a vision sensor is used to identify the object's location, and the arm goes to that position by solving to pick the object. Of course, the use of vision sensors requires the development of robust algorithms to perform object recognition and tracking, and are able to calculate the best grasping pose to pick that object. But in this section, we want to demonstrate a pick and place sequence, by defining the approaching and grasping position to pick the object and place it on another location of its workspace. We can work with this example along with Gazebo, or simply use the MoveIt! demo interface. The complete source code of this example is reported in the `seven_dor_arm_test/src/pick_place.cpp` file. As we have already seen, we first should initialize the planning scene:

```
ros::init(argc, argv, "seven_dof_arm_planner");
```

```
ros::NodeHandle node_handle;
ros::AsyncSpinner spinner(1);
spinner.start();
moveit::planning_interface::MoveGroupInterface group("arm");
moveit::planning_interface::PlanningSceneInterface
planning_scene_interface;
sleep(2);
moveit::planning_interface::MoveGroupInterface::Plan my_plan;
const robot_state::JointModelGroup *joint_model_group =
group.getCurrentState()->getJointModelGroup("arm");
```

Then, we must create the working environment of the robot, placing the grasping table and the grasping object into the scene:

```
moveit::planning_interface::PlanningSceneInterface current_scene;
geometry_msgs::Pose pose;
shape_msgs::SolidPrimitive primitive;
primitive.type = primitive.BOX;
primitive.dimensions.resize(3);
primitive.dimensions[0] = 0.03;
primitive.dimensions[1] = 0.03;
primitive.dimensions[2] = 0.08;
moveit_msgs::CollisionObject grasping_object;
grasping_object.id = "grasping_object";
pose.orientation.w = 1.0;
pose.position.y =   0.0;
pose.position.x =   0.33;
pose.position.z =   0.35;
grasping_object.primitives.push_back(primitive);
grasping_object.primitive_poses.push_back(pose);
grasping_object.operation = grasping_object.ADD;
grasping_object.header.frame_id = "base_link";
primitive.dimensions[0] = 0.3;
primitive.dimensions[1] = 0.5;
primitive.dimensions[2] = 0.32;
moveit_msgs::CollisionObject grasping_table;
grasping_table.id = "grasping_table";
pose.orientation.w = 1.0;
pose.position.y =   0.0;
pose.position.x =   0.46;
pose.position.z =   0.15;
grasping_table.primitives.push_back(primitive);
grasping_table.primitive_poses.push_back(pose);
grasping_table.operation = grasping_object.ADD;
grasping_table.header.frame_id = "base_link";
std::vector<moveit_msgs::CollisionObject> collision_objects;
collision_objects.push_back(grasping_object);
collision_objects.push_back(grasping_table);
```

```
//--- publish objects into the scene
current_scene.addCollisionObjects(collision_objects);
```

Now that the planning scene is properly configured, we can request the motion of the robot towards a pre-configured position of the workspace to bring its end effector close to the object and pick it up:

```
//---approaching
geometry_msgs::Pose target_pose;
target_pose.orientation.x = 0;
target_pose.orientation.y = 0;
target_pose.orientation.z = 0;
target_pose.orientation.w = 1;
target_pose.position.y = 0.0;
target_pose.position.x = 0.32;
target_pose.position.z = 0.35;
group.setPoseTarget(target_pose);
group.move();
//---grasping
target_pose.position.y = 0.0;
target_pose.position.x = 0.34;
target_pose.position.z = 0.35;
group.setPoseTarget(target_pose);
group.move();
```

If the grasping succeeded, we can attach the object to the end effector of the robot, in order to place it in another location of the workspace:

```
//---attach object to the robot
moveit_msgs::AttachedCollisionObject attacched_object;
attacched_object.link_name = "grasping_frame";
attacched_object.object = grasping_object;
current_scene.applyAttachedCollisionObject( attacched_object );
//---place
target_pose.position.y = -0.1;
target_pose.position.x = 0.34;
target_pose.position.z = 0.4;
group.setPoseTarget(target_pose);
group.move();
//---
target_pose.orientation.x = -1;
target_pose.orientation.y = 0;
target_pose.orientation.z = 0;
target_pose.orientation.w = 0;
target_pose.position.y = -0.1;
target_pose.position.x = 0.34;
target_pose.position.z = 0.35;
```

```
group.setPoseTarget(target_pose);
group.move();
```

Finally, we must remove the object from the robot's gripper:

```
grasping_object.operation = grasping_object.REMOVE;
attacched_object.link_name = "grasping_frame";
attacched_object.object = grasping_object;
current_scene.applyAttachedCollisionObject( attacched_object );
```

To run this example, launch the MoveIt! demo:

```
$ roslaunch seven_dof_arm_config demo.launch
```

Run the pick and place program:

```
$ rosrun seven_dof_arm_test pick_place
```

The following is the screenshot of the grasping process:

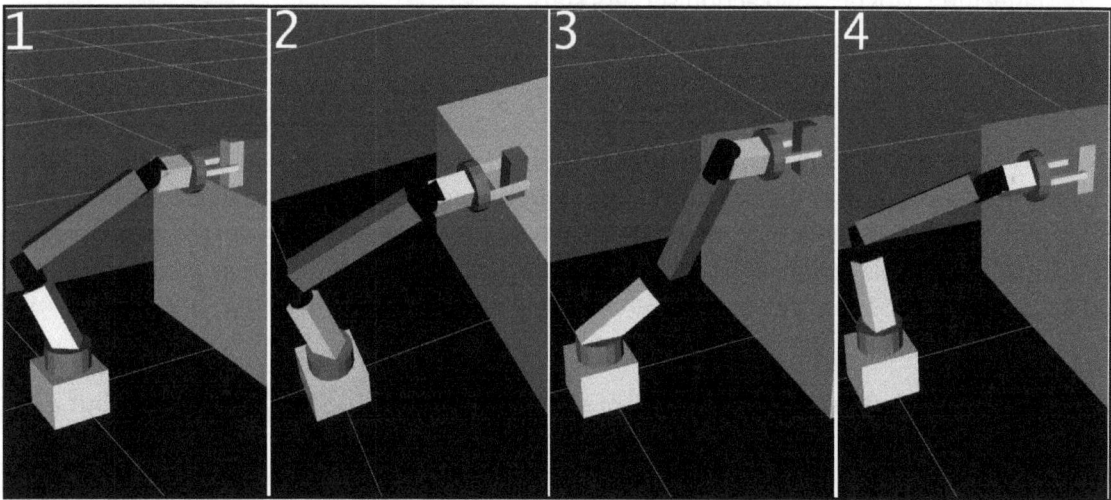

Figure 10: Pick and place sequences using MoveIt!.

The various steps in the grasping process are explained next:

- In the first step, we can see a green block, which is the object that is going to be grasped by the robot gripper. We have created this object inside the planning scene using the `pick_and_place` node. In the first part of the node, the end effector of the robot is approaching the object.
- After approaching the object, a valid trajectory to grasp the object is generated. After the grasping is completed, the green block will be attached to the robot's gripper, and will change its color to purple.
- After picking the block, the robot will transport it to another place of the workspace, before placing it on the working table. If there is a valid IK in the place pose, the gripper holds the object in the planned trajectory.
- Finally, the object is placed on the table and detached from from the robot's gripper.

Another way to perform the pick and place tasks is by using actions provided by MoveIt!. After launching MoveIt!, two action servers start:

- **pickup**: This action accepts a `moveit_msgs::PickupGoal` message in which we mainly must specify the target object to grasp, and a list of possible grasping configurations. These configurations are filled in a `moveit_msgs::Grasp` in which we have to set the complete position of the joints of the robot during the approaching and grasping actions, and the position of the end effector during the picking .
- **place**: This action is used to place an object on to a surface. It accepts a `moveit_msgs::PlaceGoal` message to specify a list of possible objects, positioning configuration.

Using MoveIt! actions assure the success of safe and complete pick and place tasks, but a lot of pre-planned information is required, making them difficult to use in advanced complex and dynamic robotic applications.

Calculating grasp poses with GPD

In this section, we will present **Grasp Pose Detector** (`https://github.com/atenpas/gpd`), a ROS package able to detect 6-DOF grasp poses for two-finger grippers, such as the one for our `seven_dof_arm` manipulator. Grasping poses are detected using 3D point clouds, so we can use the depth sensor of the robot to find object grasping poses. This package exploits deep learning and GPU calculation to detect different grasping poses for all the objects detected into the scene. To download this package, just clone the following code repository:

```
$ git clone https://github.com/atenpas/gpd.git
```

Owing to the use of GPU parallel calculation, to use this package an Nvidia video card is needed. To compile the GPD, the following libraries must be installed:

```
$ sudo apt-get install libgflags-dev libprotobuf-dev liblmdb-dev
libleveldb-dev libsnappy-dev libatlas3-base
```

In addition, GPD uses the Caffe framework (`https://github.com/BVLC/caffe`) to implement deep learning functionalities. To install this software, follow these lines of code:

```
$ git clone https://github.com/BVLC/caffe.git
$ cd caffe && mkdir build && cd build
$ cmake -DCMAKE_INSTALL_PREFIX:PATH=/usr ..
$ make && sudo make install
```

If everything goes well, we can build an ROS workspace to compile the GPD package. After completion, we we can test the Grasping Pose Detector on an example dataset, using the following command:

```
$ roslaunch gpd tutorial0.launch
```

Within the GUI that appears, press *r* to center the view, and *q* to quit the GUI and load the next visualization. The output should show several grasping poses for a point cloud test set, as shown in the next diagram:

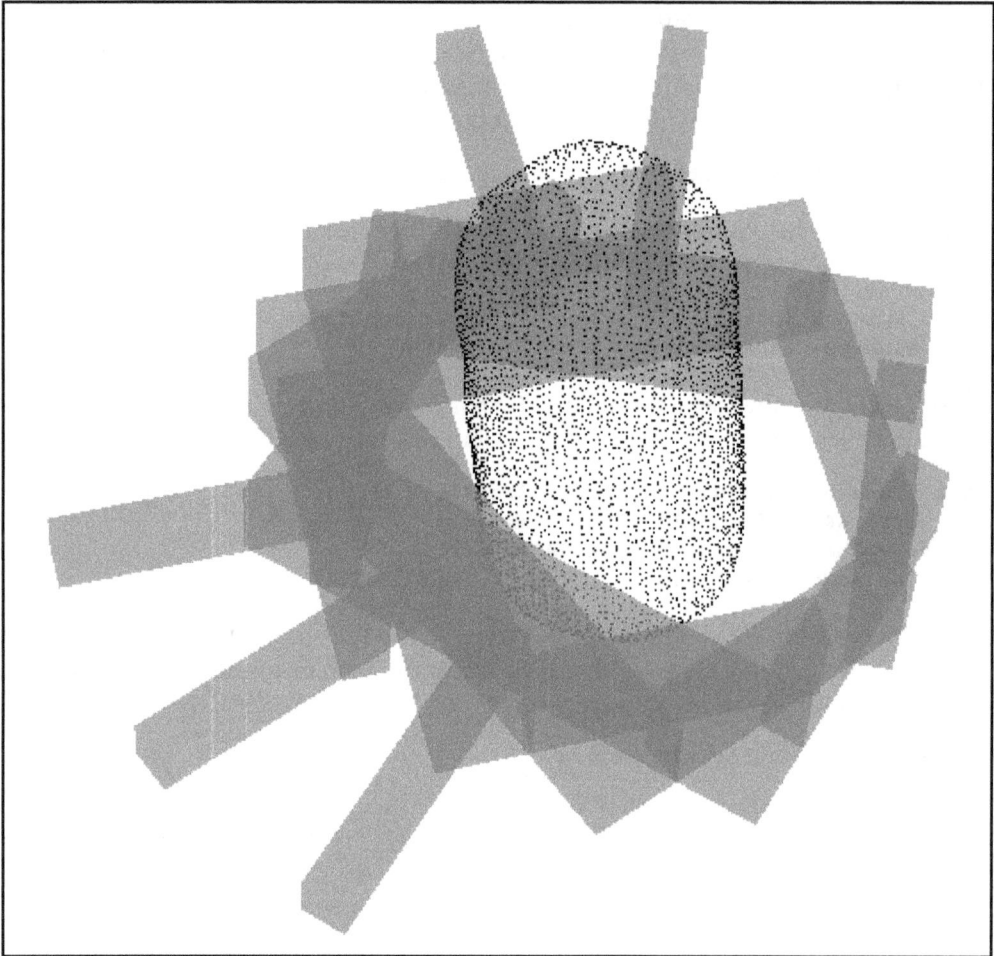

Figure 11: Grasping poses generated on a point cloud test set

To test the GPD package on our robotic system, we can use Gazebo with a simulation scene containing an object to grasp:

```
$ roslaunch seven_dof_arm_gazebo seven_dof_arm_bringup_grasping_gpd.launch
```

After we've spawned the simulation scene, we can lunch the GPD software with the following command:

```
$ roslaunch seven_dof_arm_test gpd.launch
```

We can use Rviz to visualize the possible grasping poses generated by GPD:

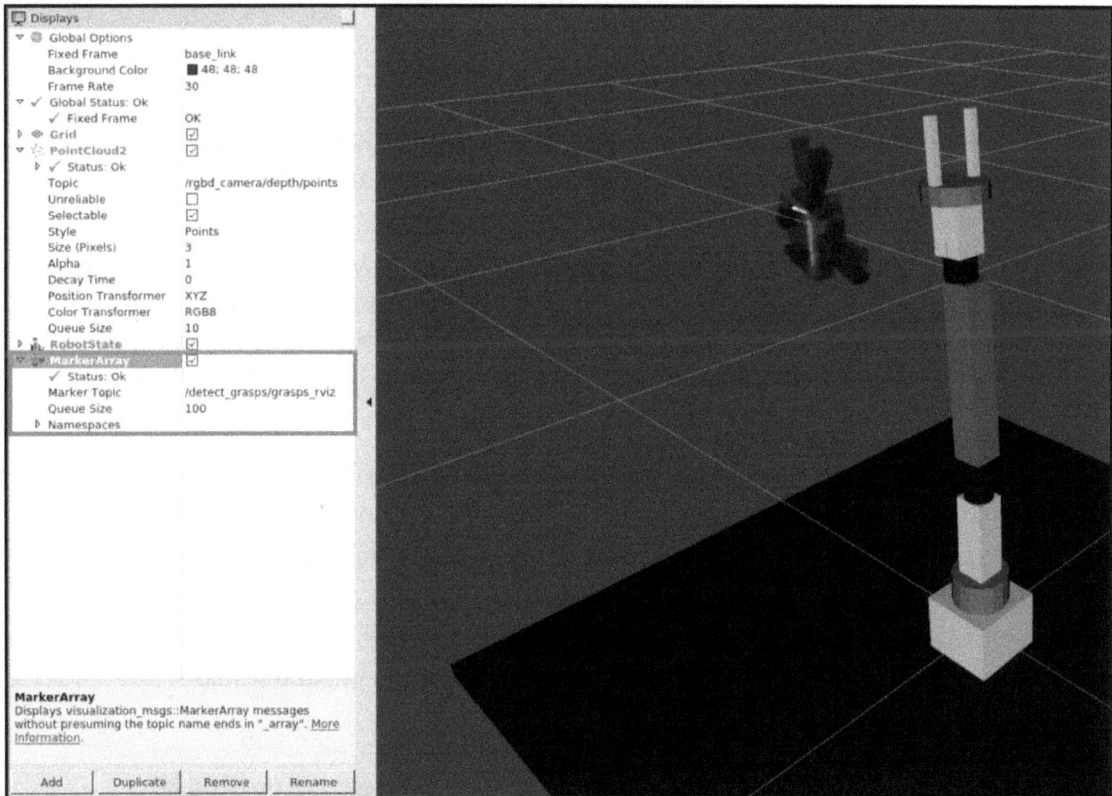

Figure 12: Grasping poses for an object in the planning scene.

In the following code, we will see some entries of the Grasping pose Detector launch file:

```
<!-- Load hand geometry parameters -->
<include file="$(find gpd)/launch/hand_geometry.launch">
    <arg name="node" value="detect_grasps" />
</include>
```

Firstly, we must inform the system of the geometry of the end effector. In the `hand_geometry` launch file, a list of parameters are included to define the width of the gripper fingers, and its depth:

```
<param name="cloud_topic" value="/rgbd_camera/depth/points" />
<param name="num_samples" value="100" />
<param name="num_threads" value="4" />
<param name="num_selected" value="10" />
```

Here, we define the topic name of the point clouds and the number of samples used to detect the grasping pose; of course, a higher number of samples requires more computation time. Finally, the `num_selected` parameter specifies the number of grasping poses to provide as output. These poses are scored, and the one with the highest score is at the top of the list.

After selecting a grasp, you can get information about where to place the robot hand from the `/detect_grasps/clustered_grasps` topic. In this message, the list of grasping configurations is published, defining the position and the orientation of the end effector during the picking action. In particular, this message contains the following field:

- `bottom`: A 3D point specifying the centred base of the robotic hand
- `top`: A 3D point specifying the centered top of the robotic hand
- `surface`: A 3D point specifying the centred position on the object surface
- `approach`: A 3D vector indicating the grasp approaching direction
- `binormal`: A 3D vector indicating the grasping surface orientation
- `axis`: A 3D vector perpendicular to the approaching direction vector
- `width`: The opening width of the gripper needed to grasp the object
- `score`: The grasping pose score

Sadly, right now no direct integration between GPD and MoveIt! are provided.

Pick and place action in Gazebo and real robot

The grasping sequence executed in the MoveIt! demo uses fake controllers. We can send the trajectory to the actual robot or Gazebo. In Gazebo, we can launch the grasping world to perform this action.

In the real hardware, the only difference is that we need to create joint trajectory controllers for the arm. One of the commonly used hardware controllers is the DYNAMIXEL controller. We will learn more about the DYNAMIXEL controllers in the next section.

Understanding DYNAMIXEL ROS Servo controllers for robot hardware interfacing

Till now, we have learned about MoveIt! interfacing using Gazebo simulation. In this section, we will see how to replace Gazebo and put a real robot interface to MoveIt!. Let's discuss the DYNAMIXEL servos and the ROS controllers.

The DYNAMIXEL servos

The DYNAMIXEL servos are smart, high-performance networked actuators for high-end robotics applications. These servos are manufactured by a Korean company called ROBOTIS (http://en.robotis.com/). These servos are very popular among robotics enthusiasts because they can provide excellent position and torque control, and also provide a variety of feedback, such as position, speed, temperature, voltage, and so on. One of their useful features is that they can be networked in a daisy chain manner. This feature is very useful in multi-joint systems, such as a robotic arm, humanoid robots, robotic snakes, and others. The servos can be directly connected to PCs using a USB to DYNAMIXEL controller, which is provided from ROBOTIS. This controller has a USB interface, and when it is plugged into the PC, it acts as a virtual COM port. We can send data to this port, and internally it will convert the RS 232 protocol to **Transistor-Transistor Logic (TTL)**, and in RS 485 standards. The DYNAMIXEL can be powered and then connected to the USB to DYNAMIXEL controller to start working with it. DYNAMIXEL servos support both TTL and RS 485 level standards. The following figure shows the DYNAMIXEL servos, called **MX-106**, and **USB To DYNAMIXEL** controller:

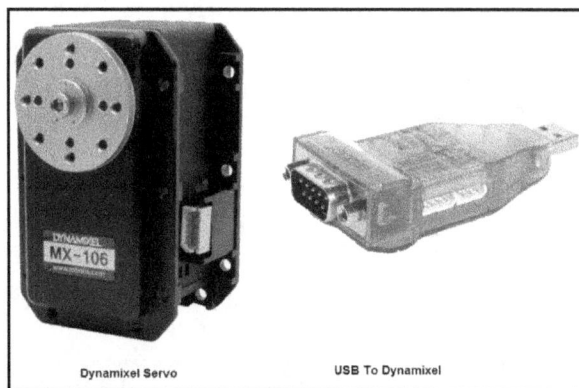

Dynamixel Servo   USB To Dynamixel

Figure 13: DYNAMIXEL Servo and USB to DYNAMIXEL controller

There are different series of DYNAMIXEL available in the market. Some of the series are MX - 28, 64 and 106, RX - 28,64, 106, and so on. The following is the connection diagram of DYNAMIXEL, USB to DYNAMIXEL to PC:

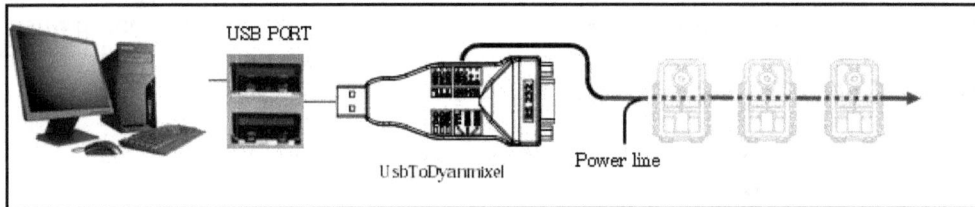

Figure 14: DYNAMIXEL Servos connected to PC using USB To DYNAMIXEL controller

Multiple DYNAMIXEL devices can be connected together in sequence (or a daisy chain), as shown in the preceding figure. Each DYNAMIXEL has a firmware setting inside its controller. We can assign the ID of servo, the joint limits, the position limits, the position commands, the PID values, the voltage limits, and so on, inside the controller. There are ROS drivers and controllers for DYNAMIXEL, which are available at:
http://wiki.ros.org/dynamixel_motor.

DYNAMIXEL-ROS interface

The ROS stack for interfacing the DYNAMIXEL motor is dynamixel_motor. This stack contains an interface for DYNAMIXEL motors, such as MX-28, MX64, MX-106, RX-28, RX64, EX106, AX-12, and AX-18. The stack consists of the following packages:

- dynamixel_driver: This package is the driver package of DYNAMIXEL, which can do low-level IO communication with DYNAMIXEL from the PC. This driver has hardware interface for the previously mentioned series of servos, and can do the read/write operation for DYNAMIXEL through this package. This package is used by high-level packages, such as dynamixel_controllers. There are only a few cases when the user directly interacts with this package.

- dynamixel_controllers: This is a higher-level package that works using the dynamixel_motor package. Using this package, we can create a ROS controller for each DYNAMIXEL joint of the robot. The package contains a configurable node, services, and spawner script to start, stop, and restart one or more controller plugins. In each controller, we can set the speed and the torque. Each DYNAMIXEL controller can be configured using the ROS parameters, or can be loaded by a YAML file. The dynamixel_controllers package supports position, torque, and trajectory controllers.

- `dynamixel_msgs`: These are the message definitions that are used inside the `dynamixel_motor` stack.

Interfacing 7 DOF DYNAMIXEL-based robotic arm to ROS MoveIt!

In this section, we will discuss a 7 DOF robot manipulator called **COOL arm-5000**, which is manufactured by a company called ASIMOV Robotics (`http://asimovrobotics.com/`), and is shown in the following figure. The robot is built using DYNAMIXEL servos. We will see how to interface a Dynamixel-based robotic arm to ROS using `dynamixel_controllers`:

Figure 15: COOL robotic Arm.

COOL arm robots are fully compatible with ROS and MoveIt!, and are mainly used in education and research. Following are the details of the arms:

- **Degree of Freedom**: 7 DOF
- **Types of Actuators**: DYNAMIXEL MX-64 and MX-28
- **List of Joints**: Shoulder Roll, Shoulder Pitch, Elbow Roll, Elbow Pitch, Wrist Yaw, Wrist Pitch, and Wrist Roll
- **Payload**: 5 Kg
- **Reach**: 1 meter
- **Work Volume**: 2.09 m3
- **Repeatability**: +/- 0.05 mm
- Gripper with 3 fingers

Creating a controller package for a COOL arm robot

The first step is to create a controller package for a COOL arm for interfacing to ROS. The COOL arm controller package is available for download along with the book codes. Before we create the package, we should install the dynamixel_controllers package:

```
$ sudo apt-get install ros-kinetic-dynamixel-controllers
```

The following command will create the controller package with the necessary dependencies. The important dependency of this package is the dynamixel_controllers package:

```
$ catkin_create_pkg cool5000_controller roscpp rospy dynamixel_controller
std_msgs sensor_msgs
```

The next step is to create a configuration file for each joint. The configuration file is called cool5000.yaml, which contains a definition of each controller's name, its type, and its parameters. We can see this file in the cool5000_controller/config folder. We have to create parameters for the seven joints in this arm. The following is a snippet of this config file:

```
joint1_controller:
    controller:
        package: dynamixel_controllers
        module: joint_position_controller
        type: JointPositionController
```

```
    joint_name: joint1
    joint_speed: 0.1
    motor:
        id: 0
        init: 2048
        min: 320
        max: 3823
joint2_controller:
    controller:
        package: dynamixel_controllers
        module: joint_position_controller
        type: JointPositionController
    joint_name: joint2
    joint_speed: 0.1
    motor:
        id: 1
        init: 2048
        min: 957
        max: 3106
```

The controller configuration file mentions the joint name, package of the controller, controller type, joint speed, motor ID, initial position, and minimum and maximum limits of the joint. We can connect as many motors as we want and can create controller parameters by including them in the configuration file. The next configuration file to create is a `joint_rajectory controller` configuration. MoveIt! can only interface if the robot has the `FollowJointTrajectory` action server. The file called `cool5000_trajectory_controller.yaml` is put in the `cool5000_controller/config` folder, and its definition is given in the following code:

```
cool5000_trajectory_controller:
    controller:
        package: dynamixel_controllers
        module: joint_trajectory_action_controller
        type: JointTrajectoryActionController
    joint_trajectory_action_node:
        min_velocity: 0.0
        constraints:
            goal_time: 0.01
```

After creating the `JointTrajectory` controller, we need to create a `joint_state_aggregator` node for combining and publishing the joint states of the robotic arm. You can find this node from the `cool5000_controller/src` folder named `joint_state_aggregator.cpp`. The function of this node is to subscribe controller states of each controller with the message type of `dynamixel::JointState`, and combine each message of the controller into the `sensor_msgs::JointState` messages and publish in the `/joint_states` topic. This message will be the aggregate of the joint states of all the DYNAMIXEL controllers. The definition of `joint_state_aggregator.launch`, which runs the `joint_state_aggregator` node with its parameters, follows. It is placed in the `cool5000_controller/launch` folder:

```
<launch>
    <node name="joint_state_aggregator" pkg="cool5000_controller"
type="joint_state_aggregator" output="screen">
    <rosparam>
            rate: 50
            controllers:
                    - joint1_controller
                    - joint2_controller
                    - joint3_controller
                    - joint4_controller
                    - joint5_controller
                    - joint6_controller
                    - joint7_controller
                    - gripper_controller
        </rosparam>
    </node>
</launch>
```

We can launch the entire controller using the following launch file, called `cool5000_controller.launch`, which is inside the `launch` folder. The code inside this launch file will start communication between the PC and the DYNAMIXEL servos, and will also start the controller manager. The controller manager parameters are serial port, baud rate, servo ID range, and update rate:

```
<launch>

    <!-- Start the Dynamixel motor manager to control all cool5000 servos -
->

    <node name="dynamixel_manager" pkg="dynamixel_controllers"
type="controller_manager.py" required="true" output="screen">
        <rosparam>
            namespace: dxl_manager
            serial_ports:
```

```
dynamixel_port:
    port_name: "/dev/ttyUSB0"
    baud_rate: 1000000
    min_motor_id: 0
    max_motor_id: 6
    update_rate: 20
    </rosparam>
</node>
```

In the next step, it should launch the controller spawner by reading the controller configuration file:

```
    <!-- Load joint controller configuration from YAML file to parameter
server -->
    <rosparam file="$(find cool5000_controller)/config/cool5000.yaml"
command="load"/>

    <!-- Start all  Cool Arm joint controllers -->
    <node name="controller_spawner" pkg="dynamixel_controllers"
type="controller_spawner.py"
        args="--manager=dxl_manager
            --port dynamixel_port
            joint1_controller
            joint2_controller
                joint3_controller
                joint4_controller
                joint5_controller
                joint6_controller
            joint7_controller
                gripper_controller"
            output="screen"/>
```

In the next section of the code, it will launch the `JointTrajectory` controller from the controller configuration file:

```
    <!-- Start the cool5000 arm trajectory controller -->
      <rosparam file="$(find
cool5000_controller)/config/cool5000_trajectory_controller.yaml"
command="load"/>
      <node name="controller_spawner_meta" pkg="dynamixel_controllers"
type="controller_spawner.py"
      args="--manager=dxl_manager
            --type=meta
            cool5000_trajectory_controller
            joint1_controller
            joint2_controller
            joint3_controller
```

```
joint4_controller
joint5_controller
joint6_controller"
output="screen"/>
```

The following section will launch the `joint_state_aggregator` node and the robot description from the `cool5000_description` package:

```
<!-- Publish combined joint info -->
<include file="$(find
cool5000_controller)/launch/joint_state_aggregator.launch" />
<param name="robot_description" command="$(find xacro)/xacro.py '$(find
cool5000_description)/robots/cool5000.xacro'" />
<node name="joint_state_publisher" pkg="joint_state_publisher"
type="joint_state_publisher" output="screen">
    <rosparam param="source_list">[joint_states]</rosparam>
    <rosparam param="use_gui">FALSE</rosparam>
</node>
```

This is all about the COOL arm controller package. Next, we need to set up the controller configuration inside the MoveIt! configuration package of the COOL arm, called `cool5000_moveit_config`.

MoveIt! configuration of the COOL Arm

The first step is to configure the `controllers.yaml`, which is inside the `cool5000_moveit_config/config` folder. The definition of this file follows. For now, we are only focusing on moving the arm, and not on handling the gripper control. So the configuration only contains the arm group joints:

```
controller_list:
  - name: cool5000_trajectory_controller
    action_ns: follow_joint_trajectory
    type: FollowJointTrajectory
    default: true
    joints:
      - joint1
      - joint2
      - joint3
      - joint4
      - joint5
      - joint6
      - joint7
```

The following is the definition of
the `cool5000_description_moveit_controller_manager.launch.xml` inside
`cool5000_moveit_config/launch`:

```
<launch>
<!--
 Set the param that trajectory_execution_manager needs to find the
controller plugin
-->
<arg name="moveit_controller_manager"
default="MoveIt_simple_controller_manager/MoveItSimpleControllerManager"/>

<param name="MoveIt_controller_manager" value="$(arg
MoveIt_controller_manager)"/>

<!--  load controller_list  -->

<rosparam file="$(find cool5000_moveit_config)/config/controllers.yaml"/>
</launch>
```

After configuring MoveIt!, we can start working on the arm. Apply a proper power supply
the arm and connect it to connect your PC to the USB of the DYNAMIXEL. We will see a
serial device generate; it may be either `/dev/ttyUSB0`, or `/dev/ttyACM0`. According to the
device, change the port name inside the controller launch file.

Start the `cool5000` arm controller using the following command:

```
$ roslaunch cool5000_controller cool5000_controller.launch
```

Start the RViz demo, and start path planning. If we press the **Execute** button, the trajectory
will execute on the hardware arm:

```
$ roslaunch cool5000_moveit_config 5k.launch
```

A random pose (which is shown in RViz) and the COOL arm is shown in the following image:

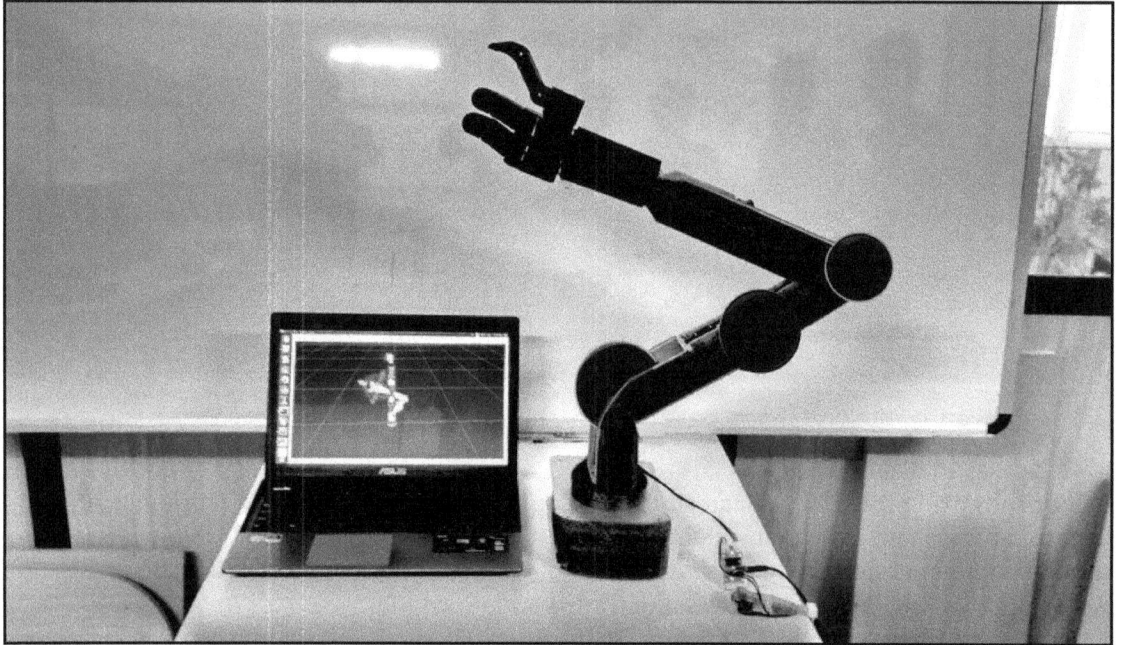

Figure 16: COOL-Arm-5000 prototype with MoveIt! visualization.

Questions

- What is the role of the FCL library in MoveIt!?
- How does MoveIt! build OctoMap of the environment?
- How could a robot avoid obstacles after grasped an object?
- What is the main aim of the GPD ROS package?
- What are the main features of DYNAMIXEL servos?

Summary

In this chapter, we explored some advanced features of MoveIt!, and how to interface it into a real hardware. The chapter started with a discussion on collision checking using MoveIt!. We saw how to add a collision object using MoveIt! APIs, and also saw the direct importing of mesh to the planning scene. We discussed a ROS node to check collision using MoveIt! APIs. After learning about collisions, we moved to perception using MoveIt!. We connected the simulated point cloud data to MoveIt! and created an OctoMap in MoveIt!. The next topic we discussed was how to perform pick and place actions to manipulate objects in the scene. We presented a ROS package to autonomously generate grasping poses starting from object point clouds. After discussing these things, we switched to hardware interfacing of MoveIt! using dynamixel servos and its ROS controllers. In the end, we saw a real robotic arm called COOL arm and its interfacing to MoveIt!, which was completely built using DYNAMIXEL controllers. In the next chapter, we will discuss how to interface *Matlab*, a world-renowned numerical computing environment with ROS.

13
Using ROS in MATLAB and Simulink

In previous chapters, we discussed how to simulate and control robots implementing ROS nodes in C++. In this chapter, we will learn how to create ROS nodes using MATLAB, a powerful piece of software that provides several toolboxes with algorithms and hardware connectivity, for developing autonomous robotic applications for ground vehicles, manipulators, and humanoid robots. In addition, MATLAB integrates Simulink: a block diagram environment for model-based design, allowing the implementation of our control programs through a graphical editor. In this chapter, we will also discuss how to implement robotic applications using Simulink.

The first part of this chapter is dedicated to a brief introduction to MATLAB and the Robotic System Toolbox. After we have learned how to exchange data between ROS and MATLAB, we will implement an obstacle avoidance system for the differential drive mobile robot, Turtlebot, showing how simple it is to use components already available in the Robotic System Toolbox and minimize the number of elements to develop in the system. In the second part of the chapter, we will introduce Simulink, showing an initial model as an example, and then discuss a publisher and a subscriber model to demonstrate the Simulink and ROS communication interface. Finally, a control system to regulate the orientation of the Turtlebot robot is developed in Simulink and tested in the Gazebo simulator.

The following are the main topics discussed in this chapter:

- Getting started with MATLAB and MATLAB-ROS and the Robotic System Toolbox
- Working with ROS topics in MATLAB
- Developing a robotic application using MATLAB and Gazebo
- Working with Simulink and the Simulink-ROS interface
- Developing a control system in Simulink and Gazebo

Getting started with MATLAB and MATLAB-ROS

MATLAB (**MATrix LABoratory**) is a multi-platform numerical computing environment widely used by industries, universities, and research centers. MATLAB was born as a mathematical software, but now it offers a lot of additional packages for different areas, such as control design, plotting, image processing, robotics, and so on. MATLAB is a proprietary product of MathWorks and it's not a free software. Usually, free licenses are distributed for student and academic institutions. You can use MATLAB on Windows, GNU/Linux, and macOS. After you have launched it, the main window of MATLAB will appear with its default layout, as shown in the following screenshot:

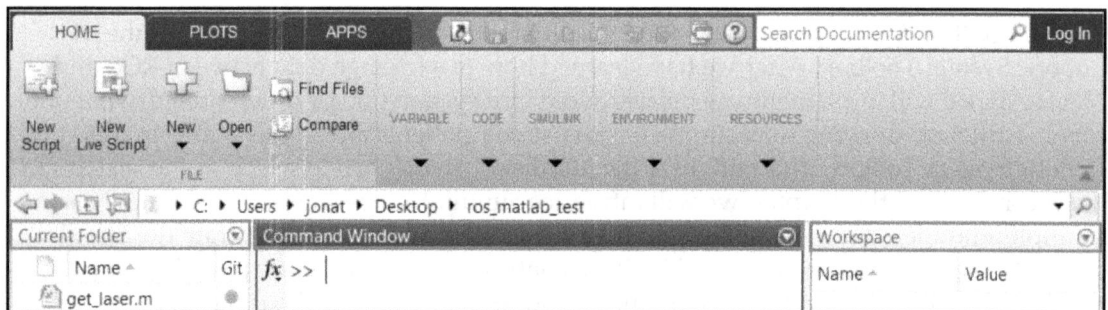

Figure 1: Main window of MATLAB in its default layout

This window includes three main panels:

- **Current Folder**: This shows local files
- **Command Window**: This is a command line to enter MATLAB commands or run MATLAB scripts
- **Workspace**: This shows data created from the **Command Window** or in the MATLAB scripts

Using the **Command Window**, you can issue mathematical commands and create variables that will be shown in the **Workspace**. The same window can be used to view MATLAB function documentation. In fact, all the built-in MATLAB functions have supporting documentation, including examples and descriptions of the function inputs, outputs, and calling syntax. You can access the documentation using `doc` or `help` commands. The first one will open an external window containing the documentation, while the second one will display the documentation in the **Command Window**. Let's see how to get the documentation about the `mean` function:

```
>> doc mean
```

You could also use this command:

```
>> help mean
```

Getting started with the Robotic System Toolbox and ROS-MATLAB interface

Beyond the standard functions provided by the default installation of MATLAB, several external toolboxes give you access to other utilities and libraries. To enable the communication between ROS and MATLAB, we need the ROS-MATLAB interface, which is part of the Robotic System Toolbox (`https://it.mathworks.com/products/robotics.html`). This toolbox provides several algorithms that help us to develop autonomous robot applications, such as path planners, obstacle avoidance methods, state estimations, kinematics, and dynamics algorithms.

In addition, this toolbox implements the interface between MATLAB and ROS that enables developers to test and port their applications on real robots and robotic simulators. You can add the Robotic System Toolbox from the packages list during the MATLAB installation, or purchase it from the toolbox website:

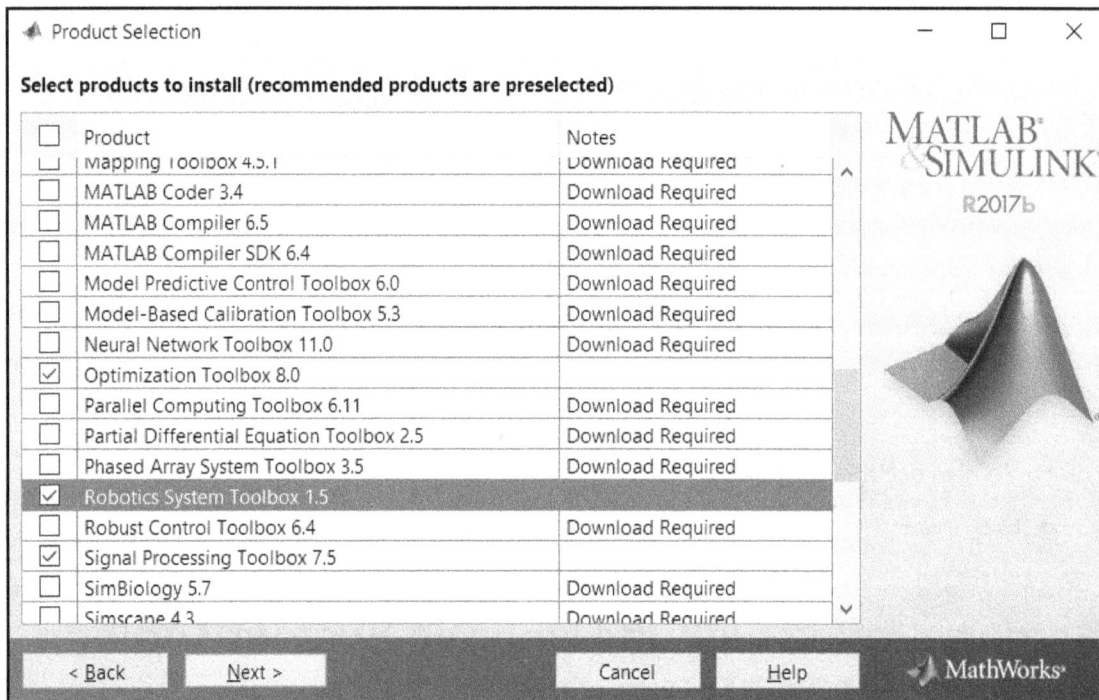

Figure 2: Robotic System Toolbox selection during MATLAB installation

Using the Robotic System Toolbox, we can transform MATLAB into a real ROS node able to exchange information with other nodes of the system and directly control simulated or real ROS-enabled robots using topics and services. The following block diagram depicts the connection between MATLAB and ROS. After connecting MATLAB to a ROS master node, it can fetch data to process from the robot or other ROS nodes. MATLAB could itself initialize a ROS master node in order to manage the communication with the nodes of the network, or it could be connected to another remote ROS master, like any other element of the ROS network. In addition, in the final version of the application, we are not forced to run MATLAB on our computer to execute it, but we can deploy the developed application as a typical C++ node:

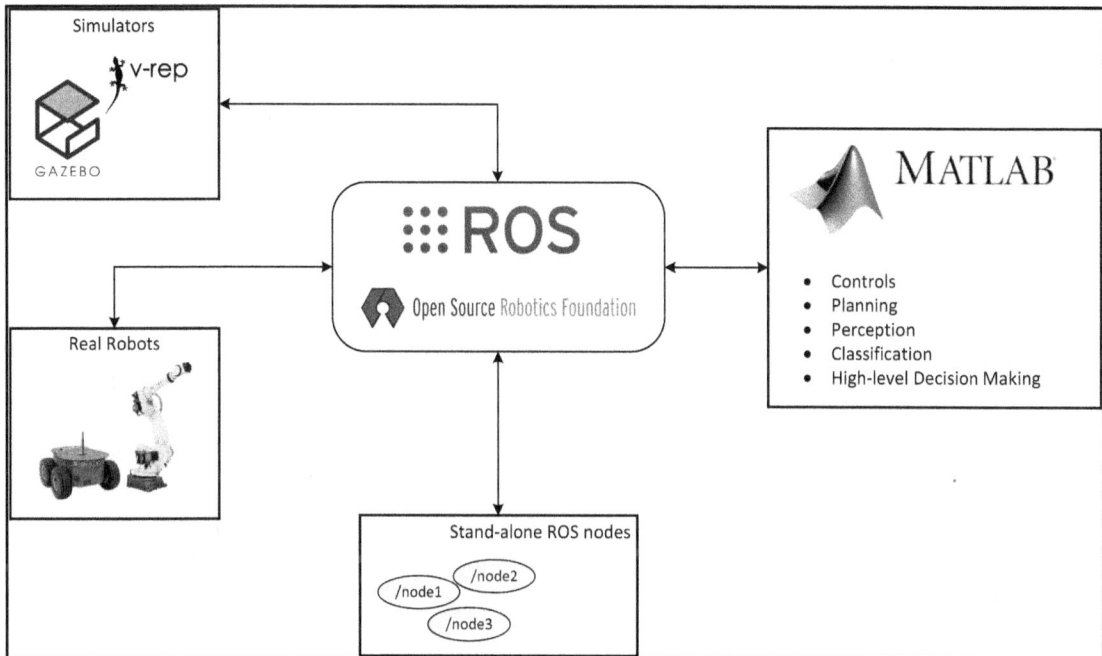

Figure 3: ROS-MATLAB interface schema

With the installation of the Robotic System Toolbox, we will have access to several ROS commands equivalent to the ones used under Linux. To list these commands, you can enter the following line in the **Command Window**:

```
>> help robotics.ros
```

The output of this command is shown in the following figure:

```
>> help robotics.ros
  ros (Robot Operating System)
    rosinit            - Initialize the ros system
    rosshutdown        - Shut down the ros system

    rosmessage         - Create a ros message
    rospublisher       - Create a ros publisher
    rossubscriber      - Create a ros subscriber
    rossvcclient       - Create a ros service client
    rossvcserver       - Create a ros service server
    rosactionclient    - Create a ros action client
    rostype            - View available ros message types

    rosaction          - Get information about actions in the ros network
    rosmsg             - Get information about messages and message types
    rosnode            - Get information about nodes in the ros network
    rosservice         - Get information about services in the ros network
    rostopic           - Get information about topics in the ros network

    rosbag             - Open and parse a rosbag log file
    rosparam           - Get and set values on the parameter server
    rosrate            - Execute loop at fixed frequency using ros time
    rostf              - Receive, send, and apply ros transformations

    rosduration        - Create a ros duration object
    rostime            - Access ros time functionality

    ros functionality is part of Robotics System Toolbox.
    Type "help robotics" for more information.
```

Figure 4: ROS-MATLAB interface commands

To initialize the ROS-MATLAB interface, we can use the `rosinit` command, while `rosshutdown` is used to stop it. By default, `rosinit` creates a ROS master node in Matlab, starting a `matlab_global_node` to communicate with the ROS network. We can see the active ROS nodes after initializing `roscore` using the `rosnode` list command:

```
>> rosinit
Initializing ROS master on http://DESKTOP-40TG18P:11311/.
Initializing global node /matlab_global_node_16208 with NodeURI http://DESKTOP-40TG18P:61762/
>> rosnode list
/matlab_global_node_16208
```

Figure 5: Default initialization of the ROS-MATLAB interface

Using the default configuration of the ROS-MATLAB interface, we must set the
ROS_MASTER_URI environmental variable on the other node of the ROS network with the IP
address of the computer running MATLAB. If you are running MATLAB on Windows, you
can easily get the IP address of your computer by using the following command:

```
>> !ipconfig
```

Or you can use the following command if you are running MATLAB on Linux:

```
>> !ifconfig
```

The output of this command in Windows is shown in the following screenshot:

```
Scheda LAN wireless Wi-Fi:

   Suffisso DNS specifico per connessione: lan
   Indirizzo IPv6 locale rispetto al collegamento . : fe80::cc11:c374:70f8:a4c4%11
   Indirizzo IPv4. . . . . . . . . . . . : 192.168.1.130
   Subnet mask . . . . . . . . . . . . . : 255.255.255.0
   Gateway predefinito . . . . . . . . . : 192.168.1.254
```

Figure 6: !ipconfig command on MATLAB, running on Windows

Otherwise, we can directly connect MATLAB to an active ROS network. In this case, we
must inform the ROS-MATLAB interface about the address of the computer/robot where
the ROS master is running. This is done with the following command:

```
>> setenv('ROS_MASTER_URI', 'http://192.168.1.131:11311')
```

```
>> setenv('ROS_MASTER_URI', 'http://192.168.1.131:11311');
>> rosinit
The value of the ROS_MASTER_URI environment variable, http://192.168.1.131:11311, will be used to connect
Initializing global node /matlab_global_node_75920 with NodeURI http://192.168.1.130:61991/
>> rosnode list
/matlab_global_node_75920
/rosout
```

Figure 7: Initializing the ROS-MATLAB interface on an external ROS network

In the next section, we will start to work with topic callbacks, initializing the ROS-MATLAB
interface and elaborating data directly from MATLAB scripts.

Starting with ROS topics and MATLAB callback functions

In this section, we will discuss how to publish and subscribe ROS messages using MATLAB scripts. The first script that we analyze defines a typical template to develop the control loop of our robot. Firstly, we will subscribe to an input topic, and, successively, we will republish its value on an output topic for a certain amount of time. The complete source code is contained in the talker.m, in the code provided with the book, or you can clone the following Git repository:

```
$ git clone https://github.com/jocacace/ros_matlab_test
```

Let's see the content of the talker.m script:

```
ros_master_ip = 'http://192.168.1.5:11311';
matlab_ip = '192.168.1.13';
rosinit(ros_master_ip, 'NodeHost', matlab_ip);
pause(2) % wait a bit the roscore initialization

talker_sub = rossubscriber( '/talker' );
[chatter_pub, chatter_msg] = rospublisher('/chatter','std_msgs/String');
r = rosrate(2); % 2 Hz loop rate

for i = 1:20
    data = talker_sub.LatestMessage;
    chatter_msg.Data = data.Data;
    send(chatter_pub, chatter_msg);
    waitfor(r);
end
rosshutdown
```

Let's see how the script works:

```
ros_master_ip = 'http://192.168.1.5:11311';
matlab_ip = '192.168.1.13';
rosinit(ros_master_ip, 'NodeHost', matlab_ip);
```

In the preceding code, we initialize the MATLAB-ROS node. In this example, we want to connect MATLAB to an external ROS network and make it able to both read and write data on topics. For this reason, we should export both ROS_MASTER_URI and ROS_HOSTNAME environmental variables. Change the IP addresses on the base of your system configuration:

```
talker_sub = rossubscriber('/talker');
[chatter_pub, chatter_msg] = rospublisher('/chatter','std_msgs/String');
```

Then, we subscribe to the /talker topic while initializing the advertiser to the /chatter topic of the std_msgs/String type:

```
data = talker_sub.LatestMessage;
send(chatter_pub, chatter_msg);
```

Finally, we use the LatestMessage function to get the last message on the input topic, while publishing the message on the /chatter topic.

At this point, you can publish the desired message on the /talker topic, using the command line from one of the computers running Linux in the same network of the MATLAB computer, and visualize the message published on the /chatter topic. Before running the MATLAB script, be sure to have correctly exported the ROS_HOSTNAME variable on the computer where you want to publish the message in order to enable MATLAB to receive the published data.

Now, you can run the script by typing its name in the **Command Window**:

```
>> talker
```

If everything has been correctly set, the output on the Linux machine should appear like in the following screenshot:

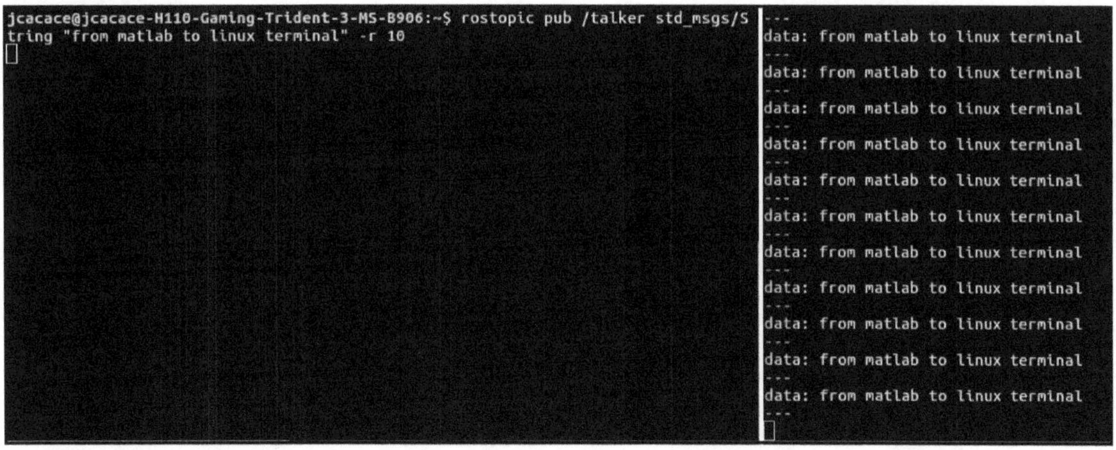

Figure 8: Communication between MATLAB and ROS.

The previous script defines a typical template to implement the control loop of an autonomous robot. Instead of continuously asking for the last message received on the topics, we can define a callback function that is called every time that a new message is received. In this way, we could write more complex control loops to handle the robot behavior, asynchronously receiving multiple information from ROS topics. In the next example, we will start to connect ROS-MATLAB to Gazebo, simulating the Turtlebot robot and plotting the value of its laser sensor using MATLAB.

To run the Gazebo simulation, we will use the turtlebot_gazebo package:

```
$ roslaunch turtlebot_gazebo turtlebot_world.launch
```

After starting Gazebo, different topics are published, among which is /scan . In this example, we need the following MATLAB functions:

- plot_laser.m: This initializes the ROS-MATLAB interface subscribing to the desired laser scanner topic and plots the laser data at a desired frame rate
- get_laser.m: This receives and stores the value of the laser scanner data

Let's look at the code of the plot_laser script:

```
function plot_laser()
    global laser_msg;
    ros_master_ip = 'http://192.168.1.5:11311';
    matlab_ip = '192.168.1.13';
    rosinit(ros_master_ip, 'NodeHost', matlab_ip);
    pause(2)
    laser_sub = rossubscriber('/scan', @get_laser );
    r = rosrate(2); % 2 Hz loop rate
    for i=1:50
        plot(laser_msg,'MaximumRange',7)
        waitfor(r);
    end
    rosshutdown
    close all
end
```

After setting up the ROS-MATLAB interface, we initialize the subscriber to the laser scan topic:

```
laser_sub = rossubscriber('/scan', @get_laser );
```

With this line, we demand, the `get_laser` function handles the data contained in the `/scan` topic. To exchange data between different MATLAB scripts, we use a global variable:

```
global laser_msg;
```

Finally, we plot the laser scanner data of the laser data for 25 seconds:

```
plot(laser_msg, 'MaximumRange', 7)
```

Let's now look at the code of the `get_laser` function:

```
function get_laser(~, message)
    global laser_msg;
    laser_msg = message;
end
```

In this function, we just save the value of the laser scanner data.

After launching the Gazebo simulation, we can run the MATLAB script:

```
>> plot_laser
```

The output of the the default placement of the scene objects is shown in the following screenshot:

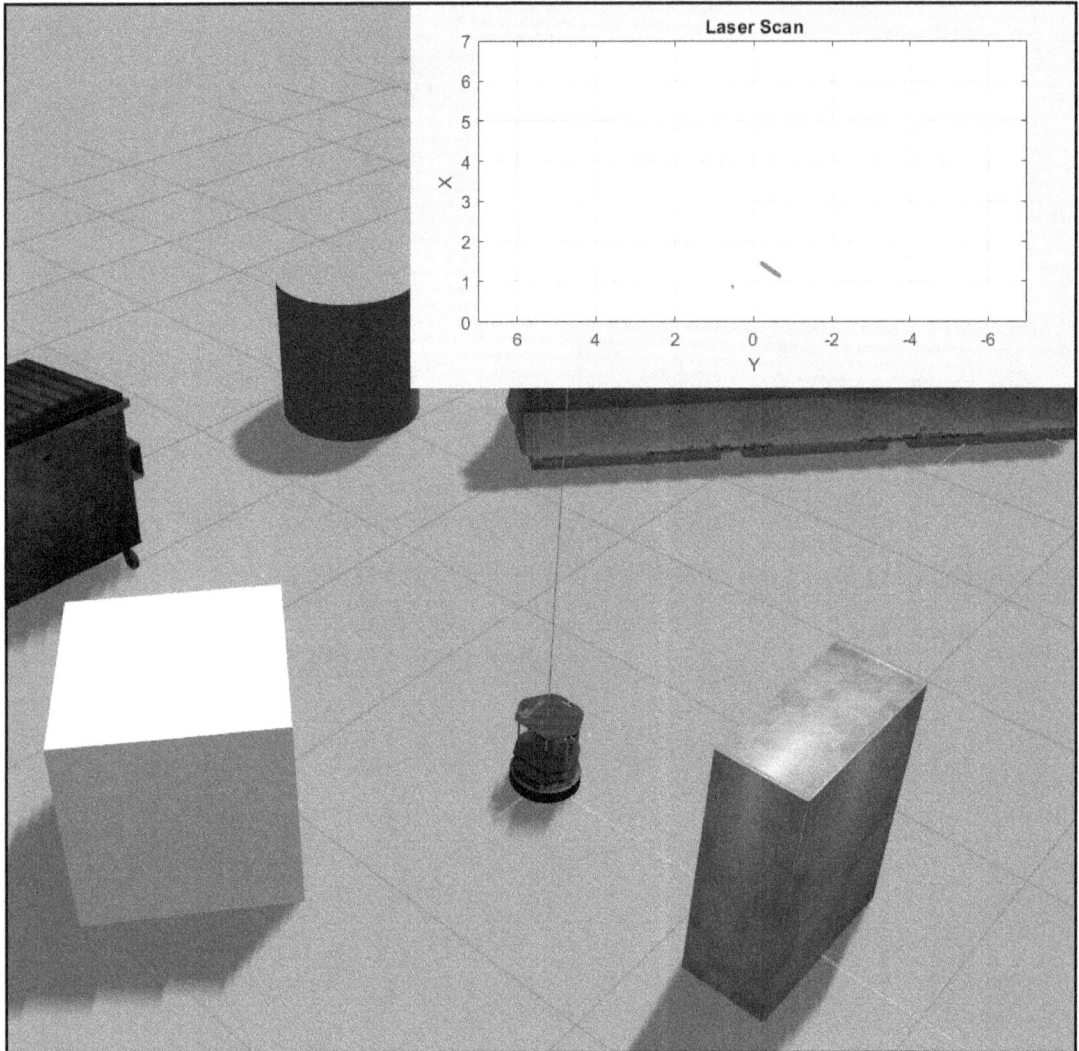

Figure 9: Gazebo laser scanner data plotted in MATLAB

Implementing an obstacle avoidance system for a Turtlebot robot

Until now, we have used MATLAB only to exchange data using ROS topics. In this section, we are going to demonstrate how easy it is to create a robotic application for a mobile robot using MATLAB and the Robotic System Toolbox. We will design an obstacle avoidance system for a differential mobile robot, that allows the Turtlebot robot to navigate a crowded environment without colliding with any obstacle. We will present a MATLAB script that will set the control velocities of the robot to generate a random movement. At the same time, the laser scanner data of the sensor of the robot will be used to avoid obstacles. To implement this behavior, we will rely on the **Vector Field Histogram** (**VFH**) algorithm to compute the obstacle-free steering directions of the robot, based on range sensor readings. This algorithm is already provided by the Robotic System Toolbox in the `robotics.VectorFieldHistogram` class. Finally, after some navigation time, some log data will be plotted, using MATLAB function. This could help developers to debug our application.

The complete source code of the script that we are going to discuss can be found in the `vfh_obstacle_avoidance.m` source file:

```matlab
function vfh_obstacle_avoidance(ros_master_ip, matlab_ip )
    rosinit(ros_master_ip, 'NodeHost', matlab_ip);
    pause(2);
    laserSub = rossubscriber('/scan');
    odomSub  =  rossubscriber('/odom');
    [velPub, velMsg] = rospublisher('/mobile_base/commands/velocity');
    vfh = robotics.VectorFieldHistogram;
    vfh.DistanceLimits = [0.05 1];
    vfh.RobotRadius = 0.1;
    vfh.MinTurningRadius = 0.2;
    vfh.SafetyDistance = 0.1;
    r_max = 6.28;
    r_min = 0.0;
    ob_dist = [];
    omod_vel = [];
    rate = robotics.Rate(10);
    odom_vel_x = [];
    odom_vel_z = [];
    odom_pos_x = [];
    odom_pos_y = [];

    while rate.TotalElapsedTime < 5
        % Get laser scan data
        laserScan = receive(laserSub);
```

```
    odom = receive(odomSub);
    ranges = double(laserScan.Ranges);
    angles = double(laserScan.readScanAngles);
    odom_vel_x = [odom_vel_x, odom.Twist.Twist.Linear.X];
    odom_vel_z = [odom_vel_z, odom.Twist.Twist.Angular.Z];
    odom_pos_x = [odom_pos_x, odom.Pose.Pose.Position.X];
    odom_pos_y = [odom_pos_y, odom.Pose.Pose.Position.Y];

    targetDir = (r_max-r_min).*rand();
    % Call VFH object to computer steering direction
    steerDir = vfh(ranges, angles, targetDir);
    ob_dist = [ob_dist, min(ranges) ];
    % Calculate velocities
    if ~isnan(steerDir) % If steering direction is valid
        desiredV = 0.2;
        w = exampleHelperComputeAngularVelocity(steerDir, 1);
    else % Stop and search for valid direction
        desiredV = 0.0;
        w = 0.5;
    end
    velMsg.Linear.X = desiredV;
    velMsg.Angular.Z = w;
    velPub.send(velMsg);
    waitfor(rate);
end
rosshutdown
figure(1);
plot( ob_dist, 'red-' );
legend('obstacle distance');
ylabel( 'm' );
grid on;
title('obstacle distance');
figure(2);
plot( odom_vel_x, 'red' );
legend('Forward velocity');
ylabel( 'm/s' );
grid on
title('forward velocity');
figure(3);
plot( odom_vel_z, 'blue' );
legend('Angular velocity');
ylabel( 'rad/s' );
grid on
title('angular velocity');
figure(4)
plot( odom_pos_x, odom_pos_y, 'red');
xlabel('x');
ylabel('y');
```

```
        title('path');
        grid on
end
```

Let's explain the previous script:

```
function vfh_obstacle_avoidance(ros_master_ip, matlab_ip )
rosinit(ros_master_ip, 'NodeHost', matlab_ip);
    pause(2) % wait a bit the roscore initialization
```

We call this script by specifying the IP address of the computer that is running `roscore` and the IP address of the MATLAB computer. In this way, we can initialize the ROS-MATLAB interface:

```
laserSub = rossubscriber('/scan');
    [velPub, velMsg] = rospublisher('/mobile_base/commands/velocity');
    odomSub =  rossubscriber('/odom');
```

Now we subscribe to the laser scan message, and declare variables to advertise the commands to control the robot. The `rospublisher` function returns both the instantiated publisher, `velPub`, and the type of the message to send via the publisher, `velMsg`. In addition, we subscribe to the odometry of the robot to track its velocity during the motion.

We are now ready to instantiate the VFH object to implement our obstacle avoidance system:

```
vfh = robotics.VectorFieldHistogram;
```

Some parameters are needed by the VFH algorithm. In particular, these are:

- `DistanceLimits`: The limits for laser readings, specified with a two-dimensional vector continuing the minimum and maximum ranges to consider a valid laser measure
- `RobotRadius`: The dimension of the robot specified in meters
- `MinTurningRadius`: The minimum turning radius, in meters, of the robot
- `SafetyDistance`: The maximum space to allow between the robot and the obstacles:

```
vfh.DistanceLimits = [0.05 1];
vfh.RobotRadius = 0.1;
vfh.MinTurningRadius = 0.2;
vfh.SafetyDistance = 0.1;
```

We are now ready to start the control loop that allows the motion of the robot. Firstly, we define the control loop rate:

```
rate = robotics.Rate(10);
```

In the following, the motion control loop is described. We want to perform the control loop for a desired amount of time. We can use `rate.TotalElapsedTime` to track the elapsed time. This function returns the elapsed time in seconds from the creation of the rate object. Inside the control loop, we will read the sensor data from the laser scanner topic:

```
while rate.TotalElapsedTime < 50
  laserScan = receive(laserSub);
         ranges = double(laserScan.Ranges);
         angles = double(laserScan.readScanAngles);
```

The `targetDir` specifies the angle direction of the robot movement. Its value must be expressed in radians, and the robot's forward direction is considered as zero radians. As already stated, the target direction in our example is randomly calculated at each control loop:

```
targetDir = (r_max-r_min).*rand();
```

Then, we can call the `vfh` method to calculate an obstacle-free steering direction on the base of the input laser scanner data and the actual desired direction of the movement:

```
steerDir = vfh(ranges, angles, targetDir);
```

If a valid steering direction exists, we need to calculate the rotation velocity to send to the robot to actuate it. To do this, we will using the following function:

```
w = exampleHelperComputeAngularVelocity(steerDir, 1);
```

This function returns the angular velocity for a differential drive robot expressed in rad/s, given a steering direction in the robot's frame, like in our case. In addition, the second parameter of the function represents a maximum velocity value in order to saturate the calculated one. Finally, we plot the minimum distance of the robot from the detected obstacles during its motion, the performed path, and the actuated angular and forward velocities:

```
figure(1);
plot( ob_dist, 'red-' );
figure(2);
plot( odom_vel_x, 'red' );
figure(3);
plot( odom_vel_z, 'blue' );
figure(4)
plot( odom_pos_x, odom_pos_y, 'red');
```

To test this example, first we need to launch the Turtlebot simulation scene on the computer where we want to run `roscore`:

```
$ roslaunch turtlebot_gazebo turtlebot_world.launch
```

Then we must invoke the MATLAB script with the correct IP address of our ROS network:

```
>> vfh_obstacle_avoidance( '192.168.1.105', '192.168.1.130' )
```

While the robot will navigate the same environment depicted in Figure 8, an example of the output of MATLAB script is shown in the following screenshot:

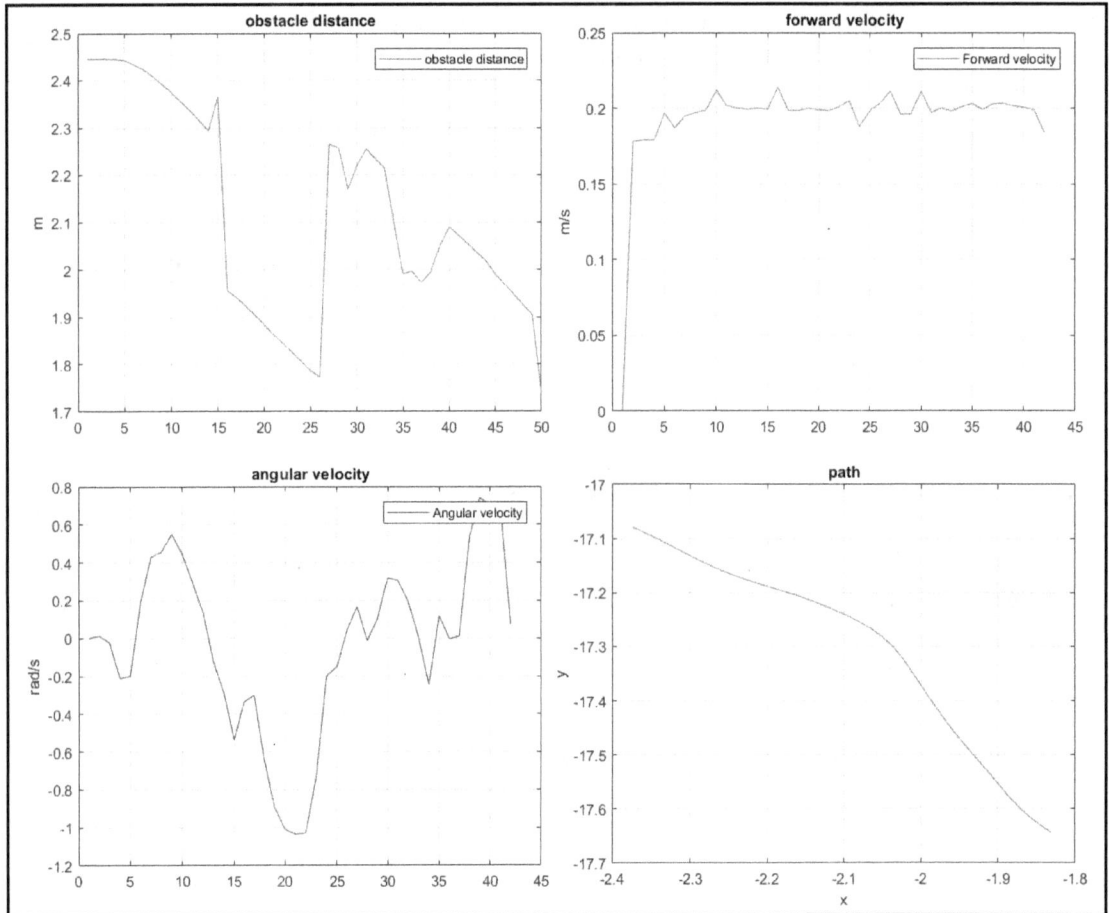

Figure 10: Log data plotted using MATLAB print functions: upper left: minimum obstacle distance, upper right: linear forward velocity, bottom left: angular velocity, bottom right: executed path

Getting started with ROS and Simulink

In the previous sections, we discussed how to interact with ROS using MATLAB. In this section, we are going to use another powerful tool of MATLAB: Simulink. Simulink is a graphical programming environment for modeling, simulating, and analyzing dynamical systems. We can use Simulink to create a model of a system and simulate its behavior over time.

In this section, we will start creating a first simple system outer from the ROS framework. We will also discuss how to develop a ROS application using Simulink.

Creating a wave signal integrator in Simulink

To model a new system, let's start by opening Simulink. We can open it by typing the following command in the **Command Window**:

```
>> Simulink
```

Then, you should choose to create a new blank model. To create a new system, we must import the desired Simulink blocks that will compose it. These blocks can be directly dragged and dropped into the model window from the **Library Browser**. To open the **Library Browser**, select **View | Library Browser** from the model pane toolbar. For our first system, we need four blocks:

- **Sine Wave**: This generates a sinusoidal signal that will represent the input of our system
- **Integrator**: This integrates an input signal
- **Bus Creator**: This combines multiple signals in one signal
- **Scope**: This graphically visualizes the input signal

After importing these blocks, your model pane should appear like in the following figure:

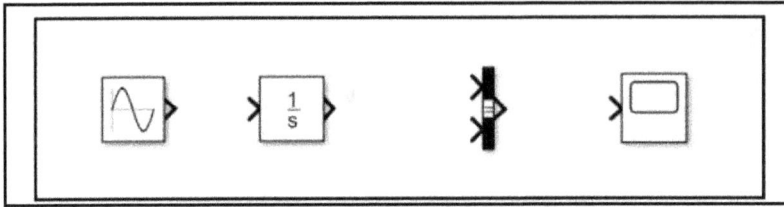

Figure 11: The sine wave, integrator, bus creator, and scope Simulink blocks

Some blocks must be properly configured with some parameters. For example, the *Sine Wave* block requires the amplitude and the frequency sinusoidal signal to generate. To set these values, we can explore block parameters with a double click on the desired block. To make the system work, we need to properly connect the Simulink blocks, as shown in this model:

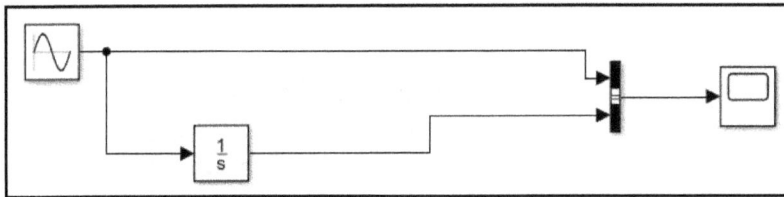

Figure 12: Sinusoidal signal integrator

Now that the model components have been connected, we can simulate the behavior of our system. First, we should configure the duration of the simulation setting the *Start* and *Stop* simulation time. Open the **Simulation | Model Configuration Parameters** window and insert the desired value. In our example, we are considering `Start time: 0` and `Stop time: 10.0`:

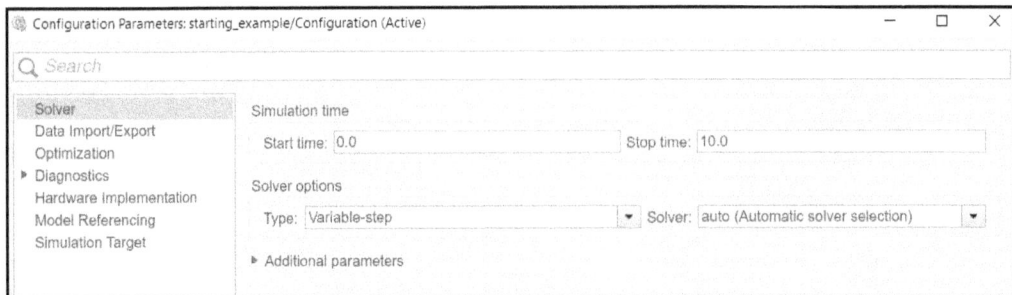

Figure 13: Simulation time for our system

Now, we can press the play button in the model pane toolbar, while we check the output by exploring the content of the Scope block, with a double click on it:

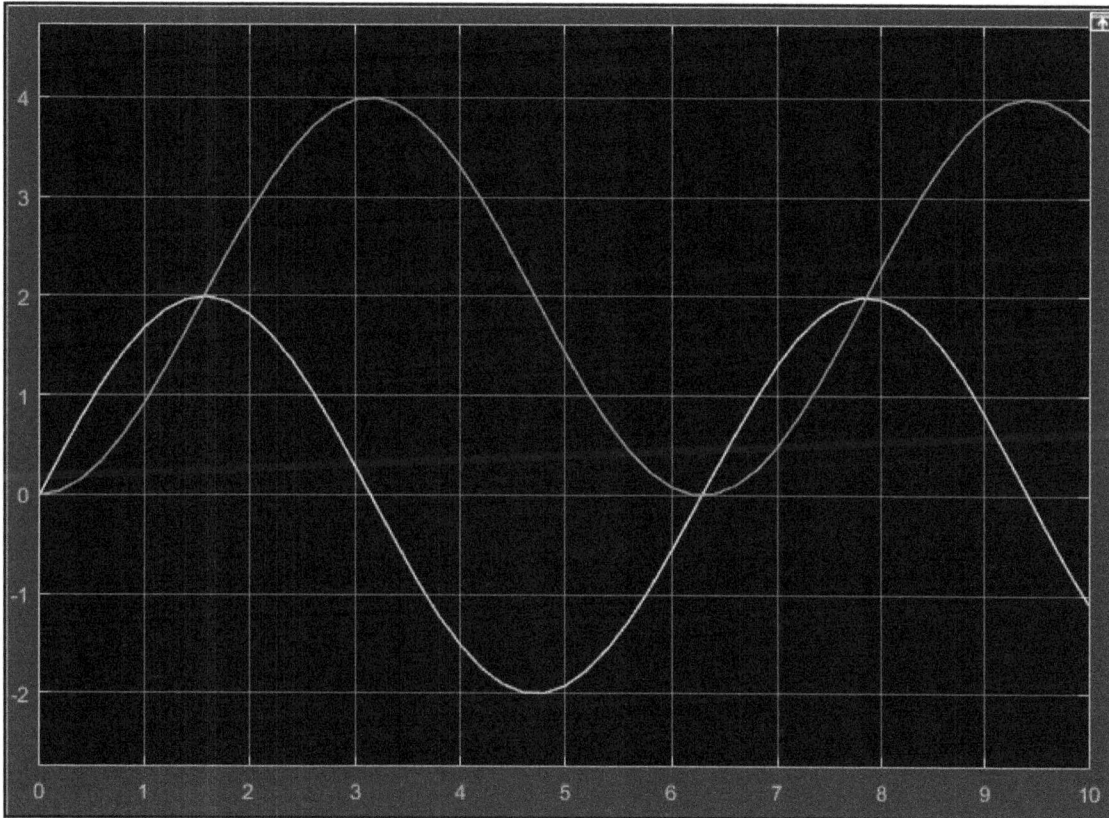

Figure 14: Sinusoidal and integrated signal

Note that, even if we inserted 10 seconds of simulation time, Simulink will not work in real time but only simulate the increment of the time steps along the simulation. In this way, the effective elapsed time during the simulation will be very short.

The model proposed in this example can be found in the book source code in the `ros_matlab_test/staring_example.mdl` model file.

Working with ROS messages in Simulink

Simulink support for ROS allows us to model systems that can be linked to other nodes of the ROS network. This support includes a library of Simulink blocks for sending and receiving messages via topics. When we start the simulation of the developed model, Simulink will try to connect to a ROS network, which can be running on the same computer where Simulink is or on another remote machine. Once this connection is established, Simulink exchanges messages with the ROS network until the simulation is terminated. As we did in the previous section, we will start by showing how to read and write data, using ROS topics, and then we will discuss how to create a more complex system to control the Turtlebot robot simulated in Gazebo.

Let's start to create two different Simulink models. In one model, we are going to develop a message publisher while in the other one we will implement a simple subscriber. These models can be found in the source code directory, `ros_matlab_test`, called `publisher.mdl` and `subscriber.mdl`, respectively.

Publishing a ROS message in Simulink

To publish a ROS message in Simulink, we mainly need two blocks:

- **Publish**: This block sends a message on the ROS network. Using block parameters, we can specify the topic name and the message type.
- **Blank message**: This block creates a blank message with the specified message type.

Let's see how to connect these blocks to publish a `geometry_msgs/Twist` message on a new topic, called `/position`. Get started by importing the blank message block from the library browser and configuring the type of message by double-clicking on it. From the block parameters pane, we can press the **Select** button to select the ROS message type from a list, as shown in the following screenshot:

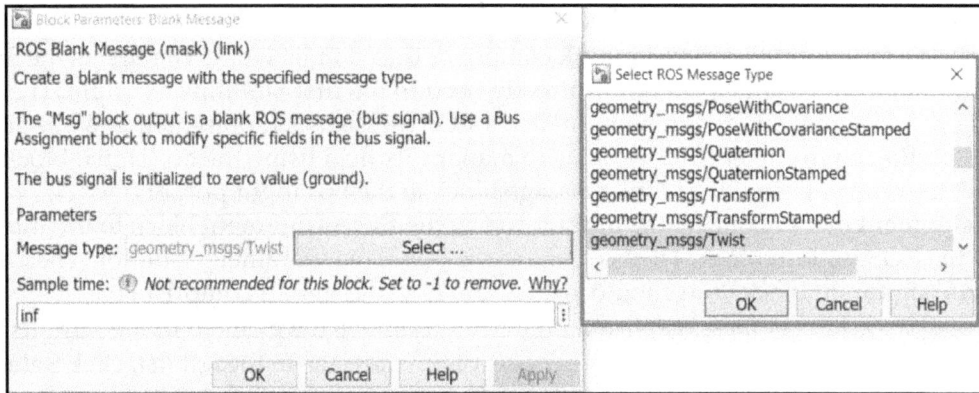

Figure 15: Parameter configuration for a Simulink ROS blank message block

Now we are ready to import the ROS publish block: drag and drop the block to the model and double click on it to configure the topic name and the message type. Select **Specify your own** for the topic source field in order to enter a desired topic name. Enter `/position` in the topic field. As we have already seen, we can select the type of the message to publish:

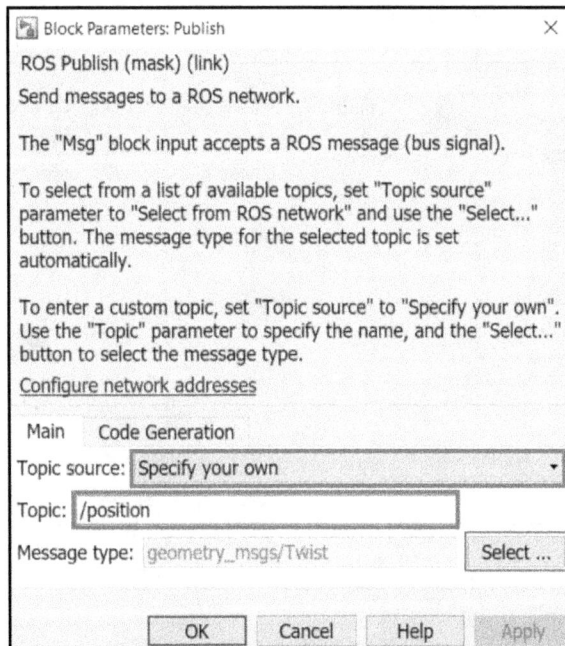

Figure 16: Parameter configuration for a Simulink ROS Publish block

Now, we must fill in the fields of the ROS message to publish before sending it into the ROS network. We will use two other Simulink components to do this work. The first is the Sine Wave, the sinusoidal signal generation already used in the first Simulink example. The second one is a signal bus assignment. In fact, a ROS message is represented as a bus signal in the Simulink environment, allowing us to manage its field using the bus signal block. Connect the output port of the blank message block to the bus input port of the **BusAssignment** block. Connect the output port of the **BusAssignment** block to the input port of the ROS publish block. Then configure the bus signal parameters: double-click on the **BusAssignment** block. You should see X, Y, and Z (the signals comprising a geometry_msgs/Twist message) listed on the left. Remove the element in the right list and select both the X and Y signals of the linear part of the message in the left list, click **Select >>**, and then click **OK** to close the block mask. In this case, we will assign only the first two components of the linear part of the Twist message:

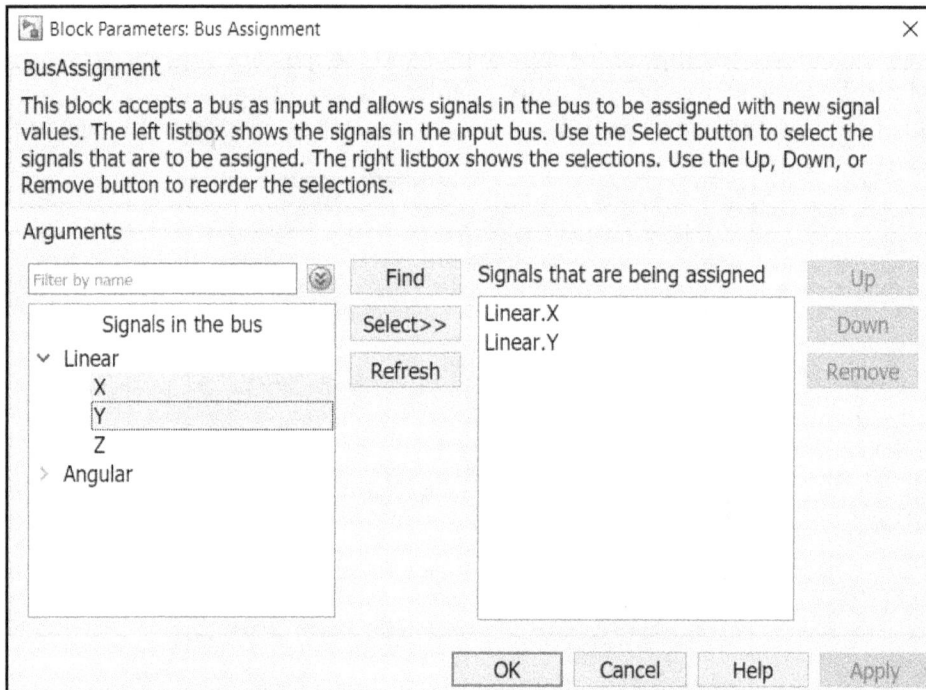

Figure 17: Bus assignment for a geometry_msgs/Twist message

After completing the parameter configuration of the bus assignment module, the shape of the block will change, accepting the value of the selected input signals. Now, we should assign the desired value to publish to these components. We can do this by using the *Sine Wave* block, as we did in the previous example. Drag and drop two sinusoidal signal generators, linking them to the bus assignment block. The final model will look as follows:

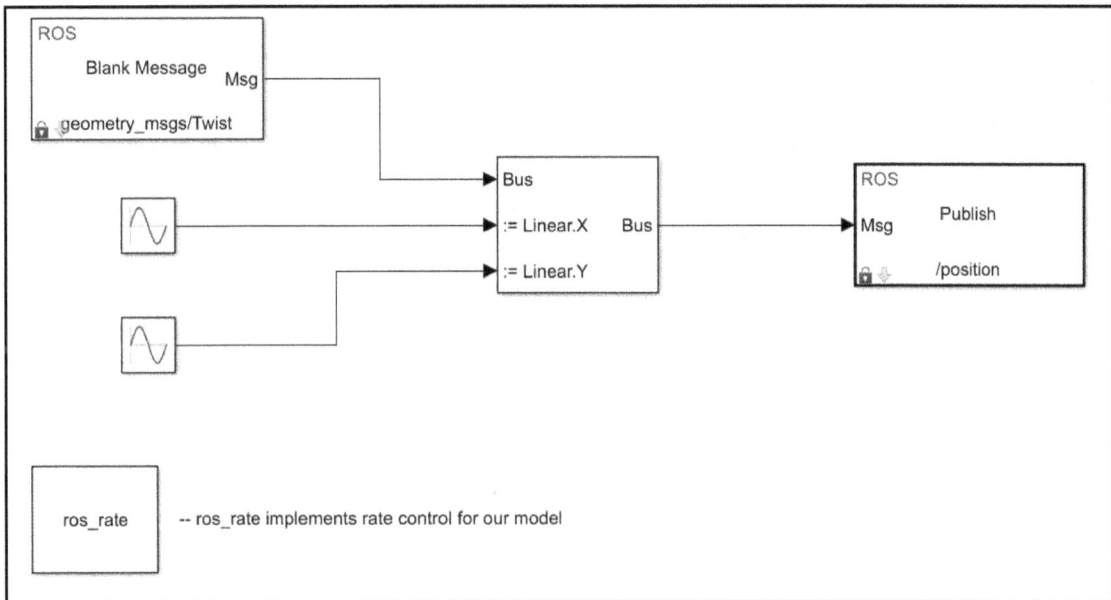

Figure 18: Publisher Simulink model

An additional block has been included in our publisher Simulink model: `ros_rate`. This block is needed to simulate a real-time behavior during the execution of our model, implementing the ROS rate mechanism. Without this module, in fact, the execution rate of this node will be very high, publishing ROS messages at its maximum frequency. The `ros_rate` block is a special module called the **MATLAB System** block and allows us to instantiate and invoke a `matlabclass` object. After importing this block into the system model, we should select the **System object name** to invoke or to create a new one:

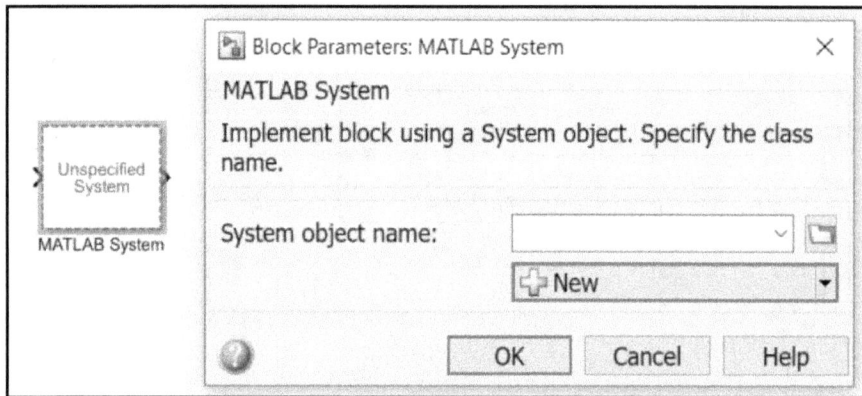

Figure 19: MATLAB system block

The code of the `ros_rate` block is in the `ros_rate.m` source file:

```
classdef ros_rate < matlab.System
    % Public, tunable properties
    properties
        RATE;
    end
    properties(DiscreteState)
    end
    % Pre-computed constants
    properties(Access = private)
        rateObj;
    end
    methods(Access = protected)
        function setupImpl(obj)
            % Perform one-time calculations, such as computing constants
            obj.rateObj = robotics.Rate(obj.RATE);
        end
        function stepImpl(obj)
            obj.rateObj.waitfor();
        end
        function resetImpl(obj)
```

```
            end
        end
    end
```

In this code, we defined the `ros_rate` class, which has two objects: the rate specifying the loop frequency, and `rateObj`, which implements the `robotics.Rate` mechanism. The most important methods of this class are the `setupImpl(obj)` method that is called at the start of the simulation and is used to initialize the class stuff, and the `stepImpl(obj)` method that is invoked at each step time in order to regulate the execution time of the simulation.

Now that our model is complete, we require a never-ending duration for our simulation setting to `inf` the `Stop time` of the simulation. In this way, we can terminate the simulation when desired by using the stop button. Now we can play the simulation and read the content published on the `/position` topic.

Subscribing to a ROS topic in Simulink

To subscribe to a ROS topic, we only need the **Subscribe** block. Even in this case, we must configure the type of the message to read and the topic name. Let's select the `/position` topic in order to read the data sent to the ROS network by the publisher Simulink model. The Subscriber block has two outputs: **IsNew**, a Boolean signal that defines if a new message is received, and **Msg**, which contains the received message:

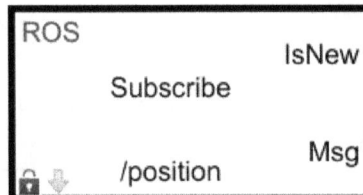

Figure 20: Simulink Subscriber block

In the publisher model, if we have used a bus creator to aggregate multiple data in one message, then we need to split the data of the message. For this, we will use a bus selector block with one input and two outputs: the X and Y fields of the linear part of the twist message. To create this block, configure it in order to have, as the selected signals, only the `Linear.X` and `Linear.Y` parts of the twist message:

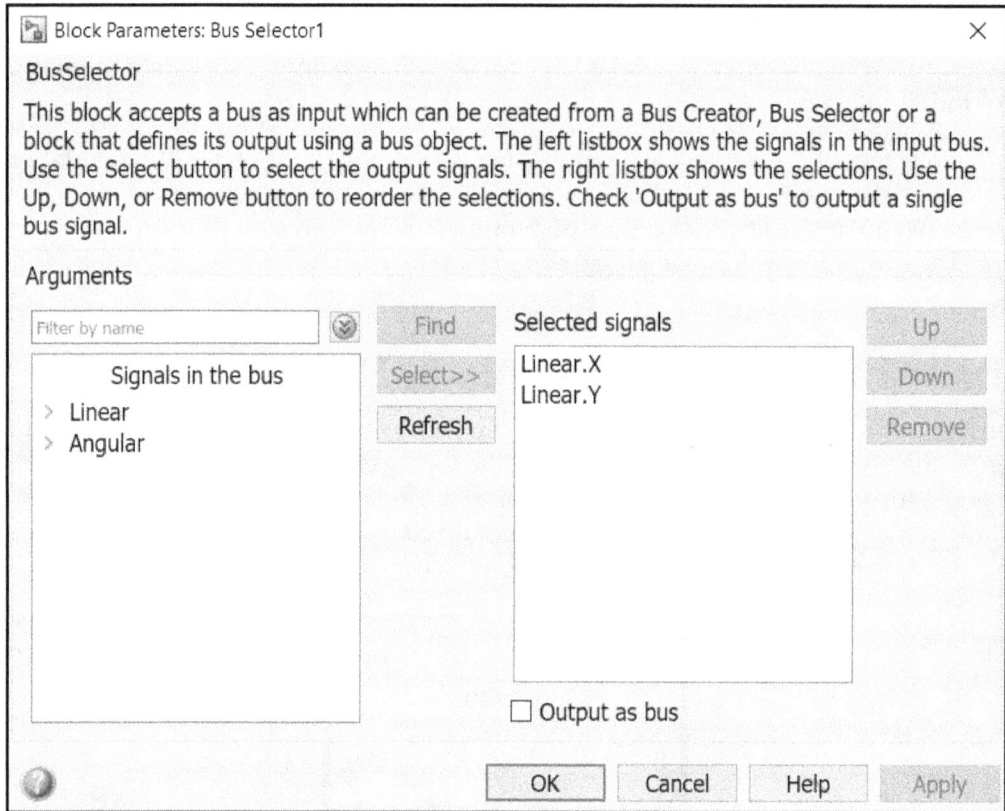

Figure 21: Bus Selector block

In our implementation, we include the bus selector into a **Subsystem**, another type of block that can be enabled/disabled with the use of an enable port. In this way, we can link the **IsNew** field of the **Subscriber** block to the **Subsystem**, and enable its output only if a new message is received. To explore the content of a subsystem, it is enough to double click on it, like any other block. Finally, we can add two scope blocks to plot the output of the subsystem. The final linked model is shown in the following figure:

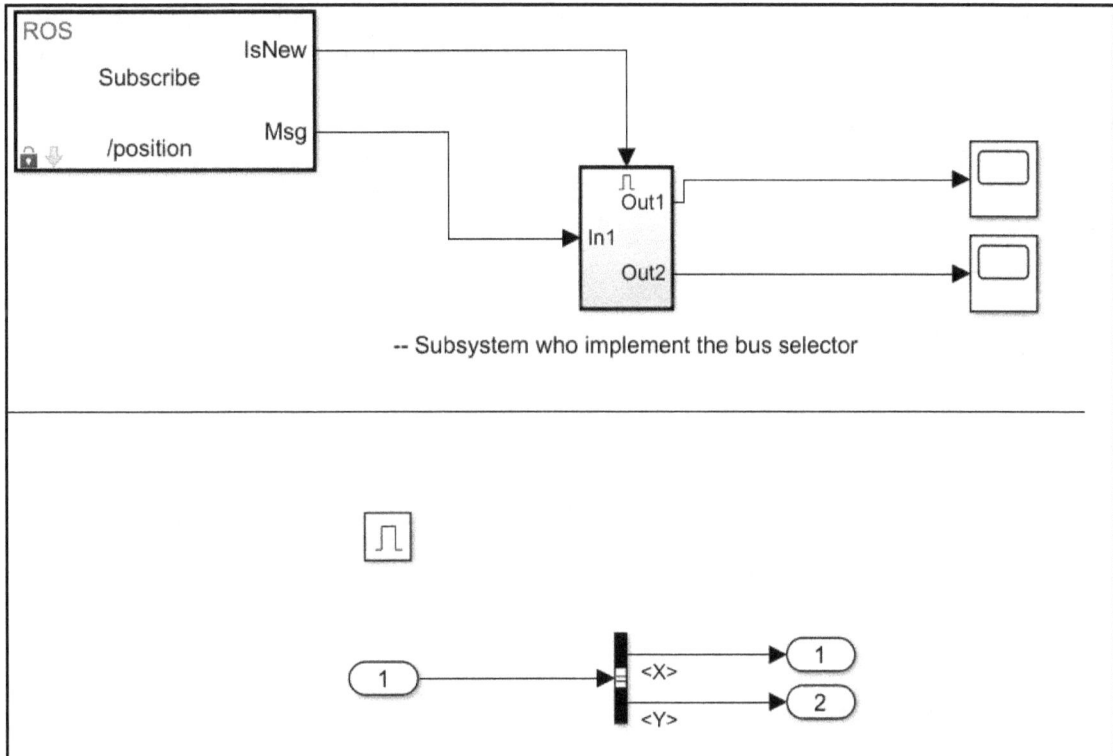

Figure 22: Subscriber system model

We can now run both the publisher and subscriber systems and check the output on the scope blocks.

Developing a simple control system in Simulink

Now that we have learned how to interface Simulink and ROS, we can try to implement a more complex system that is able to control a real or simulated robot. We will continue to work with the Turtlebot robot simulated in Gazebo, and we will see how to control its orientation in order to bring it to a desired value. In other words, we will implement a control system that will measure the orientation of the robot using its odometry, comparing this value with the desired orientation and obtaining the orientation error. We will use a PID controller to calculate the velocity to actuate the robot to reach the final desired orientation, setting the orientation error to zero. This controller is already available in Simulink, so we don't need to implement it by ourselves. Let's start to discuss all the elements of our model:

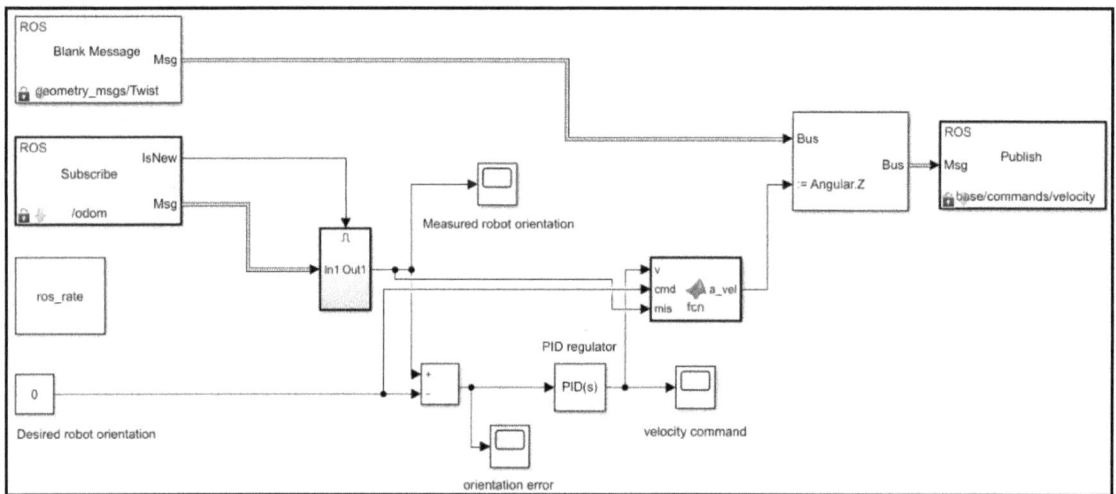

Figure 23: Turtlebot orientation control model in Simulink

The input of the system is represented by the /odom message, which contains information about the actual pose of the robot and its velocity, and the constant block, which specifies the desired orientation of the Turtlebot.

The first thing that our model does is to estimate the orientation from the /odom message. The orientation is estimated by considering the angular velocity of the robot, integrating it at each time step. We use a MATLAB function block to threshold the velocity value of the /odom message to discard noise measurements. To integrate the velocity data, we use the *Integrator* block provided by Simulink.

Again, we include this part in a subsystem:

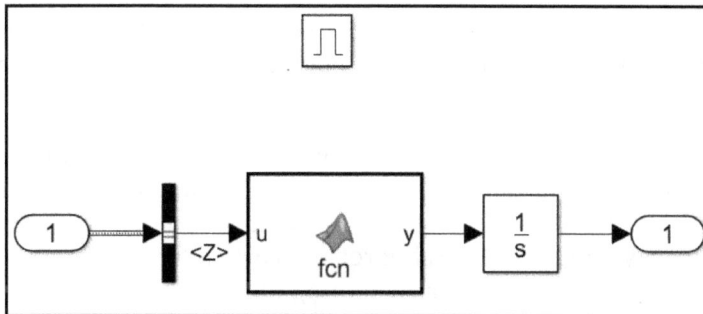

Figure 24: MATLAB function block

The MATLAB function block allows developers to translate their own MATLAB functions into Simulink blocks. In this case, the code function is as follows:

```
function y = fcn(u)
    y = 0.0;
    if abs( u ) > 0.01
        y = u;
    end
end
```

We extract the Angular.Z value from the received twist message that specifies the angular velocity with respect to the Z axes, representing which direction is rotating the robot. We consider as noise the values below 0.01 rad/s.

Now that we know how to rotate the robot, we can calculate the orientation error by considering the desired orientation (that is constant) using the Simulink sum block. To change the desired orientation, we can double click on the constant block and configure its parameters.

Finally, we can implement our robot controller. For this scope, we will use a PID controller, one of the most commonly used control loop mechanisms with feedback. This kind of controller is widely used both in industry and university settings for a variety of applications. It continuously tries to minimize the input error, applying a control output based on proportional, integral, and derivative terms, which give the controller its name. After dragging and dropping this controller in the model, its response to the input data will depends on P, I, and D terms (called gains) that can be properly tuned from the block proprieties. Finally, we must publish the data generated by the PID controller on the `/base/commands/velocity` topic to actuate the robot in the Gazebo simulation. As usual, we can check on the scope block how the orientation error decreases after starting the simulation.

Before applying the calculated velocity, we use another MATLAB function block to set the sign of the velocity. In fact, considering the sign of the velocity, the robot will rotate in two different directions: a negative velocity will make the robot rotate in a clockwise direction, while a positive velocity will make the robot rotate in a counter-clockwise direction. In our case, we want to choose the direction that will bring the robot more quickly to its direction:

```
function a_vel = fcn(v, cmd, mis)
    a_vel = 0;
     if (mis < cmd )
          a_vel = abs(v);
     elseif ( mis > cmd  )
          a_vel = -abs(v);
     end
end
```

This function block receives as input the calculated velocity, the commanded, and the actual orientation of the robot. When the measured orientation is lower than the commanded one, the robot must rotate in a clockwise direction, or otherwise in a counter-clockwise direction.

Configuring the Simulink model

Now that our model is fully connected, we only need to configure and simulate it. Firstly, we need to import the `ros_rate` module to synchronize the Simulink simulation. In this case, a higher frame rate assures a better behavior, so you can double click on the `ros_rate` block and set the rate to 100 Hz. Then, open the **Model Configuration Parameters** by clicking on **Simulation | Model Configuration Parameters** from the main menu bar of the model window or just type *Ctrl + E*. A suggested configuration is to use a **Fixed-step size** solver, specifying the desired step size (we can use `0.01` seconds):

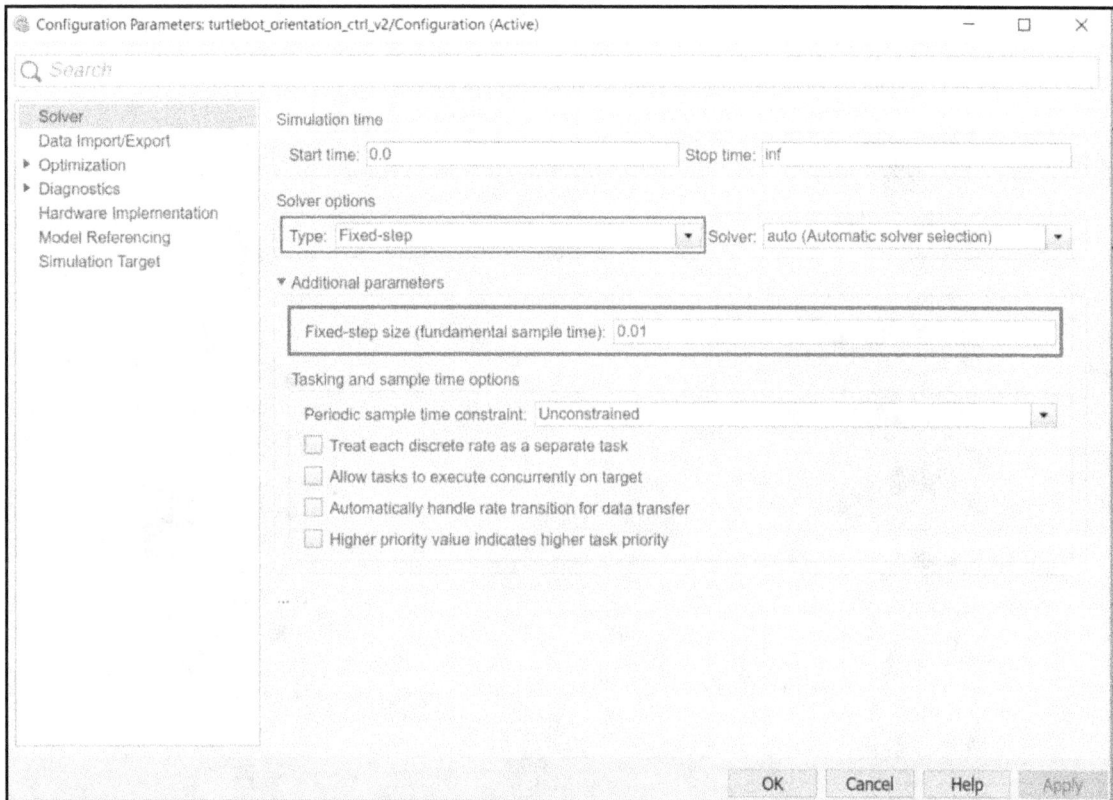

Figure 25: Model configuration parameters

Now that the model has been configured, we can simulate it. As in the last example, launch the Turtlebot simulation:

```
$ roslaunch turtlebot_gazebo turtlebot_world.launch
```

Then push the play button to start the Simulink simulation. On Gazebo, you should see the robot that tries to reach the desired orientation, while on Simulink, you can use the scope panels to monitor the orientation error and the generated velocity command:

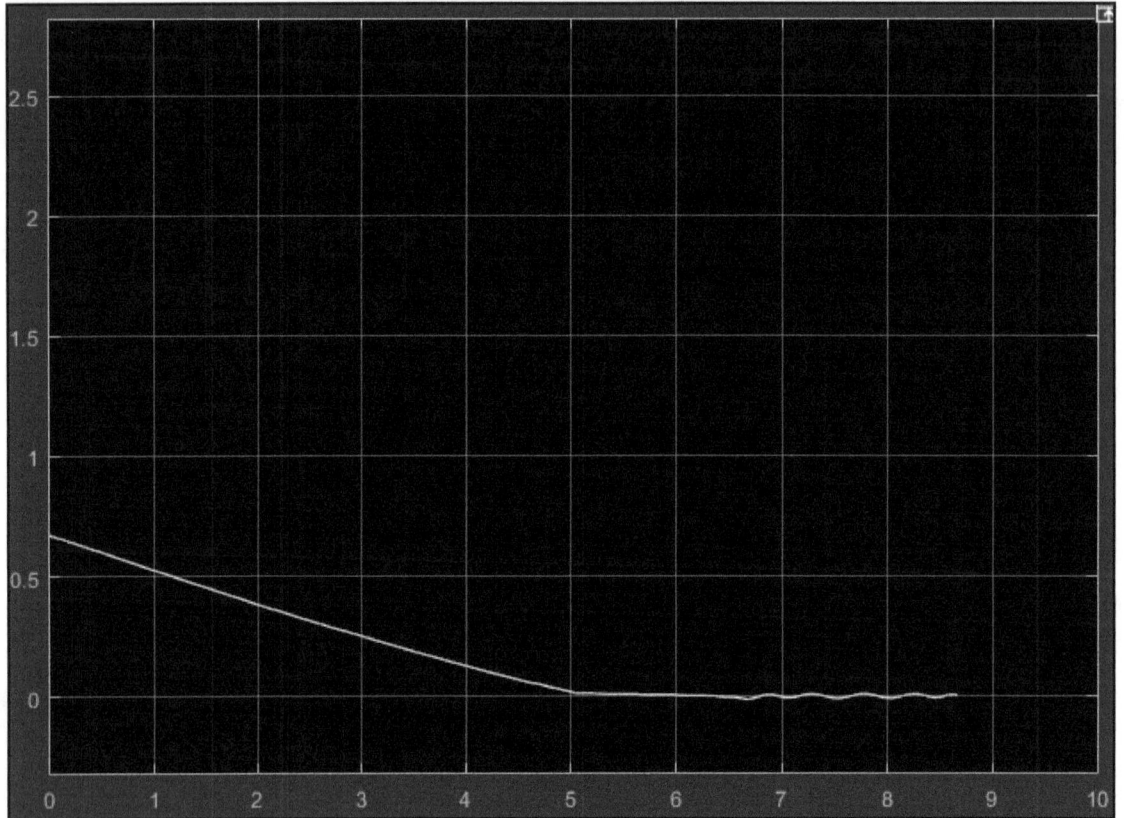

Figure 26: Orientation error evolution

Questions

- What is MATLAB and the Robotic System Toolbox?
- How can we connect MATLAB with the ROS network?
- Why is MATLAB useful to develop robotic applications?
- What is Simulink?
- What is a PID controller and how can we implement it using Simulink?

Summary

In this chapter, we learned how to use MATLAB to develop simple or complex robotic applications and how to connect MATLAB with the other ROS nodes running on the same computer or in other nodes of the ROS network. We discussed how to handle topics in MATLAB and how to develop a simple obstacle avoidance system for a differential driver robot, reusing functions already available in the MATLAB toolboxes. Then, we introduced Simulink, a graphically-based program editor that allow developers to implement, simulate, and validate their dynamic system models. We learned how to get and set data into the ROS network and how do develop a simple control system that controls the orientation of the Turtlebot robot. In the next chapter, we will present ROS-Industrial, a ROS package to interface industrial robot manipulators to ROS, and how to control it using the power of ROS, such as MoveIt!, Gazebo, RViz, and so on.

14
ROS for Industrial Robots

Until now, we have been mainly discussing interfacing personal and research robots with ROS, but one of the main areas where robots are extensively used is in industry. Does ROS support industrial robots? Are there any companies that use ROS for handling manufacturing processes? The **ROS-Industrial** package comes with a solution to interface and control industrial robot manipulators to ROS, using its powerful tools, such as MoveIt!, Gazebo, and RViz.

In this chapter, we will discuss the following topics:

- Understanding and getting started with ROS-Industrial
- Creating a URDF for an industrial robot and interfacing it with MoveIt!
- Working with MoveIt! configuration of a Universal Robots arm and ABB robots
- Understanding ROS-Industrial robot support packages
- Understanding ROS-Industrial robot client and driver packages
- Working with IKfast algorithms and the MoveIt! IKFast plugin

Let's start with a brief overview of ROS-Industrial.

Understanding ROS-Industrial packages

ROS-Industrial basically extends the advanced capabilities of ROS software to industrial robots employed in manufacturing processes. ROS-Industrial consists of many software packages, which help us to control industrial robots. These packages are **BSD** (legacy)/**Apache 2.0** (preferred) licensed programs, which contain libraries, drivers, and tools with a standard solution for industrial hardware. ROS-Industrial is now guided by the ROS-Industrial Consortium. The official website of ROS-Industrial (ROS-I) can be found at `http://rosindustrial.org/`:

Figure 1: Logo of ROS-Industrial

Goals of ROS-Industrial

The main goals behind ROS-Industrial development are as follows:

- Combining the strength of ROS with the existing industrial technologies to explore the advanced capabilities of ROS in the manufacturing process
- Developing a reliable and robust software for industrial robot applications
- Providing an easy way to do research and development in industrial robotics
- Creating a wide community supported by researchers and professionals for industrial robotics
- Providing industrial-grade ROS applications and becoming a one-stop location of industry-related applications

ROS-Industrial – a brief history

In 2012, the ROS-Industrial open source project started as the collaboration of Yaskawa Motoman Robotics (http://www.motoman.com/), Willow Garage (https://www.willowgarage.com/), and the **Southwest Research Institute (SwRI)** (http://www.swri.org/), for using ROS in industrial manufacturing. The ROS-I was founded by Shaun Edwards in January 2012.

In March 2013, the ROS-I Consortium Americas was launched, led by SwRI, and ROS-I Consortium Europe was launched, led by Fraunhofer IPA in Germany.

Benefits of ROS-Industrial

Let's look at the benefits ROS-I provides to the community:

- **Explores the features in ROS**: The ROS-Industrial packages are tied to the ROS framework so that we can use all the ROS features in industrial robots too. Using ROS, we can create custom IK solvers for each robot and implement object manipulation, using 2D/3D perception.
- **Out-of-the-box applications**: The ROS interface enables advanced perception in robots for working with picking and placing complex objects.
- **Simplifies robotic programming**: ROS-I eliminates teaching and planning paths of robots and, instead, automatically calculates a collision-free optimal path for the given points.
- **Open source**: ROS-I is open source software that allows commercial use without any restrictions.

Installing ROS-Industrial packages

Installing ROS-I packages can be done by using package managers or building from the source code. If we have installed the `ros-kinetic-desktop-full` installation, we can use the following command to install ROS-Industrial packages on Ubuntu, working with ROS Kinetic:

```
$ sudo apt-get install ros-kinetic-industrial-core
```

The preceding command will install the core packages of ROS-Industrial packages. The `industrial-core` stack includes the following set of ROS packages:

- `industrial-core`: This stack contains packages and libraries for supporting industrial robotic systems. The package consists of nodes for communicating with industrial robot controllers and industrial robot simulators, and also provides ROS controllers for industrial robots.

- `industrial_deprecated`: This package contains nodes, launch files, and so on that are going to be deprecated. The files inside this package could be deleted from the repository in the next ROS versions, so we should look for the replacement of these files before the content is going to be deleted.

- `industrial_msgs`: This package contains message definitions, which are specific to the ROS-Industrial packages.

- `simple_message`: This is a part of ROS-Industrial packages that is a standard message protocol containing a simple messaging framework for communicating with industrial robot controllers.

- `industrial_robot_client`: This package contains a generic robot client for connecting to industrial robot controllers, which is running an industrial robot server and can communicate using a simple message protocol.

- `industrial_robot_simulator`: This package simulates the industrial robot controller, which follows the ROS-Industrial driver standard. Using this simulator, we can simulate and visualize the industrial robot.

- `industrial_trajectory_filters`: This package contains libraries and plugins for filtering the trajectories, which are sent to the robot controller.

Block diagram of ROS-Industrial packages

The following diagram is a simple block diagram representation of ROS-I packages, which are organized on top of ROS. We can see the ROS-I layer on top of the ROS layers. We can see a brief description of each of the layers for better understanding. The following diagram is taken from the ROS-I wiki page (`http://wiki.ros.org/Industrial`):

- **The ROS GUI**: This layer includes the ROS plugin-based GUI tools layer, which consists of tools such as RViz, `rqt_gui`, and so on

- **The ROS-I GUI**: These GUIs are standard industrial UIs for working with industrial robots that may be implemented in the future

- **The ROS Layer**: This is the base layer in which all communications are taking place

- **The MoveIt! Layer**: The MoveIt! layer provides a direct solution to industrial manipulators in planning, kinematics, and pick and place
- **The ROS-I Application Layer**: This layer consists of an industrial process planner, which is used to plan what is to be manufactured, how it will be manufactured, and what resources are needed for the manufacturing process
- **The ROS-I Interface Layer**: This layer consists of the industrial robot client, which can be connected to the industrial robot controller using the simple message protocol
- **The ROS-I Simple Message Layer**: This is the communication layer of the industrial robot, which is a standard set of protocols that will send data from the robot client to the controller and vice versa
- **The ROS-I Controller Layer**: This layer consists of vendor-specific industrial robot controllers

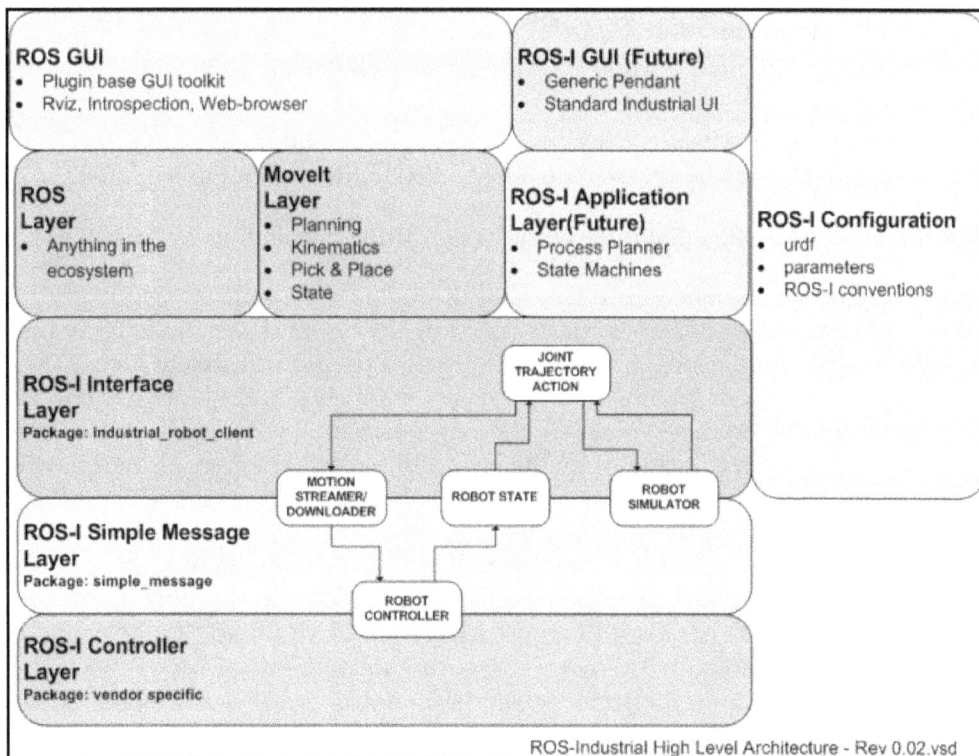

Figure 2: The block diagram of ROS-Industrial

After discussing the basic concepts, we will start to interface an industrial robot to ROS using ROS-Industrial. Firstly, we will show how to create a URDF model of an industrial robot and how to create a proper MoveIt! configuration for it. Then, we will discuss how to control real and simulated Universal Robots and Abb industrial manipulators, analyzing all the necessary elements of a ROS-I package. Finally, we will work with the Ikfast algorithm and plugin to speed up kinematic calculation with MoveIt!.

Creating a URDF for an industrial robot

Creating the URDF file for an ordinary robot and an industrial robot are the same, but industrial robots require some standards that should be strictly followed during their URDF modeling, which are as follows:

- **Simplify the URDF design**: The URDF file should be simple and readable and only need the important tags
- **Develop a common design**: Develop a common design formula for all industrial robots by various vendors
- **Modularize the URDF**: The URDF needs to be modularized using XACRO macros and it can be included in a large URDF file without much hassle

The following points are the main differences in the URDF design followed by ROS-I.

- **Collision-aware**: The industrial robot IK planners are collision-aware, so the URDF should contain an accurate collision 3D mesh for each link. Every link in the robot should export to STL or DAE with a proper coordinate system. The coordinate system that ROS-I is following is X-axes pointing forward and Z-axes pointing up when each joint is in the zero position. It is also to be noted that, if the joint's origin coincides with the base of the robot, the transformation will be simpler. It will be good if we are putting robot-based joints in the zero position (origin), which can simplify the robot design. In ROS-I, the mesh file used for visual purposes is highly detailed, but the mesh file used for collision will not be detailed, because it takes more time to perform collision checking. In order to remove the mesh details, we can use tools such as MeshLab (`http://meshlab.sourceforge.net/`), using its option (`Filters -> Remeshing, Simplification and Reconstruction -> Convex Hull`).

- **URDF joint conventions**: The orientation value of each robot joint is limited to single rotation, that is, out of the two orientation (`roll`, `pitch`, and `yaw`) values, only one value will be there.
- **Xacro macros**: In ROS-I, the entire manipulator section is written as a macro using `xacro`. We can add an instance of this macro in another macro file, which can be used for generating a URDF file. We can also include additional end-effector definitions on this same file.
- **Standards frames**: In ROS-I, the `base_link` frame should be the first link and `tool0` (tool-zero) should be the end-effector link. Also, the `base` frame should match with the `base` of the robot controller. In most cases, the transform from `base` to `base_link` is treated as fixed.

After building the `xacro` file for the industrial robot, we can convert to URDF and verify it using the following command:

```
$ rosrun xacro xacro -inorder -o <output_urdf_file> <input_xacro_file>
$ check_urdf <urdf_file>
```

Next, we can discuss the differences in creating the MoveIt! configuration for an industrial robot.

Creating the MoveIt! configuration for an industrial robot

The procedure for creating the MoveIt! interface for industrial robots is the same as the other ordinary robot manipulators, except in some standard conventions. The following procedure gives a clear idea about these standard conventions:

1. Launch the MoveIt! setup assistant by using the following command:

   ```
   $ roslaunch moveit_setup_assistant setup_assistant.launch
   ```

2. Load the URDF from the robot description folder or convert xacro to the URDF and load to the setup assistant.

3. Create a **Self-Collisiona** matrix with a **Sampling Density** of about ~ 80,000. This value can increase the collision checking in the arm.

4. Add a **Virtual Joints** matrix, as shown in the following screenshot. Here the virtual and parent frame names are arbitrary:

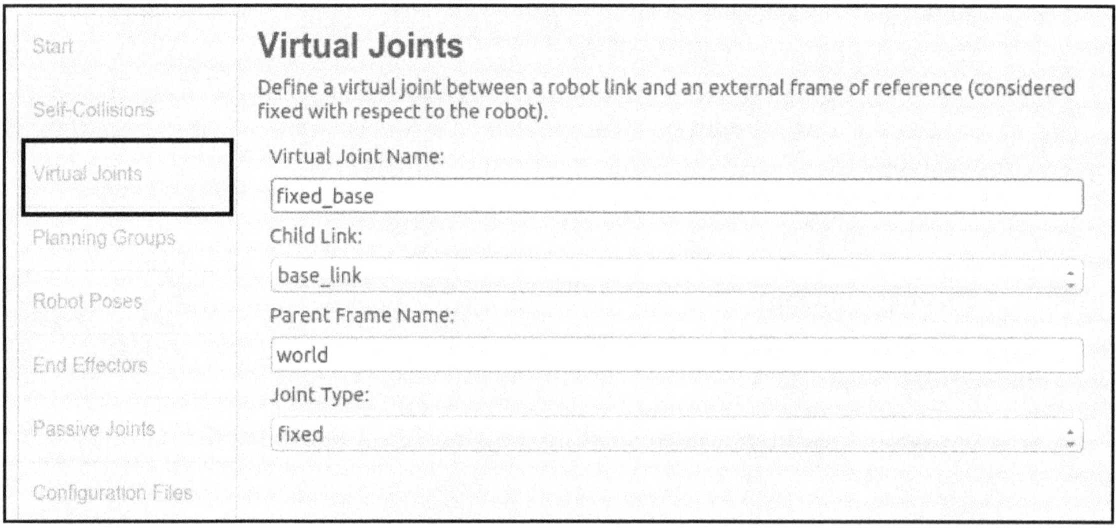

Figure 3: Adding MoveIt! - virtual joints

5. In the next step, we are adding **Planning Groups for manipulator and End Effector.** Here, also, the group names are arbitrary. The default plugin is KDL; we can change it even after creating the MoveIt! configuration:

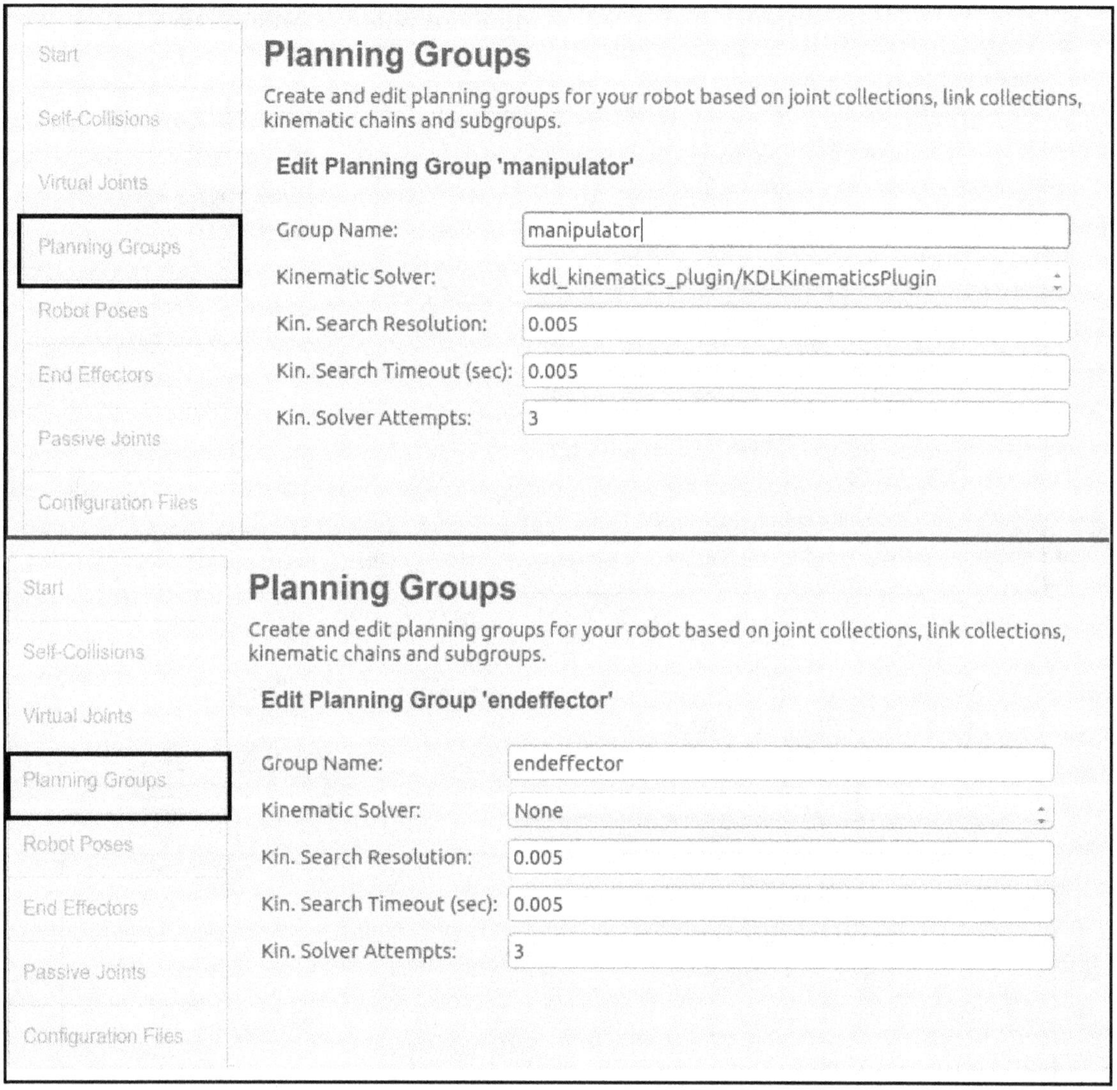

Planning Groups

Create and edit planning groups for your robot based on joint collections, link collections, kinematic chains and subgroups.

Edit Planning Group 'manipulator'

Group Name:	manipulator
Kinematic Solver:	kdl_kinematics_plugin/KDLKinematicsPlugin
Kin. Search Resolution:	0.005
Kin. Search Timeout (sec):	0.005
Kin. Solver Attempts:	3

Start
Self-Collisions
Virtual Joints
Planning Groups
Robot Poses
End Effectors
Passive Joints
Configuration Files

Planning Groups

Create and edit planning groups for your robot based on joint collections, link collections, kinematic chains and subgroups.

Edit Planning Group 'endeffector'

Group Name:	endeffector
Kinematic Solver:	None
Kin. Search Resolution:	0.005
Kin. Search Timeout (sec):	0.005
Kin. Solver Attempts:	3

Start
Self-Collisions
Virtual Joints
Planning Groups
Robot Poses
End Effectors
Passive Joints
Configuration Files

Figure 4: Creating Planning Groups in MoveIt!

6. The **Planning Groups**, that is, the **manipulator** plus the **endeffector** configuration, will be shown like this:

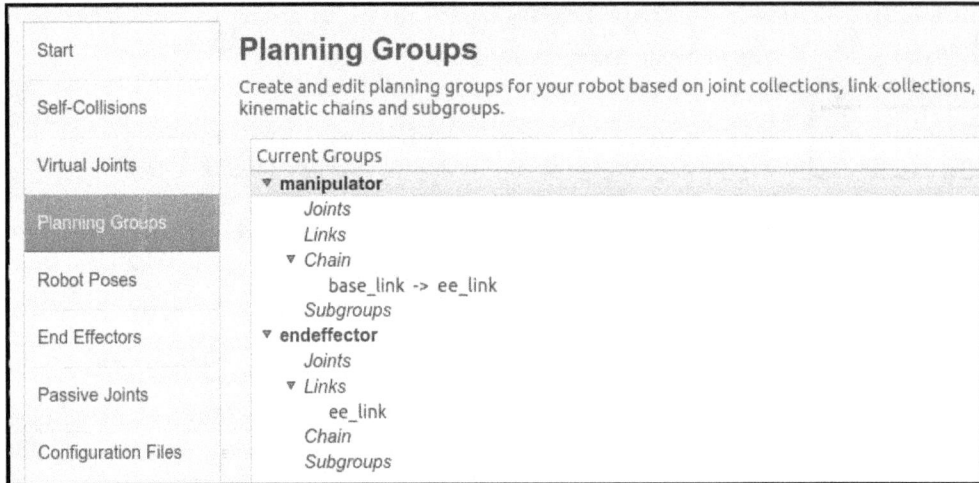

Figure 5: Planning groups of manipulators and end effectors in MoveIt!

7. We can assign **Robot Poses**, such as home position, up position, and so on. This setting is an optional one.

8. We can assign **End Effectors,** as shown in the following screenshot; this is also an optional setting:

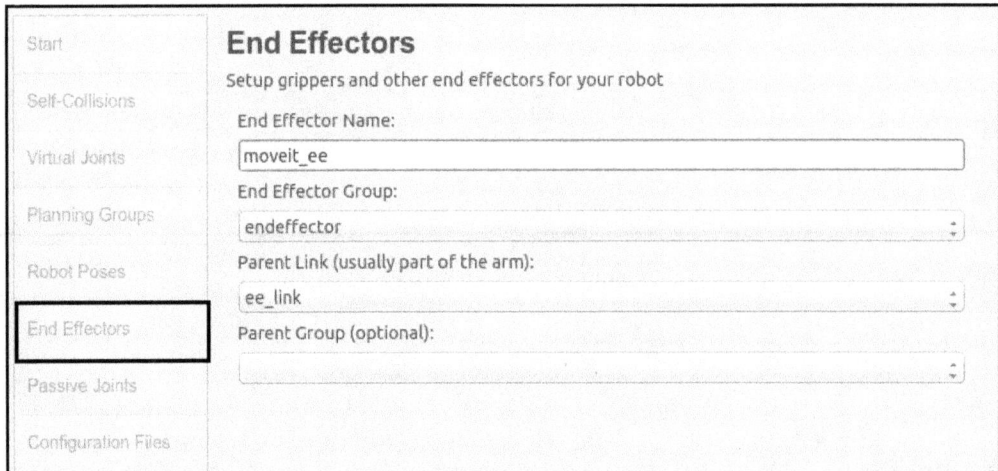

Figure 6: Setting end effectors in MoveIt! Setup Assistant

9. After setting the end effector, we can directly generate the configuration files. It should be noted that the `moveit-config` package should be named as `<robot_name>_moveit_config`, where `robot_name` is the name of the URDF file. Also, if we want to move this generated `config` package to another PC, we need to edit the `.setup_assistant` file, which is inside the `moveit` package. We should change the absolute path to the relative path. Here is an example of the `abb_irb2400` robot. We should mention the relative path of URDF and SRDF in this file, as follows:

```
moveit_setup_assistant_config:
  URDF:
    package: abb_irb2400_support
    relative_path: urdf/irb2400.urdf
  SRDF:
    relative_path: config/abb_irb2400.srdf
  CONFIG:
    generated_timestamp: 1402076252
```

Updating the MoveIt! configuration files

After creating the MoveIt! configuration, we should update the `controllers.yaml` file inside the `config` folder of the MoveIt! package. Here is an example of `controllers.yaml`:

```
controller_list:
  - name: ""
    action_ns: follow_joint_trajectory
    type: FollowJointTrajectory
    joints:
      - shoulder_pan_joint
      - shoulder_lift_joint
      - elbow_joint
      - wrist_1_joint
      - wrist_2_joint
      - wrist_3_joint
```

We should also update `joint_limits.yaml` about the joint information. Here is a code snippet of `joint_limits.yaml`:

```
joint_limits:
  shoulder_pan_joint:
    has_velocity_limits: true
    max_velocity: 2.16
    has_acceleration_limits: true
    max_acceleration: 2.16
```

We can also change the Kinematic solver plugin by editing the `kinematics.yaml` file. After editing all the configuration files, we need to edit the `controller manager launch` file (`<robot>_moveit_config/launch/<robot>_moveit_controller_manager.launch`).

Here is an example of the `controller manager.launch` file:

```
<launch>
  <rosparam file="$(find ur10_moveit_config)/config/    controllers.yaml"/>
  <param name="use_controller_manager" value="false"/>
  <param name="trajectory_execution/execution_duration_monitoring"
value="false"/>
  <param name="moveit_controller_manager" value=
"moveit_simple_controller_manager/    MoveItSimpleControllerManager"/>
</launch>
```

After creating the controller manger, we need to create the `<robot>_moveit_planning_execution.launch` file. Here is an example of this file:

```
<launch>
  <arg name="sim" default="false" />
  <arg name="limited" default="false"/>
  <arg name="debug" default="false" />

  <!-- Remap follow_joint_trajectory -->
  <remap if="$(arg sim)" from="/follow_joint_trajectory"
to="/arm_controller/follow_joint_trajectory"/>

  <!-- Launch moveit -->
  <include file="$(find ur10_moveit_config)/launch/move_group.launch">
    <arg name="limited" default="$(arg limited)"/>
    <arg name="debug" default="$(arg debug)" />
  </include>
</launch>
```

Testing the MoveIt! configuration

After editing the configuration and launch files in the MoveIt! configuration, we can start running the robot simulation and can check whether the MoveIt! configuration is working well or not. Ensure that the `ros-industrial-simulator` package is installed properly. Here are the steps to test an industrial robot:

1. Start the robot simulator.
2. Start the MoveIt! planning execution launch file using the following command line:

```
$ roslaunch <robot>_moveit_config
moveit_planning_execution.launch
```

3. Open RViz and load the RViz **Motion planning plugin,** using the **Plan and Execute** button. We can plan and execute the trajectory on the simulated robot.

Installing ROS-Industrial packages of Universal robotic arms

Universal Robots (`http://www.universal-robots.com/`) is an industrial robot manufacturer based in Denmark. The company mainly produces three arms: **UR3, UR5**, and **UR10**. The robots are shown in the following figure:

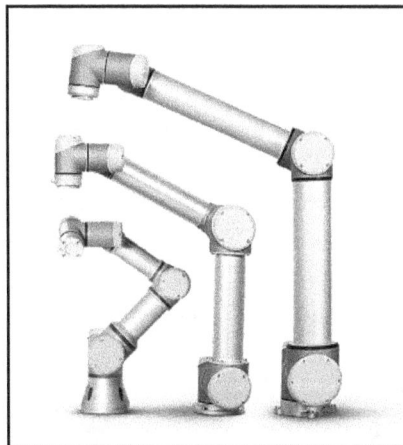

Figure 7: UR-3, UR-5, and UR-10 robots

The specifications of these robots are given in the following table:

Robot	UR-3	UR-5	UR-10
Working radius	500 mm	850 mm	1,300 mm
Payload	3 kg	5 kg	10 kg
Weight	11 kg	18.4 kg	28.9 kg
Footprint	118 mm	149 mm	190 mm

In the next section, we will install the Universal Robots packages and work with the MoveIt! interface to simulate industrial robots in Gazebo.

Installing the ROS interface of Universal Robots

We can install the Universal Robots packages by using the Ubuntu/Debian package manager:

```
$ sudo apt-get install ros-kinetic-universal-robot
```

Or, we can directly download these packages from the following repository:

```
$ git clone https://github.com/ros-industrial/universal_robot.git
```

The Universal Robot packages are:

- `ur_description`: This package consists of the robot description and Gazebo description of UR-3, UR-5, and UR-1.
- `ur_driver`: This package contains client nodes, which can communicate with the UR-3, UR-5, and UR-10 robot hardware controllers.
- `ur_bringup`: This package consists of launch files to start communication with the robot hardware controllers to start working with the real robot.
- `ur_gazebo`: This package consists of Gazebo simulations of UR-3, UR-5, and UR-10.
- `ur_msgs`: This package contains ROS messages used for communication between various UR nodes.

- urXX_moveit_config: These are the moveit config files of Universal Robot manipulators. One different package exists for each type of arm (ur3_moveit_config, ur5_moveit_config and ur10_moveit_config).
- ur_kinematics: This package contains kinematic solver plugins for UR-3, UR-5, and UR-10. We can use this solver plugin in MoveIt!

After installing or compiling the *Universal Robots* packages, we can launch the simulation in Gazebo of the UR-10 robot by using the following command:

```
$ roslaunch ur_gazebo ur10.launch
```

Figure 8: Universal Robot UR-10 model simulation in Gazebo

We can see the robot controller configuration file for interfacing into the MoveIt! package. The following YAML file defines the JointTrajectory controller. It is placed in the ur_gazebo/controller folder with the name arm_controller_ur10.yaml:

```
arm_controller:
  type: position_controllers/JointTrajectoryController
  joints:
    - shoulder_pan_joint
    - shoulder_lift_joint
    - elbow_joint
    - wrist_1_joint
    - wrist_2_joint
    - wrist_3_joint
  constraints:
```

```
        goal_time: 0.6
        stopped_velocity_tolerance: 0.05
        shoulder_pan_joint: {trajectory: 0.1, goal: 0.1}
        shoulder_lift_joint: {trajectory: 0.1, goal: 0.1}
        elbow_joint: {trajectory: 0.1, goal: 0.1}
        wrist_1_joint: {trajectory: 0.1, goal: 0.1}
        wrist_2_joint: {trajectory: 0.1, goal: 0.1}
        wrist_3_joint: {trajectory: 0.1, goal: 0.1}
    stop_trajectory_duration: 0.5
    state_publish_rate:   25
    action_monitor_rate: 10
```

Understanding the Moveit! configuration of a Universal Robot arm

The MoveIt! configuration for Universal Robot arms is in the `config` directory of each `moveit_config` package (`ur10_moveit_config` for the UR-10 configuration).

Here is the definition of the `controller.yaml` of UR-10:

```
controller_list:
  - name: ""
    action_ns: follow_joint_trajectory
    type: FollowJointTrajectory
    joints:
      - shoulder_pan_joint
      - shoulder_lift_joint
      - elbow_joint
      - wrist_1_joint
      - wrist_2_joint
      - wrist_3_joint
```

In the same directory, we can find the kinematic configuration: `kinematics.yaml`. This file specifies the IK solvers used for the robotic arm. For the UR-10 robot, the content of the kinematic configuration file is shown here:

```
#manipulator:
#   kinematics_solver: ur_kinematics/UR10KinematicsPlugin
#   kinematics_solver_search_resolution: 0.005
#   kinematics_solver_timeout: 0.005
#   kinematics_solver_attempts: 3
manipulator:
  kinematics_solver: kdl_kinematics_plugin/KDLKinematicsPlugin
  kinematics_solver_search_resolution: 0.005
  kinematics_solver_timeout: 0.005
  kinematics_solver_attempts: 3
```

The definition of `ur10_moveit_controller_manager.launch` inside the `launch` folder is given as follows. This launch file loads the trajectory controller configuration and starts the trajectory controller manager:

```
<launch>
  <rosparam file="$(find ur10_moveit_config)/config/controllers.yaml"/>
  <param name="use_controller_manager" value="false"/>
  <param name="trajectory_execution/execution_duration_monitoring"
value="false"/>
  <param name="moveit_controller_manager"
value="moveit_simple_controller_manager/MoveItSimpleControllerManager"/>
</launch>
```

After discussing these files, let's see how to plan a motion using MoveIt! and simulate it using Gazebo:

1. Start the simulation of UR-10 with joint trajectory controllers:

   ```
   $ roslaunch ur_gazebo ur10.launch
   ```

2. Start the MoveIt! nodes for motion planning. We can set `sim:=true`, to test MoveIt! only in simulation:

   ```
   $ roslaunch ur10_moveit_config
   ur10_moveit_planning_execution.launch sim:=true
   ```

3. Launch RViz with the MoveIt! visualization plugin:

```
$ roslaunch ur10_moveit_config moveit_rviz.launch config:=true
```

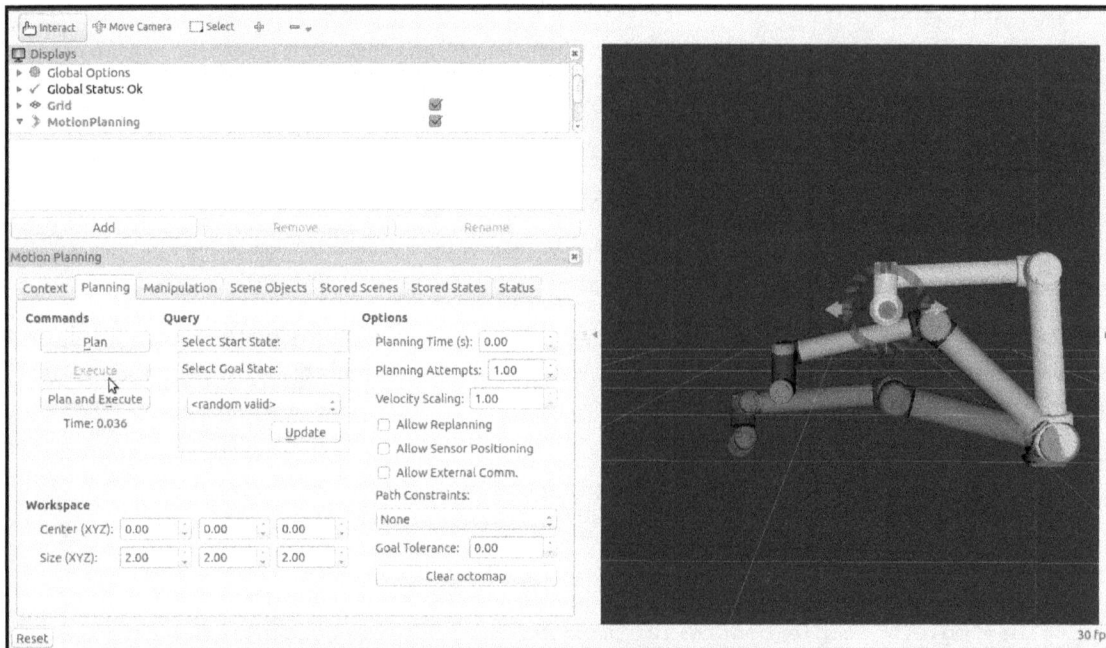

Figure 9: Motion planning in UR-10 model in RViz

We can move the end-effector position of the robot and plan the path by using the **Plan** button. When we press the **Execute** button or the **Plan and Execute** button, the trajectory should send to the simulated robot, performing the motion in the Gazebo environment.

Getting started with real Universal Robots hardware and ROS-I

After testing our control algorithms in simulation using Gazebo, we can start to perform manipulation tasks with a real Universal Robots arm. The main difference between performing a trajectory simulating the robot and using real hardware, is that we need to start the driver that will contact the arm controller to set the desired joint positions.

The default driver of Universal Robot arms is released with the `ur_driver` package of ROS-I. This driver has been successfully tested with system versions ranging from `v1.5.7` to `v1.8.2`. The last version of Universal Robot controllers is `v3.2`, so the default version of the ROS-I driver could be not fully compatible. For the newer versions of these systems (`v3.x` and up), it is recommended to use the unofficial `ur_modern_driver` package.

To download `ur_modern_driver`, use the following Git repository:

```
$ git clone ur10_moveit_config ur10_moveit_planning_execution.launch
sim:=true
```

After downloading this package, we need to compile the workspace to be able to use the driver.

The next step is to configure Universal Robots hardware to control it from our computer. Firstly, we must enable the networking capabilities of the Universal Robot, using its teach-pendant. Navigate into the **Robot -> Setup Network Menu** in order to select a proper configuration compatible with our network. If you prefer to have a fixed internet address for the robot, you must select the *Static Address* option and manually input the desired address information. Anyway, select the DHCP option, and then apply the configuration. After setting the IP address, it could be useful to check the connection status by pinging the robot controller:

```
$ ping IP_OF_THE_ROBOT
```

If the controller replies to the ping command, the connection is successfully established, and we can start to control the manipulator.

If your Universal Robots system has a version lower than `v3.x`, we can bring it up by running the following command:

```
$ roslaunch ur_bringup ur10_bringup.launch robot_ip:=IP_OF_THE_ROBOT
[reverse_port:=REVERSE_PORT]
```

Replace the `IP_OF_THE_ROBOT` with the IP address assigned to the robot controller. Then, we can test the motion of the robot by using the following script:

```
$ rosrun ur_driver IP_OF_THE_ROBOT [reverse_port:=REVERSE_PORT]
```

To operate with systems greater than `v3.x`, we can use launch files provided by the `ur_modern_driver` package:

```
$ roslaunch ur_modern_driver ur10_bringup.launch robot_ip:=IP_OF_THE_ROBOT
[reverse_port:=REVERSE_PORT]
```

The next step is to use MoveIt! to control the robot:

```
$ roslaunch ur10_moveit_config ur5_moveit_planning_execution.launch
```

```
$ roslaunch ur10_moveit_config moveit_rviz.launch config:=true
```

Note that for some desired robot configurations, MoveIt! could have difficulties with finding plans with full joint limits. There is another version with lower restrictions of the joint limits. This operative mode can be started simply by using the argument `limited` in the launch command:

```
$ roslaunch ur10_moveit_config ur5_moveit_planning_execution.launch
limited:=true
```

We have seen how to simulate and control a Universal Robot. In the next section, we will work with ABB robots.

Working with MoveIt! configuration of ABB robots

We will work with two of the most popular ABB industrial robot models: **IRB 2400** and **IRB 6640**. The following are the images of these two robots and their specifications:

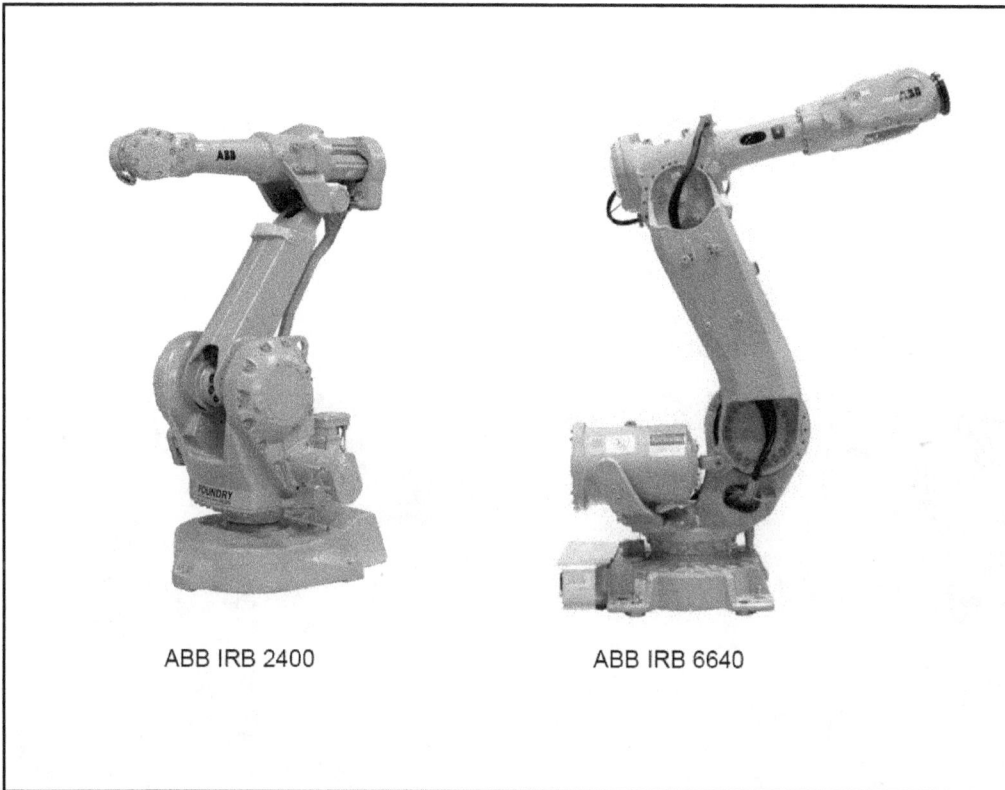

Figure 10: ABB IRB 2400 and IRB 6640

The specification of these robotic arms is given in the following table:

Robot	IRB 2400-10	IRB 6640-130
Working radius	1.55 m	3.2 m
Payload	12 kg	130 kg
Weight	380 kg	1,310-1,405 kg
Footprint	723x600 mm	1,107 x 720 mm

To work with ABB packages, clone the ROS packages of the robot into the `catkin` workspace. We can use the following command to do this task:

```
$ git clone https://github.com/ros-industrial/abb
```

Then, build the source packages using `catkin_make`. Alternatively, we can also install packages using the Ubuntu/Debian package management system. However, to follow the reminder tutorial of this chapter, it is suggested to clone the ABB repository in your ROS workspace. The following package will install the complete set of ABB robot packages:

```
$ sudo apt-get install ros-kinetic-abb
```

To launch the ABB IRB 6640 in RViz for motion planning, use the following command:

```
$ roslaunch abb_irb6640_moveit_config demo.launch
```

The RViz window will be open and we can start motion planning the robot in RViz:

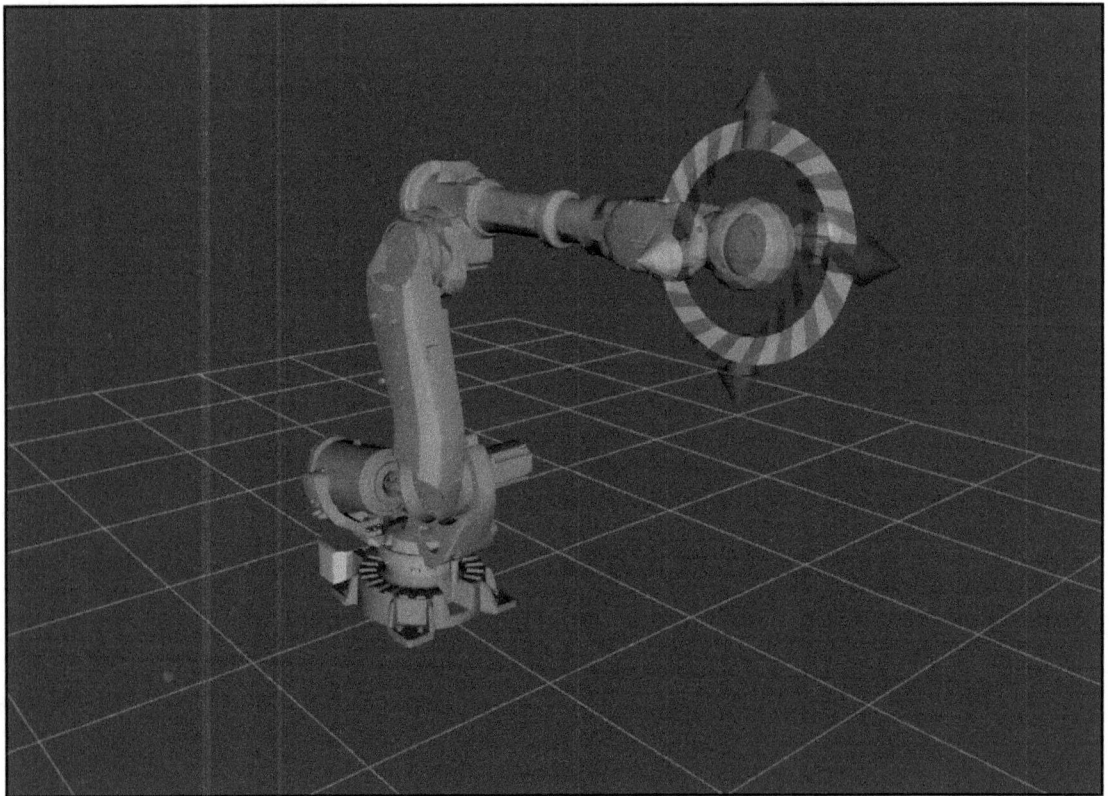

Figure 12: Motion planning of ABB IRB 6640

One of the other popular ABB robot models is the IRB 2400. We can launch the robot in RViz by using the following command:

```
$ roslaunch abb_irb2400_moveit_config demo.launch
```

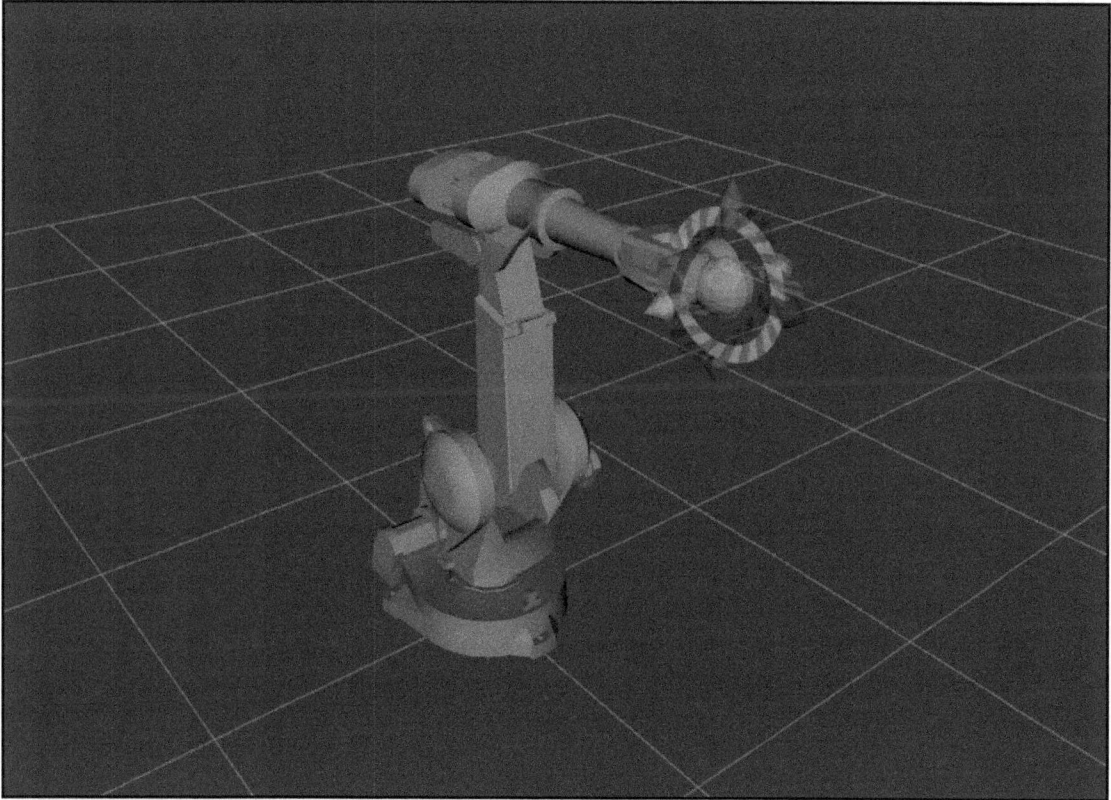

Figure 12: Motion planning of ABB IRB 2400

Understanding the ROS-Industrial robot support packages

The ROS-I robot support packages are a new convention followed for industrial robots. The aim of these support packages is to standardize the ways of maintaining ROS packages for a wide variety of industrial robot types of different vendors. Because of a standardized way of keeping files inside support packages, we don't have any confusion in accessing the files inside them. We can demonstrate a support package of an ABB robot and can see the folders and files and their uses.

We have already cloned the ABB robot packages, and inside this folder we can see three support packages that support three varieties of ABB robots. Here we are taking the ABB IRB 2400 model support package: `abb_irb2400_support`. This is the support package of the ABB industrial robot model called IRB 2400. The following list shows the folders and files inside this package:

- `config`: As the name of the folder, this contains the configuration files of joint names, RViz configuration, and robot model specific configuration.
- `joint_names_irb2400`: Inside the `config` folder, there is a configuration file, which contains the joint names of the robot that is used by the ROS controller.
- `launch`: This folder contains the launch file definitions of this robot. These files are following a common convention in all industrial robots.
- `load_irb2400.launch`: This file simply loads `robot_description` on the parameter server. According to the complexity of the robot, the number of xacro files can be increased. This file loads all xacro files in a single launch file. Instead of writing separate code for adding `robot_description` in other launch files, we can simply include this launch file.
- `test_irb2400.launch`: This launch file can visualize the loaded URDF. We can inspect and verify the URDF in RViz. This launch file includes the preceding launch files and starts the `joint_state_publisher` and `robot_state_publisher` nodes, which helps to interact with the user on RViz. This will work without the need for real hardware.
- `robot_state_visualize_irb2400.launch`: This launch file visualizes the current state of the real robot by running nodes from the ROS-Industrial driver package with appropriate parameters. The current state of the robot is visualized by running RViz and the `robot_state_publisher` node. This launch file needs a real robot or simulation interface. One of the main arguments provided along with this launch file is the IP address of the industrial controller. Also note that the controller should run a ROS-Industrial server node.

- `robot_interface_download_irb2400.launch`: This launch file starts bi-directional communication with the industrial robot controller to ROS and vice versa. There are industrial robot client nodes for reporting the state of the robot (`robot_state node`) and subscribing the joint command topic and issuing the joint position to the controller (`joint_trajectory node`). This launch file also requires access to the simulation or real robot controller and needs to mention the IP address of the industrial controllers. The controller should run the ROS-Industrial server programs too.
- `urdf`: This folder contains the set of standardized `xacro` files of the robot model.

- `irb2400_macro.xacro`: This is the xacro definition of a specific robot. It is not a complete URDF, but it's a macro definition of the manipulator section. We can include this file inside another file and create an instance of this macro.
- `irb2400.xacro`: This is the top level `xacro` file, which creates an instance of the macro, which was discussed in the preceding section. This file doesn't include any other files other than the macro of the robot. This `xacro` file will be loading inside the `load_irb2400.launch` file that we have already discussed.
- `irb2400.urdf`: This is the URDF generated from the preceding `xacro` file, using the `xacro` tool. This file is used when the tools or packages can't load `xacro` directly. This is the top-level URDF for this robot.
  - `meshes`: This contains meshes for visualization and collision checking
  - `irb2400`: This folder contains mesh files for a specific robot
  - `visual`: This folder contains STL files used for visualization
  - `collision`: This folder contains STL files used for collision checking
  - `tests`: This folder contains the test launch file to test all the preceding launch files
  - `roslaunch_test.xml`: This launch file tests all the launch files

Visualizing the ABB robot model in RViz

After creating the robot model, we can test it using the `test_irb2400.launch` file. The following command will launch the test interface of the ABB IRB 2400 robot:

```
$ roslaunch abb_irb2400_support test_irb2400.launch
```

It will show the robot model in RViz with a joint state publisher node, as shown in the following screenshot:

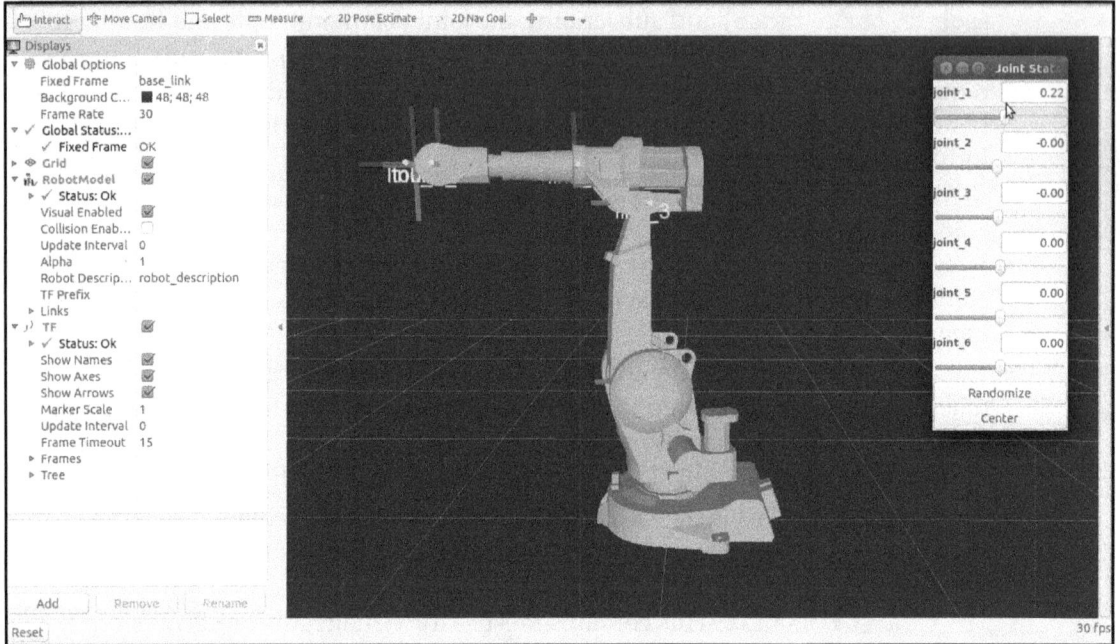

Figure 13: ABB IRB 2400 with joint state publisher on RViz

We can adjust the robot joints by adjusting the joint state publisher slider values. Using this testing interface, we can confirm whether the URDF design is correct or not.

ROS-Industrial robot client package

The industrial robot client nodes are responsible for sending robot position/trajectory data from ROS MoveIt! to the industrial robot controller. The industrial robot client converts the trajectory data to `simple_message` and communicates to the robot controller using the `simple_message` protocol. The industrial robot controller running a server and industrial robot client nodes are connecting to this server and start communicating with this server.

Designing industrial robot client nodes

The `industrial_robot_client` package contains various classes to implement industrial robot client nodes. The main functionalities that a client should have include updating the robot current state from the robot controller, and also sending joint position messages to the controller. There are two main nodes that are responsible for getting the robot state and sending joint position values:

- **The** `robot_state` **node:** This node is responsible for publishing the robot's current position, status, and so on
- **The** `joint_trajectory` **node:** This node subscribes the robot's command topic and sends the joint position commands to the robot controller via the simple message protocol

The following figure gives the list of APIs provided by the industrial robot client:

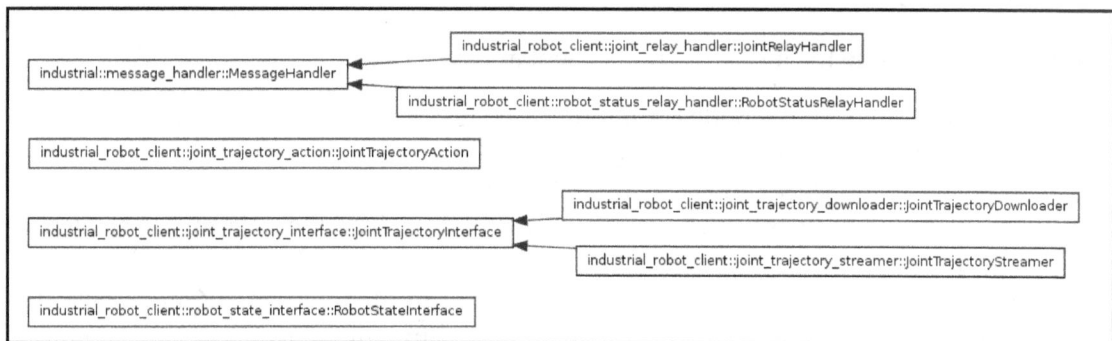

```
                                          industrial_robot_client::joint_relay_handler::JointRelayHandler
  industrial::message_handler::MessageHandler
                                          industrial_robot_client::robot_status_relay_handler::RobotStatusRelayHandler

  industrial_robot_client::joint_trajectory_action::JointTrajectoryAction

                                                  industrial_robot_client::joint_trajectory_downloader::JointTrajectoryDownloader
  industrial_robot_client::joint_trajectory_interface::JointTrajectoryInterface
                                                  industrial_robot_client::joint_trajectory_streamer::JointTrajectoryStreamer

  industrial_robot_client::robot_state_interface::RobotStateInterface
```

Figure 14: A list of the industrial robot client APIs

We can briefly go through these APIs and their functionalities, as follows:

- `RobotStateInterface`: This class contains methods to publish the current robot position and status at regular intervals after receiving the position data from the robot controller.
- `JointRelayHandler`: The `RobotStateInterface` class is a wrapper around a class called `MessageManager`. What it does is it listens to the `simple_ message` robot connection and processes each message handling, using `Messagehandlers`. The `JointRelayHandler` functionality is a `MessageHandler`, and its function is to publish the joint position in the `joint_states` topic.

- `RobotStatusRelayHandler`: This is another `MessageHandler`, that can publish the current robot status info in the `robot_status` topic.
- `JointTrajectoryInterface`: This class contains methods to send the robot's joint position to the controller when it receives a ROS trajectory command.
- `JointTrajectoryDownloader`: This class is derived from the `JointTrajectoryInterface` class, and it implements a method called `send_to_robot()`. This method sends an entire trajectory as a sequence of messages to the robot controller. The robot controller will execute the trajectory in the robot only after getting all sequences sent from the client.
- `JointTrajectoryStreamer`: This class is the same as the preceding class except in the implementation of the `send_to_robot()` method. This method sends independent joint values to the controller in separate threads. Each position command is sent only after the execution of the existing command. In the robot side, there will be a small buffer for receiving the position to make the motion smoother.

The list of nodes inside the industrial robot client are as follows:

- `robot_state`: This node is running based on `RobotStateInterface`, which can publish the current robot states
- `motion_download_interface`: This node runs `JointTrajectoryDownloader`, which will download the trajectory in sequence to the controller
- `motion_streaming_interface`: This node runs `JointTrajectoryStreamer`, which will send the joint position in parallel using threading
- `joint_trajectory_action`: This node provides a basic `actionlib` interface

ROS-Industrial robot driver package

In this section, we will discuss the industrial robot driver package. If we take the ABB robot as an example, it has a package called `abb_driver`. This package is responsible for communicating with the industrial robot controller. This package contains industrial robot clients and launches the file to start communicating with the controller. We can check what's inside the `abb_driver/launch` folder. The following is a definition of a launch file called `robot_interface.launch`:

```
<launch>
  <!-- robot_ip: IP-address of the robot's socket-messaging server -->
```

```
<arg name="robot_ip" />

<!-- J23_coupled: set TRUE to apply correction for J2/J3 parallel linkage
-->
<arg name="J23_coupled" default="false" />

<!-- copy the specified arguments to the Parameter Server, for use by
nodes below -->
<param name="robot_ip_address" type="str" value="$(arg robot_ip)"/>
<param name="J23_coupled" type="bool" value="$(arg J23_coupled)"/>

<!-- robot_state: publishes joint positions and robot-state data
                  (from socket connection to robot) -->
<node pkg="abb_driver" type="robot_state" name="robot_state"/>

<!-- motion_download_interface: sends robot motion commands by
DOWNLOADING path to robot
                                  (using socket connection to robot) -->

<node pkg="abb_driver" type="motion_download_interface"
name="motion_download_interface"/>

<!-- joint_trajectory_action: provides actionlib interface for high-level
robot control -->
<node pkg="industrial_robot_client" type="joint_trajectory_action"
name="joint_trajectory_action"/>
</launch>
```

This launch file provides a socket-based connection to ABB robots using the standard ROS-Industrial `simple_message` protocol. Several nodes are started to supply both low-level robot communication and high-level `actionlib` support:

- `robot_state`: This publishes the current joint positions and robot state data
- `motion_download_interface`: This commands the robot motion by sending motion points to the robot
- `joint_trajectory_action`: This is the `actionlib` interface to control the robot motion

Their usage is as follows:

```
$ robot_interface.launch robot_ip:=IP_OF_THE_ROBOT [J23_coupled:=false]
```

We can see the `abb_irb6600_support/launch/`
`robot_interface_download_irb6640.launch` file, and this is the driver for the ABB
IRB 6640 model. This definition of launch is given in the following code. The preceding
driver launch file is included in this launch file. In other support packages of other ABB
models, use the same driver with different joint configuration parameter files:

```
<launch>
  <arg name="robot_ip" />
  <arg name="J23_coupled" default="true" />

  <rosparam command="load" file="$(find
abb_irb2400_support)/config/joint_names_irb2400.yaml" />

  <include file="$(find abb_driver)/launch/robot_interface.launch">
    <arg name="robot_ip"    value="$(arg robot_ip)" />
    <arg name="J23_coupled" value="$(arg J23_coupled)" />
  </include>
</launch>
```

The preceding file is the manipulator-specific version of `robot_interface.launch` (of
`abb_driver`):

- Defaults provided for IRB 2400: – `J23_coupled = true`
- Usage: `robot_interface_download_irb2400.launch robot_ip:=<value>`

We should run the driver launch file to start communicating with the real robot controller.
For the ABB robot IRB 2400, we can use the following command to start bi-directional
communication with the robot controller and the ROS client:

```
$ roslaunch abb_irb2400_support robot_interface_download_irb2400.launch
robot_ip:=IP_OF_THE_ROBOT
```

After launching the driver, we can start planning by using the MoveIt! interface. It should
also be noted that the ABB robot should be configured and the IP of the robot controller
should be found before starting the robot driver.

Understanding the MoveIt! IKFast plugin

One of the default numerical IK solvers in ROS is KDL. KDL is mainly using DOF > 6. In robots DOF <= 6, we can use analytic solvers, which is much faster than numerical solvers, such as KDL. Most of the industrial arms have DOF <= 6, so it will be good if we make an analytical solver plugin for each arm. The robot will work on the KDL solver too, but if we want a fast IK solution, we can choose something such as the IKFast module to generate analytical solver-based plugins for MoveIt!. We can check which are the IKFast plugin packages present in the robot (for example, universal robots and ABB):

- `ur_kinematics`: This package contains IKFast solver plugins of UR-5 and UR-10 robots from Universal Robotics
- `abb_irb2400_moveit_plugins/irb2400_kinematics`: This package contains IKFast solver plugins for the ABB robot model IRB 2400

We can go through the procedures to build an IKFast plugin for MoveIt!. It will be useful when we create an IK solver plugin for a custom industrial robotics arm. Let's see how to create a MoveIt! IKFast plugin for the industrial robot ABB IRB 6640.

Creating the MoveIt! IKFast plugin for the ABB IRB 6640 robot

We have seen the MoveIt! package for the ABB robot IRB 6640 model. This robot works with a default numerical solver. In this section, we will discuss how to generate an IK solver plugin using IKFast, a powerful inverse kinematics solver provided within Rosen Diankov's OpenRAVE motion planning software. At the end of this section, we can run the MoveIt! demo of this robot, using our custom inverse kinematic plugin.

In short, we will build an IKFast MoveIt! plugin for robot ABB IRB 66400. This plugin can be selected during the MoveIt! setup wizard or we can mention it in the `config/kinematics.yaml` file of the `moveit-config` package.

Prerequisites for developing the MoveIt! IKFast plugin

The following is the configuration we have used for developing the MoveIt! IKFast plugin:

- Ubuntu 16.04 LTS x86_64 bit
- ROS-kinetic desktop-full
- Open-Rave 0.9

OpenRave and IK Fast modules

OpenRave is a set of command lines and GUI tools for developing, testing, and deploying motion planning algorithms in real-world applications. One of the OpenRave modules is IKFast, which is a robot kinematics compiler. OpenRave was created by a robotic researcher called Rosen Diankov. The IKFast compiler analytically solves the inverse kinematics of a robot and generates optimized and independent C++ files, which can be deployed in our code for solving IK. The IKFast compiler generates analytic solutions of IK, which is much faster than numerical solutions provided by KDL. The IKFast compiler can handle any number of DOFs, but practically it is well suited for DOF <= 6. IKFast is a Python script that takes arguments such as IK types, robot model, joint position of the base link, and end effector.

The following are the main IK types supported by IKFast:

- `Transform 6D`: This end effector should reach the commanded 6D transformation
- `Rotation 3D`: This end effector should reach the commanded 3D rotation
- `Translation 3D`: This end effector origin should reach the desired 3D translation

MoveIt! IKFast

The `ikfast` package for MoveIt! contains tools to generate a kinematic solver plugin using the OpenRave source files. We will use this tool to generate an IKFast plugin for MoveIt!.

Installing the MoveIt! IKFast package

The following command will install the `moveit-ikfast` package in ROS Indigo:

```
$ sudo apt-get install ros-kinetic-moveit-kinematics
```

Installing OpenRave on Ubuntu 16.04

Installing OpenRave on the latest Ubuntu is a tedious task. We will install OpenRave from the source itself, using the following procedure:

1. Clone the source code in the preferred folder:

   ```
   $ git clone --branch latest_stable
   https://github.com/rdiankov/openrave.git
   ```

2. For compiling the source code, we need to install the following packages:

   Install boost, Python development packages, and NumPy:

   ```
   $ sudo apt-get install libboost-python-dev
   $ python python-dev python-numpy ipython python-pip
   ```

3. Install scientific Python and its package to handle symbolic mathematics. Note that the suggested version to work with OpenRave and Ubuntu 16.04 is $v0.7.1$:

   ```
   $ sudo apt-get install python-scipy
   $ pip install -v sympy==0.7.1
   ```

4. Install the open asset import library to handle 3D file formats:

   ```
   $ sudo apt-get install libassimp-dev assimp-utils python-
   pyassimp
   ```

5. Install the `Qt4 GUI` toolkit:

   ```
   $ sudo apt-get install libsoqt4-dev
   ```

6. Install the `collada` file handling package. Clone it from the following Git repository:

   ```
   $ git clone https://github.com/rdiankov/collada-dom.git
   ```

7. Join the `collada-dom` directory, create a build folder, and compile the software:

```
$ cd collada-dom && mkdir build && cd build
$ cmake ..
$ make && sudo make install
```

8. Now, we will see how to install `cmake-gui` for configuring and generating Makefiles from `CMakeLists.txt`. The `OpenRave` project is based on CMake, so we need this tool for generating Makefiles:

```
$ sudo apt-get install cmake-qt-gui
```

The first procedure of installing `OpenRave` is to generate the Unix Makefiles from the `CMakeLists.txt` file: create a `build` folder inside the OpenRave cloned folder and open `cmake-gui` for configuring and building Makefiles. Browse the source code and the `build` folder, as shown in the following screenshot, and after configuring, uncheck the support for the MATLAB and Octave interfaces:

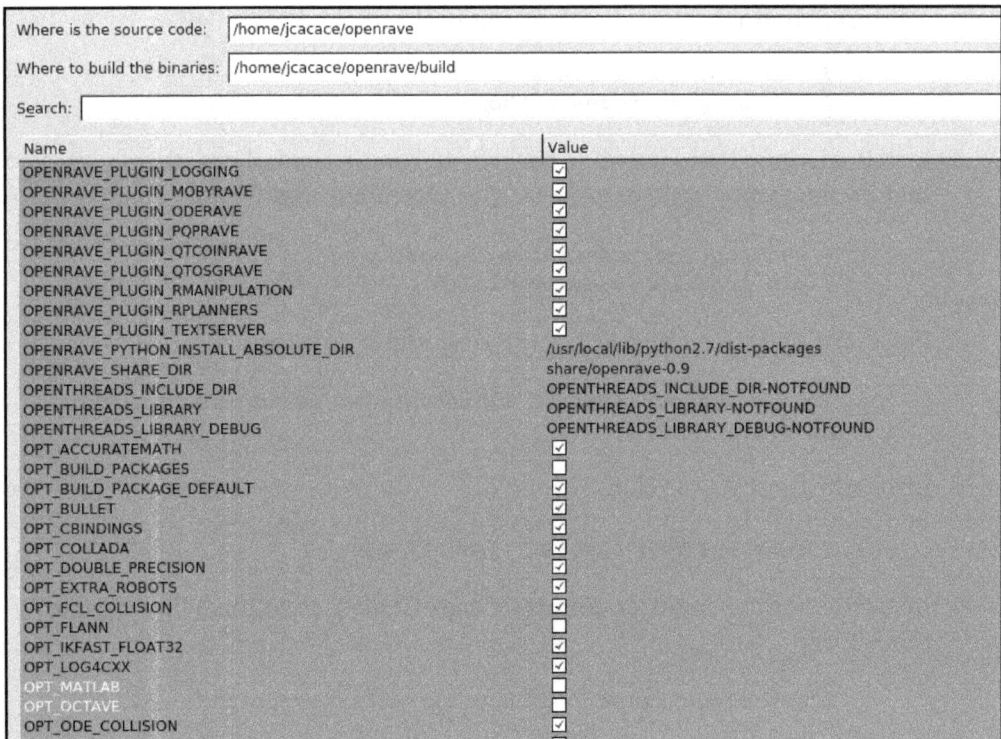

Figure 15: Configuring OpenRave with cmake-gui

Click on the **Generate** button to generate the Makefile in the selected build folder. Switch to the build folder, build the code, and install using the following command:

```
$ make
$ sudo make install
```

After installing OpenRave, execute the following command to check that OpenRave is working:

```
$ openrave
```

If everything works fine, it will open a 3D view port.

Creating the COLLADA file of a robot to work with OpenRave

In this section, we will discuss how to use URDF robot models with OpenRave. Firstly, we will see how to convert an URDF in a collada file (.dae) format; this file will be then used to generate the IKFast source file. To convert a URDF model into a collada file, we can use a ROS package, called collada_urdf.

We will work with the ABB IRB 6640 robot model, which can be found in the abb_irb6600_support package in the /urdf folder named irb6640.urdf. Alternatively, you can take this file from the ikfast_demo folder released with the book code. Copy this file into your working folder and run the following command for the conversion:

```
$ roscore && rosrun collada_urdf urdf_to_collada irb6640.urdf irb6640.dae
```

The output of the previous command is the robotic model in the collada file format.

> In most of the cases, this command fails because most of the URDF file contains STL meshes and it may not convert into DAE as we expected. If the robot meshes in the DAE format, it will work fine. If the command fails, follow this procedure:

Install meshlab tool, for viewing and editing meshes, using the following command:

```
$ sudo apt-get install meshlab
```

Open meshes present at abb_irb6600_support/meshes/irb6640/visual in Meshlab and export the file into DAE with the same name.

Edit the `irb6640.urdf` file and change the visual meshes in the STL extension to DAE. This tool only process meshes for visual purposes only, so we will get a final DAE model.

We can open the `irb6640.dae` file, using OpenRave with the following command:

```
$ openrave irb6640.dae
```

We will get the model in OpenRave, as shown in the following screenshot:

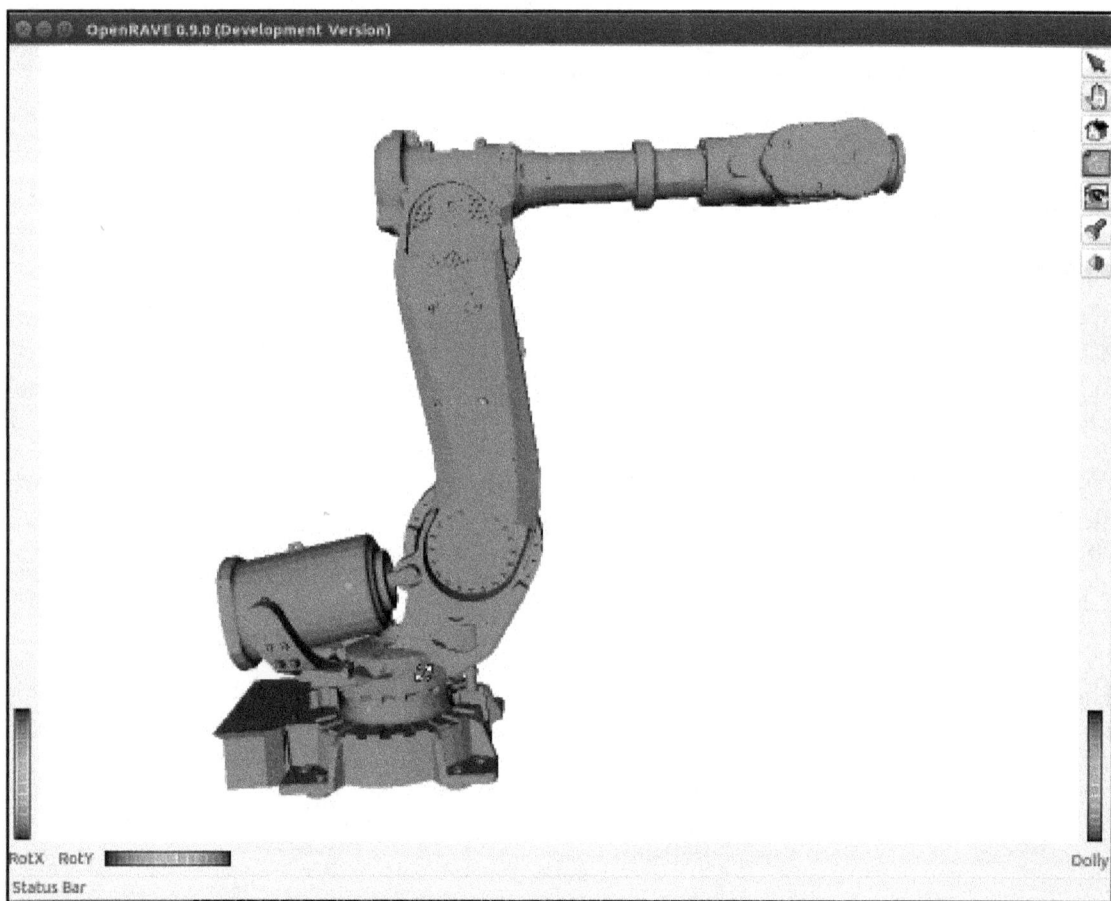

Figure 16: Viewing the ABB IRB 6640 model on OpenRave

We can check the link information of the robot by using the following command:

```
openrave-robot.py irb6640.dae --info links
```

We can get the link info about the robot in the following format:

```
name             index parents
----------------------------------
base_link        0
base             1     base_link
link_1           2     base_link
link_2           3     link_1
link_4           5     link_3
link_5           6     link_4
link_6           7     link_5
tool0            8     link_6
link_cylinder    9     link_1
link_piston      10    link_cylinder
----------------------------------
name             index parents
```

Generating the IKFast CPP file for the IRB 6640 robot

After getting the link information, we can start to generate the inverse kinematic solver source file for handling the IK of this robot. All the files needed to follow the tutorial of this section are available in the source code folder, ikfast_demo, provided with this book. Alternatively, you can download this code by cloning the following Git repository:

```
$ git clone https://github.com/jocacace/ikfast_demo.git
```

Use the following command to generate the IK solver for the ABBIRB 6640 robot:

```
$ python `openrave-config --python-dir`/openravepy/_openravepy_/ikfast.py --robot=irb6640.dae --iktype=transform6d --baselink=1 --eelink=8 --savefile=ikfast61.cpp
```

The preceding command generates a CPP file called ikfast61.cpp, in which the IK type is transform6d, the position of the baselink is 1, and the end effector link is 8. We need to mention the robot DAE file as the robot argument.

Before using this code with MoveIt!, we can test it with the ikfastdemo.cpp demo source. This ikfastdemo.cpp has been modified to include the ikfast61.cpp, as you can see from the header file list:

```
#define IK_VERSION 61
#include "output_ikfast61.cpp"
```

Compile the demo source files:

```
$ g++ ikfastdemo.cpp -lstdc++ -llapack -o compute -lrt
```

The previous command generates an executable called `compute`. If you run it without input arguments, the program displays the usage menu. To get the forward kinematic solution, given a set of joint angle values, use the following command:

```
$ ./compute fk j0 j1 j2 j3 j4 j5
```

Here, `j0 j1 j2 j3 j4 j5` represents the joint angle values in radians. To measure the average time taken by the IKFast algorithm for a set of random joint angles, use the following command:

```
$ ./compute iktiming
```

Now that we have successfully created the inverse kinematic solver CPP file, we can create a MoveIt! IKFast plugin by using this source code.

Creating the MoveIt! IKFast plugin

Creating a MoveIt! IKFast plugin is quite easy. There is no need to write code; everything can be generated using some tools. The only thing we need to do is to create an empty ROS package. The following is the procedure to create a plugin:

1. Create an empty package in which the name should contain the robot name and model number. This package is going to convert into the final plugin package, using the plugin generation tool:

   ```
   $ catkin_create_pkg abb_irb6640_moveit_plugins
   ```

2. Then, build the workspace by using the `catkin_make` command. You can also download the ROS package from here:

   ```
   $ git clone
   https://github.com/jocacace/abb_irb6640_moveit_plugins.git
   ```

3. After building the workspace, copy `ikfast.h` to `abb_irb6640_moveit_plugins/include`.

4. Copy the switch `ikfast61.cpp` previously created in the package folder, renaming it `abb_irb6640_manipulator_ikfast_solver.cpp`. This filename consists of the robot name, model number, type of robot, and so on. This kind of naming is necessary for the generating tool.

After performing these steps, open two terminals in the current path where the IK solver CPP file exists. In one terminal, start the `roscore` command. In the next terminal, move in to the `create` package and enter the plugin creation command, as follows:

```
$ rosrun moveit_kinematics create_ikfast_moveit_plugin.py abb_irb6640
manipulator abb_irb6640_moveit_plugins
abb_irb6640_manipulator_ikfast_solver.cpp
```

This command could fail due to a mismatch of the robot name specified into the URDF and SRDF files. To work around this error, we need to change the name of the robot in the SRDF file, placed into the `abb_irb6640_mveit_config/config folder`. You change line seven of this file from `<robot name="abb_irb6640_185_280">` to `<robot name="abb_irb6640">`. Or simply replace this file with the one contained in the `ikfast_demo` folder.

The `moveit_ikfast` ROS package includes the `create_ikfast_moveit_plugin.py` script for the plugin generation. The first parameter is the robot name with the model number, the second argument is the type of robot, the third argument is the package name we created earlier, and the fourth argument is the name of the IK solver CPP file. This tool needs the `abb_irb6640_moveit_config` package in order to work. It will search this package using the given name of the robot. So, if the name of the robot is wrong, the tool for raising an error will say that it couldn't find the robot `moveit` package.

If the creation is successful, the following messages will be displayed on the Terminal:

```
IKFast Plugin Generator
Loading robot from 'abb_irb6640_moveit_config' package ...
Creating plugin in 'abb_irb6640_moveit_plugins' package ...
   found 1 planning groups: manipulator
   found group 'manipulator'
   found source code generated by IKFast version 268435529

Created plugin file at '/home/jcacace/ros_ws/src/MASTERING_ROS/ch13/abb_irb6640_moveit_plugins/src/abb_irb6640_manipulator_ikfa
st_moveit_plugin.cpp'

Created plugin definition at: '/home/jcacace/ros_ws/src/MASTERING_ROS/ch13/abb_irb6640_moveit_plugins/abb_irb6640_manipulator_m
oveit_ikfast_plugin_description.xml'

Overwrote CMakeLists file at '/home/jcacace/ros_ws/src/MASTERING_ROS/ch13/abb_irb6640_moveit_plugins/CMakeLists.txt'

Modified package.xml at '/home/jcacace/ros_ws/src/MASTERING_ROS/ch13/abb_irb6640_moveit_plugins/package.xml'

Modified kinematics.yaml at /home/jcacace/ros_ws/src/abb_irb6640_moveit_config/config/kinematics.yaml

Created update plugin script at /home/jcacace/ros_ws/src/MASTERING_ROS/ch13/abb_irb6640_moveit_plugins/update_ikfast_plugin.sh
```

Figure 17: Terminal messages of successful creation of IKFast plugin for MoveIt!

As you can see from these messages, after creating the plugin, the `abb_irb6640_moveit_config/config/kinematics.yaml` file has been updated, specifying `abb_irb6640_manipulator_kinematics/IKFastKinematicsPlugin` as the kinematics solver. The updated version of the file is shown in the following code:

```
manipulator:
  kinematics_solver:
abb_irb6640_manipulator_kinematics/IKFastKinematicsPlugin
    kinematics_solver_search_resolution: 0.005
    kinematics_solver_timeout: 0.005
    kinematics_solver_attempts: 3
```

Now you can build the workspace again in order to install the plugin and start to operate with the robot and the new IKFast plugin, launching the demo scene:

```
$ roslaunch abb_irb6640_moveit_config demo.launch
```

Questions

Here are some common questions that will help you better learn and understand this chapter:

- What are the main benefits in using ROS-Industrial packages?
- What are the conventions followed by ROS-I in designing a URDF for industrial robots?
- What is the purpose of ROS' support packages?
- What is the purpose of ROS' driver packages?
- Why do we need an IKFast plugin for our industrial robot, rather than the default KDL plugin?

Summary

In this chapter, we have been discussing a new interface of ROS for industrial robots called ROS-Industrial. We have seen the basic concepts in developing the industrial packages and installed them on Ubuntu. After installation, we have seen the block diagram of this stack, and started discussing developing the URDF model for industrial robots and also creating the MoveIt! interface for an industrial robot. After covering these topics in detail, we installed some industrial robot packages of Universal Robots and ABB. We have learned the structure of the MoveIt! package and then shifted to the ROS-Industrial support packages. We have discussed in detail and switched on to concepts such as the industrial robot client and how to create the MoveIt! IKFast plugin. Finally, we used the developed plugin in the ABB robot.

In the next chapter, we will look at troubleshooting and best practices in ROS software development.

15
Troubleshooting and Best Practices in ROS

In this chapter, we will discuss how to set up an **Integrated Development Environment (IDE)** with ROS, best practices in ROS, and troubleshooting tips in ROS. This is the last chapter of this book, so before we start development in ROS, it will be good if we know the standard methods for writing the code. The following are the topics that we are going to discuss in this chapter:

- Using RoboWare Studio IDE with ROS
- Best practices in ROS
- Best coding practices in ROS using C++
- Important troubleshooting tips in ROS

Before we start coding in ROS, it will be good if we set up a ROS development environment in an IDE. Setting up an IDE for ROS is not mandatory, but it can save developers time. IDEs can provide auto completion features, as well as building and debugging tools that can make programming easy. We can use any editor, such as Sublime and VIM, or simply Gedit for coding in ROS, but it will be good if you choose IDEs when you are planning a big project in ROS. For this reason, in this chapter we will focus on RoboWare Studio, an IDE designed for ROS development. It makes the ROS development visual, simple, and manageable. Besides the facilities it has for programming, RoboWare offers useful tools to manage the ROS workspace, the creation, the handling, and the compilation of ROS nodes, and the support-running ROS tools.

Setting up RoboWare Studio in Ubuntu

Several IDEs are available in Linux—such as Net Beans (`https://netbeans.org`), Eclipse (`www.eclipse.org`), and QtCreator (`https://wiki.qt.io/Qt_Creator`)—and are suitable for different programming languages. For building and running ROS programs from IDEs, the ROS environment has to be set up. All IDEs might have a configuration file for that, but running your IDE from your ROS-sourced shell should be the easiest way to avoid inconsistency. In this section, we will discuss how to use RoboWare Studio IDE with ROS. A comprehensive list of other IDEs that are configurable with ROS can be found at `http://wiki.ros.org/IDEs`.

RoboWare Studio is an IDE especially designed for working with ROS, supporting ROS kinetic. The installation is quite easy, and automatically detects and loads an ROS environment without additional configurations. RoboWare Studio has different out-of-the-box features to help ROS developers to create their applications, such as a graphical interface to create ROS packages, source files (as well as service and message files), and list the nodes and packages.

Installing/uninstalling RoboWare Studio

To install RoboWare Studio, we need to download the installation file. Go to `http://www.roboware.me/` and download the latest version of the software. You can install it either by double-clicking on the downloaded `.deb` file to open it with the package manager GUI, or using the following commands in a terminal:

```
$ cd /path/to/deb/file/
$ sudo dpkg -i roboware-studio_<version>_<architecture>.deb
```

To remove the software, you can use the following command:

```
$ sudo apt-get remove roboware-studio
```

Getting started with RoboWare Studio

After you have installed RoboWare, you can start it from the command line:

```
$ roboware-studio
```

The main window of RoboWare will be open. In the following list, we will discuss the main elements of the RoboWare interface:

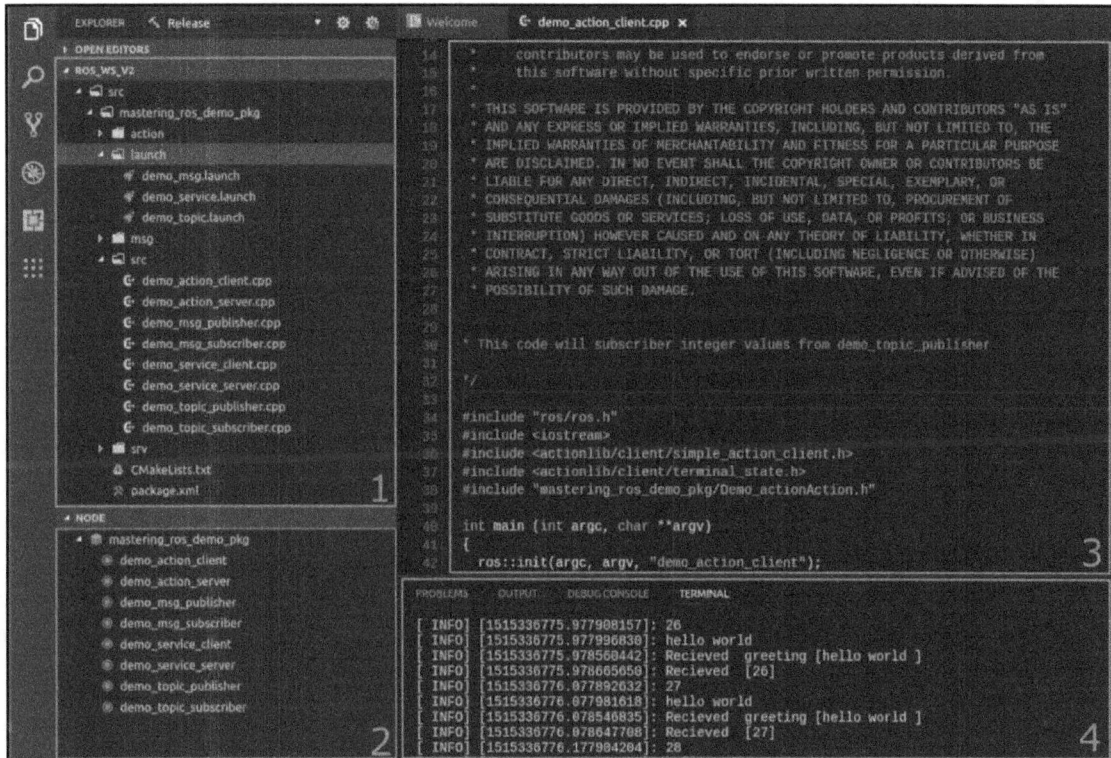

Figure 1: RoboWare Studio user interface

1. **EXPLORER** window: This panel displays the contents of the `src` directory of the ROS workspace. From this panel, you can navigate all the ROS packages installed into your ROS workspace.
2. **NODE**: In this panel, you can access all the nodes compiled inside the workspace. Nodes are folded inside packages. You can run the nodes using this panel.
3. **EDITOR**: In this panel, you can edit the source code of the packages.
4. **TERMINAL** and **OUTPUT:** This panel allows developers to use a Linux terminal integrated inside the IDE and check for possible errors during compilation.

Before we start editing our source codes, we should import the ROS workspace into RoboWare. On the main toolbar, select **File | Open Workspace**, and choose the directory representing the ROS workspace. All the packages located in the `src` directory are now shown in the explorer window:

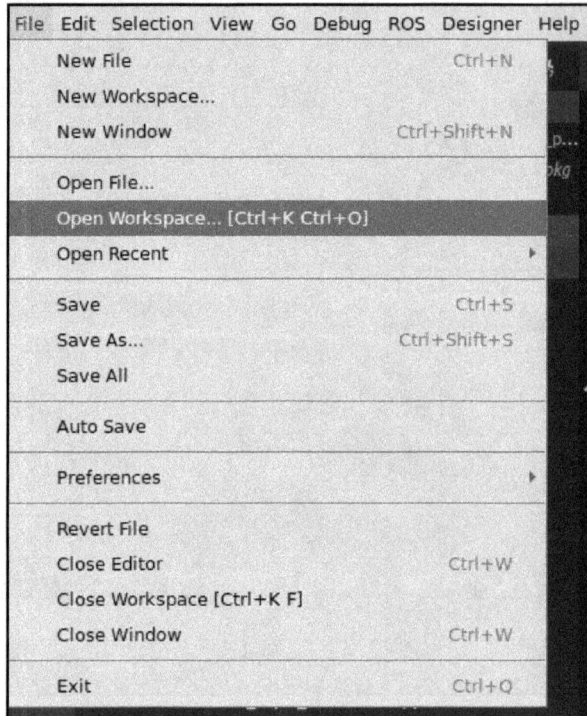

Figure 2: Importing an ROS workspace in RoboWare

Create ROS packages in RoboWare Studio

As already stated, RoboWare Studio allows developers to manage ROS projects directly from its user interface without using the Linux terminal or editing the `CMakeLists.txt` file. In this section, we will discuss how to create and handle ROS packages in RoboWare.

To create a complete ROS package with CPP executables, follow these steps:

1. Let's create the package. Right-click on the `src` folder of the ROS workspace from the explorer window and select **Add ROS Package**. Type the name for the package. A new ROS package will be created. In our case, we are creating a package called `roboware_package`:

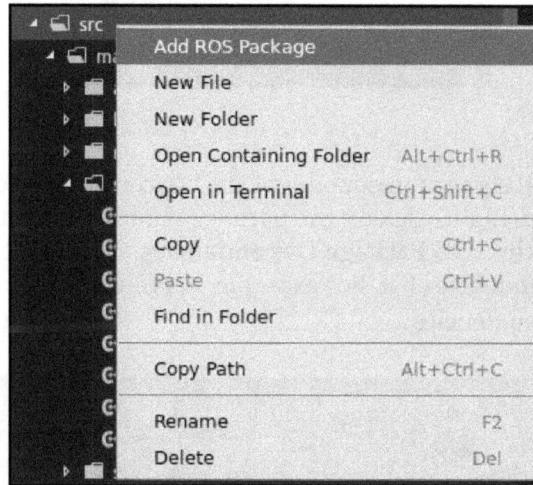

Figure 3: Adding an ROS package in RoboWare Studio

2. Now let's create the source code directory. Right-click on the package name in the explorer window and select **Add Src Folder**:

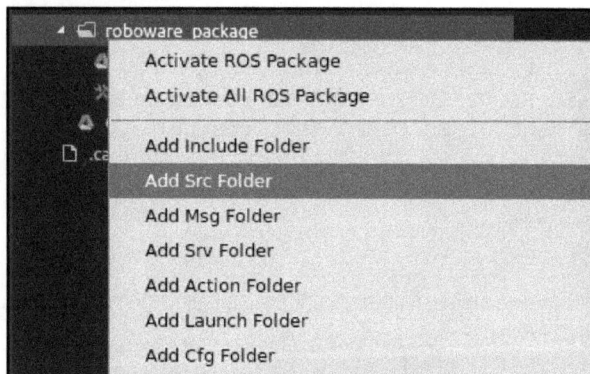

Figure 4: Adding the source code folder to an existing package in RoboWare Studio

3. Let's create the source file. Right-click on the created `src` folder and select `Add CPP File`. After you have inserted the name of the source file, RoboWare will ask you to specify whether this file is part of a system library or an executable—select the **Executable** entry:

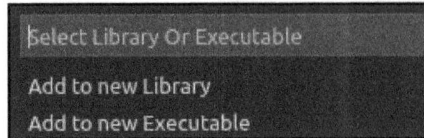

Figure 5: Selecting the type of a new CPP source file

4. Now let's add the package dependencies. We can add the desired dependencies for the package. Right-click on the package name in the explorer window and select **Edit catkin ROS Package Dependencies**. An input bar will allow us to insert the dependencies list. For example, we can add the `roscpp` and the `std_msgs` dependencies:

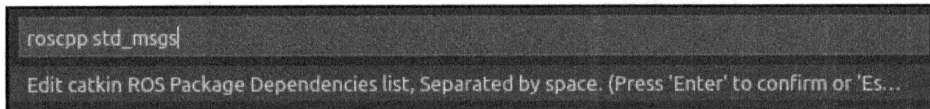

Figure 6: Specifying the dependencies of a ROS package

During these four steps, RoboWare Studio fills the `CMakeLists.txt` file in order to compile the desired executable. We can look in the updated `CMakeLists.txt` file of `roboware_package`:

```
cmake_minimum_required(VERSION 2.8.3)
project(roboware_package)
find_package(catkin REQUIRED COMPONENTS roscpp std_msgs)
find_package(catkin REQUIRED COMPONENTS roscpp)
catkin_package()
include_directories( include ${catkin_INCLUDE_DIRS} )
add_executable(roboware
  src/roboware.cpp
)
add_dependencies(roboware ${${PROJECT_NAME}_EXPORTED_TARGETS}
${catkin_EXPORTED_TARGETS})
target_link_libraries(roboware
  ${catkin_LIBRARIES}
)
```

As you can see from the generated `CMakeLists.txt` file, the executable and the additional libraries have successfully been added. Similarly, we can add ROS messages, services, and actions. We are now ready to write some code in the source file and build it.

Building ROS workspace in RoboWare Studio

RoboWare Studio supports both a release build and a debug build for local and remote compilation and deployment of ROS packages. In this tutorial, we will configure RoboWare to compile the release version of the local development mode. To select the compilation mode, use the drop-down menu from the explorer panel:

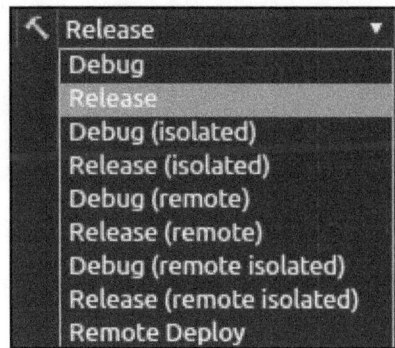

Figure 7: Selecting the build configuration of RoboWare Studio

To compile the workspace, use the main toolbar to select **ROS** | **Build entry** (or type *Ctrl + Shift + B*). The output of the compilation process is shown in the **Output** pane.

By default, RoboWare Studio compiles all packages inside the workspace (such as the `catkin_make` command). In order to manually specify one or more packages to build, we can right-click on the desired packages and select **Activate ROS Package** to activate it.

In this way, when we click the build button, only the ones that are activated will be compiled, while the deactivated packages will be marked with a strikethrough, as shown in the following figure:

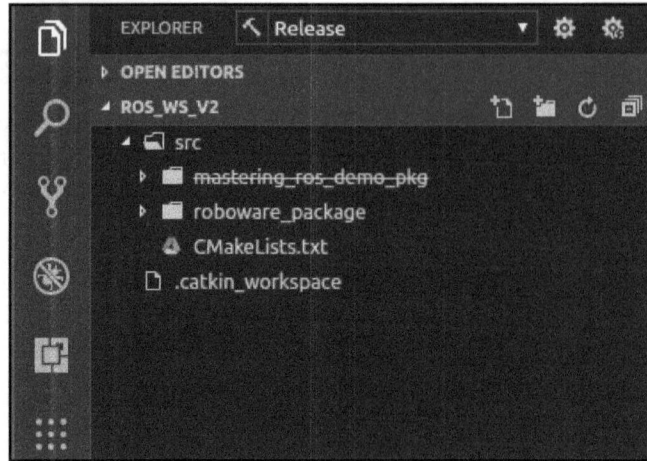

Figure 8: Activated and deactivated packages in the explorer window of RoboWare Studio

We can reset the active packages configuration by selecting **Activate All ROS Package** in the explorer window.

Executing ROS nodes in RoboWare Studio

You can run ROS nodes by using both the `roslaunch` and `rosrun` commands.

First of all, we should create a launch file for our package. To do this, right-click on the package name and select **Add Launch Folder** to create a folder named `launch`. Then, right-click on the launch folder and select **Add Launch File** to add a new file. After we have filled the launch file, we can simply right-click on the launch file's name and select **Run Launch File**:

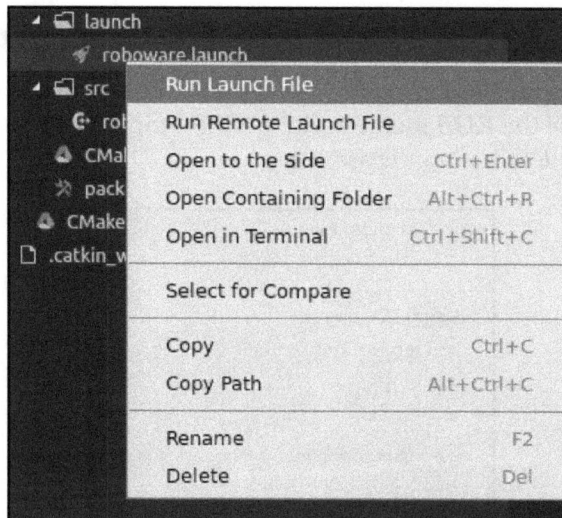

Figure 9: Running the `roslaunch` command from RoboWare Studio

To execute an ROS node using the `rosrun` command, we must select the desired executable from the node list. This will open the node window that will allow us to perform different actions on that node. For example, clicking on **Run this file** will start the execution of the node:

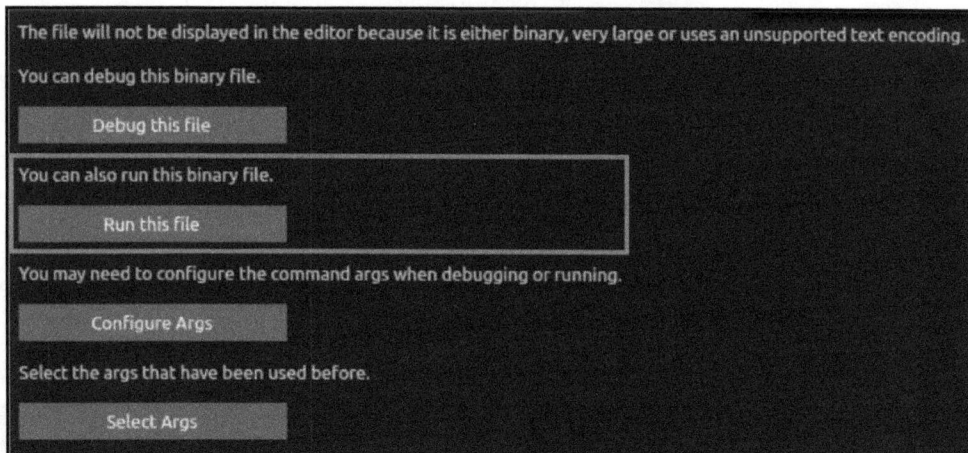

Figure 10: Running an ROS node using `rosrun`

The output of the node can be viewed by the users from the debug console window.

Starting ROS tools from the RoboWare interface

RoboWare Studio allows developers to run the some of the most commonly used ROS tools. To access these tools, use the **ROS** menu in RoboWare's top toolbar to unfold the drop-down menu shown in the following figure:

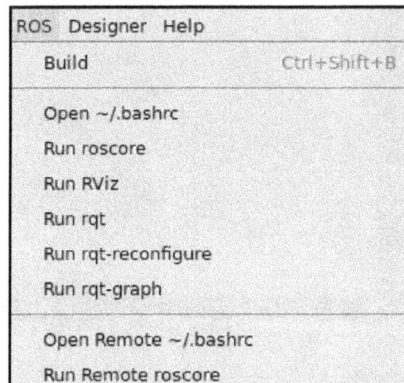

Figure 11: ROS graphical tools menu

You can directly run `roscore` from this menu or access these commonly used tools:

* `Rviz`
* `rqt`
* `rqt-reconfigure`
* `rqt-graph`

In addition, you can directly open your `.bashrc` file in the file editor and manually modify the system configuration. Moreover, you can run a remote `roscore` by selecting the **Run Remote roscore** option.

You can monitor the execution of these ROS commands from the terminal panel, where a new terminal is opened for each ROS tool and external windows are opened for the visualization tools:

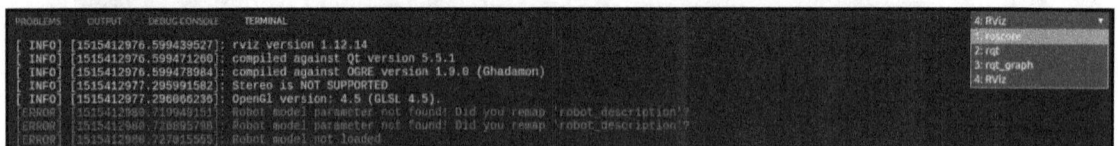

Figure 12: ROS terminal window

Handling active ROS topics, nodes, and services

To view the ROS topics, nodes, and services active in your system at a certain time, click on the ROS icon on the left-hand sidebar. The list of the information traveling along the `roscore` is shown in each box, and we can display the contents of each ROS message by clicking on the topic name:

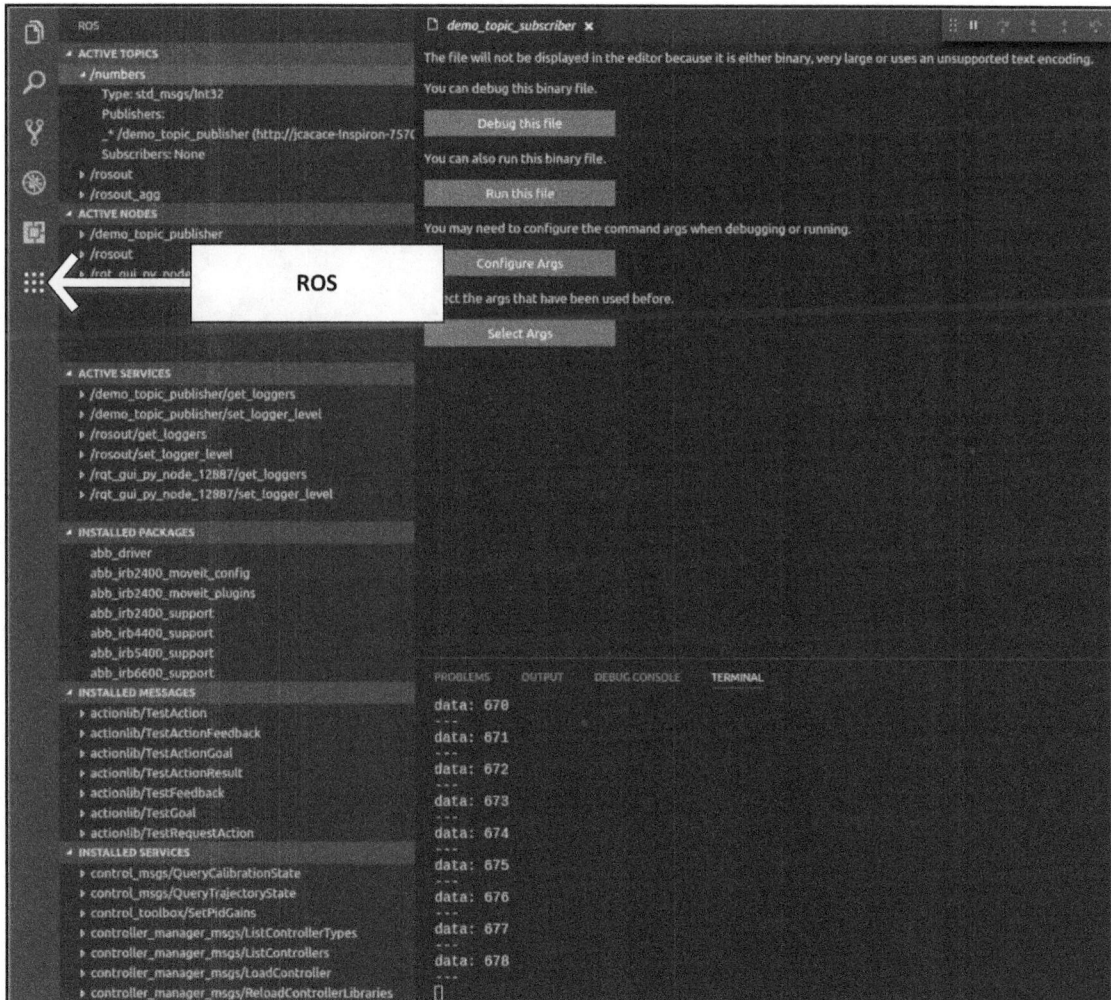

Figure 13: ROS panel in RoboWare Studio

In the example shown in the previous figure, we have chosen to display data published on the topic /numbers of type `std_msgs::Int32`.

We can even record and play ROS bagfiles from RoboWare. To start recording a bagfile, click on the **Record ROS Topic** button near the **Active Topics** panel, as shown in the following figure. Clicking on this button, all the active topics of the system will be recorded. The generated bagfile will be saved in the root directory of the workspace, with the naming format `yyyy-MM-dd-HH-mm-ss.bag`. To stop the recording, you have to type *Ctrl + C* in the Terminal window. If you want to record one or more specific topics, select them by pressing the *Ctrl* key and then clicking on the **rosbag** record button:

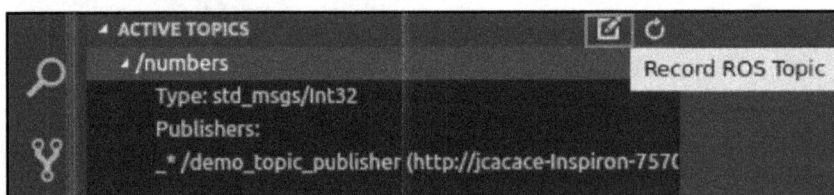

Figure 14: Recording bagfiles

To play a bagfile, you can right-click on the bagfile name from the explorer window and click on **Play Bag File**:

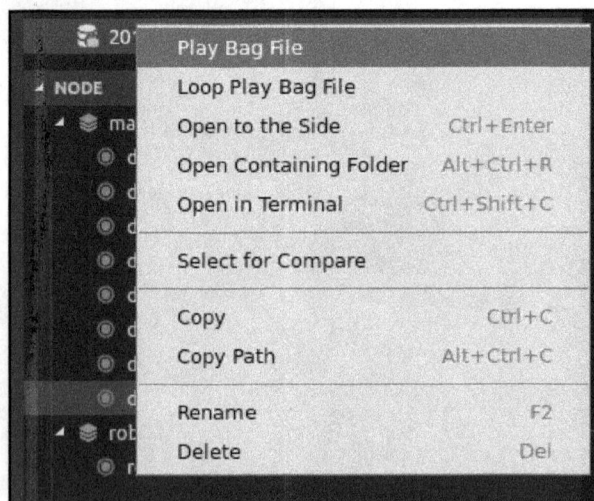

Figure 15: Playing bagfiles

Creating ROS nodes and classes with RoboWare tools

RoboWare Studio provides a wizard procedure to create C++ and Python classes and ROS nodes. To create a ROS node, do the following:

1. Right-click on the package name and select either **Add C++ ROS Node** or **Add Python ROS Node**.
2. Type the name of the package.
3. By default, two source files will be created: an example of a publisher and a subscriber node. For example, if you inserted chatter as a package name, a chatter_pub.cpp file and a chatter_sub.cpp file will be created.
4. Compile the package. The CMakeLists.txt file has already been updated according to the newly created nodes. You can remove the publisher or the subscriber in case you don't need them; the CMakeLists.txt file will be automatically updated.

As well as ROS nodes, we can create C++ classes using the following method:

1. Right-click on the package name
2. Choose **Add C++ Class**
3. Type the name of the class—for example, roboware_class
4. A header file will be created in the include directory of the package named roboware_class.h, while a CPP file named roboware_class.cpp will be added to the src directory
5. Select an executable to link the class just created, in order to import the class into another ROS node of the package
6. The CMakeLists.txt will be updated automatically

ROS package manager in RoboWare Studio

From the RoboWare Studio interface, we can install or explore the available ROS packages via the ROS package manager panel. To access this panel, click on the **ROS Packages Manager** icon in the left-hand side bar. RoboWare will automatically detect the ROS distribution in use and the list of the package already installed in the ROS package path.

From this panel, we can navigate through the packages available in the ROS repository, choosing between packages and meta-packages. You can click the package name to view its wiki page directly in RoboWare Studio, and install or uninstall the desired package:

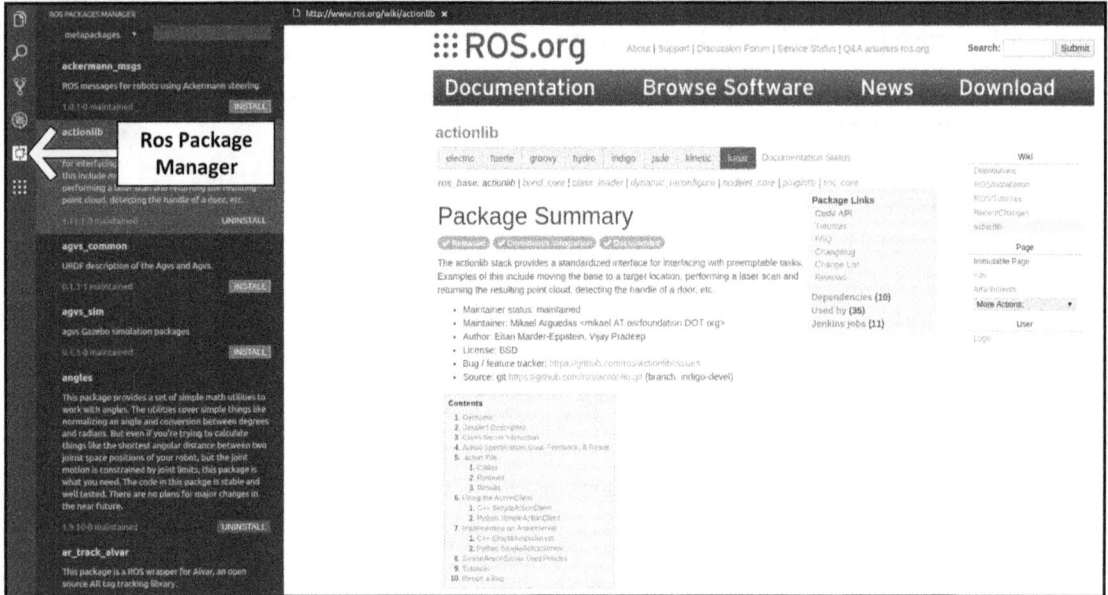

Figure 16: RoboWare Studio ROS package manager

Best practices in ROS

This section gives you a brief idea of the best practices that can be followed when we develop something with ROS. ROS provides detailed tutorials about its QA (quality assurance) process. A QA process is a detailed developer guide that includes C++ and Python code style guides, naming conventions, and so on. First, we will discuss the ROS C++ coding styles.

ROS C++ coding style guide

ROS C++ nodes follow a coding style to make the code more readable, debuggable, and maintainable. If the code is properly styled, it will be very easy to reuse and contribute to the current code. In this section, we will quickly go through some commonly used coding styles.

Standard naming conventions used in ROS

Here we are using the text HelloWorld to demonstrate the naming patterns we use in ROS:

- `HelloWorld`: This name starts with an uppercase letter, and each new word starts with an uppercase letter with no spaces or underscores.
- `helloWorld`: In this naming convention, the first letter will be lowercase, but new words will be in uppercase letters without spaces.
- `hello_world`: This only contains lowercase letters. Words are separated with underscores.
- `HELLO_WORLD`: All letters are uppercase letters. Words are separated by an underscore.

The following are the naming conventions followed by each component in ROS:

- **Packages, topics/services, files, libraries**: These ROS components follow the `hello_world` pattern
- **Classes/types**: These classes follow the `HelloWorld` naming convention—for example, `class ExampleClass`
- **Functions/methods**: Functions follow the `helloWorld` naming convention and function arguments follow the `hello_world` pattern—for example, `void exampleMethod(int sample_arg);`.
- **Variables**: Generally, variables follow the `hello_world` pattern
- **Constants**: Constants follow the `HELLO_WORLD` pattern
- **Member variables**: The member variable inside a class follows the `hello_world` pattern with a trailing underscore added—for example, `int sample_int_`
- **Global variables**: Global variables follow the `hello_world` convention with a leading g_—for example, `int g_samplevar;`
- **Namespace**: This follows the `hello_world` naming pattern

Code license agreement

We should add a license statement at the top of code. ROS is an open source software framework, and it's in the BSD license. The following is a code snippet of LICENSE, which must be inserted at the top of the code. You will get the license agreement from any of the ROS nodes from the main repository. You can check the source code from the ROS tutorial at https://github.com/ros/ros_tutorials:

```
/*********************************************************************
 * Software License Agreement (BSD License)
 *
 * Copyright (c) 2012, Willow Garage, Inc.
 * All rights reserved.
 *
 * Redistribution and use in source and binary forms, with or without
 * modification, are permitted provided that the following conditions
 * are met:
 *********************************************************************/
```

For more information about the various licensing schemes in ROS, refer to http://wiki.ros.org/DevelopersGuide#Licensing.

ROS code formatting

One thing that needs to be taken care of while developing code is its formatting. One of the basic things to remember with formatting is that each code block in ROS is separated by two spaces. The following is a code snippet showing the formatting:

```
if(a < b)
{
  // do stuff
}
else
{
  // do other stuff
}
```

The following is an example code snippet in the ROS standard formatting style:

```
#include <boost/tokenizer.hpp>
#include <moveit/macros/console_colors.h>
#include <moveit/move_group/node_name.h>

static const std::string ROBOT_DESCRIPTION = "robot_description";   //
name of the robot description (a param name, so it can be changed
```

```
externally)

namespace move_group
{

class MoveGroupExe
{
public:

  MoveGroupExe(const planning_scene_monitor::PlanningSceneMonitorPtr& psm,
bool debug) :
    node_handle_("~")
  {
    // if the user wants to be able to disable execution of paths, they can
just set this ROS param to false
    bool allow_trajectory_execution;
    node_handle_.param("allow_trajectory_execution",
allow_trajectory_execution, true);

    context_.reset(new MoveGroupContext(psm, allow_trajectory_execution,
debug));

    // start the capabilities
    configureCapabilities();
  }

  ~MoveGroupExe()
  {
```

Console output

Try to avoid `printf` or `cout` statements for printing debug messages inside ROS nodes.

We can use `rosconsole` (http://wiki.ros.org/rosconsole) for printing debug messages from ROS nodes, instead of `printf` or `cout` functions. Rosconsole offers timestamped output messages, automatically logs the printed messages, and provides five different levels of verbosity. For detailed coding styles, refer to http://wiki.ros.org/CppStyleGuide.

Best practices in the ROS package

The following are the key points to bear in mind while creating and maintaining a package:

- **Version control**: ROS supports version control using Git, Mercurial, and Subversion. We can host our code in GitHub and Bitbucket. Most of the ROS packages are in GitHub.
- **Packaging**: Inside an ROS catkin package, there will be a `package.xml`, and this file should contain the author name, description, and license.
  The following is an example of a `package.xml`:

```xml
<?xml version="1.0"?>
<package>
  <name>roscpp_tutorials</name>

  <version>0.6.1</version>

  <description>
    This package attempts to show the features of ROS step-by-step,
    including using messages, servers, parameters, etc.
  </description>

  <maintainer email="dthomas@osrfoundation.org">Dirk Thomas</maintainer>

  <license>BSD</license>

  <url type="website">http://www.ros.org/wiki/roscpp_tutorials</url>
  <url type="bugtracker">https://github.com/ros/ros_tutorials/issues</url>
  <url type="repository">https://github.com/ros/ros_tutorials</url>
  <author>Morgan Quigley</author>
```

Important troubleshooting tips in ROS

We will now look at some of the common issues that are experienced when working with ROS, as well as tips on how to solve them.

One of ROS in-built tools to find issues in an ROS system is `roswtf`. `roswtf` is a command-line tool that checks for issues in the following areas of ROS:

- Environment variables and configuration
- Packages or meta-packages configuration
- Launch files
- Online graphs

Using roswtf

We can check the issues inside an ROS package by simply going into the package and entering `roswtf`. We can also check for issues in our ROS system by entering the following command:

```
$ roswtf
```

This command generates a report about the health of the system—for example, in the case of a wrong ROS hostname and master configuration, we will have the following report:

```
Loaded plugin tf.tfwtf
============================================================================
Static checks summary:

Found 1 warning(s).
Warnings are things that may be just fine, but are sometimes at fault

WARNING ROS_HOSTNAME may be incorrect: ROS_HOSTNAME [192.168.2.23] resolves to [192.168.2.23], which does
not appear to be a local IP address ['127.0.0.1', '192.168.1.7'].


============================================================================

ROS Master does not appear to be running.
Online graph checks will not be run.
ROS_MASTER_URI is [http://192.168.2.2:11311]
```

Figure 17: `roswtf` output in the case of a wrong ROS hostname configuration

We can also run `roswtf` on launch files to search for potential issues:

```
$ roswtf <file_name>.launch
```

The wiki page of `roswtf` is available at `http://wiki.ros.org/roswtf`.

The following are some of the common issues faced when working with ROS:

- **Issue 1**:
  Error message: **Failed to contact master at [localhost:11311]. Retrying...**

```
jcacace@jcacace-Inspiron-7570:~$ rosrun roscpp_tutorials talker
[ERROR] [1515175271.173829991]: [registerPublisher] Failed to contact ma
ster at [localhost:11311].  Retrying...
```

Figure 18: Failed to contact master error message

  Solution: This message comes when the ROS node executes without running the `roscore` command or checking the ROS master configuration.

- **Issue 2**:
  Error message: **Could not process inbound connection: topic types do not match**

```
jcacace@jcacace-Inspiron-7570:~$ rostopic pub /chatter std_msgs/Int32 "data: 1"
publishing and latching message. Press ctrl-C to terminate
[WARN] [1515176143.614150]: Could not process inbound connection: topic types do not
match: [std_msgs/String] vs. [std_msgs/Int32]{'topic': '/chatter', 'tcp_nodelay': '0'
, 'md5sum': '992ce8a1687cec8c8bd883ec73ca41d1', 'type': 'std_msgs/String', 'callerid'
: '/listener'}
```

Figure 19: Inbound connection warning messages

  Solution: This happens when there is a topic message mismatch, where we publish and subscribe a topic with a different ROS message type.

- **Issue 3**:
  Error message: **Couldn't find executables**

```
jcacace@jcacace-Inspiron-7570:~$ rosrun roscpp_tutorials taker
[rosrun] Couldn't find executable named taker below /opt/ros/kinetic/sha
re/roscpp_tutorials
```

Figure 20: Couldn't find executables

  Solution: This error could occur for different reasons. One error could be the wrong name of the executable specified from the command line or the missing name of the executable in the ROS package. In this case, we should check its name inside the `CMakeLists.txt`.

- **Issue 4**:
  Error message: **roscore command is not working**

```
jcacace@jcacace-Inspiron-7570:~$ roscore
^C... logging to /home/jcacace/.ros/log/5a62571a-f2d2-11e7-9514-9cda3ea0
e939/roslaunch-jcacace-Inspiron-7570-6141.log
Checking log directory for disk usage. This may take awhile.
Press Ctrl-C to interrupt
Done checking log file disk usage. Usage is <1GB.
```

Figure 21: roscore command is not running properly

Solution: One of the reasons that can hang the `roscore` command is the definition of `ROS_IP` and `ROS_MASTER_URI`. When we run ROS on multiple computers, each computer has to assign its own IP as `ROS_IP`, and `ROS_MASTER_URI` as the IP of the computer that is running `roscore`. If this IP

is incorrect, `roscore` will not run. This error can be generated by assigning an incorrect IP on these variables.

- **Issue 5**:
  Error message: **Compiling and linking errors**

```
Base path: /home/jcacace/ros_ws
Source space: /home/jcacace/ros_ws/src
Build space: /home/jcacace/ros_ws/build
Devel space: /home/jcacace/ros_ws/devel
Install space: /home/jcacace/ros_ws/install
####
#### Running command: "make cmake_check_build_system" in "/home/jcacace/ros_ws/build"
####
####
#### Running command: "make -j8 -l8" in "/home/jcacace/ros_ws/build"
####
[ 50%] Linking CXX executable /home/jcacace/ros_ws/devel/lib/linking_error_test/linking_error
CMakeFiles/linking_error.dir/src/linking_error.cpp.o: In function `main':
/home/jcacace/ros_ws/src/linking_error_test/src/linking_error.cpp:7: undefined reference to `ros::init(int&, char**, std::__cxx
11::basic_string<char, std::char_traits<char>, std::allocator<char> > const&, unsigned int)'
collect2: error: ld returned 1 exit status
linking_error_test/CMakeFiles/linking_error.dir/build.make:104: recipe for target '/home/jcacace/ros_ws/devel/lib/linking_error
_test/linking_error' failed
make[2]: *** [/home/jcacace/ros_ws/devel/lib/linking_error_test/linking_error] Error 1
CMakeFiles/Makefile2:493: recipe for target 'linking_error_test/CMakeFiles/linking_error.dir/all' failed
make[1]: *** [linking_error_test/CMakeFiles/linking_error.dir/all] Error 2
Makefile:138: recipe for target 'all' failed
make: *** [all] Error 2
Invoking "make -j8 -l8" failed
```

Figure 22: Compiling and linking errors

Solution: If the CMakeLists.txt has no dependencies, which are required to compile the ROS nodes, it can show this error. We have to check the package dependencies in package.xml and CMakeLists.txt. Here, we are generating this error by commenting roscpp dependencies:

```
cmake_minimum_required(VERSION 2.8.3)
project(linking_error_test)

find_package(catkin REQUIRED COMPONENTS
  #roscpp
  std_msgs
)
```

Figure 23: CMakeLists.txt without package dependency

Some of the troubleshooting tips from the ROS wiki are given at http://wiki.ros.org/ROS/Troubleshooting.

Questions

- Why do we need an IDE to work with ROS?
- What are the common naming conventions used in ROS?
- Why is documentation important when we create a package?
- What is the use of the roswtf command?

Summary

In this chapter, we have seen how to work with the RoboWare Studio IDE, how to set up the ROS development environment inside the IDE, how to create nodes and packages, and how to manage ROS data. After setting up ROS in RoboWare, we discussed some of the best practices in ROS, looking at naming conventions, coding styles, best practices while creating an ROS package, and so on. After discussing best practices, we looked at ROS troubleshooting. In the troubleshooting section, we discussed various troubleshooting tips that we need to bear in mind when we work with ROS.

Other Books You May Enjoy

If you enjoyed this book, you may be interested in these other books by Packt:

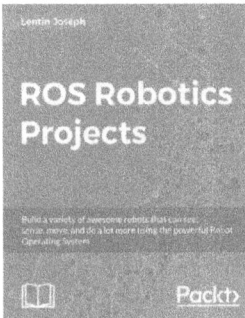

ROS Robotics Projects
Lentin Joseph

ISBN: 978-1-78355-471-3

- Create your own self-driving car using ROS
- Build an intelligent robotic application using deep learning and ROS
- Master 3D object recognition
- Control a robot using virtual reality and ROS
- Build your own AI chatter-bot using ROS
- Get to know all about the autonomous navigation of robots using ROS
- Understand face detection and tracking using ROS
- Get to grips with teleoperating robots using hand gestures
- Build ROS-based applications using Matlab and Android
- Build interactive applications using TurtleBot

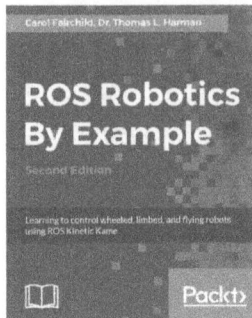

ROS Robotics By Example - Second Edition

Corey P. Schultz, Bob Perciaccante

ISBN: 978-1-78847-959-2

- Control a robot without requiring a PhD in robotics
- Simulate and control a robot arm
- Control a flying robot
- Send your robot on an independent mission
- Learning how to control your own robots with external devices
- Program applications running on your robot
- Extend ROS itself
- Extend ROS with the MATLAB Robotics System Toolbox

Leave a review - let other readers know what you think

Please share your thoughts on this book with others by leaving a review on the site that you bought it from. If you purchased the book from Amazon, please leave us an honest review on this book's Amazon page. This is vital so that other potential readers can see and use your unbiased opinion to make purchasing decisions, we can understand what our customers think about our products, and our authors can see your feedback on the title that they have worked with Packt to create. It will only take a few minutes of your time, but is valuable to other potential customers, our authors, and Packt. Thank you!

Index

E

Eclipse
  URL 524
edge-detected-images
  visualizing 323
edges
  finding, on image 323
Energia IDE
  reference link 357
  used, for flashing Chefbot firmware 357, 358
equations
  used, to find distance with ultrasonic range
    sensor 281, 283
Ethernet hotspot
  configuring, for Odroid-XU4 292, 293
  configuring, for Raspberry Pi 2 292, 293

F

Fast SLAM 195
fixed joint 76
Flexible Collision Library (FCL)
  about 171, 407
  reference link 407
floating joint 76
floating
  with URDF 78

G

Gazebo plugins
  about 225
  model plugin 225
  sensor plugin 225
  system plugin 225
  visual plugin 225
  world plugin 225
Gazebo
  controller, executing controller, executing with
    seven dof arm 243, 244
  controller, executing with seven dof arm 242
  differential wheeled robot, simulating 124
  joint state publishers, adding in launch file 129
  laser scanner, adding 126, 127
  mobile robot, moving 127, 128
  pick action 432

place action 432
robot joints moving, ROS controller used 116,
  117
used, for creating robotic arm simulation model
  107, 108, 109
used, for simulating robotic arm 106
used, for working with perception 415, 416, 417,
  418, 419, 422
gmapping node
  configuring 371, 372
  reference link 371
Grasp Pose Detector
  about 429
  reference link 429
grasp poses
  calculating, with GPD 429, 432

H

Hard Kernel 287
Hokuyo Laser scanner
  interfacing, in ROS 334, 335, 336
  reference link 334

I

IDEs
  reference link 524
IK Fast modules
  about 512
  types 512
IKFast CPP file
  generating, for IRB 6640 robot 517, 518
image processing
  CMakeLists.txt file, editing 323
  code, explanation 319
  example, building 324
  example, executing 324
  OpenCV, used 319
  ROS package, creating for experiment 319
  ROS, used 319
  source files, creating 319
images
  converting, between ROS and OpenCV using
    cv_bridge 318
  publishing, image_transport used 320, 321

Y

www.ingramcontent.com/pod-product-compliance
Lightning Source LLC
Chambersburg PA
CBHW081214220326
41598CB00037B/6779